T0155864

Lecture Notes in Computer Science

Lecture Notes in Artificial Intelligence   14473

Founding Editor

Jörg Siekmann

Series Editors

Randy Goebel, *University of Alberta, Edmonton, Canada*
Wolfgang Wahlster, *DFKI, Berlin, Germany*
Zhi-Hua Zhou, *Nanjing University, Nanjing, China*

The series Lecture Notes in Artificial Intelligence (LNAI) was established in 1988 as a topical subseries of LNCS devoted to artificial intelligence.

The series publishes state-of-the-art research results at a high level. As with the LNCS mother series, the mission of the series is to serve the international R & D community by providing an invaluable service, mainly focused on the publication of conference and workshop proceedings and postproceedings.

Lu Fang · Jian Pei · Guangtao Zhai ·
Ruiping Wang

Editors

Artificial Intelligence

Third CAAI International Conference, CICAI 2023
Fuzhou, China, July 22–23, 2023
Revised Selected Papers, Part I

Springer

Editors
Lu Fang (ID)
Tsinghua University
Beijing, China

Jian Pei
Duke University
Durham, NC, USA

Guangtao Zhai (ID)
Shanghai Jiao Tong Univeristy
Shanghai, China

Ruiping Wang (ID)
Chinese Academy of Sciences
Beijing, China

ISSN 0302-9743   ISSN 1611-3349 (electronic)
Lecture Notes in Artificial Intelligence
ISBN 978-981-99-8849-5   ISBN 978-981-99-8850-1 (eBook)
https://doi.org/10.1007/978-981-99-8850-1

LNCS Sublibrary: SL7 – Artificial Intelligence

This Springer imprint is published by the registered company Springer Nature Singapore Pte Ltd.
The registered company address is: 152 Beach Road, #21-01/04 Gateway East, Singapore 189721, Singapore

Paper in this product is recyclable.

Preface

The present book includes extended and revised versions of papers selected from the second CAAI International Conference on Artificial Intelligence (CICAI 2023), held in Fuzhou, China, during July 22–23, 2023.

CICAI is a summit forum in the field of artificial intelligence and the 2023 forum was hosted by Chinese Association for Artificial Intelligence (CAAI). CICAI aims to establish a global platform for international academic exchange, promote advanced research in AI and its affiliated disciplines, and promote scientific exchanges among researchers, practitioners, scientists, students, and engineers in AI and its affiliated disciplines in order to provide interdisciplinary and regional opportunities for researchers around the world, enhance the depth and breadth of academic and industrial exchanges, inspire new ideas, cultivate new forces, implement new ideas, integrate into the new landscape, and join the new era. The conference program included invited talks delivered by four distinguished speakers, Chenghu Zhou, Zhihua Zhou, Marios M. Polycarpou, and Xuesong Liu, as well as 17 tutorials on 8 themes, followed by an oral session of 13 papers, a poster session of 72 papers, and a demo exhibition of 16 papers. Those papers were selected from 376 submissions using a double-blind review process, and on average each submission received 2.9 reviews. The topics covered by these selected high-quality papers span the fields of AI-generated content, computer vision, machine learning, nature language processing, application of AI, and data mining, amongst others.

These two volumes contain 100 papers selected and revised from the proceedings of CICAI 2023. We would like to thank the authors for contributing their novel ideas and visions that are recorded in this book.

The proceedings editors also wish to thank all reviewers for their contributions and Springer for their trust and for publishing the proceedings of CICAI 2023.

October 2023

Lu Fang
Jian Pei
Guangtao Zhai
Ruiping Wang

Organization

General Chairs

Lu Fang   Tsinghua University, China
Jian Pei   Duke University, USA
Guangtao Zhai   Shanghai Jiao Tong University, China

Program Chair

Ruiping Wang   Chinese Academy of Sciences, China

Publication Chairs

Xiaohui Chen   University of Illinois at Urbana-Champaign, USA
Mengqi Ji   Beihang University, China

Presentation Chairs

Xun Chen   University of Science and Technology of China,
                        China
Jiantao Zhou   University of Macau, China

Demo Chairs

Jiangtao Gong   Tsinghua University, China
Can Liu   City University of Hong Kong, China

Tutorial Chairs

Jie Song   ETH Zurich, Switzerland
Tao Yu   Tsinghua University, China

Grand Challenge Chairs

David Brady   University of Arizona, USA
Haozhe Lin   Tsinghua University, China

Advisory Committee

C. L. Philip Chen   University of Macau, China
Xilin Chen   Institute of Computing Technology, Chinese
                               Academy of Sciences, China
Yike Guo   Imperial College London, China
Ping Ji   City University of New York, USA
Licheng Jiao   Xidian University, China
Ming Li   University of Waterloo, Canada
Chenglin Liu   Institute of Automation, Chinese Academy of
                               Sciences, China
Derong Liu   University of Illinois at Chicago, USA
Hong Liu   Peking University, China
Hengtao Shen   University of Electronic Science and Technology
                               of China, China
Yuanchun Shi   Tsinghua University, China
Yongduan Song   Chongqing University, China
Fuchun Sun   Tsinghua University, China
Jianhua Tao   Institute of Automation, Chinese Academy of
                               Sciences, China
Guoyin Wang   Chongqing University of Posts and
                               Telecommunications, China
Weining Wang   Beijing University of Posts and
                               Telecommunications, China
Xiaokang Yang   Shanghai Jiao Tong University, China
Changshui Zhang   Tsinghua University, China
Lihua Zhang   Fudan University, China
Song-Chun Zhu   Peking University, China
Wenwu Zhu   Tsinghua University, China
Yueting Zhuang   Zhejiang University, China

Program Committee

Boxin Shi   Peking University, China
Can Liu   City University of Hong Kong, China

Feng Xu	Tsinghua University, China
Fu Zhang	University of Hong Kong, China
Fuzhen Zhuang	Beihang University, China
Guangtao Zhai	Shanghai Jiao Tong University, China
Hao Zhao	Tsinghua University, China
Haozhe Lin	Tsinghua University, China
Hongnan Lin	Chinese Academy of Sciences, China
Jian Zhao	Institute of North Electronic Equipment, China
Jian Zhang	Peking University, China
Jiangtao Gong	Tsinghua University, China
Jiannan Li	Singapore Management University, Singapore
Jiantao Zhou	University of Macau, China
Jie Song	ETH Zurich, Switzerland
Jie Wang	University of Science and Technology of China, China
Jinshan Pan	Nanjing University of Science and Technology, China
Junchi Yan	Shanghai Jiao Tong University, China
Le Wu	Hefei University of Technology, China
Le Wang	Xi'an Jiaotong University, China
Lei Zhang	Chongqing University, China
Liang Li	Institute of Computing Technology, Chinese Academy of Sciences, China
Lijun Zhang	Nanjing University, China
Lu Fang	Tsinghua University, China
Meng Yang	Sun Yat-sen University, China
Meng Wang	BIGAI, China
Mengqi Ji	Beihang University, China
Nan Gao	Tsinghua University, China
Peng Cui	Tsinghua University, China
Qi Liu	University of Science and Technology of China, China
Qi Dai	Microsoft Research, China
Qi Ye	Zhejiang University, China
Qing Ling	Sun Yat-sen University, China
Risheng Liu	Dalian University of Technology, China
Ruiping Wang	Institute of Computing Technology, Chinese Academy of Sciences, China
Shuhui Wang	VIPL, ICT, Chinese Academic of Sciences, China
Si Liu	Beihang University, China
Tao Yu	Tsinghua University, China
Wu Liu	AI Research of JD.com, China

Xiaoyan Luo	Beihang University, China
Xiaoyun Yuan	Tsinghua University, China
Xiongkuo Min	Shanghai Jiao Tong University, China
Xun Chen	University of Science and Technology of China, China
Ying Fu	Beijing Institute of Technology, China
Yubo Chen	Institute of Automation, Chinese Academy of Sciences, China
Yuchen Guo	Tsinghua University, China
Yue Gao	Tsinghua University, China
Yue Deng	Beihang University, China
Yue Li	Xi'an Jiaotong-Liverpool University, China
Yuwang Wang	Tsinghua University, China

Contents – Part I

Contents – Part II

Multidisciplinary Research with AI

Other AI Related Topics

Robotics

Computer Vision

MARS: An Instance-Aware, Modular and Realistic Simulator for Autonomous Driving

Zirui Wu[1,2], Tianyu Liu[1,3], Liyi Luo[1,4], Zhide Zhong[1,5], Jianteng Chen[1,5], Hongmin Xiao[1,6], Chao Hou[1,7], Haozhe Lou[1,8], Yuantao Chen[1,9], Runyi Yang[1,10], Yuxin Huang[1,5], Xiaoyu Ye[1,5], Zike Yan[1], Yongliang Shi[1], Yiyi Liao[11], and Hao Zhao[1(✉)]

[1] AIR, Tsinghua University, Beijing, China
zhaohao@air.tsinghua.edu.cn
[2] System Hub, HKUST(GZ), Guangzhou, China
[3] HKUST, Hong Kong SAR, China
[4] McGill University, Montreal, Canada
[5] Beijing Institute of Technology, Beijing, China
[6] National University of Singapore, Singapore, Singapore
[7] HKU, Pokfulam, Hong Kong
[8] University of Wisconsin Madison, Madison, USA
[9] Xi'an University of Architecture and Technology, Xi'an, China
[10] Imperial College London, London, UK
[11] Zhejiang University, Hangzhou, China

Abstract. Nowadays, autonomous cars can drive smoothly in ordinary cases, and it is widely recognized that realistic sensor simulation will play a critical role in solving remaining corner cases by simulating them. To this end, we propose an autonomous driving simulator based upon neural radiance fields (NeRFs). Compared with existing works, ours has three notable features: (1) **Instance-aware.** Our simulator models the foreground instances and background environments separately with independent networks so that the static (e.g., size and appearance) and dynamic (e.g., trajectory) properties of instances can be controlled separately. (2) **Modular.** Our simulator allows flexible switching between different modern NeRF-related backbones, sampling strategies, input modalities, etc. We expect this modular design to boost academic progress and industrial deployment of NeRF-based autonomous driving simulation. (3) **Realistic.** Our simulator set new state-of-the-art photo-realism results given the best module selection. Our simulator will be **open-sourced** while most of our counterparts are not. Project page: https://open-air-sun.github.io/mars/.

H. Zhao—Sponsored by Tsinghua-Toyota Joint Research Fund (20223930097).

Supplementary Information The online version contains supplementary material available at https://doi.org/10.1007/978-981-99-8850-1_1.

Keywords: Autonomous Driving Simulator · Neural Radiance Fields

1   Introduction

Autonomous driving [10–12, 14, 22, 28] is arguably the most important application of modern 3D scene understanding [4, 23] techniques. Nowadays, Robotaxis can run in big cities with up-to-date HD maps, handling everyday driving scenarios smoothly. However, once a corner case that lies out of the distribution of an autonomous driving algorithm happens on the road unexpectedly, the lives of passengers are put at risk. The dilemma is that while we need more training data about corner cases, collecting them in the real world usually means danger and high expenses. To this end, the community believes that photorealistic simulation [5, 9, 15, 25] is a technical path of great potential. If an algorithm can experience enormous corner cases in a simulator with a small sim-to-real gap, the performance bottleneck of current autonomous driving algorithms can be potentially addressed.

Existing autonomous driving simulation methods have their own limitations. CARLA [7] is a widely used sensor simulator based upon traditional graphics engines, whose realism is restricted by asset modeling and rendering qualities. AADS [15] also exploits traditional graphics engines but demonstrates impressive photorealism using well-curated assets. On the other hand, GeoSim [5] introduces a data-driven scheme for realistic simulation by learning an image enhancement network. Flexible asset generation and rendering can be achieved through image composition with promisingly good geometry and realistic appearance.

In this paper, we take advantage of the realistic rendering ability of NeRFs for autonomous driving simulation. Training data captured from real-world environments guarantees a small sim-to-real gap. Several works also exploit NeRFs to model cars [18] and static backgrounds [9] in outdoor environments. However, the inability to model complex dynamic scenes that are composed of both moving objects and static environments limits their practical use for real-world sensor simulation. Recently, Neural Scene Graph (NSG) [19] decomposes dynamic scenes into learned scene graphs and learns latent representations for category-level objects. However, its multi-plane-based representation for background modeling cannot synthesize images under large viewpoint changes.

To be specific, our central contribution is the very first **open-source** NeRF-based modular framework for photorealistic autonomous driving simulation. The proposed pipeline models foreground instances and background environments in a decomposed fashion. Different NeRF backbone architectures and sampling methods are incorporated in a unified manner with multi-modal inputs supported. The best module combination of the proposed framework achieves state-of-the-art rendering performance on public benchmarks with large margins, indicating photorealistic simulation results.

2   Method

Overview. As illustrated in Fig. 1, we aim to provide a modular framework for constructing compositional neural radiance fields, where realistic sensor

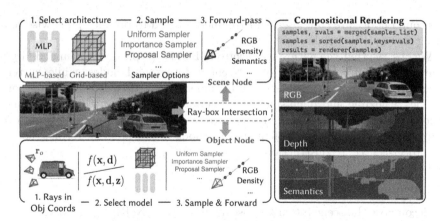

Fig. 1. Pipeline. Left: We first calculate the ray-box intersection of the queried ray
r and all visible instance bounding boxes $\{\mathcal{B}_{ij}\}$. For the background node, we directly
use the selected scene representation model and the chosen sampler to infer point-
wise properties, as in conventional NeRFs. For the foreground nodes, the ray is first
transformed into the instance frame as $\mathbf{r}_o$ before being processed through foreground
node representations (Sect. 2.1). **Right**: All the samples are composed and rendered
into RGB images, depth maps, and semantics (Sect. 2.2).

simulation can be conducted for outdoor driving scenes. A large unbounded
outdoor environment with plenty of dynamic objects is taken into consideration.

The input to the system consists of a set of RGB-images $\{\mathcal{I}_i\}^N$ (captured by
vehicle-side or roadside sensors), sensor poses $\{\mathcal{T}_i\}^N$ (calculated using IMU/GPS
signals), and object tracklets (including 3D bounding boxes $\{\mathcal{B}_{ij}\}^{N \times M}$, categories $\{\texttt{type}_{ij}\}^{N \times M}$, and instance IDs $\{\texttt{idx}_{ij}\}^{N \times M}$). N is the number of input
frames and M is the number of tracked instances $\{\mathcal{O}_j\}^M$ across the whole
sequence. An optional set of depth maps $\{\mathcal{D}_i\}^N$ and semantic segmentation
masks $\{\mathcal{S}_i\}^N$ can also be adopted as extra supervision signals during training.
By constructing a compositional neural field, the proposed framework can simulate realistic sensor perception signals (including RGB images, depth maps,
semantic segmentation masks, etc.) at given sensor poses. Instance editing on
object trajectories and appearances is also supported.

Pipeline. Our framework model each foreground instance and the background
node compositionally. As shown in Fig. 1, when querying properties (RGB, depth,
semantics, etc.) of a given ray **r**, we first calculate its intersection with all visible
objects' 3D bounding boxes to get the entering and leaving distances $[t_{\texttt{in}}, t_{\texttt{out}}]$.
Afterward, both the background node (Fig. 1 left-top) and the foreground object
nodes (Fig. 1 left-bottom) are queried, where each node samples a set of 3D points
and uses its specific neural representation network to obtain point properties
(RGB, density, semantics, etc.). Specifically, to query foreground nodes, we convert the ray origins and directions from world space into instance frames according to the object tracklets. Finally, all the ray samples from background and

foreground nodes are composed and volume-rendered to produce pixel-wise rendering results (Fig. 1 right, Sect. 2.2).

We observe that the nature of background nodes (typically unbounded large-scale scenes) differs from the object-centric foreground nodes, while current works [13, 19] in sensor simulation use unified NeRF models. Our framework provides a flexible and open-sourced framework that supports different design choices of scene representations for background and foreground nodes and can easily incorporate new state-of-the-art methods of static scene reconstruction and object-centric reconstructions.

2.1   Scene Representation

We decompose the scene into a large-scale unbounded NeRF (as the background node) and multiple object-centric NeRFs (as independent foreground nodes). Conventionally, a neural radiance field maps a given 3D point coordinate $\mathbf{x} = (x, y, z), \mathbf{x} \in \mathbb{R}^3$ and a 2D viewing direction $\mathbf{d} \in \mathbb{S}^2$ to its radiance $\mathbf{c}$ and volume density σ shown in Eq. 1. Based upon this seminal representation, many variants have been proposed for different purposes, so we take a modular design.

$$f(\mathbf{x}, \mathbf{d}) = (\mathbf{c}, \sigma) : [\mathbb{R}^3, \mathbb{S}^2] \rightarrow [\mathbb{R}^3, \mathbb{R}^+] \tag{1}$$

The challenge of modeling unbounded background scene photo-realistically lies in accurately representing far regions, so we utilize the unbounded scene warping [2] to contract the far region. For foreground nodes, we support both the code-conditioned representation $f(\mathbf{x}, \mathbf{d}, \mathbf{z}) = (\mathbf{c}, \sigma)$ ($\mathbf{z} \in \mathbb{R}^k$ denotes the instance-wise latent code) and the conventional ones, which will be explained as follows.

Architectures. In our modular framework, we support various NeRF backbones, which can be roughly categorized into two hyper-classes: MLP-based methods [1, 2, 16], or grid-based methods that store spatially-variant features in their hash grid voxel vertices [17, 21]. Although these architectures differ from each other in details, they follow the same high-level formulation of Eq. 1 and are capsuled in modules under a unified interface in MARS.

While the MLP-based representations are simple in mathematical form, we give a formal exposition of grid-based methods. The specific implementation of a multi-resolution feature grid $\{\mathcal{G}_\theta^l\}_{l=1}^L$ has layer-wise resolutions $R_l := \lfloor R_{\min} \cdot b^l \rfloor, b = \exp\left(\dfrac{\ln R_{\max} - \ln R_{\min}}{L - 1}\right)$, where $R_{\min}, R_{\max}$ are the coarsest and the finest resolution [17, 26]. The coordinates $\mathbf{x}$ are first scaled to each resolution before being processed by the ceiling and flooring operations to $\lceil \mathbf{x} \cdot R_l \rceil, \lfloor \mathbf{x} \cdot R_l \rfloor$ and hashed to obtain table indexes [17]. The extracted feature vectors are then tri-linearly interpolated and decoded through a shallow MLP.

$$(\mathbf{c}, \sigma) = f_\theta\left(\texttt{interp}(\texttt{hash\_and\_lookup}(\mathbf{x}, \{\mathcal{G}_\theta^l\}_{l=1}^L)), \mathbf{d}\right). \tag{2}$$

Sampling. We support various sampling strategies, including the recently proposed proposal network [2], which distills a density field from a radiance-free

NeRF model to generate ray samples and other sampling schemes like coarse-to-fine sampling [16] or uniform sampling [8] for flexibility.

Foreground Nodes. For rendering foreground instances, we first transform the projected rays into per-instance coordinate space and then infer the object-centric NeRFs in each instance-wise canonical space. The default setting of our framework uses code-conditioned models that exploit latent codes to encode instance features and **shared** category-level decoders to encode class-wise priors, allowing the modeling of many long tracklets with compact memory usage. Meanwhile, the conventional ones without code conditions are also supported in our framework. We detailed our modified foreground representation (denoted as 'Ours' in Sect. 3) in supplementary materials.

Background node rendering   Groundtruth

Object nodes rendering   Composed image

Fig. 2. Illustration on the compositional rendering. Some of the static vehicles in the far region are considered as background objects.

2.2 Compositional Rendering

Figure 2 demonstrates the compositional rendering results. To render an image at a given camera pose $\mathcal{T}_i$, we cast a ray $\mathbf{r} = \mathbf{o} + t\mathbf{d}$ at each rendered pixel. For each ray $\mathbf{r}$, we first calculate the intersection interval $[t_{\text{in}}, t_{\text{out}}]$ with all visible foreground nodes $\mathcal{O}_{ij}$ (Fig. 3) and transform the samples $\{P_k^{\text{obj-j}}\}$ along the ray from world space into each foreground canonical space. We also sample a set of 3D points along the ray ($\{P_k^{\text{bg}}\}$ as background samples. Samples in all nodes are first passed through their corresponding networks to obtain point-wise colors $\{\mathbf{c}_k^{\text{bg, obj}}\}$, densities $\{\sigma_k^{\text{bg, obj}}\}$, and foreground semantic logits $\{\mathbf{s}_k^{\text{bg}}\}$. Considering that the semantic properties of foreground samples are actually their category label, we create a one-hot vector as:

$$\mathbf{s}_k^{\text{obj-j}}[l] = \begin{cases} \sigma_k^{\text{obj-j}} & \text{if } l = \text{category of j's instance} \\ 0 & \text{otherwise} \end{cases}, \text{for } l \text{ in category.} \quad (3)$$

To aggregate the point-wise properties, we sort all the samples by their ray distance in world space and use the standard volume rendering process to render pixel-wise properties:

$$\hat{c}(\mathbf{r}) = \sum_{P_i} T_i \alpha_i \mathbf{c}_i + (1 - \texttt{accum}) \cdot \mathbf{c}_{\text{sky}}, \quad T_i = \exp(-\sum_{k=1}^{i-1} \sigma_k \delta_k), \tag{4}$$

$$\hat{d}(\mathbf{r}) = \sum_{P_i} T_i \alpha_i t_i + (1 - \texttt{accum}) \cdot \texttt{inf}, \quad \hat{s}(\mathbf{r}) = \sum_{P_i} T_i \alpha_i \mathbf{s}_i + (1 - \texttt{accum}) \cdot \mathbf{s}_{\text{sky}}, \tag{5}$$

where $P_i \in \texttt{sorted}(\{P_i^{\text{bg, obj}}\}), \alpha_i = 1 - \exp(-\sigma_i \delta_i), \delta_i = t_{i+1} - t_i, \texttt{accum} = \sum_{P_i} T_i \alpha_i$, $\mathbf{c}_{\text{sky}}$ is the rendered color from the Sky model (Sect. 2.3), $\texttt{inf}$ is the upper bound distance, and $\mathbf{s}_{\text{sky}}$ is the one-hot semantic logits of the $\texttt{sky}$ category.

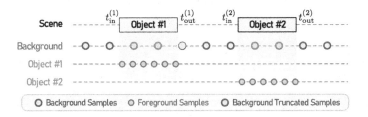

Fig. 3. Visual demonstration on our **conflict-free** sampling process. We use uniform sampling in all nodes for illustration.

2.3   Towards Realistic Rendering

Sky Modeling. In our framework, we support the usage of a sky model to deal with appearances at infinite distance, where an MLP-based spherical environment map [20] is leveraged to model the infinitely far regions that never intersect opaque surfaces:

$$f_{\text{sky}}(\mathbf{d}) = \mathbf{c}_{\text{sky}} : \mathbb{S}^2 \to \mathbb{R}^3 \tag{6}$$

However, naïvely blending the sky color $\mathbf{c}_{\text{sky}}$ with background and foreground rendering (Eq. 4) leads to potential inconsistency. Therefore, we introduce a BCE semantic regularization to alleviate this issue:

$$\mathcal{L}_{\text{sky}} = \text{BCE}(1 - \texttt{accum}, \mathcal{S}_{\text{sky}}). \tag{7}$$

Resolving Conflict Samples. Due to the fact that our background and foreground sampling are done independently, there is a chance that background samples fall within the foreground bounding box (Fig. 3 Background Truncated Samples). The compositional rendering may mistakenly classify foreground samples as background (referred to later as background-foreground ambiguity). As a result, after removing the foreground instance, artifacts will emerge in the background area (Fig. 4). Ideally, with sufficient multi-view supervision signal, the system can automatically learn to distinguish between foreground and background during the training process. However, for a data-driven simulator, obtaining abundant and high-quality multi-view images is challenging for users as vehicles move fast on the road. The ambiguity is **NOT** observed in NSG [19] as NSG only samples a few points on the ray-plane intersections, and is unlikely to have much background truncated samples.

Without regularization   With $\mathcal{L}_{\text{accum}}$

Fig. 4. We show that the background truncated samples cause background-foreground ambiguity without our regularization.

To address this issue, we devise a regularization term that minimizes the density sum of background truncated samples to minimize their influence during the rendering process as:

$$\mathcal{L}_{\text{accum}} = \sum_{P_i^{(\text{tr})}} \sigma_i, \tag{8}$$

where $\{P_i^{(\text{tr})}\}$ denotes background truncated samples.

2.4 Optimization

To optimize our system, we minimize the following objective function:

$$\mathcal{L} = \lambda_1 \mathcal{L}_{\text{color}} + \lambda_2 \mathcal{L}_{\text{depth}} + \lambda_3 \mathcal{L}_{\text{sem}} + \lambda_4 \mathcal{L}_{\text{sky}} + \lambda_5 \mathcal{L}_{\text{accum}}, \tag{9}$$

where λ_{1-5} are weighting parameters. $\mathcal{L}_{\text{sky}}$ and $\mathcal{L}_{\text{accum}}$ are explained in Eq. 7 and 8.

Color Loss: we adopt a standard MSE loss that minimizes the photo-metric errors as:

$$\mathcal{L}_{\text{color}} = ||\mathbf{c}(\mathbf{r}) - \hat{\mathbf{c}}(\mathbf{r})||_2^2. \tag{10}$$

Depth Loss: We introduce a depth loss to address textureless regions and regions that are observed from sparse viewpoints. We have devised two strategies for supervising the geometry. Given depth data, we utilize a ray distribution loss derived from [6]. On the other hand, if the depth data is not available, we utilize a mono-depth network and apply mono-depth loss following [26].

$$\mathcal{L}_{\text{depth}} = \begin{cases} \mathcal{L}_{\text{sensor\_depth}} & \text{if depth data is available} \\ \mathcal{L}_{\text{mono\_depth}} & \text{if depth data is not available} \end{cases} \tag{11}$$

Semantic Losses: We follow SemanticNeRF [29] and use a cross-entropy semantic loss $\mathcal{L}_{\text{sem}} = \texttt{CrossEntropy}(\mathbf{s}(\mathbf{r}), \mathcal{S}(\mathbf{r}))$.

3 Experiments

In this section, we provide extensive experimental results to demonstrate the proposed instance-aware, modular, and realistic simulator for autonomous driving. We evaluate our method on scenes from the KITTI [10] dataset and the Virtual KITTI-2 (V-KITTI) [3] dataset. In the following, we use **"our default setting"** to denote a grid-based NeRF with proposal sampler for the background node, and our modified category-level representation with coarse-to-fine sampler for foreground nodes.

Table 1. Quantitative results on image reconstruction task & Comparisons on the settings with baseline methods. The dataset used for evaluation is KITTI.

	NeRF [16]	NeRF+Time	NSG [19]	PNF [13]	SUDS [24]	Ours
PSNR ↑	23.34	24.18	26.66	27.48	28.31	**29.06**
SSIM ↑	0.662	0.677	0.806	0.870	0.876	**0.885**
Instance-aware	✗	✗	✓	✓	✗	✓
Modular	✗	✗	✗	✗	✗	✓
Open-sourced	✓	–	✓	✗	✓	✓

3.1 Photorealistic Rendering

We validate the photorealistic rendering performance of our simulator by evaluating image reconstruction and novel view synthesis (NVS) following [19,24].

Table 2. Quantitative results on novel view synthesis

	KITTI-75%			KITTI-50%			KITTI-25%		
	PSNR ↑	SSIM ↑	LPIPS ↓	PSNR ↑	SSIM ↑	LPIPS ↓	PSNR ↑	SSIM ↑	LPIPS ↓
NeRF [16]	18.56	0.557	0.554	19.12	0.587	0.497	18.61	0.570	0.510
NeRF+Time	21.01	0.612	0.492	21.34	0.635	0.448	19.55	0.586	0.505
NSG [19]	21.53	0.673	0.254	21.26	0.659	0.266	20.00	0.632	0.281
SUDS [24]	22.77	0.797	0.171	23.12	**0.821**	**0.135**	20.76	0.747	0.198
Ours	**24.23**	**0.845**	**0.160**	**24.00**	0.801	0.164	**23.23**	**0.756**	**0.177**
	+1.46	+0.048	-0.011	+0.88	-0.020	+0.029	+2.47	+0.009	-0.021
	VKITTI-75%			VKITTI-50%			VKITTI-25%		
	PSNR ↑	SSIM ↑	LPIPS ↓	PSNR ↑	SSIM ↑	LPIPS ↓	PSNR ↑	SSIM ↑	LPIPS ↓
NeRF [16]	18.67	0.548	0.634	18.58	0.544	0.635	18.17	0.537	0.644
NeRF+Time	19.03	0.574	0.587	18.90	0.565	0.610	18.04	0.545	0.626
NSG [19]	23.41	0.689	0.317	23.23	0.679	0.325	21.29	0.666	0.317
SUDS [24]	23.87	0.846	0.150	23.78	0.851	0.142	22.18	0.829	0.160
Ours	**29.79**	**0.917**	**0.088**	**29.63**	**0.916**	**0.087**	**27.01**	**0.887**	**0.104**
	+5.92	+0.071	-0.062	+5.85	+0.065	-0.055	+4.83	+0.058	-0.056

Baselines. We conduct qualitative and quantitative comparisons against other state-of-the-art methods: NeRF [16], NeRF with timestamp input (denoted as NeRF+Time), NSG [19], PNF [13], and SUDS [24]. Note that none of them simultaneously meet all three standards mentioned in Table 1.

Implementation Details. Our model is trained for 200,000 iterations with 4096 rays per batch, using RAdam as optimizers. The learning rate of the background node is assigned $1 * 10^{-3}$ decaying to $1 * 10^{-5}$, while that of $5 * 10^{-3}$ decaying to $1 * 10^{-5}$ in object nodes (Fig. 5).

Fig. 5. Qualitative image reconstruction results on KITTI dataset.

Experiment Settings. The training and testing image sets in the image reconstruction setting are identical, while in the NVS task, we render the frames that are not included in the training data. Specifically, we hold out every 4th frames, every 2nd and 4th frames, and training with only one in every four frames, namely 25%, 50%, and 75%.

We follow the standard evaluation protocol in image synthesis and report Peak Signal-to-Noise Ratio (PSNR), Structural Similarity (SSIM), and Learned Perceptual Image Patch Similarity (LPIPS) [27] of our default setting for quantitative evaluations. Results are shown in Table 1 for image reconstruction and Table 2 for NVS, which indicate that our method outperforms baseline methods in both settings. We can achieve 29.79 PSNR on V-KITTI using 75% training data, while the best result previously published is 23.87 (Fig. 6).

Fig. 6. Gallery of different rendering channels.

3.2   Instance-Wise Editing

Our framework separately models background and foreground nodes, which allows us to edit the scene in an instance-aware manner. We qualitatively present our capability to remove instances, add new instances, and edit vehicle trajectories. In Fig. 7, we show some editing examples of rotating and translating a vehicle, though more results can be found in our video clip.

Fig. 7. Rendering results on the edited scene.

3.3   The Blessing of Modular Design

We use different combinations of background and foreground nodes, samplers, and supervision signals for evaluation, which is credited to our modular design.

Note that some of the baseline methods in the literature actually correspond to an ablation entry in this table. For instance, PNF [13] uses NeRF as background node representation and instance-wise NeRF as foreground node representation with semantic losses. NSG [19] uses NeRF as background node representation and category-level NeRF as foreground representation, but with a multi-plane sampling strategy. Our default setting uses grid-based background node representation, and our proposed category-level method for foreground node representation.

3.4   Ablation Results

In this section, we analyze different experiment settings, verifying the necessity of our design. We reveal the impact of different design choices in background node representation, foreground node representation, etc. Specifically, we present all experiments with 50,000 iterations. Unlike prior works [13,19,24] that evaluate their method on a short sequence of 90 images, we use the full sequence from the dataset for all evaluation. Since they are not open-sourced and their exact evaluation sequences are not known, we hope our new benchmarking would standardize this important field. Quantitative evaluation can be found in Table 3.

For background and foreground nodes, we substitute our default model (ID 1 in Table 3) with MLP-based and grid-based model and list their metrics in row

2, 7–12. In the 3rd–6th row, we show the effectiveness of our model components. For model and sampler, selected modules for background and foreground nodes are noted before and after the slash, respectively.

Table 3. Quantitative evaluation for ablation studies

ID	Model	Sampler	Category	$\mathcal{L}_{sky}$	$\mathcal{L}_{depth}$	$\mathcal{L}_{sem}$	$\mathcal{L}_{accum}$	KITTI PSNR ↑	SSIM ↑	LPIPS ↓	V-KITTI PSNR ↑	SSIM ↑	LPIPS ↓
1*	Grid / Ours	prop / c2f †						**25.04**	**0.782**	**0.175**	**28.37**	**0.907**	**0.108**
2	**MLP** / Ours	**c2f** / c2f						20.14	0.589	0.476	22.19	0.664	0.409
3	Grid / Ours	prop / c2f					×	21.35	0.713	0.242	27.30	0.881	0.130
4	Grid / Ours	prop / c2f			×		×	23.68	0.774	0.181	27.32	0.881	0.129
5	Grid / Ours	prop / c2f				×		23.66	0.769	0.184	27.30	0.880	0.128
6	Grid / Ours	prop / c2f			×			20.07	0.723	0.251	27.42	0.863	0.148
7	Grid / **MLP**	prop / **c2f**						20.46	0.709	0.255	26.46	0.875	0.132
8	Grid / **Grid**	prop / **prop**						22.23	0.741	0.211	25.22	0.871	0.134
9	Grid / **MLP**	prop / **c2f**	×					20.98	0.699	0.257	27.27	0.881	0.130
10	Grid / **Grid**	prop / **prop**	×					23.71	0.763	0.193	26.65	0.882	0.125
11*	**MLP** / **MLP**	**c2f** / **c2f**						20.42	0.592	0.472	21.77	0.659	0.410

† prop stands for proposal sampler, and c2f stands for coarse-to-fine sampler.
* ID 1 is our default setting. ID 11 is similar to the setting of NSG [19] with coarse-to-fine sampler instead.

4 Conclusion

In this paper, we present a modular framework for photorealistic autonomous driving simulation based on NeRFs. Our **open-sourced** framework consists of a background node and multiple foreground nodes, enabling the modeling of complex dynamic scenes. We demonstrate the effectiveness of our framework through extensive experiments. The proposed pipeline achieved state-of-the-art rendering performance on public benchmarks. We also support different design choices of scene representations and sampling strategies, offering flexibility and versatility in the simulation process.

Limitations. Our method requires hours to train and is not capable of rendering in real-time. Besides, our method fails to consider the dynamic specular effects on glasses or other reflective materials that may cause artifacts in rendered images. Improving simulation efficiency and view-dependent effects will be our future work.

References

1. Barron, J.T., Mildenhall, B., Tancik, M., Hedman, P., Martin-Brualla, R., Srinivasan, P.P.: Mip-NeRF: a multiscale representation for anti-aliasing neural radiance fields. In: 2021 IEEE/CVF International Conference on Computer Vision (ICCV), pp. 5835–5844 (2021)
2. Barron, J.T., Mildenhall, B., Verbin, D., Srinivasan, P.P., Hedman, P.: Mip-NeRF 360: unbounded anti-aliased neural radiance fields. In: Proceedings of the IEEE/CVF Conference on Computer Vision and Pattern Recognition. arXiv (2022)

3. Cabon, Y., Murray, N., Humenberger, M.: Virtual KITTI 2. http://arxiv.org/abs/2001.10773

4. Chen, X., Zhao, H., Zhou, G., Zhang, Y.Q.: PQ-transformer: jointly parsing 3D objects and layouts from point clouds. IEEE Robot. Autom. Lett. **7**(2), 2519–2526 (2022)

5. Chen, Y., et al.: GeoSim: realistic video simulation via geometry-aware composition for self-driving. http://arxiv.org/abs/2101.06543

6. Deng, K., Liu, A., Zhu, J.Y., Ramanan, D.: Depth-supervised NeRF: fewer views and faster training for free. In: 2022 IEEE/CVF Conference on Computer Vision and Pattern Recognition (CVPR), pp. 12872–12881 (2022)

7. Dosovitskiy, A., Ros, G., Codevilla, F., Lopez, A., Koltun, V.: CARLA: an open urban driving simulator. In: Proceedings of the 1st Annual Conference on Robot Learning, pp. 1–16. PMLR (2017)

8. Fridovich-Keil, S., Meanti, G., Warburg, F., Recht, B., Kanazawa, A.: K-planes: explicit radiance fields in space, time, and appearance. In: Computer Vision and Pattern Recognition (2023)

9. Fu, X., et al.: Panoptic NeRF: 3D-to-2D label transfer for panoptic urban scene segmentation. In: 2022 International Conference on 3D Vision (3DV), pp. 1–11 (2022)

10. Geiger, A., Lenz, P., Stiller, C., Urtasun, R.: Vision meets robotics: the KITTI dataset. Int. J. Robot. Res. **32**(11), 1231–1237 (2013)

11. Hu, Y., et al.: Planning-oriented autonomous driving. In: Proceedings of the IEEE/CVF Conference on Computer Vision and Pattern Recognition, pp. 17853–17862 (2023)

12. Jin, B., et al.: ADAPT: action-aware driving caption transformer. In: 2023 IEEE International Conference on Robotics and Automation (ICRA), pp. 7554–7561 (2023)

13. Kundu, A., et al.: Panoptic neural fields: a semantic object-aware neural scene representation. In: Proceedings of the IEEE/CVF Conference on Computer Vision and Pattern Recognition, pp. 12871–12881 (2022)

14. Li, P., et al.: LODE: locally conditioned eikonal implicit scene completion from sparse LiDAR. In: 2023 IEEE International Conference on Robotics and Automation (ICRA). arXiv (2023)

15. Li, W., et al.: AADS: augmented autonomous driving simulation using data-driven algorithms. Sci. Robot. **4**(28), eaaw0863 (2019)

16. Mildenhall, B., Srinivasan, P.P., Tancik, M., Barron, J.T., Ramamoorthi, R., Ng, R.: NeRF: representing scenes as neural radiance fields for view synthesis. In: Vedaldi, A., Bischof, H., Brox, T., Frahm, J.-M. (eds.) ECCV 2020. LNCS, vol. 12346, pp. 405–421. Springer, Cham (2020). https://doi.org/10.1007/978-3-030-58452-8_24

17. Müller, T., Evans, A., Schied, C., Keller, A.: Instant neural graphics primitives with a multiresolution hash encoding. ACM Trans. Graph. **41**(4), 1–15 (2022)

18. Niemeyer, M., Geiger, A.: GIRAFFE: representing scenes as compositional generative neural feature fields. In: Proceedings of the IEEE/CVF Conference on Computer Vision and Pattern Recognition, pp. 11453–11464 (2021)

19. Ost, J., Mannan, F., Thuerey, N., Knodt, J., Heide, F.: Neural scene graphs for dynamic scenes. In: Proceedings of the IEEE/CVF Conference on Computer Vision and Pattern Recognition. arXiv (2021)

20. Rematas, K., et al.: Urban radiance fields. In: 2022 IEEE/CVF Conference on Computer Vision and Pattern Recognition (CVPR), pp. 12922–12932 (2022)

21. Tancik, M., et al.: Nerfstudio: a modular framework for neural radiance field development. ACM Trans. Graph. **1**(1) (2023)
22. Tian, B., Liu, M., Gao, H.A., Li, P., Zhao, H., Zhou, G.: Unsupervised road anomaly detection with language anchors. In: 2023 IEEE International Conference on Robotics and Automation (ICRA), pp. 7778–7785 (2023)
23. Tian, B., Luo, L., Zhao, H., Zhou, G.: VIBUS: data-efficient 3D scene parsing with VIewpoint Bottleneck and Uncertainty-Spectrum modeling. J. Photogramm. Remote Sens. **194**, 302–318 (2022)
24. Turki, H., Zhang, J.Y., Ferroni, F., Ramanan, D.: SUDS: scalable urban dynamic scenes. In: Proceedings of the IEEE/CVF Conference on Computer Vision and Pattern Recognition. arXiv (2023)
25. Yang, Z., et al.: UniSim: a neural closed-loop sensor simulator. In: Proceedings of the IEEE/CVF Conference on Computer Vision and Pattern Recognition, pp. 1389–1399 (2023)
26. Yu, Z., Peng, S., Niemeyer, M., Sattler, T., Geiger, A.: MonoSDF: exploring monocular geometric cues for neural implicit surface reconstruction. In: Advances in Neural Information Processing Systems (2022)
27. Zhang, R., Isola, P., Efros, A.A., Shechtman, E., Wang, O.: The unreasonable effectiveness of deep features as a perceptual metric. In: 2018 IEEE/CVF Conference on Computer Vision and Pattern Recognition, pp. 586–595 (2018)
28. Zheng, Y., et al.: STEPS: joint self-supervised nighttime image enhancement and depth estimation. In: 2023 IEEE Conference on Robotics and Automation (ICRA 2023) (2023)
29. Zhi, S., Laidlow, T., Leutenegger, S., Davison, A.J.: In-place scene labelling and understanding with implicit scene representation. In: Proceedings of the IEEE/CVF International Conference on Computer Vision (2021)

Concealed Object Segmentation
with Hierarchical Coherence Modeling

Fengyang Xiao[1]ⓘ, Pan Zhang[1]ⓘ, Chunming He[2(✉)]ⓘ, Runze Hu[3]ⓘ,
and Yutao Liu[4]ⓘ

[1] Sun Yat-sen University, Zhuhai 510275, China
`xiaofy5@mail2.sysu.edu.cn`
[2] Tsinghua Shenzhen International Graduate School, Tsinghua University,
Shenzhen 518055, China
`chunminghe19990224@gmail.com`
[3] Beijing Institute of Technology, Beijing 100086, China
[4] School of Computer Science and Technology, Ocean University of China,
Qingdao 266000, China

Abstract. Concealed object segmentation (COS) is a challenging task
that involves localizing and segmenting those concealed objects that are
visually blended with their surrounding environments. Despite achieving remarkable success, existing COS segmenters still struggle to achieve
complete segmentation results in extremely concealed scenarios. In this
paper, we propose a Hierarchical Coherence Modeling (HCM) segmenter
for COS, aiming to address this incomplete segmentation limitation. In
specific, HCM promotes feature coherence by leveraging the intra-stage
coherence and cross-stage coherence modules, exploring feature correlations at both the single-stage and contextual levels. Additionally, we
introduce the reversible re-calibration decoder to detect previously undetected parts in low-confidence regions, resulting in further enhancing
segmentation performance. Extensive experiments conducted on three
COS tasks, including camouflaged object detection, polyp image segmentation, and transparent object detection, demonstrate the promising
results achieved by the proposed HCM segmenter.

Keywords: Concealed object segmentation · Hierarchical coherence
modeling · Edge reconstruction

1 Introduction

Concealed object segmentation (COS) is a challenging task with the purpose of
localizing and segmenting those objects visually blended in their surrounding

F. Xiao—First Author

This work was supported by the National Science Foundation of China under
grant 62201538 and Natural Science Foundation of Shandong Province under grant
ZR2022QF006.

L. Fang et al. (Eds.): CICAI 2023, LNAI 14473, pp. 16–27, 2024.
https://doi.org/10.1007/978-981-99-8850-1_2

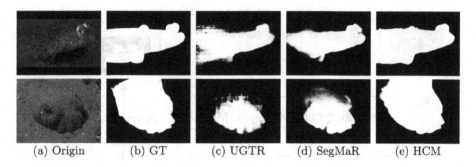

(a) Origin   (b) GT   (c) UGTR   (d) SegMaR   (e) HCM

Fig. 1. Results of UGTR [33], SegMaR [14], and the proposed HCM. It is observed that our HCM can generate more accurate and complete results.

scenarios [3,8]. COS is a general task encompassing various applications, such as camouflaged object detection (COD) [3], polyp image segmentation (PIS) [4], and transparent object detection (TOD) [22].

COS poses significant challenges due to the intrinsic similarity between foreground objects and their corresponding scenarios, making it difficult to identify discriminative cues for complete and accurate foreground-background separation. To cope with this challenge, existing COS segmenters have employed various strategies, *e.g.*, drawing inspiration from human vision [21,25], incorporating frequency clues [7], and adopting joint modeling strategies across multiple tasks [19,34]. Despite their notable achievements, existing segmenters still struggle to achieve *precise* results in some extremely concealed scenarios. As shown in Fig. 1, while UGTR [33] and SegMaR [14] manage to find the rough regions for the concealed objects, the prediction results are still incomplete.

To overcome this limitation, we propose a Hierarchical Coherence Modeling (HCM) segmenter for the COS task, which aims to generate more complete segmentation maps by promoting feature coherence. HCM incorporates two key components, namely, intra-stage coherence (ISC) and cross-stage coherence (CSC), to explore feature correlations at both single stage and contextual levels. Additionally, we develop the reversible re-calibration decoder (RRD) to detect previously undetected parts in those low-confidence regions and thus further improve segmentation performance.

Our contributions are summarized as follows:

- We propose the Hierarchical Coherence Modeling (HCM) segmenter for the COS task. HCM encourages feature coherence and thus alleviating the incomplete segmentation problem.
- We introduce RRD to detect previously undetected parts in low-confidence regions, thus improving segmentation performance.
- The proposed HCM significantly outperforms the state-of-the-art methods on three COS tasks by a large margin, *i.e.*, camouflaged object detection, polyp image segmentation, and transparent object detection.

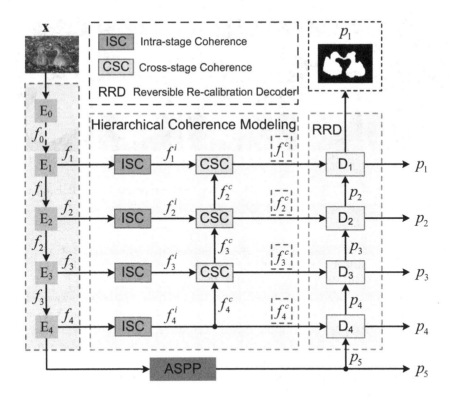

Fig. 2. Architecture of the proposed HCM.

2   Related Works

Concealed Object Segmentation. Traditional COS techniques heavily rely on manually designed feature extraction operators, which inherently suffer from limited feature extraction capacity and struggle to handle extremely complex scenarios. In contrast, learning-based approaches, facilitated by the rapid development of deep learning, have achieved remarkable success in this field. For instance, MGL [34] introduces an auxiliary edge reconstruction task and constructs a mutual graph learning strategy to generate prediction maps with clear boundaries. Inspired by human vision principles [21], PFNet leverages distraction mining techniques to achieve accurate concealed object segmentation. Recognizing the limitations of human vision, FEDER [7] introduces an adaptive decomposition approach to extract subtle yet discriminative clues that may have been overlooked. Unlike existing COS solvers, we propose HCM segmenter for the COS task, which encourages feature coherence and thus alleviates the incomplete segmentation problem. Additionally, we introduce the reversible re-calibration decoder (RRD) to detect previously undetected parts in low-confidence regions, further enhancing the segmentation performance (Fig. 2).

3   Methodology

3.1   Concealed Feature Encoder

Follow [3], we employ ResNet50 [6,11] as the default backbone of the basic encoder E for feature extraction. Given a concealed image $\mathbf{X}$, we obtain a series of feature maps $\{f_s\}_{s=0}^4$. Considering that f_4 has abundant semantic information, we further feed this feature map into an astrous spatial pyramid pooling (ASPP) module A_s [12] to generate a coarse segmentation map p_5: $p_5 = A_s(f_4)$.

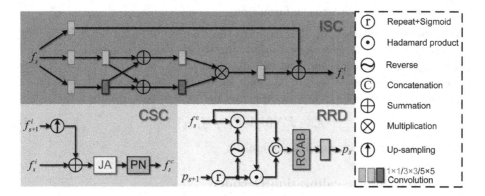

Fig. 3. Details of ISC, CSC, and RRD.

3.2   Hierarchical Coherence Modeling

Due to the inherent similarity between concealed objects and their surrounding contexts, obtaining accurate and complete segmentation results poses a significant challenge for the segmenter. To address this issue, we propose a hierarchical coherence modeling strategy that explicitly promotes feature coherence to facilitate more comprehensive predictions. Illustrated in Fig. 3, this strategy consists of two parts: intra-stage coherence (ISC) and cross-stage coherence (CSC). These parts work in conjunction to enhance the coherence of features at different stages, promoting better segmentation outcomes.

Intra-stage Coherence. ISC aims to discover feature correlations by fusing multi-scale features with different receptive fields within a single stage. This allows the aggregated features to capture scale-invariant information. As illustrated in Fig. 3, ISC comprises two primary branches with residual connections. Given the input feature f_s, we initially apply a 1×1 convolution to reduce the channel dimension. Subsequently, we process these features with two parallel convolutions using different kernel sizes, resulting in features f_s^3 and f_s^5:

$$f_s^3 = conv3(conv1(f_s)), f_s^5 = conv5(conv1(f_s)), \tag{1}$$

where $conv1, conv3, conv5$ denote $1 \times 1, 3 \times 3, 5 \times 5$ convolutions, respectively. We proceed by merging the features f_s^3 and f_s^5, which are obtained from the previous step. These merged features are then further processed using two parallel convolutions. Finally, we multiply the outputs of these convolutions in a residual connection structure to extract the scale-invariant information. This process yields the aggregated features $\{f_s^i\}_{s=1}^4$:

$$f_s^i = conv1(f_s) + conv3(conv3(f_s^3 \oplus f_s^5) \otimes conv5(f_s^3 \oplus f_s^5)), \qquad (2)$$

where $\oplus$ and $\otimes$ denote pixel-level summation and multiplication. This design facilitates the extraction of features at multiple scales and enhances the ability to capture diverse contextual information.

Cross-Stage Coherence. CSC explores the contextual feature correlations by selectively interacting cross-stage information with joint attention $JA(\cdot)$, comprising spatial attention and channel attention [2,13]. Additionally, we employ position normalization $PN(\cdot)$ to highlight the contextual similarity and eliminate discrepancy interference information across different stages, getting $\{f_s^c\}_{s=1}^4$:

$$f_s^c = PN(JA(f_s^i, up(f_{s+1}^i))), \qquad (3)$$

where $up(\cdot)$ denotes up-sampling operator.

3.3   Reversible Re-calibration Decoder

Due to the complexity of concealed object scenes, segmenters produce prediction maps that contain low-confidence and ambiguous regions. To tackle this challenge, we propose a novel module called Reversible Re-calibration Decoder (RRD). As shown in Fig. 3, RRD leverages both the previous decoder's prediction map as prior information and reverses the prediction map to extract cues from the low-confidence regions. This allows the segmenter to effectively detect previously undetected parts in these regions, leading to improved segmentation performance. Consequently, the prediction map $\{p_s\}_{s=1}^4$ is defined as follows:

$$p_s = conv3\left(RCAB\left(cat\left(f_k^s \odot S\left(rp\left(p_{s+1}\right)\right), f_k^s \odot rv\left(S\left(rp\left(p_{s+1}\right)\right)\right)\right)\right)\right), \qquad (4)$$

where $rp(\cdot)$, $S(\cdot)$, $rv(\cdot)$, $\odot$, and $conv3(\cdot)$ denote repeat, Sigmoid, reverse (element-wise subtraction with 1), Hadamard product, and 3×3 convolution. $RCAB(\cdot)$ is the residual channel attention block [15,31] and we employ this block to emphasize the noteworthy information.

3.4   Loss Functions

We follow the practice in [3,7] and employ the weighted binary cross-entropy loss L_{BCE}^w [32] and weighted intersection-over-union loss L_{IoU}^w [26] to supervised our HCM with the ground truth $\mathbf{Y}$ in a multiscale manner, which is defined as follows:

$$L = \sum_{s=1}^5 \frac{1}{2^{s-1}}\left(L_{BCE}^w\left(p_s, \mathbf{Y}\right) + L_{BCE}^w\left(p_s, \mathbf{Y}\right)\right) + L_{OH}. \qquad (5)$$

Table 1. Quantitative comparisons of our method and other 9 ResNet50-based SOTAs on COD. The best two results are in red and blue fonts.

Methods	Pub.	CAMO (250 images)				COD10K (2,026 images)				NC4K (4,121 images)			
		$M \downarrow$	$F_\beta \uparrow$	$E_\phi \uparrow$	$S_\alpha \uparrow$	$M \downarrow$	$F_\beta \uparrow$	$E_\phi \uparrow$	$S_\alpha \uparrow$	$M \downarrow$	$F_\beta \uparrow$	$E_\phi \uparrow$	$S_\alpha \uparrow$
PFANet [37]	CVPR19	0.132	0.607	0.701	0.695	0.074	0.478	0.729	0.716	0.095	0.634	0.760	0.752
CPD [29]	CVPR19	0.113	0.675	0.723	0.716	0.053	0.578	0.776	0.750	0.072	0.719	0.808	0.787
EGNet [36]	ICCV19	0.109	0.667	0.800	0.732	0.061	0.526	0.810	0.736	0.075	0.671	0.841	0.777
SINet [3]	CVPR20	0.092	0.712	0.804	0.745	0.043	0.667	0.864	0.776	0.058	0.768	0.871	0.808
PFNet [21]	CVPR21	0.085	0.751	0.841	0.782	0.040	0.676	0.877	0.800	0.053	0.779	0.887	0.829
MGL-R [34]	CVPR21	0.088	0.738	0.812	0.775	0.035	0.680	0.851	0.814	0.053	0.778	0.867	0.833
MGL-S [34]	CVPR21	0.089	0.733	0.806	0.772	0.037	0.666	0.844	0.811	0.055	0.771	0.862	0.829
LSR [20]	CVPR21	0.080	0.756	0.838	0.787	0.037	0.699	0.880	0.804	0.048	0.802	0.890	0.834
UGTR [33]	ICCV21	0.086	0.747	0.821	0.784	0.036	0.670	0.852	0.817	0.052	0.778	0.874	0.839
SegMaR [14]	CVPR22	0.072	0.772	0.861	0.805	0.035	0.699	0.890	0.813	0.052	0.767	0.885	0.835
HCM (Ours)	—	0.070	0.782	0.873	0.806	0.032	0.736	0.902	0.820	0.046	0.816	0.900	0.846

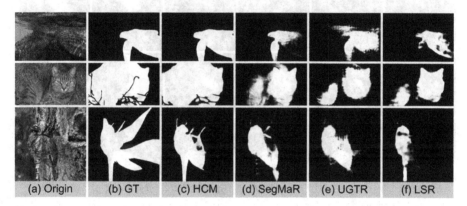

(a) Origin   (b) GT   (c) HCM   (d) SegMaR   (e) UGTR   (f) LSR

Fig. 4. Qualitative analysis on the COD task.

4   Experiments

Implementation Details. Our HCM is implemented on two RTX3090TI GPUs and is optimized by Adam with the momentum terms $(0.9, 0.999)$. Following [3], our encoder is initialized with the model pre-trained on ImageNet. During the training phase, the batch size is set to 32. The learning rate is initialized to 0.0001 and is divided by 10 every 80 epochs. The images are resized as 352×352.

4.1   Camouflaged Object Segmentation

Datasets and Metrics. Following [14], three datasets are utilized for evaluation, including *CAMO*, *COD10K*, and *NC4K*. *CAMO* comprises 1,250 camouflaged images with 8 categories. *COD10K* have 10 super-classes, containing 5,066 images. *NC4K* is the largest testing set which contains 4,121 images. Same as existing methods [3,14], our training set comprises 1,000 images from *CAMO* and 3,000 images from *COD10K*, and our test set integrates the rest of images.

Table 2. Quantitative comparisons on two benchmarks in polyp image segmentation. The best two results are in red and blue fonts.

Methods	CVC-ColonDB (380 images)						Kvasir (100 images)					
	mDice ↑	mIoU ↑	M ↓	F_β^w ↑	E_ϕ^{max} ↑	S_α ↑	mDice ↑	mIoU ↑	M ↓	F_β^w ↑	E_ϕ^{max} ↑	S_α ↑
U-Net [27]	0.512	0.444	0.061	0.498	0.776	0.712	0.818	0.746	0.055	0.794	0.893	0.858
Atten-UNet [24]	0.466	0.385	0.071	0.431	0.724	0.670	0.769	0.683	0.062	0.730	0.859	0.828
SFA [5]	0.469	0.347	0.094	0.379	0.765	0.634	0.723	0.611	0.075	0.670	0.849	0.782
PraNet [4]	0.709	0.640	0.045	0.696	0.869	0.819	0.898	0.840	0.030	0.885	0.948	0.915
MSNet [39]	0.755	0.678	0.041	0.737	0.883	0.836	0.907	0.862	0.028	0.893	0.944	0.922
TGANet [28]	0.722	0.661	0.043	0.711	0.875	0.823	0.902	0.845	0.030	0.891	0.952	0.920
LADK [35]	0.764	0.683	0.039	0.739	0.862	0.834	0.905	0.852	0.028	0.887	0.947	0.918
M²SNet [38]	0.758	0.685	0.038	0.737	0.869	0.842	0.912	0.861	0.025	0.901	0.953	0.922
HCM (Ours)	0.775	0.687	0.038	0.741	0.885	0.845	0.910	0.868	0.025	0.903	0.956	0.924

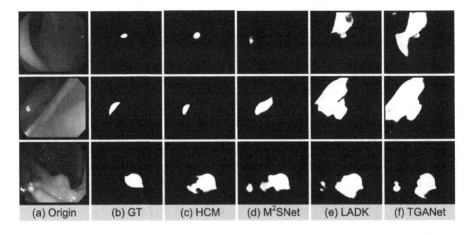

| (a) Origin | (b) GT | (c) HCM | (d) M²SNet | (e) LADK | (f) TGANet |

Fig. 5. Qualitative analysis on the PIS task.

Following [3,9], we utilize four metrics, namely mean absolute error M, adaptive F-measure F_β, mean E-measure E_ϕ, and structure measure S_α. Smaller M means better performance, yet this is reversed on F_β, E_ϕ, and S_α.

Quantitative Analysis. We compare the proposed Hierarchical Coherence Model (HCM) with nine other state-of-the-art ResNet50-based segmenters on the COD task and present the segmentation results in Table 1. As shown in the table, our HCM outperforms all other segmenters and achieves the top ranking. It surpasses the second-best COD segmenter, SegMaR [14], by a margin of 3.6%. This remarkable performance clearly showcases the superior capability of our HCM in enhancing feature coherence.

Qualitative Analysis. As shown in Fig. 4, our HCM demonstrates the capability to generate more complete and comprehensive segmentation results and reduces those uncertainty regions. This improvement can be attributed to our novel hierarchical coherence modeling strategy, which enhances feature coher-

Table 3. Quantitative comparisons on two benchmarks in transparent object detection. The best two results are in red and blue fonts.

Methods	GDD (936 images)				GSD (810 images)			
	mIoU ↑	F_β^{max} ↑	M ↓	BER ↓	mIoU ↑	F_β^{max} ↑	M ↓	BER ↓
PMD [17]	0.870	0.930	0.067	6.17	0.817	0.890	0.061	6.74
GDNet [22]	0.876	0.937	0.063	5.62	0.790	0.869	0.069	7.72
GlassNet [16]	0.881	0.932	0.059	5.71	0.836	0.901	0.055	6.12
EBLNet [10]	0.870	0.922	0.064	6.08	0.817	0.878	0.059	6.75
CSNet [1]	0.773	0.876	0.135	11.33	0.666	0.805	0.135	14.76
PGNet [30]	0.857	0.930	0.074	6.82	0.805	0.897	0.068	7.88
GDNet-B [23]	0.878	0.939	0.061	5.52	0.792	0.874	0.066	7.61
ESRNet [18]	0.901	0.942	0.046	4.46	0.854	0.911	0.046	5.74
HCM (Ours)	0.908	0.946	0.045	4.42	0.858	0.922	0.045	5.52

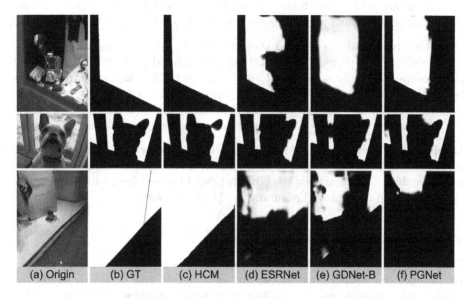

Fig. 6. Qualitative analysis on the TOD task.

ence within the segmenter. Furthermore, the proposed reversible re-calibration decoder plays a crucial role in enabling the segmenter to effectively identify previously undetected parts within these regions.

4.2 Polyp Image Segmentation

Datasets and Metrics. In line with the methodology employed in [38], we evaluate the segmentation performance on two widely-used benchmark datasets: *CVC-ColonDB* and *Kvasir*. 900 images from *Kvasir* make up the training set and the testing set comprises the remaining images. Additionally, Consistent with [38], we adopt six metrics for quantitative evaluation: namely mean dice (mDice), mean IoU (mIoU), M, weighted F-measure (F_β^w), max E-measure (E_ϕ^{max}), and

Table 4. Ablation study on *COD10K* of the COD task, where "w/o" denotes without. The best results are marked in **bold**.

Metrics	w/o HCM component	w/o RRD	Ours
$M \downarrow$	0.035	0.033	**0.032**
$F_\beta \uparrow$	0.702	0.725	**0.736**
$E_\phi \uparrow$	0.866	0.893	**0.902**
$S_\alpha \uparrow$	0.803	0.815	**0.820**

(a) Break down ablations of HCM.

Metrics	w/o ISC	w/o CSC	Ours
$M \downarrow$	0.033	0.033	**0.032**
$F_\beta \uparrow$	0.725	0.727	**0.736**
$E_\phi \uparrow$	0.895	0.888	**0.902**
$S_\alpha \uparrow$	0.812	0.815	**0.820**

(b) Effect of the HCM strategy.

S_α. For mDice and mIoU, higher values indicate better performance, whereas for the remaining four metrics, higher values indicate poorer performance.

Quantitative Analysis. Table 2 presents the quantitative comparisons on two benchmarks in polyp image segmentation. As exhibited in Table 2, our proposed HCM outperforms the second-best techniques in 0.6%. This improvement can be attributed to the introduction of our novel modules, namely the Inter-Scale Coherence (ISC) and Contextual Scale Coherence (CSC) modules, which enable the exploration of feature correlations at both single-stage and contextual levels.

Qualitative Analysis. As shown in Fig. 5, our method can capture polyp more accurately because the proposed HCM method encourages feature coherence, which enables finer discrimination of the gap between foreground and background, leading to improved accuracy in polyp segmentation.

4.3 Transparent Object Detection

Datasets and Metrics. In accordance with the experimental setup in [18], we conduct our evaluations on two datasets: *GDD* and *GSD*. To assess the segmentation results, we employ four widely-used metrics: mean intersection over union (mIoU), maximum F-measure (F_β^{max}), M, and balance error rate (BER). The training set consists of 2,980 from *GDD* and 3,202 images from *GSD*, while the remaining images are allocated to the testing set. It is important to note that a smaller value for M or BER, or a higher value for IoU and F_β^{max} indicates superior segmentation performance.

Quantitative Analysis. Table 3 demonstrates the superior performance of our HCM in transparent object detection (TOD). Our method outperforms the second-best TOD solver, ESRNet, by 1.5%. This substantial improvement further validates the effectiveness and advancement of our proposed HCM segmenter in addressing the challenges of the TOD task.

Qualitative Analysis. As depicted in Fig. 6, our HCM segmenter achieves more accurate and complete segmentation results compared to the other methods. In contrast, the comparison methods often produce incomplete segments or exhibit blurred parts. These visual comparisons provide compelling evidence of the superiority of our method in addressing the challenges of incomplete segmentation with low-confidence regions.

4.4 Ablation Study and Further Analysis

We conduct ablation studies about our HCM on *COD10K* of the COD task.

Break Down Ablations of HCM. As demonstrated in Table 4a, when examining the individual components of our HCM, namely the HCM component or RRD, the performance of HCM decreases. This observation highlights the superiority of our proposed components in contributing to the overall performance of the proposed segmenter.

Effect of the Hierarchical Coherence Modeling Strategy. We conducted additional experiments to validate the effectiveness of each component in our proposed hierarchical coherence modeling strategy. As shown in Table 4b, our results demonstrate the superiority of the ISC and CSC. These components work in synergy to form a powerful hierarchical coherence modeling strategy.

5   Conclusions

In this paper, we present a novel segmenter called HCM for COS with the aim of addressing the existing limitation of incomplete segmentation. The HCM method focuses on promoting feature coherence by utilizing both intra-stage coherence and cross-stage coherence modules, which explore feature correlations at both the single-stage and contextual levels. Moreover, we introduce the reversible re-calibration decoder to identify previously undetected parts in regions with low-confidence, thereby further improving the segmentation performance. The effectiveness of the proposed HCM segmenter is demonstrated through extensive experiments conducted on three different COS tasks: camouflaged object detection, polyp image segmentation, and transparent object detection. The results obtained from these experiments show promising outcomes, affirming the efficacy of the HCM approach.

References

1. Cheng, M.M., Gao, S.H., Borji, A., Tan, Y.Q., Lin, Z., Wang, M.: A highly efficient model to study the semantics of salient object detection. IEEE Trans. Pattern Anal. Mach. Intell. **44**(11), 8006–8021 (2021)
2. Deng, L., He, C., Xu, G., Zhu, H., Wang, H.: PcGAN: a noise robust conditional generative adversarial network for one shot learning. IEEE Trans. Intell. Transp. Syst. **23**(12), 25249–25258 (2022)
3. Fan, D.P., Ji, G.P., Sun, G., Cheng, M.M., Shen, J., Shao, L.: Camouflaged object detection. In: CVPR, pp. 2777–2787 (2020)

4. Fan, D.P., et al.: PraNet: parallel reverse attention network for polyp segmentation. In: Martel, A.L., et al. (eds.) MICCAI 2020, Part VI. LNCS, vol. 12266, pp. 263–273. Springer, Cham (2020). https://doi.org/10.1007/978-3-030-59725-2_26

5. Fang, Y., Chen, C., Yuan, Y., Tong, K.: Selective feature aggregation network with area-boundary constraints for polyp segmentation. In: Shen, D., et al. (eds.) MICCAI 2019. LNCS, vol. 11764, pp. 302–310. Springer, Cham (2019). https://doi.org/10.1007/978-3-030-32239-7_34

6. He, C., et al.: HQG-Net: unpaired medical image enhancement with high-quality guidance. arXiv preprint: arXiv:2307.07829 (2023)

7. He, C., et al.: Camouflaged object detection with feature decomposition and edge reconstruction. In: CVPR (2023)

8. He, C., et al.: Weakly-supervised concealed object segmentation with SAM-based pseudo labeling and multi-scale feature grouping. arXiv preprint: arXiv:2305.11003 (2023)

9. He, C., Wang, X., Deng, L., Xu, G.: Image threshold segmentation based on GLLE histogram. In: CPSCom, pp. 410–415. IEEE (2019)

10. He, H., et al.: Enhanced boundary learning for glass-like object segmentation. In: ICCV, pp. 15859–15868 (2021)

11. He, K., Zhang, X., Ren, S., Sun, J.: Deep residual learning for image recognition. In: CVPR, pp. 770–778 (2016)

12. Hu, R., Liu, Y., Gu, K., Min, X., Zhai, G.: Toward a no-reference quality metric for camera-captured images. IEEE Trans. Cybern. (2021)

13. Hu, R., Liu, Y., Wang, Z., Li, X.: Blind quality assessment of night-time image. Displays **69**, 102045 (2021)

14. Jia, Q., Yao, S., Liu, Y., Fan, X., Liu, R., Luo, Z.: Segment, magnify and reiterate: detecting camouflaged objects the hard way. In: CVPR, pp. 4713–4722 (2022)

15. Ju, M., He, C., Liu, J., Kang, B., Su, J., Zhang, D.: IVF-Net: an infrared and visible data fusion deep network for traffic object enhancement in intelligent transportation systems. IEEE Trans. Intell. Transp. Syst. **24**, 1220–1234 (2022)

16. Lin, J., He, Z., Lau, R.W.: Rich context aggregation with reflection prior for glass surface detection. In: CVPR, pp. 13415–13424 (2021)

17. Lin, J., Wang, G., Lau, R.W.: Progressive mirror detection. In: CVPR, pp. 3697–3705 (2020)

18. Lin, J., Yeung, Y.H., Lau, R.: Exploiting semantic relations for glass surface detection. NIPS **35**, 22490–22504 (2022)

19. Lu, Y., He, C., Yu, Y.F., Xu, G., Zhu, H., Deng, L.: Vector co-occurrence morphological edge detection for colour image. IET Image Process. **15**(13), 3063–3070 (2021)

20. Lv, Y., et al.: Simultaneously localize, segment and rank the camouflaged objects. In: CVPR, pp. 11591–11601 (2021)

21. Mei, H., Ji, G.P., Wei, Z., Yang, X., Wei, X., Fan, D.P.: Camouflaged object segmentation with distraction mining. In: CVPR, pp. 8772–8781 (2021)

22. Mei, H., et al.: Don't hit me! glass detection in real-world scenes. In: CVPR, pp. 3687–3696 (2020)

23. Mei, H., Yang, X., Yu, L., Zhang, Q., Wei, X., Lau, R.W.: Large-field contextual feature learning for glass detection. IEEE Trans. Pattern Anal. Mach. Intell. **45**, 3329–3346 (2023)

24. Oktay, O., et al.: Attention U-Net: learning where to look for the pancreas. arXiv preprint: arXiv:1804.03999 (2018)

25. Pang, Y., Zhao, X., Xiang, T.Z., Zhang, L., Lu, H.: Zoom in and out: a mixed-scale triplet network for camouflaged object detection. In: CVPR, pp. 2160–2170 (2022)

26. Rahman, M.A., Wang, Y.: Optimizing intersection-over-union in deep neural networks for image segmentation. In: Bebis, G., et al. (eds.) ISVC 2016. LNCS, vol. 10072, pp. 234–244. Springer, Cham (2016). https://doi.org/10.1007/978-3-319-50835-1_22

27. Ronneberger, O., Fischer, P., Brox, T.: U-Net: convolutional networks for biomedical image segmentation. In: Navab, N., Hornegger, J., Wells, W.M., Frangi, A.F. (eds.) MICCAI 2015. LNCS, vol. 9351, pp. 234–241. Springer, Cham (2015). https://doi.org/10.1007/978-3-319-24574-4_28

28. Tomar, N.K., Jha, D., Bagci, U., Ali, S.: TGANet: text-guided attention for improved polyp segmentation. In: Wang, L., Dou, Q., Fletcher, P.T., Speidel, S., Li, S. (eds.) Medical Image Computing and Computer Assisted Intervention – MICCAI 2022. Lecture Notes in Computer Science, vol. 13433, pp. 151–160. Springer, Cham (2022). https://doi.org/10.1007/978-3-031-16437-8_15

29. Wu, Z., Su, L., Huang, Q.: Cascaded partial decoder for fast and accurate salient object detection. In: CVPR, pp. 3907–3916 (2019)

30. Xie, C., Xia, C., Ma, M., Zhao, Z., Chen, X., Li, J.: Pyramid grafting network for one-stage high resolution saliency detection. In: CVPR, pp. 11717–11726 (2022)

31. Xu, G., He, C., Wang, H., Zhu, H., Ding, W.: DM-Fusion: deep model-driven network for heterogeneous image fusion. IEEE Trans. Neural Netw. Learn. Syst. (2023)

32. Xu, L., et al.: Multi-modal sequence learning for Alzheimer's disease progression prediction with incomplete variable-length longitudinal data. Med. Image Anal. **82**, 102643 (2022)

33. Yang, F., et al.: Uncertainty-guided transformer reasoning for camouflaged object detection. In: ICCV, pp. 4146–4155 (2021)

34. Zhai, Q., Li, X., Yang, F., Chen, C., Cheng, H., Fan, D.P.: Mutual graph learning for camouflaged object detection. In: CVPR, pp. 12997–13007 (2021)

35. Zhang, R., et al.: Lesion-aware dynamic kernel for polyp segmentation. In: Wang, L., Dou, Q., Fletcher, P.T., Speidel, S., Li, S. (eds.) Medical Image Computing and Computer Assisted Intervention - MICCAI 2022. Lecture Notes in Computer Science, vol. 13433, pp. 99–109. Springer, Cham (2022). https://doi.org/10.1007/978-3-031-16437-8_10

36. Zhao, J.X., Liu, J.J., Fan, D.P., Cao, Y., Yang, J., Cheng, M.M.: EGNet: edge guidance network for salient object detection. In: ICCV, pp. 8779–8788 (2019)

37. Zhao, T., Wu, X.: Pyramid feature attention network for saliency detection. In: CVPR, pp. 3085–3094 (2019)

38. Zhao, X., et al.: M2SNet: multi-scale in multi-scale subtraction network for medical image segmentation. IEEE Trans. Med. Imag. (2023)

39. Zhao, X., Zhang, L., Lu, H.: Automatic polyp segmentation via multi-scale subtraction network. In: de Bruijne, M., et al. (eds.) MICCAI 2021. LNCS, vol. 12901, pp. 120–130. Springer, Cham (2021). https://doi.org/10.1007/978-3-030-87193-2_12

ViT-MPI: Vision Transformer Multiplane Images for Surgical Single-View View Synthesis

Chenming Han[1], Ruizhi Shao[2], Gaochang Wu[1(✉)], Hang Shao[3], and Yebin Liu[2]

[1] State Key Laboratory of Synthetical Automation for Process Industries, Northeastern University, Shengyang, China
wugc@mail.neu.edu.cn
[2] Department of Automation, Tsinghua University, Beijing, China
[3] Zhejiang Future Technology Institute, Jiaxing, China

Abstract. In this paper, we explore the use of a single imaging device to acquire immersive 3D perception in endoscopic surgery. To solve the heavily ill-posed problem caused by the unknown depth and unseen occlusion, we introduce a Vision Transformer (ViT)-based Multiplane Images (MPI) representation, termed as ViT-MPI, for the continuous novel view synthesis using single-view input. The MPI representation provides layered depth images to explicitly decode positional relationships between tissues. Instead of using the existing full convolutional network as the backbone of our MPI representation, we exploit the ViT architecture to collect tokens output from all stages of the transformer and combine them into feature representations with different resolutions. The interactions between tokens in the ViT provide accurate predictions of local and global positional relations, ensuring reliable view synthesis of occluded regions with fine-grained details. Experiments on real-captured endoscopic surgery images from the da Vinci Surgical Robot System demonstrate that our proposed approach enables the prediction of multi-view images from a single-view input. Moreover, our method produces reasonable depth maps, further enhancing its practical applicability.

Keywords: View synthesis · Vision transformer · MPI representation · Endoscopic surgery

1 Introduction

Stereo endoscopy provides surgeons with immersive 3D perception, enabling complex surgical procedures in minimally invasive surgery. Such systems, for example, the Da Vinci surgical robot system [7], have achieved a great success in general surgery, urologic surgery, cardiac surgery, etc. The system captures binocular video with a certain baseline, thus enabling surgeons to construct 3D information in their mind while watching the binocular video.

© The Author(s), under exclusive license to Springer Nature Singapore Pte Ltd. 2024
L. Fang et al. (Eds.): CICAI 2023, LNAI 14473, pp. 28–40, 2024.
https://doi.org/10.1007/978-981-99-8850-1_3

However, the multiple imaging devices will inevitably lead to a larger surgical incision and affect the postoperative recovery of patients. Therefore, it is of great significance and necessity to provide 3D experience with a single imaging device, but it comes with additional challenges. On the one hand, it is difficult to disentangle 3D appearance of the surgery scene from the rigid movement of surgical instruments and the non-rigid deformation of tissues during the surgical process, simply by using conventional Structure from Motion (SfM). On the other hand, predicting depth information using a single image can be a heavily ill-posed problem. Multiple depth solutions can be consistent with a monocular view.

Recently, researches of depth estimation [6] and view synthesis [27] using single view input based on the deep learning technique [12] have attracted lots of attentions, making it possible to generate 3D vision from monocular input in surgical scenes. To overcome the ill-posed problem described above, these methods learn to predict positional relationships between objects in the scene rather than simply memorizing the training data, achieving generalization to unseen scenarios [11]. Among these methods, the Multiplane Images (MPIs) [20,30,31] is a more sophisticated learning-based 3D representation. It decomposes the input view(s) into multiple layered depth images, which can be further applied to rendering novel views or depth maps.

In this paper, we set our sights on the MPI representation to promote single image into immersive 3D vision for endoscopic surgery. In endoscopic applications, global contextual information may be particularly important because key structures (such as lesions) in endoscopic images may be located at any location in the image, and their reconstruction may require understanding the context of the entire image. Therefore, for better learning the positional relationships between tissues, a Vision Transformer (ViT) [3] backbone is adopted to predict the layered depth images as well as a background image for inpainting occluded regions. We term the proposed method ViT-MPI. The ViT-MPI first divides the input image into blocks and maps them into tokens, and then uses a multi-head attention mechanism to extract the local and global positional relations. Finally, a multiscale convolutional decoder is applied to fuse features of transformer layers from coarse to fine. The network is trained through end-to-end optimization using the perception loss [10] to prevent blurry artifacts caused by the mean square error loss. Experiments on dataset from a da Vinci surgical robot system demonstrates that the proposed ViT-MPI is visually and quantitatively superior to existing single-view view synthesis methods.

The contributions can be summarized as follows:

- An end-to-end solution for continuous novel view synthesis for endoscopic surgery.
- A ViT-based MPI representation for accurately predicting local and global positional relations, ensuring reliable view synthesis for the heavily ill-posed problem.
- Both visual and quantitative results demonstrate the performance of the proposed ViT-MPI.

2 Related Work

Traditional View Synthesis Methods. Traditional view synthesis methods mostly focus on interpolation of densely-sampled views, such as light field rendering [28,29], or reconstructing scene geometry from sparse views [8]. In addition, some methods involving local geometric proxies [9,15,32] have been explored. Although the final results of these methods are often satisfactory, this kind of method is only applicable to the input of multiple views.

Learning-Based View Synthesis Methods. The main advantage of learning-based methods lies in their capability to learn and generalize patterns from training data, which enables them to handle diverse and complex scenarios. Flynn et al. [5] introduced a deep learning approach to create new scene views from sparse input views, using a deep Convolutional Neural Network (CNN) to generate novel view pixel colors. Srinivasan et al. [21] introduced an innovative deep-learning algorithm employing light fields, which turns a 2D RGB image into a synthesized 4D light field. These two methods compute a representation in the coordinate of target views, requiring the execution of the trained network for each target view, thereby posing real-time rendering as a hurdle. In contrast, our approach computes the scene representation once and leverages it to produce a multitude of output views in real time.

Other techniques predict a solitary scene representation, allowing the rendering of multiple output views. Take, for example, layered depth images are initially conceived to tackle stereo-matching issues [23], they have recently gained traction in learning view interpolation and extrapolation as MPI representation [4,14,20,30]. In addition, Tucker et al. [24] extended these methods so that they can predict an MPI from a single input image.

Model Architecture. Full convolutional networks [13,17] have been widely employed for view synthesis task, and are often considered as a standard architecture. Modern architectures simultaneously handle high-resolution and lower-resolution representations throughout the network [22,26], adeptly capturing details at multiple scales, vital for realistic view synthesis.

While view synthesis has significantly benefited from convolutional networks, attention-based mechanisms, particularly transformers [25], have emerged as a powerful alternative. Originally conceived for natural language processing (NLP) tasks [2], transformers utilize a set-to-set operation paradigm built upon the self-attention mechanism. Several studies [1,18] have begun adapting these attention mechanisms for image-related tasks, including view synthesis. Intriguingly, it has been demonstrated that transformer architectures, originally successful in NLP, can also yield comparable performance in image-related tasks including image classification [3]. Therefore, our method applies the vision transformer as the backbone to predict an MPI, using only multiple views as supervision.

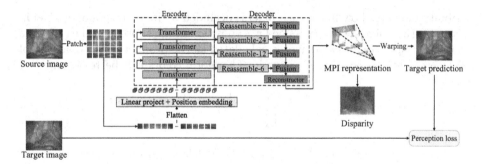

Fig. 1. Model overview. Our network based on ViT backbone generates an MPI from a single image input. The input image is decomposed into patches and flattened, followed by a linear projection and position embedding to obtain a set of tokens (white). A readout token (red) that is not grounded in the input image is added to aggregate global information. All tokens interact in pairs through multiple transformer stages. Our decoder decodes tokens from different stages into an MPI representation for subsequent rendering operations. (Color figure online)

3   Approach

3.1   MPI Representation and Rendering Using Single-View

We apply MPI [30] as a surgical scene representation with single-view input, and further to the rendering of multi-view images. We use MPI representation because of their realistic rendering of novel views and their ability to predict occluded elements, producing reliable stereo-visual effects for surgical procedures. Moreover, in our application of endoscopic scenes, this may help generate richer and more complete views from a single or small number of images. For example, it may help doctors better understand and judge the spatial structure of the lesion area.

An MPI consists of a set of D fronto-parallel planes. Every plane at fixed depths from a reference camera coordinate frame contains four channels, which are RGB channels and α channel. Here, we use c_i for the color and α_i for the alpha channels of layer i. Then the MPI can be considered as a set of RGBA layers $\{(c_1, \alpha_1), \ldots \ldots, (c_D, \alpha_D)\}$.

In this paper, we use a network f to learn the MPI representation. Consider an image I_s at viewpoint v_s is the input image of our network, then the network f outputs are a set of RGBA layers $\{(c_1, \alpha_1), \ldots \ldots, (c_D, \alpha_D)\}$ of the image I_s at viewpoint v_s:

$$f : I_s \rightarrow \{(c_1^s, \alpha_1^s), \ldots, (c_D^s, \alpha_D^s)\}. \tag{1}$$

Each layer's color is set by a blend of foreground (input image I_s) and background I_b (predicted) following Zhou et al. [30]. From the source viewpoint, we consider a point pixel to be dominated by the foreground pixel if it is visible, and conversely, if it is not visible, then the pixel is dominated by the background pixel. We use $1 - \alpha$ as the visibility for each pixel also called opacity, and the visibility indicates how much each pixel is occluded by its corresponding pixel in front of it (i.e., pixels with the same (x, y) position in the subsequent layers). The blending weight w_i for each layer is calculated as the product of the opacities of all layers that are positioned above it. Therefore, colors can be represented as follows:

$$c_i^s = w_i I_s + (1 - w_i) I_b,$$
$$w_i = \prod_{j>i} (1 - \alpha_j^s). \tag{2}$$

We adopt the method of warping each MPI layer to render a novel image. This warp operation $\mathcal{W}$ can transform an image from source viewpoint v_s to target viewpoint v_t:

$$(c_d^t, \alpha_d^t) = \mathcal{W}_{v_s \to v_t}(\delta_d, (c_d^s, \alpha_d^s)), \tag{3}$$

where δ_d denotes the amount of warping for the mth plane.

The warping operation $\mathcal{W}$ shifts the sampled pixels for each MPI layer from source viewpoint to the target viewpoint using bilinear interpolation.After the warping operation, we obtained the MPI $\{(c_1^t, \alpha_1^t), \ldots \ldots, (c_D^t, \alpha_D^t)\}$ at target viewpoint v_t.

Then the image $\hat{I}_t$ at target viewpoint is composited by the MPI at target viewpoint v_t using the over operation. The over operation uses alpha softly blending MPI layer at different depths. The specific cover operation is as follows:

$$\hat{I}_t = \sum_{i=1}^{D} (c_i^t \alpha_i^t \prod_{j=i+1}^{D} (1 - \alpha_j^t)). \tag{4}$$

3.2   Vision Transformer Backbone

Our network is based on the Vision Transformer (ViT) as the backbone [16]. We still use the encoder-decoder structure since view synthesis and depth estimation are inherently dense prediction tasks. A schematic overview of the complete architecture is shown in Fig. 1. Please refer to the supplementary materials for the implementation details.

Transformer Encoder. The Vision Transformer (ViT) encoder converts input sequence into a fixed vector, preserving spatial resolution via tokens, which correlate to patch positions. Each processed patch is referred to as a token, which takes on the role of a *word* [3]. In the ViT encoder, the token count is preserved, ensuring consistent spatial resolution for each patch across different transformer stages. The Multi-Head Self-Attention (MHSA) of ViT captures varying context within the sequence, with each attention head computing self-attention independently, enabling focus on different sequence parts. ViT achieves global receptiveness at each stage, unlike convolutional networks due to token interaction.

Furthermore, the ViT accepts position embedding obtained by processing all non-overlapping patches of size $p \times p$. The patches are initially flattened, then linearly projected. To compensate for the loss of spatial information from flattening, we incorporate location details through a position embedding operation. We also added a special token following the vanilla ViT in [3], which is dubbed *cls token*. This token serves as a sequence representation for classification task, aggregating global context information from the entire input sequence. In our view synthesis task, we refer to this special token as the *readout token* [16], which is useful to capture global information.

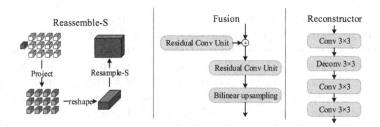

Fig. 2. *Left*: We reassemble tokens into feature maps with two spatial dimensions. *Center*: The fusion modules continuously upsample feature maps and fuse them in different scales. *Right*: The reconstructor is designed to convert the feature maps into the final MPI representation.

In the MPI representation, two pixels that are far apart may have the same disparity, i.e. they lie in the same disparity (depth) plane. The readout token can perform a self-attention operation with all the other tokens, which can better help establish a relationship between two pixels that are far apart, whereas other tokens usually pay more attention to the token information in their vicinity. The introduction of the readout token helps us construct a more reliable MPI representation. Suppose the input image size is $H \times W$ pixels, after the processing, $\left(\frac{HW}{p^2} + 1\right)$ tokens are obtained. The feature dimension of each token including the readout token is C.

Convolutional Decoder. Inspired by [16], we apply the convolutional decoder to our MPI representation task. The decoder collects the token sets output from all the transformer encoder layers to generate an MPI representation, i.e., RGBα maps. We first use linear mapping to handle the special token (see Fig. 2. (left)). Specifically, the readout token is concatenated to all other tokens along the channel dimension and fused through linear mapping to transmit information to other tokens. This step maps the tokens into image-like feature representations:

$$Project : \mathbb{R}^{\left(\frac{HW}{p^2}+1\right) \times C} \rightarrow \mathbb{R}^{\frac{HW}{p^2} \times C}. \tag{5}$$

Post special token processing, we use patch position data to reposition tokens, restoring an image-like representation. Specifically, a reshape operation generates feature maps with dimensions of $\frac{H}{p} \times \frac{W}{p} \times C$:

$$Reshape : \mathbb{R}^{\frac{HW}{p^2} \times C} \rightarrow \mathbb{R}^{\frac{H}{p} \times \frac{W}{p} \times C}. \tag{6}$$

We then perform spatial resampling on this feature representation and scale it into a $\frac{H}{s} \times \frac{W}{s}$ feature representation with $\hat{D}$ channels, i.e.:

$$Resample - s : \mathbb{R}^{\frac{H}{p} \times \frac{W}{p} \times C} \rightarrow \mathbb{R}^{\frac{H}{s} \times \frac{W}{s} \times \hat{D}}. \tag{7}$$

After the reshape operation, we map the feature representation to the $\hat{D}$ dimension through 1×1 convolution. Then we set $s = \{48, 24, 12, 6\}$ to resample the above features for each decoder layer. A strided convolution is used for spatial downsampling when $s \geq p$, while a transposed convolution is used for spatial upsampling when $s < p$. The deep transformer layer outputs are resampled at a lower resolution, whereas the shallow ones are at a higher resolution. Through the reassemble operation, our ViT is able to handle input of different resolutions. Please see the supplementary file for more details.

Using a residual structure, we sequentially fuse different resolution features over four stages, each time upsampling the input by a factor of two using bilinear interpolation (see Fig. 2. (center)). The size of feature map by the last fusion module is 1/3 of the original input image. To generate an MPI representation, we employ a reconstructor (see Fig. 2. (right)) to upscale these features back to the initial image size. The transpose convolution in the projection operation is used for this upsampling, and subsequent convolution layers resize the feature map's channel to 34.

The final output includes two types of maps, i.e., 31 alpha maps that each correspond to a disparity (depth) plane, and one background RGB image. Each type of image is scaled to match its corresponding effective range (e.g. [0, 1] for alpha images). The 31 alpha channels of the output give us $\alpha_2, \ldots, \alpha_M$. The back layer is always opaque, so $\alpha_1 = 1$ and need not be output from the network.

4   Experiments

We evaluate and demonstrate our used method on a real-captured surgical dataset by the da Vinci Surgical Robot System. We use PSNR, SSIM and LPIPS as evaluation metrics for quantitative comparisons.

4.1   Dataset and Training Objective

We evaluate our proposed method on the endoscopic stereo video clip of the distal gastric wall. We extracted a total of 2 clips, comprising 2295 frames of left and right views, with a spatial resolution of 624 × 480 for each view. We use the left view for the network input and the right view for the target prediction, i.e., label. We divided the dataset into a training set of 2254 frames and a test set of 41 frames. During the training, patches with a spatial size of 384 × 384 are extracted from the images, constructing 9016 training samples. We conduct an ablation study on our ViT modules through qualitative comparison.

For the training objective, we apply the perception loss [10] using the pretrained VGG-19 [19] to prevent blurry artifacts caused by the mean square error loss. More implementation details can be referred in the supplementary file.

4.2   Comparison

We compare two State-Of-The-Art (SOTA) MPI-based view synthesis methods by Tucker et al. [24] and Zhou et al. [30]. These two methods apply U-net backbones. For a fair comparison, we use the U-net network of the roughly equal parameters to our ViT backbone and retrain them on the same surgical training set.

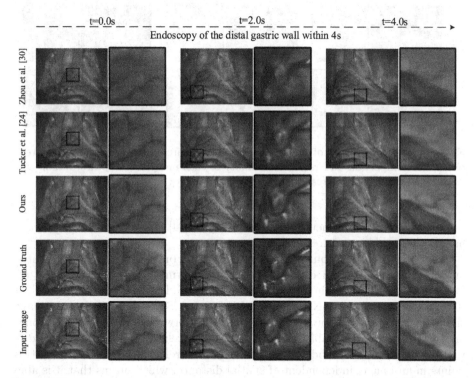

Fig. 3. Visual comparison of the synthesized results at target viewpoint with Zhou et al. [30] and Tucker et al. [24]. The results also demonstrate temporal changes within the surgical scene.

Figures 3 and 4 illustrates the qualitative results of the view synthesis of our method and the compared method. In the cases of Figs. 3 and 4, when rendering some finer blood vessels, there may be artifacts such as blurring and interruption of blood vessels. However, our method can capture global information to create a more reliable MPI representation, which alleviates these problems to a certain

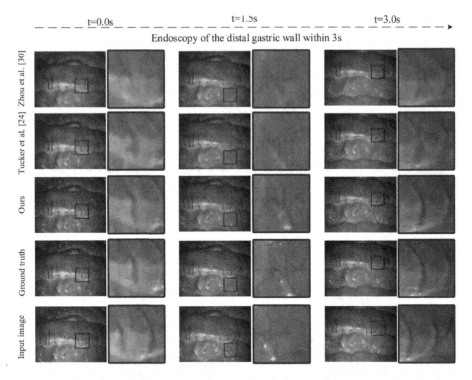

Fig. 4. Visual comparison of the synthesized results around regions with subtle textures. The comparison underscores the ability of each method to capture, retain, and reproduce the subtle textures integral.

extent. In contrast, the methods by Tucker et al. [24] and Zhou et al. [30] do not handle these thin structures well.

As shown in Table 1, our model generalizes well on the surgical dataset without any fine-tuning, and our ViT network performs better than Zhou et al. [30] (0.7892 dB increase in PSNR and 10% LPIPS drop) and Tucker et al. [24] (0.5209 dB increase in PSNR and 3% LPIPS drop). Since our ViT does not have these specific inductive biases as convolutional networks do, the convolutional networks are not as capable of building a global relationship between two distant pixels as our ViT model. The ViT learns the relationship between any two points in an image, independent of spatial distance, which means that it is able to determine pixels located in the same depth plane more accurately, regardless of whether they are far apart or close together.

4.3 Ablation Studies

In this section, we present the ablation studies on our loss function, readout token in the ViT model, and the setting of the number of depth planes.

Table 1. Quantitative comparison with SOTA methods.

Methods	PSNR ↑	SSIM ↑	LPIPS ↓
Zhou et al. [30]	26.4868±0.4904	0.8712±0.0173	0.1312±0.0355
Tucker et al. [24]	26.7531±0.5569	**0.8716**±0.0147	0.1218±0.0249
Ours	**27.2740**±0.4715	0.8599±0.0132	**0.1181**±0.0293

Table 2. Quantitative comparison with different settings of loss functions and numbers of depth planes in the MPI representation.

	PSNR ↑	SSIM ↑	LPIPS ↓
L1 loss	25.8060±1.2192	0.8515±0.0122	0.1947±0.0537
Ours w/o readout token	24.4255±2.7232	0.8537±0.0168	0.1238±0.0174
Ours ($D = 8$)	25.0054±0.8435	0.7683±0.0296	0.1692±0.0465
Ours ($D = 16$)	25.4128±0.2761	0.8074±0.0113	0.1432±0.0346
Ours ($D = 32$)	**27.2740**± 0.4715	**0.8599**±0.0132	**0.1181**±0.0293

Perceptual Loss. The influence of the perceptual loss is underscored through a comparative analysis between ViT using perceptual loss within the feature space and ViT using L1 loss within the RGB pixel space. As demonstrated in Table 2, the ViT model educated with perceptual loss demonstrates superior performance of preserving object structure and texture nuances in the view synthesis. Table 2 further provides quantitative evidence of the benefits associated with training using perceptual loss.

Readout Token in ViT. We present different ways of handing the readout token, with or without adding the readout token as shown in Table 2. From the results, it can be seen that adding a readout token greatly improves the results. The readout token can capture global information to build a more reliable MPI representation and tends to produce sharper results in the synthesized views.

Number of Depth Planes. Table 2 demonstrates that the efficacy of our model increases with the addition of more depth planes in the computed MPI representation. At present, we can only utilize 32 planes because of memory limitations, but this could be surpassed with upcoming hardware advancements or different network designs.

5   Conclusion

We present ViT-MPI, a novel vision synthesis method that combines the spatial geometric advantage of Multiplane Images (MPIs) with the powerful Vision Transformer (ViT) to provide an effective solution for single-view synthesis for surgical scenes. Experiment results show that our ViT-MPI outperforms existing single-view view synthesis methods in terms of visual quality and numerical metrics, and demonstrates preponderances in handling complex structures and nuance textures. Our approach also demonstrates how the Transformer structures can be effectively applied to the field of medical image analysis, opening up new research directions.

However, despite the remarkable progress of our approach, there are still some challenges to overcome. For example, for images with extreme perspective changes or complex backgrounds, our method may need further improvement. In the future, we will continue to explore more powerful view synthesis methods and try to apply ViT-MPI to other medical image processing tasks.

Acknowledgment. This work was supported by the Natural Science Foundation of China under Grants No. 61827805 and No. 62103092, and the Fundamental Research Funds for Central University under Grants No. N2108001.

References

1. Bello, I., Zoph, B., Vaswani, A., Shlens, J., Le, Q.V.: Attention augmented convolutional networks. In: Proceedings of the IEEE/CVF International Conference on Computer Vision, pp. 3286–3295 (2019)
2. Devlin, J., Chang, M.W., Lee, K., Toutanova, K.: BERT: pre-training of deep bidirectional transformers for language understanding. arXiv preprint: arXiv:1810.04805 (2018)
3. Dosovitskiy, A., et al.: An image is worth 16x16 words: transformers for image recognition at scale. arXiv preprint: arXiv:2010.11929 (2020)
4. Flynn, J., et al.: DeepView: view synthesis with learned gradient descent. In: Proceedings of the IEEE/CVF Conference on Computer Vision and Pattern Recognition, pp. 2367–2376 (2019)
5. Flynn, J., Neulander, I., Philbin, J., Snavely, N.: DeepStereo: learning to predict new views from the world's imagery. In: Proceedings of the IEEE Conference on Computer Vision and Pattern Recognition, pp. 5515–5524 (2016)
6. Fu, H., Gong, M., Wang, C., Batmanghelich, K., Tao, D.: Deep ordinal regression network for monocular depth estimation. In: Proceedings of the IEEE Conference on Computer Vision and Pattern Recognition, pp. 2002–2011 (2018)
7. Giulianotti, P.C., et al.: Robotics in general surgery: personal experience in a large community hospital. Arch. Surg. **138**(7), 777–784 (2003)
8. Hedman, P., Alsisan, S., Szeliski, R., Kopf, J.: Casual 3D photography. ACM Trans. Graph. (TOG) **36**(6), 1–15 (2017)
9. Hedman, P., Philip, J., Price, T., Frahm, J.M., Drettakis, G., Brostow, G.: Deep blending for free-viewpoint image-based rendering. ACM Trans. Graph. (TOG) **37**(6), 1–15 (2018)
10. Johnson, J., Alahi, A., Fei-Fei, L.: Perceptual losses for real-time style transfer and super-resolution. In: Leibe, B., Matas, J., Sebe, N., Welling, M. (eds.) ECCV 2016. LNCS, vol. 9906, pp. 694–711. Springer, Cham (2016). https://doi.org/10.1007/978-3-319-46475-6_43
11. Laina, I., Rupprecht, C., Belagiannis, V., Tombari, F., Navab, N.: Deeper depth prediction with fully convolutional residual networks. In: 2016 Fourth International Conference on 3D Vision (3DV), pp. 239–248. IEEE (2016)

12. LeCun, Y., Bengio, Y., Hinton, G.: Deep learning. Nature **521**(7553), 436–444 (2015)
13. Long, J., Shelhamer, E., Darrell, T.: Fully convolutional networks for semantic segmentation. In: Proceedings of the IEEE Conference on Computer Vision and Pattern Recognition, pp. 3431–3440 (2015)
14. Mildenhall, B., et al.: Local light field fusion: practical view synthesis with prescriptive sampling guidelines. ACM Trans. Graph. (TOG) **38**(4), 1–14 (2019)
15. Penner, E., Zhang, L.: Soft 3D reconstruction for view synthesis. ACM Trans. Graph. (TOG) **36**(6), 1–11 (2017)
16. Ranftl, R., Bochkovskiy, A., Koltun, V.: Vision transformers for dense prediction. In: Proceedings of the IEEE/CVF International Conference on Computer Vision, pp. 12179–12188 (2021)
17. Sermanet, P., Eigen, D., Zhang, X., Mathieu, M., Fergus, R., LeCun, Y.: OverFeat: integrated recognition, localization and detection using convolutional networks. arXiv preprint: arXiv:1312.6229 (2013)
18. Shao, R., Wu, G., Zhou, Y., Fu, Y., Fang, L., Liu, Y.: LocalTrans: a multiscale local transformer network for cross-resolution homography estimation. In: Proceedings of the IEEE/CVF International Conference on Computer Vision, pp. 14890–14899 (2021)
19. Simonyan, K., Zisserman, A.: Very deep convolutional networks for large-scale image recognition. arXiv preprint: arXiv:1409.1556 (2014)
20. Srinivasan, P.P., Tucker, R., Barron, J.T., Ramamoorthi, R., Ng, R., Snavely, N.: Pushing the boundaries of view extrapolation with multiplane images. In: Proceedings of the IEEE/CVF Conference on Computer Vision and Pattern Recognition, pp. 175–184 (2019)
21. Srinivasan, P.P., Wang, T., Sreelal, A., Ramamoorthi, R., Ng, R.: Learning to synthesize a 4D RGBD light field from a single image. In: Proceedings of the IEEE International Conference on Computer Vision, pp. 2243–2251 (2017)
22. Sun, K., Xiao, B., Liu, D., Wang, J.: Deep high-resolution representation learning for human pose estimation. In: Proceedings of the IEEE/CVF Conference on Computer Vision and Pattern Recognition, pp. 5693–5703 (2019)
23. Szeliski, R., Golland, P.: Stereo matching with transparency and matting. Int. J. Comput. Vision **32**(1), 45–61 (1999)
24. Tucker, R., Snavely, N.: Single-view view synthesis with multiplane images. In: Proceedings of the IEEE/CVF Conference on Computer Vision and Pattern Recognition, pp. 551–560 (2020)
25. Vaswani, A., et al.: Attention is all you need. In: Advances in Neural Information Processing Systems, vol. 30 (2017)
26. Wang, J., et al.: Deep high-resolution representation learning for visual recognition. IEEE Trans. Pattern Anal. Mach. Intell. **43**(10), 3349–3364 (2020)
27. Wiles, O., Gkioxari, G., Szeliski, R., Johnson, J.: SynSin: end-to-end view synthesis from a single image. In: Proceedings of the IEEE/CVF Conference on Computer Vision and Pattern Recognition, pp. 7467–7477 (2020)
28. Wu, G., Liu, Y., Fang, L., Chai, T.: Revisiting light field rendering with deep antialiasing neural network. IEEE Trans. Pattern Anal. Mach. Intell. **44**(9), 5430–5444 (2021)
29. Wu, G., Liu, Y., Fang, L., Dai, Q., Chai, T.: Light field reconstruction using convolutional network on epi and extended applications. IEEE Trans. Pattern Anal. Mach. Intell. **41**(7), 1681–1694 (2018)

30. Zhou, T., Tucker, R., Flynn, J., Fyffe, G., Snavely, N.: Stereo magnification: learning view synthesis using multiplane images. arXiv preprint: arXiv:1805.09817 (2018)
31. Zhou, Y., Wu, G., Fu, Y., Li, K., Liu, Y.: Cross-MPI: cross-scale stereo for image super-resolution using multiplane images. In: Proceedings of the IEEE/CVF Conference on Computer Vision and Pattern Recognition, pp. 14842–14851 (2021)
32. Zitnick, C.L., Kang, S.B., Uyttendaele, M., Winder, S., Szeliski, R.: High-quality video view interpolation using a layered representation. ACM Trans. Graph. (TOG) **23**(3), 600–608 (2004)

Dual-Domain Network for Restoring Images from Under-Display Cameras

Di Wang, Zhuoran Zheng, and Xiuyi Jia[✉]

School of Computer Science and Engineering, Nanjing University of Science and
Technology, Nanjing, China
`jiaxy@njust.edu.cn`

Abstract. With the increasing popularity of full-screen devices, phone
manufacturers have started placing cameras behind screens to increase
the percentage of the displays. However, this innovative approach, known
as under-display camera (UDC) technology, can lead to certain image
degradations. We introduce the dual-domain network (DNUDC) for
the purpose of UDC image restoration. We decompose the input into
reflection and illumination. An amplitude-phase mutual guided block is
designed to reconstruct the reflection and recover the attenuated high frequency features present in the frequency domain. Additionally, a multi-
scale hybrid dilated convolution block is also proposed to handle degradations at various scales and capture features with wide spatial extension. Our approach has been evaluated through extensive experiments,
demonstrating that our model consistently achieves superior results while
employing a relatively small number of parameters.

Keywords: Under-display camera · Retinex · Dual-domain network

1 Introduction

The UDC imaging system has emerged as a crucial technology for full-screen
smartphones. This method enables screen expansion, providing users with a
wider field of view and ultimately enhancing the user experience. Popular choices
for displays in this type of imaging systems include T-OLED and P-OLED. However, there are certain challenges associated with these displays. For instance,
T-OLED images often suffer from blur and noise [17], P-OLED images may
encounter issues such as color shift, low light, and noise. The degradation process of UDC images can be simulated by considering the convolution with a point
spread function (PSF), which represents the blurring effect, followed by the addition of noise. Based on the above modeling, some traditional deconvolution algorithms, such as Wiener Filter [4], can be applied to enhance the UDC images.
Such algorithms rely on pre-estimation of the PSFs, and finding a PSF with
universal applicability can be challenging. This difficulty arises because UDC
systems exhibit greater light diffusion compared to ordinary cameras, resulting
in more spatially dispersed PSFs [2]. Consequently, deconvolution-based algorithms often struggle to perform effectively on UDC tasks due to their limited
receptive field.

© The Author(s), under exclusive license to Springer Nature Singapore Pte Ltd. 2024
L. Fang et al. (Eds.): CICAI 2023, LNAI 14473, pp. 41–52, 2024.
https://doi.org/10.1007/978-981-99-8850-1_4

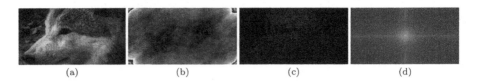

Fig. 1. (a) Clear image. (b) The amplitude information. (c) The phase information. (d) The spectrum of the image.

Recently, various computer vision processing models are continually evolving and advancing [8,13,22,27]. Nonetheless, UDC image restoration poses a greater level of complexity and challenge. Firstly, previous image-to-image mapping approaches have difficulty specializing the processing of different components. Secondly, some studies incorporate modules commonly utilized in other image enhancement tasks [23,29], without taking into account the specific degradations in UDC Systems. Thirdly, some methods introduce the domain knowledge of UDC into their models [2,29], which increases the complexity. In this paper, we introduce a novel DNUDC approach. We adopt a decomposition approach based on Retinex [10] to separate the input into illumination and reflection. The frequency domain features contain rich semantic information, as illustrated in Fig. 1. The amplitude is primarily responsible for encoding lightness and color information, while the phase provides insights into the inner structure [7], and the spectrum of the clear image exhibits sharp changes. Based on these observations, we enhance the spectrum of the reflection under the mutual guidance of amplitude and phase. In addition, it is also necessary to refine the features in the spatial domain and handle the pixel-level differences. We thus propose a multi-scale hybrid dilated convolution block to jointly restore the illumination and reflection. The dilated convolution with large receptive field can handle the degradations that span wide spatial extension. We set multi-scale processing branches to extract similar pattern information across scales. Our contributions can be outlined as follows:

- We introduce an innovative DNUDC approach, which can effectively restore degraded images captured by UDC imaging systems, and DNUDC is lightweight compared to previous models.
- An amplitude-phase mutual guided (APMG) block is introduced to reconstruct the reflection in the frequency domain, and restore the texture and color information.
- A multi-scale hybrid dilation convolution (MHDC) block is utilized to jointly enhance the illumination and reflection in the spatial domain.

2   Related Work

2.1   UDC Image Enhancement

Currently, there are relatively few studies on UDC image enhancement, and a comprehensive review [28] of UDC enhancement approaches has been provided

by Zhou et al. Many of the proposed methods improve on the U-Net structure [15,23] to restore UDC images. In addition, HrishikeshP et al. [6] utilize
dilated convolution and demonstrate its strong competitiveness. Zhou et al. [29]
use an MCIS [16] to capture paired images and design a modified version of the
U-Net model to recover the degraded images. Nevertheless, the obtained images
from their system can be unrealistic due to the lack of high dynamic range in
the monitors. Feng et al. [2] consider high dynamic range to ensure accurate representation of the data, and incorporate the domain knowledge into the model.
This approach may limit the application scenarios and increase the complexity
of the network.

2.2   Retinex-Based Visual Models

Retinex is a color vision model [10], which models the source image S as a
combination of reflection and the illumination. Mathematically, this process can
be modeled as:

$$S = R \circ I, \tag{1}$$

where R refers to the reflection map, and contains the physical properties of the
object. R should ideally contain textures and details. I denotes the illumination map, which encapsulates information regarding the brightness and contrast
resulting from external lighting conditions impacting the structure. $\circ$ represents
the multiplication operation. This theory has been widely used in image enhancement tasks. Fu et al. [3] use reflection to enhance the illumination, assuming that
the underlying structure of the illumination remains consistent across different
lighting conditions. Guo et al. [5] mine the illumination structure to refine the
enhanced results. Wei et al. [21] propose a framework that incorporates multiple
losses inspired by Retinex theory to facilitate the reconstruction process. These
methods all exploit the structure information in the degraded images, but the
artificial constraints may destroy the naturalness of the images.

2.3   Frequency Domain Enhancement Methods

Researches on combining frequency domain processing with deep learning have
been continuously raised. Mao et al. [14] connect the real and imaginary parts,
and design a residual module to capture diverse interactions. Lee-Thorp et al. [11]
use Fourier transform to replace the self-attention sublayer within Transformers [19]. Although many approaches use frequency domain information to assist
in image processing, they do not consider the semantic information provided by
phase and amplitude. Yu et al. [24] reconstruct the phase under the guidance of
amplitude, and obtain results with better texture details. Their reconstruction
process is one-way, while we further use the phase information to feed back the
enhancement of the amplitude.

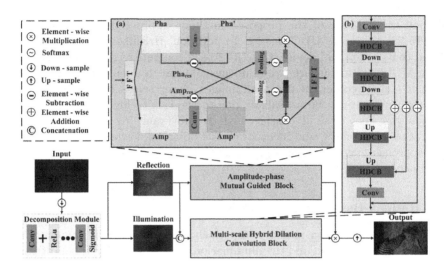

Fig. 2. Network structure of DNUDC. (a) is the amplitude-phase mutual guided block and (b) is the multi-scale hybrid dilation convolution block.

3   Methodology

We now present an overview of the architectural design of DNUDC. The overall structure is shown in Fig. 2. Given a degraded UDC image, we first decompose it into reflection R and illumination I. Next, we perform parallel frequency and spatial domain reconstruction of the reflection and illumination. Finally, the output is derived by multiplying the outputs of both branches.

3.1   Retinex-Based Image Decomposition

The structure of the decomposition network is depicted within the dashed box in Fig. 2. It uses multiple convolutional layers with the rectified linear units (ReLU) activation function to process the input. In the final convolutional layer, the channels are adjusted to 4, with the first three channels being taken as the reflection and the last channel as the illumination. We use the Sigmoid function to force the pixel intensity to be limited within the range [0,1].

3.2   Amplitude-Phase Mutual Guided Block

The frequency domain of an image encompasses both high-frequency and low-frequency components. The former contains valuable information pertaining to edges and fine details, while the latter is the approximate information of the image. Furthermore, the phase carries more detailed information about the structure and texture compared to the amplitude. It is less susceptible to noise interference and contrast distortions, ensuring the preservation of fine-scale features. The amplitude capturing the overall intensity and chromatic variations present [7]. We thus propose an amplitude-phase mutual guided (APMG) block to enhance the UDC images. For the reflection R obtained in the previous stage, APMG block first transforms it utilizing the fast Fourier transform (FFT) $\mathcal{F}(\cdot)$: $R_f = \mathcal{F}(R) = \mathcal{R} + j\mathcal{I}$, where $\mathcal{R}$ refers to the real part, $\mathcal{I}$ is the imaginary part. Then we can get the amplitude $\mathcal{A}$ and phase $\mathcal{P}$ as follows:

$$\mathcal{A}(p, q) = [\mathcal{R}^2(p, q) + \mathcal{I}^2(p, q)]^{1/2}, \tag{2}$$

$$\mathcal{P}(p, q) = arctan[\frac{\mathcal{I}(p, q)}{\mathcal{R}(p, q)}]. \tag{3}$$

Then, we refine the amplitude and phase by convolution, and obtain the corresponding residual information:

$$\mathcal{P}' = Conv(\mathcal{P}), \tag{4}$$

$$\mathcal{P}_{res} = \mathcal{P}' - \mathcal{P}, \tag{5}$$

here, $Conv$ denotes the convolution operator, $\mathcal{P}'$ is the refined phase, $\mathcal{P}_{res}$ is the residual information. We apply the same process to amplitude to obtain the refined amplitude A' and the corresponding residual information $\mathcal{A}_{res}$. We use the amplitude residual to compensate for the variations in color and brightness that may occur, and the phase residual serves as a guide in restoring the structure during the reconstruction of amplitude. Since the operations are similar, we only show the process of amplitude:

$$Pool_A = Softmax(Pooling(\mathcal{P}_{res})), \tag{6}$$

$$\mathcal{A}_{out} = \mathcal{A}' \odot Pool_A, \tag{7}$$

$$\mathcal{R}_{out}(p, q) = \mathcal{A}_{out}(p, q)cos\mathcal{P}_{out}(p, q), \tag{8}$$

$$\mathcal{I}_{out}(p, q) = \mathcal{A}_{out}(p, q)sin\mathcal{P}_{out}(p, q), \tag{9}$$

where $Pooling(\cdot)$ refers to the global average pooling, $\odot$ denotes the element-wise product. Finally, we transform $R_f' = \mathcal{R}_{out} + j\mathcal{I}_{out}$ by the inverse fast Fourier transform (IFFT) to get the reflection component R' after the amplitude-phase mutual guided enhancement. We present the degraded and the restored images, along with the corresponding frequency domain features in Fig. 3. It can be seen that our network can effectively reconstruct the phase and amplitude, and the restored spectrum is much clearer.

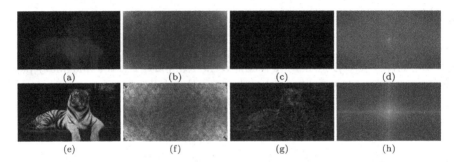

Fig. 3. The input and the output are in the first column. The remaining three columns are amplitude information, phase information, and spectrum, respectively.

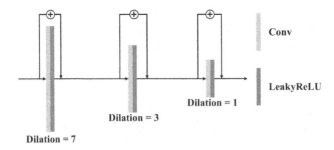

Fig. 4. Parameter settings for the original scale HDC block. The kernel size is 7×7, and the dilation rates are 7, 3, and 1, respectively.

3.3   Multi-scale Hybrid Dilation Convolution Block

The structure of MHDC block is shown at the bottom of Fig. 2. We adopt the multi-scale architecture to refine the reflection and the illumination, and the width and height ratio is maintained during processing (2048×1024). We downsample the input to 512×256 and 256×128, respectively. As mentioned in [12], the conventional dilation convolution has the drawback of sparsely sampling the feature map, which can result in grid effects and limited representation capacity. Therefore, we adopt the hybrid dilation convolution strategy [20], and design a hybrid dilation convolution (HDC) block for each scale. Figure 4 shows the architectural design of the HDC block at the original scale. For different scales, the kernel size and the dilation rates are set differently. The kernel size for medium scale (512×256) is 5×5, with dilation rates of 5, 3, and 1, respectively. The parameters for the small scale (256×128) are 3×3 and 3, 2, 1, respectively. There are residual connections between each layer in HDC block, and the sawtooth dilation rates achieve complete coverage of the receptive field. Therefore, DNUDC effectively expands the receptive field without information loss. We illustrate the visualizations of the input and output of MHDC block in Fig. 5, our network can enhance the fine-grained color and contrast using the multi-scale complementary information.

(a)   (b)   (c)   (d)

Fig. 5. Visualization of the intermediate results. (a) and (c) represent the input and output of the MHDC module, respectively. (b) and (d) are the corresponding heatmaps.

3.4   Training Loss

During training, DNUDC is trained using three loss functions. The first is the reconstruction loss $\mathcal{L}_{rec}$:

$$\mathcal{L}_{rec} = ||Y - \hat{Y}||_1, \tag{10}$$

where $\hat{Y}$ is the ground truth and Y is the output. The second is the frequency domain loss $\mathcal{L}_{fre}$:

$$\mathcal{L}_{fre} = ||\mathcal{P}(Y) - \mathcal{P}(\hat{Y})||_1 + ||\mathcal{A}(Y) - \mathcal{A}(\hat{Y})||_1, \tag{11}$$

where $\mathcal{P}(\cdot)$ denotes the phase, $\mathcal{A}(\cdot)$ is the amplitude. The third is the Retinex loss to satisfy the fundamental constraints of Retinex theory:

$$\mathcal{L}_{Ret} = ||R - \hat{R}||_1 + ||I - \hat{I}||_1 + ||\nabla I||_1, \tag{12}$$

where the first term is to ensure the reflection consistency, the third term aims to further enhance the smoothness of the illumination by considering the horizontal and vertical gradients (represented as ∇I). Thus, the total loss $\mathcal{L}$ is:

$$\mathcal{L} = \mathcal{L}_{rec} + \alpha \mathcal{L}_{fre} + \beta \mathcal{L}_{Ret}, \tag{13}$$

α is 0.1 and β is 0.01 in this paper.

4   Experiments

4.1   Datasets and Training Procedure

We train and evaluate the performance of the proposed DNUDC on two specific datasets: P-OLED and T-OLED [28]. During training, we use the Adam optimizer. Our DNUDC is trained with batch size of 4. We configure the number of epochs to be 3000 for the P-OLED and 2000 for T-OLED. We apply a decay strategy where the learning rate is reduced by a factor of 0.8 every 300 epochs for the P-OLED and every 200 epochs for T-OLED dataset with an initial learning rate set to 0.001. This decay schedule helps in fine-tuning the model over the training process to achieve better convergence and performance.

Table 1. Quantitative evaluations on two datasets. The symbol "↑" means that higher values are preferable, "↓" suggests that lower values are preferred.

Dataset	P-OLED				T-OLED				
Method	PSNR↑	SSIM↑	LPIPS↓	DISTS↓	PSNR↑	SSIM↑	LPIPS↓	DISTS↓	PARAM
PDCRN	30.68	0.9256	0.2217	0.2057	35.27	0.9637	0.1455	0.1372	4.7M
DAGF	31.19	0.9429	0.2185	0.1972	35.63	0.9679	0.1428	0.1353	1.1M
DE-UNet	29.49	0.9208	0.2359	0.2248	33.40	0.9456	0.1546	0.1428	8.9M
Restormer	30.23	0.9251	0.2307	0.2125	33.67	0.9538	0.1509	0.1417	25.31M
BNUDC	**32.04**	**0.9560**	0.1971	0.1876	**36.40**	**0.9754**	0.1362	0.1304	4.6M
DNUDC	31.82	0.9547	**0.1926**	**0.1829**	36.12	0.9742	**0.1343**	**0.1298**	**0.85**M

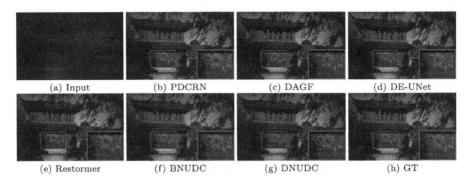

(a) Input   (b) PDCRN   (c) DAGF   (d) DE-UNet

(e) Restormer   (f) BNUDC   (g) DNUDC   (h) GT

Fig. 6. Test results on P-OLED dataset. Our method effectively restores fine details, resulting in visually pleasing outcomes.

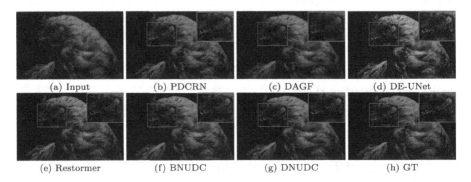

(a) Input   (b) PDCRN   (c) DAGF   (d) DE-UNet

(e) Restormer   (f) BNUDC   (g) DNUDC   (h) GT

Fig. 7. Test results on T-OLED dataset.

4.2   Results

We evaluate our DNUDC by conducting a series of experiments on the two datasets mentioned above. We select several representative methods as our comparison: PDCRN [6], DAGF [18], DE-UNet [29], BNUDC [9]. We also compare our network with the general image restoration model Restormer [25]. Several metrics are employed to assess the performance of DNUDC, including PSNR, SSIM, LPIPS [26] and DISTS [1]. All the quantitative results are reported in Table 1, and the corresponding visual comparisons can be found in Fig. 6 and 7.

Evaluation on P-OLED Dataset. According to Table 1, DNUDC has improved significantly compared to other methods, and only BNUDC achieves performance comparable to ours. DNUDC performs slightly lower in terms of PSNR and SSIM compared to BNUDC, but shows greater competitiveness in terms of LPIPS and DISTS, since the two metrics measure the perceptual simi-larity between textures of two images, and our network specifically enhances the texture details for UDC images.

Evaluation on T-OLED Dataset. All the models achieve superior results on the T-OLED dataset, which can be attributed to the slighter degradations in the T-OLED images compared to those in the P-OLED images. BNUDC and our DNUDC still achieve the best performance. PDCRN slightly changes the original color distribution of the image, DAGF still has blurred texture details, and the output of DE-UNet is not smooth, with some of the original contrast information lost during the recovery process.

Table 2. Results of the ablation experiments.

Decom	Pha-gudied	Amp-guided	APMG Block	MHDC Block	$\mathcal{L}_{fre}$	$\mathcal{L}_{Ret}$	PSNR
✓	✓			✓			30.84
✓		✓		✓			31.05
			✓	✓			30.68
✓				✓			29.84
✓			✓				30.23
✓			✓	✓			31.19
✓			✓	✓	✓		31.46
✓			✓	✓	✓	✓	**31.82**

4.3   Ablation Study

To showcase and analyze the validity of each module incorporated in DNUDC, we perform a series of experiments in the following manner:

Ablation Experiment of APMG Block. To verify the validity of APMG, we perform three ablation experiments. In the first ablation experiment we remove the phase-guided branch. For the second ablation experiment, we remove the amplitude-guided branch. In the third experiment, we remove the APMG block entirely.

Ablation Experiment of MHDC Block. We remove the MHDC block in this ablation experiment, and use the normal spatial domain convolution layers to replace the MHDC block.

Ablation Experiment of Decomposition Module. To verify the validity of our decomposition strategy, we do not decompose the input image and directly enhance it in the frequency and spatial domains in parallel with APMG block and MHDC block.

We also perform ablation experiments on the frequency domain loss $\mathcal{L}_{fre}$ and Retinex loss $\mathcal{L}_{Ret}$. The results shown in Table 2 indicate that each module of our proposed DNUDC is effective.

Table 3. Results of different scale settings in MHDC block.

Medium / Small	PSNR↑	SSIM↑	LPIPS↓	DISTS↓
768×384 / 512×256	**31.89**	0.9541	0.1959	0.1906
512×256 / 256×128	31.82	**0.9547**	**0.1926**	**0.1829**
256×128 / 128×64	31.47	0.9440	0.2008	0.1965
128×64 / 64×32	30.98	0.9329	0.2140	0.2076

Impact of Scale Settings in MHDC Block. To explore the impact of different scale settings, we down-sample the features to different resolutions in the medium-scale branch and the small-scale branch of MHDC block, as shown in Table 3. The experimental results indicate that DNUDC achieves optimal performance when the medium and small scales are set to 512×256 and 256×128, respectively. Importantly, this setup maintains the original width-to-height ratio of the image, inconsistent aspect ratio may corrupt the spatial structure in the multi-scale processing.

5   Conclusion

This paper introduces a novel dual-domain network designed specifically for the restoration of images captured using UDC imaging systems, and effectively addresses various degradations present in UDC images. Rather than learning the nonlinear mapping from the input to the output directly, we decompose the degraded image into illumination and reflection, and subsequently perform parallel dual domain enhancement of the components. We introduce the amplitude-phase mutual guided block to reconstruct the reflection, and jointly enhance the illumination and reflection utilizing the multi-scale hybrid dilation convolution block. Our DNUDC has undergone on various datasets, and the performance consistently demonstrates its extreme potential across different metrics.

Acknowledgements. This work was supported by National Natural Science Foundation of China (62176123) and Postgraduate Research & Practice Innovation Program of Jiangsu Province (KYCX22_0461).

References

1. Ding, K., Ma, K., Wang, S., Simoncelli, E.P.: Image quality assessment: unifying structure and texture similarity. IEEE Trans. Pattern Anal. Mach. Intell. **44**, 2567–2581 (2022)
2. Feng, R., Li, C., Chen, H., Li, S., Loy, C.C., Gu, J.: Removing diffraction image artifacts in under-display camera via dynamic skip connection network. In: CVPR, pp. 662–671 (2021)
3. Fu, X., Zeng, D., Huang, Y., Zhang, X.P., Ding, X.: A weighted variational model for simultaneous reflectance and illumination estimation. In: CVPR, pp. 2782–2790 (2016)
4. Goldstein, J.S., Reed, I.S., Scharf, L.L.: A multistage representation of the wiener filter based on orthogonal projections. IEEE Trans. Inf. Theory **44**, 2943–2959 (1998)
5. Guo, X., Li, Y., Ling, H.: Lime: low-light image enhancement via illumination map estimation. IEEE Trans. Image Process. **26**, 982–993 (2017)
6. HrishikeshP., S., Puthussery, D., Kuriakose, M., Jiji, C.V.: Transform domain pyramidal dilated convolution networks for restoration of under display camera images. In: ECCV, pp. 364–378 (2020)
7. Huang, J., et al.: Deep fourier-based exposure correction network with spatial-frequency interaction. In: ECCV. vol. 13679, pp. 163–180 (2022)
8. fan Jiang, Y., et al.: Enlightengan: Deep light enhancement without paired super-vision. IEEE Trans. Image Process. **30**, 2340–2349 (2021)
9. Koh, J., Lee, J., Yoon, S.: Bnudc: a two-branched deep neural network for restoring images from under-display cameras. In: CVPR, pp. 1950–1959 (2022)
10. Land, E.H.: The retinex theory of color vision. Sci. Am. **237**, 108–129 (1977)
11. Lee-Thorp, J., Ainslie, J., Eckstein, I., Ontanon, S.: FNet: Mixing tokens with fourier transforms. arXiv preprint arXiv:2105.03824 (2021)
12. Liu, P., Zhang, H., Zhang, K., Lin, L., Zuo, W.: Multi-level wavelet-cnn for image restoration. In: CVPR, pp. 773–782 (2018)
13. Liu, Y., Qin, Z., Anwar, S., Ji, P., Kim, D., Caldwell, S., Gedeon, T.: Invertible denoising network: a light solution for real noise removal. In: CVPR, pp. 13360–13369 (2021)
14. Mao, X., Liu, Y., Shen, W., Li, Q., Wang, Y.: Deep residual fourier transformation for single image deblurring. arXiv preprint arXiv:2111.11745 (2021)
15. Oh, Y., Park, G.Y., Chung, H., Cho, S., Cho, N.I.: Residual dilated u-net with spatially adaptive normalization for the restoration of under display camera images. Asia-Pacific Signal and Information Processing Association, pp. 151–157 (2021)
16. Peng, Y., Sun, Q., Dun, X., Wetzstein, G., Heidrich, W., Heide, F.: Learned large field-of-view imaging with thin-plate optics. ACM Trans. Graph. **38**, 1–14 (2019)
17. Qin, Z., Yeh, Y.W., Tsai, Y.H., Cheng, W.Y., Huang, Y.P., Shieh, H.P.D.: See-through image blurring of transparent oled display: diffraction analysis and oled pixel optimization. In: SID Symposium Digest of Technical Papers. vol. 47, pp. 393–396 (2016)
18. Sundar, V., Hegde, S., Kothandaraman, D., Mitra, K.: Deep atrous guided filter for image restoration in under display cameras. In: ECCV pp. 379–397 (2020)

19. Vaswani, A., et al.: Attention is all you need. arXiv preprint arXiv:1706.03762 (2017)
20. Wang, P., et al.: Understanding convolution for semantic segmentation. In: WACV, pp. 1451–1460 (2018)
21. Wei, C., Wang, W., Yang, W., Liu, J.: Deep retinex decomposition for low-light enhancement. arXiv preprint arXiv:1808.04560 (2018)
22. Wu, H., et al.: Contrastive learning for compact single image dehazing. In: CVPR, pp. 10546–10555 (2021)
23. Yang, Q., Liu, Y., Tang, J., Ku, T.: Residual and dense u-net for under-display camera restoration. In: ECCV, pp. 398–408 (2020)
24. Yu, H., Zheng, N., Zhou, M., Huang, J., Xiao, Z., Zhao, F.: Frequency and spatial dual guidance for image dehazing. In: ECCV. Lecture Notes in Computer Science, vol. 13679, pp. 181–198 (2022)
25. Zamir, S.W., Arora, A., Khan, S., Hayat, M., Khan, F.S., Yang, M.H.: Restormer: efficient transformer for high-resolution image restoration. In: CVPR, pp. 5728–5739 (2022)
26. Zhang, R., Isola, P., Efros, A.A., Shechtman, E., Wang, O.: The unreasonable effectivaeness of deep features as a perceptual metric. In: CVPR, pp. 586–595 (2018)
27. Zheng, Z., et al.: Ultra-high-definition image dehazing via multi-guided bilateral learning. In: CVPR, pp. 16185–16194 (2021)
28. Zhou, Y., Kwan, M., Tolentino, K., Emerton, N.: Udc 2020 challenge on image restoration of under-display camera: Methods and results. In: ECCV, pp. 337–351 (2020)
29. Zhou, Y., Ren, D., Emerton, N., Lim, S., Large, T.A.: Image restoration for under-display camera. In: CVPR, pp. 9175–9184 (2021)

Sliding Window Detection and Distance-Based Matching for Tracking on Gigapixel Images

Yichen Li[1], Qiankun Liu[1], Xiaoyong Wang[1], and Ying Fu[1,2(✉)]

[1] MIIT Key Laboratory of Complex -field Intelligent Sensing, Beijing Institute of Technology, Beijing 100081, China
{liyichen,liuqk3,wangxiaoyong,fuying}@bit.edu.cn
[2] Yangtze Delta Region Academy of Beijing Institute of Technology, Jiaxing 314019, China

Abstract. Object detection and tracking are representative tasks in the field of computer vision. Existing methods have achieved commendable results on common datasets, yet they struggle to adapt to gigapixel images that demand higher spatio-temporal resolution and offer a greater spatial visibility range. In this paper, we propose a novel method for object detection and tracking dedicated designed for gigapixel images. Specifically: 1) We devise a multi-scale sliding window for object detection, effectively tackling the constraints of hardware conditions and the wide range of object scales present in the images; 2) We introduce a region proposal-based dense crowd detection algorithm within the sliding window, significantly enhancing the detection performance in crowded and occlusion-rich scenes; 3) We propose a distance-based strategy in the online tracking algorithm, enabling the tracker to maintain high tracking accuracy and identity consistency. The experimental results demonstrate that our proposed method significantly outperforms the baseline methods in terms of both detection and tracking performance.

Keywords: Gigapixels · Object detection and tracking · Slide windows · Dense crowd detection · Online tracking

1 Introduction

Object Detection and Multi-Object Tracking (MOT) are classic tasks in the field of computer vision. Object detection aims to recognize and locate objects of interest in images or videos using bounding boxes. MOT aims at estimating the locations of interested objects in the given video while maintaining their identities consistently. Over the past few decades, thanks to the advancements in object detection, tracking-by-detection has become the mainstream approach for MOT task, dividing the MOT task into two stages: detection and tracking.

The existing datasets for object detection and tracking exhibit an inherent trade-off between wide-field coverage and high resolution, resulting in a lack of long-term analysis of crowd activities with clear local details within large-scale

L. Fang et al. (Eds.): CICAI 2023, LNAI 14473, pp. 53–65, 2024.
https://doi.org/10.1007/978-981-99-8850-1_5

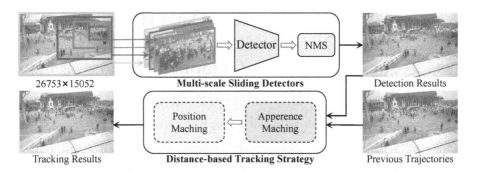

Fig. 1. Overall architecture. We divide MOT task into detection and tracking stages. In the first stage, we employ a multi-scale sliding window approach for detection, this process generates detection results for each window, which are merged through a simple post-processing step. In the second stage, we propose a distance-based tracking strategy to associate the detection results with previous trajectories.

spatio-temporal ranges. To address this limitation, the PANDA [28] dataset was introduced to advance related research in this field. Simultaneously, the introduction of the PANDA [28] dataset poses new challenges to traditional detection and tracking algorithms: 1) In terms of detection, algorithms are limited by hardware condition, and they struggle to handle gigapixel images that contain large-scale spatio-temporal information. In addition, the distribution of objects in gigapixel images is imbalanced and exhibits significant scale variations, making object detection difficult; 2) In terms of tracking, fast-moving objects with a wide range of motion are challenging to capture. These issues are particularly evident in low frame-rate gigapixel image videos, leading to object loss and identity inconsistency problems in MOT.

In response to the aforementioned difficulties faced in gigapixel images, we propose a tracking-by-detection method to address these challenges. As depicted in Fig. 1, we use sliding window for images detection, and the detection results are fed into the distance-based tracker for object trajectory association and matching. Specifically, we firstly propose a multi-scale sliding window detection method to address the issues of insufficient memory and varying object scales, than we employ a naive non-maximum suppression (NMS) pipeline for post-processing to avoid redundant predictions. Then we propose a distance-based online tracking strategy for associating object trajectories, utilizing the Euclidean distance to constrain the object trajectories and employing a lightweight online tracking method. This approach improves tracking accuracy while reducing computational costs. The contributions of this work are as follows:

– We propose a multi-scale sliding window method and introduce a dense crowd detection approach for the sliding window, which enables accurate object detection in gigapixel images.

- We propose a distance-based tracking strategy that incorporates both appearance and location information in the data association approach, which is more suitable for gigapixel image data.
- Experimental results demonstrate that the proposed method significantly outperforms the baseline methods. Particularly, our method exhibits higher recall and achieves higher accuracy in gigapixel images.

2   Related Work

This section briefly reviews related works from different aspects, including region proposal convolutional detectors and multi-object tracking.

2.1   Region Proposal Convolutional Detectors

The current mainstream methods for object detection can be categorized into one-stage [12,20,23] and two-stage [4,9,21,22,24,30] approaches. Among them, the two-stage methods strike a balance between model speed and accuracy, with Faster R-CNN [24] being the most classic example. It primarily performs object regression and classification based on region proposal networks (RPN) generated from the image. Subsequent improvements mainly focus on enhancing the performance and accuracy of the RPN. One method involves the introduction of an attention mechanism, such as CBAM [30], to improve the precision and quality of region proposals. Another approach is to combine the RPN with other techniques, such as the Cascade R-CNN [4], Libra R-CNN [22], and Grid R-CNN [21], all of which employ different strategies to improve RPN performance.

In the object detection on gigapixel images, to address the issue of computational efficiency associated with sliding window methods, we employ more lightweight region proposal convolutional detectors. Although the previous region proposal convolutional detectors [4,9,21,22,24,30] have achieved remarkable results in the field of object detection, existing methods lack research on scenarios with dense object occlusion. In this paper, we focus on dense crowd scenes and ultra-high resolution in the gigapixel images. We propose multi-scale sliding window and introduce a detector specifically designed for crowded scenarios, aiming to address the challenges posed by the gigapixe images.

2.2   Multi-object Tracking

Multi-Object Tracking (MOT) has emerged as a popular research area and has been dominated by tracking-by-detection paradigm. Existing detection and tracking methods primarily focus on data association of object detection results, and can be divided into offline and online methods. Offline methods [13,14,25,26] process the video in a batch way and can utilize the whole video information including the future frames to better handle the data association problem. While online methods [1–3,5,8,29,32] process the video frame-by-frame and generate trajectories only utilize the positional information and appearance features of the current frame's objects, resulting in lower computational complexity and reduced computational requirements compared to offline methods.

Tracking-by-detection methods primarily focus on the data association problem, and classical approaches often utilize graph-based algorithms to address such problems, including the Hungarian algorithm, network flow [7,25,31], and graph multicut [13,14,18,26]. In recent years, with the development of deep learning, lightweight online tracking methods have garnered increasing attention. Online methods typically employ the Hungarian algorithm for data association but emphasize joint learning of target detection with useful priors such as object motion [1,19,34], appearance features [5,17], occlusion maps [17], and object pose [27], these priors serve as conditions for data association.

Despite the commendable performance achieved by current MOT methods in specific scenarios, MOT tasks on gigapixel images are still limited by the significant movement range of objects. In this paper, we address this challenge by focusing on optimizing the association matching stage of the tracker to achieve improved tracking performance.

3 Methodology

The overview of the proposed detection and tracking network is shown in Fig. 1. Its workflow follows the conventional approach of tracking-by-detection. In order to address the issue of memory overflow caused by ultra-high resolution, we introduce a sliding window detection method , incorporating different scales of sliding windows based on the distribution pattern of object scales in the image. Furthermore, we propose a distance-based tracking strategy, these enhancements result in improved tracking accuracy and identity consistency.

3.1 Preliminary

Due to the challenge of highly overlapped dense objects in images, previous methods [4,9,21,22,24,30] have struggled to address this issue effectively. To tackle this problem, we introduce a dedicated detector called CrowdDet [6], which performs well in detecting dense crowds and can also generalize to less crowded scenes. The overall network structure of CrowdDet [6] closely resembles that of Faster R-CNN [24], comprising a backbone network, a region proposal network (RPN), and a classification-regression network.

Considering that multiple objects can overlap with each other, such as crowded areas, if each region proposal corresponds to single object, a set of overlapping region proposals can only be predicted as single object, leading to severe missed detections. To overcome this, CrowdDet [6] introduces instance set prediction, wherein each region proposal b_i is predicted as a set of K objects $P(b_i)$ rather than a single object. To minimize the distance between the predicted set and the ground truth, CrowdDet [6] further introduces the $EarthMover'sDistance$ (EMD) loss as

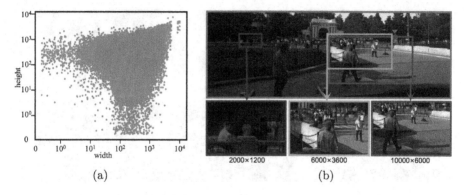

Fig. 2. Multi-scale Slide Window. (a) Distribution of object scales in gigapixel images. (b) Illustration of four scale sliding windows (Including the original image).

$$\mathcal{L}(b_i) = \min_{\pi \in \Pi} \sum_{k=1}^{K} [\mathcal{L}_{cls}(c_i^{(k)}, g_{\pi_k}) + \mathcal{L}_{reg}(l_i^{(k)}, g_{\pi_k})], \tag{1}$$

where π represents a certain permutation of $(1, 2, ..., K)$ whose k^{th} item is π_k; g_{π_k} is the π_k-th groundtruth box; $\mathcal{L}_{cls}(\cdot)$ and $\mathcal{L}_{reg}(\cdot)$ are classification loss and box regression loss respectively.

To mitigate the risk of duplicate predictions, CrowdDet [6] introduces two post-processing modules. The Set NMS is proposed to filter out duplicate predictions from different region proposals. Additionally, an optional Refinement module is incorporated in the network to eliminate duplicate predictions within the same region proposal. These post-processing modules aim to improve the precision and efficiency of the detection results by reducing duplicate outputs.

3.2   Multi-sclae Sliding Window

Different from conventional object detection, we are unable to directly input gigapixel images into the network due to computational limitations while resizing the images to fit the network's computation scale would result in a significant loss of image information. To address this challenge, we propose a multi-scale sliding window detection method.

In addition, the wide-field and ultra-high resolution also introduce significant scale variations in the objects, as depicted in Fig. 2(a). We have conducted an analysis of the object scale distribution in the PANDA dataset. The majority of objects are distributed within the range of 100×100 to 3000×3000 pixels. The largest objects in terms of scale can reach up to 3926×5068 pixels, while the smallest objects have dimensions as small as 116×155 pixels. Based on the aforementioned distribution pattern of object scales, we have designed four different scales of sliding windows, as shown in Fig. 2(b). The sliding windows are set to 2000×1200, 6000×3600, 10000×6000, and the original image size

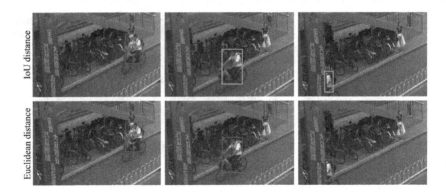

Fig. 3. Failure cases of IoU distance matching. The image shows the results of trajectory association using Euclidean distance (bottom row) and IoU distance (top row). When object (red boxes) undergo large-scale movements, the IoU distance matching fails, while the Euclidean distance provides a better solution to this problem. The different colored bounding boxes in the image represent the trajectory IDs of the objects, and a color change indicates a switch in object identity. (Color figure online)

respectively. This selection ensures that sliding windows of different scales can encompass complete objects of various sizes.

Furthermore, only using small-scale window to traverse the entire image, it would result in many sub-images without any objects and longer processing time. Hence, considering the depth variations in gigapixel images, we adopt a depth-based strategy, utilizing small-scale sliding windows in regions with higher depth and large-scale sliding windows in regions with lower depth. This approach aims to strike a balance between efficiency and accuracy while preserving the detailed features of the image to the maximum extent. Finally, we merge all the detection results from the sliding windows and perform post-processing with naive NMS to eliminate duplicate objects across different sliding windows.

3.3   Distance-Based Tracking Strategy

In online tracking algorithms, the association matching of object trajectories involves computing the affinity matrix between different objects and setting an affinity threshold to prevent incorrect associations. In this paper, we propose a distance-based tracking strategy, where trajectory association is performed by appearance features and positional information of the objects under the constraint of Euclidean distance threshold.

We have found that Euclidean distance allows for better handling of high-speed and large-scale object movements, therefore, we propose a distance-based two-stage matching approach. In the first stage, we assign detection results to existing trajectories by appearance features. Considering the possibility of large-scale object movements, we employ Euclidean distance as a constraint instead of IoU distance. This approach not only reduces computational complexity but also improves tracking performance compared to global appearance matching. To mitigate the risk of appearance matching failures, we introduce a second stage of positional information matching, where potential objects are classified as unconfirmed trajectories by Euclidean distance. The computation is

$$D_{Euclidean} = \frac{\sqrt{(x_{track} - x_{det})^2 + (y_{track} - y_{det})^2}}{D_{diag}}, \qquad (2)$$

where x_{track} and y_{track} is the center coordinates of the current trajectory in the previous frame, while D_{diag} denotes its diagonal length. x_{det} and y_{det} is the center coordinates of the detections in current frame. Additionally, we create a simplified re-identification dataset from PANDA [28], which yields appearance feature extraction models that are more compatible with gigapixel images in PANDA [28]. As illustrated in Fig. 3, our distance-based tracking strategy helps to mitigate issues associated with object loss.

4   Experiment

4.1   Datasets and Metrics

We utilize the PANDA [28] for both training and testing purposes. PANDA [28] is the first gigapixel image dataset, comprises 21 real-world scenes . The videos in PANDA [28] dataset have a resolution of 25k×14k, and cover an area exceeding $1km^2$. PANDA [28] provides 15974.6k bounding boxes, 111.8k fine-grained attribute labels and 12.7k trajectories. We select 20 scenes from the PANDA [28] and divide them equally into train and test set. Additionally, we fine-tune the ReID model using pedestrian trajectories from PANDA [28]. Following the setting of Market1501 [33], we select 100 pedestrian trajectories from each scene in the training data, with a maximum of 25 frames per trajectory, and images are resized to 128×256 pixels. In total, we obtain approximately 20,000 images, matching the scale of Market1501 [33]. For model fine-tuning, we evenly split the cropped images into train and test set.

We adopt the standard metrics of multi-object tracking for evaluation, including: Multi-Object Tracking Accuracy (MOTA), Multi-Object Tracking Precision (MOTP). Some other metrics, including Average Precision with IoU threshold (AP@0.5 and AP@0.5:0.95) and Average Recall (AR) are also introduced for the evaluation of object detection.

4.2   Implementation Details

We employ ResNet50 [11] as the backbone network and adopt the FPN [15] with RoIAlign [10] as the detection framework in CrowdDet [6], utilizing the same anchor scales as FPN [15]. During the training phase, we split the gigapixel images into sub-images using the multi-scale sliding window approach described in Sect. 3.2. We filter out images without any objects and bounding boxes with an overlap less than 50% with the ground truth at the edges of the window.

Table 1. Detection and Tracking Results Comparison.

Detector	Tracker	AP@0.5↑	AP@0.5:0.95↑	AR↑	MOTA↑	MOTP↑
Faster R-CNN [24]	DeepSORT [29]	50.5%	28.2%	34.7%	25.53%	76.67%
Cascade R-CNN [4]	DeepSORT [29]	50.4%	28.1%	35.3%	24.24%	76.31%
RetinaNet [16]	DeepSORT [29]	48.1%	26.2%	32.5%	15.57%	78.0%
Ours(single-scale)	DeepSORT [29]	53.3%	31.4%	39.2%	29.81%	80.17%
Ours	DeepSORT [29]	**70.1%**	**49.7%**	**54.3%**	35.17%	80.33%
Ours	Ours	**70.1%**	**49.7%**	**54.3%**	**40.85%**	**80.42%**

Fig. 4. Comparison of detection qualitative results under different test scenes in PANDA [28], We mark the densely crowded scenes with a yellow box and zoom in to enhance clarity. **(Best viewed on screen with zoom)**

In the detection experiments, we set the cardinality of the instance set K as 2. The threshold for Set NMS is set to 0.5, while the threshold for naive NMS is set to 0.7. The confidence threshold for the objects is set to 0.85. During the training process of the detection model, the batch size is set to 2, and the initial learning rate is set to $1e10^{-4}$. In the tracking experiments, we set the threshold for appearance affinity to 0.2 and the threshold for position affinity to 0.5. The detection model is trained for 30 epochs, and the decay factor is set to 0.1 at the 11th, 20th, and 30th epoch.

4.3 Comparsion with Other Method

We compare our method with the benchmark provided by PANDA [28], which selects Faster R-CNN [24], Cascade R-CNN [4], and RetinaNet [16] as the detectors and selects DeepSORT [29] as tracker. These detectors employed a single-scale sliding window approach and are fine-tuned on the PANDA [28] train set using pre-trained models based on COCO, while evaluation is performed on the test set. Experimental results are shown in Table 1. It can be observed that utilizing CrowdDet [6] for sliding window detection yields significant improvements. The metric AP@0.5 improved by 22%, AP@0.5:0.95 improved by 23.5%, and the AR improved by 21.8%. Compared to [4, 16, 24], employing a detector specifically designed for dense crowds is undoubtedly more suitable for capturing the localized and dense distribution of objects in gigapixel images. The higher recall rate also indicates that our method is capable of handling dense occlusion scenarios more effectively. In terms of the tracking task, the improved tracker outperforms the original DeepSORT [29], exhibiting a notable increase of 15.32% in MOTA, demonstrating the effectiveness of our proposed distance-based tracking strategy.

The qualitative detection results are shown in Fig. 4. The top two rows depict the results using single-scale sliding windows. Compared to Faster R-CNN [24], CrowdDet! [6] is less affected by crowding and occlusion. However, our proposed multi-scale sliding window approach is able to locate more interesting objects with higher precision, indicating the effectiveness of our approach. The qualitative results of MOT are presented in Fig. 5, which further demonstrate that our method ensures excellent tracking precision and identity consistency in scenarios with normal object motion and large-scale fast movements.

4.4   Ablation Study

To validate the effectiveness of the multi-scale sliding window approach, we conducted ablation experiments on detection using different scales of sliding windows, as shown in Table 2. Using small windows leads to excessively long detection times and the inability to detect large-scale objects, and even results in the segmentation of objects by multiple bounding boxes. On the other hand, using large windows reduces the detection time but sacrifices the detection of small-scale objects. Although using medium-scale windows can locate the majority of objects, it still fails to handle some extreme cases. Therefore, we combine multi-scale windows based on image depths, achieving the best detection results while maintaining a moderate processing time.

Table 2. Ablation experiments on multi-scale sliding window. The first four rows represent single-scale window detection experiments, while the last row represents multi-scale windows blended according to image depths. Time represents the average processing time on single NVIDIA RTX 3060 GPU, while Window Num denotes the average number of sliding windows per image.

Window Scale	AP@0.5↑	AR↑	Time(s)	Window Num
2000×1200	45.6%	28.4%	83.77	241
6000×3600	53.3%	31.46%	16.60	43
10000×6000	39.7%	25.1%	19.22	26
origin size	28.4%	22.3%	7.39	1
4 scale(no depth)	65.7%	52.1%	108.68	309
4 scale	70.1%	54.3%	49.8	145

Fig. 5. Comparison of visual tracking results between our method and Faster R-CNN+DeepSORT under different testing scenes in PANDA. The box color corresponds to the object ID. (**Best viewed on screen with zoom**)

Table 3. Ablation experiments on association matching. Note that we utilize the same set of detection results and perform tracking experiments by sequentially incorporating distance-based tracking strategy and fine-tuning of the ReID model.

Positional Info		Appearnce Info	MOTA↑	MOTP↑
Distance	Threshold	ReID model		
IoU	0.2	pretrain	35.17%	80.33%
Euclidean	2	pretrain	37.31%	79.99%
Euclidean	1	pretrain	38.01%	80.27%
Euclidean	0.5	pretrain	38.17%	80.35%
Euclidean	0.5	fine tune	**40.85%**	**80.42%**

The association matching is an important component of our distance-based tracking strategy. We conducted ablation experiments on the appearance and position information mentioned in the Sect. 3.3. The results in Table 3 (row $1^{st} - 2^{th}$) show that using Euclidean distance for position information association is beneficial for object tracking in gigapixel images compared to using IoU distance, and Table 3 (row $2^{nd} - 4^{th}$) show that the optimal threshold for position information affinity is found to be 0.5. Additionally, the comparison in Table 3 (row $4^{th} - 5^{th}$) demonstrates the effectiveness of fine-tuning on the ReID model.

5   Conclusion

In this paper, we focus on object detection and tracking in gigapixel images. We propose a multi-scale sliding window detection approach and utilize a crowd-aware detection algorithm as the window detector, effectively addresses the issue of insufficient GPU memory in current hardware devices, and achieves improved detection performance in gigapixel images. In terms of tracking, we propose the distance-based tracking strategy, optimize the affinity calculation in the association matching stage and utilize the Euclidean distance for association constraints, resulting in more accurate and stable tracking performance, while significantly reduces redundant computations and overheads. Experimental results demonstrate that our proposed method achieves significantly superior tracking and detection results compared to the baseline methods.

Acknowledgement. This work was supported by National Key R&D Program of China (2022YFC33 00704), and the National Natural Science Foundation of China under Grants (62171038, 62171042, and 62088101).

References

1. Bergmann, P., Meinhardt, T., Leal-Taixe, L.: Tracking without bells and whistles. In: Proceedings of the IEEE International Conference on Computer Vision, pp. 941–951 (2019)
2. Bewley, A., Ge, Z., Ott, L., Ramos, F., Upcroft, B.: Simple online and realtime tracking. In: Proceedings of the IEEE International Conference on Image Processing, pp. 3464–3468 (2016)
3. Brasó, G., Leal-Taixé, L.: Learning a neural solver for multiple object tracking. In: Proceedings of the IEEE Conference on Computer Vision and Pattern Recognition, pp. 6247–6257 (2020)
4. Cai, Z., Vasconcelos, N.: Cascade r-cnn: Delving into high quality object detection. In: Proceedings of the IEEE Conference on Computer Vision and Pattern Recognition, pp. 6154–6162 (2018)
5. Chu, P., Ling, H.: Famnet: joint learning of feature, affinity and multi-dimensional assignment for online multiple object tracking. In: Proceedings of the IEEE International Conference on Computer Vision, pp. 6172–6181 (2019)
6. Chu, X., Zheng, A., Zhang, X., Sun, J.: Detection in crowded scenes: one proposal, multiple predictions. In: Proceedings of the IEEE Conference on Computer Vision and Pattern Recognition, pp. 12214–12223 (2020)
7. Dehghan, A., Tian, Y., Torr, P.H., Shah, M.: Target identity-aware network flow for online multiple target tracking. In: Proceedings of the IEEE Conference on Computer Vision and Pattern Recognition, pp. 1146–1154 (2015)
8. Fang, K., Xiang, Y., Li, X., Savarese, S.: Recurrent autoregressive networks for online multi-object tracking. In: Proceedings of IEEE Winter Conference on Applications of Computer Vision, pp. 466–475 (2018)
9. Girshick, R.: Fast r-cnn. In: Proceedings of the IEEE International Conference on Computer Vision, pp. 1440–1448 (2015)
10. He, K., Gkioxari, G., Dollár, P., Girshick, R.: Mask R-CNN. In: Proceedings of the IEEE International Conference on Computer Vision, pp. 2961–2969 (2017)

11. He, K., Zhang, X., Ren, S., Sun, J.: Deep residual learning for image recognition. In: Proceedings of the IEEE Conference on Computer Vision and Pattern Recognition, pp. 770–778 (2016)
12. Hong, Y., Wei, K., Chen, L., Fu, Y.: Crafting object detection in very low light. In: Proceedings of the British Machine Vision Conference, p. 3 (2021)
13. Hornakova, A., Henschel, R., Rosenhahn, B., Swoboda, P.: Lifted disjoint paths with application in multiple object tracking. In: Proceedings of the IEEE International Conference on Machine Learning, pp. 4364–4375 (2020)
14. Keuper, M., Levinkov, E., Bonneel, N., Lavoué, G., Brox, T., Andres, B.: Efficient decomposition of image and mesh graphs by lifted multicuts. In: Proceedings of the IEEE International Conference on Computer Vision, pp. 1751–1759 (2015)
15. Lin, T.Y., Dollár, P., Girshick, R., He, K., Hariharan, B., Belongie, S.: Feature pyramid networks for object detection. In: Proceedings of the IEEE Conference on Computer Vision and Pattern Recognition, pp. 2117–2125 (2017)
16. Lin, T.Y., Goyal, P., Girshick, R., He, K., Dollár, P.: Focal loss for dense object detection. In: Proceedings of the IEEE International Conference on Computer Vision, pp. 2980–2988 (2017)
17. Liu, Q., et al.: Online multi-object tracking with unsupervised re-identification learning and occlusion estimation. Neurocomputing **483**, 333–347 (2022)
18. Liu, Q., Chu, Q., Liu, B., Yu, N.: Gsm: graph similarity model for multi-object tracking. In: Proceedings of the Twenty-Ninth International Joint Conference on Artificial Intelligence, pp. 530–536 (2020)
19. Liu, Q., Liu, B., Wu, Y., Li, W., Yu, N.: Real-time online multi-object tracking in compressed domain. arXiv preprint arXiv:2204.02081 (2022)
20. Liu, W., et al.: SSD: single shot multibox detector. In: Proceedings of European Conference on Computer Vision, pp. 21–37 (2016)
21. Lu, X., Li, B., Yue, Y., Li, Q., Yan, J.: Grid r-cnn. In: Proceedings of the IEEE Conference on Computer Vision and Pattern Recognition, pp. 7363–7372 (2019)
22. Pang, J., Chen, K., Shi, J., Feng, H., Ouyang, W., Lin, D.: Libra r-cnn: Towards balanced learning for object detection. In: Proceedings of the IEEE Conference on Computer Vision and Pattern Recognition, pp. 821–830 (2019)
23. Redmon, J., Divvala, S., Girshick, R., Farhadi, A.: You only look once: unified, real-time object detection. In: Proceedings of the IEEE Conference on Computer Vision and Pattern Recognition, pp. 779–788 (2016)
24. Ren, S., He, K., Girshick, R., Sun, J.: Faster r-cnn: Towards real-time object detection with region proposal networks. In: Proceedings of Advances in Neural Information Processing Systems, vol. 28 (2015)
25. Roshan Zamir, A., Dehghan, A., Shah, M.: Gmcp-tracker: global multi-object tracking using generalized minimum clique graphs. In: Proceedings of European Conference on Computer Vision, pp. 343–356 (2012)
26. Tang, S., Andriluka, M., Andres, B., Schiele, B.: Multiple people tracking by lifted multicut and person re-identification. In: Proceedings of the IEEE Conference on Computer Vision and Pattern Recognition, pp. 3539–3548 (2017)
27. Wang, M., Tighe, J., Modolo, D.: Combining detection and tracking for human pose estimation in videos. In: Proceedings of the IEEE Conference on Computer Vision and Pattern Recognition, pp. 11088–11096 (2020)
28. Wang, X., et al.: Panda: a gigapixel-level human-centric video dataset. In: Proceedings of the IEEE Conference on Computer Vision and Pattern Recognition, pp. 3268–3278 (2020)

29. Wojke, N., Bewley, A., Paulus, D.: Simple online and realtime tracking with a deep association metric. In: Proceedings of IEEE International Conference on Image Processing, pp. 3645–3649 (2017)
30. Woo, S., Park, J., Lee, J.Y., Kweon, I.S.: Cbam: convolutional block attention module. In: Proceedings of European Conference on Computer Vision, pp. 3–19 (2018)
31. Zhang, L., Li, Y., Nevatia, R.: Global data association for multi-object tracking using network flows. In: Proceedings of the IEEE Conference on Computer Vision and Pattern Recognition, pp. 1–8 (2008)
32. Zhang, Y., et al.: Bytetrack: Multi-object tracking by associating every detection box. In: Proceedings of European Conference on Computer Vision, pp. 1–21 (2022)
33. Zheng, L., Shen, L., Tian, L., Wang, S., Wang, J., Tian, Q.: Scalable person re-identification: A benchmark. In: Proceedings of the IEEE International Conference on Computer Vision, pp. 1116–1124 (2015)
34. Zhou, X., Koltun, V., Krähenbühl, P.: Tracking objects as points. In: Proceedings of European Conference on Computer Vision, pp. 474–490 (2020)

Robust Self-contact Detection Based on Keypoint Condition and ControlNet-Based Augmentation

He Zhang[1], Jianhui Zhao[1], Fan Li[1(✉)], Chao Tan[3], and Shuangpeng Sun[2]

[1] Beihang University, Beijing, China
{zhaojianhui,lifan}@buaa.edu.cn
[2] Tsinghua University, Beijing, China
[3] Weilan Tech Company, Beijing, China

Abstract. Existing self-contact detection methods have difficulty detecting dense per-vertex self-contact. Dataset collection for existing self-contact detection methods is costly and inefficient, as it requires different subjects to mimic the same pose. In this paper, we propose a generation-to-generalization approach by utilizing ControlNet to augment existing datasets. Based on that we develop a keypoint-conditioned neural network that can successfully infer per-vertex self-contact from a single image. With the extended dataset synthesized by ControlNet, our network requires only one real subject training data to achieve satisfactory individual generalization ability. Experiments verify the effectiveness of our proposed method and the improvement of the network's generalization with synthetic data.

Keywords: Self-Contact · Generation · Generalization

1 Introduction

Human self-contact plays a crucial role in various applications such as pose estimation, motion analysis, and behavior understanding. Human body parts inevitably touch each other in everyday life, yet self-contact has received limited attention in the 3D vision field. For example, current methods for pose detection only focus on aligning the human body model with the observation, neglecting the constraints of self-contact on pose ambiguity. As a result, accurately detecting self-contact is of paramount importance.

Self-contact detection faces two main challenges, the first being the insufficient availability of datasets. While existing human pose datasets [11,12,15,23] contain a limited amount of self-contact poses. Furthermore, there are few dedicated datasets for self-contact. Attempts to address this issue, Fieraru *et al.* [6] proposed HumanSC3D and FlickrSC3D, while Muller *et al.* [16] developed 3DCP and MTP. Collecting images of different people in varied scenes is a time-consuming task. These datasets still suffer from inaccurate labels and limited diversity.

L. Fang et al. (Eds.): CICAI 2023, LNAI 14473, pp. 66–77, 2024.
https://doi.org/10.1007/978-981-99-8850-1_6

With continuous development of AI Generated Content (AIGC), diffusion models have attracted widespread attention recently. Among them, Stable Diffusion [19], an influential image generation method, can synthesize high-quality images based on text descriptions. Based on Stable Diffusion, Zhang *et al.* [24] proposed ControlNet, a neural network structure to control pre-trained large diffusion models to support additional input conditions. The images synthesized by ControlNet can be conditioned by keypoints, depth map, normal map, edges, segmentation and so on. Hence, we proposed **G**eneration to **G**eneralization (G2G), which uses ControlNet instead of real subjects to mimic poses.

Constructing the mapping relationship between observations (color/depth images) and self-contact presents another challenge. Fieraru *et al.* have proposed the SCP method [6] for detecting contact region pairs in the human body mesh. While this method has shown promising results, it is only capable of detecting contact at a coarse level. Dense self-contact, which is defined on body mesh vertices, is required to more accurately describe the contact between body parts. However, dense self-contact is both sparse and high-resolution, making it difficult to establish a relationship with the image. As such, there is currently no method that can effectively detect dense self-contact with the required accuracy.

In order to address the aforementioned challenge, we present a novel approach called **R**obust **S**elf-**C**ontact **D**etection (RSCD). Our key insight is that self-contact is intricately linked to human pose. The sparsity and high resolution properties of self-contact necessitate the use of a high-resolution image feature space. Therefore, we introduce HR-Net [22] as an image encoder to obtain high-resolution features. The decoder is conditioned by 2D keypoints to associate images with self-contact constructs in a high-dimensional feature space. Cooperated with G2G, our method can achieve satisfactory generalization with training data of only one subject.

In summary, our contributions are:

- We propose G2G, which enhances the generalization of the network on the limited collected dataset.
- We propose RSCD, a novel network that detects per-vertices self-contact through keypoints-condition.

2   Related Work

2.1   Contact Detection

In recent years, contact detection has received more and more attention in computer vision. Contact is mainly divided into human-object contact, human-scene contact, and self-contact.

Human-object contact helps to analyze human behavior by understanding the interaction between individuals and objects. Gkioxari *et al.* [7] proposed detecting related objects while detecting the human body, while Chen *et al.* proposed HOT [5] for detecting full-body human-object contact.

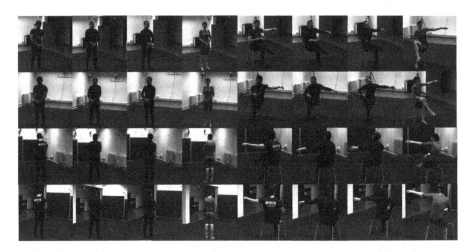

Fig. 1. Two examples of HumanSC3d. Each column contains multiview images of the same subject with the same pose. This dataset asks subjects to mimic the same poses with self-contact.

Human-scene contact reflects the interactions between individuals and their surrounding environment. In this regard, a series of methods have been proposed to detect the per-vertex contact, such as POSA [9], BSTRO [11], and HULC [20]. In pose estimation, leveraging human-scene contact plays a great role in mitigating penetration and optimizing human position.

Self-contact is an important factor in reducing pose ambiguity, as it is concerned with the intricacies of one's body language. Unlike the previous methods mentioned that required input from the surrounding scene, self-contact is solely focused on the human body itself. To detect self-contact, Fieraru *et al.* proposed SCP [6] where the body mesh is divided into several regions to help identify self-contact region pairs. Müller *et al.* [16] utilized both geodesic and Euclidean distances to calculate discrete self-contact labels, which they then used to extend SMPLify into SMPLify-DC to handle poses in self-contact. They also introduced TUCH, a method of regressing the human pose in self-contact situations. Together, these advancements in self-contact detection offer a more comprehensive approach to accurately capturing the nuances of the human pose within a given environment.

2.2   3D Body Dataset

There are many datasets available for 3D human body modeling, such as Human3.6m [12], FAUST [3], People-Snapshot [2], AMASS [15], THUman [23], ZJU-MoCap [18], PROX [8], and RICH [11], etc. However, most of these datasets lack information on body contacts, which is an important aspect of human body modeling. To address this issue, Fieraru *et al.* [6] created HumanSC3D and FlickrSC3D. The HumanSC3D dataset encompasses a collection of multiview videos featuring 172 distinct human actions. These actions are performed by a diverse group of three men and three women, as shown in Fig. 1. HumanSC3D uses 3D body scanners and 3D markers to accurately capture body shape and pose. They divided the surface of the human body into 75 regions and annotated self-contact in body part region pairs. However, this method is time-consuming and labor-intensive. FlickrSC3D collected 969 images from Flickr for further extension. But this is not able to provide satisfactory ground truth. To get a more accurate self-contact label, Muller *et al.* [16] created 3DCP and MTP. They annotated the per-vertex self-contact label on SMPL-X [17]. 3DCP needs to collect high-quality 3D scans to register SMPL-X. MTP asked subjects to mimic the pose as accurately as possible.

These data sets usually require different subjects to mimic different poses or high-quality 3D scans, as illustrated in Fig. 1. But even so, the clothing and scenes in the dataset are still relatively simple.

2.3   Generation for Generalization

A large amount of data is necessary for the model's generalization. There has been a growing interest in synthetic data to enhance the efficiency and accuracy of data collection and labeling. Sun *et al.* presented PersonX [21], which uses a pedestrian data synthesis engine to create images of individuals with various backgrounds, viewpoints, lighting conditions, and poses. For semantic segmentation tasks, SAIL-VOS [10] extracted datasets from GTA-V. Li *et al.* [13] verifies the improvement of the generalization ability of autonomous driving by using generated scenes. In 2022, NVIDIA introduced DRIVE Replicator [1], a tool for synthesizing autonomous driving data. Nevertheless, the effects of data synthesis and generation on the generalization ability of self-contact detection remain unclear.

3   Method

3.1   Definition

Similar to TUCH [16], given a mesh M with vertices M_V and two vertices $v_i \in M_V$ and $v_j \in M_V$, their Euclidean distance and geodesic distance are denoted as $Euclid(V_b^m, V_b^n)$ and $geo(V_b^m, V_b^n)$, respectively. These two vertices are in contact if $Euclid(V_b^m, V_b^n) \leq t_{euclid}$ and $geo(V_b^m, V_b^n) \geq t_{geo}$. Otherwise, these two vertices are not in contact.

We define self-contact on the SMPL [14] surface and denote self-contact as a vector $C \in \mathbb{R}^{6890}$ (6890 is the number of SMPL vertices). When the vertex v_i is in self-contact, its contact label c_i is 1, otherwise it is 0.

3.2   Self-contact Data Generation

The diversity of subjects, scenes, and poses within datasets significantly restricts the generalizability of self-contact detection. A majority of self-contact datasets

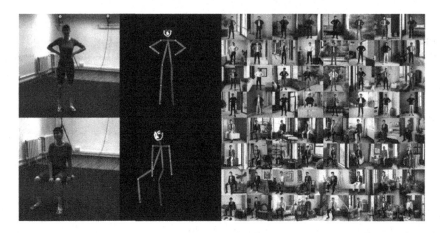

Fig. 2. ControlNet with OpenPose. ControlNet can generate images with different clothes, different scenes, and the same pose as the input image. All results are achieved with prompts: "different clothes, different scenes".

ask different subjects to perform the same poses, as seen in HumanSC3D and MTP. Such datasets present limited variability, as depicted in Fig. 1. Collecting images of subjects performing distinct actions in dissimilar surroundings is both labor-intensive and time-consuming. However, the advent of Stable Diffusion [19] and ControlNet [24] offers a viable solution for boosting detection generalization through data expansion and generation.

Stable Diffusion is capable of producing high-quality images from textual descriptions, while ControlNet enhances this large diffusion model through its ability to regulate pre-trained models based on a variety of input conditions such as normal maps, edge maps, segmentation maps, depth maps, and keypoints. To mimic a pose, we utilize the generation model instead of subjects for our task. More specifically, ControlNet operates on input images from the existing self-contact dataset. We employ the keypoints-condition mode to identify keypoints within the inputted image and generate new images with the same pose. This methodology allows us to produce a wide array of images depicting different scenes, various subjects, and the same pose, as illustrated in Fig. 2, with significant reductions in data collection costs as it no longer requires intensive pose mimicking, as was the case with practices in HumanSC3d and MTP.

To ensure high-quality source images, we have opted to use the HumanSC3d dataset. As ControlNet relies on OpenPose detection, the generation of hand poses may be suboptimal. As such, the generated images tend to better preserve limb contact semantics but may fall short in the preservation of finger contact. To ensure ample resources for our task, we generated over 10k+ images and further curated a set of 2,000 images that showcased superior contact semantics, as shown in Fig. 2.

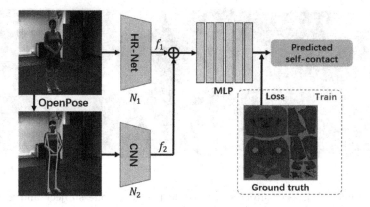

Fig. 3. Pipline. Given an input image, we first detect keypoints by OpenPose. Subsequently, the image and the keypoints are encoded by HR-Net and a convolutional neural network (CNN). The features extracted from the image and keypoints are fused. $\oplus$ is a concatenation operator. Finally, a multilayer perceptron (MLP) is employed to predict dense per-vertex contact.

3.3 Method: RSCD

In this section, we proposed a novel keypoint-conditioned self-contact detection method called RSCD. The self-contact region exclusively exists in the invisible area and has a robust correlation with the human body's keypoint position. We assert that these correlations can be learned implicitly by the network. We aim to predict the self-contact vector C from a single image I.

As the self-contact is sparse, high-resolution features are essential for per-vertex contact label prediction. Therefore, we employ HR-Net [22] as the image encoder N_1. The visual features f_1 are extracted from the input image I by network N_1. The human body's 2D keypoints depict the body's posture to a certain degree and have a strong association with self-contact. Thus, we detected the keypoints kp using OpenPose [4]. Network N_2 extracts feature f_2 from kp. By utilizing f_1 and f_2, an MLP is employed to predict the per-vertex self-contact label vector $C \in \mathbb{R}^{6890}$. We use the UV map of SMPL to mark the self-contact more clearly. The pipeline is illustrated in Fig. 3.

We train our pipeline using the mean squared error loss (MSE).

4 Experiments

4.1 Implementation Details

For network training, the whole pipeline is implemented with PyTorch. We trained the networks on two RTX3090 for 1400 epochs. The optimizer is Adam. The initial learning rate is 1e-4, which decreases every 200 epochs. The image encoder is initialized with pre-trained HR-Net weights.

Fig. 4. Results of unseen subjects. We trained on only one subject and generated images and tested on unseen subjects to evaluate the generalization. The two images in the first row are from HumanSC3D. The two images in the second row are real-world data.

We finally generated a total of 2662 images of 30 poses as the generation dataset. Due to the generative capability of ControlNet, the number of images for each pose is not the same. We selected 510 multi-view images of subject s06 in the HumanSC3D. The image in Fig. 3 shows one of the examples of subject s06. We merge these data with the generation dataset as the training set. We test the generalization of the network on subjects s01, s02, and s03 in HumanSC3D. In addition, we also did the test on real data.

We chose F1, recall, and precision as the quantitative metrics for evaluation. However, most body vertices do not have contact, and their labels are assigned as 0, the network may still produce relatively high scores even when contact is not detected. Hence we have also incorporated the contact area IOU as an additional quantitative metric, as it can be more representative of contacted area overlap accuracy.

4.2   Results

For our task, we only need images of one subject (s06 of HumanSC3D). Then ControlNet is applied to generate images with the same pose but different clothes and scenes. Our network is trained on the above images. As no prior approach has been found capable of detecting dense self-contact, our method was compared solely with the ground truth. The outcomes for previously unseen subjects are depicted in Fig. 4. Images in Fig. 4 include other subjects in HumanSC3D and real captured data. This figure serves as evidence that our algorithm demonstrates strong generalization across different individuals, regardless of clothing color or background environment. For further qualitative and quantitative results, please refer to the following sections.

4.3 Evaluation on Keypoint Condition

We present an evaluation of the impact of the keypoint condition on our method. The qualitative and quantitative results are shown in Fig. 5 and Table 1, respectively. Table 1 shows that with keypoint condition, all four metrics achieve better performances. In particular, the IOU metric achieves a quite significant improvement, which demonstrates that the contacted areas overlapped with the ground truth more accurately after keypoint conditioning. Moreover, this improvement can also be illustrated with several typical cases in Fig. 5. In which, we highlight the failed results without keypoint conditions with blue circles. This improvement can be attributed to the fact that self-contact is closely related to human poses, and the keypoint condition enables the construction of the relationship between the input image and the pose. The supervision of key points makes it easier for the network to fit onto training data, and it also plays an important role in helping network generalization.

Table 1. Quantitative comparison. Evaluation on keypoint condition.

Metrics	Overfitting on training data				Generalization			
	Precision	Recall	F1	IOU	Precision	Recall	F1	IOU
W/o	0.9997	0.9998	0.9997	0.9887	0.9646	0.9610	0.9593	0.6637
W (RSCD)	**0.9999**	**0.9999**	**0.9999**	**0.9928**	**0.9753**	**0.9634**	**0.9682**	**0.7251**

5 Ablation Studies

5.1 Generation to Generalization

In this subsection, we discuss the impact of the generation dataset. We compared five different proportions:0%, 25%, 50%, 75%, 100%. Figure 6 shows the quantitative results of different proportions. With the increase of generation data, the growth of F1, recall, precision, and IOU curves gradually slows down. With the increase of generation data, the values of F1, recall, precision, and IOU generally grow. Especially for IOU, when the generated data is not included at all (0%), the IOU value is approximately 0.2, which means the network hardly has any generalization performance. But it is boosted to 0.6 after the first 25% generated data is included. As the generated data ratio increases, the generalization becomes more and more effective. The same evidence can be also demonstrated in Fig. 7.

In our experiment, we found that by utilizing generated data, we were able to improve the generalization of the network when given images of only one subject. The experiment verified the effectiveness of generated data in improving the network's generalization capabilities. G2G makes it possible for us to improve network generalization under limited data.

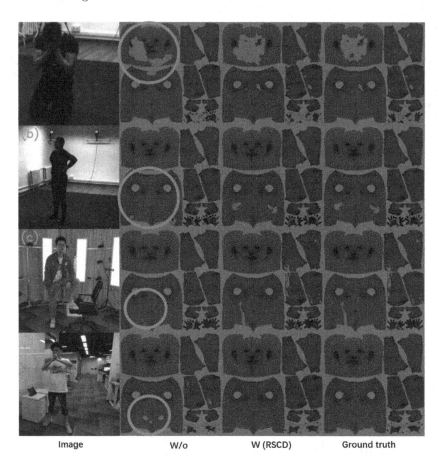

Image   W/o   W (RSCD)   Ground truth

Fig. 5. Qualitative comparison. Evaluation on keypoint condition.

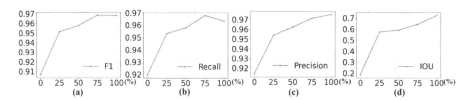

Fig. 6. Quantitative results. Ablation on generation dataset proportion. (a)–(d) represents F1, recall, precision, and IOU, respectively.

6   Limitations

Motion blur significantly impacts the accuracy of OpenPose keypoint detection, subsequently influencing the outcomes of our approach. Furthermore, it is imper-

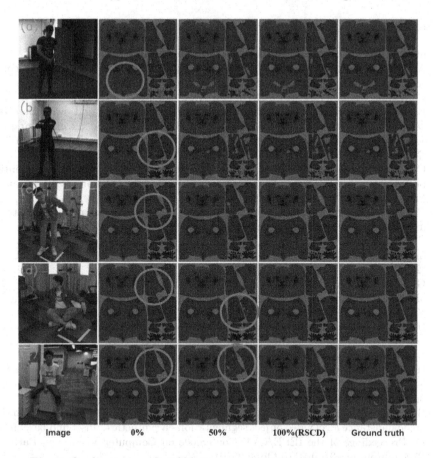

Fig. 7. Qualitative results. Ablation on generation dataset proportion.

ative to note that our method is not applicable in scenarios where body parts are excessively obstructed.

7 Conclusions

In this paper, given the scarcity of datasets, we utilize ControlNet to synthesize images for augmenting the training data. Additionally, we propose a robust self-contact detection technique, conditioned on keypoints, for identifying dense per-vertex self-contact. The generated images significantly improve generalization, enabling our network to perform well even when the training data only contains data from a single subject. Our experiments demonstrate the efficacy of our approach, highlighting the benefits of the generated data for generalization. We anticipate that our method will prove valuable for motion analysis and behavior recognition.

References

1. https://developer.nvidia.com/zh-cn/drive/drive-sim
2. Alldieck, T., Magnor, M., Xu, W., Theobalt, C., Pons-Moll, G.: Video based reconstruction of 3d people models. In: Proceedings of the IEEE/CVF Conference on Computer Vision and Pattern Recognition, pp. 8387–8397 (2018)
3. Bogo, F., Romero, J., Loper, M., Black, M.J.: Faust: dataset and evaluation for 3d mesh registration. In: Proceedings of the IEEE/CVF Conference on Computer Vision and Pattern Recognition, pp. 3794–3801 (2014). https://doi.org/10.1109/CVPR.2014.491
4. Cao, Z., Hidalgo, G., Simon, T., Wei, S.E., Sheikh, Y.: Openpose: realtime multiperson 2d pose estimation using part affinity fields. IEEE Trans. Pattern Anal. Mach. Intell. **43**(1), 172–186 (2021)
5. Chen, Y., Dwivedi, S.K., Black, M.J., Tzionas, D.: Detecting human-object contact in images. arXiv preprint arXiv:2303.03373 pp. 17100–17110 (2023)
6. Fieraru, M., Zanfir, M., Oneata, E., Popa, A.I., Olaru, V., Sminchisescu, C.: Learning complex 3d human self-contact. Proc. AAAI Conf. Artif. Intell. **35**, 1343–1351 (2021)
7. Gkioxari, G., Girshick, R., Dollár, P., He, K.: Detecting and recognizing humanobject interactions. In: Proceedings of the IEEE/CVF Conference on Computer Vision and Pattern Recognition, pp. 8359–8367 (June 2018)
8. Hassan, M., Choutas, V., Tzionas, D., Black, M.J.: Resolving 3d human pose ambiguities with 3d scene constraints. In: Proceedings of the IEEE/CVF International Conference on Computer Vision, pp. 2282–2292 (2019)
9. Hassan, M., Ghosh, P., Tesch, J., Tzionas, D., Black, M.J.: Populating 3d scenes by learning human-scene interaction. In: Proceedings of the IEEE/CVF Conference on Computer Vision and Pattern Recognition, pp. 14708–14718 (2021)
10. Hu, Y.T., Chen, H.S., Hui, K., Huang, J.B., Schwing, A.G.: Sail-vos: semantic amodal instance level video object segmentation - a synthetic dataset and baselines. In: Proceedings of the IEEE/CVF Conference on Computer Vision and Pattern Recognition, pp. 3100–3110 (June 2019)
11. Huang, C.H.P., et al.: Capturing and inferring dense full-body human-scene contact. In: Proceedings of the IEEE/CVF Conference on Computer Vision and Pattern Recognition, pp. 13274–13285 (Jun 2022)
12. Ionescu, C., Papava, D., Olaru, V., Sminchisescu, C.: Human3.6m: large scale datasets and predictive methods for 3d human sensing in natural environments. IEEE Trans. Pattern Anal. Mach. Intell. **36**(7), 1325–1339 (2014)
13. Li, Q., Peng, Z., Zhang, Q., Qiu, C., Liu, C., Zhou, B.: Improving the generalization of end-to-end driving through procedural generation. arXiv preprint arXiv:2012.13681 (2020)
14. Loper, M., Mahmood, N., Romero, J., Pons-Moll, G., Black, M.J.: Smpl: a skinned multi-person linear model. ACM Trans. Graph. (TOG) **34**(6), 248:1–248:16 (2015)
15. Mahmood, N., Ghorbani, N., Troje, N.F., Pons-Moll, G., Black, M.: Amass: archive of motion capture as surface shapes. In: Proceedings of the IEEE/CVF International Conference on Computer Vision, pp. 5441–5450 (2019)
16. Müller, L., Osman, A.A.A., Tang, S., Huang, C.H.P., Black, M.J.: On self-contact and human pose. In: Proceedings IEEE/CVF Conference on Computer Vision and Pattern Recognition, pp. 9990–9999 (Jun 2021)
17. Pavlakos, G., et al.: Expressive body capture: 3d hands, face, and body from a single image. In: Proceedings of the IEEE/CVF Conference on Computer Vision and Pattern Recognition, pp. 10975–10985 (2019)

18. Peng, S., et al.: Neural body: implicit neural representations with structured latent codes for novel view synthesis of dynamic humans. In: Proceedings of the IEEE/CVF Conference on Computer Vision and Pattern Recognition, pp. 9050–9059 (2021)
19. Rombach, R., Blattmann, A., Lorenz, D., Esser, P., Ommer, B.: High-resolution image synthesis with latent diffusion models. In: Proceedings of the IEEE/CVF Conference on Computer Vision and Pattern Recognition (CVPR), pp. 10674–10685 (2022)
20. Shimada, S., Golyanik, V., Li, Z., Pérez, P., Xu, W., Theobalt, C.: Hulc: 3d human motion capture with pose manifold sampling and dense contact guidance. In: Proceedings of the European Conference on Computer Vision, pp. 516–533 (Jun 2022)
21. Sun, X., Zheng, L.: Dissecting person re-identification from the viewpoint of viewpoint. In: Proceedings of the IEEE/CVF Conference on Computer Vision and Pattern Recognition, pp. 608–617 (2019). https://doi.org/10.1109/CVPR.2019.00070
22. Wang, J., et al.: Deep high-resolution representation learning for visual recognition. IEEE Trans. Pattern Anal. Mach. Intell. **43**(10), 3349–3364 (2020)
23. Yu, T., Zheng, Z., Guo, K., Liu, P., Dai, Q., Liu, Y.: Function4d: real-time human volumetric capture from very sparse consumer RGBD sensors. In: Proceedings of the IEEE/CVF Conference on Computer Vision and Pattern Recognition, pp. 5742–5752 (June 2021)
24. Zhang, L., Agrawala, M.: Adding conditional control to text-to-image diffusion models (2023)

Explicit Composition of Neural Radiance Fields by Learning an Occlusion Field

Xunsen Sun, Hao Zhu$^{(\boxtimes)}$, Yuanxun Lu, and Xun Cao

Nanjing University, Nanjing, Suzhou, China
`zh@nju.edu.cn`

Abstract. The neural radiance field (NeRF) is an implicit representation of the appearance and shape of objects based on neural networks. While numerous studies have shown the great performance of NeRF on tasks like free-view synthesis, it remains a challenge to composite multiple objects depicted by NeRF models. Different from previous works that focus on decomposing separate scenes from a compositional NeRF, we study how to naturally composite two trained NeRF models without combined scene images for supervision. Specifically, we propose a novel framework that learns an occlusion field (OCF) to model the occupancy property of the object. A dedicated compositional rendering equation and loss functions are then designed to learn an accurate occlusion field. With the trained occlusion field, the source object represented by NeRF can be explicitly scaled, moved, and merged into the target NeRF. Our method can synthesize plausible merged results with accurate occlusion relation and natural transition at occluding boundaries, and even work for challenging objects like hairs and leaf clusters. Experiments show that our method is superior to the previous methods, providing a new solution for the efficient and effective composition of NeRF models.

Keywords: Neural Radiance Fields · Neural Rendering · Composition

1 Introduction

Novel view synthesis from a set of calibrated images is a significant task that can be used in many applications like virtual reality and 3D simulation. Recently, neural radiance field (NeRF) [14] and its variants achieve impressive performance in synthesizing high-quality free-view images. NeRF represents the scene as a continuous volumetric scene function that predicts the volume density and radiance on the condition of spatial location and viewing direction. The follow-up works further improve its performance in rendering quality [1,7,25], speed [3,10,15,21] and feasibility [4,9,19,22,33,34]. Though huge improvements are made, the approach to merging two trained NeRF models is rarely explored, preventing NeRF from being used in interactive applications.

The straightforward way to composite two NeRF models is weighted summing the value of density and color before the volume rendering [11,27,29], or

L. Fang et al. (Eds.): CICAI 2023, LNAI 14473, pp. 78–90, 2024.
https://doi.org/10.1007/978-981-99-8850-1_7

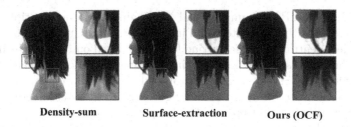

Density-sum   **Surface-extraction**   **Ours (OCF)**

Fig. 1. Density-sum-based methods generate cloud-like artifacts in composited images and surface-extraction approaches cannot produce natural transitions at the occluding boundaries, while our OCF can synthesize photo-realistic transitions at the boundaries.

extracting surface in advance for occlusion check [32]. However, these strategies may lead to unnatural transitions at the edges and cause obvious artifacts for scenes containing complex occlusion, as shown in Fig. 1. Another strategy is to train a neural network to combine two NeRF models by learning from the combined images [11,28,29], while these models require to be trained with the composited images and cannot be generalized to arbitrary trained NeRF models.

In this paper, we study how to composite two arbitrary pre-trained NeRF models realistically and efficiently. We propose to learn an occlusion field (OCF) to composite two NeRF models without knowing composited images as supervision. Given a source and target NeRF model, the MLP-based OCF could be trained by minimizing the loss function that is composed of a photometric loss, matting loss, geometric loss, and a regularization term. A novel compositional rendering equation is presented to render natural and realistic merged images from the two NeRF inputs and OCF.

Our contributions can be summarized as follows:

- We explore how to composite two arbitrary pre-trained NeRF models realistically without knowing composited images as supervision.
- The occlusion field is proposed to model the occupancy property of objects, which enables high rendering quality for complex objects like hairs and leaves.
- A novel compositional rendering equation and loss functions are designed to learn an accurate occlusion field. The experiments show the effectiveness of our method on both synthetic scenes and real-captured scenes.

2   Related Work

Neural Implicit 3D Representations: The representative works of neural implicit 3D representations include signed distance functions (SDF) [8,18], occupancy fields [5,13], and neural radiance field (NeRF) [1,11,14,30]. The 3D objects represented by implicit models are difficult to be spatially composite, while explicit models can easily do so, which is the problem that our paper focuses on. Next, we will review prior works that enhance the compositional and disentangling capabilities of NeRF.

Compositional NeRF: Compositional NeRF aims to model multiple editable objects or scenes within one integrated implicit function. Guo *et al.* [6] proposed to learn object-centric neural scattering functions based on NeRF, which models per-object light transport implicitly using lighting- and view-dependent neural networks. Similarly, Smith *et al.* [23] proposed a light field compositor module that enables reconstructing the global light field from a set of object-centric light fields. Yang *et al.* [28] proposed a two-pathway architecture, in which the scene and the object are encoded by dual branches, and each standalone object is conditioned on learnable activation codes. Niemeyer *et al.* [16] proposed compositional generative neural feature fields to disentangle the objects from the background by learning from unstructured and unposed image collections via self-supervised learning. Zhang *et al.* [31] proposed a recurrent framework that is trained across scenes and reconstructs a radiance field of a large indoor scene sequentially.

Decompositional NeRF: Decompositional NeRFs focus on parsing different factors inside the scenes separately. Rebain *et al.* [20] propose to spatially decompose a scene and dedicate smaller networks for each decomposed part, achieving efficient and GPU-friendly rendering. Tancik *et al.* [24] proposed to decompose the scene into individually trained NeRFs so that a city-level scene can be learned with NeRF. Guo *et al.* [7] modified NeRF to model scenes with reflections, which splits a scene into transmitted and reflected components and models the two components with separate neural radiance fields. To model street scenarios with moving vehicles, Ost *et al.* [17] proposed to decompose dynamic scenes into scene graphs and encode object transformation and radiance to efficiently render novel arrangements and views of the scene. Martin *et al.* [11] proposed to separately render the static scene and transient elements for modeling a high-fidelity static scene. Similarly in the task of modeling scenes with dynamic objects, Wu *et al.* [27] proposed to decompose the targets into the moving objects and the static background, each of which is represented by separate neural radiance fields with one allowing for temporal changes. Yuan *et al.* [29] presented a self-supervised framework for tracking and reconstruction of dynamic scenes with the rigid motion from multi-view RGB videos.

Different from previous work, our method focuses on synthesizing photorealistic boundaries and complex occlusion when merging two pre-trained NeRF. An additional occlusion field is learned from the pre-trained source NeRF and helps synthesize anti-aliasing boundaries between the foreground object and the occluded, and even works for complex objects like hairs and trees. Once the occlusion field is learned, the objects to be merged can be moved, rotated, and scaled with high rendering quality maintained.

3   Method

3.1   Preliminaries

Neural Radiance Field (NeRF) represents a scene as a continuous volume field with a multilayer perceptron (MLP), which takes a 3D location $\mathbf{x} = (x, y, z)$ and

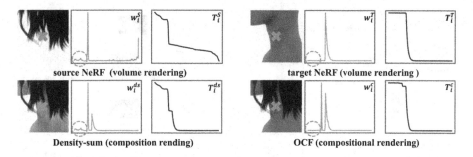

Fig. 2. We plot the distribution of weights w_i (solid red curve) and accumulated transmittance T_i (solid green curve) for each sample point along a ray in the original NeRF, density-sum-based NeRF and our OCF. NeRF predicts sample points with lower density values at semi-transparent pixels, which causes cloud-like artifacts in the combined image, while our OCF can eliminate such artifacts and results in high-quality images.

2D viewing direction $\mathbf{d} = (\theta, \phi)$ as input and outputs a volume density σ and a directional emitted color $\mathbf{c} = (r, g, b)$. To compute the color of a certain pixel, the density σ and radiance of the sample points on the projective ray are first predicted. The projective ray is formulated as $\mathbf{r}(t) = \mathbf{o} + t\mathbf{d}$, emitted from the camera center $\mathbf{o}$ and going through the given pixel on the image plane. The color $\hat{C}(\mathbf{r})$ and opacity $\hat{A}(\mathbf{r})$ of this pixel is estimated by volume rendering equation with quadrature approximation [12] used:

$$\hat{C}(\mathbf{r}) = \sum_{i=1}^{N} T_i \alpha_i \mathbf{c}_i, \quad \hat{A}(\mathbf{r}) = \sum_{i}^{N} T_i \alpha_i, \tag{1}$$

where the accumulated transmittance $T_i = \exp(-\sum_{j=1}^{i-1} \sigma_j \delta_j)$; $\alpha_i = 1 - \exp(-\sigma_i \delta_i)$; $\delta_i = t_{i+1} - t_i$, which is the interval distance between adjacent samples. The contribution of each sample point to the final accumulated color is formulated as:

$$w_i = T_i \alpha_i. \tag{2}$$

To improve the performance of representing high-resolution and complex scenes, positional encoding is adopted to map the inputs to a higher dimensional space. The NeRF is trained with the photometric loss:

$$L_{photo} = \sum_{\mathbf{r} \in \mathcal{R}} \left\| \hat{C}(\mathbf{r}) - C(\mathbf{r}) \right\|_2^2. \tag{3}$$

where $\mathcal{R}$ is the set of rays in each batch.

3.2   Occlusion Field

As shown in Fig. 2, previous methods to merge two NeRF models lead to unnatural transitions at the occlusion boundaries. To address this issue, we propose

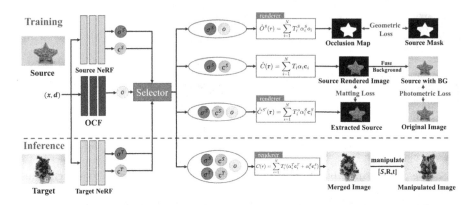

Fig. 3. Our pipeline consists of a pre-trained source NeRF, pre-trained target NeRF, and occlusion field (OCF). The OCF is trained in a self-supervised manner and can help synthesize the image of the combined scene in the inference phase.

an occlusion field (OCF) specialized in modeling an accurate object occupancy property, which helps disentangle the occlusion relationships when compositing two NeRFs, as shown in Fig. 3. Given a 3D position $\mathbf{x}$ and 2D viewing direction $\mathbf{d}$, the OCF learns the occlusion value o at a sampled point i:

$$\mathcal{F}_\phi^O : (\mathbf{x}, \mathbf{d}) \rightarrow (o_i). \tag{4}$$

where the sampling strategy of o_i is the same as that in vanilla NeRF.

3.3   Composition Rendering Equation

After obtaining the occlusion value o, a novel compositional rendering equation will be employed to generate realistic merging renderings. For clarity, we denote the foreground object as source S and the background object as target T. Their corresponding NeRF $\mathcal{F}_\theta^S$ and $\mathcal{F}_\theta^T$ could be written as follows:

$$\mathcal{F}_\theta^S : (\mathbf{x}, \mathbf{d}) \rightarrow (\sigma_i^S, \mathbf{c}_i^S), \tag{5}$$

$$\mathcal{F}_\theta^T : (\mathbf{x}, \mathbf{d}) \rightarrow (\sigma_i^T, \mathbf{c}_i^T), \tag{6}$$

where $\mathbf{x} \in \mathbb{R}^3$ is the 3D spatial coordinate, and $\mathbf{d} \in \mathbb{R}^2$ is the viewing direction. Different from Equation (1), we define the color of the source NeRF by compositing the accumulated color $\hat{C}^S(\mathbf{r})$ and the background color C_{bg}^S:

$$\hat{C}_f^S(\mathbf{r}) = \hat{C}^S(\mathbf{r}) + (1 - \hat{A}^S(\mathbf{r}))C_{bg}^S, \tag{7}$$

where the accumulated color $\hat{C}^S(\mathbf{r})$ represents the object color and the background color C_{bg}^S could be simply set as an input or learned from another network [26]. With the help of this disentangled representation, the fused color $C(\mathbf{r})$ of the composited NeRF could be calculated:

$$C(\mathbf{r}) = \sum_{i=1}^{N} T_i^c (\alpha_i^T \mathbf{c}_i^T + \alpha_i^S \mathbf{c}_i^S), \tag{8}$$

where

$$T_i^c = \exp\left(-\sum_{j=1}^{i-1}(\sigma_j^T + \sigma_j^S o_j)\delta_j\right), \tag{9}$$

and $w_i^c = T_i^c(\alpha_i^T + \alpha_i^S o_i)$ determines the contribution of each sampling point to the final accumulative color of the ray.

3.4 Model Training

The OCF is represented as a multilayer perceptron consisting of 10 fully connected layers. We follow the architecture of NeRF to introduce skip connections in our network. Positional encoding is also leveraged to map the input of $\mathbf{x}$ and $\mathbf{d}$ to a higher dimensional space. We carefully design the loss function in a self-supervised manner, which consists of four components: photometric loss $\mathcal{L}_{pm}$, matting loss $\mathcal{L}_{mat}$, geometric loss $\mathcal{L}_{geo}$, and geometric regularization $\mathcal{L}_{reg}$.

Photometric Loss. Photometric loss is used to constrain the rendering results of the updated source NeRF from being changed, which is essential for correctly compositing the source and target NeRF and rendering realistic images of the combined scene. The photometric loss is formulated as:

$$\mathcal{L}_{pm} = \sum_{r \in \mathcal{R}} \left\| \hat{C}_f^S(\mathbf{r}) - C^S(\mathbf{r}) \right\|_2^2, \tag{10}$$

where $C^S(\mathbf{r})$ is the ground truth color of source scene.

Matting Loss. Matting loss is designed to extract the objects from the source NeRF. The challenge is to disentangle the blurred transition at the occlusion boundaries, which is requisite to seamlessly composite source NeRF and target NeRF. Here we introduce occlusion map $\hat{O}(r)$, which can be rendered based on the geometry of the source NeRF via volume rendering:

$$\hat{O}^S(\mathbf{r}) = \sum_{i=1}^{N} T_i^S \alpha_i^S o_i. \tag{11}$$

Our rendering equation is based on that of vanilla NeRF to incorporate the geometric information of the occlusion field when integrating the color:

$$\hat{C}^{S'}(\mathbf{r}) = \sum_{i=1}^{N} T_i^o \alpha_i^S \mathbf{c}_i^S, \tag{12}$$

where

$$T_i^o = \exp\left(-\sum_{j=1}^{i-1} \sigma_j^S o_j \delta_j\right). \tag{13}$$

Then the matting loss is applied to extract the foreground objects with the properties of transparency or edge-excessive in the source NeRF model:

$$\mathcal{L}_{mat} = \sum_{\mathbf{r}\in\mathcal{R}} \left\| \hat{C}^{S'}(\mathbf{r}) - \hat{C}^{S}(\mathbf{r}) \right\|_2^2, \tag{14}$$

where $\hat{C}^{S}(\mathbf{r})$ is the accumulated color of source NeRF defined in Equation (7).

Geometric Loss. Considering that both OCF and source NeRF contain the geometric information of the source object, we use their corresponding rendering equations to obtain an occlusion mask and a source mask respectively. The geometric loss is formulated as:

$$\mathcal{L}_{geo} = \sum_{\mathbf{r}\in\mathcal{R}} \left\| \hat{O}^{S}(\mathbf{r}) - A^{S}(\mathbf{r}) \right\|_2^2. \tag{15}$$

Occlusion Regularization. We observed that only a small subset of sampled points along the rendering ray hit objects or background in a scene, while the rest of the points are mostly useless. And by minimizing the sum of o along each ray, the useless points are largely suppressed. Based on this observation, occlusion regularization is introduced and is formulated as:

$$\mathcal{L}_{reg} = \sum_{i=1}^{N} o_i. \tag{16}$$

The overall loss function used in our model is given by:

$$\mathcal{L} = \mathcal{L}_{pm} + \lambda_{geo}\mathcal{L}_{geo} + \lambda_{mat}\mathcal{L}_{mat} + \lambda_{reg}\mathcal{L}_{reg}, \tag{17}$$

where $\lambda_{geo}, \lambda_{mat}, \lambda_{req}$ are the weight of proposed supervision, respectively.

4 Experiment

4.1 Data Preparation

We generate 5 tuple of synthetic data with various objects and occlusion relation, including *Hair-Black*, *Hair-Blond*, *Horse&Saddle*, *Box&Fruit*, *Table&Basin*. The data of each tuple contains multi-view images of the source scene, the target scene, and the composited scene. The resolution of the rendered images is 512×512. And the images are randomly divided into 80% as the training set and 20% as the testing set. We also captured multi-view images for the scene *Tree&Star* to validate our method on real-world objects. By compositing these pre-trained neural radiance field models, we qualitatively and quantitatively evaluate our method and compare it with previous methods.

4.2   Qualitative Evaluation

As shown in Fig. 4, given a source NeRF model and a target NeRF model, our method can explicitly composite the two NeRFs with a learned occlusion field. The scenes of *Horse&Saddle*, *Box&Fruit*, *Table&Basin* contain complex occlusion relation, while our method accurately composites the two models and maintains the high rendering quality of the original NeRF. The scenes of *Hair-Black* and *Hair-Blond* contain a head and hair, which is extremely challenging to composite. There are noticeable translucency transitions at the boundaries of wisps of hair, and our method successfully synthesizes them. The scene of *Tree&Star* is a real-captured scene, which contains clusters of pine leaves. Our method can explicitly scale the star-shaped object and put it in the pine leaves cluster. In all these scenes, our method composite the two input NeRF model with correct occlusion relation and natural transition at the boundaries. The intermediate results including the occlusion map and the extracted source object are shown in the right two columns, which demonstrates that OCF is able to resolve an accurate occlusion relation. It is worth noting that our method composites the source and target neural radiance field without knowing the image of the merged scene.

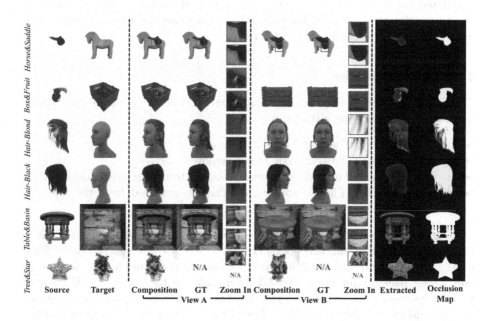

Fig. 4. Visualized results of our method on synthetic and real-captured data.

4.3   Comparison

Previous approaches for merging multiple NeRFs fall into two categories:

- (a) **Density-Sum Strategy**: merging two NeRF models by weighted summing the density σ, as adopted by NeRF-W [11], STaR [29], D2NeRF [27].
- (b) **Surface-Extraction Strategy**: to obtain the surface points, then judge the occlusion relation with the surface-to-camera distances [32].

We quantitatively evaluate the performance of our method and the fusion of these two categories of methods, as shown in Table 1. Our method outperforms two previous methods in PSNR, SSIM, and LPIPS, which indicates that our method composites two NeRFs more accurately. As shown in Fig. 5, the density-sum strategy tends to synthesize obvious cloud-like artifacts. We consider this to be due to the fact that the density field in NeRF is not suitable for direct weighted accumulation. Surface-extraction strategy tends to produce unnatural transitions at the occluding boundaries of the foreground object, which is conspicuous in the test of *Hair-Black* and *Hair-Blond*. If the multi-view constraints of the background in the source scene are not enough, a wrong background is obtained in the combined scene because the surface of the background cannot be calculated accurately, as shown in *Table&Basin*. By comparison, our methods can composite two neural radiance fields with accurate occlusion relation and natural transition at occluded boundaries.

4.4   Ablation Studies

To validate the effectiveness of each proposed module, we conduct the experiments with the following settings:

- (a) w/o mat. loss: The matting loss is removed only.
- (b) w/o geo. loss: The geometric loss is removed only.
- (c) w/o reg. term: The occlusion regularization term is removed only.
- (d) w/o view dep: The 2D viewing direction is removed from the input of OCF.

The results are visualized in Fig. 6 and quantitatively evaluated in Table 1. Our method without matting loss (a) fails to extract the source object from source NeRF accurately, resulting in cloud-like artifacts in the merged image and wrong background in the *Table&Basin* case. In the result of our method without geometric loss (b), the source object is somehow transparent with partial background fused in (see *Hair-Black*, *Box&Fruit* case), and the background of the target component is covered by the source's background (see *Table&Basin* case).

Table 1. Quantitative evaluation of comparison experiments.

PSNR↑

Method	Hair-Black	Hair-Blond	Box&Fruit	Horse&Saddle	Table&Basin
Density-sum	20.45	17.82	20.53	28.36	6.780
Surface-extraction	22.11	19.22	31.92	13.72	6.478
w/o mat. loss	21.30	19.43	29.39	33.10	7.950
w/o geo. loss	21.89	21.78	29.48	28.82	6.774
w/o reg. term	22.92	21.96	31.54	30.73	25.76
w/o view dep	22.99	**22.16**	30.60	29.95	25.47
OCF	**23.04**	22.10	**32.32**	**33.46**	**26.13**

SSIM↑

Method	Hair-Black	Hair-Blond	Box&Fruit	Horse&Saddle	Table&Basin
Density-sum	0.899	0.842	0.849	0.966	0.505
Surface-extraction	0.911	0.863	0.960	0.674	0.510
w/o mat. loss	0.907	0.857	0.955	0.978	0.526
w/o geo. loss	0.891	0.879	0.954	0.978	0.529
w/o reg. term	0.917	**0.883**	0.962	0.977	0.869
w/o view dep	0.915	0.882	0.960	0.972	0.860
OCF	**0.918**	0.877	**0.967**	**0.981**	**0.880**

LPIPS↓

Method	Hair-Black	Hair-Blond	Box&Fruit	Horse&Saddle	Table&Basin
Density-sum	0.242	0.270	0.288	0.226	0.565
Surface-extraction	0.220	0.265	0.157	0.467	0.566
w/o mat. loss	0.211	0.242	0.158	0.131	0.551
w/o geo. loss	0.211	0.239	0.160	0.130	0.555
w/o reg. term	**0.193**	0.238	0.153	0.133	0.202
w/o view dep	0.246	0.294	0.159	0.140	0.215
OCF	0.203	**0.231**	**0.152**	**0.128**	**0.182**

Our method without occlusion regularization (c) cannot model the translucent attributes of the scene accurately. As shown in *Hair-Black*, the unnatural edge transition of objects exists in the combined image. Our method without view-dependency (d) fails to synthesize natural and realistic results, especially at the edges of objects (see *Hair-Black* case for detail). By comparison, our complete method produces realistic rendering results and leads in the scoreboard.

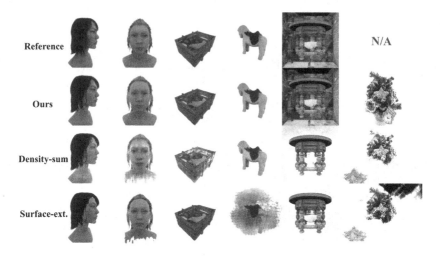

Fig. 5. The comparison of density-sum method, surface-extraction method, and ours.

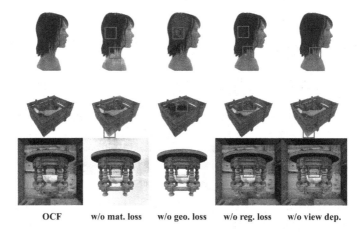

Fig. 6. Qualitative evaluation of ablation study.

5   Conclusion

We propose to composite multiple objects represented by NeRFs by learning an occlusion field. The proposed framework solves accurate occlusion relation and natural transition at occluding boundaries in a self-supervised manner, and greatly expands the application scenarios of trained NeRF models. There are still some limitations to our approach. The merging process still requires a training phase, which means it cannot be completed instantly. We only verify the performance on vanilla NeRF, and more experiments regarding recent NeRF-based frameworks like Triplane [2] and InstantNGP [15] should be studied.

Acknowledgement. This work was supported by NSFC grant 62001213, 62025108, gift funding from Huawei, and Tencent Rhino-Bird Research Program.

References

1. Barron, J.T., Mildenhall, B., Tancik, M., Hedman, P., Martin-Brualla, R., Srinivasan, P.P.: MIP-NERF: a multiscale representation for anti-aliasing neural radiance fields. In: CVPR, pp. 5855–5864 (2021)
2. Chan, E.R., et al.: Efficient geometry-aware 3d generative adversarial networks. In: CVPR, pp. 16123–16133 (2022)
3. Deng, K., Liu, A., Zhu, J.Y., Ramanan, D.: Depth-supervised nerf: fewer views and faster training for free. In: CVPR, pp. 12882–12891 (2022)
4. Gafni, G., Thies, J., Zollhofer, M., Nießner, M.: Dynamic neural radiance fields for monocular 4d facial avatar reconstruction. In: CVPR, pp. 8649–8658 (2021)
5. Genova, K., Cole, F., Sud, A., Sarna, A., Funkhouser, T.: Local deep implicit functions for 3d shape. In: CVPR, pp. 4857–4866 (2020)
6. Guo, M., Fathi, A., Wu, J., Funkhouser, T.: Object-centric neural scene rendering. arXiv preprint arXiv:2012.08503 (2020)
7. Guo, Y.C., Kang, D., Bao, L., He, Y., Zhang, S.H.: Nerfren: neural radiance fields with reflections. In: CVPR, pp. 18409–18418 (2022)
8. Jiang, C., Sud, A., Makadia, A., Huang, J., Nießner, M., Funkhouser, T., et al.: Local implicit grid representations for 3d scenes. In: CVPR, pp. 6001–6010 (2020)
9. Kim, M., Seo, S., Han, B.: Infonerf: ray entropy minimization for few-shot neural volume rendering. In: CVPR, pp. 12912–12921 (2022)
10. Liu, L., Gu, J., Zaw Lin, K., Chua, T.S., Theobalt, C.: Neural sparse voxel fields. NIPS **33**, 15651–15663 (2020)
11. Martin-Brualla, R., Radwan, N., Sajjadi, M.S., Barron, J.T., Dosovitskiy, A., Duckworth, D.: Nerf in the wild: neural radiance fields for unconstrained photo collections. In: CVPR, pp. 7210–7219 (2021)
12. Max, N.: Optical models for direct volume rendering. TVCG **1**(2), 99–108 (1995)
13. Mescheder, L., Oechsle, M., Niemeyer, M., Nowozin, S., Geiger, A.: Occupancy networks: learning 3d reconstruction in function space. In: CVPR, pp. 4460–4470 (2019)
14. Mildenhall, B., Srinivasan, P.P., Tancik, M., Barron, J.T., Ramamoorthi, R., Ng, R.: Nerf: representing scenes as neural radiance fields for view synthesis. ECCV **65**(1), 99–106 (2021)
15. Müller, T., Evans, A., Schied, C., Keller, A.: Instant neural graphics primitives with a multiresolution hash encoding. ToG **41**(4), 1–15 (2022)
16. Niemeyer, M., Geiger, A.: Giraffe: representing scenes as compositional generative neural feature fields. In: CVPR, pp. 11453–11464 (2021)
17. Ost, J., Mannan, F., Thuerey, N., Knodt, J., Heide, F.: Neural scene graphs for dynamic scenes. In: CVPR, pp. 2856–2865 (2021)
18. Park, J.J., Florence, P., Straub, J., Newcombe, R., Lovegrove, S.: Deepsdf: learning continuous signed distance functions for shape representation. In: CVPR, pp. 165–174 (2019)
19. Pumarola, A., Corona, E., Pons-Moll, G., Moreno-Noguer, F.: D-nerf: neural radiance fields for dynamic scenes. In: CVPR, pp. 10318–10327 (2021)
20. Rebain, D., Jiang, W., Yazdani, S., Li, K., Yi, K.M., Tagliasacchi, A.: Derf: decomposed radiance fields. In: CVPR, pp. 14153–14161 (2021)

21. Reiser, C., Peng, S., Liao, Y., Geiger, A.: Kilonerf: speeding up neural radiance fields with thousands of tiny MLPS. In: CVPR, pp. 14335–14345 (2021)

22. Roessle, B., Barron, J.T., Mildenhall, B., Srinivasan, P.P., Nießner, M.: Dense depth priors for neural radiance fields from sparse input views. In: CVPR, pp. 12892–12901 (2022)

23. Smith, C., et al.: Unsupervised discovery and composition of object light fields. arXiv preprint arXiv:2205.03923 (2022)

24. Tancik, M., et al.: Block-nerf: scalable large scene neural view synthesis. In: CVPR, pp. 8248–8258 (2022)

25. Verbin, D., Hedman, P., Mildenhall, B., Zickler, T., Barron, J.T., Srinivasan, P.P.: Ref-nerf: structured view-dependent appearance for neural radiance fields. In: CVPR, pp. 5481–5490. IEEE (2022)

26. Wang, Z., et al.: Learning compositional radiance fields of dynamic human heads. In: CVPR, pp. 5704–5713 (2021)

27. Wu, T., Zhong, F., Tagliasacchi, A., Cole, F., Oztireli, C.: D2nerf: self-supervised decoupling of dynamic and static objects from a monocular video. In: NIPS (2022)

28. Yang, B., Zhang, Y., Xu, Y., Li, Y., Zhou, H., Bao, H., Zhang, G., Cui, Z.: Learning object-compositional neural radiance field for editable scene rendering. In: ICCV, pp. 13779–13788 (2021)

29. Yuan, W., Lv, Z., Schmidt, T., Lovegrove, S.: Star: self-supervised tracking and reconstruction of rigid objects in motion with neural rendering. In: CVPR, pp. 13144–13152 (2021)

30. Zhang, K., Riegler, G., Snavely, N., Koltun, V.: Nerf++: analyzing and improving neural radiance fields. arXiv preprint arXiv:2010.07492 (2020)

31. Zhang, X., Bi, S., Sunkavalli, K., Su, H., Xu, Z.: Nerfusion: fusing radiance fields for large-scale scene reconstruction. In: CVPR, pp. 5449–5458 (2022)

32. Zhang, X., Srinivasan, P.P., Deng, B., Debevec, P., Freeman, W.T., Barron, J.T.: Nerfactor: neural factorization of shape and reflectance under an unknown illumination. TOG **40**(6), 1–18 (2021)

33. Zhuang, Y., et al.: Neai: pre-convoluted representation for plug-and-play neural ambient illumination. arXiv preprint arXiv:2304.08757 (2023)

34. Zhuang, Y., Zhu, H., Sun, X., Cao, X.: MoFaNeRF: morphable facial neural radiance field. In: Avidan, S., Brostow, G., Cissé, M., Farinella, G.M., Hassner, T. (eds.) ECCV 2022. LNCS, vol. 13663, pp. 268–285. Springer, Cham (2022). https://doi.org/10.1007/978-3-031-20062-5_16

LEAD: LiDAR Extender for Autonomous Driving

Jianing Zhang[1,5], Wei Li[2(✉)], Ruigang Yang[2], and Qionghai Dai[1,3,4]

[1] Department of Automation, Tsinghua University, Beijing, China
[2] Inceptio Technology, Shanghai, China
`wei.li@inceptio.ai`
[3] Beijing National Research Center for Information Science and Technology (BNRist),
Beijing, China
[4] Institute for Brain and Cognitive Science, Tsinghua University (THUIBCS), Beijing, China
[5] Department of Electronic Engineering, Fudan University, Shanghai, China

Abstract. 3D perception using sensors under vehicle industrial standards is the rigid demand in autonomous driving. MEMS LiDAR emerges with irresistible trend due to its lower cost, more robust, and meeting the mass-production standards. However, it suffers small field of view (FoV), slowing down the step of its population. In this paper, we propose LEAD, i.e., LiDAR Extender for Autonomous Driving, to extend the MEMS LiDAR by coupled image w.r.t both FoV and range. We propose a multi-stage propagation strategy based on depth distributions and uncertainty map, which shows effective propagation ability. Moreover, our depth outpainting/propagation network follows a teacher-student training fashion, which transfers depth estimation ability to depth completion network without any scale error passed. To validate the LiDAR extension quality, we utilize a high-precise laser scanner to generate a ground-truth dataset. Quantitative and qualitative evaluations show that our scheme outperforms SOTAs with a large margin.

Keywords: 3D perception · Autonomous Driving · LiDAR Extender

1 Introduction

Autonomous driving (AD) is one of the most challenging problems in computer vision and artificial intelligence, which has attracted considerable attention in recent years. Among all of the advances the AD system should achieve for mass production, 3D perception using sensors under vehicle industrial standards is the rigid demand in the near future. To meet this goal, more and more types of MEMS LiDAR emerge, with lower cost, more robust performance, and most importantly, meeting the mass production standards comparing with traditional mechanical LiDAR sensors. However, researches on 3D perception still focus on data from mechanical LiDAR sensor. In this paper, we tackle the problem of depth completion/estimation based on the MEMS LiDAR.

Despite the irresistible trend of using MEMS LiDAR, it suffers small field of view (FoV). Typical mechanical LiDAR sensors are always with 360° FoV, while MEMS LiDAR such as the one adopted in our paper is just $14.5° \times 16.2°$. A promising direction is utilizing a coupled camera with larger FoV to extend the point cloud/depth from

L. Fang et al. (Eds.): CICAI 2023, LNAI 14473, pp. 91–103, 2024.
https://doi.org/10.1007/978-981-99-8850-1_8

Fig. 1. (a) and (b) are the input pair, i.e., reference image from RGB camera and partial depth map from MEMS LiDAR. (c) is the ground truth from our LEAD dataset. (d) is our depth extension result.

MEMS LiDAR. A natural question to ask is: why do not we directly use cameras for depth estimation if an extra camera is introduced? It is true that depth estimation from monocular or stereo cameras, especially with the power of deep learning, achieves compelling results [3,6,8,9,18,27]. Nevertheless, the depth maps estimated in this line of works suffer from scale ambiguities. They may yield a plausible relative depth map, but hard to deploy in real AD systems due to the incredible scale.

Another family of works avoids the scale ambiguities with the guidance of LiDAR even only partial observations w.r.t the FoV of camera. The problem then becomes how to complete the depth maps with images [19,22]. Regarding existing depth completion approaches, the input depth maps are projected from raw point clouds from mechanical LiDAR. Thus, the depth pattern is sparse but covers the whole space of the target view (the FoV of the image). Those methods focus on *inpainting* holes of depth map using interpolation and propagation mechanism [1,17]. Oppositely, as shown in Fig. 1, our MEMS LiDAR could only produce very limit observations in a small area, which usually lies on the center of coupled images. In other words, we need to *extend/outpainting* significantly from partial depth to fill the whole space of the target image. Actually, there are few works of depth completion online sensors [12], and they are only validated on indoor scenes. To the best of our knowledge, our approach is the first one of extending such limited depth observation to large FoV with high accuracy.

The key insight of the proposed approach is to propagate partial depth from MEMS LiDAR to a larger area with the guidance of image. We introduce a multi-stage propagation to deal with this problem gradually. Eventually, we can get full of accurate depth after several stages. However, an effective extending operation between two stages is not trivial. Technically, in our approach, the output of one stage is a depth distribution set and an uncertainty map instead of one simple depth map. Then we use a novel probabilistic selection and combination operator to yield the depth for the next state. With these mechanisms, accurate depth could effectively propagate out. However, the network stays fragile even with a well-designed training strategy or parameters. Thus, we propose a teacher-student training fashion to learn depth estimation ability. We build a teacher network based on Mono2 [9] for our core depth outpainting/propagation network. Qualitative and quantitative experiments show that the proposed method

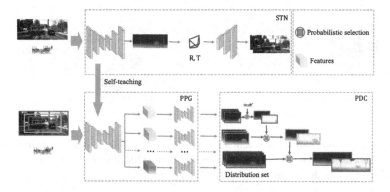

Fig. 2. Overview of our method. The pipeline consists of a self-supervised teacher network (STN), propagative probabilistic generating (PPG) module and probabilistic derivation and composition (PDC) module. STN provides the initial depth and stabilizes the training processing of PPG. PPG generates the depth probabilistic distributions for different propagation levels. With these distributions and the input partial depth map, PDC derives the final depth map with corresponding uncertainty.

outperforms SOTAs with a large margin. Additionally, to have accurate metrics, we use a 3D high-accurate long-range laser scanner to collect our dataset. In summary, the technical contributions of our work are as follows:

– We introduce a new setup focusing on extending the MEMS LiDAR by coupled image w.r.t both FoV and range. We propose a multi-stage propagation strategy based on depth distributions and uncertainty map, which shows effective propagation ability.
– We introduce a teacher-student strategy to combine monocular depth estimation and completion networks. We experimentally find such a strategy could transfer depth estimation ability to depth completion network without any scale error passed.
– To validate the LiDAR extension quality, we utilize a high-precise laser scanner to generate a ground-truth dataset. We hope such carefully collected data could benefit the community w.r.t depth researches (Fig. 2).

2   Related Work

2.1   Depth Estimation

The target of monocular depth estimation is to estimate the depth map with a single camera. This problem is ill-posed since an image can project to many plausible depths. So in practice, these methods can only provide an estimation or relative depth map. Eigen *et al.* [3] proposed the first learning-based monocular depth estimation algorithm that relies on the dense ground truth. After this work, a lot of supervised learning-based monocular depth estimation merged, such as [5] and [10]. However, acquisition of the accurate and dense ground truth is tedious. [16] tried to explore the potential of synthetic training data but the complexity of synthetic data is still not comparable

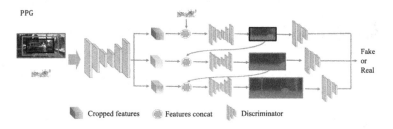

Fig. 3. Propagative probabilistic generating module. For each propagation stage, the network can fuse the output depth from last stage to generate depth map for next stage. On each stage, there is a discriminator to judge the quality of generated depth map.

with the real data. To break through the limitation of insufficient training data, Gard *et al.* [6] proposed a self-supervised learning framework that uses the stereo pair and constructs the stereo photometric reprojection warping loss to train the network. After that, Godard *et al.* [8] improved the stereo-based framework by adding a left-right consistency loss. In addition to stereo pair, Zhou *et al.* [27] only used the video sequences to estimate both the camera pose and depth map and the assumption of this method is that the scene is static so the network had to predict a mask to filter out the moving objects. Godard *et al.* [9] also improved sequence-based self-supervised framework with an auto-mask, besides, in [9], the two kinds of the self-supervised framework were used together, which also improved the monocular depth estimation result. To improve the quality of the depth map, some other tasks can be added and trained together, such as optical flow estimation [24] and image segmentation [28] [23]. To find the uncertain area, some algorithms [4] [11] [18] generate the uncertainty map while estimating the depth map.

2.2 Depth Completion

Depth completion is a relevant topic with our task, which focuses on yielding dense depth from sparse or noisy point cloud data [19]. The classical depth completion methods take only sparse or noisy depth sample from LiDAR or SLAM/SfM systems as input, which fall into the concept of depth super-resolution [13], depth inpainting [25], depth denoising [20]. In this category, Zhang *et al.* [26] proposed to predict the surface normal to estimate the dense depth map for indoor scenes in NYUv2 dataset [21]. Ma *et al.* [15] used sparse depth maps and images to first calculate the camera poses, and then train a depth completion network based on predicted poses. Those works achieve compelling results of depth densification, but they only deal with partial depth maps in the same resolution with RGB images, *i.e.* sparse depth samples are in the complete spatial space. So, the network only needs to inpaint the empty part of the depth map. However, in our setup, the input depth is only a small part w.r.t the vertical and horizontal space of our final estimated depth. Our task is more a depth outpainting problem with both the FoV and range extension are required. Instead of mechanical LiDAR, Liao *et al.* [12] adapt a line sensor to get the partial depth measurement and generate a dense depth map but limited by the setup, this method can only be applied indoor.

3 Method

3.1 Overview

Given the RGB image I and partial depth map D_s generated from MEMS LiDAR sensor, our goal is to estimate full depth map D_f with the same FoV of a camera, in other words, the same resolution of image I. The key insight of the proposed method is to propagate the partial depth to larger areas with the guidance of the image. Digging into the inputs, the partial depth D_s provides some accurate depth value, and the structure in RGB image I encodes plentiful cues for depth distribution so we want to learn a mapping $G : (I, D_s) \rightarrow p$.

However, training such a probabilistic generator faces some challenges. First, generating dense outdoor depth maps needs to face the challenge that acquiring the ground truth is hard. Even using the expensive LiDAR, there are still holes in the depth maps. Second, the training process is not stable, especially without ground truth. Besides, how to make full use of the partial depth and propagate the partial depth is also a problem.

3.2 Self-supervised Teacher Network (STN)

To stabilize the training process without ground truth, we first train a teacher network to guide the probabilistic generator. The teacher network can learn by itself to inference an initial depth map for next stage. Note that the probabilistic generator, which shares the network structure and initialization weights with teacher network, can distill the knowledge learned by the teacher network. The inputs of our teacher net are RGB and partial depth map.

Without ground truth, we adopt the self-supervised training fashion for STN. In addition to the network for depth estimation, we construct a network for pose estimation. With the estimated pose and depth, we can synthesis the target image from another viewpoint. By minimizing the photometric reprojection error, the network can be trained to generate plausible depth maps.

3.3 Propagative Probabilistic Generator (PPG)

Based on the guidance of STN, we build probabilistic generator to maximize the potential of the partial depth map in terms of full FoV depth estimation.

Multi Stage Propagation. In our experiments, we found that the straightforward mapping of $I, D_s \rightarrow p$ is unsatisfactory. This is reasonable, as D_s could provide relatively accurate depth values but only in a very limited area. Thus depth values in the remaining area heavily rely on the inference from the monocular image, which cannot guarantee accuracy. Considering the small FoV depth cannot affect the whole depth map but it can improve the nearby depth value, here we gradually expand the propagation area. During the fusion step, we adjust the scale of the unrefined larger cropped depth maps based on the median ratio,

$$D_i^s = median(D_{i-1} > 0)/median(D_i^b > 0) \cdot D_i^b,$$
$$D_i^m = (1 - \text{sgn}(D_{i-1}))D_i^s + \text{sgn}(D_{i-1})D_{i-1}, \tag{1}$$

where D_i^b is the blur depth map cropped from the output of teacher network, D_{i-1} is the refined depth map in stage $i-1$, in stage i, D_{i-1} will be padded to the same size as D_i^b, D_i^s is the depth after scale adjustment and D_i^m is the mixed depth map. Then refine depth of this stage is generated with the concatenation of cropped RGB features and depth features extracted from the D_i^m. In the next stage, the last stage depth maps will be propagated into a larger cropped depth map. Repeating this step can propagate the small FoV depth into the whole depth map. For each stage, the generated depth map is based on the refined depth map of the last stage.

Probabilistic Generating. After propagation, to generate the depth distribution, we introduce a distribution generating block to generate the distributions of each propagation stage. Figure 3 shows the details of our distribution generating block. While training, at each propagation stage, the generator can generate the depth map of this stage and the discriminator will judge the quality of the generated depth map. Like other generative adversarial networks, we introduce some noise to the input feature by randomly dropping out. While testing, we still enable the function of dropping out and generate probabilistic distribution by multiple forward sampling. Additionally, we can derive the uncertainty map $Umap$ using the standard deviation of distribution set $p(D|I, D_s)$:

$$Umap = \sigma(p) = \sqrt{\frac{1}{N} \sum_{k=1}^{N} (d_k - \mu(p))}, d_k \in p, \qquad (2)$$

where N is the size of distribution set p. $\mu(p) = \frac{1}{N} \sum_{k=1}^{N} d_k$ is the mean of p.

However, using the given small FoV RGBD values merely cannot train the discriminator well due to the limited field of view. We thus adopt the propagation strategy to train the GAN step by step. At each stage, the refined depth at the previous stage is regarded as the true samples, while the cropped depth in this stage which aligns with RGB images of the previous stage is regarded as the false samples. Besides, for better training of the discriminator, we randomly change the scale of depth maps, i.e., in stage i, for the discriminator

$$D_i^t = S \cdot D_{i-1}, D_i^f = S \cdot D_i, \qquad (3)$$

where S follows uniform distribution $S \sim U[0.8, 1.2]$, we can change the size of the RGBD image by a random scale that follows uniform distribution $S_{\text{size}} \sim U[0.5, 1.8]$. The data augment forces the discriminator to learn the structural mapping relation between RGB and depth while ignoring the different scales and sizes among different levels.

3.4   Probabilistic Derivation and Composition

With the probabilistic depth distribution, the simple way to generate the final depth map is to calculate the mean of these distributions, however, this way cannot take advantage of the partial depth map. With our special propagative probabilistic generator, we can derive the final depth map without complex post-processing. Since we generate the depth distribution at each propagation stage, we can follow the same idea to derive and compose the final depth map stage by stage. The depth map D_i in stage i can be acquired by

$$D_i = \min_{d_{k,i} \in p_i} (\|(d_{k,i} - D_{i-1}) \cdot \text{sgn}(D_{i-1})\|$$

$$+\lambda \|(d_{k,i} - D_{s,i}) \cdot \text{sgn}(D_{s,i})\|), \tag{4}$$

where p_i is the distribution set in i-th stage and in our experiment, at stage i, we run the generator for 5 times to generate the distribution set p_i, D_{i-1} is the refined depth map in stage $i - 1$, d_k is the k-th depth map in p_i, λ is the weight coefficient and $D_{s,i}$ is the cropped partial depth map whose size is the same as D_i. So in each stage, we make sure that the refined depth map is similar to the previous stage refined depth map and the partial ground truth. With D_i, the distribution of the next stage can be generated by the next generator and we use the same way to generate D_{i+1}. In this way, we can gradually propagate the partial depth information into the final result.

3.5   Network Training

For self-supervised learning, given the camera intrinsic and the relative pose between the two frames, we can use the depth map to synthesis the image of a novel view and calculate the photo-metric loss.

$$\mathcal{L}_{pe} = F(\pi(I(t'), K, R|t, D, I(t))), \tag{5}$$

$$F(I', I) = \frac{\alpha}{2}(1 - \text{SSIM}(I', I)) + \|I' - I\|. \tag{6}$$

For STN, we adopt multi-scale output and use three frames to train the network. While training with three frames,

$$\mathcal{L}_{pe} = \sum_{s=0}^{4} w_i \min_{i \in -1,1} F(I(t + i), I(t)). \tag{7}$$

The partial depth maps can supervise the output depth maps,

$$\mathcal{L}_{part} = \sum_{s=0}^{4} \|D_s - \text{sgn}(D_{part})\|. \tag{8}$$

Besides, we use edge-aware smooth loss to improve the smoothness

$$\mathcal{L}_{smooth} = |\partial_x D|e^{-|\partial_x I|} + |\partial_y D|e^{-|\partial_y I|}. \tag{9}$$

The final loss function for STN is

$$\mathcal{L}_t = w_{pe}\mathcal{L}_{pe} + w_p\mathcal{L}_{part} + w_s\mathcal{L}_{smooth}. \tag{10}$$

When training the PPG, different from the STN, the output of the network are five different size depth maps corresponding to five propagation stages. The PPG follows the GAN structure, the loss function contains a GAN loss and an appearance loss. The GAN loss is

$$
\begin{aligned}
\mathcal{L}_{GAN} = \sum_{i=0}^{5} \mathbb{E}_{I_i^t, D_i^t}[logD(I_i^t, D_i^t)] \\
+ \mathbb{E}_{I_i^t, D_i^t}[log(1 - D(G(I_i^t, D_i^t)))].
\end{aligned}
\tag{11}
$$

For appearance loss, since the STN has generated D_{blur}, we adjust the scale of the depth map to supervise the PPG

$$
s = median(D_{part} > 0)/median(D_t \cdot sgn(D_{part})),
\tag{12}
$$

$$
D_{pseudo} = s \cdot D_{blur},
\tag{13}
$$

$$
\mathcal{L}_{pseudo} = F(crop(D_{pseudo}), D_s),
\tag{14}
$$

The partial depth can adjust the scale of D_{blur} to generate D_{pseudo}. We construct the photo-metric loss of generator denoted as $\mathcal{L}_{peg}$, then the loss function of PPG is given by

$$
\mathcal{L}_s = w_{peg}\mathcal{L}_{peg} + w_{pse}\mathcal{L}_{pseudo} + w_G\mathcal{L}_{GAN}.
\tag{15}
$$

4   Experiment

4.1   Hardware and Evaluation Dataset

Hardware. We use the Tele-15 MEMS LiDAR sensor from Livox Inc.[1] as the partial depth sensor. The FoV of the MEMS LiDAR is $14.5° \times 16.2°$. The effective range is from 3 m to 200 m during our practical usage. In addition, we use an industrial camera from FLIR Inc. with 12mm focal length, $41.3° \times 31.3°$ FoV and 1536×1024 resolution.

Our LEAD Dataset. We captured around 100 h of data, in 50 streets over 500 km from the urban area in Shanghai, China. Then, we semi-automatically pick 16792 pairs of partial depth maps and their corresponding images, which are used as training and validation sets. To quantitatively evaluate the extended depth map from our setup, we utilize an additional high-accurate long-range laser scanner to capture additional 120 pairs with ground truth depth. We use Riegl Inc.'s vz-2000[2] 3D terrestrial laser scanner. The scanner has a wide FoV of $100° \times 360°$ with up to 2500 m sensing capability and 5 mm accuracy. Figure 4 shows one sample of the testing set in our LEAD dataset.

KITTI Eigen Split. To evaluate the generalizability of our proposed method, we conduct experiments on the KITTI dataset [7]. We resample a small region from the ground truth to simulate partial depth input. Note that we use the improved ground truth depth maps provided by KITTI in our experiments.

---

[1] https://www.livoxtech.com/tele-15.

[2] http://www.riegl.com/nc/products/terrestrial-scanning/produktdetail/product/scanner/58/.

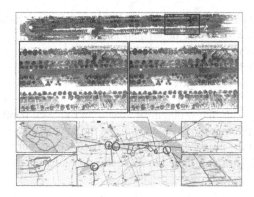

Fig. 4. Collection area and samples in LEAD dataset. The map in bottom row shows the data collection area. The point clouds in dotted box are captured from MEMS LiDAR (red) and high-accurate laser scanner (grey). (Color figure online)

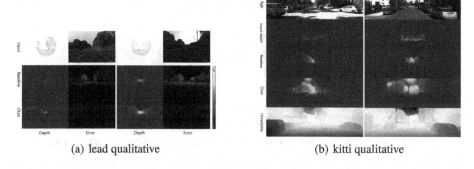

(a) lead qualitative   (b) kitti qualitative

Fig. 5. Qualitative results on LEAD and KITTIdataset .

Table 1. Quantitative results on LEAD dataset.

Method	lower is better		higher is better		
	RMSE	RMSE log	$\delta_{1.25}$	$\delta_{1.25^2}$	$\delta_{1.25^3}$
STN	15.718	0.633	0.070	0.174	0.603
Ours	**6.299**	**0.171**	**0.859**	**0.963**	**0.991**
STN (< 80)	14.446	0.633	0.072	0.176	0.604
Ours (< 80)	**6.053**	**0.172**	**0.858**	**0.963**	**0.991**
STN (> 80)	22.687	0.330	0.720	0.743	0.848
Ours (> 80)	**6.968**	**0.077**	**0.959**	**0.999**	**1.000**

4.2   Qualitative Results

Results on LEAD Dataset. Figure 5(a) shows the qualitative results on our LEAD dataset. The second row shows the depth map and its the error map for the STN module. The third row shows the results for our full pipeline.

Results on KITTI Dataset. Figure 5(b) shows the qualitative results on the KITTI dataset. Since our network is based on MonoDepth2 [9], we use it as our baseline method. We train the MonoDepth2 supervised by the input narrow FoV depth map. MonoDepth2 suffers from the problem of sparse and uneven depth distribution. The input narrow FoV depth map is not able to correct the scale even after using the ratio of the median to correct the monocular depth scale. By contrast, our propagation and distribution output modules are designed to solve this problem, resulting in more accurate wide range of depth maps.

Table 2. Quantitative results on KITTI Eigen Split with improved ground truth. "SC" means different scale correction methods: "M" means using different scales for each individual test case. The scale is the ratio between the median depth of the ground truth depth map and the median depth of the resulting depth map. "F" means using a fixed scale that is the mean scale. "P" means using the scale estimated from the input partial depth.

Method	SC	lower is better				higher is better		
		Abs Rel	Sq Rel	RMSE	RMSE log	$\delta_{1.25}$	$\delta_{1.25^2}$	$\delta_{1.25^3}$
EPC++[14]	M	0.120	0.789	4.755	0.177	0.856	0.961	0.987
Geonet[24]	M	0.132	0.994	5.240	0.193	0.833	0.953	0.985
MonoDepth2[9]	M	0.090	0.545	3.942	0.137	0.914	0.983	0.995
EPC++	F	0.153	0.998	5.080	0.204	0.805	0.945	0.982
Geonet	F	0.202	1.521	5.829	0.244	0.707	0.913	0.970
MonoDepth2	F	0.109	0.623	4.136	0.154	0.873	0.977	0.994
MonoDepth2	P	0.104	0.560	3.898	0.48	0.889	0.980	0.995
Ours (res18)	P	0.093	0.387	3.073	0.133	0.918	**0.985**	**0.996**
Ours (res50)	P	**0.090**	**0.424**	**3.419**	**0.133**	**0.916**	0.984	**0.996**

4.3 Quantitative Results

Results on LEAD Dataset. Table 1 shows the quantitative results on our LEAD dataset. We compare results for the STN module and our full pipeline.

Results on KITTI Dataset. Table 2 shows the quantitative results on the KITTI Eigen Split [2]. The first and second row blocks show results for the unsupervised monocular depth estimation methods, which need scale correction based on ground truth depth information and it is not a practical assumption. By contrast, our method only needs partial depth maps. Hence, the third-row block shows results for MonoDepth2 and our method using a partial depth map for scale correction. The results show that our method outperforms the baseline methods.

Ablation Study. Table 3 shows the ablation study results. We compare the performances among three methods: STN, STN+PPG, and STN+PPG+PDC. It can be shown that the proposed PPG and PDC modules improve the performance effectively.

Table 3. Ablation study on KITTI dataset.

Method	lower is better				higher is better		
	Abs Rel	Sq Rel	RMSE	RMSE log	$\delta_{1.25}$	$\delta_{1.25^2}$	$\delta_{1.25^3}$
STN	0.103	0.504	3.713	0.148	0.886	0.979	0.995
STN+PPG	0.106	0.486	3.635	0.144	0.904	0.983	0.996
STN+PPG+PDC	0.101	0.456	3.475	0.140	0.909	0.984	0.996

5   Conclusion

We propose a novel self-supervised learning-based method to use the small field of view solid-state MEMS LiDAR to estimate a deeper and wider depth map, a new hardware system, and a corresponding dataset for this kind of LiDAR. The experiment shows that our new setup and algorithm make full use of the depth generated by the MEMS LiDAR and generate a deeper and wider depth map. We believe that our setup and method can promote the wide application of the low-cost and miniaturized solid-state MEMS LiDAR in the field of autonomous driving.

References

1. Cheng, X., Wang, P., Yang, R.: Learning depth with convolutional spatial propagation network. IEEE Trans. Pattern Anal. Mach. Intell. (2019)
2. Eigen, D., Fergus, R.: Predicting depth, surface normals and semantic labels with a common multi-scale convolutional architecture. In: Proceedings of the IEEE International Conference on Computer Vision, pp. 2650–2658 (2015)
3. Eigen, D., Puhrsch, C., Fergus, R.: Depth map prediction from a single image using a multi-scale deep network. In: Advances in Neural Information Processing Systems, pp. 2366–2374 (2014)
4. Eldesokey, A., Felsberg, M., Holmquist, K., Persson, M.: Uncertainty-aware cnns for depth completion: uncertainty from beginning to end. In: IEEE/CVF Conference on Computer Vision and Pattern Recognition (CVPR) (June 2020)
5. Fu, H., Gong, M., Wang, C., Batmanghelich, K., Tao, D.: Deep ordinal regression network for monocular depth estimation. In: Proceedings of the IEEE Conference on Computer Vision and Pattern Recognition, pp. 2002–2011 (2018)
6. Garg, R., Vijay Kumar, B.G., Carneiro, G., Reid, I.: Unsupervised CNN for single view depth estimation: geometry to the rescue. In: Leibe, B., Matas, J., Sebe, N., Welling, M. (eds.) ECCV 2016. LNCS, vol. 9912, pp. 740–756. Springer, Cham (2016). https://doi.org/10.1007/978-3-319-46484-8_45

7. Geiger, A., Lenz, P., Urtasun, R.: Are we ready for autonomous driving? the kitti vision benchmark suite. In: 2012 IEEE Conference on Computer Vision and Pattern Recognition, pp. 3354–3361. IEEE (2012)

8. Godard, C., Mac Aodha, O., Brostow, G.J.: Unsupervised monocular depth estimation with left-right consistency. In: Proceedings of the IEEE Conference on Computer Vision and Pattern Recognition, pp. 270–279 (2017)

9. Godard, C., Mac Aodha, O., Firman, M., Brostow, G.J.: Digging into self-supervised monocular depth estimation. In: Proceedings of the IEEE International Conference on Computer Vision, pp. 3828–3838 (2019)

10. Guo, X., Li, H., Yi, S., Ren, J., Wang, X.: Learning monocular depth by distilling cross-domain stereo networks. In: Proceedings of the European Conference on Computer Vision (ECCV), pp. 484–500 (2018)

11. Johnston, A., Carneiro, G.: Self-supervised monocular trained depth estimation using self-attention and discrete disparity volume. In: Proceedings of the IEEE/CVF Conference on Computer Vision and Pattern Recognition, pp. 4756–4765 (2020)

12. Liao, Y., Huang, L., Wang, Y., Kodagoda, S., Yu, Y., Liu, Y.: Parse geometry from a line: monocular depth estimation with partial laser observation. In: 2017 IEEE International Conference on Robotics and Automation (ICRA), pp. 5059–5066. IEEE (2017)

13. Lu, J., Forsyth, D.: Sparse depth super resolution. In: Proceedings of the IEEE Conference on Computer Vision and Pattern Recognition, pp. 2245–2253 (2015)

14. Luo, C., et al.: Every pixel counts++: joint learning of geometry and motion with 3d holistic understanding. arXiv preprint arXiv:1810.06125 (2018)

15. Ma, F., Cavalheiro, G.V., Karaman, S.: Self-supervised sparse-to-dense: self-supervised depth completion from lidar and monocular camera. In: 2019 International Conference on Robotics and Automation (ICRA), pp. 3288–3295. IEEE (2019)

16. Mayer, N., et al.: What makes good synthetic training data for learning disparity and optical flow estimation? Int. J. Comput. Vision **126**(9), 942–960 (2018)

17. Park, J., Joo, K., Hu, Z., Liu, C.K., Kweon, I.S.: Non-local spatial propagation network for depth completion. In: Proceedings of European Conference on Computer Vision (ECCV) (2020)

18. Poggi, M., Aleotti, F., Tosi, F., Mattoccia, S.: On the uncertainty of self-supervised monocular depth estimation. In: Proceedings of the IEEE/CVF Conference on Computer Vision and Pattern Recognition, pp. 3227–3237 (2020)

19. Qiu, J., et al.: Deep surface normal guided depth prediction for outdoor scene from sparse lidar data and single color image. In: Proceedings of the IEEE Conference on Computer Vision and Pattern Recognition, pp. 3313–3322 (2019)

20. Shen, J., Cheung, S.C.S.: Layer depth denoising and completion for structured-light rgb-d cameras. In: Proceedings of the IEEE Conference on Computer Vision and Pattern Recognition, pp. 1187–1194 (2013)

21. Silberman, N., Hoiem, D., Kohli, P., Fergus, R.: Indoor segmentation and support inference from RGBD images. In: Fitzgibbon, A., Lazebnik, S., Perona, P., Sato, Y., Schmid, C. (eds.) ECCV 2012. LNCS, vol. 7576, pp. 746–760. Springer, Heidelberg (2012). https://doi.org/10.1007/978-3-642-33715-4_54

22. Uhrig, J., Schneider, N., Schneider, L., Franke, U., Brox, T., Geiger, A.: Sparsity invariant CNNs. In: 2017 International Conference on 3D Vision (3DV), pp. 11–20. IEEE (2017)

23. Wang, L., Zhang, J., Wang, O., Lin, Z., Lu, H.: SDC-depth: semantic divide-and-conquer network for monocular depth estimation. In: Proceedings of the IEEE/CVF Conference on Computer Vision and Pattern Recognition, pp. 541–550 (2020)

24. Yin, Z., Shi, J.: Geonet: unsupervised learning of dense depth, optical flow and camera pose. In: Proceedings of the IEEE Conference on Computer Vision and Pattern Recognition, pp. 1983–1992 (2018)

25. Zhang, H.T., Yu, J., Wang, Z.F.: Probability contour guided depth map inpainting and super-resolution using non-local total generalized variation. Multim. Tools Appl. **77**(7), 9003–9020 (2018)
26. Zhang, Y., Funkhouser, T.: Deep depth completion of a single RGB-D image. In: Proceedings of the IEEE Conference on Computer Vision and Pattern Recognition, pp. 175–185 (2018)
27. Zhou, T., Brown, M., Snavely, N., Lowe, D.G.: Unsupervised learning of depth and ego-motion from video. In: Proceedings of the IEEE Conference on Computer Vision and Pattern Recognition, pp. 1851–1858 (2017)
28. Zhu, S., Brazil, G., Liu, X.: The edge of depth: explicit constraints between segmentation and depth. In: Proceedings of the IEEE/CVF Conference on Computer Vision and Pattern Recognition, pp. 13116–13125 (2020)

Fast Hierarchical Depth Super-Resolution via Guided Attention

Yusen Hou[1], Changyi Chen[1], Gaosheng Liu[1], Huanjing Yue[1], Kun Li[2], and Jingyu Yang[1(✉)]

[1] School of Electrical and Information Engineering,
Tianjin University, Tianjin, China
{hys20,2019234356,gaoshengliu,huanjing.yue,yjy}@tju.edu.cn
[2] College of Intelligence and Computing, Tianjin University, Tianjin, China
lik@tju.edu.cn

Abstract. Depth maps captured by mainstream depth sensors are still of low resolution compared with color images. The main difficulties in depth super-resolution lie in the recovery of tiny textures from severely undersampled measurements and texture-copy artifacts due to depth-texture inconsistency. To address these problems, we propose a simple and efficient convolutional filtering approach based on guided attention, named HDSRnet-light, for high quality depth super-resolution. In HDSRnet-light, a guided attention scheme is proposed to fuse features of the pyramidal main branch with complementary features from two side-branches associated with the auxiliary high-resolution color image and a bicubic upsampled version of the input depth map. In this way, high-resolution features are progressively recovered from multi-scale information from both the depth map and the color image. Experimental results show that our method achieves state-of-art performance for depth map super-resolution.

Keywords: depth map super-resolution · guided filtering · convolutional neural network

1 Introduction

High-resolution (HR) depth maps are highly desirable in the field of 3D vision. In recent years, with rapid development of affordable and portable consumer depth cameras such as Microsoft Kinect and Time-of-Flight (TOF), consumer-level depth sensors have entered the daily life of the public. However, current depth sensors can only acquire low-resolution depth maps, which limits their applications.

Depth super-resolution methods have been developed to bridge the resolution gap between depth maps and color images. However, the super-resolution of depth maps is an under-determined problem. Fine structures are lost or distorted in LR depth maps due to under-sampling. Traditional interpolation methods would introduce blurry artifacts. So, numerous methods have been proposed to address these problems [1,2]. However, artifacts are still easily observed in

L. Fang et al. (Eds.): CICAI 2023, LNAI 14473, pp. 104–115, 2024.
https://doi.org/10.1007/978-981-99-8850-1_9

many cases. Recently, convolution neural network (CNN) had been introduced into the area of depth map super-resolution, and achieved promising results [3,4]. However, it still confronts some challenges: Due to the excessive use of color image information, texture copy artifacts still exists in some tough cases. After training to a certain level, edge information with minor variation becomes extremely difficult to reconstruct which also the main difficulty of depth map super-resolution. Besides, recent works tend to construct heavy CNN structures with huge amount of model parameters to boost objective metrics such as RMSE or MAD. The improvement in terms of such metrics are marginal with increase of model complexity. But for industrial applications, heavy models are difficult to deploy in embedded systems, and model compression would in turn sacrifice prediction precision.

Based on above observations, we propose a light and efficient CNN-based depth super-resolution approach, named HDSRnet-light, which has achieved state-of-the-art performance with a compact and fast model. Standing on the pyramidal framework, our HDSRnet-light structure has three branches: main branch for depth super-resolution, the Structure side-branch extracting depth features from $D_{bicubic}$ (Upsampling from LR depth maps via bicubic), and Detail side-branch extracting color features from HR color image. In the main branch, feature maps of the LR depth map are enhanced by an attention module with complementary features from the two side-branches, followed by an upsampling unit to magnify the size of the feature maps. The attention-and-upsampling structure is repeated twice before reaching the adder of the residual structure. The two side-branches first extract features from the auxiliary input, either bicubic depth map and color image respectively, and go through two down-sampling units to have compatible sizes with the associated attention modules. The HDSRnet-light is trained using ℓ_1 loss. Experimental results show that our method outperforms several state-of-the-art methods for most cases due to the effectiveness of the hierarchical attention mechanism. HDSRnet-light has only 287.9k parameters and is able to run at a speed of more than 300 fps under NVIDIA GeForce GTX 1080Ti with state-of-the-art performance for 8× super-resolution to the size of 1920 × 1080.

2   Related Work

2.1   Traditional Depth SR Method

Early depth super-resolution methods do not assume the RGB-D input, and are mainly based on various image filtering schemes. Lei *et al.* [5] improved the super-resolution performance by using an up-sampling filter to strengthen the view synthesis quality. Xie *et al.* [6] proposed an edge-guided method, which generates a HR edge map from LR depth map by Markov random field optimization. Park *et al.* [7] incorporated a non-local means term to preserve local structure and remove outliers.

Recent mainstream depth sensors usually output RGB-D pairs, and the associated RGB color images have a higher resolution than the depth maps. So most depth super-resolution use the HR color image or intensity image as guidance to enhance the quality of the depth map. He *et al.* [8] proposed a guided filter as a generic edge-preserving smoothing operator for depth SR. Joint Bilateral Filter [9] further applied addition guidance to improve the SR quality.

Zuo *et al.* [10] proposed a explicit edge inconsistency method for depth SR.

Yang *et al.* [11] fused the median and bilateral filtering to construct a new edge-preserving depth SR filter. Yang *et al.* [12] proposed a pixel-wise adaptive autoregressive model to utilize non-local correlation. Jiang *et al.* [13] proposed a dual domain based depth super-resolution methods, where a multi-directional total variation (MTV) prior was proposed to characterize the spatially varying geometrical structures. These methods prove that utilize HR color image as guided information can improve performance of depth SR and show strong robustness.

2.2 Deep Learning-Based Depth SR Method

Thanks to the powerful learning capability of CNN, many deep learning-based depth map SR methods have achieved some improvements. Anisotropic total generalized variation network (ATGV-Net) [14], the priority work introduced the learning framework to the variational optimization approach. Hui *et al.* [3] proposed a multi-scale guided convolutional network (MSGnet) for depth map super-resolution with RGB-D inputs. MSGnet uses multi-scale fusion strategy to capture the complementary features of LR depth map and HR color image in several scales. Riegler *et al.* [14] designed a deep convolutional network with a variational method to recover accurate HR depth map. Song *et al.* [15] utilized pixelshuffle in their method to super-resolve depth maps. Ye *et al.* [16] introduced the Progressive Multi-Branch Aggregation Network (PMBANet). PMBANet utilizes attention-based error feed-forward/backward modules in a multi-scale branch to refine depth maps and designs a guidance branch as priority knowledge to recover depth details.

As a departure of devising large models to boost performance, we propose a lightweight network which uses guided attention to fuse information. It achieves state-of-the-art performance with only 287.9k parameters.

3   Proposed Method

In this part, we first briefly introduce the framework of our method, then illustrate the details of our method. The difficulties of depth SR is how to recover the boundaries of depth map and make the model easy to deploy in the industrial environment. To address these problems, we propose a lightweight method, named HDSRnet-light, which achieves state-of-the-art performance with only significantly fewer parameters than previous models.

3.1   Framework Overview

In Fig. 1, we show the architecture of the proposed method. To be specific, HDSRnet-light consists of three branches, the top side-branch extracts structure

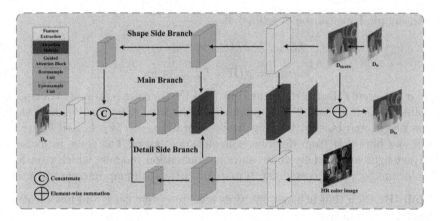

Fig. 1. Overall architecture of the proposed HDSRnet-light, consisting of three branches, *i.e.*, the main branch to reconstruct residual component from the input LR depth map, the structure side-branch to learn structural depth information from bicubic upsampled version of the depth map, and the detail side-branch to extract HR details from the HR color image.

information from the bicubic interpolated version of the LR depth map, the middle main-branch extracts depth features from the input LR depth map, and the bottom side-branch extracts edge detail information from the color image to compensate the loss of fine granular details in the LR depth map. We utilize a few number of convolutional layers to extract simple features and propose an attention scheme named guided attention (GA) to fuse features (shown in Fig. 2). The details are described in the following subsections.

3.2 Structures of Main and Side Branches

We utilize a multi-scale structure to super-resolve depth maps. Besides main-branch and detail branch, we add a structure side-branch to extract auxiliary features. Because we found that D_{bicubic} (Upsampling from LR depth map via bicubic interpolation) contains structure information, which makes the training more stable and convergence faster, especially when the size of LR depth map is much lower than HR depth map. Then, we propose to learn the residual result between the interpolated depth map and the HR depth map. Moreover, we use a few number of deconvolution and the size of convolution kernel to reduce computational complexity. We show HDSRnet-light in Fig. 1.

The downsampling unit can be described as:

$$f = \sigma(W_1 * input + b_1), \tag{1}$$

$$f_{pool} = Maxpool(f), \tag{2}$$

$$output = \sigma(W_2 * f_{pool} + b_2). \tag{3}$$

The Upsample Unit can be described as:

$$f_{deconv} = \sigma(Deconv(input)),\tag{4}$$

$$output = \sigma(W * f_{deconv} + b).\tag{5}$$

where σ represents Rectified Linear Unit (ReLU), $Deconv$ represents transposed convolution operator and "*" represents convolutional operator. W and b stand for the weight and bias in the convolution operation. W_1, W_2, b_1 and b_2 are the weight and bias that from different convolutional layers. The three branches of HDSRnet-light are built by these units and attention module, which transform HR color image, preprocessed depth map and LR depth map into several scales:

- **Main-Branch** that achieves multiple level receptive fields and fuses features from other branches;
- **Structure Side-Branch** that extracts the basic shape information of depth map in several scales;
- **Detail Side-Branch** that extracts details from HR color image in several scales, and transfer useful structure to refine depth map.

Instead of directly concatenating, we propose a guided-based attention mechanism to fuse these features, which are extracted by these branches.

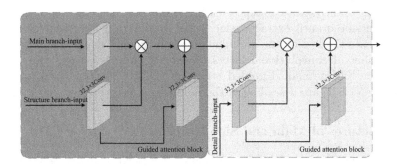

Fig. 2. Structure of the proposed attention module: the module consists of two guided attention blocks to fuse information from the main branch, structure side-branch, and the detail side-branch.

3.3   Guided Attention

Existing depth super-resolution methods have proved the effectiveness of using the color image as reference information. Inspired by He *et al.* [8], we propose guided attention to utilize the color image as guided image to regulate depth maps in feature domain. Guided filter [8] considered the pixel of guided image I_i and the pixel of output image Y_i exists a linear relationship, which can be described as

$$Y_i = \alpha_i I_i + \beta_i.\tag{6}$$

According to the characteristics of RGB-D, we consider a similar relationship between color images and depth maps exists in feature domain. So we design a guided attention to learn such a linear relationship adaptively. The proposed attention is shown in Fig. 2. It contains two steps: weight learning and bias learning.

Weight Learning: each attention module takes the features extracted from the previous convolutional layers as inputs. Taking the first guided attention block in Fig. 2 as an example, structure side-branch input (denoted by *input2*) is used to learn a series of weights via several convolutional layers for main branch input (denoted by *input1*). This operation makes sure every element in main branch input has an adaptive weight. The weight adaptive learning can be described as:

$$\alpha = \sigma(W_1 * input_2 + b_1), \tag{7}$$

where α represents the weight matrix.

Bias Adaptive Learning: we also use structure side-branch input to learn the bias via another convolutional layer. It can be described as:

$$\beta = \sigma(W_2 * input_2 + b_2), \tag{8}$$

where β represents the bias matrix.

The whole operation of the guided attention can be defined as:

$$output = \alpha \cdot \sigma(W_3 * input_1 + b_3) + \beta. \tag{9}$$

The proposed attention block helps aggregate information by adaptively attending importance to the features from multiple branches, which uses the relationship between HR color image and depth map effectively.

4   Experiments and Results

This section shows the performance of our method by comparison with state-of-the-art (SOTA) methods, attention analysis, running time and generalization ability of our method experiment on real data.

4.1   Implementation Details

We collected 58 RGB-D images from MPI Sintel [23] depth dataset, and 34 RGB-D images from Middlebury dataset (6, 10 and 18 images from 2001, 2006 and 2014 datasets, respectively) [24–26]. To evaluate the performance of our method, we test six standard depth maps (Art, Books, Moebius, Dolls, Laundry, Reindeer) from Middlebury 2005 dataset.

The patch size is set to 128×128, and we augment data by introducing random rotation by $[0°, 90°, 180°, 270°]$. We get totally $100,000$ training paired patches. LR depth maps are obtained by downsampling the HR depth maps with bicubic interpolation [4] [16].

Table 1. Quantitative depth SR results in MAD ↓ and PE ↓.

	Art			Books		
	4×	8×	16×	4×	8×	16×
JGF[1]	0.47/3.25	0.78/7.39	1.54/14.31	0.24/2.14	0.43/5.41	0.81/12.05
CDLLC[17]	0.53/2.86	0.76/4.59	1.41/7.53	0.19/1.34	0.46/3.67	0.75/8.12
EG[18]	0.48/2.48	0.71/<u>3.31</u>	1.35/**5.88**	<u>0.15</u>/1.23	0.36/3.09	0.70/7.58
MSG[3]	0.46/2.31	0.76/4.31	1.53/8.78	0.15/1.21	0.41/3.24	0.76/7.85
DGDIE[19]	0.48/2.34	1.20/13.18	2.44/26.32	0.30/3.21	0.58/7.33	1.02/14.25
DEIN[20]	0.40/2.17	0.64/3.62	1.34/6.69	0.22/1.68	0.37/3.20	0.78/8.05
CCFN[21]	0.43/2.23	0.72/3.59	1.50/7.28	0.17/<u>1.19</u>	0.36/3.07	0.69/<u>7.32</u>
GSRPT[22]	0.48/2.53	0.74/4.18	1.48/7.83	0.21/1.77	0.38/4.23	0.76/7.67
PMBANet[16]	<u>0.26</u>/<u>1.95</u>	<u>0.51</u>/3.45	<u>1.22</u>/<u>6.28</u>	**0.15/1.13**	**0.26**/<u>2.87</u>	<u>0.59</u>/**6.79**
HDSRnet-light	**0.18/1.01**	**0.37/2.44**	**0.97**/10.39	0.18/1.53	<u>0.30</u>/**2.74**	**0.57**/7.95

	Dolls			Laundry		
	4×	8×	16×	4×	8×	16×
JGF[1]	0.33/3.23	0.59/7.29	1.06/15.87	0.36/2.60	0.64/4.54	1.20/8.69
CDLLC[17]	0.31/4.61	0.53/5.94	0.79/12.64	0.30/2.08	0.48/3.77	0.96/8.25
EG[18]	0.27/2.72	0.49/5.59	0.74/12.06	0.28/1.62	0.45/2.86	0.92/7.87
MSG[3]	0.25/2.39	0.51/4.86	0.87/9.94	0.30/1.68	0.46/2.78	1.12/7.62
DGDIE[19]	0.34/4.79	0.63/9.44	0.93/11.66	0.35/2.03	0.86/3.69	1.56/16.72
DEIN[20]	0.22/1.73	0.38/3.38	0.73/9.95	0.23/1.70	0.36/3.27	0.81/7.71
CCFN[21]	0.25/1.98	0.46/4.49	0.75/9.84	0.24/1.39	0.41/2.49	0.71/<u>7.35</u>
GSRPT[22]	0.28/2.84	0.48/4.61	0.79/10.12	0.33/1.79	0.56/4.55	1.24/8.98
PMBANet[16]	<u>0.19</u>/<u>1.35</u>	<u>0.32</u>/3.22	**0.59**/8.92	<u>0.17</u>/**0.27**	<u>0.34</u>/2.41	<u>0.71</u>/**6.88**
HDSRnet-light	**0.17/1.00**	**0.31/2.39**	<u>0.60</u>/**7.62**	**0.15**/<u>1.00</u>	**0.28/2.19**	**0.69**/9.37

	Moebius			Reindeer		
	4×	8×	16×	4×	8×	16×
JGF[1]	0.25/3.36	0.46/6.45	0.80/12.33	0.38/2.27	0.64/5.17	1.09/11.84
CDLLC[17]	0.27/1.98	0.46/4.59	0.79/7.89	0.43/2.09	0.55/5.39	0.98/11.49
EG[18]	0.23/1.88	0.42/4.29	0.75/7.63	0.36/1.97	0.51/4.31	0.95/9.27
MSG[3]	0.21/1.79	0.43/4.05	0.76/7.48	0.31/1.73	0.52/2.93	0.99/7.63
DGDIE[19]	0.28/1.98	0.58/8.11	0.98/16.22	0.35/1.76	0.73/7.82	1.29/15.83
DEIN[20]	0.20/1.89	0.35/3.02	0.73/7.42	0.26/1.40	0.40/2.76	0.80/5.88
CCFN[21]	0.23/2.18	0.39/3.91	0.73/7.41	0.29/1.51	0.46/2.79	0.95/6.58
GSRPT[22]	0.24/2.02	0.49/4.70	0.80/8.38	0.31/1.58	0.61/5.90	1.07/10.35
PMBANet[16]	<u>0.16</u>/<u>1.21</u>	<u>0.28</u>/<u>2.87</u>	<u>0.67</u>/<u>6.73</u>	<u>0.17</u>/<u>1.28</u>	<u>0.34</u>/<u>2.40</u>	<u>0.74</u>/<u>5.66</u>
HDSRnet-light	**0.14/1.16**	**0.24/2.22**	**0.50/6.43**	**0.16/0.77**	**0.27/1.56**	**0.57/5.58**

We use Adam as the optimizer with $momentum = 0.9$, $\beta_1 = 0.9$, $\beta_2 = 0.99$, $eps = 10^{-8}$. Our initial learning rate is set to 0. 0001, and the decay rate is 1/10 for every 10 epochs. We train HDSRnet-light for about 80 epochs with ℓ_1

loss. Our network is implemented with the PyTorch framework on a NVIDIA 1080Ti GPU. Mean Absolute Difference (MAD), and percentage of error pixels (PE) are used to measure the difference between the predicted depth map and its ground-truth.

4.2 Comparison with SOTA Methods

We compared our method with 9 depth SR methods at three upsampling rates: 4×, 8× and 16×. Three of the compared methods are using advanced filtering or functional optimization: JGF [1], CDLLC [17], and EG [18]. Others are CNN-based SOTA methods: MSG [3], DGDIE [19], DEIN [20], CCFN [21], GSRPT [22], and PMBANet [16]. Table 1 reports objective results in terms of MAD and PE. The results show that CNN-based methods have better performance comparing to traditional filtering or optimization based methods. Our method achieves better results for most cases than the second best performer PMBANet, significantly outperforming other competing methods. Particularly, our method reduces the MAD reconstruction error below 1.0 for 16× upsampling of "Art", which is the most challenging case in the field of depth upsampling.

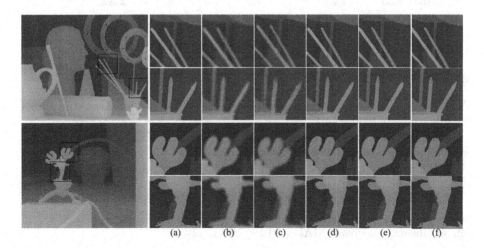

Fig. 3. Visual comparison of 8 × upsampling results on "Art" and "Reindeer": (a) GT, (b) Bicubic, (c) Depth SR [4], (d) PMBANet [16], (e) DEIN [20], and (f) our method.

Figure 3 compares the visual results of our method and other state-of-the-art methods. Comparing with the ground-truth, all these methods reconstruct similar structures in general, and our methods achieves the best visual quality. Particularly for 8× and 16× cases, the results show obvious differences around the reconstructed tiny structures. In Fig. 3, we notice some tiny objects like the tip and outline of the pencil in "Art" and the protuberance of the neck in "Reindeer" are difficult to recover.

To test generalization ability of our method, we run our model on NYU real dataset. The comparison results of other competing methods are quoted from Ye *et al.* [16], and they are trained with images from the NYU dataset. However, the training data of our HDSRnet-light does not include any image from the NYU dataset. The results in Table 2 show that our results are far superior than others, which demonstrates that the proposed HDSRnet-light can be well generalized to unseen depth maps.

Table 2. Quantitative depth SR results in RMSE on NYU dataset.

	Bicubic	EDEG [7]	DJF [27]	DGDIE [19]	GbFT [28]
4×	8.16	5.21	3.54	1.56	3.35
8×	14.22	9.56	6.2	2.99	5.73
16×	22.32	18.1	10.21	5.24	9.01

	PAC [29]	SVLRM [30]	DKN [31]	PMBANet [16]	Our method
4×	2.39	1.74	1.62	1.06	**0.76**
8×	4.59	5.59	3.26	2.28	**1.26**
16×	8.09	7.23	6.51	4.98	**2.32**

4.3   Attention Analysis

To show the effectiveness of attention module, we conduct ablation study with the following configurations:

1) **HDSRnet-light - A + ℓ_1**: keep the structure of HDSRnet-light but use concatenation to replace the attention module, and train via ℓ_1 loss.

2) **HDSRnet-light + ℓ_1**: add guided attention and train the HDSRnet-light via ℓ_1 loss.

Table 3 presents ablation results in terms of MAD and PE on five Middlebury images at 8× up-sampling rate. It can be observed that our attention mechanism can significantly decrease MAD and PE effectively.

Table 3. Ablation results in MAD/PE of our attention mechanism

	Art	Dolls	Laundry	Moebius	Reindeer	Books
Ours_wo_A	0.4/2.71	0.33/2.59	0.31/2.55	0.25/2.36	0.29/1.66	0.30/2.71
Ours_w_A	0.37/2.44	0.31/2.39	0.28/2.19	0.24/2.22	0.27/1.56	0.30/2.74

4.4 Running Time

We compared the running time of several methods on our workstation with Intel(R) Core(TM) i5-9400F CPU, 32GB RAM, and a NVIDIA GeForce GTX 1080Ti GPU. The code of Bicubic comes from Python Image Library (PIL). MSGnet [3] is implemented by Caffe, DepthSRnet [4] is implemented by TensorFlow, and our method is implemented by Pytorch.

Consider the 8× SR of a low-resolution depth map of size 135×240, the computation complexity (in FLOPs) and the running time (in ms) are reported in Table 4. The second performer PMBANet [16] has the highest complexity, and our HDSRnet-light has the lowest complexity. However, our HDSRnet-light still outperforms PMBANet (shown in Table 1). Our HDSRnet-light achieves a speed of 360 frames/second, which is comparable to the bicubic interpolation (CPU implementation).

Table 4. The results of the running time and flops

	Times (ms)	FLOPs
MSGnet [3]	405.72	4.85e11
DepthSR [4]	1639.43	4.43e12
PMBANet [16]	30.01	6.92e13
HDSRnet-light	2.61	4.62e11

5 Conclusion

In this paper, we have proposed an effective depth map super-resolution method (HDSRnet-light) with guided attention mechanism. In HDSRnet-light, we propose a guided attention scheme to fuse features of the main branch with complementary features from two side-branches associated with the auxiliary high-resolution texture information and the low-resolution depth information. In the proposed network, high-resolution features are progressively recovered from multi-scale information from both the depth map and the color image. Experimental results on benchmark datasets demonstrate that our method achieves superior performance in comparison with other state-of-the-art methods. Our HDSRnet-light has only 287.9k parameters and achieves a speed of more than 300 fps under NVIDIA GeForce GTX 1080Ti with state-of-the-art performance for the 8× super-resolution to the size of 1920×1080.

Acknowledgement. This work was supported in part by the National Natural Science Foundation of China under Grant 62231018, Grant 62171317, and Grant 62072331.

References

1. Liu, M.Y., Tuzel, O., Taguchi, Y.: Joint geodesic upsampling of depth images. In: 2013 IEEE Conference on Computer Vision and Pattern Recognition, pp. 169–176 (2013)
2. Ferstl, D., Reinbacher, C., Ranftl, R., Ruther, M., Bischof, H.: Image guided depth upsampling using anisotropic total generalized variation. In: 2013 IEEE International Conference on Computer Vision, pp. 993–1000 (2013)
3. Hui, T.-W., Loy, C.C., Tang, X.: Depth map super-resolution by deep multi-scale guidance. In: Leibe, B., Matas, J., Sebe, N., Welling, M. (eds.) ECCV 2016. LNCS, vol. 9907, pp. 353–369. Springer, Cham (2016). https://doi.org/10.1007/978-3-319-46487-9_22
4. Guo, C., Li, C., Guo, J., Cong, R., Fu, H., Han, P.: Hierarchical features driven residual learning for depth map super-resolution. IEEE Trans. Image Process. **28**(5), 2545–2557 (2019)
5. Lei, J., Li, L., Yue, H., Wu, F., Ling, N., Hou, C.: Depth map super-resolution considering view synthesis quality. IEEE Trans. Image Process. **26**(4), 1732–1745 (2017)
6. Xie, J., Feris, R.S., Sun, M.: Edge-guided single depth image super resolution. IEEE Trans. Image Process. **25**(1), 428–438 (2016)
7. Park, J., Kim, H., Tai, Y.W., Brown, M.S., Kweon, I.: High quality depth map upsampling for 3D-TOF cameras. In: 2011 International Conference on Computer Vision, pp. 1623–1630 (2011)
8. He, K., Sun, J., Tang, X.: Guided image filtering. IEEE Trans. Pattern Anal. Mach. Intell. **35**(6), 1397–1409 (2013)
9. Tomasi, C., Manduchi, R.: Bilateral filtering for gray and color images. In: International Conference on Computer Vision (2002)
10. Zuo, Y., Qiang, W., Zhang, J., An, P.: Explicit edge inconsistency evaluation model for color-guided depth map enhancement. IEEE Trans. Circuits Syst. Video Technol. **28**(2), 439–453 (2018)
11. Yang, Q., et al.: Fusion of median and bilateral filtering for range image upsampling. IEEE Trans. Image Process. **22**(12), 4841–4852 (2013)
12. Yang, J., Ye, X., Li, K., Hou, C., Wang, Y.: Color-guided depth recovery from RGB-D data using an adaptive autoregressive model. IEEE Trans. Image Process. **23**(8), 3443–3458 (2014)
13. Jiang, Z., Hou, Y., Yue, H., Yang, J., Hou, C.: Depth super-resolution from RGB-D pairs with transform and spatial domain regularization. IEEE Trans. Image Process. **27**(5), 2587–2602 (2018)
14. Riegler, G., Rüther, M., Bischof, H.: ATGV-Net: accurate depth super-resolution. In: Leibe, B., Matas, J., Sebe, N., Welling, M. (eds.) ECCV 2016. LNCS, vol. 9907, pp. 268–284. Springer, Cham (2016). https://doi.org/10.1007/978-3-319-46487-9_17
15. Song, X., Dai, Y., Qin, X.: Deeply supervised depth map super-resolution as novel view synthesis. IEEE Trans. Circuits Syst. Video Technol. **29**(8), 2323–2336 (2019)
16. Ye, X., et al.: PMBANet: progressive multi-branch aggregation network for scene depth super-resolution. IEEE Trans. Image Process. **29**, 7427–7442 (2020)
17. Xie, J., Chou, C.C., Feris, R., Sun, M.T.: Single depth image super resolution and denoising via coupled dictionary learning with local constraints and shock filtering. In: 2014 IEEE International Conference on Multimedia and Expo (ICME), pp. 1–6 (2014)

18. Xie, J., Feris, R.S., Sun, M.: Edge guided single depth image super resolution. In: 2014 IEEE International Conference on Image Processing (ICIP), pp. 3773–37777 (2014)
19. Gu, S., Zuo, W., Guo, S., Chen, Y., Chen, C., Zhang, L.: Learning dynamic guidance for depth image enhancement. In: 2017 IEEE Conference on Computer Vision and Pattern Recognition (CVPR), pp. 712–721 (2017)
20. Ye, X., Duan, X., Li, H.: Depth super-resolution with deep edge-inference network and edge-guided depth filling. In: 2018 IEEE International Conference on Acoustics, Speech and Signal Processing (ICASSP), pp. 1398–1402 (2018)
21. Wen, Y., Sheng, B., Li, P., Lin, W., Feng, D.D.: Deep color guided coarse-to-fine convolutional network cascade for depth image super-resolution. IEEE Trans. Image Process. **28**(2), 994–1006 (2019)
22. Lutio, R.D., D'aronco, S., Wegner, J.D.: Guided super-resolution as a learned pixel-to-pixel transformation (2019)
23. Butler, D.J., Wulff, J., Stanley, G.B., Black, M.J.: A naturalistic open source movie for optical flow evaluation. In: Fitzgibbon, A., Lazebnik, S., Perona, P., Sato, Y., Schmid, C. (eds.) ECCV 2012. LNCS, vol. 7577, pp. 611–625. Springer, Heidelberg (2012). https://doi.org/10.1007/978-3-642-33783-3_44
24. Scharstein, D., Szeliski, R., Zabih, R.: A taxonomy and evaluation of dense two-frame stereo correspondence algorithms. In: Proceedings IEEE Workshop on Stereo and Multi-Baseline Vision (SMBV 2001), pp. 131–140 (2001)
25. Scharstein, D., Pal, C.: Learning conditional random fields for stereo. In: 2007 IEEE Conference on Computer Vision and Pattern Recognition, pp. 1–8 (2007)
26. Scharstein, D., et al.: High-resolution stereo datasets with subpixel-accurate ground truth. In: Jiang, X., Hornegger, J., Koch, R. (eds.) GCPR 2014. LNCS, vol. 8753, pp. 31–42. Springer, Cham (2014). https://doi.org/10.1007/978-3-319-11752-2_3
27. Li, Y., Huang, J.-B., Ahuja, N., Yang, M.-H.: Deep joint image filtering. In: Leibe, B., Matas, J., Sebe, N., Welling, M. (eds.) ECCV 2016. LNCS, vol. 9908, pp. 154–169. Springer, Cham (2016). https://doi.org/10.1007/978-3-319-46493-0_10
28. AlBahar, B., Huang, J.B.: Guided image-to-image translation with bi-directional feature transformation. In: 2019 IEEE/CVF International Conference on Computer Vision (ICCV), pp. 9015–9024 (2019)
29. Su, H., Jampani, V., Sun, D., Gallo, O., Learned-Miller, E., Kautz, J.: Pixel-adaptive convolutional neural networks. In: 2019 IEEE/CVF Conference on Computer Vision and Pattern Recognition (CVPR), pp. 11158–11167 (2019)
30. Pan, J., Dong, J., Ren, J.S., Lin, L., Tang, J., Yang, M.H.: Spatially variant linear representation models for joint filtering. In: 2019 IEEE/CVF Conference on Computer Vision and Pattern Recognition (CVPR), pp. 1702–1711 (2019)
31. Kim, B., Ponce, J., Ham, B.: Deformable kernel networks for guided depth map upsampling (2019). arXiv:abs/1903.11286

A Hybrid Approach for Segmenting Non-ideal Iris Images Using CGAN and Geometry Constraints

Shanila Azhar[1], Ke Zhang[1], Xiaomin Guo[2], Shizong Yan[1], Guohua Liu[1], and Shan Chan[1(✉)]

[1] Donghua University, Shanghai, China
{415029,2171768,1222040}@mail.dhu.edu.cn, {ghliu,changshan}@dhu.edu.cn
[2] Shaanxi Provincial People's Hospital, Xi'an, Shaanxi, China
guoxiaomin@xjtu.edu.cn

Abstract. The prevalence of personal mobile devices makes iris authentication being more and more popular. Accurate iris segmentation is critical for authentication. However, it is very challenging, due to iris images captured by mobile and handheld devices may exhibit occlusion, low resolution, blur, unusual glint, ghost effect, and off-angles. Moreover, mobile devices may be equipped with visible light cameras rather than near-infrared (NIR) light cameras, which makes iris segmentation susceptible to the noise of visible light. We propose an accurate iris image segmentation approach, which takes advantages of both Conditional Generative Adversarial Network (CGAN) and geometry-based optimization. First, we design a CGAN which force the generator to produce better segmentation corresponds to the original image, a comparatively accurate prediction of iris region can be obtained. Second, a series of geometry-based optimization schemes is introduced to refine the prediction results, where elliptical Hough transform and boundary piecewise fitting are performed on the inner and outer boundary of predicted iris regions, respectively. We performed experiments on three non-ideal iris datasets of visible light and NIR environments. The segmentation accuracy is evaluated using error rate, intersection over union and F-score. Experimental results demonstrate that the proposed approach provides significant performance improvements comparing with the state-of-art methods, OSIRIS and IrisSeg.

Keywords: Mobile authentication · Iris segmentation · CGAN

1 Introduction

Iris recognition is one of the promising biometric modalities and has received much attention. The performance of iris recognition is largely dependent on the accurate isolation of iris regions from the rest of eye images [11,17]. In traditional iris recognition systems, the acquisition of iris images is commonly in near-infrared illumination environment, and requires a high degree of user cooperation. However, for mobile and handheld device authentication, non-ideal eye

L. Fang et al. (Eds.): CICAI 2023, LNAI 14473, pp. 116–129, 2024.
https://doi.org/10.1007/978-981-99-8850-1_10

images are captured in uncontrolled environmental conditions. A large amount of environmental noise can affect the quality of eye images, including reflections of visible light, motion blur, specular reflection, etc., which poses a severe challenge to iris recognition technology [1,22].

Previous works on segmenting non-ideal iris can be divided into two categories. One is to use image processing related techniques to retrieve the iris region the image based on features such as gradients and geometric relationships, and use curves to fit the contour of the iris. In this way, the anti-noise iris segmentation method based on a modified fast Hough transform is proposed, and a multi-arc and multi-line iris boundary strategy is used to define the iris boundary [6]. Subsequently, the geometric active contours are used to refine iris boundaries, and eyelash noise is suppressed by the open operation [20]. But the anti-noise ability of these methods is limited. Another is to use a deep learning approach to segment non-ideal iris images. For example, multi-scale and hierarchical convolutional neural network is proposed to segment non-ideal iris images [15]. To enhance the ability of the network to extract feature features, a deeper convolutional network has been proposed to improve segmentation accuracy [3]. Limited by the distribution of trained datasets, the segmentation results of neural network are not stable enough.

Inspired by two different ways of segmentation, we propose a combination method of learning-based and edge-based processing for segmenting non-ideal iris images. We design a conditional generative adversarial network (CGAN) in which a U-Net and a VGG network are employed as the generator and discriminator, respectively, and original iris images are fed into the generator, acting as the condition of GAN, which force the generator to make predictions of iris regions indistinguishable from real iris regions, and consistent with its original iris image as well. The prediction results of CGAN will be further refined by exploiting the natural geometry properties of iris. The outer and inner boundaries of predicted iris regions are re-fitted and smoothed, and redundant areas will be removed.

Our contributions are as follows:

- We design a hybrid approach, where the CGAN-based learning procedure and the geometry characteristic-based boundary optimization methods are aggregated together, to enable accurate and robust segmenting for non-ideal iris images captured by either NIR or visible light cameras.
- We demonstrate that introducing training constrains to the discriminator of a GAN, and geometry constrains to the boundaries of an iris region can both improve the performance of iris segmentation.
- We evaluate our approach in both ideal and non-ideal datasets using three well accepted metrics, i.e., error rate, IoU, and F1-score, and compare it with two state-of-the-art methods. Experimental results show that, for non-ideal iris images, our approach significantly outperforms both methods in all metrics.

2   Related Work

Previous iris segmentation methods usually aim at ideal iris images acquired in an ideal environment. Hough transform is used for detecting circular boundaries from iris images, and then the edge map voting based on the constraints of the iris or pupil radius is performed to determine the iris image boundary [23]. Thereafter, A new method using integral differential operators is also carried out to detect circular iris boundaries in images [7]. [10] propose an iris segmentation method based on radial suppression edge detection. They employ wavelet transform to extract the wavelet transform modulus of the iris image. According to the designed radial non-maximum suppression method, the annular edge is retained and the radial edge is removed. Finally, the threshold edge processing is used to remove the isolated edges and generate a binary edge map.

Subsequent works note the interference caused by noise on the iris segmentation, and begin to study the iris segmentation under non-ideal conditions. A novel noise detection model is designed for accurate iris segmentation. In the model, three conditions are used to determine the pixels in the eyelashes, which solves the reflection noise [14]. Alternatively, the Adaboost eye detection is performed to compensate for iris detection errors caused by two circular edge detection operations. The color segmentation method is used to solve the ghost effect noise, and the eyelid and eyelash detection is performed to reduce error [12].

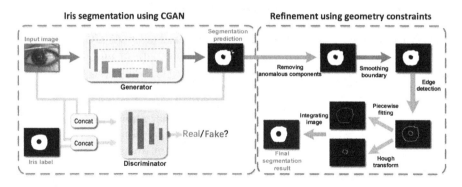

Fig. 1. The overall structure of the proposed method. Our model first feeds the input image into the neural network to produce the segmentation prediction, and then applies the refinement method to obtain the final segmentation result.

To detect iris boundaries more accurately, there are some methods using flexible contours. The active contours can be adapted to various shapes and segment multi-object at the same time, further improving the accuracy and efficiency of segmentation [21]. Considering the effects of noise, a new method combining flexible contour with Hough transform is used for iris segmentation [13].

The deep learning approaches provide a new idea for the segmentation of non-ideal iris images. Hierarchical CNN and multi-scale CNN are proposed for iris segmentation [15]. Then, a two-step segmentation method based on deep learning is proposed. Hough transform is used to locate the rough boundary, and the deep learning model is used to detect the iris image region in the rough boundary [2]. Later, [3] propose a deeper dense CNN to improve segmentation performance. Meanwhile, a new segmentation method using the graph theory to optimize the hierarchical network structure is proposed [5].

3   Methods

In our approach, we design a CGAN to generate a prediction of iris region for a non-ideal iris image. Then we use a set of boundary optimization methods based on geometry constraints to refine the prediction result, leading to an accurate segmentation of iris region. The overview of our approach is shown in Fig. 1.

3.1   Iris Segmentation Using CGAN

The small difference in boundary and gradient features in non-ideal iris images poses a challenge for iris segmentation. It is difficult to deal with complex noise interference using only image processing techniques based on gradients and geometric relationships. Since neural networks have powerful feature extraction capabilities, we choose neural network as the primary segmentation model for non-ideal iris images. In our model, we use the U-Net [19] to segment iris image. The U-Net uses a cascade structure in the up-sampling process to combine shallow features with deep features. Among them, deep features are used to locate the iris area, and shallow features are used for accurate segmentation, which is suitable for segmentation of non-ideal iris images. In the image segmentation task, the CNN constructs the loss function using only the difference between the prediction and ground truth pixels, ignoring the potential spatial continuity in the segmentation image. It is difficult to construct a loss function to force CNN to learn such constraints. However, GAN can automatically learn such a loss function that satisfies the constraint, because the goal of GAN is to train a generator that can generate predictions that are indistinguishable from ground truth. Therefore, we train an CGAN segmentation model to enable the generator to learn the statistical distribution of iris data, making the iris segmentation prediction is indistinguishable from the iris label. And we use original image as the condition, making the segmentation result corresponds to the original image under the constraint of condition.

3.2   Objective

The generator G is trained to learn a map from the original iris image x to the segmentation prediction $\hat{y}$, $G(x) \rightarrow \hat{y}$. We use $G(x)$ to denote the class probability map over 2 classes of size $H \times W \times 2$ that the segmentation model produces given an input iris image x of size $H \times W \times 3$. Unlike the standard CGAN, we do not use the noise z together as the input to the generator, the network can still use the iris image x to get the predicted segmentation result $\hat{y}$. The original image x is also used as input of the discriminator, the discriminator D learns to classify between fake (original iris image x, segmentation prediction

$\hat{y}$) and real (original iris image x, iris labels y) images. We concatenate the two images of the same spatial Resolution along the depth axis. Both the generator and discriminator observe the original iris image different from an unconditional GAN.

Adversarial Loss: We define the following adversarial loss in our model.

$$\mathcal{L}_{adv}(G, D) = \mathbb{E}_{x,y}[\log D(x, y)] + \mathbb{E}_x[\log(1 - D(x, G(x)))] \tag{1}$$

where the generator G tries to minimize this objective to fool the discriminator D. Conversely, the discriminator D tries to maximize it to distinguish between "real" and "fake" images.

Segmentation Loss: We use binary cross-entropy loss term to represent segmentation loss.

$$\mathcal{L}_{seg} = -\mathbb{E}_{x,y}[y \log G(x) + (1 - y) \log(1 - G(x))] \tag{2}$$

Training the Generator: Our goal is to locate the iris and non-iris area from a non-ideal iris image. Therefore, we employ segmentation loss to encourage the generator to correctly predict the pixel location of the iris region. And the adversarial loss is used to help the generator's predicted output closer to the real segmentation label. The objective function for the generator is defined as follows:

$$\mathcal{L}_G = \mathcal{L}_{adv} + \mathcal{L}_{seg} \tag{3}$$

Training the Discriminator: Since the adversarial loss is large if discriminator can discriminate the output of the generator from ground-truth label maps. We define the objective function for the discriminator as follows:

$$\mathcal{L}_D = -\mathcal{L}_{adv} \tag{4}$$

3.3 Network Architecture

Our network uses the architecture of U-Net as the generator, which is a convolutional encoder and decoder with skip connections. The encoder consists of a 3×3 convolution (we only use one convolution on each layer), each followed by a rectified liner unit (ReLU) and a 2×2 max pooling operation with stride 2. The decoder consists of consists of an upsampling of the Feature map followed by a 2×2 convolution, a concatenation with the correspondingly cropped Feature map from the contracting path, and a 3×3 convolution, each followed by a ReLU. The architecture of the VGG network is used in the discriminator, it contains eight convolutional layers with 3×3 filter kernel. The feature maps are followed by two dense layers and a final sigmoid activation function, which produce a probability for sample classification.

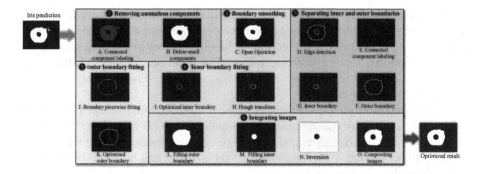

Fig. 2. Illustration of designed refinement method. The operation steps are performed in alphabetical order, and the iris prediction from neural network is as the input of refinement method. (A-B) remove the abnormal component, (C) is performed to smooth boundary, (D-O) optimize boundary shape.

3.4   Refinement Using Geometry Constraints

We observe the segmentation results from neural network appear small anomalous segmentation components and the iris boundary is rough. To solve these problems, we designed a new refinement method based on geometry constraints. The illustration of refinement method is shown in the Fig. 2.

Remove Anomalous Component. Since the anomalous segmentation area is small and discontinuous with the iris region, we first perform connected component analysis on the predicted segmentations of the neural network. Specifically, we use the 8-connected components labeling algorithm to obtain the connected regions in the graph, then calculate the size of each connected region, retain only the connected component of the largest area, and then delete other connected components. In this way, the anomalous segmentation component can be effectively removed.

Boundary Smoothing. We use the opening operation in morphology to smooth the iris boundary. The open operation consists of two operations, corrosion and expansion. The corrosion operation can eliminate the prominent boundary points and enable the boundary to shrink toward the inside. Otherwise, the expansion operation can fill the gap in the boundary and expands the entire boundary to the outside. The opening operation is first performed by etching and then expanding to remove isolated points and burrs on the boundary without causing boundary deformation. Therefore, we effectively smooth the iris boundary by the opening operation.

Boundary Shape Optimization. The boundary shape optimization is performed to further improve segmentation results. Due to the different shapes of the outer and inner boundaries, we deal with the inner and outer boundaries separately.

We first use canny edge detection algorithm to detect the inner and outer boundary curves of the iris segmentation image. After acquiring the iris boundary images, we use the connected component labeling algorithm to mark the inner and outer boundaries with different colors. The inner and outer boundaries are regarded as different connected components, and are separated according to different color markings.

The normal pupil shape of a person is nearly circular, and we hope to optimize the inner boundary by constraining the shape of the pupil boundary. Therefore, we use the elliptical Hough transform for the inner boundary image of the iris, and an ellipse on the inner boundary to replace the original pupil boundary. Such a boundary is more reasonable.

Since the outer boundary of the iris is blocked by the upper and lower eyelids, the shape of the outer contour consists of a curved portion and a straight portion. In order to smooth the outer boundary of the iris, we want to find those curved portions and then use the boundary piecewise fitting method to optimize the outer boundary. Therefore, we design an algorithm using the slope information to find the demarcation point, and optimize the shape of outer boundary.

Algorithm 1. Boundary piecewise fitting

Input: *outer boundary*
Output: *optimized outer boundary*
 1: **function** FINDCONTOUR(pic)
 2:     $SIM \leftarrow$ INITIALSIM()
 3:     $DP \leftarrow []$
 4:     $direct = [lower\_left, upper\_left, lower\_right, upper\_right]$
 5:     **for** $i = 0; i < 4; i + +$ **do**
 6:         **switch** $direct[i]$ **do**
 7:             **case** $lower\_left$
 8:                 $x, y \leftarrow$ FINDINITIALPOINT($pic, upper\_left$)
 9:             **case** $upper\_left$
10:                 $x, y \leftarrow$ FINDINITIALPOINT($pic, lower\_left$)
11:             **case** $lower\_right$
12:                 $x, y \leftarrow$ FINDINITIALPOINT($pic, upper\_right$)
13:             **case** $upper\_right$
14:                 $x, y \leftarrow$ FINDINITIALPOINT($pic, lower\_right$)
15:         $SIM \leftarrow$ SLOPEUPDATE($pic, direct[i], x, y, SIM$)
16:         $P\_start, P\_end \leftarrow$ SELECTPOINT($pic, direct[i], x, y, SIM$)
17:         $DP \leftarrow P\_start, P\_end$
18:     $optimized\ outer\ boundary \leftarrow$ POLYFIT(pic, DP)
19:     **return** $optimized\ outer\ boundary$

As shown in Algorithm 1, we first initialize a slope information matrix SIM with input image size to store the slope information of each pixel on the contour line. Initially all values Set to 0. We use the four points on the left and right ends of the top and bottom contour lines as the starting points for scanning in each direction, and whether there are valid pixels points (when scanning to lower left, the contour pixels in the left, down, and lower left directions are valid pixels) in each scanning direction as the condition for judging the termination of scanning. On the first scan, we update the slope value of SIM. For example, when scanning to the lower left, if there is a valid pixel in lower left direction, the value of the current position is updated to 1. And the other directions also update the slope value of the SIM according to similar rules. After the first scan, we need perform a second scan to update the SIM value again. The second update is to find the start and end points of the curve part in each direction. During the scanning process, We first check if the horizontal coordinate interval between two adjacent points with a SIM value of 1 is too large. If it is large, it is considered that the contour between the two points does not belong to the curve part. Then another pair of adjacent points continues to be judged until a small interval is found, the first of two adjacent points is set to 2 and is used as the starting point for the curve part. After the starting point is found, a new judgment is started. We judge whether the ordinate gap between two adjacent points with a SIM value of 1 is too large. And if so, the first of two adjacent points is set to 2 and the end point is found. After the scanning ends, if there are no adjacent points where the ordinate gap is large, the last point with a SIM value of 1 is used as the end point. After finding the start and end points of the curve section, a polynomial is used to fit the points between the start and end points.

After acquiring the new inner and outer boundaries of the iris, we need recover an iris mask image from these two boundaries images. First, we use the hole filling algorithm to fill the inside of the inner and outer boundaries, respectively. Then we inversely convert the filled inner boundary region. Finally, we integrate the two inner and outer boundary images into one iris segmentation image.

4   Experiments

In this section, we describe our experiments from datasets, evaluation metrics, implementation details, and evaluation results.

4.1   Datasets

CASIA v4 Interval. This database is a subset of CASIA Iris Image Database, which is provided by NLPR Lab [4]. It contains 2,639 iris images from 249 subjects with an image resolution of 320*280. This dataset is obtained through the camera equipped a circular NIR LED array, with suitable luminous flux. Due to the lack of corresponding ground truth in this dataset, we use the EP dataset generated by WaveLab [9], which contains the segmentation labels for the CASIA v4 Interval dataset.

UBIRIS v2. This dataset contains a total of 11,102 iris images from 261 subjects, which are 400*300 in size [18]. We select 2,250 iris images as the dataset used in our model. The iris images are captured by SOCIA Lab on non-constrained conditions, including at-a-distance, on-the-move, and on the visible wavelength. Therefore, the dataset has realistic noise factors. Similarly, the dataset contains only iris images, and the ground truth of UBIRIS v2 is from EP dataset.

Perturbed CASIA v4 Interval. The texture feature of CASIA-Iris-Interval is clear and it does not meet non-ideal condition. To obtain the various types of non-ideal iris dataset, we use the augmentation method proposed in the Shabab's study [5]. The augmentation method simulates non-ideal iris images acquired in real-life environments by reducing eye socket resolution, reducing image contrast, shading images, and blurring images. We use the perturbed CASIA dataset to verify the performance of the proposed method for non-ideal iris images.

4.2   Evaluation Metrics

We select several evaluation metrics to analyze the performance of our segmentation method for non-ideal iris image. The evaluation metrics are defined as follows:

Error Rate. We refer to the evaluation criteria of the NICE I competition to measure the performance of our proposed segmentation method. The segmentation error is represented as follows:

$$error = \frac{FP + FN}{TP + TN + FP + FN} \tag{5}$$

where TP, TN, FP, FN represent the True Positive, True Negative, False Positive, False Negative, respectively.

Intersection Over Union. IOU is often used to assess the accuracy of predictions in target detection tasks. Here we use IOU to measure the difference between the mask predictions and ground truth. The definition of IOU is as follows:

$$IOU = \frac{TP}{FP + TP + FN} \tag{6}$$

F1 Score. F1 score is an indicator used to measure the accuracy of classification model in statistics. It considers both the accuracy and the recall rate of the classification model. The F1 score is denoted as follows:

$$F1\ score = \frac{2TP}{2TP + FP + FN} \tag{7}$$

4.3   Implementation Details

Our network model is implemented in TensorFlow, and we implement refinement algorithms in Python. Our model is trained using Adam optimization algorithm, and the momentum is 0.99. We use a random normal distribution initialization to initialize the weight of the network. In experiments, the batch size is set to 10. The learning rate is 0.0001 for the first 10 epochs and linearly decay the learning rate to 0 over the next 10 epochs. The generator and the discriminator perform iterative alternation training, in which the generator performs one update after five discriminator updates. A GTX1080Ti GPU server is utilized to train the networks. For all datasets, we use 60% of the dataset as training set, 20% as validation set, and the remaining 20% as test set. To make up for the lack of data, the data augmentation is done by horizontally flipping the dataset. In addition, we cut the input image into a 128*96 size and feed it into network, which keeps the image size of different iris datasets consistent.

4.4   Comparision with the State of the Art

To compare the segmentation results of our method with other methods, we select two state-of-the-art iris segmentation methods, including the iris recognition system OSIRIS v4.1 [16] and the iris segmentation framework IrisSeg [8]. The OSIRIS is an open source iris recognition framework integrating multiple image processing methods. This framework does not require training and performs well on ideal iris images. In the experiments, we only use its iris segmentation module. To ensure that the performance of OSIRIS is not affected by unrelated factors, we set the maximum and minimum parameters of the iris radius to the appropriate values before the experiment. The IrisSeg is a segmentation framework for non-ideal iris images. This method allows for fast segmentation and does not require parameter adjustment for different iris datasets. In the experiments, we directly use the framework to test on three different datasets.

Quantitative Evaluation. In the quantitative experiment, we compare the segmentation results with the other two methods on three evaluation indicators. Table 1 is the experimental comparison results of the three datasets. In the table, we can see that our proposed method achieves the best segmentation effect on the perturbed CASIA and UBIRIS datasets. Although our segmentation results on the CASIA dataset are worse than IrisSeg, we can find it that the difference between the two is less than 1%. Meanwhile, on the other two datasets, the results of the three indicators of our method are significantly higher than the other two methods. Moreover, since the CASIA dataset is a near-infrared dataset without noise interference, and the other two datasets are non-ideal datasets containing noise. Therefore, our approach has significant advantages in segmenting non-ideal iris images. In addition, we also calculated the standard deviation of the segmentation results on each indicator. It can be seen from these figures that the standard deviation of our method is the lowest on all three datasets, indicating that the performance of our method is the most stable. Different from the other two methods, there are not many poor segmentation results in our method.

Qualitative Evaluation. We also qualitatively compare our method with the other two methods on the three datasets, which visually compares the quality of the segmentation. We randomly select a test example from each dataset to compare. Figure 3 shows the segmentation results of three different methods. Similarly, we can see that there is not much difference among the three segmentation methods for CASIA dataset, but for the other two non-ideal iris datasets,

Table 1. The quantitative comparison results of three segmentation methods.

Dataset	Method	Err%	IOU%	F1-score%
UBIRIS	OSIRIS	23.91±3.88	14.58±3.60	19.36±5.54
	IrisSeg	16.78±1.96	17.71±5.08	22.33±7.18
	Ours	**0.74±0.01**	**88.86±5.37**	**93.95±4.35**
Perturbed CASIA	OSIRIS	4.43±0.16	85.93±8.99	92.02±6.82
	IrisSeg	6.99±0.65	72.40±24.28	77.96±24.35
	Ours	**2.06±0.02**	**92.81±2.35**	**96.25±1.33**
CASIA	OSIRIS	3.54±0.07	86.91±7.12	92.77±4.80
	IrisSeg	**0.97±0.01**	**95.23±4.76**	**97.48±2.89**
	Ours	1.44±0.01	94.94±1.56	97.40±0.85

Table 2. The quantitative comparison results of ablation study.

Dataset	Method	Err%	IOU%	F1-score%
UBIRIS	w/o CGAN	0.92±0.01	86.65±6.39	92.63±5.18
	w/o refinement	0.84±0.01	87.58±7.01	93.09±6.59
	Ours	**0.74±0.01**	**88.86±5.37**	**93.95±4.35**
Perturbed CASIA	w/o CGAN	3.05±0.06	89.60±5.32	94.40±3.46
	w/o refinement	2.23±0.02	92.29±2.83	95.97±1.63
	Ours	**2.06±0.02**	**92.81±2.35**	**96.25±1.33**
CASIA	w/o CGAN	2.00±0.01	92.97±2.26	96.34±1.27
	w/o refinement	1.46±0.01	94.86±1.52	**97.48±2.89**
	Ours	**1.44±0.01**	**94.94±1.56**	97.36±0.83

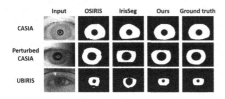

Fig. 3. The qualitative comparison results of three segmentation methods. These results are from randomly selected test samples on three iris datasets.

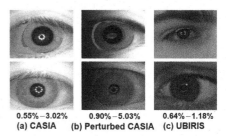

Fig. 4. The qualitative results on three iris datasets: the best (bottom) and worst (top) cases in terms of error. Green and red pixels represent the False Positives and False Negatives, respectively. (Color figure online)

the segmentation result of our method is closest to ground truth. It can effectively demonstrate that our method has the ability to segment the non-ideal iris images. Figure 4 shows the worst and best segmentation results for our method on each dataset. It can be seen that our worst results still have good accuracy and the overall results are stable.

Ablation Study. To explore the effect of the proposed CGAN model and refinement method on iris segmentation, we also design the experiments of ablation studies, and analyze the performance of our proposed method by eliminating the conditional adversarial network (w/o CGAN) and removing refinement operations (w/o refinement), separately. In the w/o CGAN setting, we choose U-Net as a benchmark. We use only the generator for iris segmentation, no longer use the discriminator and refinement method. This verifies the segmentation performance of the network model when the CGAN is not used. We retain the same hyperparameter configuration as CGAN in our experiment. In addition, we remove the entire refinement method and use the designed CGAN model to obtain the iris segmentation results, which helps to analyze the performance improvements brought by refinement method. Table 2 shows the comparison of ablation experiments. We can see that our method achieves the best performance on all three datasets. Although the standard deviation of our method on the CASIA dataset is slightly higher than w/o refinement method, the lowest standard deviation is presented on the other two datasets. It shows that the CGAN model and the designed refinement method can effectively improve the iris segmentation performance. From the comparison between the three, we can find that the segmentation model using CGAN is better than the segmentation model without CGAN, which shows that segmentation performance can be improved by CGAN structure and refinement method. Figures 5, 6, and 7 illustrate CDFs for error rate, IOU, and F1 score, respectively. Similar to the previous experiments, although our method is slightly worse than IrisSeg on CASIA dataset, the performance gap on CASIA dataset is small enough. Conversely, We have great advantages in non-ideal iris image segmentation, which demonstrates our iris segmentation method is best on the whole.

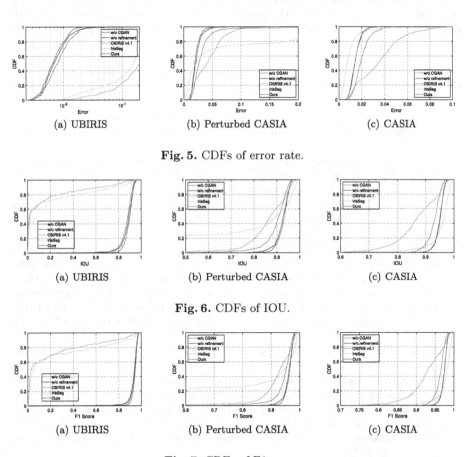

(a) UBIRIS   (b) Perturbed CASIA   (c) CASIA

Fig. 5. CDFs of error rate.

(a) UBIRIS   (b) Perturbed CASIA   (c) CASIA

Fig. 6. CDFs of IOU.

(a) UBIRIS   (b) Perturbed CASIA   (c) CASIA

Fig. 7. CDFs of F1 score.

5   Conclusion

In this paper, we propose a hybrid approach based on CGAN and geometry constraints to accurately segment non-ideal iris images. Real iris regions of eye images are introduced into a CGAN, which can guide the generator to evolve towards a stronger ability of iris region prediction. Meanwhile, we use the geometry constraints of iris shape to refine the prediction results of the CGAN. Extensive experiments on three different iris datasets demonstrate that the proposed approach achieves superior performance over the state-of-the-art methods.

Acknowledgement. This work was supported in part by the National Natural Science Foundation of China (Grant No. 61972081), and the Natural Science Foundation of Shanghai (Grant No. 22ZR1400200), the RGC RIF grant under the contract R602120, and RGC GRF grants under the contracts 16209120, 16200221 and 16207922, and Key R&D Plan of Shaanxi Province (Grant No. 2023-ZDLSF-20).

References

1. Alonso-Fernandez, F., Bigun, J.: Quality factors affecting iris segmentation and matching. In: 2013 International Conference on Biometrics (ICB), pp. 1–6. IEEE (2013)
2. Arsalan, M., et al.: Deep learning-based iris segmentation for iris recognition in visible light environment. Symmetry **9**(11), 263 (2017)
3. Arsalan, M., Naqvi, R., Kim, D., Nguyen, P., Owais, M., Park, K.: IrisDenseNet: robust iris segmentation using densely connected fully convolutional networks in the images by visible light and near-infrared light camera sensors. Sensors **18**(5), 1501 (2018)
4. of Sciences Institute of Automation, C.A.: Casia-irisv4 (2005).
5. Bazrafkan, S., Thavalengal, S., Corcoran, P.: An end to end deep neural network for iris segmentation in unconstrained scenarios. Neural Netw. **106**, 79–95 (2018)
6. Chen, Y., Adjouadi, M., Barreto, A., Rishe, N., Andrian, J.: A computational efficient iris extraction approach in unconstrained environments. In: 2009 IEEE 3rd International Conference on Biometrics: Theory, Applications, and Systems, pp. 1–7. IEEE (2009)
7. Daugman, J.: How iris recognition works. In: The Essential Guide to Image Processing, pp. 715–739. Elsevier (2009)
8. Gangwar, A., Joshi, A., Singh, A., Alonso-Fernandez, F., Bigun, J.: IrisSeg: a fast and robust iris segmentation framework for non-ideal iris images. In: 2016 International Conference on Biometrics (ICB), pp. 1–8. IEEE (2016)
9. Hofbauer, H., Alonso-Fernandez, F., Wild, P., Bigun, J., Uhl, A.: A ground truth for iris segmentation. In: 2014 22nd International Conference on Pattern Recognition, pp. 527–532. IEEE (2014)
10. Huang, J., You, X., Tang, Y.Y., Du, L., Yuan, Y.: A novel iris segmentation using radial-suppression edge detection. Signal Process. **89**(12), 2630–2643 (2009)
11. Jain, A.K., Nandakumar, K., Ross, A.: 50 years of biometric research: accomplishments, challenges, and opportunities. Pattern Recogn. Lett. **79**, 80–105 (2016)
12. Jeong, D.S., et al.: A new iris segmentation method for non-ideal iris images. Image Vis. Comput. **28**(2), 254–260 (2010)

13. Koh, J., Govindaraju, V., Chaudhary, V.: A robust iris localization method using an active contour model and hough transform. In: 2010 20th International Conference on Pattern Recognition, pp. 2852–2856. IEEE (2010)

14. Kong, W., Zhang, D.: Accurate iris segmentation based on novel reflection and eyelash detection model. In: Proceedings of 2001 International Symposium on Intelligent Multimedia, Video and Speech Processing. ISIMP 2001 (IEEE Cat. No. 01EX489), pp. 263–266. IEEE (2001)

15. Liu, N., Li, H., Zhang, M., Liu, J., Sun, Z., Tan, T.: Accurate iris segmentation in non-cooperative environments using fully convolutional networks. In: 2016 International Conference on Biometrics (ICB), pp. 1–8. IEEE (2016)

16. Othman, N., Dorizzi, B., Garcia-Salicetti, S.: Osiris: an open source iris recognition software. Pattern Recogn. Lett. **82**, 124–131 (2016)

17. Proença, H., Alexandre, L.A.: Iris recognition: analysis of the error rates regarding the accuracy of the segmentation stage. Image Vis. Comput. **28**(1), 202–206 (2010)

18. Proenca, H., Filipe, S., Santos, R., Oliveira, J., Alexandre, L.A.: The UBIRIS. v2: a database of visible wavelength iris images captured on-the-move and at-a-distance. IEEE Trans. Pattern Anal. Mach. Intell. **32**(8), 1529–1535 (2009)

19. Ronneberger, O., Fischer, P., Brox, T.: U-Net: convolutional networks for biomedical image segmentation. In: Navab, N., Hornegger, J., Wells, W.M., Frangi, A.F. (eds.) MICCAI 2015. LNCS, vol. 9351, pp. 234–241. Springer, Cham (2015). https://doi.org/10.1007/978-3-319-24574-4_28

20. Roy, K., Bhattacharya, P., Suen, C.Y.: Unideal iris segmentation using region-based active contour model. In: Campilho, A., Kamel, M. (eds.) ICIAR 2010. LNCS, vol. 6112, pp. 256–265. Springer, Heidelberg (2010). https://doi.org/10.1007/978-3-642-13775-4_26

21. Shah, S., Ross, A.: Iris segmentation using geodesic active contours. IEEE Trans. Inf. Forensics Secur. **4**(4), 824–836 (2009)

22. Thavalengal, S., Bigioi, P., Corcoran, P.: Iris authentication in handheld devices-considerations for constraint-free acquisition. IEEE Trans. Consum. Electron. **61**(2), 245–253 (2015)

23. Wildes, R.P.: Iris recognition: an emerging biometric technology. Proc. IEEE **85**(9), 1348–1363 (1997)

3D-B2U: Self-supervised Fluorescent Image Sequences Denoising

Jianan Wang[1], Hesong Li[1], Xiaoyong Wang[1(✉)], and Ying Fu[1,2]

[1] MIIT Key Laboratory of Complex-Field Intelligent Sensing,
Beijing Institute of Technology, Beijing 100081, China
wangxiaoyong@bit.edu.cn

[2] Yangtze Delta Region Academy of Beijing Institute of Technology,
Jiaxing 314019, China

Abstract. Fluorescence imaging can reveal the spatiotemporal dynamics of life activities. However, fluorescence image data suffers from photon shot noise due to a limited photon budget. Therefore, denoising fluorescence image sequences is an important task. Existing self-supervised methods solve the problem of complex parameter tuning of non-learning methods and the problem of requiring a large number of noisy-clean image pairs for supervised learning and become state-of-the-art methods for fluorescent image sequences denoising. However, they aim at 2D data, which cannot make good use of the increased time dimension information of fluorescence data compared with single image data. Besides, they still use paired noisy data to train models, and the strong prior information brought by paired data may lead to the overfitting of the model. In this work, we extend existing self-supervised methods to 3D and propose a 3D global masker that introduces a visible blind-spot structure based on 3D convolutions to avoid identity mapping while fully utilizing the input data information. Our method makes reasonable use of time dimension information and enables the task of self-supervised denoising on fluorescent images to mine information from the input data itself. Experimental results show that our method achieves a better denoising effect for fluorescent image sequences.

Keywords: Self-Supervised Learning · Fluorescence Image Sequences Denoising · 3D Global Masker

1 Introduction

Life activities are coordinated by a myriad of cellular and subcellular structures with complex spatiotemporal dynamics. Fluorescence microscopy has good molecular specificity and high spatiotemporal resolution. It is an important tool for studying cell and subcellular structures as it uses ultraviolet light or other light sources of specific wavelengths to excite objects to emit fluorescence, and then observes the shape, position, and distribution of objects.

However, the use of fluorescence microscopy also faces some challenges and problems. Due to the insufficient efficiency of existing fluorescent indicators and the susceptibility of life activities to light-induced interference [14], low photon counts inevitably generate shot noise. It greatly affects the quality of fluorescence imaging, reducing the image signal-to-noise ratio.

To improve the image quality, some researchers start with experimental equipment to obtain more photons by developing high-performance fluorescent indicators [28] or improving the performance of detection equipment [16]. However, these methods depend on the specific situation of the researcher and are difficult to be universal. In contrast, calculation-based denoising has its own merit. It does not have high requirements for researchers' equipment, so it has good compatibility and great development potential.

At present, the image denoising algorithm has been greatly developed. The earliest non-learning methods based on iterative calculation, such as NLM [4], BM3D [7], *etc.*, obtain the approximate result of denoising by looking for similar blocks of the target. However, these traditional methods usually involve complicated optimization, requiring manual adjustment of relevant parameters according to the noise situation of the data during the experiment. Therefore, although traditional methods can effectively deal with some noisy signals, such methods often require a high time cost, and it is usually difficult to achieve optimal denoising performance.

With the development of deep learning, supervised learning methods such as DNCNN [26] and FFDNet [27] have also shown good performance on denoising tasks. However, this method requires a large amount of labeled data to train the network, and the cost of obtaining noise-free images is often very high, which makes it difficult to collect effective training data sets. In order to solve the problem that supervised learning methods require a large amount of clean data, self-supervised learning represented by Noise2Noise [15] began to develop. Noise2Void [12], Neighbor2Neighbor [11], Blind2Unblind (B2U) [23] and other methods have achieved performance close to or even reached the performance of supervised learning methods.

However, current self-supervised learning methods are mainly aimed at 2D images. In the fluorescence image data, since most of the fluorescence image sequences record continuous activity information, there is a strong spatiotemporal correlation between the data frames. Therefore, self-supervised denoising algorithms in 2D are difficult to handle and exploit the spatiotemporal information inherent in fluorescence image sequences. At the same time, although DeepCAD-RT [17] uses 3D-Unet [6] to utilize the spatiotemporal information of the fluorescence image sequence, it directly uses the adjacent frames of the input data as the input and target of the model, which does not dig deep into the image information. In addition, the information correlation between the input frame and the target frame is too high, and too strong prior knowledge may also cause the model to overfit the training set.

In this work, we extend existing self-supervised methods to 3D and propose a 3D global masker that introduces a visible blind-spot structure based on 3D convolutions to avoid identity mapping while fully utilizing the input data information. Our method makes reasonable use of time dimension information and enables the task of self-supervised denoising on fluorescent images to mine information from the input data itself. Experimental results show that our method achieves better denoising effect for fluorescence data.

2   Related Work

In this section, we briefly describe the development of image denoising methods and the study of self-supervised denoising algorithms on fluorescence image data.

2.1   Image Denoising

Non-learning Image Denoising. Traditional non-learning denoising methods, such as NLM [4], BM3D [7], CBM3D [8], WNNM [9], *etc.*, perform denoising iteratively by using similar mean values as a strategy. However, these methods are often constrained by complex optimization and hyperparameter tuning, as well as long denoising inference time and limited performance improvement.

Supervised Image Denoising. In recent years, many supervised image denoising methods have been proposed. Zhang *et al.* first proposed DnCNN [26], which uses noise-clean pairs as supervision to deal with unknown noise levels. Subsequently, they further proposed FFDNet [27] with improved adaptability to different noise levels. At the same time, as a general-purpose denoiser based on multi-scale features, U-Net [21] has also achieved good results in image denoising tasks. Besides that, many improvements have also been contributed to supervised methods [1,5,10,25]. However, supervised denoising methods require a large amount of labeled data to train the network, however, the cost and difficulty of obtaining noise-free images are often very high, which makes it difficult to collect high-quality datasets and increases the difficulty of model training.

Self-supervised Image Denoising. Supervised deep learning denoising methods usually require a large number of clean images as training labels, which are difficult or cost-prohibitive to obtain in most scenarios. Therefore, a challenging and practical question is how to train effective denoising models without clean data. Noise2Noise [15] was the first to use paired noisy data to train the model, thereby alleviating the need for data. Then, Noise2Self [2] and Noise2Void [12] proposed a masking scheme for denoising a single noisy image. Since the mask covers some areas of the noisy data, this practice will cause the loss of information, thus affecting the ability to denoising. Noisier2Noise [19] introduces additional noise, but this method requires a known noise distribution, making it difficult to handle data with unknown noise distributions. Neighbor2Neighbor [11] obtains noise pairs for training by subsampling noise images, but subsampling destroys the integrity of pixel results. Recently, Wang *et al.* proposed Blind2Unblind [23], which effectively solves the information loss caused by the blind spot structure by introducing a globally aware mask mapper and re-visibility loss on top of the blind structure.

2.2 Self-supervised Denoising on Fluorescence Images

As an advanced signal processing technique, deep learning has been adopted by microscopists and achieved good performance in fluorescence imaging [3, 20, 24]. However, the highly dynamic nature of physiological activities makes it no longer feasible to collect high-quality supervised images. Li *et al.* proposed DeepCAD [18], which introduced the Noise2Noise [15] method into the fluorescence image denoising task. Subsequently, DeepCAD-RT [17] was further developed, and the speed of denoising processing was greatly accelerated by methods such as pruning. However, existing fluorescence image self-supervised algorithms still rely on paired noisy images for training, which may provide image prior information to the model due to the high similarity between input and target images, which may make it easy for the model to learn the identity mapping, making it difficult to achieve better performance [23]. In this work, our proposed 3D global masker can not only maintain the model's ability to process 3D fluorescence data, but also effectively avoid the model from being limited by the noise prior and identity mapping, thereby obtaining stronger information digging ability.

3 Method

In this section, we comprehensively introduce our research motivation, the overall framework of our method and the 3D global masker.

3.1 Motivation

Since the Noise2Noise [15] method was proposed, self-supervised denoising methods have been greatly developed and improved. For example, some methods [2, 12, 13] introduce blind spot structure, so that the model no longer needs paired data for training. On this basis, the Blind2Unblind method goes a step further. Through the introduction of a global-aware mask mapper and re-visibility loss, the model can effectively alleviate the information loss problem caused by the blind spot structure, while mining information from the input data itself.

However, we note that in the task of denoising fluorescence image data, the recently proposed DeepCAD-RT [17] method is still designed following the Noise2Noise method, using adjacent frames of the input image sequence as the input and target of the model. Therefore, we decided to propose a 3D global masker, which introduces a visible blind spot structure based on 3D convolution to avoid identity mapping while fully using the input data information, so that the model is free from information loss and identity mapping, thus improving the ability of the model to mine information from the input data.

3.2 Framework

In this work, we obtain the interpolated sequence $\Omega(y)$ through the operation of splitting-mask-interpolation-merging from the original image sequence y. We let the interpolated sequence $\mathbf{\Omega(y)}$ through the denoising network f(the 3D-Unet model is used in this work) to get $f(\mathbf{\Omega(y)})$. The $f(\mathbf{\Omega(y)})$ and the mask sequence are operated under the global mask mapper h to obtain the prediction result $h(f[\mathbf{\Omega(y)}])$. We subtract the original image sequence from the inference result to get the difference $\mathbf{d}$, and use $\mathbf{d}$ to calculate the regular constraint loss of the model. The calculation method is

$$L_{\text{reg}} = \alpha \ \text{mean}(\mathbf{d}^2). \tag{1}$$

At the same time, the original image sequence $\mathbf{y}$ directly passes through the denoising network f, and the prediction result of the non-blind spot sequence $f(\mathbf{y})$ can be obtained, which provides the missing pixel information under the blind spot structure for the learning of the model. By making the difference between $f(\mathbf{y})$ and $\mathbf{y}$, we get $\mathbf{d}_{\text{rev}}$, the revisible results ($\mathbf{r}$) obtained by the weighted combination of $\mathbf{d}_{\text{rev}}$ and $\mathbf{d}$ can be used to calculate the revisible loss of the model, the calculation method of $\mathbf{r}$ is

$$\mathbf{r} = \mathbf{d} + \beta \ \mathbf{d}_{\text{rev}}, \tag{2}$$

and the specific calculation method of the revisible loss is

$$L_{\text{rev}} = \text{mean}(\mathbf{r}^2). \tag{3}$$

The denoising network f adds the regularized constraint loss and the revisit constraint loss to obtain the loss function used to update the parameter weights. The specific calculation method is

$$L_{\text{all}} = L_{\text{reg}} + L_{\text{rev}}. \tag{4}$$

Among them, α and β are the hyperparameters preset by the experimenter, and mean is the mean value operation.

The pipeline of the whole model is shown in Fig. 1. For an input image sequence $\mathbf{y}$, we mask it with a 3D global masker $\mathbf{\Omega}$ according to a fixed order, and sample the masked result using a 3D global-aware mask mapper h to obtain $h(f[\mathbf{\Omega(y)}])$ through a denoising network f. Besides, the unmasked image sequence $\mathbf{y}$ directly passes through the denoising network f to obtain a prediction result sequence $f(\mathbf{y})$ without loss of information. The function of '⊕' is to weigh the interpolation prediction result and the direct prediction result to obtain the prediction result with heavy visible information. Through the weighted calculation results of $h(f[\mathbf{\Omega(y)}])$ and $f(\mathbf{y})$, a denoising prediction sequence with re-visibility information is obtained. For $h(f[\mathbf{\Omega(y)}])$ and revisible results, the regularization loss and the revisible loss are computed respectively with $\mathbf{y}$ to guide the parameter iteration of the model.

3.3   3D Global Masker

Through the analysis of DeepCAD-RT [17], it can be found that by applying 3D-Unet to the denoising of fluorescent image sequences and referring to the self-supervised learning idea of Noise2Noise [15], DeepCAD-RT has achieved good results in the task of denoising fluorescent image sequences. However, the idea of self-supervised learning denoising is to mine information from the unlabeled data itself. During the training process, DeepCAD-RT directly uses the adjacent frames of the image sequence as the input and target of the model. In addition to the information on the fluorescence image sequence itself, the additional supervision information brought by the high correlation between the input and the target will also guide the training of the model, which may lead to the occurrence of overfitting. To address these issues, We propose a 3D global masker.

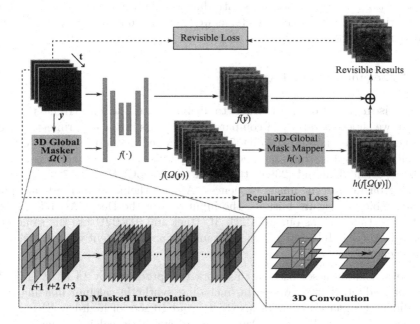

Fig. 1. An overview of our overall pipeline, where the 3D global masker uses 3D convolution to interpolate the input image sequence y. The role of '$\oplus$' is to weigh the interpolated predictions with the direct predictions. Revisibile Results are the fusion of the prediction result of the interpolated sequence and the direct prediction result.

Specifically, we made the following improvements to the 3D global masker: we rewrote the mask module in the Blind2Unblind method so that it can handle the input tensor of $[N, C, D, H, W]$, and Returns the Mask input for $[N \times c^2, C, D, H, W]$, where c is the side length of the unit that divides the image in the Blind2Unblind [23] method. In the process of interpolating the image sequence, we use 3D convolution to interpolate the input image sequence, and the pixel value of the interpolated position is provided by the neighboring pixel values of this frame and its adjacent frames. Unlike the 2D-B2U method, which interpolates only one image at a time, we interpolate the same position of the entire image sequence at a time and generate the corresponding interpolation sequence results, then stitch the interpolated image sequences together as the input of the denoising model. The specific details of our 3D Global Masker are shown at the bottom of Fig. 1.

4   Experimental Results

In this section, we comprehensively introduce the datasets, comparison methods and metrics used in our experiments, as well as the denoising results in different noisy data scenarios.

4.1   Experimental Settings

Comparison Methods. In order to demonstrate the effectiveness of our method, we choose a variety of comparative methods in the experiment, including a non-learning method (BM3D [7]), a supervised method (3D-Unet [6]) and two self-supervised learning methods. Self-supervised learning methods include the latest Blind2Unblind [23] method and the DeepCAD-RT [17] method for denoising on fluorescent image sequences. Among them, all methods are publicly available. To ensure fairness, the input size of the DeepCAD-RT method is set to be the same as our 3D-B2U, 3D-Unet and 3D-B2U use the same network as DeepCAD-RT, and all other parameters are consistent with the relevant original papers.

Datasets. The data set used in this work was produced by Li *et al.* [17], the data set is divided into two parts, including synthetic calcium imaging data with different signal-to-noise ratios (SNR) and 10 sets of high-low SNR image sequence pairs of real images. Among them, synthetic calcium imaging data was produced with silicon Neural Anatomy and Optical Microscopy (NAOMi) [22], through the use of analog methods to create images, it can provide noise-free ground truth images that cannot be obtained during normal experimental shooting. The simulated data has very similar spatio-temporal characteristics to the experimentally obtained data. By adding Poisson-Gaussian mixed noise with Poisson noise as the main noise source to the noise-free data, different SNR caused by different relative photon numbers can be simulated. Real-noise data are captured synchronously by a two-photon microscopy system. The data scenarios are real physiological activity data, including mouse dendritic activity, zebrafish brain activity, and ATP release in mouse brain, *etc.* For each physiological activity, this dataset provides high-low SNR sequence pairs. The complete data set is about 250G in total and can be downloaded from the public link.

Metrics. We follow the metrics of Li *et al.* [17], using SNR to evaluate denoising results on synthetic data, and Pearson correlation coefficient (R) to evaluate denoising results on real data.

For synthetic data, since it can provide the ground truth, we can directly calculate the SNR between the denoised result and the ground truth. For the real data, due to the lack of ground truth, we complete the denoising process on the low SNR data, and calculate the Pearson correlation coefficient between the denoising results and the corresponding high SNR data. The Pearson correlation coefficient is a statistical concept which is used to measure the degree of linear correlation between two variables, and its value range is $[-1, +1]$. The higher the result, the stronger the correlation between the two data. Its specific definition is

$$R = \frac{E[(\boldsymbol{x} - \mu_x)(\boldsymbol{y} - \mu_y)]}{\sigma_x \sigma_y},$$ (5)

where $\boldsymbol{x}$ is the data to be measured, and $\boldsymbol{y}$ is the corresponding high SNR data. μ_x and μ_y are the mean values of $\boldsymbol{x}$ and $\boldsymbol{y}$, respectively. σ_x and σ_y are the standard deviations of $\boldsymbol{x}$ and $\boldsymbol{y}$, respectively.

4.2 Synthetic Data Denoising

Due to memory limitations, we control DeepCAD-RT to use the same scale input as 3D-B2U to ensure fairness. Besides, we train the model with default settings and compare the denoising results of different denoising methods on synthetic data. All methods perform denoising inference on the last 2000 frames on the -2.51 dB data and compute the SNR with the corresponding ground truth. It is worth noting that the 3D-Unet uses the same network model as DeepCAD-RT, using noisy data and ground truth values as the input and target of the model. The comparison of inference results of each method on synthetic data is shown in Fig. 2. Table 1 shows the SNR of the inference results of each method.

For the DeepCAD-RT method, paired image pairs are used for training during training. During the training process, the model fails to fully utilize the information of the input data, moreover, the obtained information also includes strong prior information between the target and the input. When we control the size of the input data of the DeepCAD-RT method to be the same as that of 3D-B2U, the additional information between the "input-target" pairs that the model can obtain becomes less. The 3D-B2U method uses a global mask based on 3D convolution, which can focus more on mining information from the input data itself, so it can still maintain a strong denoising ability under the premise of small input data. The experimental results confirmed our inference.

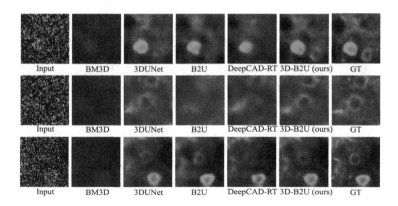

Fig. 2. Denoising results of different methods for synthetic data with the same SNR level (-2.51 dB).

Table 1. Comparison of the denoising results of each method in the scene of synthetic noise data. The denoising task is performed on the data with an initial SNR of -2.51 dB, and the denoising effect is evaluated by calculating the SNR between the denoising result and the ground truth. The higher the SNR, the better the denoising effect.

	BM3D [7]	3DUNet [6]	B2U [23]	DeepCAD-RT [17]	3D-B2U (ours)
Params (K)	0	1020	1099	1020	1020
Flops (G)	N/A	29.68	315.47	29.68	298.33
SNR (dB)↑	6.21	21.45	17.88	19.76	**21.89**

4.3   Real Data Denoising

We selected four real noise scenes such as the Zebrafish multi brain dataset to compare the denoising effects of different methods. Since the real scene data has no ground truth, we measure the quality of the denoising effect by calculating the Pearson correlation coefficient of the high SNR data and the denoising results. The comparison of inference results of each method on synthetic data is shown in Fig. 3. Table 2 shows the inference performance of different methods on the real data. It can be seen from the results that the 3D-B2U method basically achieves the same denoising ability as the state-of-the-art method.

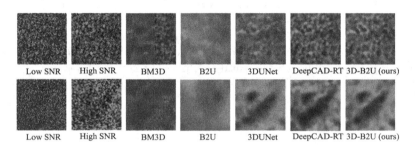

Fig. 3. Denoising results of different methods on real data scenarios. The first row is the Zebrafish multiple brain regions data, and the second row is the mouse neurites data.

Table 2. Comparison of the denoising results of each method in the real noise data scene. The denoising effect was evaluated by calculating the Pearson correlation coefficient (R) between the denoising results and the corresponding high SNR data. A higher R indicates that the denoising result is more correlated with the corresponding real high SNR data.

Data	BM3D [7]	3D-UNet [6]	B2U [23]	DeepCAD-RT [17]	3D-B2U (ours)
Zebrafish Multiple Brain	0.1449	0.7907	0.7142	**0.8044**	0.8019
Mouse Dendritic Spines	0.2227	0.4560	0.3171	0.4526	**0.4677**
Drosophila Mushroom Body	0.0437	0.8431	0.7847	0.8427	**0.8474**
ATP in Mouse Brain	0.3791	**0.5133**	0.4722	0.4982	0.5128

5 Ablation

In this work, we extend the B2U [23] method to handle 3D data, and design a 3D Global Masker to more efficiently utilize the spatiotemporal information in 3D data. We conduct ablation experiments to verify the effectiveness of our 3D extension method and the proposed 3D Global Masker.

Specifically, in the 3D extension of the B2U method, for a single frame of an image sequence, we interpolate according to a given c. After we have all the interpolated sub-images for that image, we put these interpolated results in an image stack and repeat the operation for the next image. After completing the interpolation of all the pictures in the input sequence, the obtained results are spliced together to become the input sequence $\Omega(y)$ of the model. The 3D Global Masker we proposed goes a step further and realizes a 3-dimensional visible blind spot structure through 3D convolution. To better utilize the information of the input data, we consider the input data batch as a whole. We interpolate all frames of the input sequence simultaneously according to the given c and put the result in an image stack. After all position interpolation is completed, the image sequence in the stack is the input sequence $\Omega(y)$ of the model.

3D Extension Method. Since the fluorescence data sequences we deal with have the characteristics of high dynamics and high complexity. In the image sequence, the information of adjacent frames is actually an important feature of the data itself, while the 3d extension of B2U only interpolates a single frame on the image sequence and stitches it, and the interpolation result is only provided by the pixel neighborhood in this frame. In contrast, after we extend B2U to 3D, since we use 3D-Unet as the denoising network, the interpolation results are inspired by 3D filters, and the larger data receptive field increases the ability of data to mine its own information.

3D Global Masker. Compared with the method of interpolating a single frame of the image sequence and then splicing it, the interpolation operation of the entire image sequence can better preserve the spatiotemporal information between adjacent frames of the input data. This is helpful for the model to make better use of data for training. Although the end of the previous interpolation part sequence is connected to the head of the current interpolation part at the splicing of the image sequence, for the model as a whole, most of the spatiotemporal information of the input data is "ordered". We believe that this ordered spatiotemporal information can make up for the disadvantage of unordered spatiotemporal information at the splicing, and help to improve the denoising ability of the model.

The quantitative results of the ablation experiments are shown in Table 3. From the experimental results, we can see that by extending B2U to 3D, we achieve better performance on 3D data. Besides, the introduction of 3D Global Masker further improves the model's ability to mine data information.

Table 3. Results of ablation experiments. Verified the effectiveness of B2U's 3D extension and 3D Global Masker. Among them, B2U+3D represents the 3D extension of B2U, and 3D-B2U represents the 3D extension of B2U after the introduction of 3D Global Masker.

Data	Metric	B2U	B2U+3D	3D-B2U
Synthetic Calcium Data (-2.51dB) [17]	SNR (dB)	17.88	21.77	**21.89**
Mouse Dendritic Spines [17]	R	0.3171	0.4668	**0.4677**
Mouse Neurites [17]	R	0.3676	0.4506	**0.4528**

6 Conclusion

In this work, we extend existing self-supervised methods to 3D and propose a 3D global masker that introduces a visible blind-spot structure based on 3D convolutions to avoid identity mapping while fully utilizing the input data information. Our method makes reasonable use of time dimension information and enables the task of self-supervised denoising on fluorescent images to mine information from the input data itself. Experimental results show that our method can achieve better denoising effect for fluorescent image sequences.

Acknowledgement. This work was supported by National Key R&D Program of China (2022YFC 3300704), and the National Natural Science Foundation of China under Grants (62171038, 62171042, and 62088101).

References

1. Anwar, S., Barnes, N.: Real image denoising with feature attention. In: Proceedings of the International Conference on Computer Vision, pp. 3155–3164 (2019)
2. Batson, J., Royer, L.: Noise2self: blind denoising by self-supervision. In: Proceedings of the International Conference on Machine Learning, Proceedings of Machine Learning Research, vol. 97, pp. 524–533 (2019)
3. Belthangady, C., Royer, L.A.: Applications, promises, and pitfalls of deep learning for fuorescence image reconstruction. Nat. Methods 1215–1225 (2019)

4. Buades, A., Coll, B., Morel, J.M.: A non-local algorithm for image denoising. In: Proceedings of the Conference on Computer Vision and Pattern Recognition, vol. 2, pp. 60–65 (2005)
5. Chang, M., Li, Q., Feng, H., Xu, Z.: Spatial-adaptive network for single image denoising. In: Vedaldi, A., Bischof, H., Brox, T., Frahm, J.-M. (eds.) ECCV 2020. LNCS, vol. 12375, pp. 171–187. Springer, Cham (2020). https://doi.org/10.1007/978-3-030-58577-8_11
6. Çiçek, Ö., Abdulkadir, A., Lienkamp, S.S., Brox, T., Ronneberger, O.: 3D U-net: learning dense volumetric segmentation from sparse annotation. In: Ourselin, S., Joskowicz, L., Sabuncu, M.R., Unal, G., Wells, W. (eds.) MICCAI 2016. LNCS, vol. 9901, pp. 424–432. Springer, Cham (2016). https://doi.org/10.1007/978-3-319-46723-8_49
7. Dabov, K., Foi, A., Katkovnik, V., Egiazarian, K.: Image restoration by sparse 3d transform-domain collaborative filtering. In: Image Processing: Algorithms and Systems. SPIE Proceedings, vol. 6812, p. 681207 (2008)
8. Dabov, K., Foi, A., Katkovnik, V., Egiazarian, K.O.: Color image denoising via sparse 3d collaborative filtering with grouping constraint in luminance-chrominance space. In: Proceedings of the International Conference on Image Processing, ICIP, pp. 313–316 (2007)
9. Gu, S., Zhang, L., Zuo, W., Feng, X.: Weighted nuclear norm minimization with application to image denoising. In: Proceedings of the Conference on Computer Vision and Pattern Recognition, pp. 2862–2869 (2014)
10. Guo, S., Yan, Z., Zhang, K., Zuo, W., Zhang, L.: Toward convolutional blind denoising of real photographs. In: Proceedings of the Conference on Computer Vision and Pattern Recognition, pp. 1712–1722 (2019)
11. Huang, T., Li, S., Jia, X., Lu, H., Liu, J.: Neighbor2neighbor: self-supervised denoising from single noisy images. In: Proceedings of the Conference on Computer Vision and Pattern Recognition, pp. 14781–14790 (2021)
12. Krull, A., Buchholz, T.O., Jug, F.: Noise2void-learning denoising from single noisy images. In: Proceedings of the Conference on Computer Vision and Pattern Recognition, pp. 2129–2137 (2019)
13. Krull, A., Vicar, T., Prakash, M., Lalit, M., Jug, F.: Probabilistic noise2void: unsupervised content-aware denoising. Front. Comput. Sci. 2, 5 (2020)
14. Laissue, P.P., Alghamdi, R.A., Tomancak, P., Reynaud, E.G., Shroff, H.: Assessing phototoxicity in live fluorescence imaging. Nat. Methods 14(7), 657–661 (2017)
15. Lehtinen, J., et al.: Noise2noise: learning image restoration without clean data. In: Proceedings of the 35th International Conference on Machine Learning, ICML. Proceedings of Machine Learning Research, vol. 80, pp. 2971–2980 (2018)
16. Li, B., Wu, C., Wang, M., Charan, K., Xu, C.: An adaptive excitation source for high-speed multiphoton microscopy. Nat. Methods 17(2), 163–166 (2020)
17. Li, X., et al.: Real-time denoising of fluorescence time-lapse imaging enables high-sensitivity observations of biological dynamics beyond the shot-noise limit. Nat. Biotechnol. 282–292 (2023)
18. Li, X., et al.: Reinforcing neuron extraction and spike inference in calcium imaging using deep self-supervised denoising. Nat. Methods 1395–1400 (2021)
19. Moran, N., Schmidt, D., Zhong, Y., Coady, P.: Noisier2noise: learning to denoise from unpaired noisy data. In: Proceedings of the Conference on Computer Vision and Pattern Recognition, pp. 12061–12069 (2020)
20. Ouyang, W., Aristov, A., Lelek, M., Hao, X., Zimmer, C.: Deep learning massively accelerates super-resolution localization microscopy. Nat. Biotechnol. 460–468 (2018)

21. Ronneberger, O., Fischer, P., Brox, T.: U-net: convolutional networks for biomedical image segmentation. In: Navab, N., Hornegger, J., Wells, W.M., Frangi, A.F. (eds.) MICCAI 2015. LNCS, vol. 9351, pp. 234–241. Springer, Cham (2015). https://doi.org/10.1007/978-3-319-24574-4_28

22. Song, A., Gauthier, J.L., Pillow, J.W., Tank, D.W., Charles, A.S.: Neural anatomy and optical microscopy (NAOMI) simulation for evaluating calcium imaging methods. J. Neurosci. Methods **358**, 109173 (2021)

23. Wang, Z., Liu, J., Li, G., Han, H.: Blind2unblind: self-supervised image denoising with visible blind spots. In: Proceedings of the Conference on Computer Vision and Pattern Recognition, pp. 2017–2026 (2022)

24. Weigert, M., et al.: Content-aware image restoration: pushing the limits of fluorescence microscopy. Nat. Methods 1090–10970 (2018)

25. Yue, Z., Yong, H., Zhao, Q., Meng, D., Zhang, L.: Variational denoising network: toward blind noise modeling and removal. In: Advances in Neural Information Processing Systems 32: Annual Conference on Neural Information Processing Systems, pp. 1688–1699 (2019)

26. Zhang, K., Zuo, W., Chen, Y., Meng, D., Zhang, L.: Beyond a gaussian denoiser: residual learning of deep CNN for image denoising. IEEE Trans. Image Process. **26**(7), 3142–3155 (2017)

27. Zhang, K., Zuo, W., Zhang, L.: Ffdnet: toward a fast and flexible solution for CNN-based image denoising. IEEE Trans. Image Process. **27**(9), 4608–4622 (2018)

28. Zheng, Q., et al.: Ultra-stable organic fluorophores for single-molecule research. Chem. Soc. Rev. **43**(4), 1044–1056 (2014)

Equivariant Indoor Illumination Map Estimation from a Single Image

Yusen Ai[1], Xiaoxue Chen[2], Xin Wu[1], and Hao Zhao[2(✉)]

[1] Key Laboratory of Machine Perception(MOE), School of AI,
Peking University, Beijing, China
`ysai@pku.edu.cn`
[2] Institute for AI Industry Research,
Tsinghua University, Beijing, China
`zhaohao@air.tsinghua.edu.cn`

Abstract. Thanks to the recent development of inverse rendering, photorealistic re-synthesis of indoor scenes have brought augmented reality closer to reality. All-angle environment illumination map estimation of arbitrary locations, as a fundamental task in this domain, is still challenging to deploy due to the requirement of expensive depth input. As such, we revisit the appealing setting of illumination estimation from a single image, using a cascaded formulation. The first stage predicts faithful depth maps from a single RGB image using a distortion-aware architecture. The second stage applies point cloud convolution operators that are equivariant to SO(3) transformations. These two technical ingredients collaborate closely with each other, because equivariant convolution would be meaningless without distortion-aware depth estimation. Using the public Matterport3D dataset, we demonstrate the effectiveness of our illumination estimation method both quantitatively and qualitatively. Code is available at https://github.com/Aitensa/Img2Illum.

1 Introduction

Understanding the physical properties that can be used to generate an image, which is often referred to as inverse rendering [13,32], is not only a fundamental computer vision problem but also an enabling technique of emerging A/VR applications. If this goal is finally achieved with high accuracy, we can insert any objects into captured photos without human-perceptible artifacts. But this is very challenging as the inverse rendering problem involves many sub-tasks that are difficult on their own. Among them, estimating the lighting condition is an indispensable module.

While there exist other lighting parameterizations, we choose panoramic illumination map [21,30] among alternatives due to its simplicity and expressiveness. Specifically, the task is to infer a panoramic illumination map for a certain pixel in a perspective RGB image as shown in Fig. 1. We first recap two highly related prior works as follows: (1) Neural Illumination [21] uses exactly the same setting as ours, but it's quite complicated, consisting of a geometry estimation module, a differentiable warping module and an HDR reconstruction module. (2) PointAR

L. Fang et al. (Eds.): CICAI 2023, LNAI 14473, pp. 143–155, 2024.
https://doi.org/10.1007/978-981-99-8850-1_12

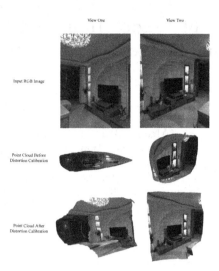

Fig. 1. The task is to infer a panoramic illumination map from a single perspective RGB image and the first step of our method is to infer a point cloud from RGB images. We want the algorithm to be equivariant to SO(3) transformations. For example, for the same point (e.g., a point on the floor) in two viewpoints shown in the left panel, we want the illumination map to be equivariant to viewpoint changes. As such, depth map distortion calibration becomes important because imposing equivariant convolution on point clouds (middle panel) is meaningless.

[30] assumes that an RGB-D image, which can be converted into a point cloud, is available as input. Then a point convolutional network directly extracts spherical harmonics that approximates the illumination map, from input point clouds.

We note that PointAR is not applicable to most cellphones without depth cameras, so we revisit the more generic single-image setting of Neural Illumination. Unfortunately, the network of Neural Illumination involves several dense prediction modules that are also inefficient for deployment. As such, we propose a new cascaded formulation that firstly predicts depth from a single RGB image and then applies a PointAR-like architecture to regress spherical harmonics from the predicted point cloud.

This new formulation is conceptually simple but successfully pushing it to the state-of-the-art performance level needs specific designs. The **first** design is introducing equivariant point convolution of [3]. The illumination map of the same point (e.g., a point on the floor in the scene shown in Fig. 1) should be equivariant to SO(3) transformation like the viewpoint changes in two rows of Fig. 1. To clarify, since the predicted point cloud needs to be re-centered to the point of interest as PointAR does, we only need to concern about SO(3) equivariance instead of SE(3) equivariance. The **second** design is introducing the distortion calibration technique proposed in [26]. It is widely known that single-view depth estimation is troubled by incorrect depth scale and bias. As shown in the middle panel of Fig. 1, without (scale/bias) distortion calibration the point clouds generated from two viewpoints are completely different. In this case, SO(3) equivariance becomes meaningless so using calibrated piont clouds (Fig. 1 right panel) is the right choice. To summarize, in this study:

- We propose a new framework that estimates panoramic illumination maps from a single RGB image, which cascades a depth estimation network and a network that estimates spherical harmonics from predicted point clouds.
- We introduce SO(3) equivariant point convolution and depth calibration into the framework. Although they are existing techniques, we are the first to show their collaboration and significant impact on illumination estimation.
- We benchmark on the large-scale public dataset Matterport3D, achieving state-of-the-art results. Through ablations, we demonstrate the impact of newly introduced modules. Codes are publicly available.

2 Related Work

Lighting Estimation has been a long-standing challenge in computer vision, and is critical for real-world AR applications like realistic relighting and object replacement. A direct way of capturing the illumination of an environment is to use a physical probe [4]. This process, though accurate, can be expensive and unsuitable for lighting estimation of different locations. Another line of works estimates illumination as a sub-task of inverse rendering [16,32], whose goal is to jointly estimate intrinsic properties of the scene, e.g. geometry, reflectance, and lighting from the input image. Classical methods formulate inverse rendering as an energy optimization problem with heuristic priors [13]. With the rapid development of deep neural networks, we could also learn generalizable models directly from single images in a data-driven fashion. Existing works estimate environment lighting in simplified problem settings, such as outdoor scenes [12,29] and objects [1,17]. In this work, we focus on more complex indoor environments, where the spatially-varying effects are not negligible.

For indoor scenes, Karsch et al. [13] recover parametric 3D lighting from a single image assuming known geometry. Gardner et al. [10] propose to learn the location and intensity of light sources in an end-to-end manner. However, their models don't handle spatially-varying lighting, i.e., different locations within the scene can have different lighting. [9] improves it by representing lighting as a set of discrete 3D lights with geometric and photometric parameters. Song et al. [21] decompose illumination prediction into several simpler differentiable sub-tasks, but suffer from spatial instability. Lighthouse [22] further proposes a multi-scale volumetric lighting representation. Wang et al. [24] leverage a holistic inverse rendering framework to guarantee physically correct HDR lighting prediction. Li et al. [16] use 360° panoramic images to obtain high-definition spatially-varying lighting. Zhan et al. [28] solve illumination estimation via spherical distribution approximation.

Meanwhile, to enable real-time AR applications on modern mobile devices, [11,30] use the spherical harmonics (SH) lighting model for fast estimation. In this work, we predict both the SH coefficients and the irradiance map.

Equivariance is a promising property of feature representation. Compared to invariance, equivariance maintains the influence of different transformations, ensuring stable and reasonable performance. In the field of computer vision, since neural networks are often sensitive to rotation transformations, a large body of work has been proposed for rotation equivariance. Existing techniques could be roughly divided into spectral and non-spectral methods.

Spectral methods usually design intrinsically rotation-equivariant basis functions [23], and develop special network architectures with these basis functions [5,14,20]. Tensor-field based networks [7,8,23] implement convolutional kernels in the spherical harmonics domain to make the features equivariant to rotations and translations. However, spherical harmonics leads to high space and time complexity. Deng et al. [5] propose a general framework built on vector activations to enable SO(3)-equivariance. Due to the nature of linear combination, [5] fails to conduct flexible vector transformations. Luo et al. [19] introduce orientations for each point to achieve equivariance based on graph neural network schemes in a fully end-to-end manner. As for non-spectral methods [3,6,15,27], they discretize the rotation group and construct a set of kernels for the group equivariant computation. EPN [3] introduces a tractable approximation to $SE(3)$ group equivariant convolution on point clouds. [27] further transfers this framework to object-level equivariance for 3D detection. Du et al. [6] proposes to construct $SE(3)$ equivariant graph neural networks with complete local frames, approximating the geometric quantities efficiently.

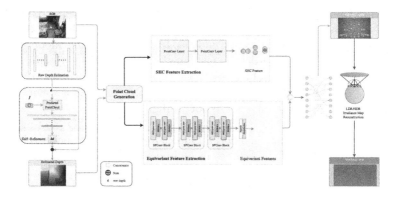

Fig. 2. The overview of our framework. We propose a cascaded illumination estimation formulation of two stages, composed of a point cloud generation module and an equivariant illumination estimation module.

3   Method

3.1   Overall Architecture

Our goal is to estimate illumination from a single perspective RGB image. This is an extremely ill-posed problem since different lighting might lead to the same appearance. Therefore, we choose to leverage geometric priors by predicting depth from the image first and then generating the corresponding point cloud at the rendered position. Following [30], we formulate the illumination estimation as a spherical harmonic coefficients regression problem, and regress spherical harmonics from the predicted point cloud.

However, such a framework still has potential issues. As shown in Fig. 1, the images of the same scenario from various perspectives may lead to different distortion of predicted depth and mislead the limited illumination estimation, especially in indoor scenes, let alone all-angle environment illumination map estimation at arbitrary locations. Moreover, there is a basic fact for image-based estimation: with light sources fixed, the illumination is consistent when the rendered point rotates or the viewpoint changes, which is namely the **equivariance of illumination**. Recently, the depth estimation from a single RGB image has made great progress [26], with a distortion-ware depth estimation paradigm and offers a precise depth estimation. In this case, the equivariance of SO(3) transformations do make sense. The precise distortion-aware depth estimation can not only guarantee the reliability of the combination of RGB and its predicted depth, but also unleash the potential of equivariance in lighting estimation.

To this end, we propose a cascaded network in Fig. 2. It contains two stages, generating point clouds with distortion-aware depth estimation and equivariant illumination estimation from different viewpoints. The model is composed of a point cloud generation module D, an equivariant feature extraction module E, a PointConv model P and a lighting estimation module R. r denotes the rendered point. The formulation of our **equivariant indoor illumination map estimation** from a single image is defined as a mapping:

$$\mathcal{F} : L(R(E(D(S,r)), P(D(S,r)))) \to I \tag{1}$$

where S is the source image, I is the target illumination map, and L is the transformation from SH coefficients to illumination map. Specifically,

$$L(I_{shc}) = I, \quad R(e_r, S_f) = I_{shc}, \tag{2}$$
$$E(P_r) = e_r, \quad P(P_r) = S_f, \tag{3}$$
$$D(S,r) = Sample(S, g(S) \circ f(S), r) = P_r. \tag{4}$$

P_r is the generated point cloud, I_{shc} is the predicted spherical harmonics, and e_r and S_f are both point features. $g(S)$ and $f(S)$ will be elaborated later.

Point Cloud Generation. In the first stage, we generate the point cloud based on the rendered point leveraging the distortion-aware depth estimation [26], which is formulated as Eq. 4. Firstly, $g(S)$ maps from an RGB image to a raw depth estimation by a Depth Prediction Model (DPM), then $f(S)$ takes the raw depth as input and estimates a refined shift for the raw depth through a Point cloud Module (PCM), $g(S) \circ f(S)$ make refinement shift on raw depth and output a corrected depth image. $Sample(S, g(S) \circ f(S), r)$ make a point cloud P_r centered at the render position r for subsequent process on the input estimated depth and corresponding image, which will be described in Sect. 3.2.

Equivariant Illumination Estimation. In the second stage, we formulate the equivariant illumination map estimation as a composite point cloud-based learning problem L that takes a predicted point cloud P_r as input and outputs a scene-consistent equivariant irradiance map. In this stage, we first simultaneously compute the raw estimate sphere harmonic coefficient (SHC) feature S_f through PointConv module P and extract the structure-aware equivariant feature e_r through the equivariant feature extraction module E, then concatenate both SHC and equivariant feature to acquire a 2nd order SH coefficients I_{shc} through Eq. 2. Finally, $L(I_{shc})$ inputs the SHC and outputs the target illumination map. More details about the modules will be described in Sect. 3.3.

3.2   Point Cloud Generation

In this section, we will describe the details of generating a point cloud recentered on the rendered point from a single RGB image.

Distortion-Aware Depth Estimation. Given an RGB image, there are two modules in order for processing. The DPM module based on PVCNN [18], generates a depth image with unknown scale and shift, and the PCM module takes the distorted point cloud as input and predicts shift refinement to the depth image.

Recentered Point Cloud Generation. Given the distortion-aware depth image Z and camera intrinsic matrix, we can easily transform the depth image into a point cloud P centered on the camera origin through:

$$x = \frac{(u - c_x)z}{f_x}, y = \frac{(u - c_y)z}{f_y}, \tag{5}$$

where u and v are the photo pixel coordinates, z is the corresponding depth value of pixel (u,v), f_x and f_y are the vertical and horizontal camera focal length, c_x and c_y are the photo-optical center, and (x,y,z) is the corresponding point of pixel (u,v).

With the rendered point r, we apply a linear translation T to P and transform the point cloud center to the observation point P_r:

$$P_r = T(P) = P - r. \tag{6}$$

Unit-Sphere Downsampling. Accounting for the efficiency of reserving the spatial structure, we exert a new technique of sphere sampling – Unit-sphere Downsampling [31]. At downsampling, for each input point cloud P_{input}, we will project the point cloud on a unit surface, and accumulate the area of the uniform surface anchor's coverage. Theoretically, let P_{data} and P_{anchor} correspondingly be the input point cloud's and the uniform surface anchors' distribution, the completeness of observation was measured by the joint entropy $H(P_{data}, P_{anchor})$,

$$H(P_{data}, P_{anchor}) = -\sum_{i \in S} \sum_{j=1}^{i} P(p'_{ij}, p_i) \log_2[P(p'_{ij}, p_i)] \tag{7}$$

where $P(p'_{ij}, p_i)$ s the joint probability of projecting points into a unit sphere with i anchor point, and S is the set of possible anchors, $\{2^k | 1 \leq k \leq 12\}$ can be accepted. In this work, we set 1280 points as the target for downsampling.

3.3 Equivariant Illumination Estimation

Equivariant Feature Extraction. For this module, we were inspired by recent works on Equivariance [3,15,19,20,27], and based on [3], we put forward the current network. For every RGB and corresponding point cloud input, we use three basic SPConv blocks whose layer channel settings are [32,32],[64,128],[128,128] and a Pointnet with channel [128,64] to output a 64-dimension Equivariant feature, which uses 60 SO(3) bases in this work. As to the other configuration of this module, the $initial\_radius\_ratio = 0.2, sampleing\_ratio = 0.4$.

SHC Feature Extraction. The module is a PointConv-based [25] backbone derived from [30]. It takes downsampled RGB and the corresponding point cloud as input, and outputs a 256-dimensional tensor, which we regard as an SHC feature because it numerically describes SHC. The two PointConvs' channel numbers are set as [64,128] and [128,256] respectively.

Concatenating the above two features, we then use a fully connected layer as the prediction head to get the predicted spherical harmonic coefficients I_{shc} and transform them into the illumination map.

3.4 Loss

To provide an auxiliary constraint on the outputs, we supervise both SH coefficients and the irradiance map, and the total loss function L is defined as:

$$\mathcal{L} = \mathcal{L}_{sh} + \mathcal{L}_{ir} \tag{8}$$

$\mathcal{L}_{sh}$ is the L2 loss of SH coefficients, which is defined in Eq. 9:

$$\mathcal{L}_{sh} = \frac{1}{9} \sum_{c=l}^{3} \sum_{l=0}^{2} \sum_{m=-l}^{l} (i_{l,c}^{m*} - i_{l,c}^{m}) \tag{9}$$

where c is the color channel (RGB), l and m are the degree and order of SH coefficients. $\mathcal{L}_{ir}$ is L2 loss for irradiance map, and defined in Eq. 10.

$$\mathcal{L}_{ir} = \frac{1}{N_{env}} \sum_{p=0}^{N_{env}} (i_p^* - i_p)^2 \tag{10}$$

where N_{env} is the number of pixels of the target image, and i is the value of the corresponding pixel.

4   Experiment

4.1   Datasets and Preprocessing

We carry out our experiments on the Matterport3D dataset [2], with illumination ground truth generated by Neural Illumination. Matterport3D is a large-scale dataset that contains RGB-D images and panoramic views for indoor scenes. Each RGB-D scene contains undistorted color and depth images (of size 1028×1024) of 18 viewpoints. The Neural Illumination dataset [21] was derived from Matterport3D and packed with additional information that associates images and the relationship between images at observation and rendering locations. We derive depth images from Matterport3D as Fig. 3 shows, whose depth images come from the DepthEst module and Unit-Sphere Downsampling module.

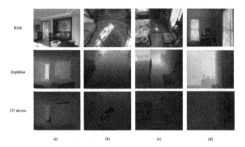

Fig. 3. Depth estimation results. The RGB images are from Matterpord3D, each column in order is RGB, predicted depth image from our DepthEst module and depth image captured from the device.

4.2   Comparison in Quality and Quantity

Quantitative Results. As shown in Table 1, We carried out our experiments based on the Matterport Dataset, we compare our solution with other illumination estimation solutions using L2 loss of SH coefficients, Irradiance map on the test set. For baseline solutions targeted at RGB-D, we keep the same setting in experiments. And we achieved superior performance compared with previous arts. We credit this to our Equivariant feature extraction module which has learned how to adjust to the transforms of the scenes and combined multiple rotation cases' tradeoffs during training, and finally calibrated and enhanced the sources for SHC regression. And the robustness will be seen in qualitative results.

Table 1. Comparison to state-of-the-art networks. Our approach achieved the lowest loss for both spherical harmonics coefficients l2 and irradiance map l2.

Method	SH coefficients l2 Loss	Irradiance map l2 Loss	United l2 Loss
Song et al. [21]	N/A	0.619	N/A
Garon et al. [11]	1.10 (±0.1)	0.63 (±0.03)	N/A
PointAR [30]	0.31 (±0.03)	0.434 (± 0.02)	0.32 (±0.02)
Ours	**0.11** (±0.05)	**0.31** (±0.04)	**0.20** (±0.04)

Also, we compare the complexity of the networks of illumination estimation stage with PointAR [30] in Table 3. Account for the difference in target task between PointAR and Ours, the increments of complexity are acceptable, so that we believe that our model can still be applied on mobile platforms.

Table 2. Comparison of loss coefficients.

Table 3. Comparison of model complexity.

Model	α	β	Valid Loss
PointAR [30]	1	10	9.04
	5	10	29.60
	10	1	5.77
Ours	1	10	**0.20**
	5	10	**0.17**
	10	1	**1.36**

Method	Parameters(M)
PointAR [30]	1.42
Ours	2.42

Qualitative Results. Here we demonstrate the quality of our method. Both PointAR and our method take RGB-D input, use unite loss as supervision for training and train 10 epochs. At test, we input the RGB-PD pairs and obtain illumination estimation results as shown in Fig. 4. It is evident that our method exhibits more detailed results. There are two main reasons for this improvement. Firstly, This optimization by DPM effectively reduces the impact of noise and enhances the level of detail in our results. Secondly, our method leverages equivariance, which enables it to effectively overcome slight perturbations. For further generalization, incorporating additional equivariance bases becomes crucial.

4.3 Ablation Study

In this section, we describe the ablation experiments performed on the model settings, sampling methods and loss function coefficients. Among them, the model setup needs to be especially noted that PointAR [30] is the degenerate model and also the method of this paper, so the ablation experiments of the equivariant module proposed in this paper will be obtained by comparing the method of this paper with PointAR. As displayed in Table 1, compared with PointAR, our

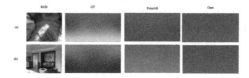

Fig. 4. Comparison of illumination estimation. Each row is a partial image of a scene and the column in order is the RGB image, GT illumination map, results of PointAR and our method.

method attained a comparative result than PointAR, which shows the efficiency of the equivariance in quantity.

Table 4. Ablation study of the sampling method in different measurements.

Method	SHC coefficients Loss	Irradiance Map Loss	Unite Loss
PointAR(w/o)	**0.417**	1.698	0.45
PointAR	0.914	**0.009**	**0.32**
Ours(w/o)	0.210	1.02	0.396
Ours	**0.11**	**0.012**	**0.204**

In Table 4, we conducted the comparative test on the use of sphere sample, which is regarded as more geometry information. Obviously, both PointAR and our method with the sphere sampling achieve better results, for instance, the SH coefficients loss decreased from 0.21 to 0.11 with sphere sampling.

As shown in Table 2, in our proposed method, the final result varies from the coefficients of the loss function. We separately conduct experiments on different parameter settings, and measures on united valid loss. It needs to be mentioned that the results are different from the Table 1. Then we can arrive at that $\alpha = 5, \beta = 10$ is a relatively optimal setting.

4.4   Application on AR

End-to-End Generation. As shown in Fig. 5, we build a pipeline for capturing, uploading and attaining the irradiance map in Fig. 5. It demonstrates the feasibility of the proposed framework.

Fig. 5. Demonstration from a snapshot RGB Image to its corresponding Irradiance map.

Rendering. As shown in Fig. 6, the rabbit is rendered at the user's preferred location. Although the rendering result seems reasonable in human's observation, it still lacks some details.

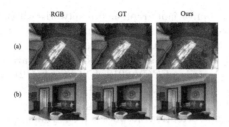

Fig. 6. AR applications. Our method is tested in indoor scenes.

5   Conclusion

In this study, we propose a novel cascaded approach for estimating illumination from a single RGB image. The first stage utilizes a distortion-aware architecture to accurately predict depth maps. In the second stage, a PointAR-like architecture is employed to regress spherical harmonics from the predicted point clouds. To ensure equivariance of the illumination map under SO(3) transformation, we introduce equivariant point convolution for estimating spherical harmonics coefficients based on distortion-aware single-frame depth estimation. These two techniques work closely together as distortion calibration is crucial to generate consistent point clouds from single images captured from different viewpoints. Experimental results demonstrate that our method achieves state-of-the-art (SOTA) performance on the large-scale Matterport3D dataset, highlighting the effectiveness of the cascaded formulation and equivariance in illumination modeling.

References

1. Boss, M., Jampani, V., Kim, K., Lensch, H., Kautz, J.: Two-shot spatially-varying BRDF and shape estimation. In: Proceedings of the IEEE/CVF Conference on Computer Vision and Pattern Recognition, pp. 3982–3991 (2020)
2. Chang, A., et al.: Matterport3D: learning from RGB-D data in indoor environments. arXiv preprint arXiv:1709.06158 (2017)
3. Chen, H., Liu, S., Chen, W., Li, H., Hill, R.: Equivariant point network for 3D point cloud analysis. In: Proceedings of the IEEE/CVF Conference on Computer Vision and Pattern Recognition, pp. 14514–14523 (2021)
4. Debevec, P.: Rendering synthetic objects into real scenes: bridging traditional and image-based graphics with global illumination and high dynamic range photography. In: ACM SIGGRAPH 2008 Classes, pp. 1–10 (2008)
5. Deng, C., Litany, O., Duan, Y., Poulenard, A., Tagliasacchi, A., Guibas, L.J.: Vector neurons: a general framework for so (3)-equivariant networks. In: Proceedings of the IEEE/CVF International Conference on Computer Vision, pp. 12200–12209 (2021)
6. Du, W., et al.: Se (3) equivariant graph neural networks with complete local frames. In: International Conference on Machine Learning, pp. 5583–5608. PMLR (2022)
7. Esteves, C., Allen-Blanchette, C., Makadia, A., Daniilidis, K.: Learning SO(3) equivariant representations with spherical CNNs. In: Ferrari, V., Hebert, M., Sminchisescu, C., Weiss, Y. (eds.) ECCV 2018. LNCS, vol. 11217, pp. 54–70. Springer, Cham (2018). https://doi.org/10.1007/978-3-030-01261-8_4
8. Fuchs, F., Worrall, D., Fischer, V., Welling, M.: Se (3)-transformers: 3D roto-translation equivariant attention networks. In: Advances in Neural Information Processing Systems, vol. 33, pp. 1970–1981 (2020)
9. Gardner, M.A., Hold-Geoffroy, Y., Sunkavalli, K., Gagné, C., Lalonde, J.F.: Deep parametric indoor lighting estimation. In: Proceedings of the IEEE/CVF International Conference on Computer Vision, pp. 7175–7183 (2019)
10. Gardner, M.A., et al.: Learning to predict indoor illumination from a single image. arXiv preprint arXiv:1704.00090 (2017)
11. Garon, M., Sunkavalli, K., Hadap, S., Carr, N., Lalonde, J.F.: Fast spatially-varying indoor lighting estimation. In: Proceedings of the IEEE/CVF Conference on Computer Vision and Pattern Recognition, pp. 6908–6917 (2019)
12. Hold-Geoffroy, Y., Athawale, A., Lalonde, J.F.: Deep sky modeling for single image outdoor lighting estimation. In: Proceedings of the IEEE/CVF Conference on Computer Vision and Pattern Recognition, pp. 6927–6935 (2019)
13. Karsch, K., Hedau, V., Forsyth, D., Hoiem, D.: Rendering synthetic objects into legacy photographs. ACM Trans. Graph. (TOG) **30**(6), 1–12 (2011)
14. Keriven, N., Peyré, G.: Universal invariant and equivariant graph neural networks. In: Advances in Neural Information Processing Systems, vol. 32 (2019)
15. Li, J., Bi, Y., Lee, G.H.: Discrete rotation equivariance for point cloud recognition. In: 2019 International Conference on Robotics and Automation (ICRA), pp. 7269–7275. IEEE (2019)
16. Li, J., Li, H., Matsushita, Y.: Lighting, reflectance and geometry estimation from 360 panoramic stereo. In: 2021 IEEE/CVF Conference on Computer Vision and Pattern Recognition (CVPR), pp. 10586–10595. IEEE (2021)
17. Li, Z., Xu, Z., Ramamoorthi, R., Sunkavalli, K., Chandraker, M.: Learning to reconstruct shape and spatially-varying reflectance from a single image. ACM Trans. Graph. (TOG) **37**(6), 1–11 (2018)

18. Liu, Z., Tang, H., Lin, Y., Han, S.: Point-voxel CNN for efficient 3D deep learning. In: Advances in Neural Information Processing Systems, vol. 32 (2019)
19. Luo, S., et al.: Equivariant point cloud analysis via learning orientations for message passing. In: Proceedings of the IEEE/CVF Conference on Computer Vision and Pattern Recognition, pp. 18932–18941 (2022)
20. Shen, W., Zhang, B., Huang, S., Wei, Z., Zhang, Q.: 3D-rotation-equivariant quaternion neural networks. In: Vedaldi, A., Bischof, H., Brox, T., Frahm, J.-M. (eds.) ECCV 2020. LNCS, vol. 12365, pp. 531–547. Springer, Cham (2020). https://doi.org/10.1007/978-3-030-58565-5_32
21. Song, S., Funkhouser, T.: Neural illumination: lighting prediction for indoor environments. In: Proceedings of the IEEE/CVF Conference on Computer Vision and Pattern Recognition, pp. 6918–6926 (2019)
22. Srinivasan, P.P., Mildenhall, B., Tancik, M., Barron, J.T., Tucker, R., Snavely, N.: Lighthouse: predicting lighting volumes for spatially-coherent illumination. In: Proceedings of the IEEE/CVF Conference on Computer Vision and Pattern Recognition, pp. 8080–8089 (2020)
23. Thomas, N., et al.: Tensor field networks: rotation-and translation-equivariant neural networks for 3D point clouds. arXiv preprint arXiv:1802.08219 (2018)
24. Wang, Z., Philion, J., Fidler, S., Kautz, J.: Learning indoor inverse rendering with 3D spatially-varying lighting. In: Proceedings of the IEEE/CVF International Conference on Computer Vision, pp. 12538–12547 (2021)
25. Wu, W., Qi, Z., Fuxin, L.: Pointconv: deep convolutional networks on 3D point clouds. In: Proceedings of the IEEE/CVF Conference on Computer Vision and Pattern Recognition, pp. 9621–9630 (2019)
26. Yin, W., et al.: Learning to recover 3D scene shape from a single image. In: Proceedings of the IEEE/CVF Conference on Computer Vision and Pattern Recognition, pp. 204–213 (2021)
27. Yu, H.X., Wu, J., Yi, L.: Rotationally equivariant 3D object detection. In: Proceedings of the IEEE/CVF Conference on Computer Vision and Pattern Recognition, pp. 1456–1464 (2022)
28. Zhan, F., et al.: Emlight: lighting estimation via spherical distribution approximation. In: Proceedings of the AAAI Conference on Artificial Intelligence, vol. 35, pp. 3287–3295 (2021)
29. Zhang, J., Sunkavalli, K., Hold-Geoffroy, Y., Hadap, S., Eisenman, J., Lalonde, J.F.: All-weather deep outdoor lighting estimation. In: Proceedings of the IEEE/CVF Conference on Computer Vision and Pattern Recognition, pp. 10158–10166 (2019)
30. Zhao, Y., Guo, T.: POINTAR: efficient lighting estimation for mobile augmented reality. In: Vedaldi, A., Bischof, H., Brox, T., Frahm, J.-M. (eds.) ECCV 2020. LNCS, vol. 12368, pp. 678–693. Springer, Cham (2020). https://doi.org/10.1007/978-3-030-58592-1_40
31. Zhao, Y., Guo, T.: Xihe: a 3D vision-based lighting estimation framework for mobile augmented reality. In: The 19th ACM International Conference on Mobile Systems, Applications, and Services (2021)
32. Zhu, R., Li, Z., Matai, J., Porikli, F., Chandraker, M.: Irisformer: dense vision transformers for single-image inverse rendering in indoor scenes. In: Proceedings of the IEEE/CVF Conference on Computer Vision and Pattern Recognition, pp. 2822–2831 (2022)

Weakly-Supervised Grounding for VQA with Dual Visual-Linguistic Interaction

Yi Liu[1,2], Junwen Pan[1], Qilong Wang[1], Guanlin Chen[1], Weiguo Nie[2],
Yudong Zhang[2], Qian Gao[2], Qinghua Hu[1], and Pengfei Zhu[1(⊠)]

[1] College of Intelligence and Computing, Tianjin University, Tianjin, China
lly_liuyi@tju.edu.cn
[2] Baidu Inc, Beijing, China

Abstract. Visual question answer (VQA) grounding, aimed at locating the visual evidence associated with the answers while answering questions, has attracted increasing research interest. To locate the evidence, most existing methods extract attention maps in an unsupervised manner from pretrained VQA models. As only the text-related objective is considered during training, the attention map coarsely depicts the grounding region, resulting in poor interpretability. A straightforward solution for improving grounding accuracy is leveraging pixel-wise masks as strong supervision. However, precise per-pixel annotation is time-consuming and labor-intensive. To address above issues, this paper presents the weakly-supervised grounding for VQA, which learns an end-to-end **D**ual **V**isual-Linguistic **I**nteraction (DaVi) network in a unified architecture with various low-cost annotations, such as click-, scribble- and box-level grounding labels. Specifically, to enable the visual mask prediction, DaVi proposes a language-based visual decoder that extends the previous VQA network. Since the visual decoder is guided with weak labels, we also present a Pseudo Grounding Refinement Module (PGRM) to refine the relatively coarse predictions as an additional constraint. Extensive experiments demonstrate that our weakly supervised DaVi significantly improves grounding performance even under the click-level supervision with one pixel annotation. Scribble-level supervision achieves 92% performance at a dramatically reduced annotation cost compared to its fully supervised counterpart. More essentially, weak visual grounding usually boosts the accuracy of text answers despite using inaccurate supervision.

Keywords: Weakly-Supervised Learning · Visual Question Answering · Visual Grounding

1 Introduction

Visual Question Answer (VQA) is a challenging task [27] that requires machines to understand visual information and questions to provide accurate answers. It has real-world applications, including aiding visually impaired individuals [7]. However, current high-performing models are complex black-box systems, which

L. Fang et al. (Eds.): CICAI 2023, LNAI 14473, pp. 156–169, 2024.
https://doi.org/10.1007/978-981-99-8850-1_13

raises concerns about answer reasoning and performance assessment [1]. VQA grounding is crucial for addressing these challenges [7], as it provides explanations for answer generation and helps evaluate answer quality and improve model performance.

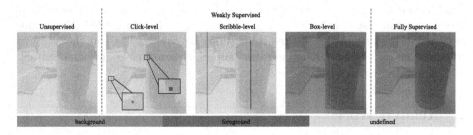

Fig. 1. VQA Grounding with different supervision types. 1) Unsupervised grounding: without any grounding labels during training. 2) Weakly supervised grounding: with click-level, scribble-level or box-level annotations. 3) Fully supervised grounding: with pixel-level ground-truth.

Previous answer grounding [12] extracted attention maps from the pretrained VQA transformers which trained with only answering loss. The absence of visual localization supervision in training leads to messy localization and clutter boundaries. To address this issue, recent advances introduced pixel-level grounding masks to provide strong supervision with spatial information. However, fully-supervised VQA grounding requires per-pixel annotations for training [3], which is expertise-demanding, labor-intensive and time-consuming. In contrast, this work introduces a weakly supervised scheme for answer grounding which leverages various low-cost grounding labels, including click-level, scribble-level, and box-level as illustrated in Fig. 1.

Meanwhile, despite the success of the vision-language Transformers has made a significant leap in the performance of VQA, there has been less improvement in the interpretability for these black-box Transformers. A typical architecture implements VQA with a visual encoder, a text encoder and a text decoder. Since the VQA model can only predict text answers but not generate grounding results, existing vision-language model can only apply post-hoc means for VQA grounding, e.g. Grad-CAM [21] is one of the most used answer grounding techniques [11]. To directly predict the grounding mask (i.e., self-explanation), we extend the existing VQA architecture with a Language-based Visual Decoder (LVD) which is learned from the additional weak labels [15]. The LVD module decodes visual features into grounding masks through cross attending to linguistic features. The LVD module along with the existing visual-based linguistic encoder form our overall model structure, named Dual Visual-Linguistic Interaction (DaVi), which generates both visual and linguistic predictions through two visual-linguistic interactions.

Since the weakly supervised LVD can only produce coarse ground masks, we propose a pseudo supervision scheme to constrain the model for cleaner predictions. Specifically, a Pseudo Grounding Refinement Module (PGRM) is designed to produce pseudo-labels, which effectively improves the performance of VQA Grounding. Our contributions are summarized as follows: i) the weakly-supervised framework learns from low-cost grounding labels, achieving remarkable grounding performance with limited budgets. ii) We propose an end-to-end Dual Visual-Linguistic Interaction (DaVi) framework for efficient execution of vision and language tasks in a single architecture. iii) Our VQA Grounding method outperforms state-of-the-art methods by over 2x IoU on the WizViz-VQA-Grounding dataset, demonstrating superior performance in IoU, accuracy, and composite metrics.

2   Related Work

2.1   Visual Question Answering

Visual Question Answering (VQA) [2] is a vital task for computer vision with real-world applications such as aiding the visually impaired [7]. Best-performing VQA models are criticized for complexity and lack of transparency, but answer grounding provides clear explanations and accurate visual evidence [3] for reasoning, enhancing interpretability and transparency. Answer grounding makes VQA models valuable tools for real-world applications.

2.2   VQA Grounding

The study of weakly supervised grounding in image phrase-grounding has received significant attention, but the equally critical task of visual question answer Grounding (VQA Grounding) has been largely overlooked. With the introduction of the concept of scene graphs, datasets containing Grounding began to be proposed, and the Visual Genome [10] and CLEVR [8] datasets contain scene graphs that represent the relationships between objects and attributes, as well as a number of clusters of objects that are typically clustered together. These representations are typically generated manually by humans for real images [16] and automatically for rendered images [8]. However, a method to automatically generate such scene graphs has recently been proposed [26]. This method uses a state-of-the-art object detection algorithm (Faster R-CNN [17]) to detect objects in images; instead of predicting local relational predicates between objects, it passes messages between different regions of the image to capture the global scene context.

AU Khan et al. [24] proposed a unsupervised approach(No pixel supervision) to localizing relevant visual entities in VQA tasks. In addition to the proposed module, [9] utilizes the visual encoder [25] to group visual tokens in the capsule, while also introducing text-guided selection using activations from the linguistic self-focus layer. The selection module masks the capsules before forwarding them to the next layer.

Existing methods use attention or gradient maps for answer grounding, while our weakly supervised framework utilizes multimodal interactions to simultaneously generate answers and answer grounding, improves the performance of VQA Grounding and overcomes the limitations of existing methods that ignore spatial modeling. These advances are critical for achieving robust and accurate VQA models for key applications.

3   Method

Our method, depicted in Fig. 2, takes as input the training images and questions and produces predictions for answer grounding and answer. To obtain pseudo-labels for the answer grounding, we select the largest class in the prediction map

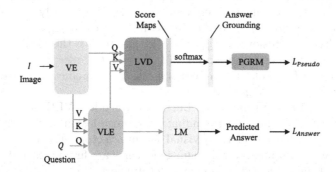

Fig. 2. Our weakly supervised VQA grounding framework, featuring four primary components: the visual encoder (VE), the visual-based language encoder (VLE), the language-based visual decoder (LVD), and the language model (LM), or answer decoder.

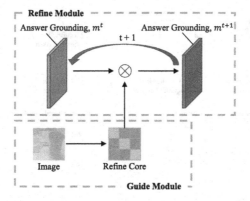

Fig. 3. Pseudo grounding refinement module(PGRM). To guide Refine Module to iteratively refine the answer grounding mask, we use Guide Module to capture pixel-level similarity information with multi-scale adaptive convolution.

generated by our network and refine it using our Pseudo Grounding Refinement Module (PGRM), shown in Fig. 3. This approach allows us to obtain supervised labels for training our model despite the lack of fully labeled data.

3.1   Architecture

The overall process is based on four primary steps: (1) Visual Encoder: We use a Vision Transformer (ViT) [25] to extract image features. The text encoder adopts the BERT [5] approach and includes the [CLS] token at the start of the text input to summarize the sentence. (2) Vision-based Language Encoder: image-question pairs are processed and visual features are linearly mapped to K_{vl}, V_{vl} and natural language features are linearly mapped to Q_{vl} features. Finally, multimodal fusion is performed to align these visual features to text features to facilitate subsequent answer generation. (3) Language-based Visual Encoder: Using the language-based visual decoder, we linearly map the visual cascade features F_v to Q_{lv} and the linguistic features to K_{lv}, V_{lv}, and finally perform multimodal fusion to align the text features to the visual features to generate the pseudo answer grounding. (4) Answer Decoder: we use a language generation model L_d similar to the bert structure, and predict the correct answer from the answer set by a classifier.

As shown in Fig. 4 Visual-based Linguistic Encoder (VLE) leverages visual features for cross-modal understanding. Our encoder maps visual features, extracted by a visual encoder, to visual feature vectors K_{vl} and V_{vl} through a separate linear mapping layer. Language features are first extracted using self-attention, and then mapped to language feature vectors Q_{vl}. A Cross-Attention (CA) layer is interleaved between the self-attention layer and the feedforward network of BERT. The CA layer attends to visual references using language features as queries and generates feature vectors F after 12 layers. These visual-

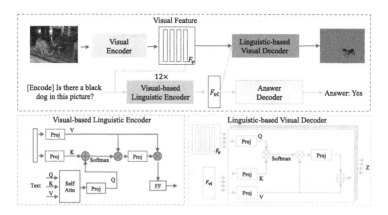

Fig. 4. Illustration of Dual Visual-Linguistic Interaction (DaVi) model, which consists of Visual Encoder, Visual-based Linguistic Encoder, Answer Decoder for answering and Linguistic-based Visual Decoder for answer grounding.

linguistic interactions in VL_e provide multimodal evidence for answer decoding. We present VL_e as a novel approach to enhance cross-modal understanding by integrating vision and language in a unified framework.

These visual-linguistic interactions in VL_e provide multimodal evidence for answer decoding in L_d, enhancing the ability of cross-modal understanding.

3.2 Language-Based Visual Decoder

To predict the answer grounding mask, the Linguistic-based Visual Decoder (LV_d) focuses on evidence-relevant regions of the visual features for answer grounding. In this implementation, visual features are mapped to image features Q_{lv} through a linear mapping layer, while language features F_{vl} are mapped to K_{lv} and V_{lv}. Cross-attention is then used to align the visual features. This approach provides an effective way to ground the answer to the visual evidence, enabling cross-modal understanding between language and vision.

3.3 Pseudo Grounding Refinement

In this section, we will describe how we utilize the Pseudo Grounding Refinement Module (PGRM) to produce high-quality supervision signals. As shown in Fig. 3 We input the training images into the network to obtain the prediction maps. Pseudo-labels are generated by selecting the largest class of the prediction map.

The core is that the neighboring pixels with similar appearance should be grounded consistently. Our implementation is derived from pixel adaptive convolution (PAC) [22]. The idea is to update the pixel labels $m :, i, j$ using convex combinations of the labels of its neighbors $\mathcal{N}(i, j)$ iteratively, and in t^{th} iterations

$$m^t_{:,i,j} = \sum_{(l,n)\in\mathcal{N}(i,j)} \alpha_{i,j,l,n} \cdot m^{t-1}_{:,l,n} \tag{1}$$

To compute α, we use the Refine Core on the pixel-level intensity I, the

$$k\left(I_{i,j}, I_{l,n}\right) = -\frac{|I_{i,j} - I_{l,n}|}{\sigma^2_{i,j}} \tag{2}$$

where we define $\sigma_{(i,j)}$ as the standard deviation of the image intensity computed locally for the Refine Core. We apply softmax to obtain the final distance $\alpha_{(i,j,l,n)}$ for each neighbor (l, n) of (i, j). For this module, we do not perform backpropagation, so it is always in "evaluation" mode,

$$L_{Pseudo} = -\frac{1}{N}\sum_{i\in n}(\hat{y}^c_i)log(y^c_i) \tag{3}$$

In summary, the model is trained in each iteration by the network using the overall loss L, which is defined as,

$$L = L_{Answer} + L_{CE} + L_{Pseudo} \tag{4}$$

3.4   Training Objectives

During training, we optimize two objectives simultaneously: one based on visual tasks and the other based on language tasks. We use different functions to calculate the two losses, as described below.

The Language Modeling Loss (LM) activates the image-grounded text decoder to generate a text description of a given image. We optimize the cross-entropy loss and train the model to maximize the likelihood of the text in an autoregressive manner. To calculate the loss, we apply label smoothing of 0.1. Compared to the widely used Masked Language Modeling (MLM) loss in Visual Language Pre-Training (VLP), LM provides the model with the ability to generalize and convert visual information into coherent captions. Let us assume a dataset C, which includes a continuous input token $x^1, ..., x^m$, and an answer label y. The maximization objective for training the network is defined as:

$$L_{Answer}(C) = \sum_{(x,y)} \log(y|x^1, ..., x^m) \tag{5}$$

The answer grounding Loss activates a Visual-based Linguistic Encoder to generate answer using fused joint-level features with a standard U-Net [18] network structure of the generative model. To calculate the loss, we train the U-Net network by minimizing the partial cross-entropy loss L_{CE} with labeled n pixels i, which is defined as:

$$L_{CE} = -\frac{1}{n} \sum_{i \in n} (\hat{y}_i^c) log(y_i^c) \tag{6}$$

Table 1. Composite metrics under weak supervision: Accuracy (50/75) measures VQA accuracy with IoU greater than 50/75, while IoU (True/False) measures IoU of correct/incorrect VQA.

Supervision	Accuracy	Accuracy (50)	Accuracy (75)	IoU	IoU (True)	IoU (False)
Unsupervised	42.97	47.16	47.05	30.29	30.41	30.16
Click-level	43.23	**57.84**	**58.53**	60.79	71.77	49.18
Scribble-level	43.76	55.71	58.50	**68.92**	**76.23**	**60.08**
Box-level	**44.38**	53.11	56.23	66.78	72.84	58.59
Full pixel	**45.80**	**57.22**	**60.70**	**73.21**	**79.00**	**64.68**

Table 2. Performance comparison of different click-level labels: $\Phi30$ pixels, 1 pixel, and 1% pixels representing dots of 30 pixels in diameter, a single pixel, and 1% of the total area of the label, respectively.

Supervision	Accuracy	Accuracy (50)	Accuracy (75)	IoU	IoU (True)	IoU (False)
$\Phi30$pixels	43.76	55.92	57.79	63.02	76.90	58.20
1 pixel	43.23	**57.84**	58.53	60.79	71.77	49.18
1%pixels	42.97	55.04	59.12	66.75	76.14	56.04
5%pixels	43.76	55.92	57.79	68.56	76.90	58.20
25%pixels	**44.12**	54.31	**59.27**	72.91	**79.74**	**64.16**
Full pixel supervision	**45.80**	**57.22**	**60.70**	**73.21**	79.00	**64.68**

Table 3. Linguistic and visual features for the evaluation of model effects. Contrast learning is pre-trained using the LAION dataset and VQA is pre-trained using the VQA-v2 dataset

	freeze		Contrast Learning		VQA	
	Visual	Text	IoU	Accuracy	IoU	Accuracy
Baseline [11]			-	35.45	–	48.18
Ours			**70.65**	**39.16**	**73.21**	45.8
Ours		✓	69.33	39.08	71.74	47.3
Ours	✓	✓	68.09	35.98	70.45	**48.27**

4 Experiments

4.1 Training Details

We use the same pre-trained model as [11] for fine-tuning. In we pre-trained the model for 40 periods using a batch of 8. We use the AdamW [14] optimizer with a weight decay of 0.05. The learning rate is pre-trained to 2e−4 and decreases linearly at a rate of 0.85, and the image resolution is increased to 512×512. In addition, we evaluate our model in the VizWiz-VQA-Grounding dataset [3]. In this dataset, the validation set is publicly available, while the test set is not. In order to evaluate the test set (Test-Dev and Test-Standard), the predictions need to be submitted to the test server. But here, we use 6494 images from the original training set as the training set and 1131 images from the validation set as the test set for our experiments and compare them with other methods.

We generate supervised data using different methods: random positioning for scribble set supervision, horizontal and vertical lines for long line generation, and external rectangles for box-level supervision. Our approach trains the model end-to-end under different weakly supervised signals.

Table 4. Dual Visual-Linguistic Interaction module. LE is language encoder, VE is visual encoder, LD is language decoder, VD is visual decoder, LVD is language-based visual decoder, and VLE is visual-based language encoder.

Method	Modules	Accuracy	IoU
LE + VE + LD + VD		17.59	60.03
LE + VE + LVD + VD	+LVD	17.77	70.31
VE + VLE + LD + VD	+VLE	35.72	61.23
VE + VLE + LVD + LD	+LVD,VLE	**39.16**	**70.65**
Mac-Caps [24]		15.76	17.42

Table 5. Effectiveness of PGRM model using different weak supervision labels.

Supervision	PGRM model	Accuracy	IoU
Unsupervised		42.97	30.29
	✓	46.59	23.67
Click-level		43.23	60.79
	✓	45.8	63.52
Scribble-level		43.76	68.92
	✓	47.83	70.44
Box-level		44.38	66.78
	✓	47.48	67.34

4.2   Ablation Study

Effect of Different Supervisory Information. To investigate the effect of different annotation signals on VQA Grounding tasks, we conduct ablation experiments and list composite index performance under different levels of supervision in Table 1. Full pixel supervision outperforms weakly supervised information. Among weakly supervised information, scribble-level supervision improves answer grounding, while box-level supervision improves VQA Grounding.

Effect of Different Percentage Labels. In order to refine more the impact of the labeling method on the performance in all directions, the click-level labels are refined in Table 2. As can be seen from the table, the greater the label coverage, the better the performance in terms of accuracy and intersection ratio, where it approaches pixel supervision in the case of 25% pixels. By looking at the two composite indices of accuracy (50) and accuracy (75) for the VQA, we can see that the two indices are not very correlated, especially the accuracy (50) for 1 pixel in accuracy (50) reaches 57.84. For the IoU, IoU(True) and IoU(False) for the answer grounding index, we can see that the model is influenced by the label coverage while is also affected by the accuracy of the VQA.

Truncated Gradient. As shown in Table 3. Controlling gradient backpropagation can tune the performance of answer grounding and visual VQA.

While our proposed method outperforms previous SOTA on LAION [20] pre-training, it underperforms Baseline on VQA pre-training. Freezing gradient back to language encoder only decreases IoU but increases accuracy, while freezing both language and visual encoder reaches optimal performance. Gradient back-propagation can thus be adjusted to tune task performance.

Table 6. Results of question and answer grounding with different pixel supervision information on the VizWiz-VQA-Grounding validation set. * indicates frozen gradient back-propagation of visual coder and vision-based language encoder while computing answer grounding.

Method	Pretrained	Supervision	Accuracy	IoU	IoU (True)
BLIP [11](Baseline)	LAION [19]	Unsupervised	37.01	–	–
BLIP(Baseline)	VQA-v2 [6]	Unsupervised	48.18	–	–
LAVT [28]	ImageNet-22K [4]	Full pixel	–	69.64	–
Ours	LAION	Unsupervised	36.78	27.72	23.30
		Scribble-level	36.78	66.15	75.70
		Box-level	37.75	64.56	71.51
		Full pixel	**39.16**	**70.65**	**77.65**
Ours	VQA-V2	Unsupervised	42.97	30.29	30.41
		Click-level	43.23	60.79	71.77
		Scribble-level	43.76	68.92	76.23
		Box-level	44.38	66.78	72.84
		Full pixel	45.80	**73.21**	**79.00**
Ours*		Full pixel	**48.27**	70.45	77.55

Table 7. Results on the VizWiz-VQA-Grounding validation and test set.

Set	Method	Pretrained	Accuracy	IoU
test	OSCAR [13]	VQA-v2	29.2	15.48
	LXMERT [23]	VizWiz-VQA	38.17	22.09
	Mac-Caps [24]	VQA-v2	15.76	17.42
	Mac-Caps [24]	VizWiz-VQA	14.83	27.43
val	BLIP [11]	LAION	37.01	–
	BLIP [11]	VQA-v2	48.18	–
	Ours	LAION	31.12	57.11
	Ours	VQA-V2	42.97	30.29
	Ours + click-level	VQA-V2	**43.23**	**60.79**

Refinement Model. As shown in Table 5, we demonstrate the effectiveness of the Refine Module in improving pseudo answer grounding masks and self-correction. Performance evaluations show significant improvements in both visual question answering and answer grounding tasks under weak supervisory signals, even under unsupervised. The IoU reaches 70.44 under scribble-level supervision, close to fully supervised VQA pre-training. Deterioration of answer grounding task performance under unsupervised signals may be due to optimization failure caused by poor quality of generated answer grounding maps.

Effect of Dual Visual-Linguistic Interaction Module. As shown in Table 4, ablation experiments on DaVi show low accuracy and IoU without interaction module, with significant improvements after adding language-based visual decoder or visual-based language encoder. Using both modules together achieves high VQA and answer grounding accuracy. Results demonstrate DaVi's ability to improve single-task performance and complement downstream tasks of different modalities.

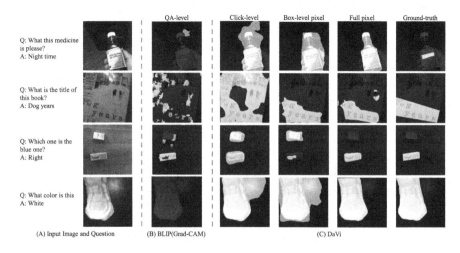

Fig. 5. This figure visualizes attention maps and answer grounding produced by models trained with different weakly supervised labels, including unsupervised.

Visualization. As can be observed from the graph Fig. 5We visualize the visual-verbal interaction feature map to validate the model's behavior. Scores are higher on regions related to linguistic expressions, guiding the model to recognize images and answer questions. The model accurately recognizes object edges and text through pixel-level answer grounding, indicating strong multimodal interaction and spatial learning capability.

5   Comparison with State-of-the-Arts

In this section, we evaluates the existing methods and our proposed method on the VizWiz-VQA-Grounding dataset, with results shown in Table 7 and Table 6. Our method outperforms others in IoU and accuracy under different weakly supervised signals, reflecting the complementary nature of VQA and answer grounding tasks. While our method has higher IoU, accuracy drops due to insufficient training data and catastrophic forgetting. Interrupting gradient back propagation can prevent catastrophic forgetting.

6   Conclusion

In this paper, we have proposed a weakly supervised approach for the VQA grounding task, which uses low-cost annotations, such as click-, scribble-, and box-level grounding labels. Moreover, we also proposed an end-to-end framework which is Dual Visual-Linguistic Interaction (DaVi) network with a language-based visual decoder and Pseudo Grounding Refinement Module (PGRM). Our approach significantly improves the performance on the VQA grounding task, achieving 92% performance with scribble-level supervision and reducing annotation cost compared to fully supervised methods. Furthermore, our approach boosts text answer accuracy despite using inaccurate supervision. These results demonstrate the effectiveness of our approach and suggest promising directions for future research on VQA grounding.

References

1. Agrawal, A., Batra, D., Parikh, D., Kembhavi, A., Don't just assume; look and answer: overcoming priors for visual question answering. In: Proceedings of the IEEE Conference on Computer Vision and Pattern Recognition, pp. 4971–4980 (2018)
2. Antol, S., et al.: VQA: visual question answering. In: Proceedings of the IEEE International Conference on Computer Vision, pp. 2425–2433 (2015)
3. Chen, C., Anjum, S., Gurari, D.: Grounding answers for visual questions asked by visually impaired people. In: Proceedings of the IEEE/CVF Conference on Computer Vision and Pattern Recognition, pp. 19098–19107 (2022)
4. Deng, J., Dong, W., Socher, R., Li, L.-J., Li, K., Fei-Fei, L.: Imagenet: a large-scale hierarchical image database. In: 2009 IEEE Conference on Computer Vision and Pattern Recognition, pp. 248–255. IEEE (2009)
5. Devlin, J., Chang, M.-W., Lee, K., Toutanova, K.: BERT: pre-training of deep bidirectional transformers for language understanding. In: North American Chapter of the Association for Computational Linguistics (2018)
6. Goyal, Y., Khot, T., Summers-Stay, D., Batra, D., Parikh, D.: Making the V in VQA matter: elevating the role of image understanding in visual question answering. In: Proceedings of the IEEE Conference on Computer Vision and Pattern Recognition, pp. 6904–6913 (2017)
7. Gurari, D., et al.: Vizwiz-priv: a dataset for recognizing the presence and purpose of private visual information in images taken by blind people. In: Proceedings of the IEEE/CVF Conference on Computer Vision and Pattern Recognition, pp. 939–948 (2019)
8. Johnson, J., Hariharan, B., Van Der Maaten, L., Fei-Fei, L., Zitnick, C.L., Girshick, R.: ClevR: a diagnostic dataset for compositional language and elementary visual reasoning. In: Proceedings of the IEEE Conference on Computer Vision and Pattern Recognition, pp. 2901–2910 (2017)

9. Khan, A.U., Kuehne, H., Gan, C., Da Vitoria Lobo, N., Shah, M.: Weakly supervised grounding for VQA in vision-language transformers. In: Avidan, S., Brostow, G., Cissé, M., Farinella, G.M., Hassner, T. (eds.) ECCV 2022. LNCS, vol. 13695, pp. 652–670. Springer, Cham (2022). https://doi.org/10.1007/978-3-031-19833-5_38

10. Krishna, R., et al.: Visual genome: connecting language and vision using crowdsourced dense image annotations. Int. J. Comput. Vision **123**(1), 32–73 (2017)

11. Li, J., Li, D., Xiong, C., Hoi, S.: Blip: bootstrapping language-image pre-training for unified vision-language understanding and generation. In: ICML (2022)

12. Li, J., Selvaraju, R., Gotmare, A., Joty, S., Xiong, C., Hoi, S.C.H.: Align before fuse: Vision and language representation learning with momentum distillation. In: Advances in Neural Information Processing Systems, vol. 34, pp. 9694–9705 (2021)

13. Li, X., et al.: OSCAR: object-semantics aligned pre-training for vision-language tasks. In: Vedaldi, A., Bischof, H., Brox, T., Frahm, J.-M. (eds.) ECCV 2020. LNCS, vol. 12375, pp. 121–137. Springer, Cham (2020). https://doi.org/10.1007/978-3-030-58577-8_8

14. Loshchilov, I., Hutter, F.: Fixing weight decay regularization in Adam (2017)

15. Pan, J., et al.: Tell me the evidence? Dual visual-linguistic interaction for answer grounding. arXiv preprint arXiv:2207.05703 (2022)

16. Ramakrishnan, S.K., Pal, A., Sharma, G., Mittal, A.: An empirical evaluation of visual question answering for novel objects. In: Proceedings of the IEEE Conference on Computer Vision and Pattern Recognition, pp. 4392–4401 (2017)

17. Ren, S., He, K., Girshick, R., Sun, J.: Faster R-CNN: towards real-time object detection with region proposal networks. In: Advances in Neural Information Processing Systems, vol. 28 (2015)

18. Ronneberger, O., Fischer, P., Brox, T.: U-net: convolutional networks for biomedical image segmentation. In: Navab, N., Hornegger, J., Wells, W.M., Frangi, A.F. (eds.) MICCAI 2015. LNCS, vol. 9351, pp. 234–241. Springer, Cham (2015). https://doi.org/10.1007/978-3-319-24574-4_28

19. Schuhmann, C., et al.: Laion-5b: an open large-scale dataset for training next generation image-text models. arXiv preprint arXiv:2210.08402 (2022)

20. Schuhmann, C., et al.: Laion-400m: open dataset of clip-filtered 400 million image-text pairs. In: NeurIPS Workshop Datacentric AI, number FZJ-2022-00923. Jülich Supercomputing Center (2021)

21. Selvaraju, R.R., Cogswell, M., Das, A., Vedantam, R., Parikh, D., Batra, D.: Grad-CAM: visual explanations from deep networks via gradient-based localization. In: Proceedings of the IEEE International Conference on Computer Vision, pp. 618–626 (2017)

22. Su, H., Jampani, V., Sun, D., Gallo, O., Learned-Miller, E., Kautz, J.: Pixel-adaptive convolutional neural networks. In: Proceedings of the IEEE/CVF Conference on Computer Vision and Pattern Recognition, pp. 11166–11175 (2019)

23. Tan, H., Bansal, M.: LxMERT: learning cross-modality encoder representations from transformers. In: Proceedings of the 2019 Conference on Empirical Methods in Natural Language Processing and the 9th International Joint Conference on Natural Language Processing (EMNLP-IJCNLP), pp. 5100–5111 (2019)

24. Urooj, A., Kuehne, H., Duarte, K., Gan, C., Lobo, N., Shah, M.: Found a reason for me? Weakly-supervised grounded visual question answering using capsules. In: Proceedings of the IEEE/CVF Conference on Computer Vision and Pattern Recognition, pp. 8465–8474 (2021)

25. Vaswani, A., et al.: Attention is all you need. In: Advances in Neural Information Processing Systems, vol. 30 (2017)

26. Xu, D., Zhu, Y., Choy, C.B., Fei-Fei, L., Scene graph generation by iterative message passing. In: Proceedings of the IEEE Conference on Computer Vision and Pattern Recognition, pp. 5410–5419 (2017)
27. Xu, K., et al.: Show, attend and tell: neural image caption generation with visual attention. In: International Conference on Machine Learning, pp. 2048–2057. PMLR (2015)
28. Yang, Z., Wang, J., Tang, Y., Chen, K., Zhao, H., Torr, P.H.S.: LAVT: language-aware vision transformer for referring image segmentation. In: Proceedings of the IEEE/CVF Conference on Computer Vision and Pattern Recognition, pp. 18155–18165 (2022)

STU3: Multi-organ CT Medical Image Segmentation Model Based on Transformer and UNet

Wenjin Zheng[1], Bo Li[1(✉)], and Wanyi Chen[2]

[1] College of Computer Science and Engineering, Chongqing University of Technology, Chongqing 400054, China
libo@cqut.edu.cn
[2] College of Science, Chongqing University of Technology, Chongqing 400054, China

Abstract. With the popularity of artificial intelligence applications in the medical field, U-shaped convolutional neural network (CNN) has garnered significant attention for their efficacy in medical image analysis tasks. However, the intrinsic limitations of convolutional operation, particularly in the receptive field since it is an end-to-end learning method, impede the establishment of long-term semantic feature dependence and holistic context information connection. This results in the edge contour details insensitive during the image segmentation task. To mitigate these shortcomings, Transformer architectures equipped with self-attention mechanism offer a potential alternative for encoding long-term semantic features and capturing global contextual information. Motivated by these insights, this paper proposes a novel U-shaped Transformer architecture, denoted as STU3, specifically engineered for medical image segmentation. Initially, a parallel training paradigm is employed that distinguishes between global fine-grained and local coarse-grained image features, optimizing the feature extraction process. Secondly, to alleviate the restrictions on fine-grained feature fusion due to peer skip connections, we propose a Residual Full-scale Feature Fusion module (RFFF) as the global decoder component. Lastly, a Global-Local Feature Fusion Block (GLFB) is implemented to seamlessly integrate the fine-grained and coarse-grained features, thereby constructing a comprehensive global information dependency network. This ensures a high level of accuracy in medical image segmentation tasks. Experimental evaluations conducted on abdominal and cervical multi-organ CT datasets substantiate the superiority of the proposed STU3 model over most current models, particularly in terms of the Dice Similarity Coefficient evaluation metric.

Keywords: Medical Image Segmentation · Swin Transformer · UNet

1 Introduction

Automatic medical image segmentation is a crucial step in medical image analysis, offering valuable diagnostic evidence in clinical practice. This technology is especially impactful for enhancing the accuracy of computer-aided diagnosis and image-guided

© The Author(s), under exclusive license to Springer Nature Singapore Pte Ltd. 2024
L. Fang et al. (Eds.): CICAI 2023, LNAI 14473, pp. 170–181, 2024.
https://doi.org/10.1007/978-981-99-8850-1_14

surgeries [1]. In recent years, CNN has emerged as the dominant paradigm in various medical image segmentation tasks [2, 3]. Notable architectures such as UNet, featuring with encoder-decoder symmetric structure [4], and its variants have illustrated superior performance. For instance, UNet++ [5] incorporates extensive skip connections to minimize the semantic gaps between feature maps, while UNet3+ [6] employs deep supervision, full-scale skip connections and classification guidance to optimize training efficiency and reduce model complexity. Similarly, DenseUNet [7] introduces the concepts of residual connection and dense connection to help information flow better in the network and promote the propagation of gradients. KiUNet [8] achieves faster convergence and captures a more subtle structure through a smaller receptive filed. Despite these advancements, U-shaped architecture suffers from the inherent limitations of convolutional operations. Specifically, the convolutional kernel can only focus on one sub-region [9]. This nature restricts their ability to capture long-term semantic dependencies and global context, rendering them less sensitive to edge and contour details in segmentation tasks [10], consequently affecting the quality of segmentation outcomes.

In the realm of natural language processing (NLP), the Transformer architecture [11] has demonstrated robust capabilities for sequence feature learning and long-term dependency modeling. This inspired the development of Vision Transformer (ViT) [12] and its adaptation from NLP to Computer Vision (CV) tasks. To mitigate training challenge associated with ViT, Touvron et al., introduced a data-efficient image Transformer (DeiT) [13], using Knowledge Distillation [14] to enhance model performance and robustness. Liu et al., proposed Swin Transformer, a hierarchical visual Transformer leveraging moving window self-attention mechanism [15]. It also implemented W-MSA and SW-MSA serial Transformer modules to reduce the computational complexity.

Given the limitations of both CNNs and Transformers in medical image segmentation, the emergence of hybrid models becomes increasingly important. TransUNet, as the first hybrid network model of Transformer and CNN [9], incorporated a global self-attention mechanism in the encoder, and benefited from jump connection and up-sampling of UNet architecture in the decoder. Other approaches such as U-shaped Swin Transformer-SwinUnet [16], DSTransUNet [17] and SwinUNETR [19] also utilize variation of Transformer modules, targeting different aspects like dual-scale feature extraction (TIE), dual-scale feature fusion (TIF) and feature up-sampling. However, there are two major obstacles, which impedes the migration of application of Transformer to medical image segmentation tasks. First [16], Transformer training requires significant computing resources and large-scale datasets. Second, Transformers, inherently being sequence-to-sequence models, exhibits limitations in capturing pixel-level spatial features and positional information compared with convolutional methods.

To address the confined receptive field in convolutional operations and the challenges in capturing pixel-level positional information inherent to Transformers, this paper proposes STU3, a novel U-shaped Transformer model for automatic medical image segmentation that leverages the strengths of both the Swin Transformer Blocks (SWTB) and the UNet architecture.

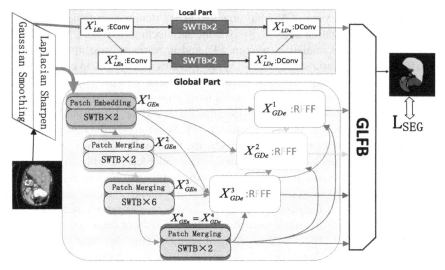

Fig. 1. The overall architecture of STU3.

2   Method

2.1   Architecture Overview

The architecture of the proposed STU3 model is depicted in Fig. 1. Due to the high grayscale level of original CT images $O \in R^{H \times W \times C}$, this paper will preprocess the original image first. The local part and the global part are both U-shaped network architectures. In the local part, the encoder initially conducts two successive down-sampling operations for feature extraction, followed by the integration of SWTB to enhance the remote dependence of the feature map, which is then fused with low-scale features. Subsequently, spatial resolution and local positional information are recovered by up-sampling twice. In the global component, the input image is partitioned into uniform pixel patches, and global semantic features are extracted via four consecutive down-samplings. A Residual Full-scale Feature Fusion module (RFFF) serves as the decoder, performing four consecutive up-sampling steps to reinstate both spatial resolution and thoroughgoing context of the feature graph. Finally, a Global-Local Feature Fusion Block (GLFB) is employed to amalgamate features from both the local and global outputs.

2.2   SWTB

The conventional Transformer encoder comprises multiple identical, standard Transformer modules, as shown in Fig. 2a. There are two core components: the Multi-Head Self-Attention mechanism (MSA) and the Multi-Layer Perceptron (MLP). Each and every component is predated by a Normalized Layer (LN) and followed by a residual link. The output of l-level standard Transformer can be mathematically expressed as:

$$\hat{M}^l = MSA(LN(M^{l-1})) + M^{l-1}$$

$$M^l = MLP(LN(\hat{M}^l)) + \hat{M}^l \tag{1}$$

Here, $\hat{M}^l$ and M^l correspond the outputs of the MSA and the MLP, respectively.

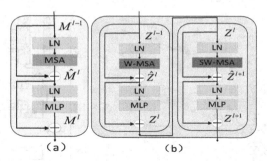

(a)   (b)

Fig. 2. (a) The architecture of the standard Transformer module; (b) The structure of SwinTransformer module.

While the standard Transformer computes relationships between all tokens in a feature map [11], its computational complexity scales quadratically with the size of the image, making it suboptimal for high-resolution feature maps. As shown in Fig. 2b, the Swin Transformer consists of two sub-modules [20], each containing the similar components and steps, except for their distinct multi-head self-attention mechanism component (W-MSA\SW-MSA). The features output by LN are divided into equal-sized and non-overlapping window sequences. Each encompasses $M \times M$ patches. W-MSA conducts intra-window multi-head self-attention mechanism, while SW-MSA shifts the original window partition to the right and down $\lfloor \frac{M}{2}, \frac{M}{2} \rfloor$ window sizes, respectively, followed by multi-head self-attention mechanism operation inside the new windows. This design mitigates the disadvantage of information isolation across windows without increasing additional computational overhead [15]. The mathematical representation of the Swin Transformer module can be expressed as:

$$\hat{S}^l = W - MSA(LN(S^{l-1})) + S^{l-1}$$
$$S^l = MLP(LN(\hat{S}^l)) + \hat{S}^l$$
$$\hat{S}^{l+1} = SW - MSA(LN(S^l)) + S^l$$
$$S^{l+1} = MLP(LN(\hat{S}^{l+1})) + \hat{S}^{l+1} \tag{2}$$

where $\hat{S}^l$ correspond the output of the W-MSA component or the SW-MSA component, and S^l is the output of the MLP. The main function of the self-attention mechanism [21] is to compute dependencies between disparate elements of the input sequence. The output of this mechanism can be formally represented as:

$$Attention(Q, K, V) = SoftMax\left(\frac{QK^T}{\sqrt{d}} + B\right)V \tag{3}$$

Among them, $B \in R^{(2M-1)^2}$ represents the relative position coding [22], M is the window size, Q represents the position information of the current concerned element, K represents the position information of other elements, and V represents the content feature and information meaning of each element.

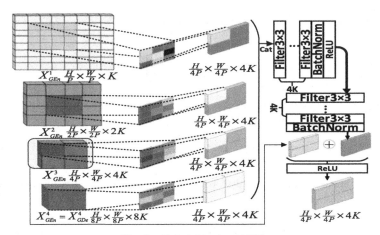

Fig. 3. Global decoder RFFF.

2.3 Local Part

The preprocessed 2D slice $X \in R^{H \times W \times C}$ is used as the input of the local part. This part has two levels, each level consists of an encoder, a skip connection, and a decoder module. The encoder downsamples the feature twice and projects the channel to $\frac{K}{4}$ dimensions. The two-stage encoder outputs X_{LEn}^i, $i = 1, 2$ resolutions of $\frac{H}{2} \times \frac{W}{2} \times \frac{K}{4}$ and $\frac{H}{4} \times \frac{W}{4} \times \frac{K}{2}$, respectively. The feature output of each level encoder will interact with the local feature information through the corresponding level of the peer-to-peer skip connection module (SWTB) [15], thereby enhancing the global information of the local features. During this phase, the size of the feature map remains invariable, and then the feature output will be merged with the output features of the lower decoder, and then deliver to the decoder to sample twice. The output X_{LDe}^i, $i = 1, 2$ resolutions of the two-stage decoder are $\frac{H}{2}, \frac{W}{2}, \frac{K}{4}$ and $\frac{H}{2} \times \frac{W}{2} \times \frac{K}{2}$ respectively, which can be expressed as:

$$X_{LDe}^i = U(H[SWTB(D(X_{LEn}^{i-1})), X_{LDe}^{i+1}]), \quad i = 1, \ldots N \quad (4)$$

Among them, $H[.]$ represents the use of convolution, batch normalization and activation function to achieve feature fusion. $U(.)$ and $D(.)$ represent up-sampling and down-sampling operations, respectively. SWTB represents the use of Swin Transformer module for feature extraction and fusion, and N represents the total series.

2.4 Global Part and RFFF

Both the global and the local parts of the model share the same image as their input $X \in R^{H \times W \times C}$. There are four hierarchical levels. The first three levels are composed of an encoder and a decoder, while the fourth level solely consists of a bottleneck layer featuring a single encoder. The first-level encoder is composed of a patch embedding layer [15] coupled with a SWTB. The patch embedding layer divides X into uniform and non-overlapping patches $X_a \in R^{\frac{H}{P} \times \frac{W}{P} \times (p^2 \times C)}$, where $\frac{H}{p} \times \frac{W}{p}$ and $p^2 \times C$ are its resolution and number of channels, respectively. p^2 is the resolution of the patch. Then, X_a is projected into a K-dimensional embedding space, with its spatial resolution preserved unchanged at $X_b = R^{\frac{H}{P} \times \frac{W}{P} \times K}$, and finally X_b will be fed into SWTB for further processing. The encoders in the latter three levels are constructed from a patch merging layer and an SWTB module. The patch merging layer down-samples the number of patches of the feature map output from the previous encoder by 4 times, while simultaneously doubling the number of channels in the feature map. The resolution and number of channels of the output X_{GEn}^i, $i = 1, 2, 3, 4$ of each stage encoder are $\frac{H}{p} \times \frac{W}{p} \times K$, $\frac{H}{2p} \times \frac{W}{2p} \times 2K$, $\frac{H}{4p} \times \frac{W}{4p} \times 4K$ and $\frac{H}{8p} \times \frac{W}{8p} \times 8K$, respectively.

In the decoder part, the RFFF module is employed. The configuration for the third-level decoder is shown in Fig. 3. Firstly, the decoder accepts feature vectors X_{GEn}^1 and X_{GEn}^2 from the low-level encoder, followed by the peer-to-peer jump connection from the same-level encoder, and finally receive the feature information X_{GDe}^4 from a high-level decoder. To clarify using the third level as an example, within the RFFF module, all feature maps with different levels of resolution are made consistent with the resolution and channel number of the corresponding level decoder output $X_{GDe}^3 \in R^{\frac{H}{4P} \times \frac{W}{4P} \times 4K}$. For the low-level features, 3-i, where i is the corresponding series, feature acquisition components are implemented for down-sampling. For same level features, the peer-to-peer jump connection is used for feature extraction. High-level features are up-sampled through i-3 feature acquisition components. In order to reduce redundancy during multi-level feature fusion, a feature aggregation component is used, effectively reducing the number of fused feature channels to 4K. Then these fused features are combined with the output features from the encoder through a residual fusion mechanism. The decoder output X_{GDe}^i, $i = 1, 2, 3$ can be expressed as:

$$X_{GDe}^i = \begin{cases} X_{GEn}^i, i=N \\ H\left[C\left(D\left(X_{GEn}^j\right)\right)_{j=1}^{i-1}, C(X_{GEn}^i), C\left(U\left(X_{GDe}^j\right)\right)_{j=i+1}^{N-1}\right], i=1,...,N-1 \end{cases} \tag{5}$$

where, $H[.]$ represents the use of convolution, batch normalization and activation function to achieve feature fusion. $U(.)$ and $D(.)$ are up-sampling and down-sampling operations, respectively. $C(.)$ stands for the use of filters to extract features, and N represents the total series.

2.5 Glfb

The GLFB is shown in Fig. 4. It receives five features with resolutions of $\frac{2H}{p} \times \frac{2W}{p} \times \frac{K}{2}$, $\frac{H}{p} \times \frac{W}{p} \times K$, $\frac{H}{2p} \times \frac{W}{2p} \times 2K$, $\frac{H}{4p} \times \frac{W}{4p} \times 4K$ and $\frac{H}{8p} \times \frac{W}{8p} \times 8K$, and uses feature the acquisition component (FAC) to up-sample the four global features, making their resolution consistent with X_{LDe}^1. Subsequently, the global features along with the local features undergo axial concatenation and are passed through a sequence of four SWTB modules. Following this, a feature aggregation group is employed to upscale the resolution by a factor of 2, while simultaneously decreasing the channel count to $\frac{K}{4}$. To complete the architecture, a segmentation head projects aggregated features into a J-dimensional embedding space, thereby providing the final segmented output. The GLFB output $X_{GLFB} \in R^{H \times W \times J}$ can be expressed as:

$$X_{GLFB} = E(SWTB([U(X_{GDe}^i)_{i=1}^N, X_{LDe}^1]))$$

(6)

where $E(.)$ represents the use of convolution, batch normalization, and activation functions to achieve extended resolution and compression channels. $U(.)$ and $[.]$ are up-sampling and axial connection, respectively. N stands for the total number of stages.

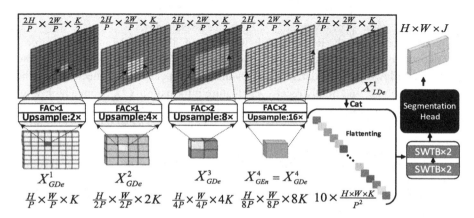

Fig. 4. Global-local feature fusion module GLFB.

3   Experiments

3.1   Implementation Details

In this paper, Dice Similarity Coefficient [26] (DSC) evaluation was performed on two distinct medical CT datasets: the abdominal multi-organ CT dataset (BTCV) and the cervical multi-organ CT dataset (CRD). BTCW focused on the six most difficult organs: gallbladder, esophagus, portal vein and splenic vein, pancreas, right adrenal gland and left adrenal gland, and CRD included four organs: bladder, uterus, rectum, and small intestine. The experiments were implemented using Python3.9 and Pytorch1.7.1. For training, rudimentary data augmentation technologies such as random flipping, rotation, and cropping were utilized, without any pre-training on external datasets. The input image and patch dimensions were set to 448 × 448 and 4, respectively. The learning rate is 1e−3, the batch size is 6, and a pre-defined iteration count of 100.

3.2 Evaluating Metric

The evaluation metric employed in this study is the DSC [26], also known as the Sorensen–Dice coefficient. This metric is widely used to quantify the overlap or similarity between two sets and is particularly pertinent for comparing image segmentation results. For each dimension of the feature map, the DSC is computed, and subsequently, the mean value is obtained to represent the resultant DSC for the given image segmentation task. The formula for DSC is provided as follows:

$$DSC = \frac{2 * |A \cap B|}{|A| + |B|} \tag{7}$$

Table 1. Accuracy comparison on BTCV

Framework	Gall	Eso	Veins	Pan	Rag	Lag	Avg
ASPP [23]	0.6358	0.7264	0.7149	0.7429	0.6361	0.6555	0.6853
TransUNet [9]	0.6549	0.7319	0.7147	0.7426	0.6376	0.6575	0.6899
SwinUnet [16]	0.6902	0.7415	0.7300	0.7496	0.6473	0.6695	0.7047
TransBTS [24]	0.685	0.7559	0.7425	0.7512	0.6795	0.6795	0.7156
UNETR [25]	0.7698	0.7401	0.7505	0.8012	0.6184	0.6361	0.7194
nnU-Net [24]	0.6658	0.7571	**0.7831**	0.7917	0.6665	0.6960	0.7267
Swin UNETR [19]	0.7712	0.7414	0.7508	0.8102	0.6396	0.6600	0.7289
CLIP [27]	**0.7952**	0.7655	0.7754	**0.8317**	0.689	0.7214	**0.7630**
STU3	0.7586	**0.7750**	0.7684	0.7933	**0.7094**	**0.7401**	0.7575

3.3 Experimental Result

So as to validate the validity of proposed STU3 model, a comprehensive comparison against SOTA is conducted on the abdominal multi-organ dataset as shown in Table 1. Table 1 presents segmentation outcomes from eight diverse models based on BTCV dataset, including ASPP, TransUNet, SwinUnet, SwinUNETR and the current optimal CLIP. It is noteworthy that STU3 achieves a DSC of 75.75%, outperforming most of the existing methods, especially on more challenging organs. Furthermore, the average DSC scores specifically for the adrenal gland is superior to that of the state-of-the-art methods. This result underscores resilience of STU3 to data imbalance and its focused attention to individual organs. Figure 5 visually substantiates these claims, displaying that the segmentation output of STU3 closely approximates the ground truth.

For the cervical multi-organ dataset, STU3 records an average DSC of 65.55%, out classing the performance of U-Unet, TransUNet, and SwinUnet models. Figure 6 reinforces the robustness generalization capabilities of STU3, as indicated by its superior segmentation outcomes. The empirical evaluations affirm the high efficacy and generalizability of the STU3 model for medical image segmentation tasks (Table 2).

Table 2. Accuracy comparison of CRD

Framework	Bladder	Uterus	Rectum	Small bowel	Avg
Unet [4]	0.7764	0.6092	0.5656	0.3123	0.5659
TransUNet [9]	0.7961	0.6766	0.6209	0.3326	0.6066
SwinUnet [16]	0.8303	**0.7515**	**0.6472**	0.3523	0.6453
STU3	**0.8375**	0.7241	0.6315	**0.4289**	**0.6555**

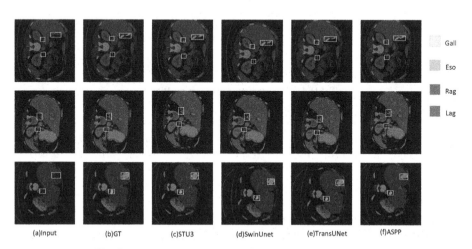

(a)Input   (b)GT   (c)STU3   (d)SwinUnet   (e)TransUNet   (f)ASPP

Fig. 5. Segmentation results of different methods on BTCV

As shown in Table 3, this paper takes the basic model STU without RFFF module and GLFB module as the benchmark model, and conducts ablation tests on the abdominal multi-organ CT dataset to evaluate the performance of RFFF module and GLFB module. The DSC segmentation accuracy of STU is 69.19%, the segmentation accuracy of STU + RFFF is 73.03%, which is increased by 3.84%, and the segmentation accuracy of STU + GLFB is 73.8%, which is increased by 4.61%. The segmentation accuracy of each organ and tissue has been improved to varying degrees, which proves that RFFF and GLFB modules can effectively extract global context information and local structural features.

Table 3. Accuracy comparison of ablation experiments on BTCV

Framework	Gall	Eso	Veins	Pan	Rag	Lag	Avg
STU	0.6882	0.6938	0.6973	0.7027	0.6725	0.6967	0.6919
STU + RFFF	0.7395	0.7414	0.7422	0.7753	0.6813	0.7023	0.7303
STU + GLFB	0.7223	0.751	0.7611	0.7628	0.6926	0.7383	0.738
STU3	**0.7586**	**0.775**	**0.7684**	**0.7933**	**0.7094**	**0.7401**	**0.7575**

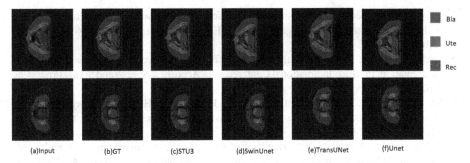

Fig. 6. Segmentation results of different methods on CRD

4 Conclusion

This paper introduces STU3, a novel model for automatic medical image segmentation that leverages the strengths of the Swin Transformer module and the UNet architecture. A parallel training scheme for global and local features is devised to optimally capture both global semantic attributes and local positional information within images. Combined with the GLFB, the model further amalgamates global coarse-grained and local fine-grained features, thereby establishing a robust link for both global information and local structural dependencies. Employing the RFFF module as the global decoder accomplishes dual objectives: it mitigates the limitations of fine-grained feature fusion and bridges the semantic gap across features at varying scales, thereby augmenting the global context across all feature maps. Experimental validation on the BTCV and CRD datasets indicates that STU3 outperforms existing SOTA in terms of accuracy. Future research will focus on the applicability to different segmentation tasks, such as tumors, polyps, and cancerous tissues. Transitioning the model from 2D to 3D to enhance segmentation precision in medical imaging also constitutes a pivotal avenue for future exploration.

References

1. Razzak, M.I., Naz, S., Zaib, A.: Deep learning for medical image processing: overview, challenges and the future. In: Classification in BioApps: Automation of Decision Making, pp. 323–350 (2018)
2. Taghanaki, S.A., Abhishek, K., Cohen, J.P., Cohen-Adad, J., Hamarneh, G.: Deep semantic segmentation of natural and medical images: a review. Artif. Intell. Rev. **54**(1), 137–178 (2020)
3. Minaee, S., Boykov, Y., Porikli, F., Plaza, A., Kehtarnavaz, N., Terzopoulos, D.: Image segmentation using deep learning: a survey. CoRR, abs/2001.05566, pp. 1–22 (2020)
4. Ronneberger, O., Fischer, P., Brox, T.: U-net: convolutional networks for biomedical image segmentation. In: International Conference on Medical Image Computing and Computer-Assisted Intervention, pp. 234–241 (2015). https://doi.org/10.1007/978-3-319-24574-4_284

5. Zhou, Z., Siddiquee, R., Tajbakhsh, N., et al.: UNet++: redesigning skip connections to exploit multiscale features in image segmentation. IEEE Trans. Med. Imaging **39**(6), 1856–1867 (2019)

6. Huang, H., Lin, L., Tong, R., et al.: Unet 3+: a full-scale connected UNet for medical image segmentation. In: IEEE International Conference on Acoustics, Speech and Signal Processing (2020)

7. Li, X., Chen, H., Qi, X., Dou, Q., Fu, C.W., Heng, P.-A.: H-Denseunet: hybrid densely connected UNet for liver and tumor segmentation from ct volumes. IEEE Trans. Med. Imaging **37**(12), 2663–2674 (2018)

8. Valanarasu, J.M.J., Sindagi, V.A., Hacihaliloglu, I., et al.: Kiu-net: overcomplete convolutional architectures for biomedical image and volumetric segmentation. IEEE Trans. Med. Imaging **41**(4), 965–976 (2021)

9. Chen, J., et al.: Transunet: transformers make strong encoders for medical image segmentation. CoRR, abs/2102.04306 (2021)

10. Gu, Z., et al.: CE-net: context encoder network for 2d medical image segmentation. IEEE Trans. Med. Imaging **38**(10), 2281–2292 (2019). https://doi.org/10.1109/TMI.2019.2903562

11. Vaswani, A., Shazeer, N., Parmar, N.: Attention is all you need. In: Advances in Neural Information Processing Systems, pp. 5998–6008 (2017)

12. Yuan, L., et al.: Tokens-to-token vit: training vision transformers from scratch on imagenet. In: Proceedings of the IEEE/CVF International Conference on Computer Vision, pp. 558–567 (2021). https://doi.org/10.48550/arXiv.2101.11986

13. Touvron, H., Cord, M., Douze, M., et al.: Training data-efficient image transformers & distillation through attention. In: International Conference on Machine Learning, pp. 10347–10357. PMLR (2021)

14. Gou, J., Yu, B., Maybank, S.J., et al.: Knowledge distillation: a survey. Int. J. Comput. Vision **129**, 1789–1819 (2021)

15. Liu, Z., et al.: Swin transformer: hierarchical vision transformer using shifted windows. CoRR, abs/2103.14030 (2021). https://arxiv.org/abs/2103.14030

16. Cao, H., et al.: Swin-unet: unet-like pure transformer for medical image segmentation. arXiv preprint arXiv:2105.05537 (2021)

17. Lin, A., Chen, B., Xu, J., et al.: DS-transunet: Dual swin transformer u-net for medical image segmentation. IEEE Trans. Instrum. Meas. **71**, 1–15 (2022)

18. Atek, S., Mehidi, I., Jabri, D., et al.: SwinT-Unet: hybrid architecture for medical image segmentation based on swin transformer block and dual-scale information. In: 2022 7th International Conference on Image and Signal Processing and their Applications (ISPA), pp. 1–6. IEEE (2022)

19. Hatamizadeh A, Nath V, Tang Y, et al. Swin UNETR: swin transformers for semantic segmentation of brain Tumors in MRI images. In: Crimi, A., Bakas, S. (eds.) BrainLes 2021. LNCS, vol. 12962, pp. 272–284. Springer, Cham (2021). https://doi.org/10.1007/978-3-031-08999-2_22

20. Bojesomo, A., Al-Marzouqi, H., Liatsis, P.: Spatiotemporal swin transformer network for short time weather forecasting. In: 1st Workshop on Complex Data Challenges in Earth Observation, 01 November 2021 (2021)

21. Shaw, P., Uszkoreit, J., Vaswani, A.: Self-attention with relative position representations. arXiv preprint arXiv:1803.02155 (2018)

22. Wu, K., Peng, H., Chen, M., et al.: Rethinking and improving relative position encoding for vision transformer. In: Proceedings of the IEEE/CVF International Conference on Computer Vision, pp. 10033–10041 (2021)

23. Chen, L.-C., Zhu, Y., Papandreou, G., Schroff, F., Adam, H.: Encoder-decoder with atrous separable convolution for semantic image segmentation, arXiv:1802.02611 (2018)

24. Isensee, F., Jaeger, P.F., Kohl, S.A.A., Petersen, J., Maier-Hein, K.H.: NNU-net: a self-configuring method for deep learning-based biomedical image segmentation. Nat. Methods **18**(2), 203–211 (2021)
25. Hatamizadeh, A., et al.: UNETR: transformers for 3D medical image segmentation. In: Proceedings of the IEEE/CVF Winter Conference on Applications of Computer Vision, pp. 574–584 (2022)
26. Dice, L.R.: Measures of the amount of ecologic association between species. Ecology **26**(3), 297–302 (1944). https://doi.org/10.2307/1932
27. Liu, J., Zhang, Y., Chen, J.N., et al.: Clip-driven universal model for organ segmentation and Tumor detection. arXiv preprint arXiv:2301.00785 (2023)

Integrating Human Parsing and Pose Network for Human Action Recognition

Runwei Ding[1], Yuhang Wen[2], Jinfu Liu[2], Nan Dai[3], Fanyang Meng[4], and Mengyuan Liu[1($\boxtimes$)]

[1] Shenzhen Graduate School, Peking University, Shenzhen, China
`nkliuyifang@gmail.com`
[2] Sun Yat-sen University, Shenzhen, China
[3] Changchun University of Science and Technology, Changchun, China
[4] Peng Cheng Laboratory, Shenzhen, China

Abstract. Human skeletons and RGB sequences are both widely-adopted input modalities for human action recognition. However, skeletons lack appearance features and color data suffer large amount of irrelevant depiction. To address this, we introduce human parsing feature map as a novel modality, since it can selectively retain spatiotemporal features of the body parts, while filtering out noises regarding outfits, backgrounds, etc. We propose an Integrating Human Parsing and Pose Network (IPP-Net) for action recognition, which is the first to leverage both skeletons and human parsing feature maps in dual-branch approach. The human pose branch feeds compact skeletal representations of different modalities in graph convolutional network to model pose features. In human parsing branch, multi-frame body-part parsing features are extracted with human detector and parser, which is later learnt using a convolutional backbone. A late ensemble of two branches is adopted to get final predictions, considering both robust keypoints and rich semantic body-part features. Extensive experiments on NTU RGB+D and NTU RGB+D 120 benchmarks consistently verify the effectiveness of the proposed IPP-Net, which outperforms the existing action recognition methods. Our code is publicly available at https://github.com/liujf69/IPP-Net-Parsing.

Keywords: Action recognition · Human parsing · Human skeletons

1 Introduction

Human action recognition is an essential task in the field of computer vision, which has great research value and broad application prospects in human-robot

R. Ding and Y. Wen—Contributed equally to this work.

This work was supported by the Basic and Applied Basic Research Foundation of Guangdong (No. 2020A1515110370) and the National Natural Science Foundation of China (No. 62203476).

L. Fang et al. (Eds.): CICAI 2023, LNAI 14473, pp. 182–194, 2024.
https://doi.org/10.1007/978-981-99-8850-1_15

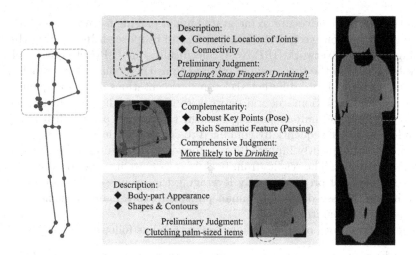

Fig. 1. An example of the modality complementarity between the human pose and the human parsing map. A more comprehensive prediction can be made by integrating robust key points from poses and rich semantic features from parsing feature maps.

interaction [26] and visual media [29,32]. Most action recognition methods take human skeletons sequences [11,13,14,24,30] or color images [23] as the input modality for the following reasons. A human skeleton can be conceptualized as an inherent topological graph, which can accurately portray body movements and is highly robust to environmental changes, thereby adopted in many studies using graph convolutional neural networks (GCNs) [2,4,5,24,28,33]. On the other hand, color images (RGB data) have rich appearance information, therefore some prior studies in action recognition employ Convolutional Neural Networks (CNNs) [6,23] to learn spatiotemporal features from video frames. In recent years, methods [6] of integrating skeletal and RGB data have emerged to make effective use of multimodal features for better action recognition.

However, both skeletal and RGB data have their respective limitations in representing human actions. Skeletons lack the capacity to convey the visual appearance of individual body parts, while RGB features are susceptible to disturbances from diverse sources, such as background interference, irrelevant elements, and changes in illumination. This naturally leads to the question: Can we explore a new modality that incorporates body-part appearance depiction while remaining noiseless and robust?

Our affirmative response is inspired by *Human Parsing*, a vision task that holds significant importance in video surveillance and human behavior analysis. This task facilitates the recognition of distinct semantic parts, such as limbs, within the human body [9]. By focusing on these semantic parts, human parsing explicitly and effectively eliminates action-irrelevant details, while retaining crucial extrinsic features of the human body. We believe this can effectively complement the skeletal data, as illustrated in Fig. 1.

In this work, we advocate to integrate human parsing feature map as a novel modality into action recognition framework, and propose an Integrating Human Parsing and Pose Network (IPP-Net). Specifically, our IPP-Net consists of two trunk branches. In the first branch, referred to as the human pose branch, pose data is transformed into different skeleton representations and subsequently fed into a graph convolutional neural network to obtain predictions. In the second branch, dubbed the human parsing branch, the human parsing features from multiple frames are sequentially combined to construct a feature map. This feature map is subsequently inputted into a convolutional neural network to derive recognition results. The results from both branches are integrated via a softmax layer to make final predictions. By leveraging the proposed IPP-Net, we effectively integrate pose data and human parsing feature maps to achieve better human action recognition.

The contributions of our work are summarized as follows:

1. We advocate to leverage human parsing feature map as a new modality for human action recognition task, which is appearance-oriented depictive and also action-relevant.
2. We propose a framework called Integrating Human Parsing and Pose Network (IPP-Net), which is the first to effectively integrates human parsing feature maps and pose data for robust human action recognition. Specifically, pose feature (representing body-part positions and connections) and human parsing feature (representing body-part contours and appearance) are learnt in two-stream approach and integrated via a late ensemble, to give comprehensive judgements about actions.
3. Extensive experiments on benchmark NTU RGB+D and NTU RGB+D 120 datasets verify the effectiveness of our IPP-Net, which outperforms most existing action recognition methods.

2   Related Work

2.1   Human Action Recognition

Prior approaches for human action recognition usually leverage skeletal data, which is a compact and sufficient representation for human actions. A significant body of work deals with more effective and efficient model architecture design for skeleton sequences [2,4,5,16,19,22,26,28,33], with the aim of exploiting more informative joints. Beyond skeleton data, several of works use multi-modal features of human actions, including RGB sequences [6] and text descriptions [27], to achieve robust recognition results. VPN [6] embeds 3D skeletons with their corresponding RGB videos, and feed them into an attention network to learn spatiotemporal relations. Empowered by Large Language Model (LLM), LST [27] conditions GCN training using the generated text descriptions of body-part motions. Compared to single modality, Multi-modal inputs provide unique information for each type of action, albeit in different forms, thereby enhancing human action understanding. However, it may contain irrelevant features

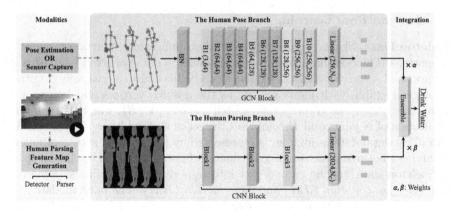

Fig. 2. Framework of our proposed Integrating Human Parsing and Pose Network.

(e.g. specific outfits, backgrounds). Our IPP-Net also leverages multi-modalities, and we argues to utilize pose data and feature map sequences of human parsing. Compared with the above approaches, human parsing filters out irrelevant information regarding illumination and backgrounds, while selectively retaining spatiotemporal features of all body parts.

2.2 Human Parsing

Human parsing involves the segmentation of a human image into finely detailed parts, including the limbs, the head, the torso, etc. Several benchmarks have been proposed for human parsing task, providing large-scale annotations of body parts [9,10]. A number of works concentrated on this problem and proposed novel models for better semantic parsing. The majority are based on ResNet architecture [8,9,17,31], while some are based on Transformer architecture [1]. Inspired by the human parsing task, we exploit the advantages of human parsing to get noiseless and concise representations, thus proposing a framework to ensemble parsing results and skeletons.

3   IPP-Net

As depicted in Fig. 2, in our proposed Integrating Human Parsing and Pose Network, we incorporate two primary branches, specifically the human pose branch and the human parsing branch. The human pose branch (Sect. 3.1) utilizes GCN to model the skeleton data, while the human parsing branch (Sect. 3.2) employs CNN to learn spatiotemporal features of the human parsing feature maps. Subsequently, the outcomes from these two branches are integrated via a late ensemble to get action predictions (Sect. 3.3).

3.1   Human Pose Learning

Skeleton Data. Skeleton data finds extensive applications in action recognition frameworks. The pose branch leverages 3D skeleton data collected by sensors. In a conceptual sense, the skeletal sequence can be likened to a naturally occurring topological graph, with joints serving as the graph's vertices and bones as its connecting edges. The graph is represented as $G = \{V, E\}$, where V represents a collection of N joints and E comprises the set of skeletal bones. When working with 3D skeletal data, a joint v_i is represented as $\{x_i, y_i, z_i\}$, with components specifying the three-dimensional coordinates of point v_i within Euclidean space.

Skeleton data can be categorized into four distinct modalities: *joint* (J), *bone* (B), *joint motion* (JM) and *bone motion* (BM). The bone modality can be derived by calculation between two physically connected joints, while joint motion and bone motion modalities can be calculated separately using joint and bone data from two successive frames respectively. We acquire the four skeleton modalities following the formula defined in [11].

Backbone. GCN-based approaches have emerged as predominant in the domain of skeleton-based action recognition for their unique advantages in modeling graph-structured data. Our IPP-Net also embraces GCN as backbone to learn pose features. A Graph Convolutional Network (GCN) consists of both graph convolutions and temporal convolutions. The typical form of a graph convolution can be formulated as:

$$H^{l+1} = \sigma \left(D^{-\frac{1}{2}} A D^{-\frac{1}{2}} H^l W^l \right), \tag{1}$$

where H^l is the joint features at layer l and σ is the activation function. $D \in R^{N \times N}$ is the degree matrix of N joints and W^l is the learnable parameter of the l-th layer. A denotes the adjacency matrix that signifies the connections between joints and can be obtained in static (predefined manually) or dynamic (initialized manually but learnable) ways. Our IPP-Net feeds the normalized four skeleton modalities defined above into the ten dynamic GCN blocks for feature extraction, followed by a linear head to obtain the recognition result.

3.2   Human Parsing Learning

Human Parsing Feature Map Generation. Inspired by the human parsing task, we propose human parsing feature maps as one novel modality representing body-part movements with appearances. The following steps shows how we generate this new modality from raw RGB videos. Given an RGB video stream $F = \{f_1, f_2, \cdots, f_N\}$ with N frames, frame-level feature is extracted by

$$I_i = E(D(f_i)), \tag{2}$$

where $1 \leq i \leq N, i \in \mathbb{N}$, then D and E denote an object detector and a feature extractor respectively. In implementation, we use YoloV5 [25] as the target

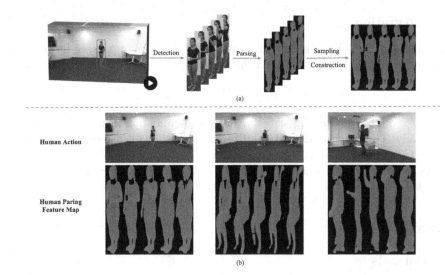

Fig. 3. (a) Illustration of human parsing feature map generation from RGB videos. (b) Visualization of human parsing feature maps for different action samples.

detector of our model, and feed the detected human maps into Resnet101 [7] to extract the features $\boldsymbol{I}_i$ of each frame.

The frame-level feature $\boldsymbol{I}_i$ gets downsampled and upsampled in PSPNet [31] for human parsing, formulated as

$$\hat{\boldsymbol{P}}_i = \mathrm{argmax}_{class}(PSPNet(\boldsymbol{I}_i)), \tag{3}$$

where $1 \leq i \leq N, i \in \mathbb{N}$. $\hat{\boldsymbol{P}}_i$ retrieves the index of the most possible body part category for each pixel.

Then the frame-level maps get resized to a standard shape [h, w]. We sample total N_{sample} frames from N frame-level maps with the random equidistant sampling strategy, denoted as

$$\tilde{\boldsymbol{P}}_k = \hat{\boldsymbol{P}}_{1+\delta \times (k-1)} \tag{4}$$

where $1 \leq k \leq N_{sample}, k \in \mathbb{N}$. Suppose $N_{sample} \leq N$, then δ is a random positive integer between 1 and $\lfloor N/N_{sample} \rfloor$. If $N_{sample} > N$, then we repeat the N maps until N_{sample} frames are sampled. The chosen N_{sample} feature maps are chronologically arranged to construct the final feature map $\boldsymbol{P}$. Figure 3 (b) visualizes the feature maps of three action samples, namely *drink water, hand waving* and *salute*.

Backbone. Intuitively the human parsing feature maps repeated in channel dimension can be viewed as 3-channel grayscale images. Therefore, a convolutional backbone is adopted to extract deep parsing features for its strong perception for locality, which is essential to percept graphic structures, such as edges and shapes in parsing feature maps $\boldsymbol{P}$.

3.3   Integration

The outcomes from the human pose branch and the human parsing branch are fused via an ensemble layer, which is formulated as:

$$S = \text{softmax}(\alpha \cdot C(V) + \beta \cdot M(P)), \tag{5}$$

where V and P denote the skeleton data and human parsing feature maps respectively. The skeleton data V and feature maps P are respectively fed into a GCN C and a CNN M. The parameters α and β represent the ensemble weights for the linear combination. After a softmax layer, we could acquire the prediction S.

4   Experiments

4.1   Datasets

Experiments are conducted on two widely-adopted large-scale human action recognition datasets, illustrated as follows:

NTU-RGB+D [18], also referred as **NTU 60**, is a extensively employed 3D action recognition dataset comprising over 56,000 video samples. These actions have been executed by 40 individuals and classified into 60 distinct categories. The original paper [18] suggests two benchmark scenarios for evaluation: (a) Cross-View (X-View), where the training set originates from cameras at $0°$ and $45°$, and the testing set is sourced from another camera at $45°$. (b) Cross-Subject (X-Sub), where the training set comprises samples from 20 subjects, while the remaining 20 subjects are reserved for testing.

NTU-RGB+D 120 [12], also referred as **NTU 120**, is derived from the NTU-RGB+D dataset. A total of 114,480 video clips across 120 daily action classes performed by 106 volunteers are recorded using 3 Kinect V2 TOF cameras. The original work [12] also suggests two criteria: (a) Cross-subject (X-Sub), where similarly the entire dataset is divided into two halves based on the number of subjects for both training and testing. (b) Cross-setup (X-Set), where the entire dataset is divided into two halves based on the parity of ID numbers for both training and testing.

4.2   Implementation Details

All experiments were carried out using four Tesla V100-PCIE-32 GB GPUs and two NVIDIA GeForce RTX 3070 GPUs. The pose branch adopts CTR-GCN [2] as the backbone. We use SGD for model training, conducting 65 epochs with a batch size of 64. The initial learning rate decayed from 0.1 by a factor of 0.1 at epochs 35 and 55. The parsing branch adopts InceptionV3 [21] as the backbone.

Table 1. Top-1 accuracy comparison with state-of-the-art methods on NTU-RGB+D and NTU-RGB+D 120 dataset.

Type	Method	Source	NTU 60 (%)		NTU 120 (%)	
			X-Sub	X-View	X-Sub	X-Set
Pose	Shift-GCN [4]	CVPR'20	90.7	96.5	85.9	87.6
	DynamicGCN [28]	MM'20	91.5	96.0	87.3	88.6
	DSTA-Net [19]	ACCV'20	91.5	96.4	86.6	89.0
	MS-G3D [15]	CVPR'20	91.5	96.2	86.9	88.4
	MST-GCN [3]	AAAI'21	91.5	96.6	87.5	88.8
	CTR-GCN [2]	ICCV'21	92.4	96.8	88.9	90.6
	GS-GCN [33]	CICAI'22	90.2	95.2	84.9	87.1
	PSUMNet [22]	ECCV'22	92.9	96.7	89.4	90.6
	InfoGCN [5]	CVPR'22	93.0	97.1	89.8	91.2
	STSA-Net [16]	Neurocomputing'23	92.7	96.7	88.5	90.7
Multi-Modality	VPN [6]	ECCV'20	93.5	96.2	86.3	87.8
	LST [27]	arXiv'22	92.9	97.0	89.9	91.1
	Ours (J+B+P)		93.4	96.8	89.4	91.2
	Ours		**93.8**	**97.1**	**90.0**	**91.7**

Similarly SGD is used to optimize the model for 30 epochs with the same batch size. The initial learning rate decayed from 0.1 by a factor of 0.0001 at epochs 10 and 25. The cross-entropy loss is employed as the training loss. During training we select 5 frames randomly to construct the feature maps of human parsing, while 5 frames at equal intervals in testing. When generating the human parsing feature map, we resize the map of each frame to a designated size of [480, 96], five frames of which are arranged in chronological order to construct the final feature with a size of [480, 480].

4.3   Comparison with Related Methods

Table 1 compares our IPP-Net with the existing human action recognition methods on the NTU 60 and NTU 120 datasets. In both of these extensive action recognition datasets, our model excels and surpasses all existing methods across virtually all evaluation metrics. Notably, our IPP-Net is the first one that combines human parsing and pose data for action recognition.

In the NTU 60 dataset, the top-1 accuracy reaches 93.8% and 97.1% on the benchmark of X-Sub and X-View respectively, which outperforms CTR-GCN [2] by 1.4% and 0.3%. On the tougher benchmark namely X-Sub, our IPP-Net outperforms LST [27] by 0.9%, even though the LST model additionally introduces texts as a new modality. In the NTU 120 dataset, the top-1 accuracy is 90.0% and 91.7% on the benchmark of X-Sub and X-View respectively, which outperforms CTR-GCN by 1.1% and 1.1%. The most related method to our work is VPN [6], which introduces RGB features besides skeletons for action recognition. On two benchmarks of NTU 120 database, our IPP-Net outperforms VPN by 3.7% and

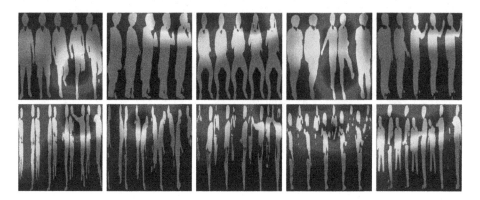

Fig. 4. Visual explanation with class activation maps on how the convolutional backbone judges the human action by the given parsing feature maps.

Table 2. Accuracy of different modalities on NTU-RGB+D and NTU-RGB+D 120.

Modality					NTU 60 (%)		NTU 120 (%)	
J	B	JM	BM	P	X-Sub	X-View	X-Sub	X-Set
✓					90.2	95.0	85.0	86.7
	✓				90.5	94.7	86.2	87.5
		✓			88.1	93.2	81.2	83.0
			✓		87.3	92.0	81.7	82.9
				✓	73.5	74.2	53.6	65.8
✓				✓	91.7	95.9	86.1	88.8
	✓			✓	91.8	95.9	87.5	89.8
✓	✓				92.2	96.2	88.7	90.2
✓	✓	✓	✓		92.4	96.5	89.0	90.5
✓	✓			✓	93.4	96.8	89.4	91.2
✓	**✓**	**✓**	**✓**	**✓**	**93.8**	**97.1**	**90.0**	**91.7**

3.9% respectively. Figure 4 visually illustrates how human parsing feature maps in our IPP-Net help recognize actions by providing semantic information about body parts. The class activation maps indicates that the human parsing branch can focus on the most informative body parts.

4.4   Ablation Study

Modality. Table 2 reports the recognition accuracy of four skeleton modalities and human parsing feature map in NTU60 and NTU120 datasets respectively. When the joint, bone and human parsing feature maps are integrated together (J+B+P), the ensemble recognition accuracy of two benchmarks in the NTU60 dataset is 93.4% and 96.8%, which outperforms the setting that combining joint

Table 3. Comparison of different numbers of frames in feature map construction.

#Frame	Parsing (%)	Ensemble (%)
3	46.7	89.8
4	50.4	89.9
5	53.6	**90.0**
6	55.6	89.9

Table 4. Accuracy of different CNN backbones in human parsing branch.

Backbone	Parsing (%)	Ensemble (%)
VGG11 [20]	49.0	89.8
VGG13 [20]	48.7	89.8
ResNet18 [7]	50.5	90.0
InceptionV3 [21]	53.6	**90.0**

and bone (J+B) by 1.2% and 0.6% respectively. Similarly, the setting (J+B+P) outperforms the setting (J+B) by 0.7% and 1.0% on the two benchmarks of the NTU120 dataset respectively. It can conclude from the experimental results that integrating human parsing as a modality into the framework can improve action recognition performance, which is attributed to the action-relevant body-part appearance provided by human parsing feature maps.

Frames for Human Parsing Feature Maps. We explore how numbers of frames for constructing human parsing feature maps affect the accuracy on NTU120 X-Sub benchmark. As depicted in Table 3, we use 3-frame, 4-frame, 5-frame and 6-frame settings respectively to make up feature maps. The shapes of the four maps are all generated as [480,480] and then resized to [299,299] to meet InceptionV3's demand. We observe that the ensemble accuracy is 90.0% when using 5-frame parsing maps, which is the highest among the four settings.

Backbones to Learn Parsing Features. On NTU120 X-Sub benchmark, we implement four different CNN backbones to learn parsing features. Results in Table 4 indicate that InceptionV3 gets the highest ensemble accuracy among all the CNN backbones.

5   Conclusions

This work proposes an Integrating Human Parsing and Pose Network (IPP-Net) for human action recognition, which introduces the human parsing feature maps as a new modality to represent human actions. Human parsing can selectively preserve spatiotemporal body-part features while filtering out action-irrelevant information in RGB data. As a multi-modal action recognition framework, our IPP-Net is the first to leverage both skeletons and human parsing feature maps, considering both robust keypoints and rich semantic body-part features. The effectiveness of IPP-Net is verified on the NTU-RGB+D and NTU-RGB+D 120 datasets, where our IPP-Net outperforms most existing methods.

References

1. Chen, W., et al.: Beyond appearance: a semantic controllable self-supervised learning framework for human-centric visual tasks. In: Proceedings of the IEEE Conference on Computer Vision and Pattern Recognition (CVPR) (2023)
2. Chen, Y., Zhang, Z., Yuan, C., Li, B., Deng, Y., Hu, W.: Channel-wise topology refinement graph convolution for skeleton-based action recognition. In: Proceedings of the IEEE International Conference on Computer Vision (CVPR) (2021)
3. Chen, Z., Li, S., Yang, B., Li, Q., Liu, H.: Multi-scale spatial temporal graph convolutional network for skeleton-based action recognition. In: Proceedings of the AAAI Conference on Artificial Intelligence (AAAI) (2021)
4. Cheng, K., Zhang, Y., He, X., Chen, W., Cheng, J., Lu, H.: Skeleton-based action recognition with shift graph convolutional network. In: Proceedings of the IEEE Conference on Computer Vision and Pattern Recognition (CVPR) (2020)
5. Chi, H.G., Ha, M.H., Chi, S., Lee, S.W., Huang, Q., Ramani, K.: InfoGCN: representation learning for human skeleton-based action recognition. In: Proceedings of the IEEE Conference on Computer Vision and Pattern Recognition (CVPR) (2022)
6. Das, S., Sharma, S., Dai, R., Brémond, F., Thonnat, M.: VPN: learning video-pose embedding for activities of daily living. In: Vedaldi, A., Bischof, H., Brox, T., Frahm, J.-M. (eds.) ECCV 2020. LNCS, vol. 12354, pp. 72–90. Springer, Cham (2020). https://doi.org/10.1007/978-3-030-58545-7_5
7. He, K., Zhang, X., Ren, S., Sun, J.: Deep residual learning for image recognition. In: Proceedings of the IEEE Conference on Computer Vision and Pattern Recognition (CVPR) (2016)
8. Li, P., Xu, Y., Wei, Y., Yang, Y.: Self-correction for human parsing. IEEE Trans. Pattern Anal. Mach. Intell. **44**(6), 3260–3271 (2020)
9. Liang, X., Gong, K., Shen, X., Lin, L.: Look into person: joint body parsing & pose estimation network and a new benchmark. IEEE Trans. Pattern Anal. Mach. Intell. **41**(4), 871–885 (2019)
10. Liang, X., et al.: Deep human parsing with active template regression. IEEE Trans. Pattern Anal. Mach. Intell. **37**(12), 2402–2414 (2015)
11. Liu, J., Wang, X., Wang, C., Gao, Y., Liu, M.: Temporal decoupling graph convolutional network for skeleton-based gesture recognition. IEEE Trans. Multimedia (2023)
12. Liu, J., Shahroudy, A., Perez, M., Wang, G., Duan, L.Y., Kot, A.C.: NTU RGB+D 120: a large-scale benchmark for 3D human activity understanding. IEEE Trans. Pattern Anal. Mach. Intell. **42**(10), 2684–2701 (2020)
13. Liu, M., Meng, F., Chen, C., Wu, S.: Novel motion patterns matter for practical skeleton-based action recognition. In: AAAI Conference on Artificial Intelligence (AAAI) (2023)
14. Liu, M., Meng, F., Liang, Y.: Generalized pose decoupled network for unsupervised 3D skeleton sequence-based action representation learning. Cyborg Bionic Syst. **2022**, 0002 (2022)

15. Liu, Z., Zhang, H., Chen, Z., Wang, Z., Ouyang, W.: Disentangling and unifying graph convolutions for skeleton-based action recognition. In: Proceedings of the IEEE Conference on Computer Vision and Pattern Recognition (CVPR) (2020)
16. Qiu, H., Hou, B., Ren, B., Zhang, X.: Spatio-temporal segments attention for skeleton-based action recognition. Neurocomputing **518**, 30–38 (2023)
17. Ruan, T., Liu, T., Huang, Z., Wei, Y., Wei, S., Zhao, Y.: Devil in the details: towards accurate single and multiple human parsing. In: Proceedings of the AAAI Conference on Artificial Intelligence (AAAI) (2019)
18. Shahroudy, A., Liu, J., Ng, T.T., Wang, G.: NTU RGB+D: a large scale dataset for 3D human activity analysis. In: Proceedings of the IEEE Conference on Computer Vision and Pattern Recognition (CVPR) (2016)
19. Shi, L., Zhang, Y., Cheng, J., Lu, H.: Decoupled spatial-temporal attention network for skeleton-based action-gesture recognition. In: Proceedings of the Asian Conference on Computer Vision (ACCV) (2020)
20. Simonyan, K., Zisserman, A.: Very deep convolutional networks for large-scale image recognition (2015)
21. Szegedy, C., Vanhoucke, V., Ioffe, S., Shlens, J., Wojna, Z.: Rethinking the inception architecture for computer vision. In: Proceedings of the IEEE Conference on Computer Vision and Pattern Recognition (CVPR) (2016)
22. Trivedi, N., Sarvadevabhatla, R.K.: PSUMNet: unified modality part streams are all you need for efficient pose-based action recognition. In: Karlinsky, L., Michaeli, T., Nishino, K. (eds.) Computer Vision – ECCV 2022 Workshops. ECCV 2022. LNCS, vol. 13805. Springer, Cham (2023). https://doi.org/10.1007/978-3-031-25072-9_14
23. Tu, Z., Li, H., Zhang, D., Dauwels, J., Li, B., Yuan, J.: Action-stage emphasized spatiotemporal VLAD for video action recognition. IEEE Trans. Image Process. **28**(6), 2799–2812 (2019)
24. Tu, Z., Zhang, J., Li, H., Chen, Y., Yuan, J.: Joint-bone fusion graph convolutional network for semi-supervised skeleton action recognition. IEEE Trans. Multimedia **25**, 1819–1831 (2022)
25. Ultralytics: ultralytics/yolov5: v7.0 - YOLOv5 SOTA Realtime Instance Segmentation (2022)
26. Wen, Y., Tang, Z., Pang, Y., Ding, B., Liu, M.: Interactive spatiotemporal token attention network for skeleton-based general interactive action recognition. In: IEEE/RSJ International Conference on Intelligent Robots and Systems (IROS) (2023)
27. Xiang, W., Li, C., Zhou, Y., Wang, B., Zhang, L.: Language supervised training for skeleton-based action recognition. arXiv:2208.05318 (2022)
28. Ye, F., Pu, S., Zhong, Q., Li, C., Xie, D., Tang, H.: Dynamic GCN: context-enriched topology learning for skeleton-based action recognition. In: Proceedings of the ACM International Conference on Multimedia (ACM MM) (2020)
29. Zhang, F.L., Wu, X., Li, R.L., Wang, J., Zheng, Z.H., Hu, S.M.: Detecting and removing visual distractors for video aesthetic enhancement. IEEE Trans. Multimedia **20**(8), 1987–1999 (2018)
30. Zhang, J., Jia, Y., Xie, W., Tu, Z.: Zoom transformer for skeleton-based group activity recognition. IEEE Trans. Circuits Syst. Video Technol. **32**(12), 8646–8659 (2022)
31. Zhao, H., Shi, J., Qi, X., Wang, X., Jia, J.: Pyramid scene parsing network. In: Proceedings of the IEEE Conference on Computer Vision and Pattern Recognition (CVPR) (2017)

32. Zheng, Z.H., Zhang, H.T., Zhang, F.L., Mu, T.J.: Image-based clothes changing system. Comput. Visual Media **3**, 337–347 (2017)
33. Zhu, S., Zhan, Y., Zhao, G.: Multi-model lightweight action recognition with group-shuffle graph convolutional network. In: Proceedings of the CAAI International Conference on Artificial Intelligence (CICAI) (2022)

Lightweight Rolling Shutter Image Restoration Network Based on Undistorted Flow

Binfeng Wang[1], Yunhao Zou[1], Zhijie Gao[1,2(✉)], and Ying Fu[1,2]

[1] MIIT Key Laboratory of Complex-field Intelligent Sensing,
Beijing Institute of Technology, Beijing 100081, China
[2] Yangtze Delta Region Academy of Beijing Institute of Technology,
Jiaxing 314019, China
gzj@bit.edu.cn

Abstract. Rolling shutter(RS) cameras are widely used in fields such as drone photography and robot navigation. However, when shooting a fast-moving target, the captured image may be distorted and blurred due to the feature of progressive image collection by the rs camera. In order to solve this problem, researchers have proposed a variety of methods, among which the methods based on deep learning perform best, but it still faces the challenges of poor restoration effect and high practical application cost. To address this challenge, we propose a novel lightweight rolling image restoration network, which can restore the global image at the intermediate moment from two consecutive rolling images. We use a lightweight encoder-decoder network to extract the bidirectional optical flow between rolling images. We further introduce the concept of time factor and undistorted flow, calculate the undistorted flow by multiplying the optical flow by the time factor. Then bilinear interpolation is performed through the undistorted flow to obtain the intermediate moment global image. Our method achieves the state-of-the-art results in several indicators on the RS image dataset Fastec-RS with only about 6% of that of existing methods.

Keywords: Rolling Shutter Image Restoration · Undistorted Flow · Optical Flow

1 Introduction

Depending on the type of shutter, cameras can be divided into two types, rolling shutter(RS) camera and global shutter(GS) camera. As shown in Fig. 1(left), the GS camera scans each line of the image in parallel when shooting, while the RS camera scans line by line when shooting. The RS camera can obtain images with a higher frame rate and higher definition at a lower cost and has a wide range of applications in the fields of motion capture, machine vision, and consumer electronics. However, due to the progressive imaging mechanism

L. Fang et al. (Eds.): CICAI 2023, LNAI 14473, pp. 195–206, 2024.
https://doi.org/10.1007/978-981-99-8850-1_16

of the RS camera, when the subject or the camera is moving rapidly, the images captured will be distorted and blurred. Consequently, as shown in Fig. 1(right), in the first row of images, the door in the RS image is heavily skewed compared to the GS image.

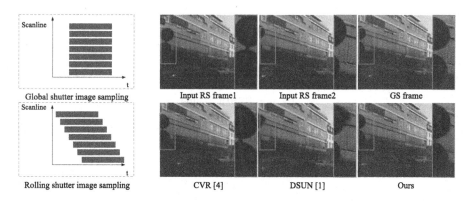

Fig. 1. Our model inputs two consecutive RS images and outputs the GS image corresponding to the intermediate moment. As can be seen from the second row of results, the restoration results of our method have higher geometric similarity to the real GS image than other models.

In order to solve the RS effect, researchers have proposed many solutions, which can be roughly divided into two categories: hardware-based and calculation-based. Hardware-based solutions implement global functionality by placing additional memory nodes on the RS sensor to store charge, voltage, and even pixels in the digital domain. But hardware-based solutions have significant disadvantages in terms of sensor size, cost, and noise.

The calculation-based method corrects the captured RS image through statistics, formulas, models and other methods. Through the combination of image deblurring, video frame interpolation, optical flow and other methods in the field of computer vision, the RS image correction based on deep learning has made great breakthroughs. Liu *et al.* [1] first proposed DSUN, which inputs two consecutive RS images, restores the GS image corresponding to the second frame, and constructs the first synthetic datasets Fastec-RS for the RS image correction. Zhong *et al.* [8] constructed the first real-world dataset BS-RSCD for the RS image correction problem, and proposed a deep learning model JCD combined with image deblurring. Fan *et al.* [2–4,10] combined RS image correction and video frame interpolation to predict the GS image at the intermediate moment from two consecutive rolling images. Other models including CVR [4], SUNet [3], RSSR [2] predict the bidirectional optical flow and undistorted flow between the RS images, and then use the undistorted flow to warp the RS images into the GS. VRS [10] uses trained video frame interpolation models to interpolate a large number of RS image interpolation frames between two RS images, and combines these frames into a GS image. Among them, CVR [4] and VRS [10] perform best, which is the current state-of-the-art. However, to predict a GS image, VRS [10] needs to generate thousands of candidate frames, which wastes a lot of memory and computing power. CVR [4] uses multiple U-Nets for superposition, yet the model occupies too much memory, making it difficult to deploy in practical applications. Cao *et al.* [7] constructed another real-world RS image dataset BS-RSC, and proposed adaptive warping and multiple displacement fields to capture complex motions of objects. Zhou *et al.* [5,6,9] modified the form of input data to obtain additional information, Wang *et al.* [6] proposed RS global features, and built an optical instrument to acquire datasets RSGR-GS. Zhong *et al.* [9] restores the intermediate GS image through two RS images scanned from top to bottom and bottom to top, respectively, on the synthetic dataset RS-GOPRO. Zhou *et al.* [5] uses the event camera to obtain the event signal of the RS image, and corrects the RS image through the additional event signal. EvUnroll [5], IFED [9], RSGR [6] require the use of new types of camera that is expensive, making it difficult to popularize.

Considering the above situation, we design a lightweight rolling shutter image restoration model that restores the GS image at the intermediate moment from two consecutive RS images with undistorted flow. Our method achieves the best results in several indicators on the RS image dataset Fastec-RS while the number of parameters of our model is only about 6% of that of CVR [4].

2   Related Works

In this section, we present related works on our method, the most important of which is video frame interpolation.

Video frame interpolation [17–19] increases the frame rate of a video by inserting a new frame between two known frames. With recent advances in optical flow estimation [11–13,15], flow-based VFI methods have been actively studied to exploit motion information explicitly. Some methods employ off-the-shelf flow models [20,21] for interpolation, and estimate task-specific flows as guidance for pixel-level motion [14,22,23]. In addition, in order to improve the practicability of the VFI model, some methods [16] supervise the intermediate results of the interpolation, and realize efficient video frame interpolation with fewer parameters. VFI is often interpolated between two GS images. We have learned its idea and interpolated GS image from RS image.

3   Approach

3.1   Problem Formulation

When a RS camera acquires an image, all its scanlines are exposed sequentially with different timestamps. Therefore, each scan line corresponds to a different GS image frame. Let the number of lines in the image be h and the constant inter-line delay time be t_d, the rolling shutter imaging model can be obtained as follows:

$$[\boldsymbol{I}^r(x)]_s = [\boldsymbol{I}^g_s(x)]_s, \tag{1}$$

where s is the row number corresponding to the extracted pixel in the rolling shutter image, and $[]_s$ means to extract the pixel from the sth row of the image. Assuming that the acquisition time corresponding to the first row of the image is 0, and the total number of rows of the image is h, then, $\boldsymbol{I}^g_s$ is the GS image at time $t_d \cdot s$.

Reversing the above process, we can use the RS image to restore the GS image.

$$\boldsymbol{I}^g(x) = \boldsymbol{I}^r(x + \boldsymbol{U}_{g \to r}(x)), \tag{2}$$

where $\boldsymbol{U}_{g \to r}$ is the displacement field from each pixel in the GS image to the corresponding pixel in the RS image, called undistorted flow. However, the undistorted flow is difficult to predict directly, in this paper, we combine optical flow and temporal factors to predict the undistorted flow.

Our task is to restore the GS image at the intermediate moment from two consecutive RS images. And we make the following assumptions: 1. The acquisition time interval of each line of the rolling screen image is constant. 2. After the last line of the RS image of the previous frame is collected, the first line of the RS image of the next frame will be collected immediately. In practical applications, the speed of the RS camera can even start to capture the next frame before the previous frame is captured. Therefore, this assumption is reasonable and easy to implement.

3.2   Architecture Overview

We propose a lightweight rolling shutter image restoration network based on undistorted flow. Our model uses a lightweight encoder-decoder network to extract the bidirectional optical flow between two consecutive frames of RS images, and then multiplies the optical flow by a time factor to calculate the undistorted flow. Then, we use the undistorted flow to warp the RS image to calculate the candidate frames. Finally, we multiply the candidate frames by the mask to obtain the GS image at the intermediate moment. We will introduce these parts separately next. The overall structure of our model is shown in Fig. 2.

3.3   Extract Feature Pyramid

To obtain a contextual representation from each input rolling image frame, our model first extracts a feature pyramid with a compact encoder network. It should be noted that we use the same set of encoder parameters for each RS image, which greatly reduces the parameter amount of the encoder network.

The encoder network inputs a RS image and outputs a four-level feature pyramid of the image. For the feature extraction of each layer, two $3 \cdot 3$ convolution blocks are used. The step sizes of the convolution blocks are 2 and 1, respectively, and the activation function used is PReLU.

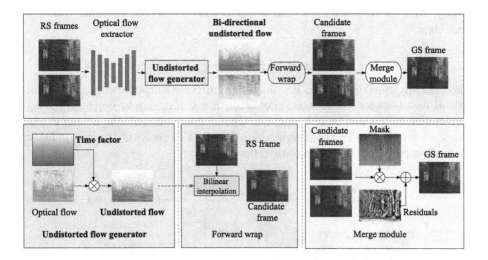

Fig. 2. The overall structure of our model.

3.4   Generate Bidirectional Optical Flow

To reconstruct the bidirectional optical flow between rolling images from the feature pyramid, we use a multi-level decoder network for decoding. The decoder network inputs the feature pyramids of two RS images and outputs the bidirectional optical flow, mask and residuals.

The main body of the decoder network is composed of four levels of progressively increasing decoders. The first level decoder inputs the features at the bottom of the two feature pyramids, and outputs the bidirectional optical flow and intermediate features of the next level. The second and third levels decoders respectively input the intermediate features, bidirectional optical flow, and context features of this level, and outputs the intermediate features and bidirectional optical flow residuals of the next level. By upsampling the bidirectional optical flow of this layer, added with bidirectional optical flow residuals, we can calculate the bidirectional optical flow of the next level, this method makes our training process more stable. The fourth layer decoder does not generate intermediate features, instead, it generates a GS image residual and a mask, which are used to synthesize a GS image from candidate frames later. The formulation of the decoders are:

$$(\Delta F_i^{j+1}, O^{j+1}) = D^j(G_i^j); i = 0, 1; j = 1, \tag{3}$$

$$(\Delta F_i^{j+1}, O^{j+1}) = D^j(F_i^j, O^j, G_i^j); i = 0, 1; j = 2, 3, \tag{4}$$

$$(\Delta F_i, M, Res) = D^j(F_i^j, O^j, G_i^j); i = 0, 1; j = 4, \tag{5}$$

where F_i^j is the optical flow from image i to image $1 - i$ at level j, O^j is the intermediate feature at level j, G_i^j is the feature extracted from RS image at level j, M and Res are mask and residual used to merge candidate frames in next step.

3.5　Time Factor and Undistortion Flow

Theoretically speaking, if two RS images are directly warped using bidirectional optical flow between RS images, the result of warping should be the RS image corresponding to the middle frame, not the GS image. In order to obtain the GS image corresponding to the intermediate frame, it is necessary to first generate the undistorted flow from the optical flow.

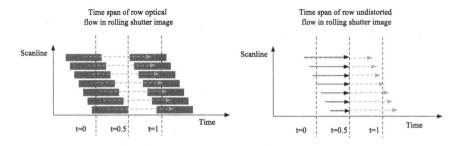

Fig. 3. Comparison of the time span of optical flow and undistorted flow.

In a RS image, the acquisition time of pixels in the same row is the same. Figure 3 is a comparison of the time span of optical flow and undistorted flow. The green dotted line in the left figure is the time period spanned by the optical flow of each row of pixels. Since the optical flow between two RS images is predicted, the length of each time period is the same. But their start times are different, the start time of the first row is the earliest, and the start time of the last row is the latest. Assuming that the image has h lines in total, the acquisition time interval of each line of image is $1/h$, the acquisition time of the middle line of the first frame image is $t = 0$, and the acquisition time of the middle line of the second frame image is $t = 1$, then for the sth line image, the start time of its optical flow span is $(s - h/2)/h$, and the end time is $(s + h/2)/h$. And if the first frame image is to be warped to the GS image at the middle moment, the actual optical flow span end time should be $1/2$. As shown in the right figure, the black line is the time span of undistorted flow. The length of he undistorted flow span should be $(1/2 - ((s - h/2)/h) = 1 - s/h)$. From this, the transformation formula between undistorted flow and optical flow can be derived:

$$U_{r_{0 \to 0.5}}^s = F_r^s \cdot T^s, \tag{6}$$

$$T^s = 1 - s/h, \tag{7}$$

where F_r^s is the optical flow corresponding to the sth row, $U_{r\to0.5}^s$ is the undistorted flow corresponding to the sth row, T^s is the time factor corresponding to the sth row.

Similarly, the reverse undistorted flow formula is:

$$U_{r\to0.5}^s = F_r^s \cdot (s/h). \tag{8}$$

After obtaining the undistorted flow, we can use the undistorted flow to warp the two RS images respectively to obtain two candidate frames. The warping method we use is bilinear interpolation.

When synthesizing two candidate GS images into a global image at an intermediate moment, we use the mask and residual combination method commonly used in video frame interpolation this method can effectively reduce the occurrence of synthesizing GS frames pixel overlap, black hole problem. The formula for this method is as follows:

$$\hat{I}_{0.5}^g = M_0 \cdot \hat{I}_{0\to0.5}^g + M_1 \cdot \hat{I}_{1\to0.5}^g + Res. \tag{9}$$

3.6   Losses

In terms of loss function, we use two losses: image reconstruction loss and undistorted flow smoothing loss.

The image reconstruction loss limits the final image generated by the model to be as close as possible to the GS image at the intermediate moment. The performance of the traditional L1 loss in this task is relatively poor. Therefore, we use a new image reconstruction loss. The loss is the sum of the two parts of the loss, and the calculation formula is:

$$L_r = \sigma(\hat{I}_{0.5}^g - I_{0.5}^{gt}) + L_{cen}(\hat{I}_{0.5}^g, I_{0.5}^{gt}), \tag{10}$$

where $\sigma(x) = (x^2 + \epsilon^2)^\alpha$, where $\alpha = 0.5, \epsilon = 10^{-3}$, this loss is an alternative to the traditional L1 loss called Charbonnier loss, L_{cen} is a statistical loss for Computes the soft Hamming distance between census-transformed image patches of size $7 \cdot 7$.

In order to add a smoothing term to the estimated undistorted flow to make the restoration result smoother, a smoothing loss function L_s can be defined based on the idea of full variational regularization:

$$L_s = (\|\nabla \hat{U}_{0\to0.5}\|_2 + \|\nabla \hat{U}_{1\to0.5}\|_2), \tag{11}$$

where λ_s is the hyperparameter controlling the weight of the smoothing term, ∇ is the gradient operator, and U is the undistorted flow.

The overall losses function are:

$$L = \lambda_1 L_r + \lambda_2 L_s, \tag{12}$$

where λ_1, λ_2 are parameters that can be adjusted manually. According to the experiment, we set these two parameters to 1 and 0.3 respectively.

4   Experiment

In this section, we compare with the baseline approaches and provide analysis and insight into our method.

4.1   Datasets

In the experiment, we use Fastec-RS [1], which is a real-world RS image synthesized by a high frame rate GS camera installed on a ground vehicle dataset to evaluate all compared methods. The dataset is divided into three parts: train, val, and test. Each part of data consists of several segments of video. Each video has 34 continuous time images corresponding to the RS image. The dataset provides the GS image annotation signals of the first row and the central scanning line of the RS image, so in two consecutive frames of RS images, the GS annotation image at the time t = 0.5 can be obtained, We uses it as labeled data to train the network.

In this experiment, We use the training set to train all deep learning based methods. Both the verification set and the test set are given, which are used to evaluate the performance of the model. In order to make evaluation of the model more convincing, we use the results on both the validation set and the test set as the evaluation index.

4.2   Evaluation Strategies

We use two traditional evaluation indicators PSNR (Peak Signal-to-Noise Ratio) and SSIM (Structural Similarity Index Measurement) in the field of RS image restoration. In addition, the parameter amount of the model is also one of our evaluation indicators.

4.3   Comparison with SOTA Methods

We cmopare our model with CVR [4], SUNet [3], RSSR [2] and DSUN [1] on the Fastec-RS-test dataset and Fastec-RS-val dataset. SUNet did not provide the original code, and the experimental data was the original data in the paper without parameter information. Our model can flexibly tune parameters according to performance and memory footprint requirements. LRRN_L, LRRN, and LRRN_S in the table correspond to the models with encoder-decoder network parameters from large to small.

The comparison results are shown in Table 1. In the Fastec-RS-val data, the PSNR and SSIM of LRRN_L reached the highest while LRRN reached the second highest and LRRN_S were the third highest. On the Fastec-RS-test dataset, the PSNR performance of the model in this paper is second only to CVR, and the SSIM index is still the top three. In terms of parameter quantity, the parameters of LRRN_S, LRRN, and LRRN_L in this paper are 10.1, 19.0 and 79.2. Under the condition of achieving similar PSNR and SSIM indicators, the parameter

Table 1. Comparison with the state-of-the-art Methods.

model	PSNR (test)	SSIM (test)	PSNR (val)	SSIM (val)	param(M)
DSUN [1]	26.52	0.792	30.77	0.851	14.9
SUNet [3]	28.34	0.837	-	-	-
CVR [4]	**28.72**	0.847	32.85	0.868	166
RSSR [2]	21.23	0.776	26.32	0.789	101.5
LRRN_S(ours)	28.03	0.848	33.11	0.881	**10.1**
LRRN(ours)	28.26	0.851	33.35	0.902	19.0
LRRN_L(ours)	28.35	**0.852**	**33.52**	**0.912**	79.2

quantity of our model is only 6% of the CVR model, which means our model has greater practical application value.

We use our large-parameter model LRRN_L and small parameter model LRRN_S to restore the RS image respectively, and visualize the restoration results, and compare the restoration results with the previous state-of-the-art method CVR. The visualization results are shown in Fig. 4. In the face of complex situations such as occlusion, the image restored by our method is closer to the real GS image, and a good restoration result can also be obtained when using a model with small parameters. This further illustrates the practicability and superiority of our method.

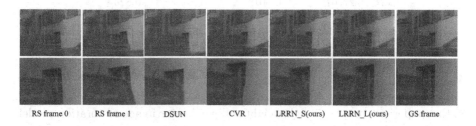

RS frame 0   RS frame 1   DSUN   CVR   LRRN_S(ours)   LRRN_L(ours)   GS frame

Fig. 4. In this situation that the window is framed in the first RS image and blocked in the second RS image, our large-parameter model LRRN_L can still restore images very similar to the GS image, and the small-parameter model LRRN_S restores better results, while the CVR model for comparison is seriously distorted.

4.4   Ablation Studies

Loss Function. We first conducted an ablation experiment on the loss function. Results are shown in Table 2. LRRN, ΔL_r, and ΔL_s are the cases where the loss function parameter λ_1, λ_2 are set to $1, 0.3; 0, 1; 1, 0$ respectively. It can be seen that the image reconstruction loss L_r has the greatest impact on the model. And the flow smoothing loss L_s can also improve the performance of the model.

Undistorted Flow. We compare undistorted flow to a method that reduces the steps of multiplying the time factor with optical flow with the original model. ΔU in Table 2 is the result of using only optical flow. It can be seen that the PSNR and SSIM indicators of the model using the undistorted flow method are much higher, which verifies effectiveness of undistorted flow in RS image restoration.

Mask. We compare our method with the method that directly uses the linear weighted average of the values of the two candidate frames to obtain the GS image. ΔM in Table 2 is the result of the linear weighting method. Compared with the method of linear weighted average, the method of using mask has achieved a very large improvement in PSNR and SSIM indicators, which proves that when combining two candidate GS images into one, the mask can effectively improve the quality of the composite result.

Table 2. Ablation Studies.

model	PSNR (test)	SSIM (test)	PSNR (val)	SSIM (val)
LRRN	**28.26**	**0.851**	**33.35**	**0.902**
Δl_r	24.13	0.688	28.21	0.712
Δl_s	27.99	0.844	33.14	0.869
ΔU	27.87	0.838	32.14	0.854
ΔM	27.16	0.801	31.45	0.823

5   Conclusion

In this paper, we propose a lightweight rolling shutter image restoration model, which can effectively extract the undistorted flow from two consecutive frames of rolling shutter images, and then restore the global image at the intermediate moment. For the calculation of distortion-free flow, we innovatively proposed the method of multiplying the optical flow by the time factor, and achieved effective results. Our method achieves SOTA results on multiple indicators on the Fastec-RS dataset with parameter greatly reduced. Through further research on the method in this paper, there will be great hope that it will be extended to practical applications in the future.

Acknowledgments. This work was supported by the National Natural Science Foundation of China under Grants (62171038, 62171042, and 62088101), and the R&D Program of Beijing Municipal Education Commission (Grant No. KZ202211417048).

References

1. Peidong, L., Zhaopeng. C., Viktor. L.: Deep shutter unrolling network. In: CVPR, pp. 10–22 (2020)
2. Bin, F., Yuchao, D.: Deep shutter unrolling network. In: ICCV, pp. 4228–4237 (2021)
3. Bin, F., Yuchao, D.: Sunet: symmetric undistortion network for rolling shutter correction. In: ICCV, pp. 4541–4550 (2021)
4. Bin, F., Yuchao, D.: Context-aware video reconstruction for rolling shutter cameras. In: CVPR, pp. 17572–17582 (2022)
5. Xinyu, Z., Peiqi, D., Yi, M.: EvUnroll: neuromorphic events based rolling shutter image correction. In: CVPR, pp. 17751–17784 (2022)
6. Zhixiang, W., Xiang, J., Jia-Bin H.: Neural global shutter: learn to restore video from a rolling shutter camera with global reset feature. In: CVPR, pp. 17794–17803 (2022)
7. Mingdeng, C., Zhihang, Z., Jiahao, W.: Learning adaptive warping for real-world rolling shutter correction. In: CVPR, pp. 17785–17793 (2022)
8. Zhihang, Z., Yinqiang, Z., Imari, S.: Towards rolling shutter correction and deblurring in dynamic scenes. In: CVPR, pp. 9219–9228 (2020)
9. Zhihang, Z., Mingdeng, C., Xiao, S.: Bringing rolling shutter images alive with dual reversed distortion. In: Avidan, S., Brostow, G., Cissé, M., Farinella, G.M., Hassner, T. (eds.) ECCV 2022. LNCS, vol. 13667, pp. 223–249. Springer, Cham (2022). https://doi.org/10.1007/978-3-031-20071-7_14
10. Naor, E., Antebi, I., Bagon, S., Irani, M.: Combining internal and external constraints for un-rolling shutter in videos. In: Avidan, S., Brostow, G., Cissé, M., Farinella, G.M., Hassner, T. (eds.) ECCV 2022. LNCS, vol. 13677, pp. 119–134. Springer, Cham (2022). https://doi.org/10.1007/978-3-031-19790-1_8
11. Alexey, D., Philipp, F., Eddy, I.: FlowNet: learning optical flow with convolutional networks. In: ICCV, pp. 2758–2766 (2015)
12. Deqing, S., Xiaodong, Y., Ming-Yu, L.: PWC-Net: CNNs for optical flow using pyramid, warping, and cost volume. In: CVPR, pp. 8934–8943 (2018)
13. Teed, Z., Deng, J.: RAFT: recurrent all-pairs field transforms for optical flow. In: Vedaldi, A., Bischof, H., Brox, T., Frahm, J.-M. (eds.) ECCV 2020. LNCS, vol. 12347, pp. 402–419. Springer, Cham (2020). https://doi.org/10.1007/978-3-030-58536-5_24
14. Junheum, P., Chul, L., Chang-Su, K.: Asymmetric bilateral motion estimation for video frame interpolation. In: ICCV, pp. 3703–3712 (2021)
15. Shihao, J., Dylan, C., Yao, L.: Learning to estimate hidden motions with global motion aggregation. In: ICCV, pp. 9772–9781 (2021)
16. Zhewei, H., Tianyuan, Z., Wen, H.: Real-time intermediate flow estimation for video frame interpolation. In: Avidan, S., Brostow, G., Cissé, M., Farinella, G.M., Hassner, T. (eds.) ECCV 2022. LNCS, vol. 13674, pp. 624–642. Springer, Cham (2022). https://doi.org/10.1007/978-3-031-19781-9_36
17. Zou, Y., Zheng, Y., Takatani, T., Fu, Y.: Learning to reconstruct high speed and high dynamic range videos from events. In: CVPR, pp. 2024–2033 (2021)
18. Zeng, Y., Zou, Y., Fu, Y.: 3D²Unet:3D deformable Unet for low-light video enhancement. In: PRCV, pp. 66–77 (2021)
19. Zhang, F., Li, Y., You, S., Fu, Y.: Learning temporal consistency for low light video enhancement from single images. In: CVPR, pp. 4967–4976 (2021)

20. Niklaus, S., Liu, F.: Context-aware synthesis for video frame interpolation. In: CVPR, pp. 1701–1710 (2018)
21. Xu, X., Siyao, L., Sun, W., Yin, Q., Yang, M.H.: Quadratic video interpolation. In: NeurIPS, pp. 1645–1654 (2019)
22. Jiang, H., et al.: Super slomo: High quality estimation of multiple intermediate frames for video interpolation. In: CVPR, pp. 9000–9008 (2018)
23. Liu, Z., Yeh, R.A., Tang, X., Liu, Y., Agarwala, A.: Video frame synthesis using deep voxel flow. In: ICCV, pp. 4473–4481 (2017)

An Efficient Graph Transformer Network for Video-Based Human Mesh Reconstruction

Tao Tang[1,2], Yingxuan You[1(✉)], Ti Wang[1], and Hong Liu[1]

[1] Key Laboratory of Machine Perception, Shenzhen Graduate School, Peking University, Shenzhen, China
{taotang,youyx,tiwang}@stu.pku.edu.cn, hongliu@pku.edu.cn
[2] School of Computer Science and Engineering, Central South University, Changsha, China

Abstract. Although existing image-based methods for 3D human mesh reconstruction have achieved remarkable accuracy, effectively capturing smooth human motion from monocular video remains a significant challenge. Recently, video-based methods for human mesh reconstruction tend to build more complex networks to capture temporal information of human motion, resulting in a large number of parameters and limiting their practical applications. To address this issue, we propose an **E**fficient **G**raph **T**ransformer network to **R**econstruct 3D human mesh from monocular video, named EGTR. Specifically, we present a temporal redundancy removal module that uses 1D convolution to eliminate redundant information among video frames and a spatial-temporal fusion module that combines Modulated GCN with transformer framework to capture human motion. Our method achieves better accuracy than the state-of-the-art video-based method TCMR on 3DPW, Human3.6M and MPI-INF-3DHP datasets while only using 8.7% of the parameters, indicating the effectiveness of our method for practical applications.

Keywords: Transformer · Graph Convolutional Network · Temporal Redundancy Removal · Video-based 3D Human Mesh Reconstruction

1 Introduction

Estimating 3D human pose and shape from a single image or video has significant practical applications in computer graphics, virtual reality, physical therapy and so on [1]. This task typically involves taking an image or a sequence of video frames as input and generating pose and shape parameters of human model [2] as output.

While existing image-based methods [3–7] can generate reasonably accurate 3D human mesh from individual images, they often struggle to estimate smooth 3D human motion from videos due to the absence of temporal information. To tackle this challenge, some methods [8–11] have extended image-based methods to video scenarios. These approaches primarily leverage Recurrent Neural Networks (RNNs) [12] to capture temporal information (i.e., the continuity of human motion) and achieve coherent 3D human motion estimation. However, these methods have several limitations. For instance, VIBE [9] uses a bidirectional Gated Recurrent Unit (GRU) that lacks sufficient temporal information because GRU only transmits temporal information between

L. Fang et al. (Eds.): CICAI 2023, LNAI 14473, pp. 207–219, 2024.
https://doi.org/10.1007/978-981-99-8850-1_17

adjacent frames, resulting in excessive motion jitter in the reconstructed human mesh sequence. TCMR [11] employs three GRUs to capture past, future, and global temporal

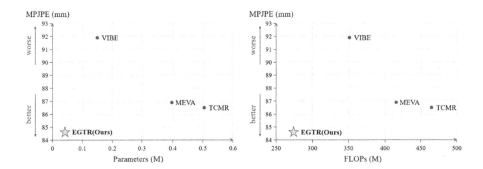

Fig. 1. Comparision between accuracy (MPJPE) and parameters (left), FLOPs (right) of video-based methods. All methods are evaluated on the 3DPW dataset.

information. It constrains neighboring three frames to the intermediate frame, causing the network to reconstruct the average human mesh within adjacent frames and resulting in over-smoothed 3D human mesh reconstruction with insufficient accuracy. Nevertheless, methods based on RNNs suffer from difficulties in parallelization and have a large number of model parameters, significantly limiting their practical applications.

To address the above issues, we propose an **E**fficient **G**raph **T**ransformer network for video-based human mesh **R**econstruction (EGTR). Our method mainly consists of three modules: Temporal Redundancy Removal (TRR), Spatial-Temporal Fusion (STF), and Multi-Branch Integration (MBI). As shown in Fig. 1, EGTR has better 3D human body reconstruction accuracy than other video-based methods while significantly reducing the parameters and FLOPs. Our main contributions are as follows:

- We propose an efficient network EGTR for 3D human mesh reconstruction from a monocular video that combines Modulated GCN with transformer framework. EGTR not only improves reconstruction accuracy, but also significantly reduces the parameters and FLOPs.
- We introduce novel modules namely Temporal Redundancy Removal (TRR) which decreases the local redundancies present in video frames and Spatial-Temporal Fusion (STF) which uses GCN to replace multi-head attention in transformer framework, significantly reducing the model parameters.
- Experiments show that our EGTR achieves better accuracy with fewer parameters. For instance, despite having only 8.7% of the parameters compared to TCMR, EGTR achieves a 2.2% improvement in MPJPE on the 3DPW dataset.

2   Related Work

2.1   Human Mesh Reconstruction

Reconstructing 3D human mesh from an image or video is a challenging task, which has gained significant attention in recent years due to its efficiency and convenience. Many previous methods utilize parametric human models, such as SCAPE [13], SMPL [2], SMPL-X [14], and STAR [15], to reconstruct human mesh by regressing human pose and shape parameters.

Image-Based Human Mesh Reconstruction. For methods that use a single image as input, HMR [3] proposed an end-to-end trainable 3D human reconstruction network that introduces an adversarial training approach and minimizes the reprojection loss of 2D keypoints, allowing the network can be trained using in-the-wild images with only 2D annotations. SPIN [4] introduced a self-improving network that consists of an SMPL parameter regressor and an iterative fitting framework, then trained a ResNet [16] to extract static features of the human body from images. Some methods [5–7] used prior knowledge such as joint interdependencies, body parts segmentation, and mesh alignment to assist the regression of SMPL parameters. However, when applying image-based methods to videos, reconstruction errors between different frames lead to inconsistent human motion (i.e., motion jitter), due to the absence of temporal information.

Video-Based Human Mesh Reconstruction. For methods that use a sequence of frames as input, HMMR [8] introduced using acceleration error to evaluate the smoothness of the reconstructed human motion. VIBE [9] employed a bidirectional GRU-based motion generator and an adversarial motion discriminator. It trained the discriminator with an actual human motion dataset AMASS [17], assisting the generator in generating more realistic human motion. MEVA [10] also used a bidirectional GRU-based generator, and it added a residual estimation to estimate the details of person-specific motion. However, VIBE and MEVA still suffer from inadequate temporal information extracted by bidirectional GRU, resulting in the persistence of motion jitter. Therefore, TCMR [11] proposed a three-branch network that utilizes a bidirectional GRU and two unidirectional GRUs to extract temporal information from past and future frames to constrain the target frame. However, the large number of parameters in the network composed of three GRUs makes it hard to deploy on practical applications.

2.2   Graph Convolutional Networks

Graph Convolution Networks (GCNs) generalize the capabilities of CNNs by performing convolution operations on graph-structured data. Recently, GCNs have been widely applied to 3D human pose and mesh reconstruction [18–23], primarily for extracting and integrating information from various body joints or meshes. Thanks to the natural graph structures of the human skeleton and body mesh, GCNs are appropriate to model human topology. GraphCMR [18] utilized GCNs to regress the position of mesh vertices without using the parametric model (SMPL [2]). Pose2Mesh [19] employed GCNs to estimate human mesh from 2D and 3D poses. GATOR [21] utilized GCN to assist in capturing the multiple relations between the skeleton and human mesh. Modulated GCN [22] addressed the issue of sharing feature transformations among different nodes while keeping relatively small parameters. Modulated GCN can be expressed as:

$$Y = sigmoid(D^{-\frac{1}{2}}\tilde{A}D^{-\frac{1}{2}}X(W \odot M)), \tag{1}$$

where X represents the input features of all nodes in the graph, $\tilde{A}$ donates the learnable adjacency matrix, D is the degree matrix, W is the fusion matrix that needs to be learned, M represents modulation vectors, and Y is the output of Moudulated GCN.

3　Method

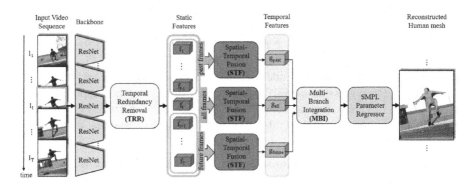

Fig. 2. The overview of efficient graph transformer network for video-based human mesh reconstruction (EGTR). Given a video sequence, ResNet [16] is utilized to extract the static features and TRR reduces the redundancy of neighboring frames. Then, the static features are separated into three sequences and respectively fused by STF into temporal features of the past, future and all frames. After that, MBI integrates the temporal features into a feature of the target frame. Finally, the SMPL parameter regressor outputs the human mesh.

3.1　Overview of EGTR

The overview of EGTR is shown in Fig. 2. Given a video sequence $V = \{I_t\}_{t=1}^{T}$ with T frames, we firstly use ResNet [16] pretrained by SPIN [4] to extract static features sequence $F = \{f_t\}_{t=1}^{T}$ of all frames, where $f_t \in \mathbb{R}^{2048}$. We consider $(\lfloor T/2 \rfloor + 1)_{th}$ frame as the target frame, $1, ..., (\lfloor T/2 \rfloor)_{th}$ frames as past frames and $(\lfloor T/2 \rfloor + 2)_{th}, ..., T_{th}$ frames as future frames. Then, the Temporal Redundancy Removal (TRR) module and three branches of Spatial-Temporal Fusion (STF) modules are sequentially applied to obtain the temporal feature of past frames g_{past}, future frames g_{future}, and global frames g_{all}, where $g_* \in \mathbb{R}^{2048}$. Multi-Branch Integration (MBI) module integrates the extracted temporal features and gets $g_{int} \in \mathbb{R}^{2048}$. Finally, g_{int} is fed to the pretrained SMPL regressor to obtain the human mesh vertices. We introduce each module in EGTR as follows.

3.2　Temporal Redundancy Removal

Due to the small temporal interval between consecutive video frames, the variations in human body actions are subtle. Consequently, the static features extracted by ResNet exhibit similarities, impeding the subsequent network focus on crucial human motion information. This draws a challenge in acquiring comprehensive temporal features from videos. The Temporal Redundancy Reduction (TRR) module employs 1D convolution to capture the differential features among neighboring frames in the static features sequence. This effectively decreases the local redundancies in video frames and enables the following network to capture global dependencies. Specifically, a 1D convolution layer with a kernel size of 3, a stride of 1, and padding of 1 is utilized within this module, which considers the static features of neighboring three frames, effectively reducing the redundancy in the static features of neighboring frames.

3.3   Spatial-Temporal Fusion

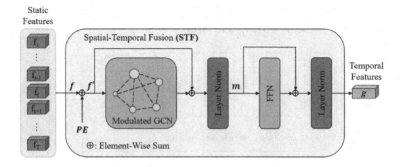

Fig. 3. Pipeline of the Spatial-Temporal Fusion module.

Given a static features sequence $F = \{f_t\}_{t=1}^{T}$ after TRR, we extract temporal features for the target frame from the past and future frames by employing three branches of STF with the same architecture. For the reconstruction of the target frame, the static features of $T = 16$ frames consisting of 8 frames before and 7 frames after the target frame are input to the three branches of STF module. Previous methods for video-based human mesh reconstruction [9–11] use GRU to capture temporal features by sequentially inputting video frames into the network, preserving the temporal order of the frames. As we simultaneously take the spatial features of all frames as input, resulting in the loss of the inherent temporal order of the frames in the original sequence. Consistent with the transformer [24], we employ sine and cosine functions for position encoding of the input sequence. A 2048-dimensional position encoding (PE) is generated for each frame.

For each branch, as shown in Fig. 3, We employ Modulated GCN [22] within the transformer framework to fuse the static features for the temporal feature of the target frame. Instead of the multi-head attention in the transformer encoder, Modulated GCN is used in EGTR to add temporal constraints, which enhances the smoothness of reconstructed 3D human motion. Specifically, we consider each video frame as a graph node and the adjacency matrix of the graph is a learnable matrix obtained by training on large mixed 3D and 2D human motion datasets. This significantly reduces the parameters and FLOPs of the network. The STF can be expressed as the following equations:

$$f' = f + PE, \tag{2}$$

$$m = Norm(Modulated\ GCN(f')), \tag{3}$$

$$g = Norm(FFN(m) + m), \tag{4}$$

where $Norm$ demotes the layer normalization [25], FFN denotes feedforward networks.

3.4 Multi-branch Integration

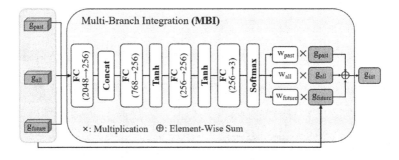

Fig. 4. Pipeline of the Multi-Branch Integration module.

After separating the original 16-frame sequence into three subsequences: past 8 frames, future 7 frames, and the global 16 frames, we input each subsequence to the STF to generate g_{past}, g_{future} and g_{all}. As shown in Fig. 4, the multi-branch integration module passes the temporal information through four fully connected layers with the Tanh activation function, and utilizes a softmax to output weights that represent the influence of past, future, and global temporal information on the target frame: w_{past}, w_{future} and w_{all}. Finally, the temporal features of three branches are fused by weighted summation to obtain the temporal feature of the target frame, which can be calculated as the following equation:

$$g_{int} = w_{past}g_{past} + w_{all}g_{all} + w_{future}g_{future}. \tag{5}$$

By separating into three sub-sequences, this module significantly reduces the training difficulty of the highly non-linear reconstruction task. It assists the STF in focusing on the accuracy and smoothness of the reconstructed human motion.

3.5   Loss Function

For training, we utilize the following loss functions: 3D joint position loss $\mathcal{L}_{3D}$, 2D joint reprojection loss $\mathcal{L}_{2D}$, SMPL body shape parameter loss $\mathcal{L}_{shape}$ and SMPL pose parameter loss $\mathcal{L}_{pose}$. L2 losses between predicted and ground-truth SMPL parameters and 2D/3D joint coordinates are used. Due to each loss function having a different scale, the total loss is calculated as the weighted sum of the four losses above. This can be formulated as:

$$\mathcal{L} = \lambda_1\mathcal{L}_{3D} + \lambda_2\mathcal{L}_{2D} + \lambda_3\mathcal{L}_{shape} + \lambda_4\mathcal{L}_{pose}. \tag{6}$$

The experimental settings for the hyperparameters are $\lambda_1 = 300$, $\lambda_2 = 300$, $\lambda_3 = 0.06$ and $\lambda_4 = 60$.

4   Experiments

4.1   Experimental Settings

Implementation Details. Following previous methods [9, 11] we configure the input sequence length (T) to be 16. The ResNet and SMPL parameter regressor are initialized by the pretrained SPIN [4]. We employ the Adam optimizer [26] for weight updates. Static features are precomputed from the images using the ResNet [16] to optimize training time and memory consumption. We set the initial learning rate to 5×10^{-5}, with a reduction factor of 10 applied when accuracy has no improvement after 5 epochs. The network is trained for 50 epochs using a single NVIDIA RTX 2080Ti GPU. The PyTorch [27] framework is utilized for code implementation.

Evaluation Metrics and Datasets. To evaluate reconstruction accuracy, we consider the Mean Per Joint Position Error (MPJPE), Procrustes-Aligned MPJPE (PA-MPJPE), and Mean Per Vertex Position Error (MPVPE). These metrics measure the positional differences between predicted and ground truth in millimeters (mm). To evaluate reconstruction smoothness, we utilize the acceleration error proposed in HMMR [9], which is measured in (mm/s^2). Our training dataset includes 3DPW [28], Human3.6M [29], MPI-INF-3DHP [30], PoseTrack [31], InstaVariety [9], and Penn Action [32]. 3DPW is the only dataset that provides accurate ground truth SMPL parameters. Following previous methods [9, 11], 3DPW, Human3.6M, and MPI-INF-3DHP are used for evaluation, which have annotation for 3D keypoints.

4.2   Comparison with State-of-the-Art Methods

To compare our approach with state-of-the-art video-based 3D human mesh reconstruction methods that report the acceleration error in Table 1. The result shows that EGTR outperforms the current state-of-the-art video-based 3D human reconstruction methods in most metrics and datasets.

Table 1. Evaluation of state-of-the-art methods on 3DPW, Human3.6M, and MPI-INF-3DHP Datasets. All methods use 3DPW training set while training, but do not use the SMPL parameters of Human3.6M from Mosh [33]. The top two best results are highlighted in **bold** and <u>underlined</u>, respectively.

Method	3DPW				Human3.6M			MPI-INF-3DHP			input frames
	PA-MPJPE↓	MPJPE↓	MPVPE↓	ACC-ERR↓	PA-MPJPE↓	MPJPE↓	ACC-ERR↓	PA-MPJPE↓	MPJPE↓	ACC-ERR↓	
HMMR [8]	72.6	116.5	139.3	15.2	56.9	–	–	–	–	–	16
VIBE [9]	57.6	91.9	–	25.4	53.3	78.0	27.3	68.9	103.9	27.3	16
MEVA [10]	54.7	86.9	–	11.6	53.2	76.0	15.3	65.4	**96.4**	11.1	90
TCMR [11]	<u>52.7</u>	<u>86.5</u>	<u>102.9</u>	**6.8**	<u>52.0</u>	<u>73.6</u>	**3.9**	<u>63.5</u>	<u>97.3</u>	**8.5**	16
EGTR (Ours)	**52.3**	**84.6**	**100.2**	<u>9.1</u>	**47.5**	**68.9**	<u>5.1</u>	**62.2**	97.5	<u>10.6</u>	16

Comparison of Accuracy and Smoothness. In terms of reconstruction accuracy, EGTR achieves results closest to the ground truth compared to other methods. The Spatial-Temporal Fusion (STF) module extract information from adjacent frames for human body reconstruction, significantly improving the robustness and stability of human mesh reconstruction from images. While MEVA outperforms all other methods in MPJPE on MPI-INF-3DHP dataset, it requires at least 90 frames for reconstruction, limiting its applicability for short videos.

Regarding the smoothness of reconstructed human motion, although our approach is not as smooth as the TCMR, it shows substantial improvement compared to the previous methods such as HMMR, VIBE and MEVA. Moreover, qualitative evaluations indicate that TCMR seems to be too focused on generating over-smoothed 3D human motion, which limits its reconstruction accuracy.

Table 2. Comparison of the network parameters and FLOPs.

Method	Parameters (M)	FLOPs (M)
VIBE [9]	15.01	351.19
MEVA [10]	39.70	415.43
TCMR [11]	50.43	464.80
EGTR (Ours)	**4.39**	**274.43**

Comparison of Parameters and FLOPs. As shown in Table 2, we compare the model sizes of the previous methods. "Parameters" represents the number of model parameters, which indicates the model size. "FLOPs" represents the floating-point operations, which indicates the computational complexity of method. Compared to TCMR, EGTR achieves a reduction of 91.3% (from 50.43 M to 4.39 M) in parameters and 41.0% (from 464.80 M to 274.43 M) in FLOPs. Furthermore, on the 3DPW dataset, EGTR shows a further decrease of 2.2% (from 86.5 mm to 84.6 mm) in MPJPE and 2.6% (from 102.9 mm to 100.2 mm) in MPVPE. These results indicate that EGTR has better real-time performance and broader applications.

4.3 Qualitative Evaluation

In addition to quantitative evaluation, the qualitative evaluation of human mesh reconstruction methods is also an important consideration in comparison.

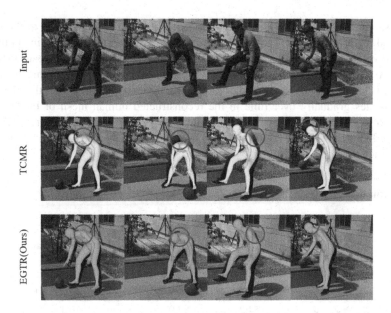

Fig. 5. Qualitative comparison of TCMR and EGTR on 3DPW dataset.

Comparison on the Continuous Video. As shown in Fig. 5, we utilize the EGTR and TCMR to reconstruct the video from the 3DPW dataset. The first column represents some input frames, and the second and third columns show the reconstructed human meshes of TCMR and EGTR, respectively. We can observe that compared to TCMR, our EGTR achieves significantly higher reconstruction accuracy in terms of limb positions, body shape, and back torso. Moreover, we find that TCMR tends to produce over-smoothed human motion, resulting in smaller body proportions and insufficient accuracy.

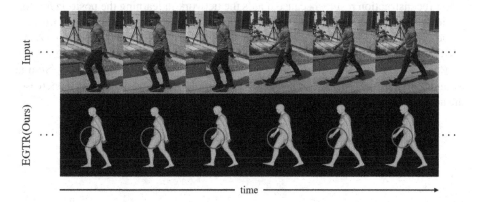

Fig. 6. Qualitative results of EGTR on a stitched video.

Analysis on the Stitched Video. To provide a more intuitive reflection of the strong temporal feature extraction capability of our EGTR, we conduct an experiment using a stitched video. We repeat two different frames 20 times respectively to create a stitched video. As shown in Fig. 6, frames 18_{th} to 23_{nd} are displayed. The 20_{th} frame introduces a sudden change in body shape and pose. We can note that the motion of the hands and legs changes gradually over time in the reconstructed human mesh of EGTR rather than abruptly changing between the 20_{th} and 21_{st} frames. This demonstrates that our EGTR effectively alleviates the problem of motion jitter in the video-based human mesh reconstruction.

4.4 Ablation Analysis

Table 3. Ablation results for different modules of EGTR on 3DPW dataset.

TRR	PE	MBI	STF	3DPW			
				PA-MPJPE ↓	MPJPE ↓	MPVPE ↓	ACC-ERR ↓
✗	✓	✓	✓	54.2	87.9	103.8	10.1
✓	✗	✓	✓	53.5	86.9	102.9	9.5
✓	✓	✗	✓	55.7	90.2	105.9	**7.4**
✓	✓	✓	✗	54.1	91.1	106.7	27.5
✓	✓	✓	✓	**52.3**	**84.6**	**100.2**	9.1

As shown in Table 3, the results demonstrate the effects of modules in Sect. 3 on estimating accurate and smooth human meshes. Without TRR module, The redundant information from neighboring frames prevents the subsequent network from focusing on crucial human motion information, leading to decreased reconstruction accuracy and smoothness. Moreover, position encoding also plays a crucial role in achieving better reconstruction results because it aids the network in learning the positional information of each frame within the video sequence. The MBI module can significantly reduce reconstruction accuracy errors, albeit at the cost of a slight decrease in ACC-ERR. Additionally, paying attention to 4_{th} row, directly using static features extracted by ResNet treats the reconstruction of each video frame as independent tasks. Similar to image-based methods, without using STF module not only significantly decreases the accuracy but also results in a large decrease in smoothness.

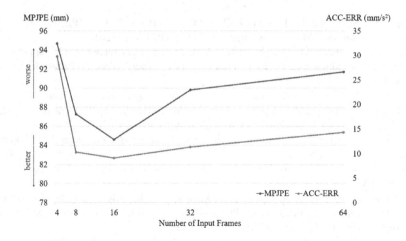

Fig. 7. Ablation results for different number of input frames of EGTR on 3DPW dataset.

We also conduct ablation experiments to investigate the impact of different number of input frames on the performance of EGTR. As shown in Fig. 7, we conduct experiments by setting the input length to 4, 8, 16, 32, and 64. The results indicate that EGTR achieves the best performance when the input length is 16 frames. When the input is fewer than 16 frames, it fails to capture sufficient temporal information. In addition, when the input exceeds 16 frames, the lightweight Graph Transformer network struggles to model excessively long temporal dependencies.

5   Conclusions

In this paper, we propose an efficient graph transformer network for video-based human mesh reconstruction (EGTR). We introduce the temporal redundancy removal module to remove redundant spatial features from adjacent video frames. We also propose the spatial-temporal fusion module, which utilizes Modulated GCN combined with transformer framework to propagate and fuse temporal features. Compared to TCMR, we achieve a reduction of 91.3% in model parameters and 41.0% in FLOPs, while further improving the MPJPE and MPVPE by 2.2% and 2.6% on the 3DPW dataset. Experiments evaluate the efficiency of our EGTR for human mesh reconstruction, which shows its potential for practical applications.

Acknowledgement. This paper is funded by National Natural Science Foundation of China (No.62073004), National Key R&D Program of China (No.2020AAA0108904), and Shenzhen Fundamental Research Program (No. GXWD20201231165807007-20200807164903001).

References

1. Tian, Y., Zhang, H., Liu, Y., Wang, L.: Recovering 3D human mesh from monocular images: a survey. arXiv preprint arXiv:2203.01923 (2022)

2. Loper, M., Mahmood, N., Romero, J., Pons-Moll, G., Black, M.J.: SMPL: a skinned multi-person linear model. ACM Trans. Graphics (TOG) **34**(6), 1–16 (2015)
3. Kanazawa, A., Black, M.J., Jacobs, D.W., Malik, J.: End-to-end recovery of human shape and pose. In: Proceedings of the IEEE Conference on Computer Vision and Pattern Recognition (CVPR), pp. 7122–7131 (2018)
4. Kolotouros, N., Pavlakos, G., Black, M.J., Daniilidis, K.: Learning to reconstruct 3D human pose and shape via model-fitting in the loop. In: Proceedings of the IEEE International Conference on Computer Vision (ICCV), pp. 2252–2261 (2019)
5. Georgakis, G., Li, R., Karanam, S., Chen, T., Košecká, J., Wu, Z.: Hierarchical kinematic human mesh recovery. In: Vedaldi, A., Bischof, H., Brox, T., Frahm, J.-M. (eds.) ECCV 2020. LNCS, vol. 12362, pp. 768–784. Springer, Cham (2020). https://doi.org/10.1007/978-3-030-58520-4_45
6. Kocabas, M., Huang, C. H. P., Hilliges, O., Black, M. J.: PARE: part attention regressor for 3D human body estimation. In: Proceedings of the IEEE International Conference on Computer Vision (ICCV), pp. 11127–11137 (2021)
7. Zhang, H., Tian, Y., Zhou, X., Ouyang, W., Liu, Y., Wang, L., Sun, Z.: Pymaf: 3d human pose and shape regression with pyramidal mesh alignment feedback loop. In: Proceedings of the IEEE International Conference on Computer Vision (ICCV), pp. 11446–11456 (2021)
8. Kanazawa, A., Zhang, J.Y., Felsen, P., Malik, J.: Learning 3D human dynamics from video. In: Proceedings of the IEEE Conference on Computer Vision and Pattern Recognition (CVPR), pp. 5614–5623 (2019)
9. Kocabas, M., Athanasiou, N., Black, M.J.: VIBE: video inference for human body pose and shape estimation. In: Proceedings of the IEEE Conference on Computer Vision and Pattern Recognition (CVPR), pp. 5253–5263 (2020)
10. Luo, Z., Golestaneh, S.A., Kitani, K.M.: 3D human motion estimation via motion compression and refinement. In: Ishikawa, H., Liu, C.-L., Pajdla, T., Shi, J. (eds.) ACCV 2020. LNCS, vol. 12626, pp. 324–340. Springer, Cham (2021). https://doi.org/10.1007/978-3-030-69541-5_20
11. Choi, H., Moon, G., Chang, J.Y., Lee, K.M.: Beyond static features for temporally consistent 3D human pose and shape from a video. In: Proceedings of the IEEE Conference on Computer Vision and Pattern Recognition (CVPR), pp. 1964–1973 (2021)
12. Cho, K., Merrienboer, B., Gulcehre, C., Bahdanau, D., Bougares, F., Schwenk, H.: Learning phrase representations using RNN encoder-decoder for statistical machine translation. arXiv preprint arXiv:1406.1078 (2014)
13. Anguelov, D., Srinivasan, P., Koller, D., Thrun, S., Rodgers, J., Davis, J.: Scape: shape completion and animation of people. In: ACM SIGGRAPH, pp. 408–416 (2005)
14. Pavlakos, G., Choutas, V., Ghorbani, N., Bolkart, T., Osman, A.A.A., Tzionas, D.: Expressive body capture: 3d hands, face, and body from a single image. In: Proceedings of the IEEE Conference on Computer Vision and Pattern Recognition (CVPR), pp. 10975–10985 (2019)
15. Osman, A.A.A., Bolkart, T., Black, M.J.: STAR: sparse trained articulated human body regressor. In: Vedaldi, A., Bischof, H., Brox, T., Frahm, J.-M. (eds.) ECCV 2020. LNCS, vol. 12351, pp. 598–613. Springer, Cham (2020). https://doi.org/10.1007/978-3-030-58539-6_36
16. He, K., Zhang, X., Ren, S., Sun, J.: Deep residual learning for image recognition. In: Proceedings of the IEEE Conference on Computer Vision and Pattern Recognition (CVPR), pp. 770–778 (2016)
17. Mahmood, N., Ghorbani, N., Troje, N.F., Pons-Moll, G., Black, M.J.: AMASS: archive of motion capture as surface shapes. In: Proceedings of the IEEE International Conference on Computer Vision (ICCV), pp. 5442–5451 (2019)

18. Kolotouros, N., Pavlakos, G., Daniilidis, K.: Convolutional mesh regression for single-image human shape reconstruction. In: Proceedings of the IEEE Conference on Computer Vision and Pattern Recognition (CVPR), pp. 4501–4510 (2019)

19. Choi, H., Moon, G., Lee, K.M.: Pose2Mesh: graph convolutional network for 3D human pose and mesh recovery from a 2D human pose. In: Vedaldi, A., Bischof, H., Brox, T., Frahm, J.-M. (eds.) ECCV 2020. LNCS, vol. 12352, pp. 769–787. Springer, Cham (2020). https://doi.org/10.1007/978-3-030-58571-6_45

20. Lin, K., Wang, L., Liu, Z.: Mesh graphormer. In: Proceedings of the IEEE International Conference on Computer Vision (ICCV), pp. 12939–12948 (2021)

21. You, Y., Liu, H., Li, X., Li, W., Wang, T., Ding, R.: Gator: graph-aware transformer with motion-disentangled regression for human mesh recovery from a 2D Pose. In: IEEE International Conference on Acoustics, Speech and Signal Processing (ICASSP), pp. 1–5 (2023)

22. Zou, Z., Tang, W.: Modulated graph convolutional network for 3D human pose estimation. In: Proceedings of the IEEE International Conference on Computer Vision (ICCV), pp. 11477–11487 (2021)

23. Wang, T., Liu, H., Ding, R., Li, W., You, Y., Li, X.: Interweaved graph and attention network for 3D human pose estimation. In: IEEE International Conference on Acoustics, Speech and Signal Processing (ICASSP), pp. 1–5 (2023)

24. Vaswani, A., Shazeer, N., Parmar, N., Uszkoreit, J., Jones, L., Gomez, A.N.: Attention is all you need. In: Conference on Neural Information Processing Systems (NIPS) (2017)

25. Ba, J.L., Kiros, J.R., Hinton G.E.: Layer normalization. arXiv preprint arXiv:1607.06450 (2016)

26. Kingma, D.P., Ba, J.: Adam: A method for stochastic optimization. arXiv preprint arXiv:1412.6980 (2014)

27. Paszke, A., Gross, S., Chintala, S., Chanan, G., Yang, E., DeVito, Z.: Automatic differentiation in pytorch (2017)

28. Marcard, T., Henschel, R., Black, M.J., Rosenhahn, B., Pons-Moll, G.: Recovering accurate 3d human pose in the wild using imus and a moving camera. In: Proceedings of the European Conference on Computer Vision (ECCV), pp. 601–617 (2018)

29. Ionescu, C., Papava, D., Olaru, V., Sminchisescu, C.: Human3.6m: large scale datasets and predictive methods for 3D human sensing in natural environments. IEEE Trans. Pattern Anal. Mach. Intell. (TPAMI) 36(7), 1325–1339 (2013)

30. Mehta, D., Rhodin, H., Casas, D., Fua, P., Sotnychenko, O., Xu, W.: Monocular 3D human pose estimation in the wild using improved CNN supervision. In: International Conference on 3D Vision (3DV), pp. 506–516 (2017)

31. Andriluka, M., Iqbal, U., Insafutdinov, E., Pishchulin, L., Milan, A., Gall, J.: Posetrack: a benchmark for human pose estimation and tracking. In: Proceedings of the IEEE Conference on Computer Vision and Pattern Recognition (CVPR), pp. 5167–5176 (2018)

32. Zhang, W., Zhu, M., Derpanis, K.G.: From actemes to action: A strongly-supervised representation for detailed action understanding. In: Proceedings of the IEEE International Conference on Computer Vision (ICCV), pp. 2248–2255 (2013)

33. Loper, M., Mahmood, N., Black, M.J.: MoSh: motion and shape capture from sparse markers. ACM Trans. Graphics (TOG) 33(6), 220:1-220:13 (2014)

Multi-scale Transformer with Decoder for Image Quality Assessment

Shuai Zhang and Yutao Liu[✉]

School of Computer Science and Technology, Ocean University of China,
Qingdao 266100, China
zhangshuai8775@stu.ouc.edu.cn, liuyutao@ouc.edu.cn

Abstract. Blind image quality assessment (BIQA) is of great significance in image processing field. However, due to diverse image content and complex types of distortions, the issue of BIQA has not been fully resolved. To address this issue more effectively, in this paper, we propose a framework based on Vision Transformer for BIQA called MSIQT. This model aims to extract image features more effectively and achieve a more accurate representation of quality. Specifically, at the input end, we adopt a multi-scale input approach to enrich the image features and utilize ResNet-50 for feature extraction. At the output end, a decoder is introduced to interpret quality-aware vectors obtained from image features. Experiments on four image quality assessment datasets prove that the proposed method outperforms or is comparable to state-of-the-art approaches.

Keywords: blind image quality assessment · vision transformer · multi-scale

1 Introduction

Image quality assessment is critical in both production and living. Its purpose is to allow machines to automatically assess image quality from a human perception perspective. Accurate and efficient image quality assessment can drive other tasks in image processing towards more advanced directions, such as image enhancement and image dehaze. Image quality evaluation can be roughly classified according to whether there are reference images auxiliary evaluation, including FR-IQA [18], RR-IQA [19] and NR-IQA [20]. Both FR-IQA and RR-IQA require reference images which are generally high-quality images corresponding to the distorted images. However, it can be luxury to obtain reference images on many occasions, and FR-IQA and RR-IQA methods are subject to various limitations. On the contrary, NR-IQA methods, which do not need reference images, have a wider range of applications.

Traditional blind image quality assessment methods evaluate image quality by detecting specific types of distortions, including blur, block artifacts, various forms of noise, etc. NIQE [1], extracts quality features from the test images

L. Fang et al. (Eds.): CICAI 2023, LNAI 14473, pp. 220–231, 2024.
https://doi.org/10.1007/978-981-99-8850-1_18

and fits them to a multivariate Gaussian model to evaluate quality of the test images. The advent of deep learning has provided many different solutions to BIQA. In recent years, CNN and ViT have shined brilliantly, and most advanced BIQA algorithms are based on these two networks. CNN-based methods primarily extract features from images through operations like convolution and pooling. These features are mapped to final quality scores using several fully connected layers. Le et al. [2] designed a five-layer CNN, including one convolution layer, one pooling layer, and three fully connected layers, to predict image scores. Zhang et al. [3] proposed two CNN structures specifically designed for synthetic and real distortion images, respectively. CNN-based blind image quality assessment methods performed well, however, the local perception characteristic of CNNs may make it challenging to extract global features from images, which can potentially impact the final evaluation results. Methods based on Vision Transformer divide images into several fixed-size patches and encode them. These encoded patches are then fed into a Transformer for attention computation, and the final evaluation result is obtained using the CLS token. BIQA methods based on ViT can be generally categorized into two types in terms of implementation. One is to combine with CNN, first use CNN to get feature map, and then input the feature map into ViT. Golestaneh et al. [21] used CNN to extract local features of images, and input the features into ViT to obtain global representation of images, and used the ranking between images to improve the monotonic correlation between different evaluation indicators. Another ViT-based implementation method is to directly divide the image into fixed-size patches, input them into ViT, and extract the global features of the image for evaluation [10].

Since there are no reference images to compare in BIQA, it is necessary to extract as many features in images as possible. Existing methods generally use CNN to extract features or directly input the original image, but these features may not be rich, or the model may ignore some features during processing, making the final evaluation biased. We use a multi-scale method when inputting images, zoom the original image while maintaining the aspect ratio, and input images of multiple scales, so that the features that the model can analyze are more abundant. Recently, BIQA methods based on ViT have achieved good results. However, most of the methods only use the encoder. We introduce a decoder to further analyze and process the output of encoder, so that the quality evaluation results more precise.

This paper's key contributions can be summed into three points:

1. We designed a multi-scale image quality assessment transformer (MSIQT) that enables multi-scale feature extraction.
2. We introduced a decoder and attention panels into the model to help the Transformer better map features to the score domain.
3. We tested MSIQT on four large-scale quality evaluation datasets, including TID2013 [14], LIVE [12], LIVEC [15], and CSIQ [13]. Our suggested model's results are comparable to advanced quality evaluation approaches.

The subsequent chapters of this paper are organized as follows. The second section covers relevant work on BIQA, the third section explains our suggested method framework, the fourth section gives experimental data and analysis, and the fifth section is a conclusion.

2   Related Work

Traditional BIQA approaches and deep learning BIQA methods are the two types of BIQA approaches. Deep learning methods are further classified into CNN-based methods and ViT-based methods. Several types of blind image quality evaluation methods are introduced in detail below.

2.1   Traditional Blind IQA

Traditional BIQA methods mainly extract color, contrast and other features in images through mathematical or physical modeling, and performs the final quality evaluation [27]. Mathematical methods and machine learning algorithms have played a big role in traditional fields. Anish et al. [22] proposed a BIQA model based on natural scene statistics operating in spatial domain. They calculated the naturalness by counting the local brightness differences of pictures in a large number of scenes. Zhang et al. [25] built a Gaussian model for picture patches using a set of raw natural images, then utilized the acquired model to assess the quality of each image patch and average pooling to produce a global score. Xu et al. [26] proposed a BIQA algorithm based on high-order statistical aggregation. Local image patches are extracted as local features and codebooks are constructed, which are subsequently used to construct global quality-aware image representations. Finally, a regression algorithm in machine learning is used to calculate the correlation between human subjective perception and objective indicators.

2.2   CNN-Based Blind IQA

Benefiting from the feature extraction and representation capabilities of CNN [17], CNN-based methods have achieved considerable success. Some CNN-based image quality assessment methods leverage the remarkable feature expression abilities of CNN. Le et al. [2] proposed a five-layer CNN, employs simple convolution and pooling operations to extract image features. Bosses et al. [4] designed an end-to-end CNN-based BIQA method that includes convolution layers, five pooling layers, and two fully connected layers. This architecture makes it deeper compared to other coherent IQA models. Su et al. [9] proposed an adaptive hypernetwork architecture for evaluating the quality of real-world outdoor photographs. The architecture first utilizes ResNet-50 to extract features from images. Subsequently, a content-aware hypernetwork is employed to train different weights and biases for each image, and finally, a simple network is used to obtain the final score.

BIQA is often limited by the size of datasets. Some CNN methods address this issue by tackling the problem of small datasets to improve model performance. Liu et al. [5] suggested a ranking-based NR-IQA approach. They used a Siamese network to rank photos according to their quality by using synthetic distortions generated with known relative image quality. The feature representation from the Siamese network was then sent to a CNN for individual image quality evaluation. CNN models often require pretraining on large datasets and then further fine-tuning on downstream tasks. However, these pretrained networks are widely used in other vision tasks, which can lead to generalization issues when evaluating different types of distortions. Zhu et al. [6] developed a NR-IQA metric that learns shared meta-knowledge from people while evaluating the quality of photos with varied distortions. This enables the model to adapt easily to unknown distortions.

2.3   ViT-Based Blind IQA

Transformer [7] was initially introduced and widely applied in the field of natural language processing (NLP). Its outstanding performance in various NLP tasks, such as machine translation and language modeling, drew attention from the computer vision community. Vision Transformer (ViT) [8] is one of the most representative examples of applying the Transformer model in the field of computer vision. It has performed admirably in image classification tasks. ViT separates the input picture into numerous patches, each of which is projected onto a fixed-length vector. The Transformer model is then given these vectors. To allow image classification, a specific token indicating the image classification job is introduced to the input sequence. The final projected class corresponds to the output corresponding to this token.

The global attention of Vision Transformer on images helps capture global features of images, which may be advantageous for evaluating image quality. Manri et al. [24] proposed a framework with ViT as backbone for FR-IQA. The method first uses CNN to extract perceptual features of the image, which are then input to ViT to compare distorted image with reference image. Currently, BIQA algorithms based on ViT can be mainly categorized into two types: hybrid methods and pure ViT-based methods. Hybrid methods first extract image features using pre-trained CNN models and then process the feature maps using ViT. You et al. [10] first utilize ResNet-50 to extract image features. The feature maps are then projected and pooled before being inputted into the ViT structure. Finally, a MLP head is employed to obtain the quality distribution. Pure ViT-based methods directly divide the input image into patches and feed them into the ViT for processing. Ke et al. [11] focused on addressing the limitation of CNNs, which can only handle fixed-size images. They achieved this by inputting images of different scales into the ViT structure.

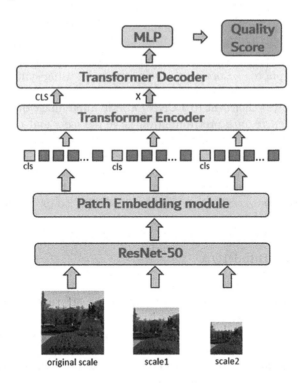

Fig. 1. Model overview of MSIQT. We employ multi-scale inputs to enrich the image features, including the original size of the image and two smaller sizes obtained through downsampling. Each image is fed into ResNet-50 to extract feature maps, which are then fed into a patch generation module to segment them into fixed-size patches. The generated patches of different scales are augmented with a CLS token and position embeddings. Subsequently, these tokens are inputted into a Transformer encoder for attention computation. Afterwards, the CLS tokens from the three scales are summed up to form a single token, and the remaining vectors are concatenated and inputted together into the decoder. The decoder further processes the cls token and feeds it into MLP to obtain the final quality score.

3   Proposed Method

3.1   Overall Architecture

ViT divides the input image into fixed-sized patches, which may overlook some distortions across patches and affect the final evaluation results. To address this issue and extract image features more comprehensively, we use multi-scale input in our model. Most previous ViT-based methods only include an encoder, where the encoder's output, the CLS token, is directly fed into an MLP to obtain the final output. We incorporate a decoder into our structure to provide further interpretation of the output vectors. Figure 1 depicts the general design of our suggested model.

3.2   Multi-scale Input

Using multi-scale inputs is beneficial for enriching image features and strengthening the representation of cross-patch features that may be overlooked in single-scale inputs. In our approach, we employ three scales of inputs, including the original image and two downsampled scales, scale 1 and scale 2. According to human visual perception, resizing an image while changing its aspect ratio can result in a degradation of visual quality. Therefore, when downsampling the image, we maintain its original aspect ratio to preserve the maximum amount of inherent features on the smaller scales. Specifically, we start by adjusting the width of the image to a given size. Then, based on the original aspect ratio of the image, we calculate the corresponding height after the width modification. The new image height is calculated as follows:

$$H = h * (W/w) \tag{1}$$

where h is the original image's height, w is the original image's width, W is the image's width in the new scale, and H is the image's new height in the new scale. Finally, we perform downsampling on the image according to the generated new dimensions. By preserving the original aspect ratio and maintaining proportional adjustments, we aim to retain the maximum amount of original features on the downscaled image.

3.3   Attention Aggregation in Transformer Encoder

Given an image $I \in \mathcal{R}^{C \times H \times W}$, we use ResNet-50 [16] to extract image features at three different scales, resulting in three sets of feature maps with a dimension of $d = 2048 \times h \times w$, where h and w are proportional to the original image size. C represents the number of channels. The patch embedding module is used to generate embeddings corresponding to the three scales. Assuming each image is divided into N patches, each patch is transformed into embedding having a dimension of D. We appended a CLS token $T_{cls} \in \mathcal{R}^{1 \times D}$ to each of the N embeddings yielding to $N + 1$ embeddings, like the original ViT. The learnable CLS token is used to aggregate both global and local quality-aware features of images, which are used for subsequent quality assessment. A positional embedding, used to encode position information, is also added to these N+1 embeddings. The multi-scale inputs of the image are eventually transformed into three sequences as follows:

$$T = \{T_{cls}, T_1, T_2, \ldots T_N\} \tag{2}$$

These sequences are then input into the encoder for attention computation. The encoder consists of several multi-head attention modules (MHSA). T is first transformed into three matrices: Q, K, and V. The computation process of the encoder is as follows:

$$
\begin{aligned}
MHSA(Q, K, V) = &cat(Attention(Q_1, K_1, V_1), \ldots, \\
&Attention(Q_g, K_g, V_g))W_H \\
Y_M = &MHSA(Q, K, V) + T \\
Y_O = &MLP(Norm(Y_M)) + Y_M,
\end{aligned} \tag{3}
$$

where $Attention(Q_g, K_g, V_g) = softmax(\frac{Q_g K_g^T}{\sqrt{d}})V_g$, W_H represents the weights of the linear projection layer and $Norm()$ refers to the layer normalization.

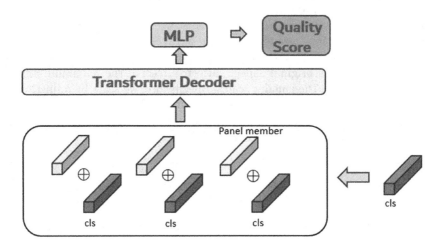

Fig. 2. The specific structure of the Attention panel. The cls token output from the encoder is expanded into N shares, and N depends on the number of panel members. Each cls token is combined with a panel member, and then sent to the decoder for processing.

3.4   Decoder and Quality Score Generation

The output Y_O obtained from the encoder can be represented as:

$$Y_O = \{Y_O[0], Y_O[1], \dots, Y_O[N]\} \in \mathcal{R}^{(N+1) \times D} \tag{4}$$

Since we input images of three scales, we get $Z = \{Y_{O-original}, Y_{O-scale1}, Y_{O-scale2}\}$ from encoder. Then, we merge the CLS tokens in three scales as follows:

$$Z_O[O] = Y_{O-original}[0] + Y_{O-scale1}[0] + Y_{O-scale2}[0], \tag{5}$$

and concatenate the remaining vectors, so that the information in all scales can be processed in the decoder.

The new CLS token, $Z_O[0]$, is first put through a multi-head attention module to represent the relationship of one element with the others. The multi-head attention output is then followed by a residual connection to construct the decoder's query. We use the remaining part of Z_O as the key and value of the decoder, use them and the query to calculate the cross-attention, and send the output to MLP to calculate the final score. In order to obtain a more robust evaluation score and reduce possible model prediction bias, inspired by DEIQA [23], we add an attention panel at the decoder side. The structure is shown in Fig. 2. The CLS token at the input of the decoder is copied N copies and added to the learnable vector. The number of N is a hyperparameter. This vector participates in the calculation of multi-head attention, and the output of cross-attention is also expanded to N. We feed N outputs into MLP and average the outputs to get the final score.

Fig. 3. Some images in LIVEC.

4   Experimental Results

4.1   Datasets and Evaluation Protocols

MSIQT's performance was examined using four datasets, which comprised LIVE [12], CSIQ [13], TID2013 [14] and LIVEC [15]. LIVE consists of a total of 779 distorted images, which were generated by applying 5 to 6 levels of degradation using five distortion operations on reference images. CSIQ contains 30 original images and 866 synthetic distorted images, encompassing six different types of distortions. TID2013 comprises 25 reference photos without distortion, and every reference image is distorted with 24 different types of distortions, each having five levels of distortion. Common distortion types in the synthetic datasets include Gaussian blur, JPEG compression, and random noise, among others. LIVEC consists of 1162 images captured using modern mobile devices under a wide range of real-world distortion conditions. These photos are taken by different photographers using various cameras, resulting in images with complex and realistic distortions. Figure 3 shows some images in LIVEC.

As a model for evaluating image quality, the accuracy of evaluation results is undoubtedly the most important indicator. In our experiments, we utilized two commonly used metrics for evaluation, namely SRCC and PLCC. These evaluation metrics are used to evaluate the accuracy of our model due to its wide application in other domains as well as BIQA. And their absolute values range from 0 to 1, with values closer to 1 indicating superior performance.

4.2 Implementation Details

The number of multi-scale inputs of MSIQT is set to 3, and the usual scale sizes are the original image size, 384, 224. The image patch size is 16 and the token dimension is 384. The encoder depth is 12 and the number of heads is also 12. The depth of the decoder is 1 and the size of attention panel is set to 6.

MSIQT was trained for 100 epochs on each of the four quality assessment datasets. The learning rate is set to 1e-4, and the batch size is generally 16. The datasets were randomly split into two sections for training and testing, with four-fifths of the data used as the training set, and one-fifth of the data used as the test set. We perform the training on each dataset ten times to increase the accuracy of the findings, and the mean values of the evaluation index are used as the experimental result.

4.3 Comparison of Quality Evaluation Results

Table 1 compares our suggested method to several state-of-the-art BIQA methods on four datasets. These advanced methods include both traditional methods and some methods based on deep learning. Our proposed method outperforms or matches state-of-the-art methods on four datasets, especially on TID2013. Our proposed model achieved better results on TID2013 dataset. The reason may be that TID2013 dataset has more pictures than other datasets, and our model extracts more sufficient features when facing with more images, thus exhibiting superior performance over other methods. These experimental findings show that our proposed strategy is effective. To a certain extent, it shows that the multi-scale input and the use of decoder can extract rich features in images and perform effective representation and mapping. As a non-synthetic image dataset, LIVEC imposes stricter requirements on the model's ability to extract features and fit scores. It can be seen that compared to the three synthetic datasets, the test results of the model on LIVEC are slightly lower. This illustrates some shortcomings of our model in the face of non-synthetic datasets, and points the way for future research, that is, to make the model better evaluate images from non-synthetic datasets.

4.4 Ablation Experiment

We conducted ablation tests to confirm the precise role of each component of the model. First, we replaced the decoder part of the model with ordinary MLP.

Table 1. MSIQT's SRCC and PLCC results on four datasets, and comparisons with other state-of-the-art methods. The red mark is the finest among them, and the blue mark is the second best.

Method	LIVE		CSIQ		TID2013		LIVEC	
	SRCC	PLCC	SRCC	PLCC	SRCC	PLCC	SRCC	PLCC
BRISQUE [22]	0.926	0.935	0.866	0.893	0.367	0.475	0.316	0.369
WaDIQaM [4]	0.885	0.887	0.851	0.842	0.837	0.851	0.680	0.674
DBCNN [3]	0.919	0.918	0.946	0.959	0.816	0.865	0.837	0.863
HyperIQA [9]	0.964	0.962	0.926	0.942	0.859	0.874	0.846	0.873
TReS [21]	0.949	0.954	0.932	0.943	0.850	0.882	0.852	0.880
MSIQT(ours)	0.951	0.955	0.956	0.955	0.947	0.956	0.849	0.879

Table 2. Ablation experiments on LIVEC and CSIQ. The red mark is the finest among them, and the blue mark is the second best.

Method	LIVEC		CSIQ	
	SRCC	PLCC	SRCC	PLCC
MSIQT(without decoder)	0.824	0.841	0.919	0.921
MSIQT(without multi-scale input)	0.840	0.860	0.955	0.953
MSIQT(ours)	0.849	0.879	0.956	0.955

After comparing the two results, we found that the results on both datasets decreased after replacing it with MLP, indicating that the decoder does play a role in further processing and mapping the features obtained from the encoder. Then, we remove the multi-scale input and replace it with a single-scale original image input, and the rest of the model is the same as the original model. The findings reveal that the model's performance deterioration is not noticeable, indicating that the impact of multi-scale input on the performance of the model is not as large as imagined. The results predicted by the model are slightly lower. This indicates that multi-scale input plays a role in enriching image features. The specific experimental results are shown in the Table 2.

5   Conclusion

In this paper, we propose a BIQA transformer (MSIQT). It aims to extract image features more comprehensively for quality evaluation purposes. We explore quality-aware features from the multi-scale representation of the image and further extract them using a pre-trained model. The transformer encoder is utilized for aggregating attention mechanisms, while the decoder is employed to refine perceptual information, thereby achieving a more accurate assessment of image quality. The results of experiments on four datasets show that MSIQT is superior in terms of prediction accuracy.

Acknowledgement. This work was supported by the National Science Foundation of China under grant 62201538 and Natural Science Foundation of Shandong Province under grant ZR2022QF006.

References

1. Mittal, A., Soundararajan, R., Bovik, A.C.: Making a "Completely Blind" image quality analyzer. IEEE Signal Process. Lett. **20**(3), 209–212 (2013). https://doi.org/10.1109/LSP.2012.2227726
2. Kang, L., Ye, P., Li, Y., Doermann, D.: Convolutional neural networks for no-reference image quality assessment. In: 2014 IEEE Conference on Computer Vision and Pattern Recognition, Columbus, OH, USA, 2014, pp. 1733–1740 (2014). https://doi.org/10.1109/CVPR.2014.224
3. Zhang, W., Ma, K., Yan, J., Deng, D., Wang, Z.: Blind image quality assessment using a deep bilinear convolutional neural network. IEEE Trans. Circuits Syst. Video Technol. **30**(1), 36–47 (2020). https://doi.org/10.1109/TCSVT.2018.2886771
4. Bosse, S., Maniry, D., Müller, K.-R., Wiegand, T., Samek, W.: Deep neural networks for no-reference and full-reference image quality assessment. IEEE Trans. Image Process. **27**(1), 206–219 (2018). https://doi.org/10.1109/TIP.2017.2760518
5. Liu, X., Van De Weijer, J., Bagdanov, A.D.: RankIQA: learning from rankings for no-reference image quality assessment. In: 2017 IEEE International Conference on Computer Vision (ICCV), Venice, Italy, 2017, pp. 1040–1049 (2017). https://doi.org/10.1109/ICCV.2017.118
6. Zhu, H., Li, L., Wu, J., Dong, W., Shi, G.: MetaIQA: deep meta-learning for no-reference image quality assessment. In: 2020 IEEE/CVF Conference on Computer Vision and Pattern Recognition (CVPR), Seattle, WA, USA, 2020, pp. 14131–14140 (2020). https://doi.org/10.1109/CVPR42600.2020.01415
7. Vaswani, A., et al.: Attention is all you need. In: NIPS (2017)
8. Dosovitskiy, A., et al.: An image is worth 16x16 words: transformers for image recognition at scale. In: International Conference on Learning Representations. Virtual Event, Austria (2021)
9. Su, S., et al.: Blindly assess image quality in the wild guided by a self-adaptive hyper network. In: 2020 IEEE/CVF Conference on Computer Vision and Pattern Recognition (CVPR), Seattle, WA, USA, 2020, pp. 3664–3673 (2020). https://doi.org/10.1109/CVPR42600.2020.00372
10. You, J., Korhonen, J.: Transformer for image quality assessment. In: 2021 IEEE International Conference on Image Processing (ICIP), Anchorage, AK, USA, 2021, pp. 1389–1393 (2021). https://doi.org/10.1109/ICIP42928.2021.9506075
11. Ke, J., Wang, Q., Wang, Y., et al.: MUSIQ: multi-scale image quality transformer. In: International Conference on Computer Vision (2021). https://doi.org/10.1109/ICCV48922.2021.00510
12. Sheikh, H.R., Sabir, M.F., Bovik, A.C.: A statistical evaluation of recent full reference image quality assessment algorithms. IEEE Trans. Image Process. **15**(11), 3440–3451 (2006). https://doi.org/10.1109/TIP.2006.881959
13. Larson, E.C., Chandler, D.M.: Most apparent distortion: full-reference image quality assessment and the role of strategy. J. Electron. Imaging **19**(1), 011006 (2010)

14. Ponomarenko, N., et al.: Image database TID2013: peculiarities, results and perspectives. Signal Process. Image Commun. **30**, 57–77 (2015)

15. Ghadiyaram, D., Bovik, A.C.: Massive online crowdsourced study of subjective and objective picture quality. IEEE Trans. Image Process. **25**(1), 372–387 (2016). https://doi.org/10.1109/TIP.2015.2500021

16. He, K., Zhang, X., Ren, S., Sun, J.: Deep residual learning for image recognition. In: 2016 IEEE Conference on Computer Vision and Pattern Recognition (CVPR), Las Vegas, NV, USA, 2016, pp. 770–778 (2016). https://doi.org/10.1109/CVPR. 2016.90

17. Lecun, Y., Bottou, L., Bengio, Y., Haffner, P.: Gradient-based learning applied to document recognition. Proc. IEEE **86**(11), 2278–2324 (1998). https://doi.org/10. 1109/5.726791

18. Wang, Z., Bovik, A.C., Sheikh, H.R., Simoncelli, E.P.: Image quality assessment: from error visibility to structural similarity. IEEE Trans. Image Process. **13**(4), 600–612 (2004). https://doi.org/10.1109/TIP.2003.819861

19. Liu, Y., Zhai, G., Gu, K., Liu, X., Zhao, D., Gao, W.: Reduced-reference image quality assessment in free-energy principle and sparse representation. IEEE Trans. Multimedia **20**(2), 379–391 (2018). https://doi.org/10.1109/TMM.2017.2729020

20. Moorthy, A.K., Bovik, A.C.: Blind image quality assessment: from natural scene statistics to perceptual quality. IEEE Trans. Image Process. **20**(12), 3350–3364 (2011). https://doi.org/10.1109/TIP.2011.2147325

21. Golestaneh, S.A., Dadsetan, S., Kitani, K.M.: No reference image quality assessment via transformers, relative ranking, and self-consistency. In: Proceedings of the IEEE/CVF Winter Conference on Applications of Computer Vision, pp. 1220–1230 (2022)

22. Mittal, A., Moorthy, A.K., Bovik, A.C.: No-reference image quality assessment in the spatial domain. IEEE Trans. Image Process. **21**(12), 4695–4708 (2012). https:// doi.org/10.1109/TIP.2012.2214050

23. Qin, G., et al.: Data-efficient image quality assessment with attention-panel decoder. arXiv:abs/2304.04952 (2023)

24. Cheon, M., Yoon, S.-J., Kang, B., Lee, J.: Perceptual image quality assessment with transformers. In: 2021 IEEE/CVF Conference on Computer Vision and Pattern Recognition Workshops (CVPRW), Nashville, TN, USA, 2021, pp. 433–442 (2021). https://doi.org/10.1109/CVPRW53098.2021.00054

25. Zhang, L., Zhang, L., Bovik, A.C.: A feature-enriched completely blind image quality evaluator. IEEE Trans. Image Process. **24**(8), 2579–2591 (2015). https://doi. org/10.1109/TIP.2015.2426416

26. Xu, J., Ye, P., Li, Q., Du, H., Liu, Y., Doermann, D.: Blind image quality assessment based on high order statistics aggregation. IEEE Trans. Image Process. **25**(9), 4444–4457 (2016). https://doi.org/10.1109/TIP.2016.2585880

27. Liu, Y., et al.: Unsupervised blind image quality evaluation via statistical measurements of structure, naturalness, and perception. IEEE Trans. Circuits Syst. Video Technol. **30**(4), 929–943 (2020). https://doi.org/10.1109/TCSVT.2019.2900472

Low-Light Image Enhancement via Unsupervised Learning

Wenchao He and Yutao Liu[✉]

School of Computer Science and Technology, Ocean University of China,
Qingdao 266100, China
hwc@stu.ouc.edu.cn, liuyutao@ouc.edu.cn

Abstract. The models based on unsupervised learning methods have achieved prominent achievement in several low-level tasks such as image restoration and low-light enhancement. Many of them are based on generative adversarial networks such as EnlightenGAN. Although EnlightenGAN can be trained without the need for paired images, there are still existing some issues such as insufficient illumination and color distortion. Inspired by the achievement in visual tasks made by Vision Transformer(ViT), we propose a discriminator based on ViT to replace the original fully convolutional network to solve this problem. Furthermore, to improve the illumination enhancement effect, we devise a new loss function enlightened by the luminance in SSIM and multi-scale SSIM. Our method surpasses the state-of-the-art on mainstream testing datasets.

Keywords: Low-Light image Enhancement · Unsupervised Learning · Vision Transformer · Generative Adversarial Network

1 Introduction

In the real-world environment, capturing high-quality images in insufficient illumination is challenging. This is due to the poor shooting environment, the limitation of the photographic devices, and incorrect operation by the photographer. It will cause low ISO, high noise, and poor visibility that will not only impact the visual experience but also diminish the performance of numerous downstream high-level vision algorithms. To suppress the degradation, there are various algorithms that have been proposed for decades, such as Histogram equalization(HE) [1,2]and Retinex theory methods [3–6].

With the tremendous progress in deep neural networks, methods based on deep learning have made brilliant success in a series of low-level tasks, including super-resolution [9], denoising [7,8], and dehazing [10]. However, various deep learning-based methods heavily depend on the low-normal image pairs, which raises a series of challenges [11,12]. For the low/normal image pairs gathering, capturing them in the same place is extremely difficult and impracticable [13,14]. Although the synthesized dataset obtained by adjusting gamma values

L. Fang et al. (Eds.): CICAI 2023, LNAI 14473, pp. 232–243, 2024.
https://doi.org/10.1007/978-981-99-8850-1_19

to normal-light images can alleviate the problem, the dataset obtained in this way does not take into account the specific situation of the real world [15,16].

To mitigate the problem of lacking paired images, unsupervised learning methods are proposed. EnlightenGAN [17] is the first work that introduced unsupervised learning to the low-light enhancement domain with Generative adversarial network(GAN) [18]. EnlightenGAN is formed of two components: U-net [19] architecture generator, global-local discriminator. Although EnlightenGAN achieves outstanding enhancement effects on low-light images, there are still existing some issues with it, such as somewhere lack of enhancement and color distortion.

Benefiting by the global attention mechanism, Vision Transformer(ViT) can effectively extract image features for classification [20]. We consider what discriminators do to be essentially a classification task. Inspired by this motivation, we propose to replace the vanilla discriminator with the pure ViT to extract the features to discriminate the image whether real normal-light image or not. And it will help the generator to improve itself for enhancing. Moreover, to address the issue of insufficient enhancement in some areas, we propose single-scale and multi-scale illumination loss for enhancement. We find that the illuminance is extremely similar between the normal-light image and the enhanced image. Extensive experiments are conducted on mainstream datasets and outcomes indicate that our method outperforms other methods we compared.

2 Related Work

2.1 Traditional Method

In the past few decades, research on low-light enhancement has a long tradition, various algorithms have been proposed to boost the visual quality for both subjective and objective. Histogram equalization(HE) [1,2] is a famous classic technique in image enhancement, which is wide-used in several tasks. By redistributing the pixel intensities of an image's histogram, HE and its variants make the distribution more uniform across the entire intensity range and thus can improve the image's contrast efficaciously.

Another category of low-light image enhancement technique is Retinex theory [3,4], which assumes that the image is composed of two components, illumination, and reflectance. The first algorithm of Retinex theory was Single Scale Retinex (SSR), which only manipulates the reflectance. And then, Multi-Scale Retinex (MSR) was proposed by Jobson et al. to suppress the degradation of the image by linearly combining multi-scale enhancement results [5,6]. The outputs from those early attempts look somewhere over-exposure and strange. Wang et al. proposed an improved algorithm called NPE, which keeps the balance between naturalness and enhancement by manipulating the illumination [21]. Fu et al. proposed a weighted variational algorithm named SRIE to simultaneously provide an estimation of both reflectance and illumination and then adjust the illumination [22]. Guo et al. proposed a method named LIME, which accelerates the illumination map estimation through ALM [23]. Those works substantially suppose that the images don't exist color distortion and all are noise-free. However, the real circumstance is a bit more complex.

2.2   Deep Learning Method

Full Supervised Method. With the achievement made by deep learning in other vision tasks, deep learning is introduced into low-light enhancement. Lore et al. proposed the LLNet to utilize Sparse Autoencoder to enhance the contrast and denoise simultaneously, which was the first work applying convolutional neural networks in the low-light enhancement domain [24]. Inspired by the Retinex theory, Chen et al. proposed an end-to-end framework RetinexNet that combines Retinex theory with deep network [25]. GladNet divided the enhancement task into two steps–illumination estimation and detail reconstruction [26]. MBLLEN proposed using 3D convolution instead of 2D convolution for video low-light image enhancement [27]. However, training these models extremely requires low/normal image pairs, which are difficult for collecting.

Unsupervised Method. Unsupervised learning had achieved progress in other low-level tasks. EnligthenGAN was the first work to introduce unsupervised learning to low-light enhancement, which was an adversarial network including global-local discriminator [17]. Guo et al. presented an unsupervised model named Zero-DCE, which formulated the enhancement task as an illumination curve learning [28]. Although those methods solve the problem of requiring paired dataset training, they still remain the drawbacks of color distortion and image noise.

3   Proposed Method

As shown in the model in Fig. 1, the architecture of the proposed work is composed of an attention-guided generator and global-local discriminators. The U-Net style generator is the same as the generator in EnlightenGAN [17]. And each attention module of the generator is to multiply the feature map with a (resized) attention map. However, we proposed a pure Vision Transformer to replace the vanilla discriminators. Moreover, we propose illumination loss and MSI loss as supplements for the loss function.

3.1   Vision Transformer Discriminator

Same as the EnlightenGAN, we also adopt global-local discriminator structure. However, instead of the vanilla full convolutional network, we adopt the Vision Transformer(ViT) for image discrimination.

Intuitively speaking, identifying whether an image is an enhanced image by a discriminator is essentially an image classification problem. Because both real and fake can be analogized as two labels for image classification. Although both vanilla global and local discriminators employ the same PatchGAN [29] architecture for real/fake discrimination, limited by the convolutional neural network itself, the vanilla PatchGAN can't extract the features to direct the generator to improve itself better. Inspired by the huge success made by ViT in image classification, we propose replacing the vanilla full convolutional network with pure ViT. The structure of the pure ViT discriminators is shown on the right of Fig. 1.

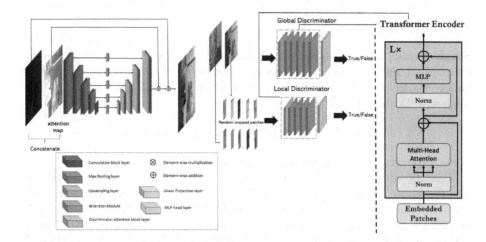

Fig. 1. Total structure of our model. The generator is on the left side. Each convolutional block of the generator consists two 3×3 convolutional layers and then through the operation of the batch normalization and the LeakyRelu. On the right side is global-local discriminator, which consists of transformer blocks. The blue dashed line indicates the transformer encoder. (Color figure online)

For the global ViT discriminator, we apply five transformer attention blocks to build up the network. The original standard function of the discriminator is the same as the one in EnlightenGAN [17]:

$$D_{Re}(x_r, x_f) = \sigma((R(x_r)) - \mathbb{E}_{x_f \sim \mathbb{P}_{fake}}[R(x_f)]) \tag{1}$$

$$D_{Re}(x_f, x_r) = \sigma((R(x_f)) - \mathbb{E}_{x_r \sim \mathbb{P}_{real}}[R(x_r)]) \tag{2}$$

where R denotes the discriminator, x_r and x_f are sampled from the real and fake distribution, σ stands for the sigmoid function. As for the generative adversarial loss of our model, we also adopt the least-square GAN (LSGAN) to take the place of the original sigmoid function.

$$\mathcal{L}_D^{Global} = \mathbb{E}_{x_r \sim \mathbb{P}_{real}}[(D_{Re}(x_r, x_f) - 1)^2] + \mathbb{E}_{x_f \sim \mathbb{P}_{fake}}[D_{Re}(x_f, x_r)]^2 \tag{3}$$

$$\mathcal{L}_G^{Global} = \mathbb{E}_{x_f \sim \mathbb{P}_{fake}}[(D_{Re}(x_f, x_r) - 1)^2] + \mathbb{E}_{x_r \sim \mathbb{P}_{real}}[D_{Re}(x_r, x_f)]^2 \tag{4}$$

Also, we utilize four attention blocks to build up the local discriminator. We also randomly crop 5 patches from both the real images and the outputs each time, here is the local adversarial loss:

$$\mathcal{L}_D^{Local} = \mathbb{E}_{x_f \sim \mathbb{P}_{fake-patches}}[(D(x_f) - 0)^2] + \mathbb{E}_{x_r \sim \mathbb{P}_{real-patches}}[(D(x_r) - 1)^2] \quad (5)$$

$$\mathcal{L}_G^{Lobal} = \mathbb{E}_{x_f \sim \mathbb{P}_{fake-patches}}[(D(x_f) - 1)^2] \quad (6)$$

3.2 Loss Function

Single-Scale and Multi-scale Illumination Loss. Structure Similarity Index Measure(SSIM) [30] is one of the well-known visual quality metrics, which mainly considers three key features, luminance, contrast, and structure. The original SSIM function is:

$$SSIM(x, y) = [l(x, y)^\alpha \cdot c(x, y)^\beta \cdot s(x, y)^\gamma] \quad (7)$$

where exponents α, β, γ are all set to 1 by default.

Usually, when we determine the similarity between two images, we need to combine those three variables into SSIM. In our task, we should improve the illumination of the low-light image intuitively. We find that the two normal-light images are almost identical in luminance, while there is a significant difference between a low-light image and a normal-light image. Therefore, the Single-scale illumination loss(SSI) $\mathcal{L}_{SSI}$ is defined as:

$$\mathcal{L}_{SSI} = \frac{2\mu_x \mu_y + c_1}{\mu_x^2 + \mu_y^2 + c_1} \quad (8)$$

where μ_x, μ_y denote the mean value of the two input images' pixels separately. By default, we set $c_1 = 1e-4$.

The illumination perception of an image also depends on the distance from the image to the observer. Based on this, we used Multi-scale illumination(MSI) loss as a constraint, which is the illuminance in MS-SSIM [31]. We define it as:

$$\mathcal{L}_{MSI} = [\mathcal{L}_{SSI}]^{\alpha_M} \quad (9)$$

where the α_M depends on the scale you choose. By default, we choose $M = 5$ and the $\alpha_M = 0.1333$.

Self Feature Preserving Loss. Johnson et al. [32] proposed perceptual loss by modeling the feature space distance between images using a pre-trained VGG model for maintaining the perceptual similarity of images before and after enhancement. Brandon et al. [33] observed that pre-trained VGG models are not susceptible when adjusting the input image's pixel intensity range. For the sake of this, our self feature preserving loss is the same as the EnlightneGAN's loss:

$$L_{SFP}(I^L) = \frac{1}{W_{i,j}Hi,j} \sum_{x=1}^{W_{i,j}} \sum_{y=1}^{H_{i,j}} (\Phi_{i,j}(I^L) - \Phi_{i,j}(G(I^L)))^2 \quad (10)$$

where I^L represents the input images for enhancement. $G(I^L)$ represents results through the generator. $\Phi i, j(\cdot)$ represents the feature maps extracted from images by the pre-trained VGG-16 model. $W_{i,j}$ denotes the width of the extracted feature maps and the $H_{i,j}$ denotes the height of the extracted feature maps. i represents the VGG-16's i-th max pooling layer, and j represents the j-th convolutional layer after the maxpooling layer. By default, we choose $i = 5$, $j = 1$.

Same to the generative adversarial loss, we also define the self feature preserving loss into two parts. For the local discriminator, the local self feature preserving Loss is defined as $\mathcal{L}_{SFP}^{Local}$, while the global one is defined as $\mathcal{L}_{SFP}^{Global}$. The total loss function for training the whole model is described as follows:

$$Loss = \mathcal{L}_{SFP}^{Local} + \mathcal{L}_{SFP}^{Global} + \mathcal{L}_{G}^{Global} + \mathcal{L}_{G}^{Local} + \mathcal{L}_{SSI} + \mathcal{L}_{MSI} \quad (11)$$

4 Experiment

4.1 Datasets and Implementation Details.

Unpaired Enhancement Dataset Jiang et al. [17] have collected an unpaired enhancement dataset for training the model. The training dataset contains 1016 normal-light images and 914 low-light images which are obtained from public datasets. All of them are in PNG format and then resized to 400 × 600 for training and testing.

Testing Dataset. For the testing images, we choose the LOL dataset [25] and VE-LOL [34] dataset to measure the model performance. The LOL dataset includes 15 low/normal light image pairs and the VE-LOL contains 100 low/normal light image pairs. All of them perform the same operations as the training dataset.

Implementation Details. Input images are randomly cropped to 256 × 256 for training while the testing images retain the initial size. In the first 100 epochs, the initial learning rate is 1e-4, then gradually decays to 0 in the last 100 epochs. Adam is used as the optimizer and the training batch size is set to 32. The model is trained under two Nvidia RTX 3090 for nearly two hours.

Table 1. Objective results in VE-LOL and LOL datasets among all the methods

Method	VE-LOL			LOL		
	SSIM ↑	MS-SSIM↑	PSNR↑	SSIM↑	MS-SSIM↑	PSNR ↑
LIME	0.4674	0.4598	16.9714	0.4822	0.4747	17.1812
SRIE	0.5204	0.5203	14.4505	0.4937	0.4942	11.8552
NPE	0.4617	0.4543	17.3324	0.4818	0.4744	16.9697
Dong et al.	0.4757	0.4692	17.2553	0.4792	0.4722	16.7165
RetinexNet	0.4092	0.4007	16.0971	0.3373	0.3268	14.9774
GladNet	0.6871	0.6820	19.8200	0.5636	0.5570	16.9419
MBLLEN	0.6947	0.6943	17.8690	0.7270	0.7266	17.8583
EnlightenGAN	0.6794	0.6755	18.6396	0.5337	0.5284	15.3080
Zero-DCE	0.5770	0.5736	18.0587	0.5615	0.5588	14.8607
ours	0.7393	0.7359	19.5355	0.5928	0.5866	16.6105

4.2   Performance Evaluation

Objective Measurement. For objective measurement, we choose three visual quality metrics: SSIM [30], MS-SSIM [31], and PSNR to assess the performance of our model. As the results shown in Table 1, we compare several competing models ranging from traditional to deep learning-based methods: NPE [21], SRIE [22], LIME [23], dong et al. [35], RetinexNet [25], GladNet [26], MBLLEN [27], EnligthenGAN [17] and Zero-DCE [28]. In the LOL dataset, our method's performance is only behind the MBLLEN in SSIM and MS-SSIM and the performance in PSNR also falls behind many methods. However, among all the methods, our method performs best in both SSIM and MS-SSIM on the VE-LOL dataset, and only below GladNet on PSNR.

Subjective Measurement. As shown in Fig. 2, although our method falls behind the MBLLEN and performs mediocrely in objective visual metrics in LOL dataset, our method greatly suppresses color distortion and is more natural than other methods. As we can see, SRIE and Zero-DCE can not sufficiently enhance the brightness of images. In addition, from LIME to EnlightenGAN, all of them make the background of the enhanced image greener than the normal-light image, which means that they still exist color distortion issues. In contrast, our method not only increases higher brightness but also suppresses color distortion.

Figure 3 displays the enhancement outcomes in the VE-LOL dataset. Our method's results are more approaching the ground-truth and are looking more natural. The results of RetinexNet exists severe image noise. LIME and NPE lead to over-exposure results, while Zero-DCE and SRIE lead to under-exposure. Also as the bounding box shows in Fig. 3, the outcome of EnlightenGAN occurs color distortion, because the leaves turn yellow, not green. Compared to other enhancement methods, our method provides a more natural and realistic visual performance on those two datasets.

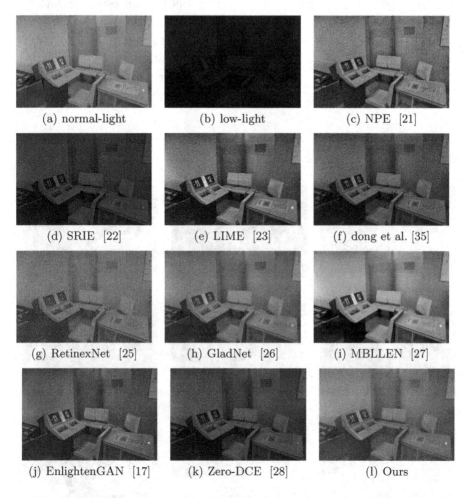

(a) normal-light   (b) low-light   (c) NPE [21]

(d) SRIE [22]   (e) LIME [23]   (f) dong et al. [35]

(g) RetinexNet [25]   (h) GladNet [26]   (i) MBLLEN [27]

(j) EnlightenGAN [17]   (k) Zero-DCE [28]   (l) Ours

Fig. 2. Visual comparison with other enhancement methods in LOL dataset

Table 2. Objective visual quality results in VE-LOL dataset for ablation study

pure Vision Transformer	SSI Loss	MSI Loss	VE-LOL		
			SSIM↑	MS-SSIM↑	PSNR↑
✓	✓	✓	0.7393	0.7359	19.5355
✓	✗	✓	0.7257	0.7213	19.6525
✓	✓	✗	0.7374	0.7335	19.5075
✓	✗	✗	0.6553	0.6499	18.0113
✗	✓	✓	0.6673	0.6649	17.0985

Table 3. Objective visual quality results in LOL dataset for ablation study

pure Vision Transformer	SSI Loss	MSI Loss	LOL		
			SSIM↑	MS-SSIM↑	PSNR↑
✓	✓	✓	0.5928	0.5866	16.6105
✓	✗	✓	0.5554	0.5503	15.5048
✓	✓	✗	0.5855	0.5791	16.7426
✓	✗	✗	0.6553	0.6499	18.0113
✗	✓	✓	0.5823	0.5764	16.3229

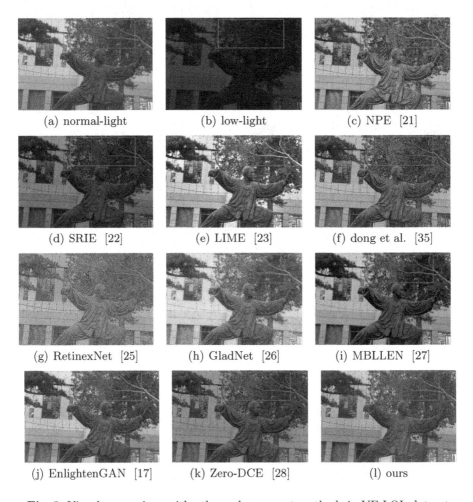

(a) normal-light　　　　　(b) low-light　　　　　(c) NPE [21]

(d) SRIE [22]　　　　　(e) LIME [23]　　　　　(f) dong et al. [35]

(g) RetinexNet [25]　　　　(h) GladNet [26]　　　　(i) MBLLEN [27]

(j) EnlightenGAN [17]　　(k) Zero-DCE [28]　　　　(l) ours

Fig. 3. Visual comparison with other enhancement methods in VE-LOL dataset

4.3 Ablation Study

A group of ablation experiments are conducted to test the effectiveness of the modules we proposed. Firstly, we focus on the visual quality measurements, which are shown in Tables 2 and 3. For each table, the first three columns list our proposed modules and the last three are the visual quality metrics. According to Table 2 and Table 3, the SSIM and MS-SSIM significantly drop while without illumination or MS-SSIM loss, especially the former. Although replacing the vanilla discriminator with ViT will lead to a decrease in visual metrics, as shown in Fig. 4, the ViT discriminator structure can effectively suppress color distortion. As the image is shown in Fig. 4(c), the cabinet color is slightly green without the ViT, but in Fig. 4(f) the cabinet color remains white.

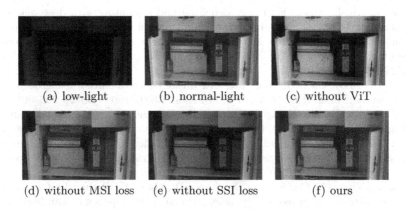

(a) low-light   (b) normal-light   (c) without ViT

(d) without MSI loss   (e) without SSI loss   (f) ours

Fig. 4. Visual comparison from the ablation study of our method

5   Conclusion

In this paper, a new unsupervised low-light image enhancement model is proposed. By replacing the fully convolutional network with ViT, it cultivates both subjective and objective visual qualities. Moreover, with the illumination loss and MS-SSIM constraint, our model shows superiority among the compared models.

However, the computational complexity of pure ViT greatly limits the speed of model training. In the future, we'd upgrade the structure of the discriminator for reducing computational complexity and improving visual quality.

Acknowledgements. This work was supported by the National Science Foundation of China under grant 62201538 and Natural Science Foundation of Shandong Province under grant ZR2022QF006.

References

1. Pizer, S.M., et al.: Adaptive histogram equalization and its variations. Comput. Vis. Graphics Image Process. **39**(3), 355–368 (1987)
2. Zuiderveld, K.: Contrast Limited Adaptive Histogram Equalization, p. 474–485. Academic Press Professional Inc, USA (1994)
3. Land, E.H., McCann, J.J.: Lightness and retinex theory. JOSA **61**(1), 1–11 (1971)
4. Land, E.H.: The retinex. Am. Sci. **52**(2), 247–264 (1964)
5. Rahman, Z.U., Jobson, D.J., Woodell, G.A.: Multi-scale retinex for color image enhancement. In: Proceedings of 3rd IEEE International Conference on Image Processing, vol. 3, pp. 1003–1006. IEEE (1996)
6. Jobson, D.J., Rahman, Z.U., Woodell, G.A.: A multiscale retinex for bridging the gap between color images and the human observation of scenes. IEEE Trans. Image Process. **6**(7), 965–976 (1997)
7. Xie, J., Xu, L., Chen, E.: Image denoising and inpainting with deep neural networks. In: Advances in Neural information Processing Systems, vol. 25 (2012)
8. Zhang, K., Zuo, W., Chen, Y., Meng, D., Zhang, L.: Beyond a gaussian denoiser: residual learning of deep CNN for image denoising. IEEE Trans. Image Process. **26**(7), 3142–3155 (2017)
9. Dong, C., Loy, C.C., He, K., Tang, X.: Image super-resolution using deep convolutional networks. IEEE Trans. Pattern Anal. Mach. Intell. **38**(2), 295–307 (2015)
10. Cai, B., Xu, X., Jia, K., Qing, C., Tao, D.: DehazeNet: an end-to-end system for single image haze removal. IEEE Trans. Image Process. **25**(11), 5187–5198 (2016)
11. Liu, Y.: Unsupervised blind image quality evaluation via statistical measurements of structure, naturalness, and perception. IEEE Trans. Circuits Syst. Video Technol. **30**(4), 929–943 (2020)
12. Liu, Y., Zhai, G., Gu, K., Liu, X., Zhao, D., Gao, W.: Reduced-reference image quality assessment in free-energy principle and sparse representation. IEEE Trans. Multimedia **20**(2), 379–391 (2018)
13. Liu, Y., Gu, K., Wang, S., Zhao, D., Gao, W.: Blind quality assessment of camera images based on low-level and high-level statistical features. IEEE Trans. Multimedia **21**(1), 135–146 (2019)
14. Liu, Y., Gu, K., Li, X., Zhang, Y.: Blind image quality assessment by natural scene statistics and perceptual characteristics. ACM Trans. Multimedia Comput. Commun. Appl. (TOMM) **16**(3), 1–91 (2020)
15. Hu, R., Liu, Y., Gu, K., Min, X., Zhai, G.: Toward a no-reference quality metric for camera-captured images. IEEE Trans. Cybern. **53**(6), 3651–3664 (2023). https://doi.org/10.1109/TCYB.2021.3128023
16. Min, X., Zhai, G., Gu, K., Liu, Y., Yang, X.: Blind image quality estimation via distortion aggravation. IEEE Trans. Broadcast. **64**(2), 508–517 (2018)
17. Jiang, Y., et al.: Enlightengan: deep light enhancement without paired supervision. IEEE Trans. Image Process. **30**, 2340–2349 (2021)
18. Goodfellow, I., et al.: Generative adversarial networks. Commun. ACM **63**(11), 139–144 (2020)
19. Ronneberger, O., Fischer, P., Brox, T.: U-Net: convolutional networks for biomedical image segmentation. In: Navab, N., Hornegger, J., Wells, W.M., Frangi, A.F. (eds.) MICCAI 2015. LNCS, vol. 9351, pp. 234–241. Springer, Cham (2015). https://doi.org/10.1007/978-3-319-24574-4_28
20. Dosovitskiy, A., et al.: An image is worth 16x16 words: transformers for image recognition at scale. arXiv preprint arXiv:2010.11929 (2020)

21. Wang, S., Zheng, J., Hu, H.M., Li, B.: Naturalness preserved enhancement algorithm for non-uniform illumination images. IEEE Trans. Image Process. **22**(9), 3538–3548 (2013)
22. Fu, X., Zeng, D., Huang, Y., Zhang, X.P., Ding, X.: A weighted variational model for simultaneous reflectance and illumination estimation. In: Proceedings of the IEEE Conference on Computer Vision and Pattern Recognition, pp. 2782–2790 (2016)
23. Guo, X., Li, Y., Ling, H.: Lime: low-light image enhancement via illumination map estimation. IEEE Trans. Image Process. **26**(2), 982–993 (2016)
24. Lore, K.G., Akintayo, A., Sarkar, S.: LLNet: a deep autoencoder approach to natural low-light image enhancement. Pattern Recogn. **61**, 650–662 (2017)
25. Wei, C., Wang, W., Yang, W., Liu, J.: Deep retinex decomposition for low-light enhancement. arXiv preprint arXiv:1808.04560 (2018)
26. Wang, W., Wei, C., Yang, W., Liu, J.: GladNet: low-light enhancement network with global awareness. In: 2018 13th IEEE International Conference on Automatic Face & Gesture Recognition (FG 2018), pp. 751–755. IEEE (2018)
27. Lv, F., Lu, F., Wu, J., Lim, C.: MBLLEN: low-light image/video enhancement using CNNs. In: BMVC, vol. 220, p. 4 (2018)
28. Guo, C., et al.: Zero-reference deep curve estimation for low-light image enhancement. In: Proceedings of the IEEE/CVF Conference on Computer Vision and Pattern Recognition, pp. 1780–1789 (2020)
29. Zhu, J.Y., Park, T., Isola, P., Efros, A.A.: Unpaired image-to-image translation using cycle-consistent adversarial networks. In: Proceedings of the IEEE International Conference on Computer Vision, pp. 2223–2232 (2017)
30. Wang, Z., Bovik, A.C., Sheikh, H.R., Simoncelli, E.P.: Image quality assessment: from error visibility to structural similarity. IEEE Trans. Image Process. **13**(4), 600–612 (2004)
31. Wang, Z., Simoncelli, E.P., Bovik, A.C.: Multiscale structural similarity for image quality assessment. In: The Thrity-Seventh Asilomar Conference on Signals, Systems & Computers, 2003. vol. 2, pp. 1398–1402. IEEE (2003)
32. Johnson, J., Alahi, A., Fei-Fei, L.: Perceptual losses for real-time style transfer and super-resolution. In: Leibe, B., Matas, J., Sebe, N., Welling, M. (eds.) ECCV 2016, Part II. LNCS, vol. 9906, pp. 694–711. Springer, Cham (2016). https://doi.org/10.1007/978-3-319-46475-6_43
33. RichardWebster, B., Anthony, S.E., Scheirer, W.J.: Psyphy: a psychophysics driven evaluation framework for visual recognition. IEEE Trans. Pattern Anal. Mach. Intell. **41**(9), 2280–2286 (2018)
34. Liu, J., Xu, D., Yang, W., Fan, M., Huang, H.: Benchmarking low-light image enhancement and beyond. Int. J. Comput. Vision **129**, 1153–1184 (2021)
35. Dong, X., Pang, Y., Wen, J.: Fast efficient algorithm for enhancement of low lighting video. In: ACM SIGGRAPH 2010 Posters, pp. 1–1 (2010)

GLCANet: Context Attention for Infrared Small Target Detection

Rui Liu[1,2], Qiankun Liu[2], Xiaoyong Wang[2(✉)], and Ying Fu[1,2]

[1] Yangtze Delta Region Academy of Beijing Institute of Technology,
Jiaxing 314019, China
[2] MIIT Key Laboratory of Complex-field Intelligent Sensing,
Beijing Institute of Technology, Beijing 100081, China
{liurui20,liuqk3,wangxiaoyong,fuying}@bit.edu.cn

Abstract. Infrared small target detection (IRSTD) refers to extracting small targets from infrared images with noisy interference and blurred background. Due to their small size and low contrast in the image, infrared targets are easily overwhelmed, which requires the network to have a wider receptive field for images and better ability to process local information. How to extract contextual information simply and efficiently remains challenging. In this paper, we propose a global and local context attention network (GLCANet), where the global context extraction module (GCEM) and the local context attention module (LCAM) are devised to address this problem. Specifically, GCEM transforms the feature map from the spatial domain to the frequency domain for feature extraction. Since updating a single value in the frequency domain affects all raw data globally, GCEM enables the network to consider the global context at an early stage and obtain a wider receptive field. LCAM fuses multiple layers of features, where we devise a local context-oriented down-sampling block (LCDB). LCDB transforms the planar dimension of the original feature map into the spatial dimension, which can extract more local contextual information while down-sampling the feature. Experiments on public datasets demonstrate the superiority of our method over representative state-of-the-art IRSTD methods.

Keywords: infrared image · target detection · contextual information

1 Introduction

Infrared small target detection (IRSTD) is widely used in various fields, including military reconnaissance [1,2], security monitoring [3], fire early warning [4,5] and so on. Different from general visible light target detection, there are several difficulties in infrared small target detection: 1)Dim: Since infrared images usually have a lot of noise and background clutter, small targets are not obvious in the image and are easily overwhelmed by the background. 2)Small: The size of the target is very small, accounting for less than 0.15% of the entire image.

L. Fang et al. (Eds.): CICAI 2023, LNAI 14473, pp. 244–255, 2024.
https://doi.org/10.1007/978-981-99-8850-1_20

3)Changeable shape: The shape and size of infrared small targets will change in different scenes.

To detect small infrared targets, various IRSTD methods have been proposed. Typical methods include filter based methods [6–8], local information based methods [9,10] and low-rank based methods [11,12]. These methods have some limitations in complex backgrounds, target changes, low contrast and noise processing, etc.

Different from these typical methods, deep learning based methods achieve better performance due to their unique characteristics,*e.g.*, data-driven learning, automatic feature learning, and end-to-end learning. Among them, CNN-based methods are developing most rapidly. Liu *et al.* [13] proposed the pioneer CNN-based method for IRSTD. After this, the work of Wang *et al.* [14] achieved a balance between miss detection and false alarm. However, small and dim infrared targets are easily overwhelmed by noise, background interference, and other similar hotspots, which requires the network to have a wider receptive field for images and a better ability to process local information. Dai *et al.* proposed ACM-Net [15] and ALCNet [20] to leverage contextual information, which achieved good performance. Subsequently, lots of methods focusing on the extraction of contextual information have been proposed [16–19,21–24]. When extracting global contextual information, the receptive field of these module-based methods depends too much on the deepening of the network level, and cannot effectively extract global contextual information in the early stage, leading to the failure to achieve good performance. Meanwhile, global contextual information is easily lost during feature conduction in deep networks, leading to the inaccurate positioning of small targets. As for the extraction of local context information, deepening the network tends to lead to information loss, and complex modules also perform poorly. How to extract contextual information simply and efficiently remains challenging.

To address this problem, we propose a global and local context attention network (GLCANet) with two key modules. First, we devise a global context extraction module (GCEM) to efficiently extract global contextual information at an early stage. Specifically, GCEM transforms the feature map from the spatial domain to the frequency domain for feature extraction. Since updating a single value in the frequency domain affects all raw data globally, GCEM can effectively extract global information at any layer in the network, which enables the network to consider the global context from early layers and obtain a wider receptive field. Then, we devise a local context attention module (LCAM) to extract more local contextual information. LCAM fuses multiple layers of features, where we devise a local context-oriented down-sampling block (LCDB). LCDB transforms the planar dimension of the original feature map into the spatial dimension, which can extract more local contextual information while down-sampling the feature. By combining GCEM and LCAM in the network, the contextual information of the target is efficiently extracted. Results on the two public datasets of IRSTD-1k [29] and NUAA-SIRST [15] demonstrate that our GLCANet outperforms other SOTA methods on metrics intersection over union (IoU) ratio, probability detection (P_d) rate and false-alarm (F_a) rate.

The main contributions of this paper are summarized as follows:

- We propose a global context extraction module which can extract global contextual information at any layer in the network and more accurately locate small infrared targets.
- We propose a local context attention module to effectively extract more local contextual information and obtain a more complete target shape.
- Experiments on the two public datasets of IRSTD-1k and NUAA-SIRST demonstrate the superior performance of our method.

2   Related Work

2.1   Infrared Small Target Detection

So far, various IRSTD methods have been proposed. Typical methods include filter based methods [6–8], local information based methods [9,10] and low-rank based methods [11,12]. These traditional methods have some limitations in complex backgrounds, target changes, low contrast and noise processing, etc.

In contrast, deep learning based methods are characterized by automatic feature learning, high-level feature representation, large-scale data training, contextual information utilization, and end-to-end learning. This leads to better performance of CNN-based methods on IRSTD. Liu *et al.* [13] proposed a multilayer perception (MLP) network, which is the pioneer CNN-based method for IRSTD. After this, the work of Wang *et al.* [14] achieved a balance between miss detection and false alarm.

Although these methods improve the detection effect of infrared small targets, the loss of small target information remains, which is limited by noise and clutter interference in infrared images and information loss during feature extraction in CNN-based methods.

2.2   Global Contextual Information

Researchers have done a lot of work to extract the global contextual information of infrared small targets. An asymmetric contextual modulation module is proposed by Dai *et al.* [15] to extract multi-layer contextual information. Zhang *et al.* [16] computed global associations between semantics through joint work between multiple modules. However, the receptive field of these methods depends too much on the deepening of the network level, and cannot effectively extract global contextual information in the early stage, leading to the failure to achieve good performance. Wu *et al.* [18] proposed a network with a skip-connected feature pyramid network (SCFPN) to fuse small object features and contextual multi-scale features. Ju *et al.* [19] proposed an end-to-end CNN-based target detector ISTDet to achieve a better trade-off between speed and accuracy. As a result, global contextual information is easily lost during feature conduction, leading to inaccurate positioning of small targets.

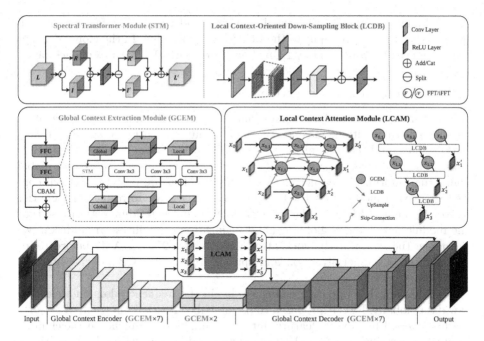

Fig. 1. Overview of the proposed GLCANet and the structure of GCEM and LCAM.

2.3 Local Contextual Information

Existing methods for extracting local contextual information are mainly classified into module based methods and network based methods. Dai *et al.* [20] proposed a cross-layer bottom-up local attentional modulation (BLAM) module. Inspired by this, Tong *et al.* [21] proposed a BAA block to achieve dynamic perception of fine details. Yu *et al.* [22] proposed a simplified bilinear interpolation attention module (SBAM) to speed up inference. However, when the network level deepens, small infrared targets are easily overwhelmed by noise and clutter, and these specific modules achieve poor performance. There are also some works trying to design networks for local information. Qi *et al.* [23] usesd a U-Net with skip connections to obtain low-level local details of small targets. Lv *et al.* [24] proposed a specially crafted feature pyramid aggregation module to process local information. Unfortunately, these complex modules do not efficiently extract local information after greatly increasing the amount of computation, not achieving the expected good performance.

3 Method

3.1 Overall Architecture

We show an overview of our GLCANet in Fig. 1. As can be seen, the network backbone is a U-Net structure [25]. After expanding the number of channels, the infrared image is input to the global context encoder part. The features of each layer in the encoder are input to the LCAM for processing. In the global decoder part, the features processed by LCAM are fused with the features of each layer.

3.2 Global Context Extraction Module

Infrared images have a lot of noise and clutter, and small targets are often submerged. In addition, most of the high-resolution feature maps are useless backgrounds, and the recognition targets only occupy a small part of them, thus wasting a lot of computation. All of these require the network to extract global contextual information earlier. To solve this problem, we propose a global context extraction module (GCEM). As shown in Fig. 1, we introduce fast Fourier convolution [26] (FFC) to replace the convolution in the residual network, so that the module has stronger global context acquisition capabilities. In addition, we introduce the convolution block attention module [27] (CBAM) before residual addition. Channel attention and spatial attention in CBAM can suppress unnecessary regional features.

Considering that updating a single value in the frequency domain affects all raw data globally, FFC is proposed to use global contextual information at early feature layers. FFC divides features into local and global branches at the channel level for processing. The local branch is processed by conventional convolutions, while the global branch is processed by Fourier transform through a spectral transformer module (STM). The operation steps of STM are as follows:

a) Apply a 2-D FFT operation to the input tensor $\mathbf{L}$:

$$\mathbf{R}^{H \times \frac{W}{2} \times C}, \mathbf{I}^{H \times \frac{W}{2} \times C} = FFT(\mathbf{L}^{H \times W \times C}), \tag{1}$$

where $FFT(\cdot)$ denotes the fast Fourier transform. $\mathbf{R}$ and $\mathbf{I}$ are the real part and imaginary part of the result.

b) Apply 1×1 convolution, batch normalization and ReLU on $\mathbf{L}_1$ obtained by concatenating the real part and the imaginary part along the channel dimension:

$$\mathbf{L}_2^{H \times \frac{W}{2} \times 2C} = ReLU(Bn(Conv(\mathbf{L}_1^{H \times \frac{W}{2} \times 2C}))), \tag{2}$$

where $ReLU(\cdot)$ denotes the ReLU function. $Bn(\cdot)$ and $Conv(\cdot)$ denote batch normalization and convolutional layers, respectively.

c) Apply the inverse 2-D FFT operation to the re-split real part $\mathbf{R}'$ and imaginary part $\mathbf{I}'$ from $\mathbf{L}_2$:

$$\mathbf{L}'^{H \times W \times C} = iFFT(\mathbf{R}'^{H \times \frac{W}{2} \times C}, \mathbf{I}'^{H \times \frac{W}{2} \times C}), \tag{3}$$

where $iFFT(\cdot)$ denotes the inverse fast Fourier transform.

After FFC processing, the feature map integrates more contextual information, but not all information is conducive to the detection of small targets. To this end, we introduce a convolution block attention module (CBAM) to combine the channel and spatial attention of the feature map, so as to strengthen the effective feature contribution while weakening the invalid.

3.3 Local Context Attention Module

GCEM's extraction of global context provides more accurate positioning for small targets, but good detection results also require a more complete target shape. The simple skip connection in the U-Net structure cannot effectively pay attention to the local context for small and dim infrared targets, leading to the loss of shape information. To solve the problem, a local context attention module (LCAM) is proposed to extract more local contextual information. As shown in Fig. 1, the LCAM fuses multiple layers of features, where we devise a local context-oriented down-sampling block (LCDB). LCDB transforms the planar dimension of the original feature map into the spatial dimension, which can extract more local contextual information while down-sampling the feature. The operation of LCDB can be expressed as:

$$\mathbf{R}' = ReLU(SPD(\mathbf{R}) + Short(\mathbf{R})), \tag{4}$$

where $ReLU(\cdot)$ denotes the ReLU function. $Short(\cdot)$ stands for a 1×1 convolution with a stride of 2 to retain more discriminative feature information. $SPD(\cdot)$ [28] represents a structure with two convolutional layers to convert the plane information of the feature map into depth information, and can be expressed as:

$$\mathbf{R}^* = Conv_1(\mathbf{R}), \tag{5}$$

$$SPD(\mathbf{R}) = Conv_2(ReLU(Cat(\mathbf{R}_{0,0}^*, \mathbf{R}_{0,1}^*, \mathbf{R}_{1,0}^*, \mathbf{R}_{1,1}^*))), \tag{6}$$

where $Conv_1(\cdot)$ and $Conv_2(\cdot)$ denote convolutional layer. $Cat(\cdot)$ denotes the concatenation operation. $\mathbf{R}_{0,0}^*, \mathbf{R}_{0,1}^*, \mathbf{R}_{1,0}^*, \mathbf{R}_{1,1}^* \in \mathbf{R}^{*H \times W \times C}$, and $\mathbf{R}_{0,0}^*$ can be obtained as:

$$\mathbf{R}^* = \begin{bmatrix} a_{11} & a_{12} & \cdots & a_{1j} \\ a_{21} & a_{22} & \cdots & a_{2j} \\ \vdots & \vdots & \ddots & \vdots \\ a_{i1} & a_{i2} & \cdots & a_{ij} \end{bmatrix}, \mathbf{R}^*{}_{0,0} = \begin{bmatrix} a_{11} & a_{13} & \cdots & a_{1(j-1)} \\ a_{33} & a_{33} & \cdots & a_{3(j-1)} \\ \vdots & \vdots & \ddots & \vdots \\ a_{(i-1)1} & a_{(i-1)3} & \cdots & a_{(i-1)(j-1)} \end{bmatrix}. \tag{7}$$

Compared with interpolation, this operation can retain more local context information of small targets. As can be seen, although LCDB is a learnable block, we use the same LCDB block at the same resolution layer. Such a setting is inspired by the attention mechanism. When down-sampling the feature map of the same layer, the features that need to be paid attention are roughly the same. Therefore we choose to use the same LCDB to down-sample the same layer features.

4 Experiment

4.1 Datasets and Evaluation Metrics

Datasets. We choose the IRSTD-1k [29] and NUAA-SIRST [15] as experimental datasets. IRSTD-1k includes 1,001 infrared images, while NUAA-SIRST contains 427 infrared images. For each dataset, we take 50% of the images as the training set, 30% of them as the validation set, and 20% of them as the test set.

Table 1. Quantitative comparisons with state-of-the-art methods.

Method	IRSTD-1k			NUAA-SIRST		
	IoU	P_d	F_a	IoU	P_d	F_a
Top-Hat [8]	10.06	75.11	1432	7.143	79.84	1012
Max-Median [30]	6.998	65.21	59.73	4.172	69.20	55.33
WSLCM [31]	3.452	72.44	6619	1.158	77.95	5446
TLLCM [32]	3.311	77.39	6738	1.029	79.09	5899
IPI [11]	27.92	81.37	16.18	25.67	85.55	11.47
NRAM [33]	15.25	70.68	16.93	12.16	74.52	13.85
RIPT [34]	14.11	77.55	28.31	11.05	79.08	22.61
PSTNN [35]	24.57	71.99	35.26	22.40	77.95	29.11
MSLSTIPT [36]	11.43	79.03	1524	10.30	82.13	1131
MDvsFA [14]	49.50	82.11	80.33	60.30	89.35	56.35
ACM [15]	60.97	90.58	21.78	72.33	96.33	**9.325**
ALCNet [20]	62.05	92.19	31.56	74.31	97.34	20.21
Ours	**67.97**	**93.88**	**12.22**	**78.24**	**99.98**	10.29

Evaluation Metrics. We evaluate the proposed GCEM and LCDM modules using several common metrics as follows:

a) *Intersection over Union (IoU)*: It is the ratio of the intersecting area to the union area:

$$IoU = \frac{A_{inter}}{A_{union}}, \tag{8}$$

where A_{inter} and A_{union} denote the intersection areas and union areas.

b) *Probability of Detection (P_d)*: It is the ratio of the number of correctly predicted targets N_{pred} to the total number of targets N_{total}:

$$P_d = \frac{N_{pred}}{N_{total}}. \tag{9}$$

c) *False-Alarm Rate (F_a)*: It is the ratio of the false predicted target pixels P_{false} to all pixels in the image P_{all}:

$$F_a = \frac{P_{false}}{P_{all}}. \tag{10}$$

4.2 Implementation Details

AdaGrad is adopted as the optimizer and we set the learning rate to be constant at 0.05. We set the training epoch and batch size of the model to 500 and 4, respectively. ALCNet [20], ACMNet [15], and MDvsFA [14] are selected as representative CNN-based methods for comparison. For traditional methods, Top-Hat [8], Max-Median [30], WSLCM [31], TLLCM [32], IPI [11], NRAM [33], RIPT [34], PSTNN [35], and MSLSTIPT [36] are selected.

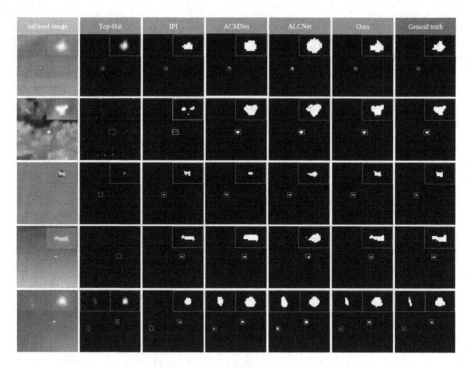

Fig. 2. Visual comparison of detection performance on several representative infrared images. The box in the upper right corner is a close-up view of the target. Correctly detected targets, missed detected targets, and falsely detected targets are framed by red, blue, and yellow boxes, respectively. (Color figure online)

4.3   Quantitative Results

As can be seen from Table. 1, compared to SOTA methods, our method performs best on most metrics on both datasets. Traditional methods have limited ability in challenging cases and thus perform poorly. Moreover, as can be seen from the results, other CNN-based methods do not pay enough attention to contextual information, resulting in inaccurate positioning and shape detection of the target. In contrast, the IoU of our method reaches as high as 67.97% on the IRSTD-1k dataset, which means that our method can detect the object shape more completely. The performance on P_d and F_a also demonstrates that our method is more accurate for target localization.

4.4   Visual Results

We selected several representative infrared images in the NUAA-SIRST dataset to compare the visual effects of different methods. As shown in Fig. 2, traditional methods frequently produce false detection and missed detection, other CNN-based methods cannot effectively use contextual information, which leads to insufficient target localization accuracy and loss of edge information. However, our method can accurately locate the target and detect a more complete target shape. We attribute this success to the unique modules, *i.e.* the GCEM and LCAM, where the former can effectively extract global contextual information and fuse it into features to accurately locate small targets, and the latter can take advantage of local contextual information after localization to maintain the details of small targets.

Table 2. Ablation study of the GCEM and the LCAM.

Modules	IoU	P_d	F_a
UNet	64.98	89.46	15.71
UNet+GCEM	66.89	90.82	**9.03**
UNet+LCAM	66.71	89.22	9.11
UNet+GCEM+LCAM	**67.97**	**93.88**	12.22

Table 3. Ablation study of FFC blocks in GCEM.

Blocks	IoU	P_d	F_a
Conv+Conv	65.76	90.13	12.98
FFC+Conv	66.48	90.14	9.34
Conv+FFC	65.95	**91.50**	13.06
FFC+FFC	**66.89**	90.82	**9.03**

Table 4. Ablation study of CBAM in GCEM.

Methods	IoU	P_d	F_a
GCEM w/o CBAM	64.99	88.44	12.45
GCEM	**66.89**	**90.82**	**9.03**

4.5   Ablation Study

To investigate the effectiveness of the proposed GCEM and LCAM, we conduct several ablation studies on the IRSTD-1k dataset. As can be seen from Table 2, GCEM and LCAM each improve the model performance, and using both of them achieves the best balance of detection metrics.

Impact of GCEM. We investigate the influence of different numbers and positions of FFC blocks in GCEM. As shown in Table 3, the FFC block has a significant improvement effect. Specifically, GCEM achieves the best balance among all metrics when using two FFC blocks at the same time. Moreover, as shown in Table 4, when not using CBAM, GCEM produces more false predictions, and the IoU is significantly reduced. We choose two FFC blocks with CBAM as the default setting.

Impact of LCAM. We also performe ablation study on the proposed LCAM. As shown in Table 5, when not using GCEM, LCAM produces more false predictions and achieves poor performance on the *IoU* metric. The *IoU* is also significantly reduced when not using LCDB. The best balance is delivered when using both of them. Meanwhile, as can be seen from Table 6, the one-to-many connection of LCDB achieves the best balance among all metrics. We choose to use GCEM to extract features and use LCDB in a one-to-many manner in LCAM as the default setting.

Table 5. Ablation study of the blocks in LCAM.

Methods	IoU	P_d	F_a
LCAM w/o GCEM	64.67	**91.84**	24.82
LCAM w/o LCDB	65.21	89.45	**6.91**
LCAM	**66.71**	89.22	9.11

Table 6. Ablation study of the connection mode of LCDB in LCAM.

Modes	IoU	P_d	F_a
One-to-One	66.06	**90.14**	**8.20**
One-to-Many	**66.71**	89.22	9.11

5   Conclusion

In this paper, we propose a novel GLCANet to accurately locate small infrared targets while preserving more shape details. Specifically, we devise two novel modules, *i.e.*, the global context extraction module and local context attention module to better exploit contextual information, where the former uses Fourier transform to extract global contextual information at an early stage and the latter fuses multiple layers of features paying more attention to local contextual information. Extensive experiments on public datasets verify the effectiveness and superiority of our GLCANet over SOTA methods.

Acknowledgment. This work was supported by the National Natural Science Foundation of China under Grants (62171038, 62171042, and 62088101), and the R&D Program of Beijing Municipal Education Commission (Grant No. KZ202211417048).

References

1. Hudson, R.D., Hudson, J.W.: The military applications of remote sensing by infrared. Proc. IEEE **63**(1), 104–128 (1975)

2. Harney, R.C.: Military applications of coherent infrared radar. In: Society of Photo-Optical Instrumentation Engineers on Physics and Technology of Coherent Infrared Radar I (1982)
3. Huang, H., Yu, H., Xu, H., et al.: Near infrared spectroscopy for on/in-line monitoring of quality in foods and beverages: a review. J. Food Eng. **87**(3), 303–313 (2008)
4. Robinson, J.M.: Fire from space: global fire evaluation using infrared remote sensing. Int. J. Remote Sens. **12**(1), 3–24 (1991)
5. Arrue, B.C., Ollero, A., De Dios, J.R.M.: An intelligent system for false alarm reduction in infrared forest-fire detection. IEEE Intell. Syst. Appl. **15**(3), 64–73 (2000)
6. Jia-xiong, P., Wen-lin, Z.: Infrared background suppression for segmenting and detecting small target. Acta Electron. Sin. **27**(12), 47–51 (1999)
7. Azimi-Sadjadi, M.R., Pan, H.: Two-dimensional block diagonal LMS adaptive filtering. IEEE Trans. Signal Process. **42**(9), 2420–2429 (1994)
8. Bai, X., Zhou, F.: Analysis of new top-hat transformation and the application for infrared dim small target detection. Pattern Recogn. **43**(6), 2145–2156 (2010)
9. Chen, C.L.P., Li, H., Wei, Y., et al.: A local contrast method for small infrared target detection. IEEE Trans. Geosci. Remote Sens. **52**(1), 574–581 (2013)
10. Deng, H., Sun, X., Liu, M., et al.: Infrared small-target detection using multiscale gray difference weighted image entropy. IEEE Trans. Aerosp. Electron. Syst. **52**(1), 60–72 (2016)
11. Gao, C., Meng, D., Yang, Y., et al.: Infrared patch-image model for small target detection in a single image. IEEE Trans. Image Process. **22**(12), 4996–5009 (2013)
12. Wang, X., Peng, Z., Kong, D., et al.: Infrared dim and small target detection based on stable multisubspace learning in heterogeneous scene. IEEE Trans. Geosci. Remote Sens. **55**(10), 5481–5493 (2017)
13. Liu, M., Du, H., Zhao, Y., et al.: Image small target detection based on deep learning with SNR controlled sample generation. Curr. Trends Comput. Sci. Mech. Autom. **1**, 211–220 (2017)
14. Wang, H., Zhou, L., Wang, L.: Miss detection vs. false alarm: adversarial learning for small object segmentation in infrared images. In: Proceedings of the IEEE/CVF on International Conference on Computer Vision, pp. 8508–8517 (2019)
15. Dai, Y., Wu, Y., Zhou, F., et al.: Asymmetric contextual modulation for infrared small target detection. In: Proceedings of the IEEE/CVF on Winter Conference on Applications of Computer Vision, pp. 950–959(2021)
16. Zhang, T., Li, L., Cao, S., et al.: Attention-guided pyramid context networks for detecting infrared small target under complex background. IEEE Trans. Aerosp. Electron. Syst. **59**, 1–13 (2023)
17. Hong, Y., Wei, K., Chen, L., et al.: Crafting object detection in very low light. In: Proceedings of the British Machine Vision Virtual Conference, pp. 3 (2021)
18. Wu, D., Cao, L., Zhou, P., et al.: Infrared small-target detection based on radiation characteristics with a multimodal feature fusion network. Remote Sens. **14**(15), 3570 (2022)
19. Ju, M., Luo, J., Liu, G., et al.: ISTDet: an efficient end-to-end neural network for infrared small target detection. Infrared Phys. Technol. **114**, 103659 (2021)
20. Dai, Y., Wu, Y., Zhou, F., et al.: Attentional local contrast networks for infrared small target detection. IEEE Trans. Geosci. Remote Sens. **59**(11), 9813–9824 (2021)
21. Tong, X., Sun, B., Wei, J., et al.: EAAU-Net: enhanced asymmetric attention U-Net for infrared small target detection. Remote Sens. **13**(16), 3200 (2021)

22. Yu, C., Liu, Y., Wu, S., et al.: Pay attention to local contrast learning networks for infrared small target detection. IEEE Geosci. Remote Sens. Lett. **19**, 1–5 (2022)
23. Qi, M., Liu, L., Zhuang, S., et al.: FTC-Net: fusion of transformer and CNN features for infrared small target detection. IEEE J. Sel. Top. Appl. Earth Observations Remote Sens. **15**, 8613–8623 (2022)
24. Lv, G., Dong, L., Liang, J., et al.: Novel asymmetric pyramid aggregation network for infrared dim and small target detection. Remote Sens. **14**(22), 5643 (2022)
25. Ronneberger, O., Fischer, P., Brox, T.: U-Net: convolutional networks for biomedical image segmentation. In: International Conference on Medical Image Computing and Computer-Assisted Intervention, pp. 234–241 (2015)
26. Chi, L., Jiang, B., Mu, Y.: Fast fourier convolution. Adv. Neural. Inf. Process. Syst. **33**, 4479–4488 (2020)
27. Woo, S., Park, J., Lee, J.Y., et al.: CBAM: convolutional block attention module. In: Proceedings of the European Conference on Computer Vision, pp. 3–19 (2018)
28. Sunkara, R., Luo, T.: No more strided convolutions or pooling: a new CNN building block for low-resolution images and small objects. In: European Conference on Machine Learning and Principles and Practice of Knowledge Discovery in Databases, pp. 443–459 (2022)
29. Zhang, M., Zhang, R., Yang, Y., et al.: ISNET: shape matters for infrared small target detection. In: Proceedings of the IEEE/CVF Conference on Computer Vision and Pattern Recognition, pp. 867–876 (2022)
30. Deshpande, S.D., Er, M.H., Venkateswarlu, R., et al.: Max-mean and max-median filters for detection of small targets. In: Society of Photo-Optical Instrumentation Engineers on Signal and Data Processing of Small Targets (1999)
31. Han, J., Moradi, S., Faramarzi, I., et al.: Infrared small target detection based on the weighted strengthened local contrast measure. IEEE Geosci. Remote Sens. Lett. **18**(9), 1670–1674 (2020)
32. Han, J., Moradi, S., Faramarzi, I., et al.: A local contrast method for infrared small-target detection utilizing a tri-layer window. IEEE Geosci. Remote Sens. Lett. **17**(10), 1822–1826 (2019)
33. Zhang, L., Peng, L., Zhang, T., et al.: Infrared small target detection via nonconvex rank approximation minimization joint l 2, 1 norm. Remote Sens. **10**(11), 1821 (2018)
34. Dai, Y., Wu, Y.: Reweighted infrared patch-tensor model with both nonlocal and local priors for single-frame small target detection. J. Sel. Top. Appl. Earth Observations Remote Sens. **10**(8), 3752–3767 (2017)
35. Zhang, L., Peng, Z.: Infrared small target detection based on partial sum of the tensor nuclear norm. Remote Sens. **11**(4), 382 (2019)
36. Sun, Y., Yang, J., An, W.: Infrared dim and small target detection via multiple subspace learning and spatial-temporal patch-tensor model. IEEE Trans. Geosci. Remote Sens. **59**(5), 3737–3752 (2020)

Fast Point Cloud Registration for Urban Scenes via Pillar-Point Representation

Siyuan Gu and Ruqi Huang$^{(\boxtimes)}$

Tsinghua Shenzhen International Graduate School, Tsinghua -Berkeley Shenzhen Institute, Shenzhen, China
ruqihuang@sz.tsinghua.edu.cn

Abstract. Efficient and robust point cloud registration is an essential task for real-time applications in urban scenes. Most methods introduce keypoint sampling or detection to achieve real-time registration of large-scale point clouds. Recent advances in keypoint-free methods have succeeded in alleviating the bias and error introduced by keypoint detection via coarse-to-fine dense matching strategies. Nevertheless, the running time performance of such a strategy turns out to be far inferior to keypoint methods. This paper proposes a novel framework that adopts a pillar-point representation based feature extraction pipeline and a three-stage semi-dense keypoint matching scheme. The scheme includes global coarse matching, anchor generation and local dense matching for efficient correspondence matching. Experiments on large-scale outdoor datasets, including KITTI and NuScenes, demonstrate that the proposed feature representation and matching framework achieve real-time inference and high registration recall.

Keywords: Point cloud registration · Pillar-point representation · Semi-dense keypoint matching

1 Introduction

Point cloud registration plays a fundamental role in various applications including indoor scene reconstruction, drone mapping, autonomous driving, to name a few. In general, it aims to estimate the optimal rigid transformation between a pair of unaligned point clouds. Early axiomatic approaches cast point registration as minimizing certain types of geometric residuals (e.g., Euclidean distance [21], or normal distribution [18]). On the other hand, recent trends in learning-based methods [2,6,10,16] follow a generalized correspondence-based workflow, which consists of feature extraction, keypoint sampling, correspondence matching, outlier rejection, and pose estimation.

This work was supported in part by the National Natural Science Foundation of China under contract No. 62171256, in part by Shenzhen Key Laboratory of next-generation interactive media innovative technology (No. ZDSYS20210623092001004).

When dealing with large-scale point clouds, such as those generated by scanning devices like LiDARs at a rate of hundreds of thousands of points per second, most axiomatic methods and learning-based methods alleviate computational burden by utilizing keypoint sampling. In particular, modern learning-based methods typically obtain keypoints through either plain Furthest Point Sampling (FPS) [16] or learned saliency [2]. However, keypoint-based methods are not only influenced by the sampling scheme but also often rely on the assumption that a sufficient number of repeatable keypoints across input point clouds are available. Methods like [2,12] attempt to enhance keypoint repeatability by employing deep learning-based keypoint detectors, but they still face challenges associated with detection errors.

By contrast, the recent keypoint-free paradigm [19,27] proposes to perform dense point matching in a coarse-to-fine manner. This paradigm tackles the challenge of dense matching in large-scale point clouds by breaking point clouds down into local dense matching within multiple matched patches (i.e., superpoints). The keypoint-free approach has demonstrated excellent performance in terms of accuracy and robustness. Despite the employment of hierarchical matching strategies and the avoidance of time-consuming RANSAC pose estimators, these keypoint-free methods have not yet achieved runtime efficiency comparable to methods that utilize keypoint sampling or detection [7,16] in large-scale outdoor scenes.

Motivated by the aforementioned observations, we propose a pipeline that incorporates a novel matching scheme, which involves sampling anchor points on only one side of input point cloud pairs, referred to as semi-dense keypoint sampling. The corresponding candidates to anchor points are searched in feature space and the coarse matching stage can help to reduce the search space to ensure robustness. Virtual corresponding points as weighted sum of candidates are generated and used as centers of mini patches in local fine matching. Compared to keypoint-free methods, anchor correspondence generation narrows the distance between mini patches, leading to a higher inlier ratio and smaller neighborhood size.

Experimental results demonstrate that our pipeline achieves comparable registration performance with the state-of-the-art methods, including both keypoint-based and keypoint-free approaches. Additionally, our pipeline exhibits excellent generalization performance when applied to unseen scenes. Furthermore, as a pipeline that eliminates the need for keypoint detection, we significantly improve the runtime efficiency by a large margin, typically performing four times faster than the keypoint-free counterpart [19].

The main contributions of our work are listed as follows:

- An efficient and robust registration network for large-scale urban point clouds based on pillar-point representations.
- A three-stage correspondence matching scheme with semi-dense anchor correspondence generation.
- Extensive experiments on large-scale urban datasets have proved the high efficiency of our proposed network with comparable registration accuracy.

2   Related Works

Learned 3D Feature Descriptor. Early works in 3D feature learning most belong to patch-based methods. [28] proposes the representative 3DMatch benchmark and a neural network utilizing voxel-based Truncated Distance Function as local patch descriptors. [1] proposes 3D cylindrical convolution layers to extract features from spherically voxelized point cloud. [6] first suggests to learn dense descriptors (FCGF) from full voxelized point cloud via sparse 3D convolutions and gains enormous speedup. [26] proposes KPConv which defines convolution on precomputed kernel points to adapt to irregularity of point clouds. KPConv is utilized by several registration methods including [2,19,27].

Works in object detection area also propose some generic represent learning concepts. [14,23,25] construct feature extract modules with keypoint-to-voxel set abstraction. This kind of modules first query keypoint features via trilinear interpolation from multi-scale voxel features or directly from independent point MLP and then fuse all the features. [11] and related [22] divide scenes into pillar structure with infinite length in vertical direction and achieve significant breakthrough in inference speed.

Correspondence-based Registration Methods. Point cloud registration methods which utilize a common correspondence step can be summarized into two main categories, *i.e.*, with or without keypoints. The former, such as [13,16], use uniform grid sampling or farthest point sampling to extract a few interest points and construct a keypoint set for training. Similar to our work, [7] suggests a pillar-based method to construct patches based on filtered salient keypoints and utilizes graph neural network to search correspondences. These methods reduce storage for interest points from the beginning but are easily influenced by keypoint sampling strategies.

On the other hand, keypoint-free methods including [6,27], inspired by classical image matching method [20], perform hierarchical matching on point cloud. They utilize patch overlaps to supervise superpoint matching and solve patchwise point matching with optimal transport techniques. Though they can achieve more stable results than the keypoint-based counterparts, they suffer from efficiency issue when the input point clouds become larger.

3   Methodology

Given a pair of input clouds denoted as $\mathcal{P} \in \mathbb{R}^{m \times 3}$ and $\mathcal{Q} \in \mathbb{R}^{n \times 3}$ respectively, we aim to estimate rigid rotation $\mathbf{R} \in SO(3)$ and translation $\mathbf{t} \in \mathbb{R}^3$ that align $\mathcal{P}$ and $\mathcal{Q}$. As shown in Fig. 1, our pipeline first learns a two-scale feature representation with a shared encoder-decoder, then solves for point correspondences and finally predicts rigid transformation.

3.1   Pillar-Point Based Feature Extractor

Pillar Feature Embedding. Common scenes perceived from ground LiDAR have such uniqueness that the variances of the roll and pitch components of transformations are significantly smaller than that of the yaw component, or $Var(\theta_z) \gg Var(\theta_x), Var(\theta_y)$ under Euler angle form. Therefore the pillar-based feature embedding, previously utilized in [11], is introduced into our registration pipeline for efficiency.

A pillar structure is organized by uniformly dividing the whole scene into regular grids with full height in z-axis. For each pillar with center $\mathbf{x}_c^i = (x_c^i, y_c^i, z_c^i)$, point set $\{\mathbf{x}_j^i\}$ and its arithmetic mean $\overline{\mathbf{x}}^i\}$, we calculate a 6-dimensional vector $F_{pt} = \{x_j^i - x_c^i, y_j^i - y_c^i, z_j^i - z_c^i, x_j^i - \overline{x}^i, y_j^i - \overline{y}^i, z_j^i - \overline{z}^i\}$ as the initial input for every single point in the pillar. Then a two-layer shared MLP is applied to encode the statistics into pillar features $F_{pl} = \mathrm{MLP}(F_{pt})$. In the embedding process, dynamic voxelization strategy from [30] is adopted in our pillar partition step and hence no points are truncated.

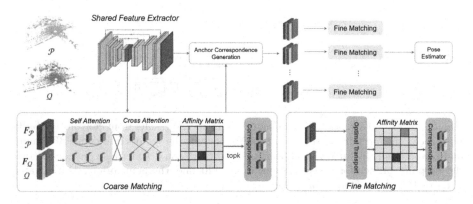

Fig. 1. The proposed point cloud registration pipeline is mainly composed a shared feature extractor, a hierarchical feature scheme and a pose estimator. The shared pillar-point based feature extractor extracts coarse-scale feature (marked in red) in downsampling and fine-scale feature (marked in purple) in upsampling. The feature matching scheme is composed of three stages, namely coarse matching, anchor generation and fine matching, which generate correspondences at different levels. The details of proposed feature matching scheme is stated in Sect. 3.2. Finally, a pose estimator based on an iterative proposal and verification scheme filters out outliers and outputs final transformation. (Color figure online)

Convolutional Backbone. We adopt a Residual U-Net backbone like that in [6], which is built with sparse 2D convolution block to aggregate pillar features. The backbone has two output features, coarse-level features F_c at the bottleneck of backbone and fine-level features F_f. It should be noticed that a proposed point feature decoder is appended to last convolutional layer to revert tensors located on 2D grids to point-wise features by interpolation.

Point Feature Decoder. In our case, a pillar contains multiple points, inconsistent to the output feature map F_{bev} of last convolutional layer. To convert the feature map into point-wise features F_f suitable for fine matching among points, we incorporate the concept of set abstraction in [14] to further increase the separability of points. The final point feature F_f is calculated by $F_f = \text{MLP}(\text{Concat}[\mathbf{x}, F_{pl}, F_{bev}])$. The grid set abstraction procedure is illustrated in Fig. 2. It simultaneously reserves the scalability of voxel/pillar-based methods and the compatibility with point-based methods.

3.2 Hierarchical Matching Scheme

Coarse Matching. Following [20], we adopt a transformer to learn patch features at a coarse-level. The transformer structure consists of a sequence of self- and cross- attention modules.

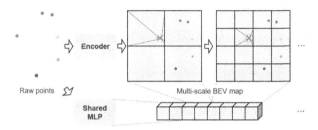

Fig. 2. Grid set abstraction based decoder. The middle results from convolution backbone are in the form of sparse 2D vectors. We convert the vectors into dense BEV maps and retract point features via bilinear interpolation. The decoder also includes a standalone point branch for compensation. In our pipeline, the point branch is integrated with MLP in pillar embedding layer.

We first aggregate coarse features F_c for each point cloud with a geometric-aware self-attention block. For attention mechanism, the query $\mathbf{Q}$, key $\mathbf{K}$ and value $\mathbf{V}$ by projecting input $\mathbf{x}_i, \mathbf{x}_j$ with learnable weight matrixs $\mathbf{W^Q}, \mathbf{W^K}, \mathbf{W^V} \in \mathbb{R}^{b \times b}$. The self attention matrix $\mathbf{A}_{SA}$ can be expressed as $\mathbf{A}_{SA} = \mathbf{Q}(\mathbf{K} + \mathbf{G})^T / \sqrt{b}$, where $\mathbf{G} = \mathbf{g} \cdot \mathbf{W^G}$ is projected geometric embedding. The output feature $F_{SA}^{\mathcal{P}}$ is calculated by $F_{SA}^{\mathcal{P}} = \mathbf{A}_{SA} \cdot \mathbf{V}$, where $\mathbf{A}_{SA}$ is first normalized by softmax function as in [19]. The updated feature $F_{SA}^{\mathcal{Q}}$ is calculated by the same formula. The proposed geometric embedding $\mathbf{g}$ serves as positional hints to enhance the self attention. For each point $\mathbf{x}$, its neighborhood embedding $\mathbf{g}$ is constructed by its nearest k neighbours $\{\mathbf{x_1}, ..., \mathbf{x_k}\}$.

$$\mathbf{g} = \text{MLP}(\text{Concat}[\|\mathbf{x}_i - \mathbf{x}\|, \angle(\mathbf{x}_i - \bar{\mathbf{x}}, \mathbf{x} - \bar{\mathbf{x}})/(2\pi)]). \tag{1}$$

The geometric embedding vector $\mathbf{g}$ is concatenated by Euclidean distance between $\mathbf{x}$ and its neighbours and angles with neighbourhood center $\bar{\mathbf{x}}$ as reference point.

The attention matrix of cross attention block is similarly computed as $\mathbf{A}_{CA}^{\mathcal{P}} = \mathbf{Q}^{\mathcal{P}}(\mathbf{K}^{\mathcal{Q}})^T/\sqrt{b}$, ,where we use subscripts $:^{\mathcal{P}},:^{\mathcal{Q}}$ to distinguish variables from two point clouds. The output cross attention feature $F_{CA}^{\mathcal{P}}$ is calculated as $F_{CA}^{\mathcal{P}} = \mathbf{A}_{CA}^{\mathcal{P}} \cdot \mathbf{V}^{\mathcal{Q}}$, where attention matrix is also first normalized by softmax function. The attention matrix $\mathbf{A}_{CA}^{\mathcal{Q}}$ and cross attention feature $F_{CA}^{\mathcal{Q}}$ is calculated in the symmetric formula.

After performing inter- and intra- point cloud attention aggregation, we got aggregated coarse-level feature $F_c'^{\mathcal{P}}$ and $F_c'^{\mathcal{Q}}$. The entries of similarity matrix $S' \in \mathbb{R}^{|\mathcal{P}| \times |\mathcal{Q}|}$ is computed as dual Softmax function of patch features. We refer readers to [19] for details. We select top N_c entries of similarity matrix S' with minimum values as confident sparse correspondences.

Anchor Correspondence Generation. Points in overlapping pillars tend to have larger spatial distribution compared to points in the knn-grouped node stated in previous works [19,27]. Therefore, we propose to sample anchor points inside sparse correspondences and adopt virtual correspondence generation inspired by HRegNet [16]. Figure 3 shows the scheme for generating a pair of anchors. First for each selected coarse pair $(P^{\mathcal{P}}, P^{\mathcal{Q}})$ in the coarse matching stage, we sample max to M_0 anchor points $\mathbf{X_q} \subset P^{\mathcal{Q}}$ per pair. Then for each anchor point $x_q \in \mathbf{X_q}$, we search for M_1 nearest points in feature space as candidates.

Next, we incorporate original point feature F_p, feature similarity F_d and structure similarity F_s to learn the attentive weights of candidate points. For calculation of feature similarity F_d, we use common cosine similarity $F_d = <F_p, F_p^i> / (|F_p| \cdot |F_p^i|)$. For calculation of structure similarity, we search for K nearest neighbours of anchor points $\mathbf{x}_i \in \mathbf{X_q}$ in sampled anchor points, denoted as $\{\mathbf{x}_k\}_{k=1}^K \subset \mathbf{X_q}$. We calculate the distances between x_i and x_i^j and also distances between their candidate points x_i^m, x_k^n. The entry d_{imk} of final structure similarity F_d is calculated by

$$d_{imk} = \min_n \left| \|\mathbf{x}_i - \mathbf{x}_k\|_2 - \|\mathbf{x}_i^m - \mathbf{x}_k^n\|_2 \right|. \tag{2}$$

Finally, we concatenate F_p, F_d, F_s and input them into a three-layer shared-MLP as HRegNet and SDMNet [15,16]. A maxpool and softmax layer is then applied to get final weights w_{ik} of candidate points. The final virtual correspondence $\mathbf{x}_i' \in \mathbf{X_v}$ is calculated as weighted sum of candidate points $\mathbf{x}_i' = \sum_k w_{ik}\mathbf{x}_k$. In addition, MLP and sigmoid function is applied to learned weights w_{ik} to get confidence score c_i for each pair of $(\mathbf{x}_i, \mathbf{x}_i')$. In testing stage, we utilize learned confidence score to filter anchor correspondences with confidence score below a predefined threshold c_0.

The output coordinates and confidence score of anchor correspondence generation module is respectively regularized by classification loss and probabilistic distance.

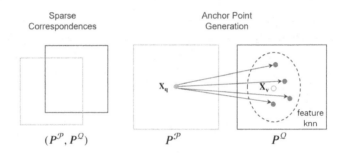

Fig. 3. Scheme for anchor correspondence generation.

Fine Matching. At the fine-scale level, we seek for learning point-wise correspondence using optimal transport algorithm [20].

For each anchor correspondence $(\mathbf{x}, \mathbf{x}')$, we group knn neighbours of both into mini patches and carry out local fine matching. The initial batched similarity matrix is constructed by calculation of unnormalized cosine similarity $s'_{ij} = <F_{\mathbf{x},i}, F_{\mathbf{x}',j}>/\sqrt{b}$ where $F_{\mathbf{x},i}$ denotes feature of ith neighbour of $\mathbf{x}$ and likewise for $F_{\mathbf{x}',j}$, b is the feature dimension length of $F_{\mathbf{x}}$. The feature similarity matrix is enhanced with an additional row and column serving as dustbins as in [20] and denoted as $\tilde{S}'$. Then Sinkhorn algorithm [24] is applied to solve the extended assignment matrix $\tilde{Z}$ on $\tilde{S}'$. The final assignment matrix Z is obtained by discarding the last row and column of $\tilde{Z}$. Finally, same as coarse-scale matcher, entries of S'_{ij} with top k maximum similarity are chosen as final point correspondences. We refer readers to [20] for more details.

3.3   Pose Estimator

Finally, we adopt parametric-free weighted SVD algorithm [3] as our pose estimator in a iterative proposal and verification scheme. We calculate a set of $\mathbf{R}_i, \mathbf{t}_i$ for each mini-patch generated from confident anchor correspondences as N'_c proposals. For each iteration in pose verification, we select $\mathbf{R}_i, \mathbf{t}_i$ with most inliers whose residuals are less than a predefined distance threshold d_0 and use the inlier points as input of next iteration. Experiments show that the pose estimator can guarantee accuracy while outperforming RANSAC on efficiency.

3.4   Loss Function

For the supervision of coarse matching stage, an overlap-aware circle loss function from [19] is utilized. Each pair of patch correspondence is seen as positive sample only if point correspondences account for at least 10%. We denote patch from point cloud $\mathcal{P}$ as $P^{\mathcal{P}}$ and its positive and negative correspondence from point cloud $\mathcal{Q}$ as $P^{\mathcal{Q}+}$ and $P^{\mathcal{Q}-}$. The overlap-aware circle loss is defined as following:

$$\mathcal{L}_c^{\mathcal{P}} = \frac{1}{|\mathcal{N}|} \sum_{P^{\mathcal{P}} \in \mathcal{N}} \log[1 + \sum_{P^{\mathcal{Q}+}} e^{\sqrt{\lambda}\beta^+ (d-\Delta^+))} \cdot \sum_{P^{\mathcal{Q}-}} e^{\beta^- (\Delta^- - d))}], \qquad (3)$$

where λ represents the overlap ratio, d is feature space distance. $\beta^+ = \gamma(d - \Delta^+)$ and $\beta^- = \gamma(\Delta^+ - d)$ are weights for positive samples and negative samples respectively. Loss $\mathcal{L}_c^{\mathcal{Q}}$ is calculated in the same way and final loss is $\mathcal{L}_c = (\mathcal{L}_c^{\mathcal{P}} + \mathcal{L}_c^{\mathcal{Q}})/2$.

For anchor generation stage, the coordinates $(\mathbf{x}_q, \mathbf{x}_v)$ and confidence c of generated anchor correspondences is supervised by distance loss and classification loss borrowed from [15].

$$\mathcal{L}_{a1} = \sum_i (\ln(\alpha - c_i) + \frac{d}{\alpha - c_i}), d = \|\mathbf{R}_{gt}\mathbf{x}_q + \mathbf{t}_{gt} - \mathbf{x}_v\|_2, \qquad (4)$$

$$\mathcal{L}_{a2} = BCE(c, \exp(-d/d_0)), d = \|\mathbf{R}_{gt}\mathbf{x}_q + \mathbf{t}_{gt} - \mathbf{x}_v\|_2. \qquad (5)$$

Fine-level loss is a negative log-likelihood loss defined on ground truth correspondence set $\mathcal{M}$ with matching radius τ and unmatched point sets $\mathcal{I}, \mathcal{J}$ from two point clouds as in [19, 20].

$$\mathcal{L}_f = -\sum_{(i,j)\in\mathcal{M}} \log \tilde{Z}_{ij} - \sum_{i\in\mathcal{I}} \log \tilde{Z}_{i,N+1} - \sum_{j\in\mathcal{J}} \log \tilde{Z}_{M+1,j}, \qquad (6)$$

where $\tilde{Z} \in \mathbb{R}^{(M+1)\times(N+1)}$.

The overall loss is $\mathcal{L} = \lambda_c\mathcal{L}_c + \lambda_{a1}\mathcal{L}_{a1} + \lambda_{a2}\mathcal{L}_{a2} + \lambda_f\mathcal{L}_f$.

4 Experiments

4.1 Implementation Details

We implement our pipeline with a GTX 2080Ti GPU and a Intel Xeon Platinum 8255C @ 2.50 GHz CPU. We train our model for 15 epochs using an Adam optimizer with an initial learning rate $1e-4$ and an exponential decaying rate 0.9. The batch size is set to 1 for all experiments. The width for pillar embedding is set to 0.3m. In both training and testing phases, we select up to 128 coarse correspondences but accept those only with overlap ratios > 0.1 for training phase. We randomly sample 12 anchor points per patch and select 4 candidates for each anchor points in generation of virtual correspondence. For data augmentation, we apply random rotation within $4°$ in pitch and roll and within $360°$ in yaw, and random translation within 0.5m and random scale within $[0.95, 1.05]$.

We evaluate our pipeline and the baselines on two large-scale urban datasets: KITTI Odometry dataset [9] and NuScenes dataset [4]. We follow the split settings of [16] to organize point cloud pairs and refine the point cloud pair poses from original KITTI Odometry dataset with ICP registration.

4.2 Results on KITTI and NuScenes

We evaluate registration result with three metrics following [6, 27]. The first is Relative Rotation Error (RRE), *i.e.*, the geodesic distance between estimated and ground truth rotation matrices $\hat{\mathbf{R}}$ and $\mathbf{R}_{gt}$, which is computed as $RRE = \arccos(Tr(\mathbf{R}_{gt}^{-1}\hat{\mathbf{R}} - I)/2)$. The second is Relative Translation Error (RTE), the Euclidean distance between estimated and ground truth translation $\hat{\mathbf{t}}$ and $\mathbf{t}_{gt}$, which is $RTE = \|\mathbf{t}_{gt} - \hat{\mathbf{t}}\|_2$. And the last is Registration Recall (RR), defined as the fraction of point cloud pairs with RRE and RTE below certain thresholds. Following prior works [2,6,10,19,27], we set the threshold as RRE< 5° and RTE< 2m throughout.

Regarding baselines, we compare our methods with both axiomatic methods **FGR** [29], **RANSAC** [8] and learning-based methods **DGR** [5], **HRegNet** [16], and **GeoTrans** [19]. Part of results are borrowed from [16]. Apart from the three metrics, we also report the mean inference time (in seconds) on the test point cloud pairs. Note that DGR and HRegNet distinct from the rest as they explicitly take ground truth transformations into loss function and regress transformation.

Table 1. Registration results on KITTI and Nuscenes dataset.

Model	KITTI dataset				NuScenes dataset			
	RRE(°)	RTE(m)	RR(%)	T(s)	RRE(°)	RTE(m)	RR(%)	T(s)
FGR	0.96± 0.81	0.93± 0.59	39.43	0.506	1.01± 0.92	0.71± 0.62	32.24	0.285
RANSAC	0.54± 0.40	0.13± 0.70	91.90	0.550	0.74± 0.70	0.21± 0.19	60.86	0.268
DGR	0.37± 0.30	0.32± 0.32	98.71	1.497	0.48± 0.43	0.21± 0.18	98.4	0.523
HRegNet	**0.18± 0.08**	0.056± 0.075	99.77	0.106	**0.27± 0.20**	**0.12± 0.11**	100.0	0.087
GeoTrans	0.18± 0.13	0.063± 0.045	**100.0**	0.368	OOM[a]			
Ours	0.26± 0.20	**0.046± 0.034**	**100.0**	**0.092**	0.31± 0.25	0.14± 0.13	100.0	**0.082**

[a] Out of memory during training phase.

Table 2. Generalized registration results on Apollo SouthBay Dataset.

Sequence	Model	RRE(°)	RTE(cm)	RR(%)	T(s)
SanJoseDowntown	HRegNet	0.15± 0.34	9.9± 22.2	90.0	0.108
	GeoTrans	0.13± 0.20	5.5± 8.9	99.9	0.321
	Ours	**0.13± 0.15**	**3.2± 4.8**	**100.0**	**0.092**
BaylandsToSeafood	HRegNet	0.37± 0.67	29.6± 42.9	81.4	0.108
	GeoTrans	**0.11± 0.14**	**8.8± 10.2**	**93.6**	0.293
	Ours	0.17± 0.25	9.9± 13.9	93.3	**0.092**

Table 1 shows that though relative rotation error of our work is in midstream, our method achieves comparable performance to state-of-art methods in registration recall and relative translation error. Compared with the state-of-art keypoint-free approach [19], our runtime is significantly smaller. Moreover, in the case of NuScenes dataset, we observe an out-of-memory breakdown in implementing **GeoTrans**, while **Ours** deliver the best or second best results in comparison. Compared with the state-of-art keypoint-free approach **HRegNet**, the recall rate of the proposed method is higher on KITTI dataset and it is proved in Sect. 4.3 that our performance downgrades less than **HRegNet** on unseen datasets. The runtime of our method achieves best on both datasets.

4.3   Generalization to Apollo Southbay Dataset

We further test the generalization ability of our method and the baselines on the 'SanJoseDowntown' and 'BaylandsToSeafood' sequence from Apollo SouthBay Dataset [17]. The test point cloud pairs are constructed in the same way as NuScenes. For each method, we directly apply pretrained weight trained on KITTI Odometry dataset.

Table 2 reports the generalization performance. When encountering unseen dataset, **HRegNet** suffers a significant drop in registration recall while detection-free works like **GeoTrans** and ours still perform well.

4.4   Ablation Study

We conduct ablation experiments to study the effectiveness of the key component within our pipeline. Table 3 shows ablation result on different modules. We directly initialize the candidates points for anchors in the whole point cloud range to ablate coarse matching. We test the setting similar to [19] where no anchor points are required and dense points are randomly sampled inside patches to ablate anchor generation. We ablate fine matching by comparing the estimated pose using filtered anchor correspondences with original estimated poses. Results show that our individual modules keep the our performance the best.

Table 3. Comparison of our modules on KITTI dataset.

Model	IR(%)	RRE(°)	RTE(cm)	RR(%)	T(s)
ours	**96.1**	**0.26**	**4.6**	100	0.092
w/o coarse	86.7	1.18	23.6	73	0.101
w/o anchor	87.8	0.36	5.9	100	0.109
w/o fine	92.4	0.31	8.2	100	**0.081**

Table 4. Comparison of different sampling density on KITTI dataset.

Hyperparameters	PIR(%)	IR(%)	RRE(°)	RTE(cm)	RR(%)	T(s)
$N_c = 256, N_a = 12$	97.7	95.5	0.246	**4.2**	100	0.103
$N_c = 128, N_a = 12$	98.9	96.1	0.258	4.6	100	0.092
$N_c = 64, N_a = 12$	**99.2**	**96.5**	**0.284**	5.1	100	0.086
$N_c = 128, N_a = 16$	98.9	95.9	0.260	4.6	100	0.098
$N_c = 128, N_a = 8$	98.9	96.2	0.259	4.6	100	**0.084**

The selection of hyperparameters, particularly selected sparse correspondence numbers N_c and max anchor points per pair N_a has influence on final result. We change N_c and N_a to search for a balanced setting. Table 4 shows the impact of sampling density. The accuracy increases with density while runtime decreases.

We also ablate the choice of superpoint representation in feature extractor. Table 5 shows that superpoint in pillar form achieves a little inferior performance in exchange for 30% improvement in inference time.

Table 5. Comparison of different representations on KITTI dataset.

Setting	Length	RRE(°)	RTE(cm)	RR(%)	T(s)	Model Size
Voxel	0.3m	**0.244**	**4.3**	**100**	0.131	11.2M
Pillar	0.3m	0.259	4.6	**100**	0.092	**5.4M**
Pillar	0.5m	0.291	5.1	**100**	**0.086**	**5.4M**

5 Conclusion

We have proposed an efficient network for point cloud registration in the urban scenes. By utilizing efficient feature extraction modules and hierarchical matching strategy, we make a step towards real-time robust deep learning based point cloud registration. Experiments show that our pipeline, being compact and light, achieves comparable inference speed and accuracy with state-of-art methods in urban scenes.

In the future work, we will further look into works like [13] and study the potential of our pipeline on multi-task learning. Our pipeline is suitable for more universal scene understanding by integration with other downstream task such as object detection and semantic segmentation.

References

1. Ao, S., Hu, Q., Yang, B., Markham, A., Guo, Y.: SpinNet: learning a general surface descriptor for 3d point cloud registration. In: IEEE Conference on Computer Vision and Pattern Recognition, pp. 11748–11757 (2021)
2. Bai, X., Luo, Z., Zhou, L., Fu, H., Quan, L., Tai, C.L.: D3Feat: joint learning of dense detection and description of 3D local features. In: IEEE Conference on Computer Vision and Pattern Recognition, pp. 6358–6366 (2020)
3. Besl, P.J., McKay, N.D.: A Method for registration of 3-D shapes. IEEE Trans. Pattern Anal. Mach. Intell. **14**, 239–256 (1992)
4. Caesar, H., et al.: NuScenes: a multimodal dataset for autonomous driving. In: IEEE Conference on Computer Vision and Pattern Recognition, pp. 11618–11628 (2020)
5. Choy, C.B., Dong, W., Koltun, V.: Deep global registration. In: IEEE Conference on Computer Vision and Pattern Recognition, pp. 2511–2520 (2020)

6. Choy, C.B., Park, J., Koltun, V.: Fully convolutional geometric features. In: IEEE International Conference on Computer Vision, pp. 8957–8965 (2019)
7. Fischer, K., Simon, M., Olsner, F., Milz, S., Gross, H.M., Mader, P.: Stickypillars: robust and efficient feature matching on point clouds using graph neural networks. In: IEEE Conference on Computer Vision and Pattern Recognition, pp. 313–323 (2021)
8. Fischler, M.A., Bolles, R.C.: Random sample consensus: a paradigm for model fitting with applications to image analysis and automated cartography. Commun. ACM **24**(6), 381–395 (1981)
9. Geiger, A., Lenz, P., Urtasun, R.: Are we ready for autonomous driving? the KITTI vision benchmark suite. In: IEEE Conference on Computer Vision and Pattern Recognition, pp. 3354–3361 (2012)
10. Huang, S., Gojcic, Z., Usvyatsov, M.M., Wieser, A., Schindler, K.: PREDATOR: registration of 3D point clouds with low overlap. In: IEEE Conference on Computer Vision and Pattern Recognition, pp. 4265–4274 (2021)
11. Lang, A.H., Vora, S., Caesar, H., Zhou, L., Yang, J., Beijbom, O.: PointPillars: fast encoders for object detection from point clouds. In: IEEE Conference on Computer Vision and Pattern Recognition, pp. 12689–12697 (2019)
12. Li, J., Lee, G.H.: USIP: unsupervised stable interest point detection from 3D point clouds. In: IEEE International Conference on Computer Vision, pp. 361–370 (2019)
13. Liu, C.J., Guo, J., Yan, D., Liang, Z., Zhang, X., Cheng, Z.L.: SARNet: semantic augmented registration of large-scale urban point clouds (2022), arXiv preprint arXiv:2206.13117
14. Liu, Z., Tang, H., Lin, Y., Han, S.: Point-voxel CNN for efficient 3D deep learning. In: Advances in Neural Information Processing Systems, pp. 963–973 (2019)
15. Lu, F., et al.: Sparse-to-dense matching network for large-scale LiDAR point cloud registration. IEEE Trans. Pattern Anal. Mach. Intell. 1–13 (2023)
16. Lu, F., et al.: HRegNet: a hierarchical network for large-scale outdoor LiDAR point cloud registration. In: IEEE International Conference on Computer Vision, pp. 15994–16003 (2021)
17. Lu, W., Zhou, Y., Wan, G., Hou, S., Song, S.: L3-net: towards learning based lidar localization for autonomous driving. In: IEEE Conference on Computer Vision and Pattern Recognition, pp. 6382–6391 (2019)
18. Magnusson, M., Lilienthal, A.J., Duckett, T.: Scan registration for autonomous mining vehicles using 3D-NDT. J. Field Rob. **24**(10), 803–827 (2007)
19. Qin, Z., Yu, H., Wang, C., Guo, Y., Peng, Y., Xu, K.: Geometric transformer for fast and robust point cloud registration. In: IEEE Conference on Computer Vision and Pattern Recognition, pp. 11133–11142 (2022)
20. Sarlin, P.E., DeTone, D., Malisiewicz, T., Rabinovich, A.: SuperGlue: learning feature matching with graph neural networks. In: IEEE Conference on Computer Vision and Pattern Recognition, pp. 4937–4946 (2020)
21. Segal, A.V., Hähnel, D., Thrun, S.: Generalized-ICP. In: Robotics: Science and Systems (2009)
22. Shi, G., Li, R., Ma, C.: PillarNet: real-time and high-performance pillar-based 3D object detection. In: European Conference on Computer Vision. Springer, Heidelberg (2022). https://doi.org/10.1007/978-3-031-20080-9_3
23. Shi, S., et al.: PV-RCNN: point-voxel feature set abstraction for 3D object detection. In: IEEE Conference on Computer Vision and Pattern Recognition, pp. 10526–10535 (2020)
24. Sinkhorn, R., Knopp, P.: Concerning nonnegative matrices and doubly stochastic matrices. Pac. J. Math. **21**, 343–348 (1967)

25. Tang, H., Liu, Z., Zhao, S., Lin, Y., Lin, J., Wang, H., Han, S.: Searching efficient 3D architectures with sparse point-voxel convolution. In: Vedaldi, A., Bischof, H., Brox, T., Frahm, J.-M. (eds.) ECCV 2020. LNCS, vol. 12373, pp. 685–702. Springer, Cham (2020). https://doi.org/10.1007/978-3-030-58604-1_41

26. Thomas, H., Qi, C., Deschaud, J.E., Marcotegui, B., Goulette, F., Guibas, L.J.: KPConv: flexible and deformable convolution for point clouds. In: IEEE International Conference on Computer Vision, pp. 6410–6419 (2019)

27. Yu, H., Li, F., Saleh, M., Busam, B., Ilic, S.: CoFiNet: reliable coarse-to-fine correspondences for robust point cloud registration. In: Advances in Neural Information Processing Systems, vol. 29, pp. 23872–23884 (2021)

28. Zeng, A., Song, S., Nießner, M., Fisher, M., Xiao, J., Funkhouser, T.A.: 3DMatch: learning local geometric descriptors from RGB-D reconstructions. In: IEEE Conference on Computer Vision and Pattern Recognition, pp. 199–208 (2017)

29. Zhou, Q.-Y., Park, J., Koltun, V.: Fast global registration. In: Leibe, B., Matas, J., Sebe, N., Welling, M. (eds.) ECCV 2016. LNCS, vol. 9906, pp. 766–782. Springer, Cham (2016). https://doi.org/10.1007/978-3-319-46475-6_47

30. Zhou, Y., et al.: End-to-End multi-view fusion for 3D object detection in LiDAR point clouds. In: Conference on Robot Learning, vol. 100, pp. 923–932 (2019)

PMPI: Patch-Based Multiplane Images for Real-Time Rendering of Neural Radiance Fields

Xiaoguang Jiang[1], You Yang[1], Qiong Liu[1(✉)], Changbiao Tao[2], and Qun Liu[2]

[1] Huazhong University of Science and Technology, Wuhan, China
q.liu@hust.edu.cn
[2] ZTE Corporation, Shenzhen, China

Abstract. Neural radiance fields (NeRFs) have made it possible to synthesize novel views in a photo-realistic manner. However, real-time view synthesis with superior quality and low consuming remains a challenge due to the dense but uniform sampling of NeRFs. This paper proposes Patch-based Multiplane Images (PMPIs) for real-time view synthesis. PMPI is an adaptive combination of 3D patches, each encodes an implicit 2D neural radiance field. We then propose a method to learn our PMPI. The structure of our PMPI is periodically updated during training. Patches of PMPI are thus assembled around visible contents. We compare our method with six the state-of-the-art techniques, including other plane-based methods. The proposed method achieves the highest PSNR, SSIM and LPIPS scores and enables real-time over 50fps rendering. We also prove the adaptability of PMPI with an ablation study on the number of sampling points.

Keywords: View synthesis · Scene representation · Multiplane images · Neural radiance field

1 Introduction

Novel view synthesis techniques are crucial to a variety of fascinating applications, including virtual reality and metaverse. Recently, one representative work by Mildenhall *et al.* [1] learned a neural radiance field (NeRF) from input images. NeRF encodes the geometry and appearance of the entire space of a scene. NeRF dramatically outperforms previous work and makes photo-realistic results possible. Despite the significant progress in rendering quality, NeRF in practice still shows artifacts when it comes to extremely complex geometry and detailed textures.

To improve the rendering quality, subsequent works tried to use explicit models as guidance for computing implicit representations. Explicit 3D geometric models are generally used, such as voxel grids [6,8,9], point clouds [2,10,11] and meshes [5,12,13]. Explicit plane-based models are also used to extend NeRF for detailed results and real-time rendering. Instead of slow volume rendering used by original NeRF, plane-based model is naturally suitable for real-time rendering

L. Fang et al. (Eds.): CICAI 2023, LNAI 14473, pp. 269–280, 2024.
https://doi.org/10.1007/978-981-99-8850-1_22

via fast warping and alpha compositing. One typical plane-based model is multiplane images (MPIs) [14–18]. For example, NeX [15] is a plane-based NeRF. It represents a scene with an MPI and then learns a NeRF which is only fine-tuned in the planes. Although the plane-based NeRFs [7,15] are efficient in learning and rendering, the plane-based models suffer from inefficient modeling of scenes. For NeX, repeated texture artifacts are frequently seen when it comes to detailed textures. The planes in an MPI are fixed and placed equidistantly in the depth space or inverse depth space. As a result, many pixels of an MPI are placed in empty space and have no contribution to rendering results. The inefficient sampling of MPIs leads to repeated texture artifacts [18]. Real-time view synthesis with superior quality and low consuming remains a challenge.

To solve this challenge, we propose a new representation model, Patch-based Multiplane Images (PMPIs) for real-time novel view synthesis. Our PMPI describes a collection of fronto-parallel patches. The direction of each patch is fixed, while the position of each patch in our PMPI changes for better surface fitting. In this way, more dense and effective samplings are produced without using more computational resources by assembling patches around visible contents. The collection of patches is semi-structured. To learn a PMPI from images for each scene, we have addressed three problems. First, we propose an end-to-end method. Unlike previous approaches which got 3D geometry priors in advance [2–4,7], we extract coarse geometry during training because extra geometry priors are often too noisy and hard to obtain. Second, we take the extracted coarse geometry as a guidance and propose a strategy to optimize the structure of our PMPI via feedback updating. The feedback style ensures the convergence of the position of each patch. Third, we employ a simplified rendering process for PMPI to speed up the training process and enable real-time rendering.

The contributions of this work can be concluded as follows:

- We propose Patch-based Multiplane Images (PMPIs), a new 3D scene representation with a flexible structure to depict 3D surfaces and appearance efficiently.
- To make full use of the flexibility of our PMPI for different scenes, we propose a end-to-end method to optimize the structure and the values of the proposed PMPI simultaneously. The experimental results show that a PMPI with a flexible structure can effectively reduce repeated texture artifacts and recover more complete geometry. Extensive ablation experiments validate the efficiency of the proposed PMPI.

2   Related Work

2.1   Neural Implicit Representations for View Synthesis

Mildenhall *et al.* [1] proposed neural radiance fields (NeRFs) for view synthesis. NeRF is implicit and continuous, parameterized as a multi-layer perceptron (MLP). This method represents a scene as a 5D radiance field and directly regresses the volume density and RGB values. NeRF was then enhanced in two

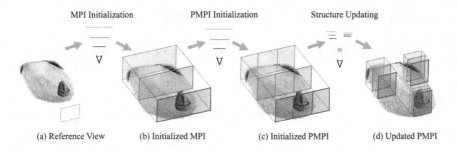

MPI Initialization   PMPI Initialization   Structure Updating

(a) Reference View   (b) Initialized MPI   (c) Initialized PMPI   (d) Updated PMPI

Fig. 1. Illustration of our PMPI in normalized device coordinate (NDC) space. For each target scene given (a), we first initialize an MPI for scene representing (b). We take a step forward to split each plane of the MPI into patches whose depths are variable (c). The patches in each grid are then updated and gathered around the visible content (d).

major areas: greater visual quality and faster rendering. Some works improve the visual quality by using additional 3D supervision or sampling more densely around surfaces with the help of geometry information. For example, depth-supervised NeRF [3] learned a NeRF under not only color supervision, but also depth supervision from a corresponding sparse point cloud. NSVF [8] and Point-nerf [2] use a voxel grid and a point cloud respectively, which are combined with local implicit features to preserve fine details. The above depth-supervised methods require very dense sampling points to show sharp results with detailed thin structures, which result in extremely high computational complexity. NeX [15] learns an enhancement of multiplane images(MPIs), which can be rendered efficiently through simple warping and alpha compositing.

2.2   Representations of Multiplane Images

Multiplane images (MPIs) is a scene representation that consists of a set of fronto-parallel planes at a fixed range of depths with respect to a reference view. Each sampling point in an MPI contains RGB and alpha values representing the scene appearance and geometry respectively. Compared to neural implicit representations, an MPI can be rendered in real time via planar warping and alpha compositing.

Original MPI [14] is proposed for view synthesis from small-baseline stereo and learned with a convolutional neural network (CNN). Mildenhall *et al.* [19] learned an MPI for each input observation via a CNN. Novel views are then rendered by blending adjacent MPIs. Flynn *et al.* [16] produced MPIs using learned gradient descent. One recent work based on MPI is NeX [15] by Sutti-sak Wizadwongsa *et al.* This method enables view-dependent effects modeling by parameterizing the RGB values as a function of the viewing direction and approximates this function with a linear combination of learnable basis functions. NeX views an MPI as discrete samplings of implicit, volumetric representation like NeRF and directly regresses the values of each sampling through a implicit modeling framework.

3   Representation of Patch-Based Multiplane Images

To solve the issue caused by inefficient sampling of MPIs, we propose a new scene representation, called patch-based multiplane image (PMPI). Our PMPI contains a set of fronto-parallel patches in a reference frustum, as shown in (d) of Fig. 1. Similar to the planes of an MPI, each patch of our PMPI contains an RGB image and an alpha map. At the position of the corresponding pixel, the RGB image and alpha map encode the texture and transparency respectively. Figure 1 illustrates an example of generating a PMPI. Given the images of a scene and a reference view of our PMPI, we construct a PMPI from an initialized MPI via splitting and rearrangement. We first place a set of planes to initialize an MPI by placing fronto-parallel planes in the reference viewing frustum. Then we split every plane into patches to obtain an initialized PMPI. As shown in Fig. 1, each patch is a rectangle part of the original plane. The splitting of planes can also be viewed as splitting the reference viewing frustum into small grids. The patches in each grid form an minor MPI. Note that the depth range of the minor MPI in each grid can change in accordance with visible scene contents.

Specifically, assume that an initialized MPI $\mathcal{M}$ has $N_{\mathcal{M}}$ planes. The dimension of each plane is $H_{\mathcal{M}} \times W_{\mathcal{M}} \times 4$, where the last dimension contains the RGB and alpha values. We then split every plane into patches, as shown in Fig. 1. Each patch is a rectangular part of the original plane and the dimension of each patch is $H_{\mathcal{P}} \times W_{\mathcal{P}} \times 4$. Thus the number of patches of our PMPI $\mathcal{P}$ is:

$$N_{\mathcal{P}} = \frac{N_{\mathcal{M}} \times H_{\mathcal{M}} \times W_{\mathcal{M}}}{H_{\mathcal{P}} \times W_{\mathcal{P}}}. \tag{1}$$

Let $\mathbf{c}_i \in \mathbb{R}^{H_{\mathcal{P}} \times W_{\mathcal{P}} \times 3}$ and $\boldsymbol{\alpha}_i \in \mathbb{R}^{H_{\mathcal{P}} \times W_{\mathcal{P}}}$ denote the RGB image and alpha map respectively of the ith patch. Let (u_i, v_i, d_i) describe the position of the ith patch, where (u_i, v_i) is the reference image coordinates of the center of the ith patch and d_i is the depth of the ith patch from the reference camera. Note that (u_i, v_i) is fixed while d_i changes in accordance with the scene's content. A PMPI can thus be described as a collection of RGBA patches $\{\mathcal{P}_1, \mathcal{P}_2, ..., \mathcal{P}_{N_{\mathcal{P}}}\}$, where $\mathcal{P}_i = (\mathbf{c}_i, \boldsymbol{\alpha}_i, u_i, v_i, d_i)$ denotes the ith patch and $N_{\mathcal{P}}$ is the total number of patches. In relation to MPI, the patches in each grid of our PMPI can be thought of as a minor MPI with dynamic depth range, or an MPI can be thought of as a special case of a PMPI.

4   Training of Adaptive PMPI

4.1   Initialization of Patches

As illustrated in Fig. 2, initialization takes a given reference view and the specified resolution of patches $H_{\mathcal{P}} \times W_{\mathcal{P}}$ as input. This process ends up with an initialized PMPI as the scene representation. Figure 1 illustrates this process in detail. We first initialize the structure of an MPI by placing planes in the reference viewing frustum. Then the resolution of patches $H_{\mathcal{P}} \times W_{\mathcal{P}}$ is taken as

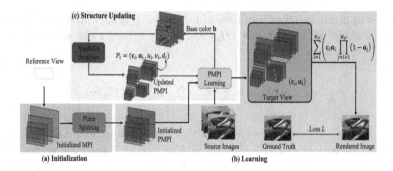

Fig. 2. An overview of our end-to-end method. (a) We initialize a PMPI by splitting each plane of an MPI into $N_{\mathcal{P}}$ patches. Each patch $\mathcal{P}_i = (\mathbf{c}_i, \boldsymbol{\alpha}_i, u_i, v_i, d_i)$ contains an RGB image $\mathbf{c}_i$ and an alpha map $\boldsymbol{\alpha}_i$. The position of patch $\mathcal{P}_i$ is denoted as u_i, v_i, d_i. (b) In Learning process, we calculate the loss between rendered image and ground truth. Then the weights of neural networks and base color $\mathbf{b}$ are learned via backpropagation. (c) We update the structure of a PMPI periodically.

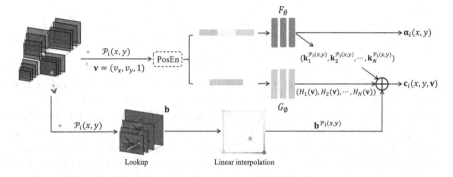

Fig. 3. An Illustration of Learning PMPI. We obtain alpha value $\alpha_i(x, y)$ and RGB color $\mathbf{c}_i(x, y, \mathbf{v})$ of each pixel $\mathcal{P}_i(x, y)$ via two MLPs and explicitly stored base color. "PosEn" indicates positional encoding [1];

a guidance for splitting the planes. Each plane in an MPI is split into patches, each with a resolution of $H_{\mathcal{P}} \times W_{\mathcal{P}} \times 4$. Each patch $\mathcal{P}_i$ contains a RGB color image $\mathbf{c}_i \in \mathbb{R}^{H_{\mathcal{P}} \times W_{\mathcal{P}} \times 3}$ and an alpha map $\boldsymbol{\alpha}_i \in \mathbb{R}^{H_{\mathcal{P}} \times W_{\mathcal{P}}}$.

4.2 Learning Appearance and Geometry

In the learning process of a PMPI, the alpha value and RGB color vector of each pixel are learned through multilayer perceptrons(MLPs). Specifically, we follow the learning process used by NeX [15]. Let $\mathcal{P}_i(x, y)$ denote a pixel in patch $\mathcal{P}_i$ with a patch coordinate (x, y). To allow for view-dependent modeling, we also parameterize the color of each pixel $\mathcal{P}_i(x, y)$ in a PMPI as a function of position and viewing direction $\mathbf{v} = (v_x, v_y, 1)$ in the camera coordinate system [15]. The function is approximated with a base color vector $\mathbf{b} \in \mathbb{R}^3$ and a linear combination of learnable basis functions $\{H_n(\mathbf{v}) : \mathbb{R}^3 \to \mathbb{R}\}$ over the spherical domain described by vector $\mathbf{v}$:

$$c_i(x, y, \mathbf{v}) = \mathbf{b}^{\mathcal{P}_i(x,y)} + \sum_{n=1}^{N} \mathbf{k}_n^{\mathcal{P}_i(x,y)} H_n(\mathbf{v}) \tag{2}$$

where $c_i(x, y, \mathbf{v}) \in \mathbb{R}^3$ is a vector of RGB color values in pixel $\mathcal{P}_i(x, y)$ over the viewing direction $\mathbf{v}$, $\mathbf{b}^{\mathcal{P}_i(x,y)} \in \mathbb{R}^3$ is a vector of base color values in pixel $\mathcal{P}_i(x, y)$, $\mathbf{k}_n^{\mathcal{P}_i(x,y)} \in \mathbb{R}^3$ is a vector of the nth RGB coefficients of N global basis functions in pixel $\mathcal{P}_i(x, y)$, $H_n(\mathbf{v}) \in \mathbb{R}$ is the nth learnable basis function under viewing direction $\mathbf{v}$ and N is the number of basis functions. In this way, the color in each pixel varies when changing viewing directions.

For pixel $\mathcal{P}_i(x, y)$, base color $\mathbf{b}^{\mathcal{P}_i(x,y)}$ is stored explicitly while RGB coefficients $\mathbf{k}_n^{\mathcal{P}_i(x,y)}$, alpha value $\alpha_i(x, y)$ and basis functions $H_n(\mathbf{v})$ are learned using two MLPs:

$$F_\theta : (\mathcal{P}_i(x, y)) \to (\alpha_i(x, y), (\mathbf{k}_1^{\mathcal{P}_i(x,y)}, \mathbf{k}_2^{\mathcal{P}_i(x,y)}, ..., \mathbf{k}_N^{\mathcal{P}_i(x,y)})) \tag{3}$$

$$G_\phi : (\mathbf{v}) \to (H_1(\mathbf{v}), H_2(\mathbf{v}), ..., H_N(\mathbf{v})) \tag{4}$$

where $\mathcal{P}_i(x, y)$ is a pixel in the patch coordinate system and $\mathbf{v}$ is the normalized viewing direction. The process of learning PMPI is illustrated in Fig. 3.

To optimize the base color and the weights of MLPs, we render our PMPI into target views and compute loss for backpropagation. Specifically, we employ a variant of Axis Aligned Bounding Box intersection test [20] instead of planar warping to find out the accurate intersections of rays with the patches. Then the color and alpha values (RGBA) in intersecions are evaluated using bilinear interpolation and inference of MLPs. The color of target pixel is calculated by compositing the color and alpha values of intersections:

$$\hat{\mathbf{I}}_t = \sum_{i=1}^{N_{\mathcal{P}}} \left(\mathbf{c}_i \alpha_i \prod_{j=i+1}^{N_{\mathcal{P}}} (1 - \alpha_j) \right) \tag{5}$$

where $N_{\mathcal{P}}$ is the number of patches of a PMPI, $\mathbf{c}_i \in \mathbb{R}^{H_{\mathcal{P}} \times W_{\mathcal{P}} \times 3}$ and $\alpha_i \in \mathbb{R}^{H_{\mathcal{P}} \times W_{\mathcal{P}}}$ denote the color image and alpha map in the ith patch $\mathcal{P}_i$, respectively.

After rendering, we then calculate the loss between rendered results and ground truth. The weights of the two MLPs and base colors k are optimized by minimizing the following loss function:

$$L = \left\| \hat{\mathbf{I}}_t - \mathbf{I}_t \right\|^2 + \omega \left\| \nabla \hat{\mathbf{I}}_t - \nabla \mathbf{I}_t \right\|_1 + \gamma \mathbf{TV}(\mathbf{b}) \tag{6}$$

where $\hat{\mathbf{I}}_t$, $\mathbf{I}_t$ are the rendered image and the ground-truth image respectively, ∇ denotes the gradient operator, $\mathbf{TV}(\mathbf{b})$ denotes the total variation loss of base color images, ω and γ are balancing weights.

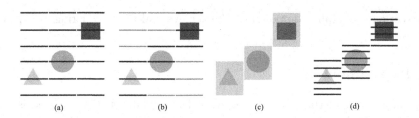

Fig. 4. An illustration of the first structure updating of a PMPI in the vertical view of normalized device coordinates. (a) An initialized PMPI with patches (black). (b) Patches are determined to be preserved (black) or pruned (gray). (c) Updated depth ranges. (d) Updated PMPI with rearranged patches. (Color figure online)

4.3   Updating Structure of PMPI

In order to gather the sampling points around the space with relevant scene contents, the depth of each patch needs to be optimized during training. However, gradient-based optimization procedure is computationally expensive. Besides, it is hard to find a proper loss function which is convex over the depth of each patch.

Inspired by neural sparse voxel fields [8], we update the structure of PMPI periodically during training based on learned coarse geometry. Instead of 3D priors or implicit alpha values, we reason coarse geometry from the explicitly stored base color k. We find that, in practice, the normalized base color values are optimized extremely close to $\mathbf{B} = (0.5, 0.5, 0.5)$ for the sampling points which are invisible in all observations. Therefore, we define the ith patch $\mathcal{P}_i$ to be invisible under the condition as follows:

$$\text{if} \max_{\substack{0 \le x < W_{\mathcal{P}} \\ 0 \le y < H_{\mathcal{P}}}} \left\| \mathbf{b}^{\mathcal{P}_i(x,y)} - \mathbf{B} \right\|^2 < \delta \tag{7}$$

where $\mathbf{b}^{\mathcal{P}_i(x,y)} \in \mathbb{R}^3$ is a vector of base color values in pixel $\mathcal{P}_i(x,y)$ and δ is a threshold ($\delta = 6 \times 10^{-4}$ in all our experiments).

The above formula enables us to identify the invisible patches efficiently. After a certain period of training, a patch is pruned if both itself and its neighbors are invisible. Then the ranges of depths are updated according to the depths of the nearest and farthest patches. Depths of all the patches in each grid are then reset equidistantly in inverse depth space, according to the updated range of depths. The operation is illustrated in Fig. 4.

5   Real-Time Rendering with Customized CUDA Kernel

After training, we inference MLPs and compute the color and alpha values on all pixels of PMPI. Then the color images and alpha maps are stored for real-time rendering. Explicitly stored images can be fast rendered. To further accelerate the rendering process, we implement a custom CUDA kernel for ray-plane intersection and alpha composition. We achieve real-time rendering of captured scenes.

6   Experiments

We evaluate our method on Real Forward-Facing dataset. Our method is compared to a bunch of state-of-the-art methods. In addition, we conduct an ablation study to demonstrate the advantage of PMPI over MPI in a more direct way. To validate the efficiency of PMPI, we render the a baked PMPI model using an NVIDIA RTX 3090. We reduce the number of planes $N_{\mathcal{M}}$ in the initialized MPI and compare our method to NeX [15].

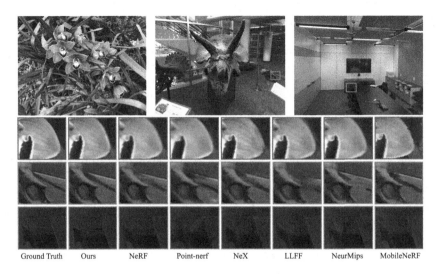

Fig. 5. Qualitative comparisons between Ours, NeRF [1], Point-nerf [2], NeX [15], LLFF [19], NeurMips [7] and MobileNeRF [5].

Table 1. Quantitative comparisons between our method, NeRF [1], Point-nerf [2], NeX [15], LLFF [19], NeurMips [7] and MobileNeRF [5]. All scores are averaged across the test images of Real Forward-Facing dataset. Bold numbers represent the best scores. The results shows that our model is rendered in real-time.

	Ours	NeRF	Point-nerf	NeX	LLFF	NeurMips	MobileNeRF
PSNR↑	**27.33**	26.76	20.61	27.26	24.41	21.52	25.91
SSIM↑	**0.905**	0.883	0.738	0.904	0.863	0.718	0.825
LPIPS↓	**0.174**	0.246	0.358	0.178	0.212	0.291	0.183
Real-time	✓	✗	✗	✓	✓	✓	✓

6.1   Training Details of Our Method

The number of planes $N_{\mathcal{M}}$ is set to 192. Each plane contains a RGB image and an alpha map with a resolution of 1440×1188 pixels. The planes are then split into patches, each with a resolution of 36×36. In order to model view-dependent effects, the RGB values in each pixel of a PMPI are parameterized as a function of the viewing direction, as shown in Formula 2, where N is set to 8. The weights of the two MLPs and base color k are optimized using Adam optimizer [21] by minimizing the loss function as shown in Formula 6. To compute the loss, we randomly sample and render 8000 pixels in the training view and compare them to the corresponding pixels in the ground truth. Same as NeX [15], we set $\omega = 0.05, \gamma = 0.03$ and train the networks and base color for 4000 epochs. The learning rates of base color and networks are set to 0.01 and 0.001, respectively. The learning rates decrease with a decay factor of 0.1 every 1333 epochs. We update the structure of PMPI at 1k, 1.5k, 2k and 2.5k epochs.

6.2   Comparisons

Quantitative Evaluation. To show the superior quality of our method, we evaluate our method and the state-of-the-art methods using the common PSNR, SSIM [22] and LPIPS [23] metrics. We report the quantitative results in Table 1. The results show that our method achieves the highest average scores across all metrics. By the way, we implement a rendering software for our PMPI model. We achieve real-time over 50fps rendering using an NVIDIA RTX 3090 at this high quality.

Qualitative Evaluation. The qualitative results are presented in Fig. 5. Our results have sharper boundaries and more details than the other methods, especially in the backgrounds. For the first row in Fig. 5, our method recovers greater texture of the petal. For the second and third row, our method preserves sharp boundaries while other methods show repeated texture or much noise.

Table 2. Quantitative evaluation of our method and NeX [15] on different numbers of planes. All scores are averaged across the test images of Real Forward-Facing dataset. Bold numbers represent the best scores. $N_{\mathcal{M}}$ is the number of planes in the initialized MPI.

	$N_{\mathcal{M}}=192$		$N_{\mathcal{M}}=128$		$N_{\mathcal{M}}=64$	
	Ours	NeX	Ours	NeX	Ours	NeX
PSNR↑	**27.33**	27.26	**27.03**	26.94	**26.57**	26.11
SSIM↑	**0.905**	0.904	**0.902**	0.899	**0.890**	0.880
LPIPS↓	**0.174**	0.178	**0.180**	0.184	**0.202**	0.225

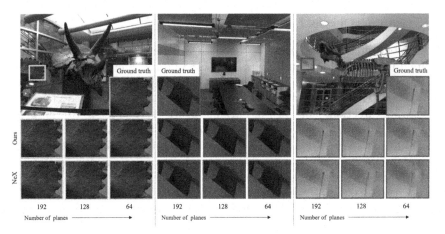

Fig. 6. Qualitative comparisons between our method and NeX [15] while varying the number of planes. Our results stay at high quality but NeX shows much more blurriness and broken boundaries when the number of planes decreases, such as on the pattern on the skull of a dinosaur and on the boundaries of the chair in the second column.

6.3   Ablation Study

To demonstrate the advantage of PMPI over MPI in a more direct way, we compare our method to NeX [15] and set the number of planes $N_{\mathcal{M}}$ in the initialized MPI to 192, 128 and 64. The MPI used by NeX shares the same number and resolution of planes as our initialized MPI. In this way, our method and NeX share the same number of sampling points. Quantitative results are presented in Table 2 and qualitative comparisons are illustrated in Fig. 6.

The results prove that updating structures improves the performance of PMPI greatly. When the number of plane decreases, NeX has a much lower PSNR and produces increasingly blurriness and broken boundaries while our results stay at high quality. For example, our method preserves straight boundaries while NeX shows bent boundaries, as shown in Fig. 6. By gathering the patches around visible contents in scenes, our method reduces the negative effects of decreasing planes.

7   Conclusions

We propose a new scene representation, patch-based multiplane images (PMPIs) for novel view synthesis. Based on the proposed model, we construct a method for fast and photo-realistic rendering. Our PMPIs capture and produce detailed textures with less repeated texture artifacts and allow real-time rendering. We compare our method to other state-of-the-art methods in real scenes and our method outperforms other state-of-the-art methods in both qualitative and quantitative metrics. Besides, we conduct extensive studies on the effects of varying numbers of planes. Our PMPIs remain effective when the number of planes decreases.

References

1. Mildenhall, B., Srinivasan, P., Tancik, M., Barron, J., Ramamoorthi, R., Ng, R.: Nerf: representing scenes as neural radiance fields for view synthesis. In: European Conference on Computer Vision (2020)
2. Xu, Q., et al.: Point-nerf: Point-based neural radiance fields. In: Proceedings of the IEEE/CVF Conference on Computer Vision and Pattern Recognition, pp. 5438–5448 (2022)
3. Deng, K., Liu, A., Zhu, J.-Y., Ramanan, D.: Depth-supervised nerf: fewer views and faster training for free. In: Proceedings of the IEEE/CVF Conference on Computer Vision and Pattern Recognition, pp. 12882–12891 (2022)
4. Roessle, B., Barron, J.T., Mildenhall, B., Srinivasan, P.P., Nießner, M.: Dense depth priors for neural radiance fields from sparse input views. In: Proceedings of the IEEE/CVF Conference on Computer Vision and Pattern Recognition, pp. 12892–12901 (2022)
5. Chen, Z., Funkhouser, T., Hedman, P., Tagliasacchi, A.: Mobilenerf: exploiting the polygon rasterization pipeline for efficient neural field rendering on mobile architectures. In: Proceedings of the IEEE/CVF Conference on Computer Vision and Pattern Recognition, pp. 16569–16578 (2023)
6. Hedman, P., Srinivasan, P.P., Mildenhall, B., Barron, J.T., Debevec, P.: Baking neural radiance fields for real-time view synthesis. In: Proceedings of the IEEE/CVF International Conference on Computer Vision, pp. 5875–5884 (2021)
7. Lin, Z.-H., Ma, W.-C., Hsu, H.-Y., Wang, Y.-C.F., Wang, S.: Neurmips: neural mixture of planar experts for view synthesis. In: Proceedings of the IEEE/CVF Conference on Computer Vision and Pattern Recognition, pp. 15702–15712 (2022)
8. Liu, L., Gu, J., Zaw Lin, K., Chua, T.-S., Theobalt, C.: Neural sparse voxel fields. In: Advances in Neural Information Processing Systems, vol. 33, pp. 15651–15663 (2020)
9. Fridovich-Keil, S., Yu, A., Tancik, M., Chen, Q., Recht, B., Kanazawa, A.: Plenoxels: radiance fields without neural networks. In: Proceedings of the IEEE/CVF Conference on Computer Vision and Pattern Recognition, pp. 5501–5510 (2022)
10. Aliev, K.-A., Ulyanov, D., Lempitsky, V.S.: Neural point-based graphics. In: ECCV (2020)
11. Rückert, D., Franke, L., Stamminger, M.: ADOP: approximate differentiable one-pixel point rendering. ACM Trans. Graph. **41**(4), 1–14 (2022)
12. Riegler, G., Koltun, V.: Free view synthesis. In: Vedaldi, A., Bischof, H., Brox, T., Frahm, J.-M. (eds.) ECCV 2020. LNCS, vol. 12364, pp. 623–640. Springer, Cham (2020). https://doi.org/10.1007/978-3-030-58529-7_37
13. Riegler, G., Koltun, V.: Stable view synthesis. In: Proceedings of the IEEE/CVF Conference on Computer Vision and Pattern Recognition, pp. 12216–12225 (2021)
14. Zhou, T., Tucker, R., Flynn, J., Fyffe, G., Snavely, N.: Stereo magnification: learning view synthesis using multiplane images. ACM Trans. Graph. **37**(4), 1–12 (2018)
15. Wizadwongsa, S., Phongthawee, P., Yenphraphai, J., Suwajanakorn, S.: Nex: real-time view synthesis with neural basis expansion. In: 2021 IEEE/CVF Conference on Computer Vision and Pattern Recognition (CVPR), pp. 8530–8539 (2021)
16. Flynn, J., et al.: DeepView: view synthesis with learned gradient descent. In: 2019 IEEE/CVF Conference on Computer Vision and Pattern Recognition (CVPR), pp. 2362–2371 (2019)
17. Tucker, R., Snavely, N.: Single-view view synthesis with multiplane images. In: 2020 IEEE/CVF Conference on Computer Vision and Pattern Recognition (CVPR), pp. 548–557 (2020)

18. Srinivasan, P.P., Tucker, R., Barron, J.T., Ramamoorthi, R., Ng, R., Snavely, N.: Pushing the boundaries of view extrapolation with multiplane images. In: 2019 IEEE/CVF Conference on Computer Vision and Pattern Recognition (CVPR), pp. 175–184 (2019)
19. Mildenhall, B., et al.: Local light field fusion: practical view synthesis with prescriptive sampling guidelines. ACM Trans. Graph. **38**(4), 1–14 (2019)
20. Haines, E.: Essential ray tracing. Glas **89**, 33–77 (1989)
21. Kingma, D.P., Ba, J.: Adam: a method for stochastic optimization. CoRR, vol. abs/1412.6980 (2015)
22. Wang, Z.: Image quality assessment: from error visibility to structural similarity. IEEE Trans. Image Process. **13**(4), 600–612 (2004)
23. Zhang, R., Isola, P., Efros, A.A., Shechtman, E., Wang, O.: The unreasonable effectiveness of deep features as a perceptual metric. In: Proceedings of the IEEE Conference on Computer Vision and Pattern Recognition, pp. 586–595 (2018)

EFPNet: Effective Fusion Pyramid Network for Tiny Person Detection in UAV Images

Ruichen Zhang, Qiong Liu[✉], and Kejun Wu

School of Electronic Information and Communications,
Huazhong University of Science and Technology, Wuhan, China
q.liu@hust.edu.cn

Abstract. Unmanned Aerial Vehicles (UAVs) have found extensive applications in the field of rescue and navigation scenarios. The objects in UAV images are generally with small sizes, which rises a serious challenge of object detection. Most existing methods address this issue by constructing multi-scale feature pyramids to integrate deep semantic information with shallow layer, but these networks fail to effectively extract and learn features of tiny objects in the shallow layer. In this paper, we propose an Effective Fusion Pyramid Network (EFPNet) for tiny person detection in UAV images. EFPNet consists of a Multi-Dimensional Attention Module (MDAM) and an Effective Feature Fusion Module (EFFM). The MDAM learns the weighted combination of features in both channel and spatial dimensions, which generates attention maps. It enriches semantic information in features. The EFFM utilizes the information from attention maps of different layers, which guides feature fusion between adjacent layers. It maintains consistency between deep and shallow features. Our proposed model achieves an Average Precision (AP) of 60.72% on the TinyPerson dataset, which demonstrate our model outperforms other state-of-the-art detectors.

Keywords: Tiny object detection · Self-attention · Feature pyramid network · Unmanned aerial vehicles

1 Introduction

Due to their exceptional mobility, large field-of-view, and cost-effectiveness, unmanned aerial vehicles (UAVs) have found widespread application in various tasks such as environmental monitoring [25] and maritime rescue [3,28]. UAVs are typically deployed at a distance from the objects of interest, enabling them to capture images with a large field-of-view. Consequently, these images encompass targets exhibiting significant scale variations, including a substantial number of tiny objects(less than 20 pixels), thus tiny objects often suffer from low signal-to-noise ratios, making it challenging to detect them in the background [27]. As a result, the performance of most detectors in detecting such tiny objects is unsatisfactory, the detection precision of tiny objects in many public datasets is

L. Fang et al. (Eds.): CICAI 2023, LNAI 14473, pp. 281–292, 2024.
https://doi.org/10.1007/978-981-99-8850-1_23

less than half that of larger objects [20]. Hence, there exists significant scope for improvement in the field of tiny object detection.

Generally, detectors continuously perform downsampling and pooling operations on input images. In this process, the features of tiny objects gradually get overwhelmed and drown in the background [2], resulting in the detector's inability to detect tiny objects effectively. To solve the issue of feature disappearance, some methods generate additional small targets in the dataset [5,13] to achieve a better balance between positive and negative samples. However, the performance of these methods varies significantly on different datasets, indicating limited generalization capability. Most existing detectors utilize Feature Pyramid Network [16] (FPN) to combine deep and shallow features, though it allows the shallow features to acquire richer semantic information for performance enhancement, it fails to fully address the semantic conflict arising from the disappearance of tiny object features. As the feature information of tiny objects gradually gets submerged within the background information during forward propagation, the majority of anchor points in deep layers are mistakenly assigned as negative samples. This results in semantic conflict between deep and shallow features, leading to inconsistent gradient computation within the network [19]. Consequently, deep features do not enrich the semantics of shallow features but instead have a negative impact, ultimately causing the detector to fail in detecting tiny objects. Guo et al. [9] proposed a consistency supervision method to reduce the semantic gap between different layers, Gong et al. [8] proposed a statistical-based feature fusion method to alleviate the negative influence of deep features on shallow features. Nevertheless, these methods are limited in improving precision when detecting tiny objects due to the noisier semantic information and inadequate mitigation of semantic conflict during feature fusion, resulting in minimal accuracy improvement.

In this paper, we propose an Effective Fusion Pyramid Network (EFPNet) to improve the detection precision of tiny person. To address the issue of tiny object features being lost during downsampling and pooling processes in the network, we propose a Multi-Dimensional Attention Module (MDAM). By learning the weighted combination of features in both channel and spatial dimensions, MDAM generates attention maps that carry rich semantic information. By utilizing the self-attention mechanism and maintaining a higher internal resolution during attention map generation, MDAM effectively strengthens the semantic information of tiny objects across different layers, preventing them from being lost in background noise. To resolve the semantic conflict and inconsistent gradient computation in FPN, we propose a Effective Feature Fusion Module (EFFM). EFFM guides the fusion of deep and shallow features by statistically analyzing the number of responsive pixels and connected regions in the attention maps from different layers. It utilizes the effective information from deep layers while suppressing conflicting information from shallow features. This method effectively prevents semantic conflicts and enables the network to learn tiny features accurately. The experimental results demonstrate that our method significantly improves the accuracy of tiny person detection.

Our contribution can be summarized as follows:

- We propose EFPNet for tiny person detection in UAV images. The proposed Multi-Dimensional Attention Module (MDAM) utilizes both channel and spatial information and maintain a high internal resolution to avoid semantic information loss. Effective Feature Fusion Module (EFFM) guidies feature fusion in the FPN using pixel-level information to mitigate semantic conflicts and relieve the inconsistency in gradient computation.
- The proposed EFPNet significantly improves the performance of the detector due to the introduction of the proposed MDAM and EFFM. It outperforms state-of-the-art detectors on the TinyPerson benchmark.

2   Related Works

Multi-scale Feature Fusion. Objects in UAV images often exhibit tiny sizes and extreme scale variations, causing significant challenges for object detection. Lower-level features in deep networks lack semantic information but contain rich texture and geometric details, while higher-level features exhibit the opposite characteristics. Fusion of multi-scale features can transfer high-level semantic information to lower-level features, improving the expressive ability of features. FPN [16] constructs a feature pyramid by using outputs from different layers of the backbone and performs feature fusion through a top-down pathway. NAS-FPN [7] designs a novel connection method based on neural architecture search. CE-FPN [23] designs a context enhancement method for extracting stronger features. To address the semantic conflict issue in the fusion of higher-level and lower-level features, FaPN [12] employs deformable convolutions for implicit compensation to enhance feature consistency. A2-FPN [11] aggregates information from adjacent features. These works have partially alleviated the feature loss problem for small objects, but the detection performance is still not ideal for extremely tiny objects.

Attention Mechanism. Attention mechanisms are considered a potential means of optimizing features by selectively focusing on the most important regions in an image and ignoring other regions. In object detection tasks, channel attention and spatial attention are frequently used. In channel attention methods, SK-Net [15] employs channel attention to adaptively adjust the receptive field size of different feature channels, ABNet [21] captures cross-channel interaction to extract fine-grained features. In spatial attention methods, Dai *et al.* [4] proposes a deformable convolution approach to adapt to different objects. Some methods combine channel attention and spatial attention. CBAM [26] introduces a module that cascades channel attention and spatial attention to compute attention maps, while Liu *et al.* [18] propose a module that can cascade and parallelize both types of attention. These attention modules have shown improvements in general visual tasks, but their effectiveness is limited for tiny object detection tasks where features are hard to extract.

3   The Proposed Method

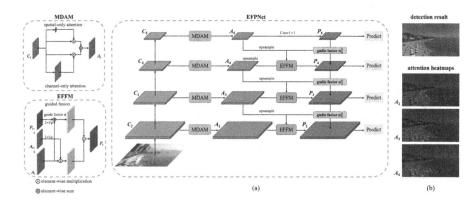

Fig. 1. Overview of our EFPNet. (a)EFPNet architecture, Multi-Dimensional Attention Module (MDAM) generates attention maps with rich semantics, Effective Feature Fusion Module (EFFM) guides the fusion of features from adjacent layers. (b)Visualization of detection result and attention heatmaps.

3.1   Overview of the Proposed EFPNet

This chapter will introduce the architecture of our EFPNet. In order to obtain higher-quality feature maps, we adopt Swin-T [22] as the backbone of our network. As shown in Fig. 1. $\{C_2, C_3, C_4, C_5\}$ denotes the feature maps of different levels after input images being down-sampled by $\{4, 8, 16, 32\}$ times, these features are used to construct the feature pyramid. Then, they are input into the MADM to generate semantically enriched attention maps $\{A_2, A_3, A_4, A_5\}$. $\{P_2, P_3, P_4\}$ are generated from the attention maps of adjacent layers by EFFM, which are further used to enhance the features of tiny objects. P_5 is obtained by applying convolution to A_5. The EFPNet is mainly composed of the MADM and EFFM. MADM learns the weighted combination of features in both the channel and spatial dimensions to generate enhanced attention maps. EFFM guides the fusion of features from adjacent layers based on the information of tiny objects, it prevents the loss of tiny objects information. In the following chapters, we will describe the specific implementation details of the main modules.

3.2   Multi-dimensional Attention Module

It is challenging for general detectors to extract high-quality features for tiny objects due to their limited amount of pixels. Inspired by the attention model used in pixel-level regression tasks, we designed MADM to generate attention maps containing high-quality features of tiny objects. The structure of MADM is illustrated in Fig. 2. This module divides the input feature map into two branches to further highlight features in different dimension: one branch learns the channel-only weighted combination, and the other branch learns the spatial-only weighted combination. The output of two branches are then multiplied with the original feature and added to obtain the final attention map.

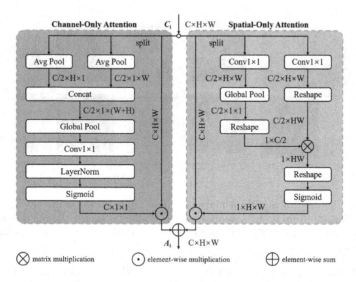

Fig. 2. The structure of Multi-Dimensional Attention Module (MDAM). Input features are divided into two branches to generate channel-only attention tensor and spatial-only attention tensor.

To calculate the channel-only attention tensor, the input feature $(C \times H \times W)$ is split in the channel dimension, 1D horizontal global pooling and 1D vertical global pooling is performed on the H and W dimensions of each split. This pooling strategy in different dimensions preserves more positional information. Then we use global pooling and convolution to make the concatenated feature tensor match the channel dimension of input. After normalization and sigmoid activation, the channel-only attention tensor A^{ch} is obtained.

For spatial-only attention tensor calculation, we also split the input along the channel dimension. The two split branches undergo global pooling and reshaping, and then their element-wise product generates the feature tensor. This approach allows for higher internal resolution preservation without significantly increasing computational complexity, thereby preserving more tiny object features. After reshaping and sigmoid activation, the spatial-only feature tensor A^{sp} is obtained.

The channel-only feature tensor A^{ch} and spatial feature tensor A^{sp} are multiplied to the original feature map and added to obtain the final attention map A_i according to the following equation:

$$A_i = C_i^{ch} \odot C_i + C_i^{sp} \odot C_i, \tag{1}$$

where C_i^{ch} and C_i^{sp} denotes channel-only feature tensor and spatial-only feature tensor at i^{th} layer, $\odot$ is element-wise multiplication, and C_i is the input feature at i^{th} layer.

3.3   Effective Feature Fusion Module

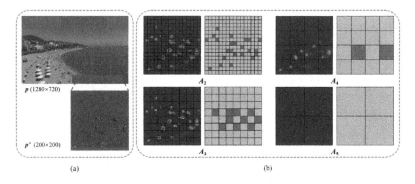

Fig. 3. Visualization of attention maps. (a) The input image $p(1280 \times 720)$ and one patch $p'(200 \times 200)$ from p. (b) Attention maps of different layers, the red points denotes pixels with values above 20% of the maximum value of the input attention map. (Color figure online)

The downsampling and pooling processes in the network cause the features of tiny objects to gradually drown in the background noise. As shown in Fig. 3, we visualized the attention maps at different layers, and it is clear that the features of tiny objects are visible in the lower layers. However, in the higher layers, most of the features of tiny objects vanish. These deep features tend

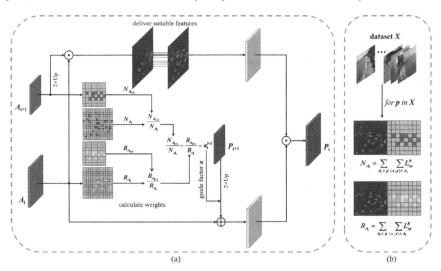

Fig. 4. (a) The structure of EFFM, feature fusion is guided by a factor α calculated by statistical analysis. (b) The calculation of N_{A_i} and R_{A_i}.

to indicate the absence of tiny objects in the image, while the corresponding positions in the shallow features still contain the features of tiny objects. When fusing features from different layers, a semantic conflict arises, where the features of tiny objects cannot be distinguished from the background features, resulting in poor performance in tiny object detection.

To alleviate the semantic conflicts during the feature fusion process, we designed EFFM to guide the fusion of adjacent layers' features. EFFM allows the appropriate target features from deeper layers to propagate to shallower layers while suppressing potentially conflicting features. This selective feature fusion approach preserves the features of tiny objects in the lower layers while reducing the negative impact of higher-layer features on the lower-layer features. In the fusion process, we introduced a fusion factor, α, to control the weights of different layers. This factor enhances the guiding role of EFFM. The calculation of α is illustrated in Fig. 4.

We first compute two pixel-level statistics, N_{A_i} and R_{A_i}, based on the attention maps A_i generated at different layers using training images. N_{A_i} represents the number of pixels with values above 20% of the maximum value of the input attention map, and R_{A_i} represents the number of connected regions formed by these pixels. These statistics reflect the quantity of tiny objects at different layers. The formulas for calculating N_{A_i} and R_{A_i} are as follows:

$$N_{A_i} = \sum_{A_i in p} \sum_{(x,y) in A_i} L_{xy}^N, \tag{2}$$

$$R_{A_i} = \sum_{A_i in p} \sum_{(x,y) in A_i} L_{xy}^R, \tag{3}$$

where p denotes input images form dataset X, (x,y) denotes coordinate in A_i, L_{xy}^N is the activated pixels which value is above 20% of the maximum value of A_i, and L_{xy}^R is the connected regions formed by L_{xy}^N. This approach of separately counting pixels and connected regions enables a reasonable allocation of weights during the fusion of neighboring layers' features and avoids incorrect calculations for partially occluded targets. The fusion factor α_i^{i+1}, which is derived from N_{A_i} and R_{A_i}, is calculated using the following fonction:

$$\alpha_i^{i+1} = \frac{N_{A_{i+1}}}{N_{A_i}} + \frac{R_{A_{i+1}}}{R_{A_i}}, \tag{4}$$

where $N_{A_{i+1}}$ and N_{A_i} denotes the number of activated pixels in different layers, $R_{A_{i+1}}$ and R_{A_i} denotes the number of connected regions in different layers.

To ensure consistent gradient computation and mitigate the effects of semantic conflicts, we multiply the attention maps by the upsampled features from higher layers. This strengthens the regions that are simultaneously detected in adjacent layers while suppressing the negative impact of regions that only appear in the higher layers on the lower layers. This approach ensures that more objects can be detected in each layer during subsequent multi-scale detection and also helps alleviate issues caused by occlusion. The feature fusion process in EFFM can be represented as follows:

$$P_i = (A_i + \alpha_i^{i+1} f_{up}(A_{i+1})) \odot (A_i \odot f_{up}(A_{i+1})), \tag{5}$$

where $\odot$ denotes element-wise multiplication, f_{up} is the nearest upsampling operation, and P_i is the output of EFFM.

4   Experiments and Results

4.1   Experimental Settings

Datasets and Evaluation Metrics. Our EFPNet is evaluated on TinyPerson [27], which is a public dataset for seaside tiny person detection. There are around 1600 images with more than 70k bounding boxes are annotated. The size range of person is divided into 5 intervals: $tiny[2, 20]$, $tiny1[2, 8]$, $tiny2[8, 12]$, $tiny3[12, 20]$, and $small[20, 32]$. In order to keep consistent with the TinyPerson benchmark [27], we also adopt AP (average precision) as evaluation metrics.

Implementation Details. We choose Swin-T and ResNet-50 pre-trained on ImageNet as the backbone respectively. To prevent GPU being out of memory during training, we cropped the input images into patches of size 680×510 with a 40 pixel overlap. Our network was developed based on the MMDetection toolkit [1]. All models were trained for 12 epochs on two 24GB RTX 3090 GPUs. We employed the stochastic gradient descent optimizer with an initial learning rate of 0.002, which was decreased by a factor of 0.1 after 6 epochs. For anchor generation, we used aspect ratios of 0.5, 1.2, and 2.0.

4.2   Visualization Analysis

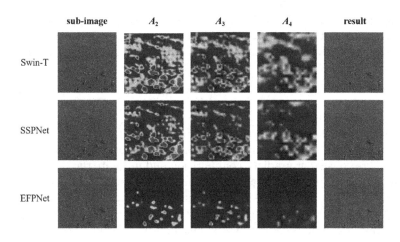

Fig. 5. Qualitative comparison of attention maps generated by different method. Sub-image(200×200) is cropped from the input image, The A2, A3, and A4 are the attention maps in different layers and result is the detection result of the sub image.

To demonstrate the effectiveness of MDAM, we compared visualization of the attention heatmaps generated by MDAM with those generated by state-of-the-art method (SSPNet). As shown in Fig. 5, the attention heatmaps generated by MDAM exhibit higher quality and fewer noise compared to other methods. These high-quality feature maps enable more accurate detection of tiny person and reduce the number of missed targets. Thus, our approach is highly effective for detecting tiny person.

Fig. 6. Visualization of detection results.

To further validate the effectiveness of EFPNet, we present the detection results of several images in Fig. 6. These images contain densely crowded scenes, significant scale variations among crowds and sparsely scattered person. It can be observed that results retain the features of correct targets while suppressing the features of incorrect targets. Our EFPNet is also capable of accurately detecting partially occluded objects. While there are occasional misclassifications of tiny objects such as buoys, we believe that these issues will be resolved as the dataset becomes more abundant. Overall, our EFPNet can accurately detect tiny targets while maintaining the performance in detecting larger targets.

4.3 Comparison to State-of-the-arts

In Table 1, we present a comparison of our EFPNet with state-of-the-art methods on TinyPerson. We measure the performance using the standard criterion Average Precision (AP). The superscript of AP represents the IOU threshold, while the subscript represents size of tiny objects. A higher AP indicates better performance of the detector. During the training process, we applied the same configuration to all models and utilized consistent data augmentation and multi-scale training methods for all detectors. From the table, we can observe

Table 1. APs of different methods on TinyPerson. The best result in each AP is highlighted in bold.

Detector	AP_{50}^{tiny}	AP_{50}^{tiny1}	AP_{50}^{tiny2}	AP_{50}^{tiny3}	AP_{50}^{small}	AP_{25}^{tiny}	AP_{75}^{tiny}
RetinaNet [17]	51.19	35.44	54.53	60.89	66.83	70.68	6.21
Faster RCNN-FPN [24]	51.46	35.65	55.96	61.51	67.02	71.05	6.38
FoveaNet [14]	54.18	37.97	57.27	64.84	71.63	74.81	7.12
RetinaNet+SM with S-α [8]	54.64	41.32	57.35	64.22	67.43	73.59	6.78
Swin-T [22]	55.55	42.39	58.64	64.71	68.91	75.56	7.24
Faster RCNN-SSPNet [10]	58.86	47.25	61.82	66.47	72.14	77.98	8.92
Swin-T-AEFNet [6]	59.82	47.59	61.74	68.43	72.23	78.09	9.21
Faster RCNN-EFPNet	60.35	48.33	62.96	69.14	72.20	78.16	9.16
Cascade RCNN-EFPNet	59.19	47.82	61.77	68.35	72.14	77.96	8.99
Swin-T-EFPNet	**60.72**	**48.85**	**63.18**	**69.43**	**72.52**	**78.48**	**9.34**

that while using the Faster-RCNN framework, our EFPNet improves the performance by 8.89% compared to FPN of AP_{50}^{tiny}, 1.49% compared to the latest SSPNet. Moreover, while employing the Swin-T framework, our method outperforms Swin-T by 5.17% and AEFNet by 0.90%. These results strongly demonstrate the effectiveness and superiority of EFPNet in tiny object detection task.

4.4 Ablation Experiments

To demonstrate the effectiveness of MADM and EFFM, we conducted ablation experiments by integrating MADM and EFFM separately on Swin-T. The experimental results are shown in Table 2, it can be observed that both MADM and EFFM contribute to performance gains. Specifically, EFFM achieves larger improvements due to its ability to address more severe semantic conflicts in feature fusion. The combination of MADM and EFFM allows the two modules to complement each other and leads to significant performance gains.

Table 2. Ablation experiments on TinyPerson.

Detector	AP_{50}^{tiny}	AP_{50}^{tiny1}	AP_{50}^{tiny2}	AP_{50}^{tiny3}	AP_{50}^{small}	AP_{25}^{tiny}	AP_{75}^{tiny}
Swin-T [22]	55.55	42.39	58.64	64.71	68.91	75.56	7.24
Swin-T+MADM	58.26	45.15	60.85	67.08	70.11	77.02	8.44
Swin-T+EFFM	58.92	46.07	61.54	67.73	70.74	77.46	8.59
Swin-T+MADM+EFFM	60.72	48.85	63.18	69.43	72.52	78.48	9.34

5   Conclusions

We propose a feature pyramid network to accurately detect tiny objects in large-scale scenes by generating high-quality attention maps and guiding feature fusion effectively. Two major components are designed to improve the detection performance, namely the Multi-Dimensional Attention Module (MDAM) and the Efficient Feature Fusion Module (EFFM). MDAM extracts information from both the channel and spatial dimensions to generate attention maps with rich semantic information. EFFM guides feature fusion by statistically analyzing the pixel-level object information in the attention maps, effectively alleviating semantic conflicts and ensuring gradient consistency during the fusion process. Visualization results and comparative experiments demonstrate that our network can effectively extract features of tiny objects and achieve high-precision detection for complex tiny objects, with average precision of 60.72% on the public dataset TinyPerson. In future work, we will explore the application of our proposed model in occluded scenes and multi-class tiny object detection tasks.

References

1. Chen, K., et al.: MMDetection: Open MMLab detection toolbox and benchmark. arXiv:1906.07155 (2019)
2. Cheng, G., Yuan, X., Yao, X., Yan, K., Zeng, Q., Han, J.: Towards large-scale small object detection: Survey and benchmarks. arXiv:2207.14096 (2022)
3. Cheng, Y., Xu, H., Liu, Y.: Robust small object detection on the water surface through fusion of camera and millimeter wave radar. In: 2021 IEEE/CVF International Conference on Computer Vision (ICCV), pp. 15243–15252 (2021)
4. Dai, J., et al.: Deformable convolutional networks. In: 2017 IEEE International Conference on Computer Vision (ICCV), pp. 764–773 (2017)
5. Duan, C., Wei, Z., Zhang, C., Qu, S., Wang, H.: Coarse-grained density map guided object detection in aerial images. In: 2021 IEEE/CVF International Conference on Computer Vision Workshops (ICCVW), pp. 2789–2798 (2021)
6. Gao, S., Liu, C., Zhang, H., Zhou, Z., Qiu, J.: Multiscale attention-based detection of tiny targets in aerial beach images. Front. Mar. Sci. **9**, 1073615 (2022)
7. Ghiasi, G., Lin, T.Y., Pang, R., Le, Q.V.: NAS-FPN: learning scalable feature pyramid architecture for object detection. In: 2019 IEEE/CVF Conference on Computer Vision and Pattern Recognition (CVPR), pp. 7029–7038 (2019)
8. Gong, Y., Yu, X., Ding, Y., Peng, X., Zhao, J., Han, Z.: Effective fusion factor in FPN for tiny object detection. In: 2021 IEEE Winter Conference on Applications of Computer Vision (WACV), pp. 1159–1167 (2020)
9. Guo, C., Fan, B., Zhang, Q., Xiang, S., Pan, C.: AugFPN: improving multi-scale feature learning for object detection. 2020 IEEE/CVF Conference on Computer Vision and Pattern Recognition (CVPR), pp. 12592–12601 (2019)
10. Hong, M., Li, S., Yang, Y., Zhu, F., Zhao, Q., Lu, L.: SSPNet: scale selection pyramid network for tiny person detection from UAV images. IEEE Geosci. Remote Sens. Lett. **19**, 1–5 (2021)
11. Hu, M., Li, Y., Fang, L., Wang, S.: A2-FPN: attention aggregation based feature pyramid network for instance segmentation. In: 2021 IEEE/CVF Conference on Computer Vision and Pattern Recognition (CVPR), pp. 15338–15347 (2021)
12. Huang, S., Lu, Z., Cheng, R., He, C.: FaPN: feature-aligned pyramid network for dense image prediction. In: 2021 IEEE/CVF International Conference on Computer Vision (ICCV), pp. 844–853 (2021)
13. Kisantal, M., Wojna, Z., Murawski, J., Naruniec, J., Cho, K.: Augmentation for small object detection. arXiv:1902.07296 (2019)

14. Kong, T., Sun, F., Liu, H., Jiang, Y., Li, L., Shi, J.: FoveaBox: beyound anchor-based object detection. IEEE Trans. Image Process. **29**, 7389–7398 (2019)
15. Li, X., Wang, W., Hu, X., Yang, J.: Selective kernel networks. In: 2019 IEEE/CVF Conference on Computer Vision and Pattern Recognition (CVPR), pp. 510–519 (2019)
16. Lin, T.Y., Dollár, P., Girshick, R.B., He, K., Hariharan, B., Belongie, S.J.: Feature pyramid networks for object detection. In: 2017 IEEE Conference on Computer Vision and Pattern Recognition (CVPR), pp. 936–944 (2016)
17. Lin, T.Y., Goyal, P., Girshick, R.B., He, K., Dollár, P.: Focal loss for dense object detection. IEEE Trans. Pattern Anal. Mach. Intell. **42**, 318–327 (2017)
18. Liu, H., Liu, F., Fan, X., Huang, D.: Polarized self-attention: towards high-quality pixel-wise regression. arXiv:2107.00782 (2021)
19. Liu, S., Huang, D., Wang, Y.: Learning spatial fusion for single-shot object detection. arXiv:1911.09516 (2019)
20. Liu, W., et al.: SSD: single shot multibox detector. In: European Conference on Computer Vision (2015)
21. Liu, Y., Li, Q., Yuan, Y., Du, Q., Wang, Q.: ABNet: adaptive balanced network for multi-scale object detection in remote sensing imagery. IEEE Trans. Geosci. Remote Sens. **60**, 1–14 (2021)
22. Liu, Z., et al.: Swin transformer: hierarchical vision transformer using shifted windows. In: 2021 IEEE/CVF International Conference on Computer Vision (ICCV), pp. 9992–10002 (2021)
23. Luo, Y., et al.: CE-FPN: enhancing channel information for object detection. Multimedia Tools Appl. **81**, 30685–30704 (2021)
24. Ren, S., He, K., Girshick, R.B., Sun, J.: Faster R-CNN: towards real-time object detection with region proposal networks. IEEE Trans. Pattern Anal. Mach. Intell. **39**, 1137–1149 (2015)
25. Varga, L.A., Kiefer, B., Messmer, M., Zell, A.: SeaDronesSee: a maritime benchmark for detecting humans in open water. In: 2022 IEEE/CVF Winter Conference on Applications of Computer Vision (WACV), pp. 3686–3696 (2021)
26. Woo, S., Park, J., Lee, J.Y., Kweon, I.S.: CBAM: convolutional block attention module. In: European Conference on Computer Vision (2018)
27. Yu, X., Gong, Y., Jiang, N., Ye, Q., Han, Z.: Scale match for tiny person detection. In: 2020 IEEE Winter Conference on Applications of Computer Vision (WACV), pp. 1246–1254 (2019)
28. Zhang, R., et al.: Automatic detection of earthquake-damaged buildings by integrating UAV oblique photography and infrared thermal imaging. Remote. Sens. **12**, 2621 (2020)

End-to-End Object-Level Contrastive Pretraining for Detection via Semantic-Aware Localization

Long Geng and Xiaoming Huang[✉]

Computer School, Beijing Information Science and Technology University, Beijing 100029, People's Republic of China
huangxm0556@163.com

Abstract. Pretraining on a large dataset is the first stage of many computer vision tasks such as classification, detection, and segmentation. A conventional pretraining approach is performed on large datasets with human annotation. In this context, self-supervised learning, which uses unlabeled datasets to pretrain models, shows increasing promise for applications. Throughout the development of self-supervised learning, image-level contrastive representation learning has emerged as a highly effective approach for general transfer learning. However, it may lack specificity when applied to a specific downstream task, compromising performance in that task. Recently, an object-level self-supervised pretraining framework called SoCo is proposed for object detection. To achieve object-level pretraining, they adopt the traditional selective search algorithm to generate object proposals, which needs high space and time cost and also hinders end-to-end training to achieve global optimization. In this work, we propose an end-to-end object-level contrastive pretraining for detection, which obtains object proposals using the pretraining network itself. Specifically, we adopt the heat map from the features at the last backbone convolutional layer as semantic information to roughly localize objects, then generate promised proposals with center-suppressed sampling and multiple cropping strategies. The experimental results show that our method displays better performance with significantly less training space and time cost.

Keywords: Object Detection · Self-Supervised Learning · Semantic-aware Localization · Contrastive Learning · Pretraining

1 Introduction

Object detection aims at finding objects in images or videos, and labeling them with bounding boxes and the corresponding categories. Object detection methods based on deep learning can be categorized into two classes, namely single-stage and two-stage approaches, based on the generation of proposal windows [1]. Examples of single-stage methods include YOLO [2] and SSD [3], while Faster R-CNN [4] is an example of a two-stage method. This classification is based on whether these methods generate proposal windows or not. Both single-stage and two-stage object detection algorithms require pretraining on large datasets, such as ImageNet, to initialize the network effectively. Pretraining on such extensive datasets is a crucial step for both types of algorithms.

© The Author(s), under exclusive license to Springer Nature Singapore Pte Ltd. 2024
L. Fang et al. (Eds.): CICAI 2023, LNAI 14473, pp. 293–304, 2024.
https://doi.org/10.1007/978-981-99-8850-1_24

A conventional pretraining approach is carried out on large labeled datasets, while self-supervised learning methods alleviate the dependence of model pretraining on labeled data. The visual representations learned by image-level contrastive learning are generalizable and can perform quite well in many downstream tasks. However, it is also this generality that makes the initialization of the model sacrifice the specificity it deserves when we focus on a specific downstream task. Recent research has observed that the representations learned through image-level contrastive learning may not be optimal for dense labeling tasks, such as object detection and instance segmentation. This indicates a significant representation gap between image-level contrastive learning and object-level bounding boxes in the context of object detection. In detection tasks, it is common to use bounding boxes to represent the detected object and to reflect the relevant properties of object detection by the position and size of the bounding boxes.

To address the representation gap, a novel object-level self-supervised pre-training framework called Selective Object COntrastive learning (SoCo) has been proposed [5]. SoCo introduces a design principle that emphasizes aligning the self-supervised pretext task with the downstream task, aiming to bridge the representation gap effectively. SoCo uses selective search [6], a traditional algorithm, to complete the generation of object proposals, thus introducing an object-level representation, while treating each object proposal in an image. SoCo performs scale and position data enhancement on the same image to obtain multiple augmented views, and learns object-level visual representations by maximizing similarity through contrastive learning, enabling the acquisition of important properties like translation invariance and scale invariance, which are crucial for object detection tasks. Additionally, SoCo performs pretraining on all network modules used in the detector, ensuring well-initialized layers throughout the detector.

SoCo [5] should be the first to achieve pretraining of the entire object detection network, and the task alignment approach used to achieve this goal is highly innovative and inspiring. However, the object proposals in SoCo pretraining are generated offline using selective search [6], which needs high space and time cost. The traditional proposal generation usually shows worse performance than deep learning-based methods. Besides, it does not allow end-to-end training to achieve global optimization.

To conquer the shortcomings of SoCo [5], we consider the object proposals generation using the pretraining network itself. Specifically, we adopt the heat map from the features at the last convolutional layer of the backbone network as semantic information to roughly localize objects in the image, then generate promised proposals with center-suppressed sampling and multiple cropping strategies. To evaluate the effectiveness of our method, we conducted pretraining on the ImageNet dataset [7] followed by fine-tuning on the MS COCO dataset [8]. This two-step process allowed us to validate the performance and efficacy of our approach.

The main contributions of this work can be summarized as follows:

(1) Introduction of an end-to-end object-level contrastive pretraining approach for object detection. This approach leverages the pretraining network itself to obtain object proposals, eliminating the need for separate proposal generation methods.
(2) Comparative evaluation against the SoCo method [5] on the ImageNet dataset, demonstrating that our proposed approach achieves superior performance while requiring significantly less training space and time.

Section 2 provides a comprehensive review of relevant self-supervised learning methods, establishing the context for our proposed approach. In Sect. 3, we present our method along with the enhancements made to improve its effectiveness. The experimental evaluation of our approach is detailed in Sect. 4, showcasing its performance and comparative analysis against existing methods. Finally, Sect. 5 concludes the paper, summarizing the key findings and contributions of our work.

2   Related Work

Learning effective visual representations in the absence of supervision is a long-standing topic. In this section, we begin by reviewing self-supervised learning techniques for classification and object detection tasks, then introduce the recent object-level self-supervised pretraining framework SoCo [5].

2.1   Self-supervised Learning for Classification

In the field of image classification, self-supervised learning has been a powerful alternative to supervised pretraining, especially in image-rich but sparsely annotated domains.

The backbone pretraining strategies can be categorized into contrastive, clustering-based, and self-distillation [9]. Contrastive learning approaches (e.g., MoCo [10] and SimCLR [11]) use InfoNCE loss to compare sample pairs. In general, a common practice involves obtaining multiple views of each image through data augmentations. This is done by maximizing the similarity between different augmented views of the same image while simultaneously minimizing the similarity between augmented views of different images. This approach aims to enhance the robustness and generalization capabilities of the learned representations by encouraging consistency across different views of the same image while emphasizing the differences between different images. Clustering-based approaches generate pseudo-labeling by unsupervised clustering techniques. The paper introduced a method called Swapping Assignments between multiple Views of the same image (SwAV) [12]. SwAV aims to predict cluster assignments for one view based on an augmented view of the same image. Unlike contrastive learning, self-distillation methods focus on maximizing the similarity between predictions made by a teacher and student model. In the BYOL (Bring Your Own Latent) [13] method, the student model is optimized using gradient descent, while the teacher model's weights are updated using an exponential moving average of the student weights. This approach facilitates knowledge transfer and improves the performance of the student model.

Conceptually, several problems exist in transferring a classification-based representation to detection. The presence of an untrained detection head is one aspect to consider. Model architecture differences lead to the omission of pre-training for the detection heads used in object detection. Conversely, there exists a task mismatch between ImageNet Top-1 classification accuracy and object detection performance. Although certain attributes are utilized in classification, they may hinder accurate object localization, which can lead to imperfect positive correlation.

2.2 Self-supervised Learning for Object Detection

Self-supervised object detection methods can be broadly classified into three categories: predictive, contrastive, and self-distillation.

In predictive methods (e.g., UP-DETR [14]), pretraining of the detection head is achieved by having the head re-predict the location of the autogenerated "ground truth" crop. Contrastive methods (e.g., DenseCL [155]) attempt to train the box head of the Faster RCNN by minimizing the InfoNCE loss such that the output of positive sample pairs is close and the output of negative sample pairs is far. Self-distillation methods, such as SoCo, are significantly different from contrastive methods because they do not require the use of negative samples. SoCo employs a simultaneous training approach to pretrain the backbone, feature pyramid, and RoI head of the Faster R-CNN model. This involves training two networks in parallel, allowing for comprehensive pretraining of these key components in object detection.

These methods not only try to compensate for the shortcomings of classification methods but also attempt pretraining the dedicated modules used for object detection on unsupervised pretext tasks as well.

2.3 Selective Object COntrastive Learning (SoCo)

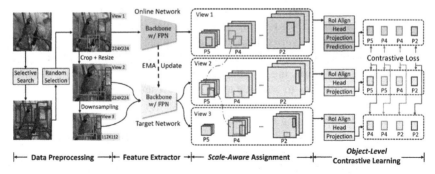

Fig. 1. Overview of SoCo. SoCo utilizes selective search for object proposals and creates multiple views with varying scales and locations. It uses a backbone network with FPN and RoIAlign for feature encoding. Contrastive learning is performed at the object level to learn invariant representations. The target network is updated using exponential moving average.

The main flowchart of SoCo is illustrated in Fig. 1. In this section, we will cover it in detail in several parts.

Object Proposal Generation. To generate object proposals, SoCo employs the use of selective search [6], an unsupervised algorithm that takes into consideration factors such as color similarity. This allows SoCo to generate accurate and diverse object proposals for further processing.

View Construction. SoCo uses three views, namely V_1, V_2, and V_3, where V_1 is obtained by resizing the original image, V_2 is obtained by randomly cropping V_1, and V_3

is obtained by downsampling V_2. Each view undergoes independent and random augmentation. By introducing variations in scale and location for the same object proposal across the augmented views, the model can effectively learn translation-invariant and scale-invariant object-level representations.

Scale-Aware Assignment. To facilitate the learning of scale-invariant object-level representations, SoCo assigns object proposals with areas falling within specific ranges $\{0 - 48^2, 49^2 - 96^2, 97^2 - 192^2, 193^2 - 224^2\}$ to different pyramid levels $\{P_2, P_3, P_4, P_5\}$ respectively. This approach ensures that object proposals of varying scales are encouraged to learn scale-invariant representations through contrastive learning. By considering proposals at different scales, SoCo can effectively capture object-level information across different size ranges.

Architecture. Object proposals address the architectural discrepancy between pretraining and downstream detection finetuning. Mask R-CNN [16] evaluates transfer performance, utilizing ResNet-50 with FPN as the image-level feature encoder. RoIAlign extracts RoI features from the feature map. SoCo employs both the online and target networks, sharing a common architecture but with different weights.

3 Method

In this section, we present the proposed end-to-end object-level contrastive pretraining for detection, which obtains object proposals using the pretraining network itself, includingsemantic-aware localization, center-suppressed sampling, and multiple crop strategies.

From the Introduction, it can be seen that the current self-supervised learning method SoCo [5], which performs well in object detection, has certain shortcomings: object proposals generation by selective search [6] wastes a lot of time and storage space, traditional proposal generation usually shows worse performance than deep learning-based methods, and it cannot achieve end-to-end training. By observing the excellent performance of the semantic-aware localization strategy [17] to obtain heat maps and the multiple cropping idea [12] in self-supervised learning, this paper innovatively uses the above strategies for object proposal generation to achieve end-to-end self-supervised object detection. We refer to the improved method as SoCo-E2E.

As shown in Fig. 2, SoCo-E2E uses the semantic-aware localization strategy to obtain the bounding box, followed by several object proposal boxes by the center-suppressed sampling strategy. During each training step, k proposals are randomly chosen to create three views that exhibit variations in scale and location. The backbone network is employed to encode image-level features, while RoI Align is utilized to extract object-level features. Based on the area of the object proposals, they are assigned to different pyramid levels, and contrastive learning is conducted at the object-level to facilitate the learning of translation invariance and scale invariance for detection. The target network is updated by performing an exponential moving average of the online network. This approach helps stabilize the learning process and ensures that the target network benefits from the accumulated knowledge of the online network.

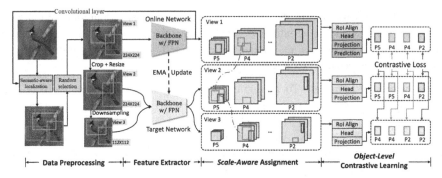

Fig. 2. Overview of SoCo-E2E.

3.1 Semantic-Aware Localization

The semantic-aware localization strategy [17] enables the model to learn semantic information in the image in an unsupervised manner so that the generated object proposals are reasonably framed to objects. In this research paper, the heat map is computed by aggregating features at the final convolutional layer across channels and subsequently normalizing them within the range of [0,1]. Figure 3 provides visual representations of the heat maps generated at different training milestones, including the 20th, 40th, 60th, and 80th epochs.

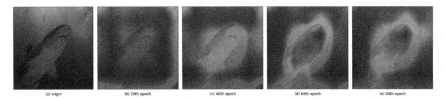

Fig. 3. Heat map for different training epochs

Based on the above analysis, we use the information in the heat map to locate objects during the training process. Specifically, a random generation method is used to initialize the object proposals at the early stage of training, as a way to make the network learn the semantic information of the whole image. Then, the bounding box of object B is obtained from the heat map by a threshold function, as shown in Eq. 1.

$$B = L(I[M > thresh]) \tag{1}$$

where M denotes the heat map, $thresh \in [0,1]$ is the threshold of activation, I is the indicator function, and L computes the rectangular closure of the activation position.

Throughout the training process, the object proposals undergo periodic and progressive updates to leverage the latest learned features from the mode l. It is important to note that the objective of this method is not precise localization, but rather guiding the bounding box generation by identifying the object of interest. The threshold parameter, denoted as $thresh \in [0, 1]$, controls the proportion of the bounding box.

3.2 Center-Suppressed Sampling

The semantic-aware localization strategy generates a bounding box containing the objects of interest. To avoid that the object proposals generated based on this bounding box are too concentrated and contain approximate semantic content, in this subsection, we introduce the center-suppressed sampling strategy [17] to solve this problem.

The primary objective is to minimize the concentration of object proposals around the center by dispersing them. To achieve this, the paper proposes the utilization of a beta distribution $\beta(\alpha, \alpha)$ with identical parameters α. By adjusting α, the shape of the distribution can be controlled effectively. We expand the variance of the object proposals by setting $\alpha < 1$ so that the probability is lower near the center and higher at other locations. In this way, the object proposals are more easily dispersed near the boundary line of the operable region and the overlap can be largely avoided.

(a) Random Sampling   (b) Center-Suppressed Sampling

Fig. 4. Example of center-suppressed sampling

As shown in Fig. 4, based on the bounding box obtained by the semantic-aware localization strategy in Sect. 3.1, random sampling leads to too much similarity among object proposals, which is not conducive to model learning. When generating object proposals in this paper, the central suppression sampling strategy will be used to make the object proposals overlap as little as possible to obtain differentiated semantic information, so that the model can be learned better.

3.3 Multiple Crop

In SwAV [12], the data enhancement strategy of multiple-crop was first proposed. In previous self-supervised contrastive learning methods, such as MoCo [10], and SimCLR [11], all of them crop two random views of 224×224 size from the original image, while the multi-crop strategy includes two standard random crops and V small views.

The larger area crops reflect the features of the whole scene and only enable the model to learn the global features. If we want the model to learn the local features of these objects, we need to add multiple additional small area crops. To keep the model from paying extra computational cost, the authors of SwAV [12] proposed using 2 crops of 160×160 size to learn the image's global features. Also to add additional positive samples to learn local features, 4 crops of size 96×96 were selected. By adjusting the size of the crops, a trade-off is made between the area of the crops and the number of crops to add additional views to learn local features without increasing the computational cost.

(a) Random Sampling   (b) Multi-crop Sampling

Fig. 5. Multi-crop sampling example

As shown in Fig. 5, when generating object proposals in this paper, the multiple cropping strategy will be used to control the size of the object proposals so that they can extract global features and local features as much as possible to better learn the semantic information of the images.

4   Experiment

4.1   Pretraining Settings

Similar to SoCo [5], we also use Mask R-CNN to evaluate transfer performance, ResNet-50 with FPN for image-level feature encoding, and RoIAlign to extract RoI features. The difference lies in the generation phase of object proposals, where we obtain the convolutional layer output of the backbone network during training. Same to SoCo [5], ImageNet [7] was used as the dataset for self-supervised pretraining. Data enhancement was performed on all constructed views using the process used in BYOL [13], including random level flipping, color dithering, Gaussian blur, exposure, and grayscale operations. In all experiments, we adopt a training schedule consisting of 100 epochs, and the reported results in the comparisons with SoCo methods are based on 100 epochs. The LARS optimizer is utilized, along with a cosine decay learning rate schedule. The weight decay is set to $1.0 \times e^{-5}$, and the total batch size is configured as 256 across 4 Nvidia V100 GPUs.

4.2   Finetuning Settings

For transfer learning, the COCO datasets are employed. Specifically, we use the COCO train2017 set, which consists of approximately 118,000 images.

In our approach, we utilize the Mask R-CNN detector [166] with the R50-FPN backbone. The evaluation metrics include AP^{bb}, AP^{bb}_{50} and AP^{bb}_{75} for object detection, as well as AP^{mk}, AP^{mk}_{50} and AP^{mk}_{75} for instance segmentation.

To ensure consistency, synchronized batch normalization is implemented across all layers, including the newly initialized batch normalization layers during finetuning, following the approach in [18].

For the COCO datasets, we adopt stochastic gradient descent with a batch size 8 on 4 GPUs. Weight decay and base learning rate are selected as of $2.5 \times e^{-5}$ and 0.02. The learning rate increases linearly for the first 1000 iterations and then decreases twice by a factor of 10 after 2/3 and 8/9 of the total training time, as described in [18].

4.3 Training Time and Space Cost

We carry a series of experiments to verify the feasibility of the object proposal generation scheme proposed in this paper, including runtime and storage space comparison, performance evaluation, and ablation study.

Table 1. Comparison of runtime and storage space

Method	Time				Storage space
	selective search	pretrain	fine-tune	total	
SoCo [5]	36 h	13.5 h	10 h	59.5 h	291 G
SoCo-E2E (Ours)	-	14 h	10 h	24 h	1 G

As shown in Table 1, with a 10% ImageNet dataset, the SoCo method requires about 36 h of selective search, 13.5 h of pretraining and 10 h of fine-tuning. The total time required is 59.5 h. The SoCo-E2E method proposed in this paper requires only 14 h of pretraining and 10 h of fine-tuning. The total time required is 24 h. The total training time is 60% lower than that of the SoCo method. In terms of storage space, SoCo requires 291 G, while the SoCo-E2E proposed requires less than 1 G. Therefore, the SoCo-E2E method has a great improvement in both runtime and storage space.

4.4 Performance Comparison

Table 2 shows the results for Mask R-CNN with R50-FPN backbone. We compare the proposed method with SoCo [5] on the COCO 1 × schedules. Due to hardware limitations, we use batch size 256 over 4 Nvidia V100 16G GPUs in the proposed method (denoted as SoCo-E2E#). For a fair comparison, we also run the author's code with batch size 256 over 4 Nvidia V100 16G GPUs (denoted as SoCo#).

As shown in the bottom two rows of Table 2, compared with SoCo# [5], the proposed SoCo-E2E# shows about 1%-2% performance improvement, reflecting the effectiveness of our work. Additionally, the proposed method can achieve end-to-end training, which is more convenient to use, and improve efficiency, avoiding a large amount of time and storage space occupied when using the selective search, and also reducing the hardware requirements when applying the method to other datasets.

Table 2. Comparison with SoCo [5] on COCO by using Mask R-CNN with R50-FPN.

Methods	Epoch	AP^{bb}	AP^{bb}_{50}	AP^{bb}_{75}	AP^{mk}	AP^{mk}_{50}	AP^{mk}_{75}
SoCo[#] [5]	100	32.9	51.4	35.3	30.1	48.6	32.1
SoCo-E2E[#] (Ours)	100	**34.2**	**52.7**	**37.1**	**31.1**	**49.9**	**33.2**

4.5 Ablation Study

To further analyze the advantages of SoCo-E2E, we conduct an ablation study that examines the effectiveness of the semantic-aware localization strategy. We carry pretraining experiments on 0%, 10% and 100% ImageNet datasets, the results are shown in Table 3. The result with 0% ImageNet datasets which means object detection without pretraining, shows significantly worse performance and indicates the importance of pretraining in object detection tasks. Our work shows a little worse performance than SOCO [5] on pretraining with 10% ImageNet datasets while achieving better results on pretraining with 100% ImageNet datasets.

We analyze that the semantic-aware localization strategy has the property of benefiting from larger datasets, while the performance of traditional selective search algorithms is independent of dataset size. This also indicates that semantic-aware localization methods have more performance advantages in the field of self-supervised learning using large datasets.

Table 3. Evaluation results on COCO by using Mask R-CNN with R50-FPN.

method	ImageNet	AP^{bb}	AP^{bb}_{50}	AP^{bb}_{75}	AP^{mk}	AP^{mk}_{50}	AP^{mk}_{75}
None	0%	26.65	43.15	28.11	24.65	40.59	26.08
SoCo[#] [5]	10%	32.09	50.34	34.72	29.16	47.24	30.90
	100%	32.89	51.35	35.29	30.14	48.63	32.08
SoCo-E2E[#] (Ours)	10%	31.85	49.74	34.46	29.03	47.06	31.03
	100%	**34.15**	**52.72**	**37.10**	**31.14**	**49.89**	**33.19**

5   Conclusion

In this paper, we propose an end-to-end object-level contrastive pretraining for detection. To this end, we use semantic-aware localization to learn semantic information for generating bounding boxes during training, then apply center-suppressed sampling and multiple cropping to increase the diversity and plausibility of object proposals. The comparative experiments demonstrate that the proposed method shows better performance with significantly less training space and time cost. By observing the experimental results on datasets of different sizes, it is found that the semantic-aware localization strategy can learn better semantic information on larger datasets. The phenomenon reflects that semantic-aware localization has a good prospect in the field of self-supervised learning on large datasets.

Acknowledgments. This work was supported by Scientific Research Project of Beijing Educational Committee (KM202011232014).

References

1. Zaidi, S.S.A., Ansari, M.S., Aslam, A., Kanwal, N., Asghar, M., & Lee, B.: A survey of modern deep learning based object detection models. Digital Signal Process. **126** 103514. (2022)
2. Redmon, J., Divvala, S., Girshick, R., Farhadi, A.: You only look once: unified, real-time object detection. In: Proceedings of the IEEE Conference on Computer Vision and Pattern Recognition, pp. 779–788 (2016)
3. Liu, W., et al.: SSD: single shot multibox detector. In: Leibe, B., Matas, J., Sebe, N., Welling, M. (eds.) ECCV 2016. LNCS, vol. 9905, pp. 21–37. Springer, Cham (2016). https://doi.org/10.1007/978-3-319-46448-0_2
4. Ren, S., He, K., Girshick, R., Sun, J.: Faster R-CNN: towards real-time object detection with region proposal networks. In: Advances in Neural Information Processing Systems, vol. 28 (2015)
5. Wei, F., Gao, Y., Wu, Z., Hu, H., Lin, S.: Aligning pretraining for detection via object-level contrastive learning. Adv. Neural. Inf. Process. Syst. **34**, 22682–22694 (2021)
6. Uijlings, J.R., Van De Sande, K.E., Gevers, T., Smeulders, A.W.: Selective search for object recognition. Int. J. Comput. Vision **104**(2), 154–171 (2013)
7. Everingham, M., Van Gool, L., Williams, C.K., Winn, J., Zisserman, A.: The pascal visual object classes (VOC) challenge. Int. J. Comput. Vis. **88**(2), 303–338 (2010)
8. Lin, T.-Y., et al.: Microsoft coco: common objects in context. In: Fleet, D., Pajdla, T., Schiele, B., Tuytelaars, T. (eds.) ECCV 2014. LNCS, vol. 8693, pp. 740–755. Springer, Cham (2014). https://doi.org/10.1007/978-3-319-10602-1_48
9. Huang, G., Laradji, I., Vazquez, D., Lacoste-Julien, S., Rodriguez, P.: A survey of self-supervised and few-shot object detection (2021). arXiv preprint arXiv:2110.14711
10. He, K., Fan, H., Wu, Y., Xie, S., Girshick, R.: Momentum contrast for unsupervised visual representation learning. In: Proceedings of the IEEE/CVF Conference on Computer Vision and Pattern Recognition, pp. 9729–9738 (2020)
11. Chen, T., Kornblith, S., Norouzi, M., Hinton, G.: A simple framework for contrastive learning of visual representations. In: International Conference on Machine Learning (PMLR), pp. 1597–1607 (2020)
12. Caron, M., Misra, I., Mairal, J., Goyal, P., Bojanowski, P., Joulin, A.: Unsupervised learning of visual features by contrasting cluster assignments. Adv. Neural. Inf. Process. Syst. **33**, 9912–9924 (2020)
13. Grill, J.B., et al.: Bootstrap your own latent-a new approach to self-supervised learning. Adv. Neural. Inf. Process. Syst. **33**, 21271–21284 (2020)
14. Dai, Z., Cai, B., Lin, Y., Chen, J.: UP-DETR: unsupervised pretraining for object detection with transformers. In: Proceedings of the IEEE/CVF Conference on Computer Vision and Pattern Recognition, pp. 1601–1610 (2021)

15. Wang, X., Zhang, R., Shen, C., Kong, T., Li, L.: Dense contrastive learning for self-supervised visual pretraining. In: Proceedings of the IEEE/CVF Conference on Computer Vision and Pattern Recognition, pp. 3024–3033 (2021)
16. He, K., Gkioxari, G., Dollár, P., Girshick, R. Mask R-CNN. In: Proceedings of the IEEE International Conference on Computer Vision, pp. 2961–2969 (2017)
17. Peng, X., Wang, K., Zhu, Z., Wang, M., You, Y.: Crafting better contrastive views for siamese representation learning. In: Proceedings of the IEEE/CVF Conference on Computer Vision and Pattern Recognition, pp. 16031–16040 (2022)
18. Chen, X., Fan, H., Girshick, R., He, K.: Improved baselines with momentum contrastive learning (2020). arXiv preprint arXiv:2003.04297

PointerNet with Local and Global Contexts for Natural Language Moment Localization

Linwei Ye[1](✉) , Zhi Liu[2] , and Yang Wang[3]

[1] College of Computer Science and Artificial Intelligence, Wenzhou University,
Wenzhou, China
ylw@wzu.edu.cn
[2] School of Communication and Information Engineering, Shanghai University,
Shanghai, China
[3] Department of Computer Science and Software Engineering, Concordia University,
Montreal, Canada

Abstract. We consider the problem of natural language moment localization. Given an untrimmed video and a natural language query, we aim
to automatically retrieve a semantically relevant moment in the video
referred by the query sentence. Most existing methods work by projecting
visual and linguistic data into feature embedding space, then matching
the semantic similarity or ranking a set of pre-defined segments to select
the moment. In this paper, we propose a novel PointerNet with local and
global contexts to solve this problem. Our proposed model first uses a
recurrent network over words to interact visual and linguistic features
in a fine-grained fashion. The word recurrence represents each clip as a
multimodal feature that captures the fine-grained interaction of each clip
with all words in the query sentence. It then uses another bi-directional
recurrent network that processes all clips in the video. The clip recurrence refines the local context information of each clip and produces a
global context representation of the entire video. Finally, the global video
context and the local context of each clip are jointly used to determine
the start and the end positions of the moment. Extensive experimental
results demonstrate the effectiveness of our proposed method.

Keywords: Vision and Language · Deep Learning · Moment
Localization

1 Introduction

Video understanding is an important problem in computer vision with many
potential applications, such as intelligent video retrieval, browsing, recommendation, etc. A lot of existing work in video understanding focuses on activity
detection. There has been fruitful progress [2,22,24] in recent years. However,
previous work in video activity detection requires a set of pre-defined activity

L. Fang et al. (Eds.): CICAI 2023, LNAI 14473, pp. 305–316, 2024.
https://doi.org/10.1007/978-981-99-8850-1_25

classes such as eating, dancing and washing. This has limited its applications in the real world. In addition, a video with long duration may contain complex activities that cannot be described as a simple action class. For example, Fig. 1 shows an example of a complex video with different activities ("open refrigerator" and "pour milk"). It is more appealing to use the free-form natural language as the query for video understanding. In this paper, we address the problem of natural language moment localization in unconstrained videos. Specifically, given a video and a natural language sentence, our goal is to automatically determine the start and end positions of a moment in the video that corresponds to semantic meaning of the query.

Some works [5,8,13,18–21] have been proposed to solve the natural language moment localization problem. These methods usually treat the video and language modalities individually and extract visual and linguistic features separately from each modality. Then they use different fusion strategies to integrate these features to obtain multimodal feature representation by addition and multiplication [5], concatenation [16], pooling [9] or attentive weights [19], etc.

Most existing methods [1,5,8,19,23] for this task also require generating candidate segments in the form of video segments. The moment localization is then treated as a matching or ranking problem. In this way, they are able to reduce the search space of all clips in the video to the candidate video segments and utlize the multimodal features within these video segments. However, in order to precisely localize the moment, these works usually need to generate dense segments. This is time-consuming for long videos in practice. In addition, the multimodal feature representations for these generated segments have limited contexts since the feature extraction process only considers the information within the segment. The independent matching of each candidate segment is suboptimal without considering the global context of the whole video.

Fig. 1. An illustration of natural language moment localization. Given an input video and a natural language query sentence, the goal is to localize the moment in the video referred by the query sentence. The moment (shown in blue) can potentially involve complex activities, such as "opens a refrigerator" shown in red and "pour milk" shown in green. (Color figure online)

What is the strategy that humans use in order to solve the natural language moment localization problem? Given an input video and a sentence query, people often follow a vision-language-vision reading order and go back-and-forth several times between the video and sentence before making the prediction [7,14]. Motivated by this observation, we propose a novel PointerNet-based model [15] for moment localization in this paper. Our model produces an effective multimodal representation for every clip in the video. It also captures the global video context of the entire video and the local context of each clip. Specifically, we introduce word recurrence that computes multimodal feature for each clip in the video by taking into account the interaction of this clip with each word in the query sentence. This multimodal clip feature representation captures fine-grained interaction between words in the sentence and clips in the video. In addition, we develop temporal clip recurrence of all clips to refine local context information for each clip and build global video context by going forward and backward over the whole video. Then the generated global video context is used together with the local context of each clip to localize the moment. Finally, we use PointerNet to predict soft positions for the start and the end positions of the moment. Our network does not require segment proposals and can be trained in an end-to-end fashion.

Our contributions can be summarized as follows. (1) We propose a novel PointerNet with local and global video contexts for natural language moment localization. (2) We introduce word recurrence to recurrently interact visual and linguistic information for an effective multimodal representation in a sequential order. (3) We further introduce clip recurrence to refine local context information for each clip to build relationships of individual clips and generate global video context of the whole video to directly predict the start and end positions of the moment of interest.

2 Our Approach

Let X denote an input video with a sequence of T clips as $X = \{x_t\}_{t=1}^{T}$. A set of moment and natural language annotations $\{S, p_s, p_e\}$ is associated with the video X for a specific moment, where S is a natural language sentence describing the content of a moment that we want to retrieve. The sentence S consists of a sequence of L words. Here p_s and p_e are the start position and the end position of the corresponding moment in the video, respectively. Specifically, the input to our network is a video X and a natural language sentence S. Our task is to predict the start position p_s and the end position p_e of the moment according to the query sentence. The overall architecture of our proposed model is illustrated in Fig. 2.

2.1 Word Recurrence for Multimodal Clip Features

We propose a word recurrence network for multimodal clip feature extraction in this section. The goal is to represent each clip in the video as a feature vector that captures the information about the query sentence.

Visual Encoder: For a given clip x_t in the long video X, we first extract the visual feature of this clip using the inflated 3D ConvNet (I3D) [3]. I3D inflates filters and kernels of 2D ConvNet to 3D and uses these filters to extract spatio-temporal features on a clip x_t. We then summarize raw spatio-temporal I3D

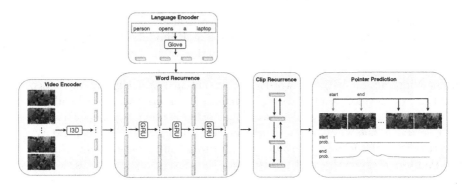

Fig. 2. An overview of our approach. The proposed network consists of several components, including video and language encoders, word recurrence for multimodal clip features, clip recurrence, and pointer prediction for moment localization. Our model first extracts visual features for clips in the video and linguistic features for words in the sentence. Then a multimodal feature representation for each clip is generated by the word recurrence. Video clip recurrence is further used to refine local context information for each clip and build global video context of the whole video. Finally, a PointNet uses the global video context and the local context of each clip to predict the start and the end positions of the moment in the video.

features over spatial regions as a visual feature vector v_t by a global average pooling.

$$v_t = \mathrm{SpatialPool}(\mathrm{I3D}(x_t)), \quad t = 1, 2, ..., T \tag{1}$$

where $\mathrm{I3D}(x_t)$ extracts the spatial-temporal I3D features from the clip x_t and $\mathrm{SpatialPool}(\cdot)$ denotes the global average pooling over spatial regions. We use d_v to denote the dimension of v_t, i.e. $v_t \in \mathbb{R}^{d_v}$.

Language Encoder: In order to capture fine-grained word-level representations, we represent each word by its Glove [11] word embedding vector and then use a fully connected layer to transform the original word embedding to the final word-level representations. The query sentence is represented as $\{w_l\}_{l=1}^{L} \in \mathbb{R}^{d_w}$, where L is the total number of words in the sentence and d_w is the dimension of the word vector representation.

Multimodal Clip Features: When people solve the moment localization task, they usually examine the language words and the video in a back and forth manner and gradually correlate linguistic semantics with visual contents [14]. Inspired by this, we propose to combine the visual feature of each clip with the linguistic feature of every word using a sequential process. Concretely, we first concatenate every clip feature v_t and every word feature w_l along the channel dimension to result in a multimodal representation as follows:

$$f_{t,l} = [v_t, w_l] \in \mathbb{R}^{d_v+d_w}, \ \forall t \in \{1, 2, ..., T\} \ \forall l \in \{1, 2, ..., L\} \tag{2}$$

The feature vector $f_{t,l}$ contains both the visual information of the t-th clip v_t and the linguistic information of the l-th word w_l. For a particular clip v_t, we use gated recurrent units (GRU) [4] to recurrently aggregate multimodal features over all words in the sentence as:

$$z_{t,l} = \sigma(W_z f_{t,l} + U_z h_{t,l-1} + b_z) \tag{3a}$$
$$r_{t,l} = \sigma(W_r f_{t,l} + U_r h_{t,l-1} + b_r) \tag{3b}$$
$$h_{t,l} = z_{t,l} \odot h_{t,l-1} + (1 - z_{t,l}) \odot \tag{3c}$$
$$\tanh(W_h f_{t,l} + U_h(r_{t,l} \odot h_{t,l-1}) + b_h) \tag{3d}$$
$$\text{where} \quad l = 1, 2, ..., L \tag{3e}$$

where W_z, U_z, W_r, U_r, W_h, U_h, b_z, b_z and b_h are parameters of the GRU. σ denotes the sigmoid function and $\odot$ is the Hadamard product. $z_{t,l}$ and $r_{t,l}$ are the update gate and reset gate, respectively. $h_{t,l}$ is the hidden state also known as the output after finishing reading the l-th word in the sentence. When sequentially taking the multimodal features over words, the hidden state $h_{t,l}$ is updated for every clip t in the video at the same time according to the current input $f_{t,l}$ and the previous hidden state $h_{t,l-1}$ by controlling the information flow through gates $z_{t,l}$ and $r_{t,l}$. The recurrence of GRU is performed over words to make each clip interact with each word in order to capture fine-grained interaction between each clip in the video and each word in the query sentence. The final output of the GRU $h_{t,L}$ at the last time step L has read all words in the sentence and is used as the multimodal feature representation for the clip. We use $c_t = h_{t,L}$ to denote this multimodal feature for the clip t.

2.2   Clip Recurrence and Global Video Context

The generated multimodal clip representation in Sect. 2.1 only depends on the local context within a single clip. However, people tend to look over the entire video to get a comprehensive context of the video first in order to localize the moment associated with the query sentence. Inspired by this observation, In this section, we first employ clip recurrence of all clips in the entire video to refine local context information for each clip and obtain a global context representation of the entire video. Then the global video context as well as the refined local context of each clip is jointly used to accurately localize the moment as shown in Fig. 3.

For a sequence of multimodal clip representations $\{c_t\}_{t=1}^{T}$ over clips in the video, we first encode all clips of the video via clip recurrence by a temporal GRU which updates the hidden state along the video clip order as:

$$\overrightarrow{z_t'} = \sigma(\overrightarrow{W_{z'}}c_t + \overrightarrow{U_{z'}}\overrightarrow{h_{t-1}'} + \overrightarrow{b_{z'}}) \tag{4a}$$
$$\overrightarrow{r_t'} = \sigma(\overrightarrow{W_{r'}}c_t + \overrightarrow{U_{r'}}\overrightarrow{h_{t-1}'} + \overrightarrow{b_{r'}}) \tag{4b}$$
$$\overrightarrow{h_t'} = \overrightarrow{z_t'} \odot \overrightarrow{h_{t-1}'} + (1 - \overrightarrow{z_t'}) \odot \tag{4c}$$
$$\tanh(\overrightarrow{W_{h'}}c_t + \overrightarrow{U_{h'}}(\overrightarrow{r_l'} \odot \overrightarrow{h_{t-1}'}) + \overrightarrow{b_{h'}}) \tag{4d}$$
$$\text{where} \quad t = 1, 2, ..., T \tag{4e}$$

Similarly, $\overrightarrow{W_{z'}}$, $\overrightarrow{U_{z'}}$, $\overrightarrow{W_{r'}}$, $\overrightarrow{U_{r'}}$, $\overrightarrow{W_{h'}}$, $\overrightarrow{U_{h'}}$, $\overrightarrow{b_{z'}}$ and $\overrightarrow{b_{h'}}$ are parameters of this GRU. $\overrightarrow{z'_{t,L}}$ and $\overrightarrow{r'_{t,L}}$ are the update and reset gates of the temporal GRU. The final hidden state at the last time step T (i.e. $\overrightarrow{h'_T}$) has gone over all clips in the forward direction.

We use another temporal GRU to produce backward hidden state $\overleftarrow{h'_t}$ in the opposite direction in the video as follows:

$$\overleftarrow{z'_t} = \sigma(\overleftarrow{W_{z'}}c_t + \overleftarrow{U_{z'}}\overleftarrow{h'_{t+1}} + \overleftarrow{b_{z'}}) \tag{5a}$$

$$\overleftarrow{r'_t} = \sigma(\overleftarrow{W_{r'}}c_t + \overleftarrow{U_{r'}}\overleftarrow{h'_{t+1}} + \overleftarrow{b_{r'}}) \tag{5b}$$

$$\overleftarrow{h'_t} = \overleftarrow{z'_t} \odot \overleftarrow{h'_{t+1}} + (1 - \overleftarrow{z'_t}) \odot \tag{5c}$$

$$\tanh(\overleftarrow{W_{h'}}c_t + \overleftarrow{U_{h'}}(\overleftarrow{r'_l} \odot \overleftarrow{h'_{t+1}}) + \overleftarrow{b_{h'}}) \tag{5d}$$

$$\text{where} \quad t = T, T-1, ..., 1 \tag{5e}$$

The multimodal clip feature with local context is updated by the combination of the forward and backward hidden states at each clip t as $h'_t = [\overrightarrow{h'_t}, \overleftarrow{h'_t}]$. The encoded h'_t contains the progressive context information over time steps, which is essential for moment boundary identification [10,17]. Then the global video context can be obtained as $G = [\overrightarrow{h'_T}, \overleftarrow{h'_1}]$. G gathers the final hidden states in both directions for global contextual multimodal information through all clips and words.

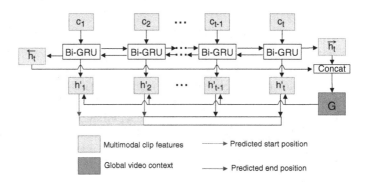

Fig. 3. Clip Recurrence and global video context. The multimodal features of clips in the video recurrently interact with other clips via a bi-directional GRU to refine local context information for each clip. The final hidden states of the bi-directional GRU are used as the global video context representation.

2.3   PointerNet-Based Moment Localization

PointerNet [15] is introduced to predict discrete positions based on the input sequence. It first proposes to use a pointer to indicate the potential position over the input sequence to solve tasks such as convex hull and Delaunay triangulation. Inspired by the pointer mechanism, we utlize the global video context of the video and the local context of each clip to produce two pointers (i.e. start position and end position) corresponding to the localized moment. In the following, we use the process of the start position prediction as an example. The same technique can also be applied for the end position prediction. To localize the start position, the pointer function is calculated as follows:

$$s_t = w^T \tanh(W_a h'_t + W_b G), \quad \forall t \tag{6}$$

where W_a, W_b and w are learnable parameters of the pointer function. s_t denotes the score of a specific clip t being the start position of the moment. We then calculate the probability of the clip being the start position by normalizing the responses predicted by Eq. 6 across all clips in the video by:

$$e_t = \frac{\exp(s_t)}{\sum_{t'=1}^{T} \exp(s'_t)}, \quad \forall t \tag{7}$$

We propose to use a soft position prediction instead of the hard selection strategy for position prediction. Specifically, we generate a sequence of integers as the same length as the video, i.e., $\{1, 2, ..., T\}$, which represent possible clip positions in the video. We can then calculate the weighted average for a start position as follows:

$$p_s = \sum_{t=1}^{T} t \cdot e_t \tag{8}$$

where p_s can be interpreted as a "soft pointer" indicating the start position of the moment. We use another pointer function (with its own learnable parameters) similar to Eq. 6 to generate the end position scores of all clips. We then predict the end position p_e by Eq. 7 and Eq. 8.

2.4   Training

Given a pair of predicted positions (p_s, p_e) and ground truth positions (p_s^{gt}, p_e^{gt}), we design a normalized mean square error (MSE) loss to directly regress the predicted positions defined as: $L_{mse} = \frac{(p_s - p_s^{gt})^2 + (p_e - p_e^{gt})^2}{p_e^{gt} - p_s^{gt}}$. The MSE loss measures the absolute difference at the start and the end positions between the prediction and the ground truth. However, only using MSE loss may fail to evaluate a moment that has a reasonable overlap with ground truth. Therefore, we additionally define an IoU loss: $L_{iou} = -\log\left(\frac{[p_s, p_e] \cap [p_s^{gt}, p_e^{gt}]}{[p_s, p_e] \cup [p_s^{gt}, p_e^{gt}]}\right)^2$, to measure whether the predicted moment matches with the ground truth. where $[p_s, p_e]$ denotes the temporal interval with p_s and p_e as the start and the end positions, respectively. $[p_s^{gt}, p_e^{gt}]$ is similarly defined. The overall loss of our network is composed of these two loss functions with a weight parameter α to balance between two losses as: $L = L_{mse} + \alpha L_{iou}$.

3   Experiments

We evaluate our approach on three publicly available natural language moment localization datasets, including Charades-STA [5], ActivityNet Captions [6], and TACoS [12]. We follow the evaluation metrics used in [20] ("R@1 IoU@σ" and "mean IoU") to measure the performance of the proposed network.

Implementation Details: We truncate input sentences to keep the maximum length as 20 words and embed each word into a 300 dimensional Glove word vector. Then each word vector is transformed to $d_w = 512$ with a fully connected layer and concatenated with the visual feature of each clip of dimension $d_v = 1024$ to result in a 1536 dimensional multimodal feature representation. The whole network is trained in an end-to-end fashion by Adam optimization algorithm with an initial learning rate at $1e^{-4}$ and a weight decay of $1e^{-3}$.

Table 1. Ablation study on the Charades-STA dataset.

Methods	R@1, IoU@0.3	R@1, IoU@0.5	R@1, IoU@0.7	mIoU
Baseline	62.82	46.07	21.34	41.57
Baseline+WR	64.49	47.23	23.06	42.93
Baseline+GVC	65.00	48.41	25.08	44.10
Baseline+WR+GVC (Ours)	**69.87**	**55.75**	**30.22**	**47.83**
Ours w/iou	55.12	36.52	19.17	36.33
Ours w/mse	65.23	48.11	23.06	43.54
Ours w/mse+iou	**69.87**	**55.75**	**30.22**	**47.83**

3.1   Ablation Study

To verify the effectiveness of each component of our network, we conduct ablation experiments on the Charades-STA dataset with different variants of the proposed method as follows:

- *Baseline*: this model does not have the word recurrence for multimodal clip features and global video context. Instead, it uses a LSTM to encode the whole sentence as a single sentence vector and then concatenates the sentence vector with the visual feature of each clip for multimodal representation. It predicts the start and end positions based on the local context of each video clip only.
- *Baseline+WR*: this model adds the word recurrence (WR) to the baseline model.

- *Baseline+GVC*: this model adds the global video context (GVC) to the baseline model.
- *Baseline+WR+GVC (i.e. ours)*: this is our proposed model that uses both WR and GVC.

The experimental results are shown in Table 1. It can be observed that either word recurrence for multimodal clip features or global video context improves the moment localization performance on its own compared with the baseline. The complete model with both WR and GVC further improves the performance. The results demonstrate the effectiveness of the proposed multimodal representation and the global video context for the moment localization problem. Meanwhile, the network trained with both MSE loss and IoU loss achieves the best performance compared with using either one.

3.2   Comparison with State-of-the-art

We compare our network with several competitive methods including moment contextual network (MCN) [1], cross-model temporal regression localizer (CTRL) [5], multilevel integration and multi-task loss (MIML) [19], moment alignment network (MAN) [21], attention based localization (ABLR) [20], semantic matching reinforcement learning (SMRL) [16], Boundary proposal network (BPnet) [18] and span-QA net (VSLNet) [22].

Table 2. Comparison of different methods on the Charades-STA dataset, the ActivityNet Captions dataset and the TACoS dataset, respectively.

Methods	Charades-STA		ActivityNet Caption		TACoS	
	R@1, IOU@0.5	R@1, IOU@0.7	R@1, IoU@0.3	R@1, IoU@0.5	R@1, IOU@0.3	R@1, IOU@0.5
MCN [1]	17.46	8.01	21.37	9.58	10.06	5.70
CTRL [5]	21.42	7.15	28.70	14.00	17.40	12.90
ABLR [20]	24.36	9.01	55.67	**36.79**	19.50	9.40
SMLR [16]	24.36	11.17	–	–	20.25	15.95
MIML [19]	35.60	15.80	45.30	27.70	–	–
MAN [21]	46.53	22.72	–	–	–	–
BPNet [18]	50.75	31.64	42.07	24.69	25.96	20.96
VSLNet [22]	54.19	**35.22**	43.22	26.16	29.61	**24.27**
Ours	**55.75**	30.22	**56.12**	34.53	**31.46**	17.59

Table 2 show the comparisons on the Charades-STA dataset, the ActivityNet Captions dataset and the TACoS dataset, respectively. Our network outperforms these approaches in most cases. Our method obtains better results in R@1,IoU@0.5 on the Charades-STA dataset and in R@1,IoU@0.3 on the TACoS dataset, but worse results with higher IOU compared with VSLNet. It is probably because the VSLNet incorporates the concept of multi-paragraph QA for boosting their performance on long videos. For the results on the ActivityNet Captions dataset, our network achieves superior performance in terms of R@1,IoU@0.3 but slightly behind ABLR in terms of R@1,IoU@0.5. However, their method is much more unstable and the results varies dramatically over different datasets where the performance degenerates on the Charades-STA dataset and TACoS dataset.

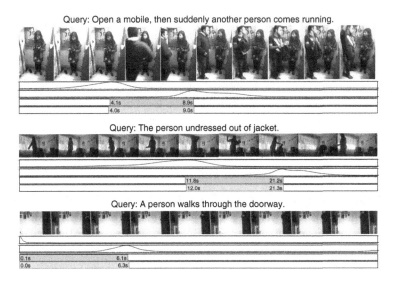

Fig. 4. Qualitative examples of our proposed network. The two curve graphs show the probabilities of the start and the end positions of clips over a video, respectively. The moment in red is our predicted moment and the moment in grey is the ground truth for the given query shown at the top of the video. (Color figure online)

Some qualitative examples are presented in Fig. 4. In the top example, our proposed network correctly localizes the moment involving two activities "open a mobile" and "another person comes running". In the second example, our network localizes an entire process of a long continuous activity "undressed out of jacket". The third example shows the situation where the background of the scene remains unchanged after the moment "walks through the doorway". Our model successfully localizes the precise moment once the activity ends. In addition, we visualize the probabilities defined in Eq. 7 of the start and the end positions of clips over a video, respectively. The two curve graphs below each corresponding video in Fig. 4 show how our network responses to the input and identifies the localized moment.

4   Conclusion

In this paper, we have presented a novel PointNet-based model with local and global contexts for natural language moment localization. The proposed network uses word recurrence or an effective multimodal feature representation of each clip. It then uses clip recurrence to refine local context information for each clip and build global video context. Finally, the PointerNet is adopted to produce start and end positions over clips for the moment of interest. Experimental results on three datasets shows that the supervisor performance of the proposed method.

Acknowledgments. This work was supported in part by the National Natural Science Foundation of China (Grant No. 62102289) and in part by the Zhejiang Provincial Natural Science Foundation (Grant No. LQ22F020005).

References

1. Anne Hendricks, L., Wang, O., Shechtman, E., Sivic, J., Darrell, T., Russell, B.: Localizing moments in video with natural language. In: IEEE International Conference on Computer Vision, pp. 5803–5812 (2017)
2. Caba Heilbron, F., Escorcia, V., Ghanem, B., Carlos Niebles, J.: ActivityNet: a large-scale video benchmark for human activity understanding. In: IEEE Conference on Computer Vision and Pattern Recognition, pp. 961–970 (2015)
3. Carreira, J., Zisserman, A.: Quo vadis, action recognition? A new model and the kinetics dataset. In: IEEE Conference on Computer Vision and Pattern Recognition, pp. 6299–6308 (2017)
4. Cho, K., et al.: Learning phrase representations using RNN encoder-decoder for statistical machine translation. In: Conference on Empirical Methods in Natural Language Processing (2014)
5. Gao, J., Sun, C., Yang, Z., Nevatia, R.: TALL: temporal activity localization via language query. In: IEEE International Conference on Computer Vision, pp. 5267–5275 (2017)
6. Krishna, R., Hata, K., Ren, F., Fei-Fei, L., Niebles, J.C.: Dense-captioning events in videos. In: International Conference on Computer Vision (2017)
7. Liu, C., Lin, Z., Shen, X., Yang, J., Lu, X., Yuille, A.L.: Recurrent multimodal interaction for referring image segmentation. In: IEEE International Conference on Computer Vision (2017)
8. Liu, M., Wang, X., Nie, L., He, X., Chen, B., Chua, T.S.: Attentive moment retrieval in videos. In: ACM SIGIR Conference on Research & Development in Information Retrieval, pp. 15–24 (2018)
9. Liu, M., Wang, X., Nie, L., Tian, Q., Chen, B., Chua, T.S.: Cross-modal moment localization in videos. In: ACM International Conference on Multimedia, pp. 843–851 (2018)
10. Ma, S., Sigal, L., Sclaroff, S.: Learning activity progression in LSTMs for activity detection and early detection. In: IEEE Conference on Computer Vision and Pattern Recognition, pp. 1942–1950 (2016)
11. Pennington, J., Socher, R., Manning, C.: GloVe: global vectors for word representation. In: Conference on Empirical Methods in Natural Language Processing, pp. 1532–1543 (2014)
12. Regneri, M., Rohrbach, M., Wetzel, D., Thater, S., Schiele, B., Pinkal, M.: Grounding action descriptions in videos. Trans. Assoc. Comput. Linguist. **1**, 25–36 (2013)
13. Tunguturi, M.: Moment localization using multi-scale 2D temporal adjacent networks and natural language. Int. J. Mach. Learn. Sustain. Dev. **4**(3), 1–10 (2022)
14. Underwood, G., Jebbett, L., Roberts, K.: Inspecting pictures for information to verify a sentence: Eye movements in general encoding and in focused search. Q. J. Exp. Psychol. Sect. A **57**(1), 165–182 (2004)

15. Vinyals, O., Fortunato, M., Jaitly, N.: Pointer networks. In: Advances in Neural Information Processing Systems, pp. 2692–2700 (2015)

16. Wang, W., Huang, Y., Wang, L.: Language-driven temporal activity localization: a semantic matching reinforcement learning model. In: IEEE Conference on Computer Vision and Pattern Recognition,

17. Wei, Z., et al.: Sequence-to-segment networks for segment detection. In: Advances in Neural Information Processing Systems, pp. 3507–3516 (2018)

18. Xiao, S., et al.: Boundary proposal network for two-stage natural language video localization. In: Proceedings of the AAAI Conference on Artificial Intelligence. vol. 35, pp. 2986–2994 (2021)

19. Xu, H., He, K., Plummer, B.A., Sigal, L., Sclaroff, S., Saenko, K.: Multilevel language and vision integration for text-to-clip retrieval. In: AAAI Conference on Artificial Intelligence. vol. 33, pp. 9062–9069 (2019)

20. Yuan, Y., Mei, T., Zhu, W.: To find where you talk: Temporal sentence localization in video with attention based location regression. In: AAAI Conference on Artificial Intelligence. vol. 33, pp. 9159–9166 (2019)

21. Zhang, D., Dai, X., Wang, X., Wang, Y.F., Davis, L.S.: MAN: moment alignment network for natural language moment retrieval via iterative graph adjustment. In: IEEE Conference on Computer Vision and Pattern Recognition, pp. 1247–1257 (2019)

22. Zhang, H., Sun, A., Jing, W., Zhen, L., Zhou, J.T., Goh, R.S.M.: Natural language video localization: A revisit in span-based question answering framework. IEEE Trans. Pattern Anal. Mach. Intell. 44(8), 4252–4266 (2021)

23. Zhang, L., Radke, R.J.: Natural language video moment localization through query-controlled temporal convolution. In: Proceedings of the IEEE/CVF Winter Conference on Applications of Computer Vision, pp. 682–690 (2022)

24. Zheng, M., Huang, Y., Chen, Q., Liu, Y.: Weakly supervised video moment localization with contrastive negative sample mining. In: AAAI Conference on Artificial Intelligence. vol. 36, pp. 3517–3525 (2022)

Self-supervised Meta Auxiliary Learning for Actor and Action Video Segmentation from Natural Language

Linwei Ye$^{(\boxtimes)}$ and Zhenhua Wang

College of Computer Science and Artificial Intelligence, Wenzhou University,
Wenzhou, China
ylw@wzu.edu.cn

Abstract. This paper addresses the problem of actor and action video segmentation from natural language. Given a video and a language query, the goal is to segment the actor and its action described by the query. Existing methods focus on exploring elaborated multimodal feature fusion networks to combine visual and linguistic features for an effective multimodal representation directly learnt from this labeled segmentation task. In this paper, we propose a novel self-supervised meta auxiliary learning method to improve the primary segmentation task by adding an auxiliary task for better generalization. The auxiliary task is established to reconstruct the input sentence representation so that the multimodal representation can be adapted to a specific query. In addition, the auxiliary task does not require additional labels. It can also be used in test time to update a multimodal representation according to a specific query in a self-supervised way.

Keywords: Language and vision · Auxiliary learning · Actor and action video segmentation

1 Introduction

Understanding actors and their actions in a video is a fundamental problem in video understanding. There has been lots of existing work in action detection [2,19] and segmentation [17]. However, these studies rely on a list of predefined action classes to recognize specific human activities such as "jumping", "walking" and "standing". This greatly restricts the potential applications of these methods in the real world. In contrast, a natural language sentence provides a richer and more flexible way of specifying actors and actions in a video. In this paper, we consider the problem of actor and action video segmentation from natural language as [4]. The goal is to segment a specific actor and his/her action referred by an arbitrary natural language query. Figure 1 shows an example of this task.

A general way of solving vision and language segmentation problem is to design an elaborated fusion strategy for a multimodal representation. These

L. Fang et al. (Eds.): CICAI 2023, LNAI 14473, pp. 317–328, 2024.
https://doi.org/10.1007/978-981-99-8850-1_26

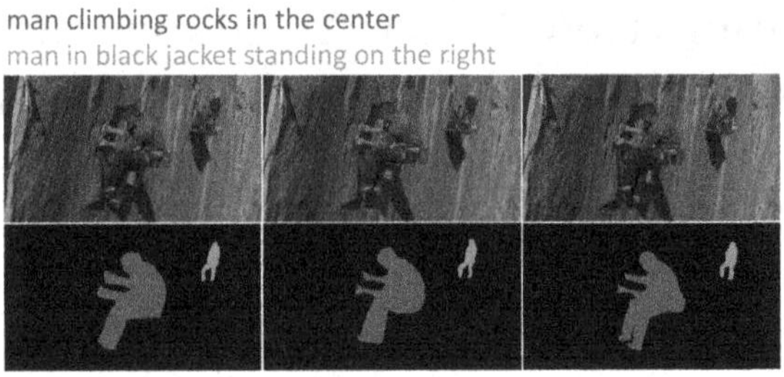

man climbing rocks in the center
man in black jacket standing on the right

Fig. 1. Illustration of actor and action video segmentation from natural language. Given an input video and a natural language query. The language query refers an actor and his/her action. The goal is to generate the pixel-level segmentation mask specified by the query. In this figure, the masks colored with red and green correspond to the query sentences with the same color at the top of each video. (Color figure online)

methods generally use convolutional neural networks to extract visual features and recurrent neural networks to encode linguistic features. Then they combine the visual features with linguistic features for a multimodal representation by different strategies such as concatenation [1,5], dynamic filters [4] or cross-guided attention [14,20]. Afterwards, a segmentation mask is produced based on the multimodal representation. The linguistic information is implicitly learned alongside the segmentation task. Different from these previous methods, we argue that the knowledge of visual and linguistic representations should be able to transfer between both visual and linguistic domains in order for an effective multimodal representation.

Learning to reconstruct the language sentence from the input has been shown to be effective for constructing a more robust multimodal representation in vision and language tasks (e.g. [10,12]). In addition, the recent progress of auxiliary learning shows its ability of improving the generalization of a primary task [9,13]. The input language query in our task can potentially serve as a natural supervision signal without any additional labeling.

Motivated by these observations, we propose a novel self-supervised auxiliary learning method for actor and action video segmentation from natural language. The proposed model consists of a feature extraction network, a primary segmentation network and an auxiliary language reconstruction network. The feature extraction network is a backbone network used to extract visual and linguistic features from the input. The primary segmentation network leverages the visual and linguistic features to build the spatial attention and language-context vision attention, which drives the network to focus on important spatial regions corresponding to the natural language query. The auxiliary language reconstruction network integrates visual contexts with word-level linguistic features to generate vision-context language attention. The visually attentive features are then used to reconstruct the input sentence representation as the auxiliary task. This self-supervised auxiliary task allows the network to optimize the shared feature extraction parameters for a better multimodal representation. Then the updated shared parameters can be used for the primary segmentation task. The self-supervised learning strategy does not require additional labels and can also be deployed during test time to adapt the model parameters to a specific test example. An overview of our approach is presented in Fig. 2.

The main contributions of our work are threefold: (1) We propose a self-supervised meta auxiliary learning method to improve the primary segmentation task for the problem of actor and action video segmentation from natural language. (2) We introduce spatial attention and language-context vision attention to generate effective multimodal feature representation. We also introduce vision-context language attention to reconstruct the sentence representation for the auxiliary task in a self-supervised fashion. (3) The experimental results on two actor and action video segmentation datasets demonstrate that the effectiveness of the proposed method.

2   Our Approach

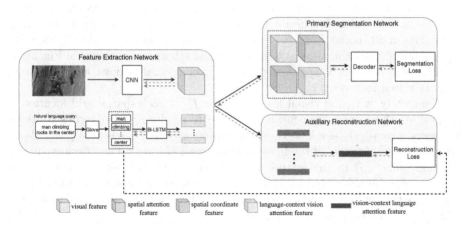

Fig. 2. Overview of our approach. The proposed model consists of a feature extraction network, a primary segmentation network and an auxiliary language reconstruction network. The auxiliary language reconstruction network is used to reconstruct the input sentence representation in a self-supervised way. It adapts the multimodal representation and the network parameters to the specific input query in the meta auxiliary training (green dash lines). The updated parameters will be used for training the primary segmentation task (red dash lines) or producing segmentation masks in testing. (Color figure online)

2.1   Feature Extraction Network

Let I denote an input frame from a video. We first use a convolutional neural network (i.e. DeepLab [3]) to extract visual features from I represented as

$f^v \in \mathbb{R}^{(H \cdot W) \times C_v}$, where $H \cdot W$ is the spatial size of the feature map and C_v is the feature channel dimension. We use $f_i^v \in \mathbb{R}^{C_v}$ to denote the feature vector corresponding to a particular spatial grid location i where $i \in \{1, 2, ..., H \cdot W\}$.

For a given natural language query with L words, we represent each word in the query with a pre-trained Glove word embedding vector [11] as $\{e_l\}_{l=1}^L$ where $e_l \in \mathbb{R}^{C_e}$ is the word vector of the l-th word and C_e is the dimension of the word embedding. Then a bidirectional LSTM is adopted to encode both forward and backward relations between words.

We use $f_l^w \in \mathbb{R}^{C_w}$ to denote the final word-level feature representation of the l-th word, which is the concatenation of the bidirectional hidden vectors of LSTM at the corresponding time step. Finally, we use $f^w \in \mathbb{R}^{L \times C_w}$ to denote the feature representation of all L words in the query sentence.

2.2 Primary Segmentation Network

The visual and linguistic features in Sect. 2.1 are only extracted in their own modalities separately. For the problem of actor and action video segmentation from natural language, the task requires more detailed understanding of visual and linguistic inputs. Self-attention mechanism [15] has been proven useful to capture meaningful task-relevant features and suppress unimportant ones from redundant multimodal features. Specifically, we propose spatial attention (as shown in Fig. 3(a)) and language-context visual attention (as shown in Fig. 3(b)) to effectively extract long-range relations over spatial regions and language-context visual features.

Concretely, with the visual feature vector f_i^v at each spatial grid location i, we first use three linear transformation layers to produce a set of representations for query $q_i = W_q f_i^v$, key $k_i = W_k f_i^v$ and value $v_i = W_v f_i^v$, where $W_q, W_k, W_v \in \mathbb{R}^{C_a \times C_v}$ are parameters of the linear transformation layers. Then for any spatial location pair (i, j) in the feature map f^v, the similarity between key k_i and query q_j can be calculated by $q_j^T k_i$. Afterwards, we use a softmax function to normalize the similarity and aggregate similarity values over all spatial locations. The operation can be summarized as:

$$f_i^{sa} = \sum_j \text{softmax}(q_j^T k_i) v_j \tag{1}$$

The resultant spatial attention features f_i^{sa} capture correlations between different spatial locations in the visual features.

In order to combine the linguistic context information with the visual feature representation for guiding the segmentation, we further propose language-context vision attention to explore correlations between visual features and corresponding words. Given the visual feature map $f^v \in \mathbb{R}^{(H \cdot W) \times C_v}$ and the linguistic features $f^w \in \mathbb{R}^{L \times C_w}$, we project the visual and linguistic features to the same semantic space using a 1×1 convolution layer and a linear layer, respectively. It results in $\tilde{f}^v \in \mathbb{R}^{(H \cdot W) \times C_a}$ and $\tilde{f}^w \in \mathbb{R}^{L \times C_a}$. Then we transpose $\tilde{f}^w$ and multiply it with $\tilde{f}^v$ to generate a similarity matrix of size $(H \cdot W) \times L$. Similarly, a softmax function is applied along the L axis to measure the correlations of each word to different spatial regions. Finally, we collect the weighted correlation values over all words as follows:

$$f^{va} = \text{softmax}\left(\tilde{f}^v(\tilde{f}^w)^T\right)\tilde{f}^w \qquad (2)$$

where $f^{va} \in \mathbb{R}^{(H \cdot W) \times C_a}$ denotes the language-context vision attention features. The overall process is visualized in Fig. 3(a).

Following previous work in referring segmentation [5,8], we also extract spatial coordinate features $f^{sc} \in \mathbb{R}^{(H \cdot W) \times 8}$ to capture the spatial information which is crucial for handling query sentences with relative position words, such as "left" and "right". To produce the final segmentation mask, we concatenate the visual features f^v, spatial attention features f^{sa}, the language-context vision attention features f^{va} and the spatial coordinate features f^{sc} to form a multimodal feature representation $f^m = \text{Concat}(f^v, f^{sa}, f^{va}, f^{sc})$.

In addition, we extract visual features at three levels from ResNet-based DeepLab blocks (*Res3*, *Res4* and *Res5*) and use above spatial attention and language-context vision attention methods to get multimodal feature representations $\{f_s^m\}_{s=1}^S (s = 1, 2, 3)$ corresponding to three different levels. Then a convolutional LSTM (ConvLSTM) [16] is adopted to refine multi-level features as follows:

$$(H_s^m, C_s^m) = \text{ConvLSTM}(f_s^m, H_{s-1}^m, C_{s-1}^m) \qquad (3)$$

where H_s^m and C_s^m represent the hidden state and the cell state of each time step over different level s. The final hidden state H_S^m of ConvLSTM is then used to as the final multimodal feature representation. Finally, we feed H_S^m to another convolutional layer to produce a segmentation mask M for the input frame. We learning the primary segmentation network using a binary cross entropy loss with a ground truth segmentation mask.

2.3   Auxiliary Language Reconstruction Network

In this section, we propose an auxiliary task to help improve the segmentation performance. Here we propose to reconstruct the linguistic sentence representation from the multimodal feature representation as the auxiliary task.

We align the channel dimension of visual and linguistic features by applying a 1×1 convolution layer to transform f^v to $\bar{f}^v \in \mathbb{R}^{(H \cdot W) \times C_a}$ and applying a linear layer to transform f^w to $\bar{f}^w \in \mathbb{R}^{L \times C_a}$ as shown in Fig. 3(c). A vision-context similarity matrix can be calculated by $\bar{f}^w(\bar{f}^v)^T$. We then use a softmax function along the $H \cdot W$ axis to normalize the correlation between each spatial grid location of the visual features and each word. The vision-context language attention features are obtained by aggregating all weighted visual information as $f^{wa} = \text{softmax}\left(\bar{f}^w(\bar{f}^v)^T\right)\bar{f}^v$, where $f_l^{wa} \in \mathbb{R}^{1 \times C_a}$ to denote the corresponding feature for the l-th word in the sentence.

We use the vision-context language attention features to reconstruct the sentence representation by averaging over words and projecting it into the same

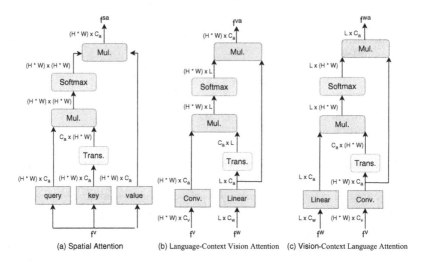

(a) Spatial Attention   (b) Language-Context Vision Attention   (c) Vision-Context Language Attention

Fig. 3. Illustration of the proposed attention methods. (a) Spatial attention and (b) Language-context vision attention are used to effectively extract long-range relations over spatial regions and language-context visual features for the primary segmentation network. (c) Vision-context language attention incorporate visual features into linguistic features to reconstruct the input sentence representation for learning an adaptive multimodal representation.

dimension of C_e with a linear layer as:

$$S^r = W\Big(\frac{1}{L}\sum_{l=1}^{L} f_l^{wa}\Big) + b \tag{4}$$

where $S^r \in \mathbb{R}^{C_e}$ is the reconstructed sentence representation and $W \in \mathbb{R}^{C_e \times C_a}$. We also average the word embedding vectors $\{e_l\}_{l=1}^{L}$ as a ground truth sentence representation $S \in \mathbb{R}^{C_e}$. The loss function of the auxiliary reconstruction network can be written as $L_{\text{aux}}(I, S) = ||S^r - S||^2$, where $||\cdot||$ denotes the L_2 norm. The mean square error loss trains the network to learn a multimodal representation that can be used to reconstruct the original language query sentence.

2.4   Meta Auxiliary Training

Assume that we have a set of training instances $(I^{(n)}, S^{(n)}, Y^{(n)})$ $(n = 1, 2, ..., N)$, where $I^{(n)}$ and $S^{(n)}$ are a video frame and a sentence representation of a language query, respectively. Note that $S^{(n)}$ represents an averaged pre-trained Glove word vectors here for brevity instead of raw text. $Y^{(n)}$ is a ground truth segmentation mask. Let θ^m denote the parameters of the feature extraction network. The output of the feature extraction network is used as the input to both the primary and auxiliary tasks. Let θ^{pri} and θ^{aux} represent the task-specific parameter sets for the primary segmentation network and auxiliary language reconstruction network, respectively. We use $\Theta = \{\theta^m, \theta^{\mathrm{pri}}, \theta^{\mathrm{aux}}\}$ to denote the entire model parameters. A straightforward way of learning the parameters is to optimize one of the following two loss functions:

$$\min_{\Theta} \frac{1}{N} \sum_{n=1}^{N} L_{\mathrm{pri}}(I^{(n)}, Y^{(n)}; \Theta) \tag{5}$$

$$\min_{\Theta} \frac{1}{N} \sum_{n=1}^{N} \left(L_{\mathrm{pri}}(I^{(n)}, Y^{(n)}; \Theta) + L_{\mathrm{aux}}(I^{(n)}, S^{(n)}; \Theta) \right) \tag{6}$$

We call Eq. 5 and Eq. 6 the *primary training* and the *joint training*, respectively. Note that the primary training does not consider the network branch for the auxiliary task, so it only learns the parameters $\{\theta^m, \theta^{\mathrm{pri}}\}$ corresponding to the feature extraction network and the primary segmentation network. The joint training can be seen as a form as multi-task learning.

In this paper, we propose a meta auxiliary training approach to learn the model parameters. During testing, the model parameters are fine-tuned by the network given a specific input (i.e. video frame and language query).

We treat the language query as a self-supervised label for the auxiliary task (i.e. language reconstruction). During testing, we use this auxiliary task to adapt the model parameters for each test example. This gives our model more flexibility to adapt to each test example. During training, we use a meta-learning paradigm to learn model parameters that facilitate such adaptation during testing.

We first describe how to adapt the learned model parameters Θ during testing. Let I and S denote a frame and a language representation during testing. We perform a small number of gradient updates of the model parameters Θ using the loss L_{aux}, i.e.

$$\widetilde{\Theta} \leftarrow \Theta - \alpha \nabla_{\Theta}(L_{\mathrm{aux}}(I, S); \Theta) \tag{7}$$

Note that since $L_{aux}(I, S; \Theta)$ only involves $\{\theta^m, \theta^{\mathrm{pri}}\}$, the update in Eq. 7 will only change $\{\theta^m, \theta^{\mathrm{aux}}\}$, but not θ^{pri}. We use $\widetilde{\theta}^m$ and $\widetilde{\theta}^{\mathrm{aux}}$ to denote the corresponding parameters after this update. We can consider $\widetilde{\Theta}$ from Eq. 7 as the model parameters specifically tuned to the test example (I, S). We then predict the segmentation mask for (I, S) using $\widetilde{\Theta}$.

During meta-training, our goal is to learn Θ that has the following property. For a given training example $(I^{(n)}, S^{(n)}, Y^{(n)})$, we first apply Eq. 7 on $(I^{(n)}, S^{(n)})$ so Θ becomes $\widetilde{\Theta}^{(n)}$. We would like $\widetilde{\Theta}^{(n)}$ to produce a segmentation mask that matches $Y^{(n)}$. In other words, the performance of $\widetilde{\Theta}$ is measured by $L_{\mathrm{pri}}(I^{(n)}, Y^{(n)}; \widetilde{\Theta})$. During meta-training, the model parameters Θ are trained by optimizing $L_{\mathrm{pri}}(I^{(n)}, Y^{(n)}; \widetilde{\Theta})$ across all training examples as follows:

$$\min_{\Theta} \sum_{n=1}^{N} L_{\mathrm{pri}}(I^{(n)}, Y^{(n)}; \widetilde{\Theta}^{(n)}) \tag{8}$$

Note that the optimization in Eq. 8 is performed over Θ, but $L_{\mathrm{pri}}(I^{(n)}, Y^{(n)}; \widetilde{\Theta}^{(n)})$ is defined in terms of $\widetilde{\Theta}^{(n)}$ which are the parameters obtained after performing the update in Eq. 7 on $(I^{(n)}, S^{(n)})$ of the n-th training example.

Algorithm 1 shows an outline of the meta auxiliary learning.

Algorithm 1: Meta Auxiliary Training

Data: Network parameters: $\Theta = \{\theta^m, \theta^{\mathrm{pri}}, \theta^{\mathrm{aux}}\}$; learning rate: α, β

while *not done* **do**

    Sample a batch of training data $\{(I^{(n)}, S^{(n)}, Y^{(n)})\}_{n=1}^{N}$

    for *each training sample n* **do**

        Compute adapted parameters $\widetilde{\Theta}^{(n)}$ from Θ as:

        $\widetilde{\Theta}^{(n)} \leftarrow \Theta - \alpha \nabla_{\Theta} L_{\mathrm{aux}}(I^{(n)}, S^{(n)}; \Theta)$

        Update: $\Theta \leftarrow \Theta - \beta \sum_n \nabla_{\Theta} L_{\mathrm{pri}}(I^{(n)}, Y^{(n)}; \widetilde{\Theta}^{(n)})$

    end

end

---

3   Experiments

Datasets: We perform comprehensive evaluations on two public actor and action video segmentation datasets including Actor-Action Dataset (A2D) dataset [17] and Joint- annotated HMDB (JHMDB) dataset [6]. They are originally collected for actor and action video segmentation. The nature language descriptions are complemented by [4] for the task in this paper.

Evaluation Metrics: To fairly compare with other methods, we follow previous work [4,14] to use overall and mean intersection-over-union (Overall IoU and Mean IoU) and Precision@X ($prec@X$) to evaluate the performance of methods.

Implementation Details: We truncate input sentences to keep the maximum length as 20 words and embed each word into a pre-trained Glove word vector with $C_e = 300$. Then the hidden size of the bidirectional LSTM used to encode words is 500, which results in $C_w = 1000$ dimensional feature for each word. The dimension of the visual feature is also set to $C_v = 1000$ and the dimension of the projected space for attention is $C_a = 500$. We set the learning rate α for auxiliary reconstruction network as $5e^{-5}$ and the learning rate β of training for the primary segmentation network as $2.5e^{-4}$.

3.1   Ablation Study

We verify the effectiveness of the proposed meta auxiliary learning. We compare our method with two alternative learning methods: (1) training only with

Table 1. Ablation study of auxiliary learning on A2D Sentences dataset in terms of prec@X, meanIoU and Overall IoU.

Method	Overlap					IoU	
	prec@0.5	prec@0.6	prec@0.7	prec@0.8	prec@0.9	Overall	Mean
Primary	51.5	44.3	34.3	19.5	2.8	61.2	44.9
Primary+Auxiliary (joint train)	53.5	46.2	34.9	20.1	3.0	62.1	46.8
Primary+Auxiliary (meta train only)	54.0	46.2	35.1	20.3	3.0	62.3	46.9
Primary+Auxiliary (meta train and test)	**55.0**	**47.4**	**35.8**	**20.7**	**3.4**	**63.0**	**47.3**

the primary segmentation network as Eq. 5, denoted as "Primary"; (2) training primary and auxiliary networks jointly as multi-task learning in Eq. 6, denoted as "Primary+Auxiliary (joint learning)". Table 1 presents the comparisons of different learning approaches. It can be observed that adding the self-supervised auxiliary task can improve the primary segmentation task. In addition, our meta auxiliary training consistently outperforms the primary only method and the joint training method with the same training network and data.

3.2 Comparison with the State-of-the-art

Table 2. Comparison of segmentation performance with the state-of-the-art methods on A2D Sentences dataset in terms of prec@X, Overall IoU and Mean IoU.

Method	Overlap					mAP	IoU	
	prec@0.5	prec@0.6	prec@0.7	prec@0.8	prec@0.9	0.5:0.95	Overall	Mean
Hu et al. [5]	34.8	23.6	13.3	3.3	0.1	13.2	47.4	35.0
Li et al. [7]	38.7	29.0	17.5	6.6	0.1	16.3	51.5	35.4
Gavrilyuk et al. [4]	50.0	37.6	23.1	9.4	0.4	21.5	55.1	42.6
Wang et al. [14]	55.7	45.9	31.9	16.0	2.0	27.4	60.1	49.0
Ye et al. [20]	48.7	43.1	35.8	**23.1**	5.2	–	61.8	43.2
Yang et al. [18]	**65.2**	**58.0**	**44.5**	20.8	1.6	**34.8**	58.8	**51.3**
Bellver et al. [1]	49.5	–	–	–	**6.4**	–	59.9	43.0
Ours	55.0	47.4	35.8	20.7	3.4	29.6	**63.0**	47.3

Quantitative Results: We compare our method with several state-of-the-art approaches in actor and action video segmentation from natural language, including [1,4,14,18,20] with RGB input for visual features. Following previous methods [4,14], we also involve one referring image segmentation model [5] and one lingual specification model [7] for comparison.

The experimental results on the A2D Sentences dataset and the JHMDB sentences dataset are shown in Table 2 and Table 3, respectively. Although our method only achieves best result in overall IoU, it still generates comparable

Table 3. Comparison of segmentation performance with the state-of-the-art methods on JHMDB Sentences dataset in terms of prec@X, Overall IoU and Mean IoU.

Method	Overlap					mAP	IoU	
	prec@0.5	prec@0.6	prec@0.7	prec@0.8	prec@0.9	0.5:0.95	Overall	Mean
Hu et al. [5]	63.3	35.0	8.5	0.2	0.0	17.8	54.6	52.8
Li et al. [7]	57.8	33.5	10.3	0.6	0.0	17.3	52.9	49.1
Gavrilyuk et al. [4]	69.9	46.0	17.3	1.4	0.0	23.3	54.1	54.2
Wang et al. [14]	75.6	56.4	28.7	3.4	0.0	28.9	57.6	58.4
Ye et al. [20]	76.4	62.5	**38.9**	**9.0**	**0.1**	–	62.8	58.1
Yang et al. [18]	74.6	57.3	25.6	1.5	0.0	27.8	55.6	56.3
Ours	**78.4**	**63.8**	37.9	7.3	0.0	**33.3**	**62.9**	**59.7**

results with other methods in the other metrics. Note that our method does not require temporal proposals as [18] which relies on an external detector. In addition, the proposed method shows superior performance on the JHMDB Sentences dataset over most metrics. It should be noted that this dataset is used only for testing. We use the network trained on A2D Sentences dataset without fine-tuning as previous methods. The remarkable improvement on the JHMDB Sentences dataset shows the better generalization ability of our method from our meta auxiliary learning.

Fig. 4. Qualitative examples of our method. For each example, we show the language query, video frames, our segmentation result and the ground truth from top to bottom. Different colored segmentation masks correspond to queries with the same color.

Qualitative Results: Figure 4 shows qualitative examples produced by our network to present the scenarios where actors are specified by different sentence queries. The moving actor ("car is flying") and static actor ("guy in black sitting") are accurately identified in the left example. In the right example, the fine-grained segmentation masks are produced for two neighboring and moving actors ("cat" and "ball").

4   Conclusion

We have presented a novel self-supervised auxiliary learning method for actor and action video segmentation from natural language. The proposed approach produce spatial attention, language-context vision attention and vision-context language attention for this task. We also design a meta auxiliary training method in a self-supervised way, to improve the primary segmentation task.

Acknowledgments. This work was supported in part by the National Natural Science Foundation of China (Grant No. 62102289) and in part by the Zhejiang Provincial Natural Science Foundation (Grant No. LQ22F020005).

References

1. Bellver, M., Ventura, C., Silberer, C., Kazakos, I., Torres, J., Giro-i Nieto, X.: A closer look at referring expressions for video object segmentation. Multimedia Tools Appl. **82**(3), 4419–4438 (2023)
2. Caba Heilbron, F., Escorcia, V., Ghanem, B., Carlos Niebles, J.: Activitynet: a large-scale video benchmark for human activity understanding. In: IEEE Conference on Computer Vision and Pattern Recognition, pp. 961–970 (2015)
3. Chen, L.C., Papandreou, G., Kokkinos, I., Murphy, K., Yuille, A.L.: Deeplab: semantic image segmentation with deep convolutional nets, atrous convolution, and fully connected crfs. IEEE Trans. Pattern Anal. Mach. Intell. **40**(4), 834–848 (2017)
4. Gavrilyuk, K., Ghodrati, A., Li, Z., Snoek, C.G.: Actor and action video segmentation from a sentence. In: IEEE Conference on Computer Vision and Pattern Recognition, pp. 5958–5966 (2018)
5. Hu, R., Rohrbach, M., Darrell, T.: Segmentation from natural language expressions. In: Leibe, B., Matas, J., Sebe, N., Welling, M. (eds.) ECCV 2016. LNCS, vol. 9905, pp. 108–124. Springer, Cham (2016). https://doi.org/10.1007/978-3-319-46448-0_7
6. Jhuang, H., Gall, J., Zuffi, S., Schmid, C., Black, M.J.: Towards understanding action recognition. In: IEEE International Conference on Computer Vision, pp. 3192–3199 (2013)
7. Li, Z., Tao, R., Gavves, E., Snoek, C.G., Smeulders, A.W.: Tracking by natural language specification. In: IEEE Conference on Computer Vision and Pattern Recognition, pp. 6495–6503 (2017)
8. Liu, C., Lin, Z., Shen, X., Yang, J., Lu, X., Yuille, A.L.: Recurrent multimodal interaction for referring image segmentation. In: IEEE International Conference on Computer Vision (2017)
9. Liu, S., Davison, A., Johns, E.: Self-supervised generalisation with meta auxiliary learning. In: Advances in Neural Information Processing Systems, pp. 1677–1687 (2019)
10. Mao, J., Huang, J., Toshev, A., Camburu, O., Yuille, A.L., Murphy, K.: Generation and comprehension of unambiguous object descriptions. In: IEEE Conference on Computer Vision and Pattern Recognition (2016)
11. Pennington, J., Socher, R., Manning, C.: Glove: global vectors for word representation. In: Conference on Empirical Methods in Natural Language Processing, pp. 1532–1543 (2014)

12. Rohrbach, A., Rohrbach, M., Hu, R., Darrell, T., Schiele, B.: Grounding of textual phrases in images by reconstruction. In: Leibe, B., Matas, J., Sebe, N., Welling, M. (eds.) ECCV 2016. LNCS, vol. 9905, pp. 817–834. Springer, Cham (2016). https://doi.org/10.1007/978-3-319-46448-0_49

13. Sun, Y., Wang, X., Liu, Z., Miller, J., Efros, A.A., Hardt, M.: Test-time training for out-of-distribution generalization. arXiv:1909.13231 (2019)

14. Wang, H., Deng, C., Yan, J., Tao, D.: Asymmetric cross-guided attention network for actor and action video segmentation from natural language query. In: IEEE International Conference on Computer Vision, pp. 3939–3948 (2019)

15. Wang, X., Girshick, R., Gupta, A., He, K.: Non-local neural networks. In: IEEE Conference on Computer Vision and Pattern Recognition, pp. 7794–7803 (2018)

16. Xingjian, S., Chen, Z., Wang, H., Yeung, D.Y., Wong, W.K., Woo, W.C.: Convolutional lstm network: a machine learning approach for precipitation nowcasting. In: Advances in Neural Information Processing Systems, pp. 802–810 (2015)

17. Xu, C., Hsieh, S.H., Xiong, C., Corso, J.J.: Can humans fly? action understanding with multiple classes of actors. In: IEEE Conference on Computer Vision and Pattern Recognition, pp. 2264–2273 (2015)

18. Yang, J., Huang, Y., Niu, K., Huang, L., Ma, Z., Wang, L.: Actor and action modular network for text-based video segmentation. IEEE Trans. Image Process. **31**, 4474–4489 (2022)

19. Yang, Y., Deng, C., Gao, S., Liu, W., Tao, D., Gao, X.: Discriminative multi-instance multitask learning for 3d action recognition. IEEE Trans. Multimedia **19**(3), 519–529 (2016)

20. Ye, L., Rochan, M., Liu, Z., Zhang, X., Wang, Y.: Referring segmentation in images and videos with cross-modal self-attention network. IEEE Trans. Pattern Anal. Mach. Intell. **44**(7), 3719–3732 (2021)

RsMmFormer: Multimodal Transformer Using Multiscale Self-attention for Remote Sensing Image Classification

Bo Zhang[1], Zuheng Ming[2], Yaqian Liu[1], Wei Feng[3], Liang He[1(✉)], and Kaixing Zhao[1(✉)]

[1] School of Software, Northwestern Polytechnical University, Xi'an, China
{2021050018,kaixing.zhao}@nwpu.edu.cn
[2] Laboratoire L2TI, Institut Galilée, Université Sorbonne Paris Nord, Villetaneuse, France
[3] School of Electronic Engineering, Xidian University, Xi'an, China

Abstract. Remote Sensing (RS) has been widely utilized in various Earth Observation (EO) missions, including land cover classification and environmental monitoring. Unlike computer vision tasks on natural images, collecting remote sensing data is more challenging. To fully exploit the available data and leverage the complementary information across different data sources, we propose a novel approach called Multimodal Transformer for Remote Sensing (RsMmFormer) for image classification, which utilizes both Hyperspectral Image (HSI) and Light Detection and Ranging (LiDAR) data. In contrast to the conventional Vision Transformer (ViT), which does not incorporate the inherent biases and assumptions of convolutions, we improve our RsMmFormer model by incorporating convolutional layers. This allows us to integrate the favorable characteristics of convolutional neural networks (CNNs). Next, we introduce the Multi-scale Multi-head Self-Attention (MSMHSA) module, which enables learning detailed representations, facilitating the detection of small targets occupying only a few pixels in the remote sensing image. The proposed MSMHSA module facilitates the integration of Hyperspectral Imaging (HSI) and LiDAR data in a progressive and detailed manner, effectively attending to both global and local contexts using self-attention mechanisms. Comprehensive experiments conducted on popular benchmarks such as Trento and MUUFL showcase the effectiveness and superiority of our proposed RsMmFormer model for remote sensing image classification.

Keywords: Multimodal Transformer · Multi-Scale Multi-head self-attention · Convolutions · Remote sensing image classification

1 Introduction

Remote Sensing (RS) has been significantly contributing to a wide range of Earth Observing (EO) tasks, playing a crucial role in their execution because of its

L. Fang et al. (Eds.): CICAI 2023, LNAI 14473, pp. 329–339, 2024.
https://doi.org/10.1007/978-981-99-8850-1_27

rapid imaging feature and wide application prospect. Generally, RS can be used (but not limited) in different tasks, such as landcover classification [1–3], mineral and forest resources exploration [4], object/target detection [5,6], environmental monitoring [7], urban planning [8], biodiversity conservation, as well as disaster response and management. As Remote Sensing (RS) data becomes increasingly accessible, research in RS has transitioned towards data-driven approaches, employing a variety of Machine Learning (ML) and Deep Learning (DL) models in RS systems. However, in the past few years, most studies focused only on single EO sensors, such as HSI sensors, rather than combining different types of sensor data. Although HSI acquired from different sensors can provide more rich spectral information, It is unable to distinguish land cover objects, such as roads and roofs, that share similar materials. [9]. On the other hand, LiDAR data provides valuable elevation information, allowing for the discrimination of objects with similar spectral signatures but different elevations. This capability enables the distinction between features like roads and roofs that are constructed using materials like cement [10]. Integrating multimodal data for remote sensing classification can serve as a solution to this dilemma. Over the past few years, DL methods have gained significant popularity in the fusion of multimodal data for RS image classification [11,12]. More recently, Vision Transformers (ViT) [13] model has emerged as a new leading approach in RS image classification. It leverages self-attention mechanisms to capture both local and global features of an image or image sequence, gaining traction in the field. SpectralFormer [14] learned the spectral representation of neighboring bands using a cross-layer encoder module of ViT. However, it neglected spatial information and only uses spectral information. Swalpa et al. proposed MFT [10] which incorporates HSI and other source data to construct a multimodal ViT for RS image classification. Nevertheless, MFT did not consider the compatibility problem when fusing the data with a large resolution gap such as HSI and LiDAR data which may affect the landcover classification in complex scenes [15]. To leverage the complementary information between the different modalities, we propose a multimodal transformer using self-attention between two modalities HSI and LiDAR data for RS image classification. Instead of using a vanilla ViT as in MFT or SpectralForm, we propose a MSMHSA module using different heads of transformer aiming to better fuse the feature representations with different resolutions of heterogeneous data from different modalities. Besides, we also introduce convolutions to our RsMmFormer using Convolutional Tokenization to tokenize HSI and LiDAR, instead of employing linear projection to generate the Query, Key, and Value feature tensors for self-attention.

The primary contributions of this paper can be summarized as follows: 1) We design a Multimodal Transformer (RsMmFormer) for RS image classification using HSI and LiDAR data. 2) A MSMHSA module implemented on a single transformer allows better fusing of multimodal data of different resolutions. 3) To incorporate the desirable properties of convolutions into RsMmFormer, we introduce convolutions as a means of integration. 4) The exceptional performance achieved by the proposed RsMmFormer validates its effectiveness as a state-of-the-art backbone for multimodal RS image classification.

2   Related Works

Over the past few decades, various traditional methods have been investigated to derive more relevant and informative features from multi-modal RS data, such as random forest (RF), morphological profiles (MPs) [16], attribute profiles (APs) [17], extinction profiles (EPs) [18] and subspace learning [19]. Ham et al. investigated hierarchical classifiers based on RF to improve the generalization in analysis of quantity limited hyperspectral data [21]. Recently, deep learning techniques have gained significant attention and have been extensively applied in the field of multi-modal data fusion for RS data classification. These techniques have demonstrated remarkable capabilities in extracting and learning informative features from RS data. In [11], Makantasis et al. exploited a CNN2D based network to encode pixels' spectral and spatial information. Vision Transformers methods used attention mechanism to learn the local and global features of an HSI data. SpectralFormer [14] used a cross-layer encoder module of ViT to learn the spectral features between HSI bands. And Swalpa et al. proposed MFT [10] which leverage the complementary information between the different modalities to construct a multi-modal ViT for RS image classification. Inspired by the former methods, we propose a MSMHSA transformer to improve the overall fusion and classification accuracy.

3   Methodology

3.1   Overall Architecture

An overview of the architecture of RsMmFormer is illustrated in Fig. 1. To balance the performance and the parameters of model, we set the proposed transformer depth to 2.

Convolutional Tokenization. Unlike the vanilla Transformer, we use convolutional embedding to tokenize $\mathbf{Q}uery/\mathbf{K}ey/\mathbf{V}alue \in \mathbb{R}^{H_A \times W_A \times C_A}$ feature tensors. Firstly, the 11*11 data cubes are padding to 16*16. And sequential layers Conv3D [12] and HetConv2D [20] are used to extract and learn the informative features of HSI cube and reduce the HSI spectral channels down to 64. A Conv2D layer is used to extract LiDAR cube's feature map and expend the band to 64. After that, the feature maps, concatenated in the last dimension, act as the input of convolutional embedding to get the $\mathbf{Q}$, $\mathbf{K}$ and $\mathbf{V}$.

Subsequently the $\mathbf{Q}$, $\mathbf{K}$ and $\mathbf{V}$ obtained from the previous step are passed into the MSMHSA module to facilitate the learning of both local and global dependencies in the fused data. In the output layer of the MSMHSA module, we replace the linear layer and layer normalization with a convolution layer,

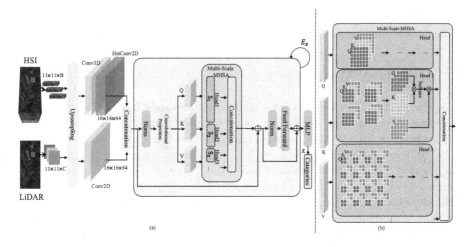

Fig. 1. (a) The overall architecture of the Multimodal Transformer Using Multiscale Self-Attention for RS image classification (RsMmFormer) is presented, which introduces convolutions to the transformer. (b) The proposed MSMHSA module integrated into a single transformer architecture.

utilizing a kernel size of 3 and padding of 1. Additionally, a LeakyReLU activation function is applied. The mentioned modules could be defined as follow:

$$\mathbf{Q}, \mathbf{K}, \mathbf{V} = Conv2D(\mathbf{X_{in}}, k = (1,1)) \tag{1}$$

$$\begin{cases} X_{out} = Conv2D(X_{in}, k = (3,3), p = (1,1)) \\ X = LeakyReLU(\mathbf{X_{out}}, 0.2) \end{cases} \tag{2}$$

A comprehensive description of the MSMHSA module can be located in Sect. 3.2. Finally, at the conclusion of the transformer, we introduce a Feed-Forward Network (FFN) with Norm layers. In this study, we further enhance the FFN by substituting the linear projection layers with convolution layers. Similar to the approach used in ViT [22], After the transformer architecture, we incorporate a residual MLP module to encode the classification embeddings.

3.2   Multi-scale Multi-Head Self-Attention (MSMHSA)

The objective of MSMHSA, illustrated in Fig. 1(b), is to introduce a pyramid structure into the self-attention module. This structure facilitates the generation of multi-scale feature maps, enabling pixel-level feature fusion with complementary features. The proposed MSMHSA is applied to different heads within each layer of the transformer. All the heads adhere to a uniform procedure for computing self-attention.

Specifically, the feature tensors Query, Key, and Value are evenly split among these heads along the corresponding dimension prior to being fed into the MSMHSA module.

In the context of a transformer model, there exists a set of heads whose number is determined by the scales' number, represented by $\mathbf{N}$. And the shape of $\mathbf{i}$-th scale is $H_i \times W_i$. These heads are responsible for processing fed feature tensors $\mathbf{Query}, \mathbf{Key}$ and $\mathbf{Value}$ of size $H_A \times W_A \times C_A$, and the feature tensors for each head are $\mathbf{Q_i}/\mathbf{K_i}/\mathbf{V_i} \in \mathbb{R}^{H_A \times W_A \times \frac{C_A}{N}}$. The feature maps will be divided into $\mathbf{n_i}$ patches, where $\mathbf{n_i}$ is determined by $\frac{H_A}{H_i} \times \frac{W_A}{W_i}$. For the first head $Head_1$, with W_1 and H_1 being equal to W_A and H_A respectively, we utilize a full-size patch $\mathbf{q_1}/\mathbf{k_1}/\mathbf{v_1} \in \mathbb{R}^{H_A \times W_A \times \frac{C_A}{N}}$ to compute the global attention feature tensor. By following the aforementioned steps, we can generate the self-attention feature map $\mathbf{h_1} \in \mathbb{R}^{H_A \times W_A \times \frac{C_A}{n}}$ of $Head_1$. Then for $Head_2$, we divide $\mathbf{Q_2}/\mathbf{K_2}/\mathbf{V_2}$ into n_2 patches, where n_2 equals $\frac{H_A}{H_2} \times \frac{W_A}{W_2}$, each patch $\mathbf{q_2}/\mathbf{k_2}/\mathbf{v_2}$ of size $n_2 \times H_2 \times W_2 \times \frac{C_A}{N}$ and then obtain $\mathbf{h_2} \in \mathbb{R}^{n_2 \times H_2 \times W_2 \times \frac{C_A}{N}}$ of $Head_2$. We continue to divide $\mathbf{Q_3}/\mathbf{K_3}/\mathbf{V_3}$ into $\mathbf{n_3}$ patches, where $\mathbf{n_3}$ equals $\frac{H_A}{H_3} \times \frac{W_A}{W_3}$, to generate the self-attention feature map $\mathbf{h_3} \in \mathbb{R}^{n_3 \times H_3 \times W_3 \times \frac{C_A}{N}}$ of $Head_3$. The remaining heads are also processed in the same way as before. Finally, we concatenate the resulting attention feature tensors of each scale $\{\mathbf{h_1}, \mathbf{h_2}, \mathbf{h_3}, ...\}$ together to create the resultant multi-scale attention feature tensor $\mathbf{H} \in \mathbb{R}^{H_A \times W_A \times C_A}$ (We need to transform the shape of $\mathbf{h_{i \geq 2}}$ to be match the same format as $\mathbf{h_1}$ for consistency):

$$\mathbf{H} = \mathbf{Concat}(\mathbf{h_1}, \mathbf{Reshape}(\mathbf{h_2}), \mathbf{Reshape}(\mathbf{h_3}), ..., \mathbf{Reshape}(\mathbf{h_i})). \qquad (3)$$

The attention feature tensor $\mathbf{h_i}$ is defined as follows:

$$\mathbf{h_i} = \Sigma_m^C \Sigma_n^C \mathbf{Softmax}(\frac{\mathbf{q_{i,m}} \mathbf{k_{i,n}^T}}{\sqrt{d_{head_{i,n}}}}) \mathbf{v_{i,n}}, \qquad (4)$$

Here, the attention feature tensor h_i is calculated using the following components: $\mathbf{q_{i,m}}$ represents the m-th patch obtained from feature tensor $\mathbf{Q_i}$ for the i-th head ($Head_i$), while $\mathbf{k_{i,n}}$ and $\mathbf{v_{i,n}}$ denotes the n-th patches obtained from the feature tensors $\mathbf{K_i}$ and $\mathbf{V_i}$ respectively for the i-th head ($Head_i$). Then, just like what was mentioned earlier, $\mathbf{q_{i,m}}, \mathbf{k_{i,n}}$ and $\mathbf{v_{i,n}} \in \mathbb{R}^{H_i \times W_i \times \frac{C_A}{N}}$. $d_{head_{i,n}}$ represents the dimension of the $\mathbf{q_{i,m}}$. In every head $Head_i$, we join the obtained patches $\mathbf{q_i}, \mathbf{k_i}$ and $\mathbf{v_i}$ from all pictures together to generate the attention feature map of a single scale $\mathbf{h_i}$. Thus, The self-attention mechanism of each head always incorporates both local attention, which focuses on local spatial information, simultaneously., i.e., utilizing $\mathbf{q_{i,m}}$ and $\mathbf{k_{i,n}}$ generated from the neighborhood to compute self-attention, and global attention focusing on the global context information calculated by $\mathbf{q_{i,m}}/\mathbf{k_{i,n}}$ from far regions within the image. In this work, rather than appending an additional token like ViT does for image classification, we utilize a sequence-based representation, denoted as the result of residual MLP Head $\mathbf{Z}$, which learns from all the tokens in the input. We also employ a cross-entropy loss for the final land-cover classification task.

4 Experiments and Analysis

4.1 Experimental Setup

(1) Data Description In order to assess the effectiveness of our proposed RsMmFormer, we perform experiments on two commonly employed datasets that involve the integration of HSI and LiDAR data.

Trento Dataset: This dataset consists of a pair of data, namely hyperspectral imaging and LiDAR, collected from a rural area located Trento, Italy. The HSI data comprises 63 bands, while the LiDAR data consists of a single band. Both the hyperspectral imaging and LiDAR data in this dataset have a size of 166 × 600 pixels, with a spatial resolution of 1 m, encompassing a total of 6 different classes.

MUUFL Dataset: This dataset was gathered at the University of Southern Mississippi Gulf Park. Both the hyperspectral imaging and LiDAR data in the dataset encompass 325 × 220 pixels. The hyperspectral imaging initially comprised 72 bands, but four bands at the beginning and end were discarded due to noise problems. Thus, the experiment utilized the remaining 64 bands. The LiDAR data consisted of 2 bands. The dataset comprises 11 distinct classes.

(2) Experimental Setup The experiments were conducted on a CentOS Linux server (release 7.9.2009) with a single Nvidia 3090 GPU, which has 24576 MB of VRAM.

The models under consideration were trained and tested with batch sizes of 64 for training phase and 500 for testing phase. The models were trained using an Adam optimizer with a learning rate of 5e–4 and weight decay of 5e–3. A step scheduler with a step size of 50 and a gamma value of 0.9 was also employed. Each experiment was performed for 500 epochs, repeated three times, and the results reported include the average values and standard deviations. The source code was implemented using PyTorch 1.12.1 and Python 3.8.7.

(3) Evaluation metrics The classification performance of our model is evaluated quantitatively using three commonly used metrics: overall accuracy (OA), average accuracy (AA), and statistical Kappa (κ) coefficients.

4.2 Quantitative Analysis

Table 1 and Table 2 report the quantitative OA, AA, *kappa* and each class accuracy on two widely used datasets Trento and MUUFL to compare the proposed RsMmFormer with other state-of-art methods, i.e., RF [21], CNN2D [11], ViT [22], SpectralFormer [14] and MFT [10]. Our model RsMmFormer obtains the best performance on all three indices on both two benchmarks, such as 99.18% and 94.73% OA, 97.91% and 84.57% AA and 98.90% and 93.02% Kappa on Trento and MUUFL datasets. Our model has also achieved the best performance for almost each class accuracy, and even it has gained 20% improvement on landcover Yellow-Curb (class 10) compared to the latest MFT on MUUFL data.

Table 1. Classification Performance on Trento Data (HSI and LiDAR) - OA, AA, and Kappa Values (in %). The Best is shown in **bold**.

Class No.	RF [21]	CNN2D [11]	ViT [22]	Spectral-Former [14]	MFT [10]	RsMmFormer
1	83.73 ± 00.06	96.98 ± 00.21	90.87 ± 00.77	96.76 ± 01.71	98.23 ± 00.38	**99.71 ± 0.25**
2	96.30 ± 00.06	97.56 ± 00.14	99.32 ± 00.77	97.25 ± 00.66	**99.34 ± 00.02**	98.06 ± 0.80
3	70.94 ± 01.55	55.35 ± 00.00	92.69 ± 01.53	58.47 ± 11.54	89.84 ± 09.00	**94.47 ± 1.77**
4	99.73 ± 00.07	99.66 ± 00.03	**100.0 ± 00.00**	99.24 ± 00.21	99.82 ± 00.26	99.96 ± 0.02
5	95.35 ± 00.25	99.56 ± 00.07	97.77 ± 00.86	93.52 ± 01.75	**99.93 ± 00.05**	99.90 ± 0.07
6	72.63 ± 00.90	76.91 ± 00.15	86.72 ± 02.02	73.39 ± 06.78	88.72 ± 00.94	**95.34 ± 1.32**
OA	92.57 ± 00.07	96.14 ± 00.03	96.47 ± 00.49	93.51 ± 01.27	98.32 ± 00.25	**99.18 ± 0.02**
AA	86.45 ± 00.32	87.67 ± 00.04	94.56 ± 00.57	86.44 ± 02.96	95.98 ± 01.64	**97.91 ± 0.25**
κ	90.11 ± 00.09	94.83 ± 00.04	95.28 ± 00.65	91.36 ± 01.67	97.75 ± 00.00	**98.90 ± 0.02**

Table 2. Classification Performance on MUUFL Data (HSI and LiDAR) - OA, AA, and Kappa Values (in %). The Best is shown in **bold**.

Class No.	RF [21]	CNN2D [11]	ViT [22]	Spectral-Former [14]	MFT [10]	RsMmFormer
1	95.42 ± 00.09	95.79 ± 00.11	97.85 ± 00.29	97.30 ± 00.83	97.90 ± 00.39	**98.88 ± 0.15**
2	74.03 ± 00.11	72.76 ± 00.58	76.06 ± 02.40	69.35 ± 05.16	**92.11 ± 01.58**	88.84 ± 1.66
3	75.81 ± 00.38	78.92 ± 00.52	87.58 ± 03.46	78.48 ± 03.41	**91.80 ± 00.82**	90.00 ± 0.80
4	68.59 ± 00.77	83.59 ± 00.99	92.05 ± 02.31	82.63 ± 03.68	91.59 ± 02.25	**95.19 ± 0.24**
5	88.17 ± 00.18	78.29 ± 01.12	94.73 ± 00.60	87.91 ± 02.97	**95.60 ± 01.21**	95.28 ± 0.48
6	77.28 ± 00.93	50.34 ± 02.13	82.02 ± 01.13	58.77 ± 02.76	88.19 ± 03.49	**88.48 ± 0.97**
7	64.83 ± 00.97	79.70 ± 00.26	87.11 ± 01.54	85.87 ± 00.62	90.27 ± 02.13	**92.94 ± 1.14**
8	93.29 ± 00.27	71.95 ± 01.10	97.60 ± 00.16	95.60 ± 01.26	97.26 ± 00.53	**97.84 ± 0.53**
9	19.15 ± 01.37	43.92 ± 01.24	57.83 ± 04.45	53.52 ± 04.32	61.35 ± 03.80	**65.02 ± 1.79**
10	04.41 ± 00.72	12.45 ± 00.27	31.99 ± 08.86	08.43 ± 02.22	17.43 ± 04.63	**36.97 ± 3.39**
11	71.88 ± 00.84	26.82 ± 02.60	58.72 ± 03.85	35.29 ± 06.00	72.79 ± 09.25	**80.85 ± 5.58**
OA	85.32 ± 00.09	83.40 ± 00.04	92.15 ± 00.19	88.25 ± 00.56	**94.34 ± 00.07**	94.73 ± 0.20
AA	66.62 ± 00.16	63.14 ± 00.21	78.50 ± 01.28	68.47 ± 01.44	81.48 ± 00.70	**84.57 ± 0.35**
κ	80.39 ± 00.12	77.94 ± 00.06	89.56 ± 00.27	84.40 ± 00.77	92.51 ± 00.10	**93.02 ± 0.26**

4.3 Ablation Study

Ablation studies are performed exclusively on the Trento dataset. The tables highlight the best results, which are presented in bold.

Evaluation of the Effectiveness of Multimodal Fusion. In order to evaluate the effectiveness of multimodal fusion, we trained the proposed model respectively on single modality and multimodalities. Only one branch has been used to input the data when training the model in single modality as shown in Fig. 1. In Table 3, we can see that the performance of multimodal model is superior to single-modal either HSI or LiDAR for all three indices, i.e., OA, AA, κ and almost for each class accuracy, which demonstrate the effectiveness of our multimodal transformer RsMmFormer for RS image classification.

Table 3. Multimodal v.s. single-modal RsMmFormer.

Class	LiDAR only	HSI only	Multimodal
1	97.93 ± 0.56	99.21 ± 0.27	**99.71 ± 0.25**
2	74.47 ± 4.60	91.20 ± 2.48	**98.06 ± 0.80**
3	58.11 ± 5.98	93.58 ± 2.18	**94.47 ± 1.77**
4	93.79 ± 0.43	99.83 ± 0.20	**99.96 ± 0.02**
5	96.67 ± 0.56	**99.96 ± 0.03**	99.90 ± 0.07
6	67.03 ± 3.18	77.34 ± 4.60	**95.34 ± 1.32**
OA	90.29 ± 0.45	96.56 ± 0.60	**99.18 ± 0.02**
AA	81.33 ± 1.47	93.52 ± 1.35	**97.91 ± 0.25**
κ	86.99 ± 0.61	95.39 ± 0.81	**98.90 ± 0.02**

Table 4. Effectiveness of multiscale RsMmFormer.

16*16	8*8	4*4	2*2	OA	AA	κ
✓				99.04	97.29	98.71
	✓			98.46	97.03	97.94
		✓		98.89	97.50	98.51
			✓	98.97	96.93	98.62
✓	✓			99.06	96.72	98.74
✓		✓		99.18	97.61	98.90
✓			✓	99.17	97.58	98.89
	✓	✓		98.78	96.96	98.36
	✓		✓	98.70	96.11	98.26
		✓	✓	99.06	98.09	98.74
✓	✓	✓		99.13	97.21	98.83
✓	✓		✓	99.05	97.42	98.73
✓		✓	✓	**99.18**	**97.91**	**98.91**
	✓	✓	✓	98.71	97.28	98.27
✓	✓	✓	✓	99.14	97.22	98.85

Evaluation of the Effectiveness of Multi-scale MHSA. In Table 4, it can be observed that the model using MSMHSA performs always better than the one using single-scale MHSA, e.g., the model using 16×16, 4×4, 2×2 gains 0.3%, 0.7% and 0.5% improvement in terms OA, AA and κ respectively.

4.4   Visualization

Figure 2 demonstrates a qualitative assessment by visually presenting the classification maps generated by different models on the Trento dataset, utilizing HSI and LiDAR data. The MSMHSA module helps to learn the features in a fine-to-coarse manner, which obtains a classification map with less noise and finer details.

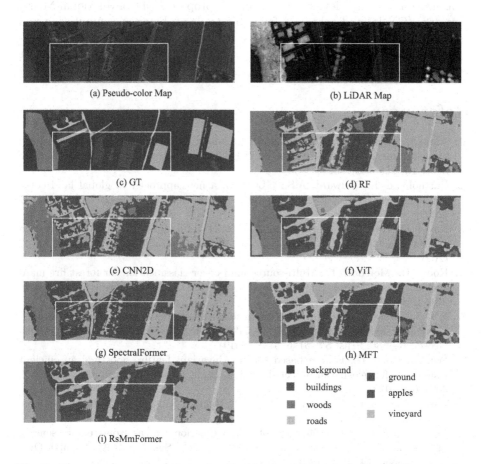

Fig. 2. The visual representations for the Trento dataset include: (a) Pseudo-color Map, (b) LiDAR, (c) Ground truth, along with the classification maps inferred by various models: (d) RF, (e) CNN2D, (f) ViT, (g) SpectralFormer [14], (h) MFT, and (i) RsMmFormer, based the HSI and LiDAR data on the Trento dataset.

5   Conclusion

We have designed a Multi-modal Transformer (RsMmFormer), which allows us to explore the complementary information between the spectral information in HSI and the spatial information in LiDAR for RS image classification. The proposed MSMHSA module in the Transformer aims to better fuse the multi-modal data with very different resolutions. Additionally, we have incorporated convolutions into our model to leverage the favorable properties of Convolutional Neural Networks (CNNs) and achieve a favorable trade-off between computation and accuracy. The demonstrated effectiveness and state-of-the-art performance highlight that the model RsMmFormer can serve as a valuable backbone for Remote Sensing (RS) image classification.

References

1. Ahmad, M., Shabbir, S.: Hyperspectral image classification-traditional to deep models: a survey for future prospects. IEEE J. Sel. Topics Appl. Earth Obs. Remote Sens. **15**, 968–999 (2021)
2. Bartholome, E., Belward, A.S.: GLC2000: a new approach to global land cover mapping from Earth observation data. Int. J. Remote Sens. **26**(9), 1959–1977 (2005)
3. Roy, S.K., Kar, P.: Revisiting deep hyperspectral feature extraction networks via gradient centralized convolution. IEEE Trans. Geosci. Remote Sens. **60**, 1–19 (2021)
4. Koetz, B., Morsdorf, F.: Multi-source land cover classification for forest fire management based on imaging spectrometry and LiDAR data. Forest Ecol. Manag. **256**, 263–271 (2008)
5. Wu, X., Hong, D.: ORSIm detector: a novel object detection framework in optical remote sensing imagery using spatial-frequency channel features. IEEE Trans. Geosci. Remote Sens. **57**, 5146–5158 (2019)
6. Wu, X., Hong, D.: Fourier-based rotation-invariant feature boosting: an efficient framework for geospatial object detection. IEEE Geosci. Remote Sens. Lett. **17**, 302–306 (2019)
7. Ustin, S.L.: Manual of Remote Sensing, Remote Sensing for Natural Resource Management and Environmental Monitoring. John Wiley & Sons, Hoboken (2004)
8. Chen, C., Yan, J.: Classification of urban functional areas from remote sensing images and time-series user behavior data. IEEE J. Sel. Topics Appl. Earth Obs. Remote Sens. **14**, 1207–1221 (2020)
9. Ghamisi, P., Benediktsson, J.A., Phinn, S.R.: Land-cover classification using both hyperspectral and LiDAR data. Int. J. Image Data Fusion **6**, 189–215 (2015)
10. Roy, S.K., Deria, A.: Multimodal fusion transformer for remote sensing image classification. arXiv preprint arXiv:2203.16952 (2023)
11. Makantasis, K., Karantzalos, K., Doulamis, A., Doulamis, N.: Deep supervised learning for hyperspectral data classification through convolutional neural networks. In: International Geoscience and Remote Sensing Symposium (2015)
12. Hamida, A.B., Benoit, A., Lambert, P., Amar, C.B.: 3-D deep learning approach for remote sensing image classification. IEEE Trans. Geosci. Remote Sens. **56**(8), 4420–4434 (2018)

13. Vaswani, A., Shazeer, N.: Attention is all you need. Adv. Neural Inf. Process. Syst. **30** (2017)
14. Hong, D., et al.: SpectralFormer: rethinking hyperspectral image classification with transformers. In: Computer Vision and Pattern Recognition (2021)
15. Gao, L., Hong, D., Yao, J., Zhang, B., Gamba, P., Chanussot, J.: Spectral super-resolution of multispectral imagery with joint sparse and low-rank learning. IEEE Trans. Geosci. Remote Sens. **59**, 2269–2280 (2021)
16. Benediktsson, J.A., Palmason, J.: Classification of hyperspectral data from urban areas based on extended morphological profiles. IEEE Trans. Geosci. Remote Sens. **43**, 480–491 (2005)
17. Dalla Mura, M., Benediktsson, J.A.: Morphological attribute profiles for the analysis of very high resolution images. IEEE Trans. Geosci. Remote Sens. **48**, 3747–3762 (2010)
18. Ghamisi, P., Souza, R.: Extinction profiles for the classification of remote sensing data. IEEE Trans. Geosci. Remote Sens. **54**, 5631–5645 (2016)
19. De La Torre, F., Black, M.J.: A framework for robust subspace learning. Int. J. Comput. Vision **54**, 117–142 (2003)
20. Singh, P., Verma, V.K., et al.: Hetconv: heterogeneous kernel-based convolutions for deep CNNs. In: Proceedings of the IEEE/CVF Conference on Computer Vision and Pattern Recognition, pp. 4835–4844 (2019)
21. Ham, J., Chen, Y.: Investigation of the random forest framework for classification of hyperspectral data. IEEE Trans. Geosci. Remote Sens. **43**, 492–501 (2005)
22. Dosovitskiy, A., Beyer, L.: An image is worth 16x16 words: transformers for image recognition at scale. arXiv preprint arXiv:2010.11929 (2010)

Fashion Label Relation Networks for Attribute Recognition

Tongyang Wang, Yan Huang, and Jianjun Qian[✉]

PCA Lab, Key Lab of Intelligent Perception and Systems for High-Dimensional Information of Ministry of Education, and Jiangsu Key Lab of Image and Video Understanding for Social Security, School of Computer Science and Engineering, Nanjing University of Science and Technology, Nanjing, China
{tongyangwang,arvohy,csjqian}@njust.edu.cn

Abstract. Clothes attribute recognition has played a distinguished role in the fashion industry. A large number of attributes and the intrinsic relations between attributes make this task challenging. Most prior methods employ the landmark detection to improve performance. However, there has been little research devoted to analyzing the relationships between fashion labels. To address the above problem, this paper proposes an effective Fashion Label Relation (FLR) network, including the local label relation (LLR) and the global label relation (GLR). LLR uses an attention mechanism to focus on local label relations in conjunction with a predicted label correlation matrix for refining the label representation. To fully characterize the relationships among all attributes, GLR performs a pairwise label co-occurrence prediction task in label co-occurrence prediction (LCP) module and constructs a new label feature distribution in label relation smoothing (LRS) module to avoid overfitting. The comprehensive experimental results strongly demonstrate that our proposed framework outperforms state-of-the-art algorithms.

Keywords: Fashion recognition · label relation · attention mechanism

1 Introduction

Fashion, as a visual domain, has gained significant interest from computer vision researchers in recent years. In the field of computer vision, there are various areas of research related to fashion, such as fashion recommendation [1], clothing classification [2], and fashion trend prediction [2,3]. Among these areas, our primary focus is on traditional fashion attribute recognition.

As an outfit has multiple attributes, fashion attribute recognition is essentially a multi-label classification task. The previous works combine auxiliary tasks together to achieve better performance. Liu et al. [4] proposed a Fashion-Net to jointly predict attributes and the location of landmarks. [5,6] also learn jointly with landmark detection and category classification. However, these works expand the model complexity and increase the amount of computation load. Meanwhile, the most previous methods ignore the implicit associations between labels.

L. Fang et al. (Eds.): CICAI 2023, LNAI 14473, pp. 340–351, 2024.
https://doi.org/10.1007/978-981-99-8850-1_28

In the field of conventional multi-label classification, researchers have started to focus on modeling the correlation between labels. Recently, several works have employed Graph Convolutional Network (GCN) to map label representations [7,8]. However, these methods still lack the ability to establish correlations in many complex scenarios. Transformers have shown success in various computer vision tasks, as we all known it include object detection [9,10] and image classification [11]. The attention mechanism, a key component of transformers, models relationships within data and has been used in many multi-label classification works [12,13]. Previous studies have achieved significant results but typically considered fewer than 100 labels in their tasks. In contrast, our task involves hundreds to thousands of labels.

To overcome this difficulty, we wander to build label relationships from local-wise and global-wise orientations, respectively. The local-wise part mainly aims to model label relations by focusing on several labels with high correlation and ignoring other irrelevant labels. And the other part is responsible to improve global correlation learning by using a label distribution constraint and a label co-occurrence prediction constraint.

Based on the ideas mentioned above, we propose a Fashion Label Relation Network for fashion attribute recognition. This network consists of an LLR module and a GLR module. In LLR, we predict a correlation matrix to refine label embedding according to its local guidance and attention mechanism. After that, we perform cross-attention to pool image features for downstream steps. In our approach, we utilize the VGG-16 model [14] to extract image features. The co-occurrence relationships among labels play a significant role in revealing label correlations, and the advantage is that it doesn't require additional manual annotation and has low computational complexity. In the proposed method, called GLR (Graph-based Label Relationship), we go beyond just considering co-occurrence and capture label correlations by leveraging a given partially relevant label set to predict the relevance of unknown labels. This helps in incorporating the relationships between labels into the classification process. In multi-label classification tasks, true labels are often represented using a multi-hot vector, where each label is indicated by a binary value (0 or 1) denoting its presence or absence. However, relying solely on the multi-hot vector may not fully capture the intricate relationships between objects and labels. Therefore, if we heavily rely on the multi-hot vector during training, it can lead to overconfidence of the model and potentially affect its performance. Therefore, a new label distribution is generated in GLR to replace the original multi-hot vector. This new distribution is then compared with the predicted distribution to compute the loss. Extensive experiments show that our model significantly outperforms the compared methods. The main contributions are listed as follows:

- A local label relation (LLR) module is proposed to predict a correlation matrix, combing attention mechanism to build local-wise attribute relationships.

- A global label relation (GLR) module is developed with a co-occurrence prediction constraint and a label distribution constraint, which can model the global-wise attribute relationships dynamically.
- Based on LLR and GLR, the proposed Fashion Label Relation (FLR) network achieves state-of-the-art performance on four fashion datasets.

2   Related Work

Fashion Image Recognition. In recent years, because of the improvement of deep learning and the appearance of large-scale fashion datasets [4,15,16], many convolutional neural networks have been introduced to dig more discriminative representation and obtain more superior performance. In 2016 the paper FashionNet [4] is proposed, and it contained a deep model designed for joint prediction of clothing category classification and landmark localization prediction. Instead, [5,6] tended to combine a-priori information like grammar knowledge when training models for achieving better performance. However, although these methods achieved good performance, they ignored the relationship between the fashion attributes, thereby hindering the further improvement of the recognition accuracy.

Label Relationship Modeling. For multi-label classification tasks, from the previous study we find that building label relations is a critical problem, which further motivates us to model the relationship between labels. Attention mechanism strategy [17] has been widely used in the deep-learning fields, such as natural language processing (NLP) task and computer vision (CV) task. It was first brought to vision in Vision Transformer (ViT) [18] when the study use it to split an image into a sequence of visual tokens. Many works [9,10,19] introduces it as an effective architecture for relationship digging and have demonstrated better results. Though the attention mechanism is expert in obtaining the relationship, it will not work well when the number of entities is huge. With the objective of reducing the effects mentioned, we apply a correlation matrix to assist with it. Nevertheless, label co-occurrence characteristics were analyzed as primary in multi-label classification problems [20], due to it can help with enhancing label correlation learning. Label smoothing(LS) is another relation modeling method and it was first introduced in the image classification task [21], they take it as a regularization technique to stop the model from predicting the training inputs too confidently, and has been applied widely in many other works [17,22]. Naturally, it is not hard for us to attain some inspiration from these mentioned works, that is, we can forge several constraints to dynamically model the correlation between labels from a global perspective.

3   Methodology

In this section, we will introduce our Fashion Label Relation (FLR) network in detail. The overview of FLR is shown in Fig. 1.

3.1 Framework

Suppose we have a dataset consisting of images that can be classified into C different classes. The label space is denoted as $y = [y_1, y_2, ..., y_C]$, where each y_c represents whether the image belongs to the c-th class or not. If the image contains the c-th category label, then y_c is 1, otherwise, it is 0. Our task is to learn a predictive function that can assign predicted probabilities to each class for a given input image I. We aim to obtain the probabilities $p = [p_1, p_2, ..., p_C]$ corresponding to each class. These probabilities represent the model's confidence in predicting the presence or absence of each class in the image.

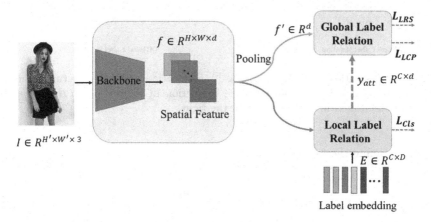

Fig. 1. The overall architecture of our proposed Fashion Label Relation (FLR) network consists of two essential structures. The LLR structure enables the label embeddings to refine themselves and capture image features. The GLR structure uses the output from LLR to predict label co-occurrence probability and a new label distribution.

Feature Extraction. Let's consider an input image denoted as $I \in R^{H' \times W' \times 3}$. To extract spatial features from this image, we can use the VGG-16 network [14] as the backbone network. The spatial feature $f \in R^{H \times W \times d}$, where $H' \times W'$ represent the height and weight of feature map respectively, and d represents the dimension of the extracted features.

Local Label Relation. An illustration of local relation construction is shown in Fig. 2(a). Firstly, we utilize a random initialization label embedding $E \in R^{C \times D}$ to predict K relation positions, so that attain a correlation matrix A^p reflecting the labels that each label is interested in. Then, both E and A^p are feed to the label attention block and acquire a refined label representation E'. In practical

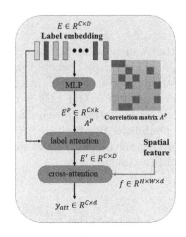 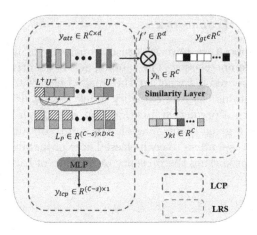

a)Local Label Relation

b)Global Label Relation

Fig. 2. a) Illustration of LLR structure. b) Illustration of GLR structure, which is composed of a basic Label Co-occurrence Prediction(LCP) module on the left and a Label Relation Smooth(LRS) module on the right.

terms, we define the formula as follows.

$$
\begin{aligned}
A^p &= MLP(E), \\
A &= softmax(\frac{EW_Q(EW_K)^T}{\sqrt{C}} * A^p), \\
E' &= AEW_V,
\end{aligned}
\tag{1}
$$

where A^p is the correlation matrix, and $W_{\{Q\}}$, $W_{\{K\}}$, $W_{\{V\}}$ are represented as the learnable weights of query, key and value projections. A is the attention matrix. Subsequently, we adopt the cross-attention mechanism to encourage the label to query interested class-related region features for the subsequent binary classification. After the LLR construction processed the inputs via two consecutive attention stages, the original label embedding E obtains an appropriate class-related representation y_{attr} and updates itself iteratively. To address the class imbalance issue in the classification task, we employ the asymmetric loss [23] as our classification loss function:

$$
\mathcal{L}_{CLs} = \frac{1}{C} \sum_{i=1}^{C} \begin{cases} (1-p_i)^{\gamma+} log(p_i), & y_{gt}^i = 1. \\ (p_i)^{\gamma-} log(1-p_i), & y_{gt}^i = 0. \end{cases}
\tag{2}
$$

where $p = [p_1, ..., p_C]$ is the predicted results of y_{attr}. y_{gt} is the ground truth.

Global Label Relation.

Label Co-occurrence Prediction. In order to enhance the label correlation learning globally, we add an auxiliary label co-occurrence prediction branch named

LCP. Firstly, let's assume that the label set for the dataset is denoted as U, and the attribute set corresponding to each image is denoted as U^+, where U^+ belongs to U. The strategy begins by randomly selecting s attributes from the label set U^+ and form a new set L^+. These selected attributes are guaranteed to exist in the corresponding images. Then, we pair the remaining labels from the total label set with these s selected labels L^+. In this approach, the average feature vector serves as a representation of the selected s labels. It is combined with each of the remaining label vectors one by one to form pairs for further processing. Ultimately, the goal is to predict whether these pairs of labels will appear together in an image. From Fig. 2(b), we can see the overview of GLR. We use the binary cross-entropy loss to calculate the label co-occurrence prediction loss:

$$\mathcal{L}_{LCP} = -\sum_{i=1}^{C-s} [y_{pair}^i \ln(y_{lcp}^i) + (1 - y_{pair}^i) \ln(1 - y_{lcp}^i)] \tag{3}$$

we denote y_{pair}^i as the ground-truth, $y_{pair}^i = 1$ only if the i-th label pair will be co-occurrence.

Label Relation Smooth. Moreover, the LRS module overcomes the limitations of inflexible techniques like uniform label smoothing, which treat all labels equally. By considering the individual similarities between objects and labels, the module provides a more adaptable and fine-grained approach to capturing label dependencies. We employ a Multi-Layer Perceptron (MLP) layer to construct the similarity layer shown in Fig. 2 (b). Specifically, this similarity layer takes the output of LLR named y_{attr} and the pooled image features f' as the inputs, and then computes their similarity values. In order to preserve the primary label distribution information, we add the multi-hot vector ground truth to help with the new label distribution building. So far, we have received the ultimate predicted new label distribution y_{kl}. To measure the dissimilarity between the predicted classification result p and the ground truth label distribution y_{kl}, we employ the Kullback-Leibler divergence (KL-divergence) [24] as the loss function. The loss can be formulated as follows:

$$\begin{aligned} \mathcal{L}_{LRS} &= KL(y_{kl}\|p), \\ &= \sum_{i=1}^{C} y_{kl}^i \log \frac{y_{kl}^i}{p_i}, \end{aligned} \tag{4}$$

3.2   Learning Objective

In this subsection, three constraints term defined above are employed to improve the robustness of the recognition task. The total training loss function is as follows:

$$\mathcal{L}_{sum} = \mathcal{L}_{CLs} + \lambda\mathcal{L}_{LCP} + \alpha\mathcal{L}_{LRS} \tag{5}$$

where λ and α are hyperparameters, which denote the weight of L_{LCP} and L_{LRS} loss respectively. We minimize the loss by using the adaptive moment estimation [25] optimization.

4 Experiment

4.1 Benchmark Dataset and Evaluation Metrics

DeepFashion-C [4] is a comprehensive and big clothing dataset that contains rich annotations for clothing items. Each image in this dataset is extensively labeled with 1,000 attributes. The attribute labels set are divided into five distinct groups, which characterize various aspects of the clothing items. These groups include 'texture', 'fabric', 'shape', 'part', and 'style'. In terms of dataset split, 209,222 fashion images from dataset are allocated for training purposes. Another set of 40,000 images is designated for validation, while the rest 40,000 images serve as test samples.

iFashion (iMaterialist Fashion Attribute) [16] is a large-scale fashion dataset constructed from a collection of over one million fashion images. It boasts a comprehensive label space consisting of eight groups, encompassing a total of 228 fine-grained attributes. These attribute groups are categorized as 'category', 'color', 'gender', 'material', 'neckline', 'pattern', 'sleeve', and 'style'.

Evaluation Metrics. In accordance with the evaluation protocol established in [4], the performance of the model is assessed using the top-k recall rate metric. This metric measures the accuracy of attribute predictions by ranking the classification scores and determining the number of attributes that are correctly matched within the top-k predictions. Specifically, in iFashion dataset, the attributes amount of 'gender' and 'sleeve' are less than 5, so we choose to evaluate them with accuracy.

4.2 Implementation Details

We adopt the settings described below for all experiments. Following [6], we leverage vgg-16 [14] pre-trained on ImageNet [26] as our backbone. In the training stage, we resize the input images into 224×224. And the vgg-16 output feature's size is defined as $H \times W \times d = 14 \times 14 \times 512$, the hidden dimension is seted as $D = 512$ and $d = 512$. Moreover, we use image normalization technology to normalize the input images, and set mean as $[0, 0, 0]$ and set std as $[1, 1, 1]$. And then for data augmentation, we use RandAugment [27]. We set $\lambda = 0.5$, $\alpha = 0.5$ in Eq.(5). All the experiments are implemented on PyTorch using NVIDIA TITAN RTX GPU. We trained the model for 30 epochs with batch size=64, and employ the Adam [25] as the optimizer with the learning rate equals to 1×10^{-4}, and with True-weight-decay [28] of $1e - 2$, $\beta 1 = 0.9$ and $\beta 2 = 0.999$.

4.3 Comparison with the Benchmarking Methods

Comparisons on DeepFashion-C. As shown in Table 1, we compare our approach on DeepFahsion-C benchmark with some state-of-the-art methods. For fair

Table 1. Comparisons with state-of-the-art methods on the Deepfashion-C dataset. Best:**bold**.

Methods	Texture		Fabric		Shape		Part		Style		All	
	Top-3	Top-5	Top-3	Top-5	Top-3	Top-5	Top-3	Top-5	Top-3	Top-5	Top-3	Top-5
WTBI [29]	24.21	32.65	25.38	36.06	23.39	31.26	26.31	33.24	49.85	58.68	27.46	35.37
DARN [30]	36.15	48.15	36.64	48.52	35.89	46.93	39.17	50.17	66.11	71.36	42.35	51.95
FashionNet [4]	37.46	49.52	39.30	49.84	39.47	48.59	44.13	54.02	66.43	73.16	45.52	54.61
BCRNN [5]	50.31	49.52	40.31	48.23	53.32	61.05	40.65	56.32	68.70	**74.25**	51.53	60.95
Lu et al. [31]	56.17	65.83	43.20	53.52	58.28	67.80	46.97	57.42	**68.82**	74.13	**54.69**	**63.74**
re-impl of BCRNN [6]	56.48	65.85	44.10	54.40	61.30	70.30	49.24	59.36	33.58	42.44	49.19	58.80
Ts-fashionNet [6]	**58.52**	**68.19**	**46.44**	**57.02**	**61.86**	**70.81**	**49.82**	**60.36**	34.40	43.44	50.58	60.43
re-impl of [31]	56.49	66.31	43.69	53.96	57.74	67.21	46.40	56.80	31.59	40.25	26.80	34.84
re-impl of [6]	59.16	68.79	46.28	56.75	60.05	69.31	48.58	59.16	35.50	44.22	28.87	37.28
ML-GCN [7]	58.09	67.40	44.54	54.75	56.86	65.98	45.64	55.96	33.95	42.16	27.75	35.72
Vgg16 [14]	57.02	66.51	42.58	52.78	54.98	64.48	41.37	51.69	30.25	39.29	25.97	33.40
Ours	**62.66**	**72.31**	**51.08**	**61.48**	**63.30**	**72.14**	**54.10**	**64.29**	**43.27**	**51.38**	**32.43**	**42.09**

Table 2. Comparisons with state-of-the-art methods on the ifashion dataset. Best:**bold**.

Methods	category		color		gender	material		neckline		pattern		sleeve	style		All	
	Top-3	Top-5	Top-3	Top-5	Acc	Top-3	Top-5	Top-3	Top-5	Top-3	Top-5	Acc	Top-3	Top-5	Top-3	Top-5
Lu et al. [31]	82.52	90.50	72.75	85.78	90.77	85.87	93.25	87.72	95.91	88.38	93.47	82.03	77.96	88.13	38.25	53.36
Ts-FashionNet [6]	82.92	90.67	74.41	86.97	91.06	86.51	93.54	89.18	96.42	87.69	93.08	82.66	79.28	88.98	39.63	55.35
Vgg16 [14]	80.55	88.71	69.84	83.74	90.49	84.67	92.21	88.36	95.97	85.02	91.14	82.10	77.42	87.81	38.85	53.81
ML-GCN [7]	80.65	88.68	73.43	86.05	90.67	85.01	92.45	88.53	96.07	86.18	91.84	82.06	77.85	87.84	39.00	54.41
Ours	**85.07**	**92.08**	**76.38**	**88.53**	**91.65**	**88.76**	**94.63**	**90.11**	**96.78**	**90.09**	**94.35**	**83.49**	**81.09**	**90.3**	**40.44**	**56.96**

comparisons, we follow their resolution settings [5, 6] and use the same backbone. From the top half of Table 1, we find that the results within the 'style' group are quite different. According to [5, 6], the previous works utilized additional fashion-related data or the attributes' annotations might have been modified or updated over time. In addition, the all top-3 and top-5 recall rates also have discrepancies between the previous and our experiments. We infer they may directly average the results of all attribute groups before separately. So for fairness and reality, we imitate [6] and utilize the re-implementation experiment results for comparison, the results are presented in the bottom half of the Table 1. Our FLR significantly outperforms all the benchmarking methods. On average, FLR produces better recognition results than the best benchmarking results (shown in bold) around 4.73% and 4.70% on top-3 recall and top-5 recall respectively.

Comparisons on iFashion. Furthermore, we utilize the same experimental methods as described above to train on the iFashion dataset, and the results are presented in Table 2. It can be seen from the table that our method exceeds all other methods. According to the above results, it is easy to find that our method is very effective for fashion image attribute recognition task, which achieves state-of-the-art performance and can generalize to other database.

Table 3. Ablation experiments on the Deepfashion-C dataset. Best:**bold**.

Model	Texture		Fabric		Shape		Part		Style		All		Avg
	Top-3	Top-5	Top-3	Top-5	Top-3	Top-5	Top-3	Top-5	Top-3	Top-5	Top-3	Top-5	
FLR	**62.66**	72.31	**51.08**	61.48	63.30	**72.14**	**54.10**	64.29	**43.27**	51.38	**32.43**	**42.09**	**55.88**
w/o GLR	62.34	**72.35**	50.83	**61.55**	63.37	72.06	53.91	**64.42**	42.50	50.94	32.33	41.86	55.70
w/o LLR	62.11	71.76	50.73	61.26	**63.40**	72.06	53.85	63.78	43.25	**51.51**	32.18	41.61	55.62
w/o GLR & LLR	61.82	71.50	50.32	60.76	63.00	71.72	53.70	63.65	42.13	50.41	32.15	41.46	55.21

Table 4. Results on clothes retrieval datasets. Best:**bold**.

Methods	Inshop		Consumer-to-shop	
	Top-30	Top-50	Top-20	Top-50
BCRNN [5]	74.91	83.86	67.07	76.51
TS-FashionNet [6]	78.45	86.69	70.40	79.71
TS-FashionNet (pre-trained) [6]	79.04	87.13	69.33	78.66
Ours	**85.62**	**92.03**	**71.33**	**80.45**

4.4 Performance Analysis

Ablation Experiment. To deeply evaluate the effectiveness of our proposed GLR module and LLR module, we reconstruct our model with different ablation factors in Table 3 on the DeepFashion-C dataset. First, we study the baseline framework (i.e. FLR without LLR and GLR) with the identical training protocol, and the results, presented in the last row, show that it reaches a high baseline performance. Though all key components are deleted, our proposed baseline framework still outperforms the aforementioned SOTA methods, which shows the adaptability and superiority of our base model. Second, to intuitively compare results, we average each line to add an extra 'Avg' column. Note that each component in our study has its own benefits, particularly the proposed LLR module, which brings the most substantial performance improvement. On average, it achieves a gain of 0.49% compared to the baseline model. Furthermore, our proposed FLR module brings the best performance. This obviously demonstrates that the advantages of the individual components are complementary, and their combination leads to superior overall results.

Visualization and Analysis. To further demonstrate the role of our relational understanding network FLR. We utilize Grad-CAM [32] to exhibit the visualization of cross-attention maps in Fig. 3. The first column contains the input images, while the rest display the results of object location, with each attribute accurately located. It validates that our approach could precisely perceive small objects such as 'V-neck' and 'zip' while capturing the whole big objects like 'life' and 'sheath'.

4.5   Results on Clothes Retrieval Datasets

Experimental Setup. DeepFashion provides two benchmarks for evaluating clothing retrieval tasks: In-shop Clothes Retrieval and Consumer-to-Shop Clothes Retrieval. Every clothing item in both datasets has around 7 images. As for In-shop Clothes Retrieval, it has 7,982 clothing items and contains 52,712 images together with 463 attributes in total. Consumer-to-Shop Clothes Retrieval has 33,881 clothing items and 239,557 images in all and contains 303 attributes. Exactly as [6], we use the split methods like them. Similarly, We fairly choose the top-30 and top-50 recall rates for In-shop Clothes Retrieval and the top-20 and top-30 recall rate for Consumer-to-Shop Clothes Retrieval to align with [6].

Performance Evaluation. The experiment results are shown in Table 4, where the bold values indicate the best performance. We can see that our method clearly outperforms all the others across all of the evaluation metrics. Due to the numerous attributes in the In-Shop dataset, our model is required to effectively mine label correlations to achieve optimal performance. As a result, our model plays a more significant role in improving performance on the In-Shop dataset when compared to that on the Consumer-to-Shop Clothes dataset.

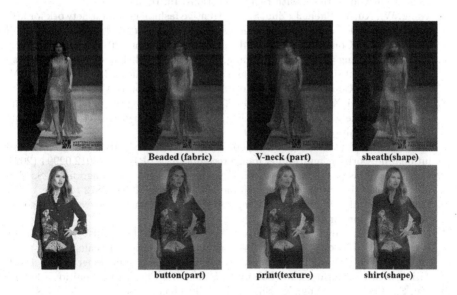

Fig. 3. Visualization of cross-attention maps.

5   Conclusion

In this paper, we propose the Fashion Label Relation (FLR) network for fashion image attribute recognition. Our method utilizes attention mechanisms to extract correlations between labels based on a correlation matrix. To further improve global label relation learning, we introduce a label co-occurrence prediction branch and create a new smooth label distribution, which served as two loss constraints to make the model more robust. Experimental results on multiple datasets demonstrate the effectiveness of our approach. In the future, we plan to further explore label relationships in depth to achieve higher performance.

Acknowledgments. This work was supported by the National Science Fund of China under Grant Nos. 62176124,61876083.

References

1. Vaccaro, K., Shivakumar, S., Ding, Z., Karahalios, K., Kumar, R.: The elements of fashion style. In: Symposium (2016)
2. Al-Halah, Z., Stiefelhagen, R., Grauman, K.: Fashion forward: Forecasting visual style in fashion. IEEE (2017)
3. Mall, U., Matzen, K., Hariharan, B., Snavely, N., Bala, K.: Geostyle: discovering fashion trends and events. In: 2019 IEEE/CVF International Conference on Computer Vision (ICCV) (2020)
4. Liu, Z., Luo, P., Qiu, S., Wang, X., Tang, X.: Deepfashion: powering robust clothes recognition and retrieval with rich annotations. In: IEEE (2016)
5. Wang, W., Xu, Y., Shen, J., Zhu, S.C.: Attentive fashion grammar network for fashion landmark detection and clothing category classification. In: 2018 IEEE/CVF Conference on Computer Vision and Pattern Recognition (2018)
6. Zhang, Y., Zhang, P., Yuan, C., Wang, Z.: Texture and shape biased two-stream networks for clothing classification and attribute recognition. In: 2020 IEEE/CVF Conference on Computer Vision and Pattern Recognition (CVPR) (2020)
7. Chen, Z.M., Wei, X.S., Wang, P., Guo, Y.: Multi-label image recognition with graph convolutional networks. In: 2019 IEEE/CVF Conference on Computer Vision and Pattern Recognition (CVPR) (2019)
8. Ye, J., He, J., Peng, X., Wu, W., Qiao, Y.: Attention-driven dynamic graph convolutional network for multi-label image recognition. CoRR, abs/2012.02994 (2020)
9. Carion, N., Massa, F., Synnaeve, G., Usunier, N., Kirillov, A., Zagoruyko, S.: End-to-end object detection with transformers. CoRR, abs/2005.12872 (2020)
10. Zhang, H., et al.: Dino: Detr with improved denoising anchor boxes for end-to-end object detection. arXiv e-prints (2022)
11. Dosovitskiy, A., Beyer, L., Kolesnikov, A., Weissenborn, D., Houlsby, N.: An image is worth 16×16 words: transformers for image recognition at scale (2020)
12. Lanchantin, J., Wang, T., Ordonez, V., Qi, Y.: General multi-label image classification with transformers. In: Computer Vision and Pattern Recognition (2021)
13. Liu, S., Zhang, L., Yang, X., Su, H., Zhu, J.: Query2label: a simple transformer way to multi-label classification (2021)
14. Simonyan, K., Zisserman, A.: Very deep convolutional networks for large-scale image recognition. Computer Science (2014)
15. Ge, Y., Zhang, R., Wang, X., Tang, X., Luo, P.: Deepfashion2: a versatile benchmark for detection, pose estimation, segmentation and re-identification of clothing images. In: 2019 IEEE/CVF Conference on Computer Vision and Pattern Recognition (CVPR) (2019)
16. Guo, S., et al.: The imaterialist fashion attribute dataset (2019)

17. Vaswani, A., et al.: Attention is all you need. arXiv (2017)
18. Dosovitskiy, A., et al.: An image is worth 16×16 words: transformers for image recognition at scale. In: International Conference on Learning Representations (2021)
19. Sun, C., Liu, F., Xiang, T., Hospedales, T.M., Yang, W.: Semantic regularisation for recurrent image annotation (2016)
20. Xue, X., Wei, Z., Jie, Z., Wu, B., Yao, L.: Correlative multi-label multi-instance image annotation. In: International Conference on Computer Vision (2011)
21. Zoph, B., Vasudevan, V., Shlens, J., Le, Q.V.: Learning transferable architectures for scalable image recognition (2017)
22. Chorowski, J., Jaitly, N., Chorowski, J., Jaitly, N.: Towards better decoding and language model integration in sequence to sequence models (2017)
23. Ben-Baruch, E., Ridnik, T., Zamir, N., Noy, A., Zelnik-Manor, L.: Asymmetric loss for multi-label classification (2020)
24. Kullback, S., Leibler, R.A.: On information and sufficiency. Ann. Math. Stat. **22**(1), 79–86 (1951)
25. Kingma, D.P., Ba, J.: Adam: a method for stochastic optimization. In: International Conference on Learning Representations (2014)
26. Jia, D., Wei, D., Socher, R., Li, L.J., Kai, L., Li, F.F.: Imagenet: a large-scale hierarchical image database, pp. 248–255 (2009)
27. Cubuk, E.D., Zoph, B., Shlens, J., Le, Q.V.: Randaugment: practical automated data augmentation with a reduced search space. In: 2020 IEEE/CVF Conference on Computer Vision and Pattern Recognition Workshops (CVPRW) (2020)
28. Loshchilov, I., Hutter, F.: Decoupled weight decay regularization (2017)
29. Chen, H., Gallagher, A., Girod, B.: Describing clothing by semantic attributes. In: Fitzgibbon, A., Lazebnik, S., Perona, P., Sato, Y., Schmid, C. (eds.) ECCV 2012. LNCS, vol. 7574, pp. 609–623. Springer, Heidelberg (2012). https://doi.org/10.1007/978-3-642-33712-3_44
30. Huang, J., Feris, R.S., Chen, Q., Yan, S.: Cross-domain image retrieval with a dual attribute-aware ranking network. IEEE (2015)
31. Liu, J., Lu, H.: Deep fashion analysis with feature map upsampling and landmark-driven attention. In: Leal-Taixé, L., Roth, S. (eds.) ECCV 2018. LNCS, vol. 11131, pp. 30–36. Springer, Cham (2019). https://doi.org/10.1007/978-3-030-11015-4_4
32. Selvaraju, R.R., Cogswell, M., Das, A., Vedantam, R., Parikh, D., Batra, D.: Grad-cam: visual explanations from deep networks via gradient-based localization. In: IEEE International Conference on Computer Vision (2017)

A Modified Fuzzy Markov Random Field Incorporating Multiple Features for Liver Tumor Segmentation

Laquan Li[✉] and Yan Jiang

School of Science, Chongqing University of Posts and Telecommunications, Chongqing 400065, People's Republic of China
lilq@cqupt.edu.cn

Abstract. Automated segmentation of liver tumors from computerized tomography (CT) images plays a crucial role in computer-aided pathological diagnosis, surgical planning, and postoperative assessment. However, liver tumors exhibit significant variations in size, shape, and location, often low contrast and blurry boundaries with surrounding tissues, making the segmentation task highly challenging. To address this problem, this study proposes a novel and powerful segmentation method based on fuzzy Markov Random Fields(fMRF). Without the need for preprocessing steps, the method utilizes superpixel blocks to form coarse-grained features and intensity, gradient information, and texture information to create enhanced feature vectors representing the tumors. Meanwhile, a new potential function is designed by combining the affiliation distance and multi-feature information in the prior energy function of the model, as a way to further improve the judgment performance of the method for label classification. Finally, morphological processing is applied to refine the segmentation results and obtain the final tumor segmentation outcome. The proposed method is applied to the 3Dircadb dataset. The results demonstrate that this method achieves superior overall segmentation performance compared to many existing approaches, particularly in scenarios involving low contrast and blurry boundaries in tumor segmentation.

Keywords: fuzzy Markov Random Field · tumors segmentation · CT images

1 Introduction

Hepatocellular carcinoma (HCC) represents a highly prevalent malignancy on a global scale, exerting a substantial toll in terms of mortality [1, 2]. Timely identification, precise diagnosis, and effective management of hepatocellular carcinoma play a pivotal role in enhancing patient survival outcomes and optimizing their overall well-being. In the realm of clinical application, computed tomography (CT) has emerged as a widely utilized modality for the detection and characterization of hepatic neoplasms owing to its favorable attributes such as superior signal-to-noise ratio, exceptional spatial resolution, expedited scanning capabilities, and favorable cost-effectiveness. By furnishing

© The Author(s), under exclusive license to Springer Nature Singapore Pte Ltd. 2024
L. Fang et al. (Eds.): CICAI 2023, LNAI 14473, pp. 352–363, 2024.
https://doi.org/10.1007/978-981-99-8850-1_29

meticulous details encompassing tumor morphology, dimensions, and spatial coordinates, CT empowers clinicians with invaluable data to discern and deliberate upon optimal therapeutic approaches. Nonetheless, the process of segmentation is commonly executed through manual intervention by radiologists, a practice characterized by its protracted duration, laborious nature, and significant reliance on individual operators. Consequently, the imperative to develop automatic or semi-automatic methodologies for liver tumor segmentation has become exceedingly urgent, garnering escalating research interest and scrutiny [3].

Precisely and reliably delineating liver tumors from CT images continues to pose formidable challenges attributable to the following factors: (1) substantial anatomical heterogeneity exhibited by tumors in terms of their spatial distribution, dimensions, and morphologies; (2) indistinct demarcation of tumor boundaries with adjacent hepatic tissues; and (3) inherent noise artifacts stemming from CT acquisition and contrast injection protocols. To mitigate these challenges, a plethora of methodologies have been devised and introduced, aiming to offer effective solution. The methodologies employed for segmentation can be classified into distinct categories, namely traditional image segmentation approaches [4–7], theory-driven methodologies [8, 9] and machine learning-based techniques [10–12]. In the realm of medical image processing, machine learning has assumed a progressively pivotal role in recent years, manifesting as a potent paradigm for advanced data analysis and decision-making. A substantial body of research endeavors has been dedicated to the development of machine learning-based methodologies for liver tumor segmentation. These approaches, broadly classified into two primary categories, encompass traditional learning techniques and deep learning paradigms. Each of these approaches has its own characteristics, but there is still much room for improvement in their performance in tumor segmentation.

Markov Random Field (MRF) model is a machine learning method with a solid theoretical foundation. It is widely used in image segmentation due to their ability to describe the spatial information of an image well [13, 14]. However, classical MRF models are defined only on deterministic classes, which poses challenges in CT image segmentation such as grayscale overlap, grayscale blurring, low contrast, and partial volume effects. For the problems existing in medical images, many scholars use fuzzy logic and statistics to describe the uncertainty of segmentation to accomplish the segmentation task [15–17]. The fuzzy MRF model is the result of introducing fuzzy set theory into the model, which can deal with both uncertainties in medical image segmentation - ambiguity and randomness - without losing the spatial information of the image and overcoming the effects of uncertainty due to grey-scale overlap, blurring and partial volume effects, thus improving the image segmentation accuracy.

We are aware that hepatic lesions in CT images often exhibit highly fuzzy boundaries. In such cases, we consider applying a fuzzy MRF-based approach for liver tumor segmentation of CT images. However, the conventional fuzzy MRF method utilizes only the pixel intensity information of the image. Therefore, we construct an enhanced feature vector of the tumor from the perspective of characterizing the tumor properties, using intensity, gradient, texture information, and coarse-grained features. Based on the enhanced vector, a new potential function is proposed by combining the affiliation distance metric. It makes the method not only consider the dissimilarity judgment on the labels, but also combine the difference distance on the features, which further enhances the accuracy of the tumor segmentation. In addition, our segmentation process was subjected to morphological post-processing to refine the tumor results of the proposed method. We performed the validation of our method on the public dataset 3Dircadb, and its evaluation demonstrated the effectiveness of the proposed method.

2   Proposed Method

The proposed method is a probabilistic model based on fuzzy Markov Random Field(fMRF) theory. Figure 1 illustrates the flowchart of the segmentation method. A detailed description of the proposed method is provided below.

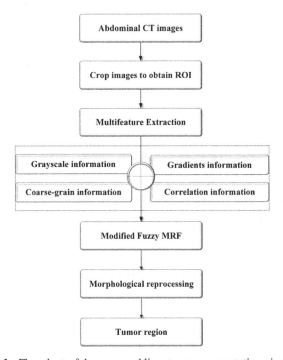

Fig. 1. Flowchart of the proposed liver tumor segmentation pipeline.

2.1   Feature Extraction

We traverse the CT scans of cases and select the ROI containing tumors. Then, the simple linear iterative clustering technique (SLIC) [18] is used to generate region blocks to form coarse-grained information and calculate the average of the region blocks as coarse-grained features. The Kirsch operator is used to obtain the image gradient information. The grey scale co-generation matrix (GLCM) is calculated in parallel. To reduce the computational effort, we visualize each feature map of the GLCM and select the feature that most clearly represents tumors, i.e. the correlation feature. In order to incorporate features in different scales, all the features are extracted in both 11×11 patches. These features are incorporated into the feature vector as input to the next step.

2.2 The Modified Fuzzy Markov Random Field Model

Fuzzy segmentation of an image is based on allowing each pixel to belong simultaneously to more than one class. Then, the fuzzy segmentation problem is to associate to the pixel at location a vector $x_s = (u_{s1}, u_{s2}, ..., u_{sk}, ..., u_{sK})$ with $u_{sk} \in [0, 1]$, $\sum_k u_{sk} = 1$, where u_{sk} represents the degree of membership of the pixel s to class k, and K is the number of classes.

In the modified multi-feature fuzzy MRF(MFMRF), three fields are used for the description. Let $S = \{(i, j)|1 \le i \le M, 1 \le j \le N\}$ be an input image where $M \times N$ denotes the size of the image. $Y = \{y_s|s \in S\}$ is the observed random field which represents the observed image. $X = \{x_s|s \in S\}$ is the fuzzy random field defined on S. $Z = \{z_s|s \in S\}$ is the label random field defined on S, which corresponds to the final segmentation results and takes value from the set $\Lambda = \{1, 2, ..., K\}$. X, as a fuzzy random field, is introduced to replace a classical random variable. When X loses its fuzziness, it degenerates to the classical Markov random field Z.

We model the above three random fields to achieve segmentation of liver tumors. The prior knowledge of the image is obtained by fuzzy random fields, updated by maximum the posterior probability(MAP), and ultimately the tumor segmentation is achieved by eliminating the ambiguity for X. From MRF theory, it is clear that the image segmentation problem based on MRF model will eventually be transformed into a combinatorial optimization problem of the following equation:

$$X^* = \underset{x}{argmax} P(Y|X)P(X) \tag{1}$$

$P(Y|X)$ is the likelihood function, and $P(X)$ is a joint priori distribution. Therefore, the MFMRF model can be obtained by giving the prior energy and the likelihood energy.

Determination of the Degree of Affiliation. We proceed the classical fuzzy MRF approach [17] by defining the affiliation at pixel point s as

$$\begin{aligned} \tilde{U} &: K \to [0, 1] \\ k &\to \tilde{U}(k) = \frac{|N_k|}{\sum_k |N_k|} \end{aligned} \tag{2}$$

$|N_k|$ is the number of pixels in its neighborhood that belong to class k. $\tilde{U}(k)$ is the affiliation of pixel s to class k.

Establishment of the Distribution of Fuzzy Prior. X is the random field that blurs the label field, and the value of each pixel in X is only relevant to its neighborhood. According to the Hammersley–Clifford theorem [13], $P(X)$ obeys the Gibbs distribution which is given by

$$P(X) = \frac{1}{Z(X)} exp\{-\frac{U(X)}{T}\} \tag{3}$$

where $Z(X)$ is the normalizing factor and $U(X)$ is called the fuzzy priori energy function defined on the potential group, T can be considered as a constant and is usually taken as 1.

In MRF prior distribution, its potential function is typically defined in terms of the Potts model [13], which only makes use of the dissimilarity of the labels in the neighborhood. For the tumor characteristics in CT images, we introduce the distance of affiliation in soft segmentation theory and incorporate the multi-feature information in the image. So a novel fuzzy prior energy function $U(X)$ is proposed as follows

$$U(X) = \sum_s \frac{\beta}{2}(||x_s - x_t||)\frac{(Y_c + \sigma_k^2)}{\sigma_k^2} \tag{4}$$

Here,

$$||x_s - x_t|| = \sum_{t \in N_s}\sum_k |u_{sk} - u_{tk}| \tag{5}$$

And

$$Y_c = \sqrt{\sum_{t \in N_s}\left|y_s^{feat} - y_t^{feat}\right|} \tag{6}$$

where $y_s^{feat} = (y_s^{pixel}, y_s^{gradi}, y_s^{text}, y_s^{cgrain})$ denotes the grayscale feature, gradient feature, correlation feature and coarse-grained feature vector at pixel point s. Y_c represents the feature difference between a point and its neighboring points. This distance function delineates subtle distinctions between pixels and provides a more refined description of prior information, whereas the classical model only considers the similarity and dissimilarity between pixels.

Establishment of the Fuzzy Likelihood Distribution. As for the likelihood term $P(Y|X)$, we assume that different Y_s are independent given the labels and each $P(y_s|x_s)$ obeys a Gaussian distribution, that is

$$P(Y|X) = \prod_s P(y_s|x_s)$$
$$= \prod_s \frac{1}{\sqrt{2\pi}\sigma}exp\{-\frac{(y_s-\mu)^2}{2\sigma^2}\} \tag{7}$$

Compared to the classical MRF model, the likelihood distribution energy in this approach incorporates fuzzy weights, denoted as

$$\mu = \sum_k u_{sk}\mu_k$$
$$\sigma^2 = \sum_k u_{sk}\sigma_k^2 \tag{8}$$

μ_k and σ_k^2 are the mean and variance of the kth class. Applying a negative logarithmic transformation to Eq. (8), the likelihood energy function can be defined as

$$U(Y|X) = \sum_s[\frac{(y_s - \mu)^2}{2\sigma^2} + ln\sigma] \tag{9}$$

By taking the negative logarithm of Eq. (1), it can be simplified into a form of energy function minimization, which is expressed as $X^* = \underset{x}{argmin} U(X, Y) = \underset{x}{argmin}\{U(Y|X) + U(X)\}$. Correspondingly, the optimization objectives of the modified multi-featured fuzzy MRF model is denoted as

$$X^* = \underset{x}{argmin} U(X, Y)$$
$$= \underset{x}{argmin}\{\sum_s [\frac{(y_s - \mu)^2}{2\sigma^2} + ln\sigma] + \sum_s \frac{\beta}{2}(||x_s - x_t||)\frac{(Y_c + \sigma_k^2)}{\sigma_k^2}\} \tag{10}$$

In this paper, we use the iterated conditional modes (ICM) approach to perform the final solution to Eq. (10). Algorithm 1 shows the steps of proposed practical implementation.

Algorithm 1. The Proposed Method

Input: the observed image, Parameters {K, β, ε, the Maximum number of iterations t_max}
Output: the segmentation label Z

---

1. Extraction features;
2. Get the initial label field Z by using the k-means algorithm to cluster the features into K classes;
3. Fuzzification of Z. The affiliation is calculated according to Eq. (2) to obtain the fuzzy field X;
4. Defuzzification of the fuzzy field X. According to the principle of maximum subordination, the algorithm obtain an updated deterministic label field Z;
5. From the label field Z, updating the mean and variance according to Eq. (8);
6. Calculate the characteristic field energy from Eq. (9) and bring Eq. (5)(6) into Eq.(4) to find the fuzzy random field energy;
7. Update the label field Z according to equation (10) using the ICM;
8. Determining iteration termination. If $U^{t+1} - U^t < \varepsilon$, the iteration is terminated. Otherwise, repeat steps 3)-7) until the maximum number of iterations is satisfied.

2.3 Post-processing

To obtain the tumor region, morphological post-processing was performed. In order to eliminate isolated points and smooth the segmentation results, an opening operation with a disk-shaped structuring element of width 1 pixel was applied to refine the tumor segmentation. This morphological operation helps in removing small isolated regions and improving the overall segmentation accuracy by enhancing the connectivity and smoothness of the segmented tumor region.

3 Experimental Results

3.1 Dataset and Evaluation Measures

Like most scholars, we perform the application and comparison of segmentation methods in the public dataset 3Dircadb and LiTs. They are widely recognized and utilized within the research community for benchmarking and validating liver-related algorithms and techniques. The LiTs dataset is composed of 131 contrast-enhanced 3D abdominal CT scans obtained from different scanners and protocols at six different clinical sites. The 3Dircadb dataset consists of 20 contrast-enhanced CT volumes obtained from different European hospitals. It is worth mentioning that the LiTs dataset contains 3Dircadb data.

To evaluate the performance of the proposed method quantitatively, four metrics were computed to measure the volumetric overlap of the segmentation result compared to ground truth. The four metrics are dice similarity coefficient (DICE), volumetric overlap error (VOE), relative volume difference (RVD) and average symmetric surface distance(ASD). For the detailed definitions of these statistic measures, please refer to [19]. The value of DICE ranges from 0 to 1, with a value of 0 indicating no overlap and 1 representing perfect segmentation. For the other metrics, a value of 0 represents perfect segmentation. A negative value of RVD indicates under-segmentation.

3.2 Experimental Details

In our experiments, the parameter settings for generating coarse-grained blocks using the SLIC method were automatically set to the total number of image pixels divided by 100. For the setting of category K, we set K to 3 as the selected ROIs usually contain tumors, liver tissue and background areas. The parameter β in the priori energy function is empirically set to 0.5. Additionally, we set the maximum number of iterations to 400 to ensure timeliness.

In the comparison experiments, we refer to the setup of [3, 20]. Among the several methods compared, the deep learning based method is applied on LiTs data. These methods split the LiTs dataset into a dataset containing 3Dircadb and the remaining data as test and training sets, respectively. Therefore, our method only utilizes the 3Dircadb dataset for comparison.

3.3 Results and Discussion

We perform the implementation and analysis of the proposed segmentation method on the public dataset 3Dircadb. Figure 2 shows some example results of our proposed method with and without post-processing. Its numerical evaluation results are displayed in Table 1, and these results show that our method has good tumor results without post-processing. After the post-processing step, our tumor segmentation results are more reliable and stable.

Table 1. Performance evaluation of segmentation methods without post-processing on 3Dircadb dataset

Method	Dice	VOE	RVD	ASD
fMRF[17]	0.73 ± 0.10	0.40 ± 0.15	0.15 ± 0.25	1.90 ± 1.05
Ours	0.77 ± 0.04	0.36 ± 0.08	-0.02 ± 0.16	1.65 ± 1.24

Figure 3 gives some segmentation results of fMRF and the modified fMRF. As seen in the ground truth contour in the third column, the boundary between the tumor and the liver tissue is blurred. In such a context, the comparison between the result of fMRF in the first column and the result of our method in the second column demonstrates the superiority of our method. The segmentation results of liver tumors at vague boundaries are closer to the gold standard. Figure 4 demonstrates the overlap between our method and ground truth tumor contours. It can be seen that the proposed method is also very close to the ground truth in low contrast, especially in the case of the fourth column.

Table 2 presents the segmentation outcomes on the 3Dircadb public dataset, evaluated using the Dice coefficient along with three error measures. As anticipated, the proposed method consistently surpasses the fMRF approach across all indices, substantiating the efficacy of the modified fMRF framework for liver tumor segmentation. Reference to the setup and comparison of [3, 20], we performed quantitative evaluations with currently available deep learning methods U-Net [21], Deeplabv3+ [22], Trans-Unet [23], H-DUNET [24], mU-Net [25] and two other automatic methods [3, 26], whose results are also presented in Table 2. The table reveals that the averaged Dice values attained by the alternative approaches are comparatively lower. However, the enhanced fMRF model, which integrates multiple features, exhibits significantly improved overall performance in liver tumor segmentation, as evidenced by higher Dice and lower VOE, RVD, ASD scores. Also, the comparison of the variance data results in the table shows that our method has better stability. The numerical results of these four indicators are almost always better than the compared methods. Combining the results of these indicators, we can know the effectiveness of the proposed method. From the visualization results presented in Figs. 2, 3, and 4, we can see that the CT image tumor regions have different intensities and vary greatly in shape and size, yet our method still demonstrates good segmentation results on these morphologically diverse tumors. Again, as far as training time(Tr.t) and test time(Te.t) analysis are concerned, we refer to the comparison of [3],

Table 2. Comprehensive evaluation of the segmentation performance of our method compared to other existing approaches using the 3Dircadb dataset.

Method	Dice	VOE	RVD	ASD	Tr.t(h)	Te.t(s)
U-Net [21]	0.68 ± 0.11	0.40 ± 0.13	-0.09 ± 0.31	2.78 ± 1.05	22.3	4.5
Deeplabv3 + [22]	0.67 ± 0.18	0.47 ± 0.19	-0.12 ± 0.39	2.94 ± 0.88	26.7	3.7
TransUnet [23]	0.70 ± 0.13	0.44 ± 0.14	-0.19 ± 0.27	4.04 ± 3.20	30.2	7.3
H-DUNET [24]	0.65 ± 0.02	0.49 ± 0.05	0.33 ± 0.10	5.29 ± 6.15	–	–
mU-Net [25]	0.68 ± 0.06	0.36 ± 0.14	-0.01 ± 0.18	1.58 ± 0.51	–	–
Di et al. [3]	0.71 ± 0.07	0.31 ± 0.12	-0.35 ± 0.14	1.74 ± 1.24	0.8	25.1
Moghbel et al. [26]	0.75 ± 0.15	0.23 ± 0.12	0.09 ± 0.19	–	–	–
fMRF [17]	0.75 ± 0.13	0.38 ± 0.05	0.12 ± 0.30	1.84 ± 1.15	–	10.8
Ours	0.78 ± 0.02	0.35 ± 0.03	-0.02 ± 0.14	1.62 ± 1.20	–	12.2

whose results are placed in the last two columns of Table 2. In contrast to automated methods for deep learning, we do not require training time. The experimental results data show that our method spends an average of 12.2 s per tumor. Although higher than the comparison method, we do not need training time. So, the time consumed is within acceptable limits.

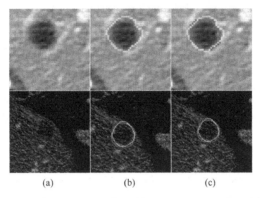

(a)   (b)   (c)

Fig. 2. (a) Original image, (b) Tumor results without post-processing, (c) Tumor results with post-processing. Segmentation results and Ground truth are shown as red and green outlines, respectively (Color figure online)

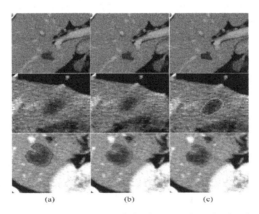

(a)   (b)   (c)

Fig. 3. Visual comparison between fMRF and the improved method. The tumors are shown in blue, red and green outlines in each column, respectively. (Color figure online)

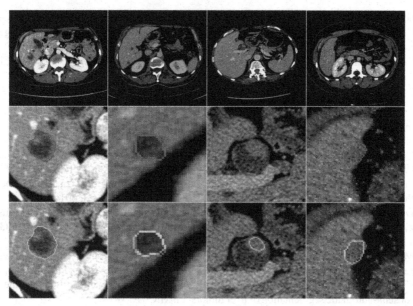

Fig. 4. Segmentation results for some tumors. The first row shows the original CT images. The second row shows a partial enlargement of the segmentation of the proposed method, and is shown with a red outline. The third row shows a comparison of the proposed method with ground-truth, where the split contours are in red, the ground-truth contours in green and the overlapping part of contours in yellow. (Color figure online)

4   Conclusion

In this paper, we have presented a modified multi-feature fuzzy MRF model for hepatic lesion segmentation. It improves upon the fMRF by incorporating the pixel feature, the coarse-grained feature, the gradient information and the correlation feature that can adequate representation of tumor characteristics and friendly to classification of pixels with blurred boundaries for segmenting hepatic lesions or liver tumors. The proposed method eliminates the need for pre-segmentation of the liver and avoids the use of complex and cumbersome training procedures. By incorporating enhanced characteristic information, we have developed an improved fuzzy Markov Random Field model that effectively minimizes and accurately identifies tumor regions.

The improved method was tested on the 3Dircadb dataset and compared with existing methods. The results substantiate the effectiveness of the proposed method in accurately segmenting tumors with challenging characteristics such as low contrast, blurred boundaries, and variations in shape, location, and intensity. It surpasses existing methods in terms of segmentation accuracy and reduces the need for manual interaction, thus achieving superior overall performance.

Acknowledgement. This work was supported in part by the National Natural Science Foundation of China (Grant No. 61901074) and the Science and Technology Research Program of Chongqing Municipal Education Commission (Grant Nos. KJQN201900636 and KJZD-K202200606) and the Natural Science Foundation of Chongqing (Grant No. 2022NSCQ-MSX3746) and China Postdoctoral Science Foundation (Grant No. 2021M693771).

References

1. Camilla, M., Giuseppe, L.: Cancer statistics: a comparison between world health organization (WHO) and global burden of disease (GBD). Eur. J. Publ. Health **30**(5), 1026–1027 (2020)
2. Pilleron, S., Soto-Perez-De-Celis, E., Vignat, J., et al.: Estimated global cancer incidence in the oldest adults in 2018 and projections to 2050. Int. J. Cancer **148**(3), 601–608 (2021)
3. Di, S., Zhao, Y., Liao, M., et al.: Automatic liver tumor segmentation from ct images using hierarchical iterative superpixels and local statistical features. Expert Syst. Appl. **203**(3), 117347 (2022)
4. Moghe, A., Singhai, J., Shrivastava, S., et al.: Automatic threshold based liver lesion segmentation in abdominal 2D-CT images. Int. J. Image Process. **5**(2), 2011–2166 (2011)
5. Choudhary A., Moretto N., Ferrarese F.P., et al.: An entropy based multi-thresholding method for semi-automatic segmentation of liver tumors. In: MICCAI Workshop, vol. 41(43), pp. 43–49(2008)
6. Anter, A.M., Azar, A.T., Hassanien, A.E., et al.: Automatic computer aided segmentation for liver and hepatic lesions using hybrid segmentations techniques. In: 2013 Federated Conference on Computer Science and Information Systems, pp. 193–198. IEEE, Krakow (2013)
7. Krishnakumar, S., Manivannan, K.: Effective segmentation and classification of brain tumor using rough k means algorithm and multi kernel svm in mr images. J. Ambient. Intell. Humaniz. Comput. **12**(6), 6751–6760 (2020)
8. Li, C., Wang, X., Eberl, S., et al.: A likelihood and local constraint level set model for liver tumor segmentation from ct volumes. IEEE Trans. Biomed. Eng. **60**(10), 2967–2977 (2013)
9. Siriapisith, T., Kusakunniran, W., Haddawy, P.: Pyramid graph cut: Integrating intensity and gradient information for grayscale medical image segmentation. Comput. Biol. Med. **126**, 103997 (2020)
10. Pesapane, F., et al.: Abdominal imaging. In: Amalou, H., Suh, R.D., Wood, B.J. (eds.) The Radiology Survival Kit, pp. 95–146. Springer, Cham (2021). https://doi.org/10.1007/978-3-030-84365-6_5
11. Aghamohammadi, A., Ranjbarzadeh, R., Naiemi, F., et al.: Tpcnn: two-path convolutional neural network for tumor and liver segmentation in ct images using a novel encoding approach. Expert Syst. Appl. **183**, 115406 (2021)
12. Gul, S., Khan, M.S., Bibi, A., et al.: Deep learning techniques for liver and liver tumor segmentation: a review. Comput. Biol. Med.. Biol. Med. **147**, 105620 (2022)
13. Li, S.Z.: Markov random field modeling in image analysis, 3rd edn. Springer-Verlag, Berlin (2009)
14. Chen, S.Y., Tong, H., Cattani, C.: Markov models for image labeling. Math. Probl. Eng.Probl. Eng. **2012**, 1–18 (2012). https://doi.org/10.1155/2012/814356
15. Salzenstein, F., Pieczynski, W.: Parameter estimation in hidden fuzzy Markov random fields and image segmentation. Graph. Models Image Process. **59**(4), 205–220 (1997)
16. Ruan S., Moretti B., Fadili J., et al.: Segmentation of magnetic resonance images using fuzzy markov random fields. In: Proceedings 2001 International Conference on Image Processing, vol. 3, pp. 1051–1054, IEEE, Piscataway (2001)

17. Liu, X., Langer, D.L., Haider, M.A., et al.: Prostate cancer segmentation with simultaneous estimation of markov random field parameters and class. IEEE Trans. Med. Imaging **28**(6), 906–915 (2009)
18. Achanta, R., Shaji, A., Smith, K., et al.: Slic superpixels compared to state-of-the-art superpixel methods. IEEE Trans. Pattern Anal. Mach. Intell. **34**(11), 2274–2282 (2012)
19. Heimann, T., Van Ginneken, B., Styner, M.A., et al.: Comparison and evaluation of methods for liver segmentation from ct datasets. IEEE Trans. Med. Imaging **28**(8), 1251–1265 (2009)
20. Wu, W., Wu, S., Zhou, Z., Zhang, R., Zhang, Y.: 3D liver tumor segmentation in CT images using improved fuzzy C-means and graph cuts. BioMed Res. Int. **2017**, 1–11 (2017). https://doi.org/10.1155/2017/5207685
21. Ronneberger, O., Fischer, P., Brox, T.: U-net: convolutional networks for biomedical image segmentation. In: Navab, N., Hornegger, J., Wells, W.M., Frangi, A.F. (eds.) Medical Image Computing and Computer-Assisted Intervention — MICCAI 2015. LNCS, vol. 9351, pp. 234–241. Springer, Cham (2015). https://doi.org/10.1007/978-3-319-24574-4_28
22. Chen, L.-C., Zhu, Y., Papandreou, G., Schroff, F., Adam, H.: Encoder-decoder with Atrous separable convolution for semantic image segmentation. In: Ferrari, V., Hebert, M., Sminchis-escu, C., Weiss, Y. (eds.) Computer Vision – ECCV 2018. LNCS, vol. 11211, pp. 833–851. Springer, Cham (2018). https://doi.org/10.1007/978-3-030-01234-2_49
23. Chen, J., Lu, Y., Yu, Q., et al.: Transunet: Transformers make strong encoders for medical image segmentation. arXiv preprint, arXiv:210204306 (2021)
24. Li, X., Chen, H., Qi, X., et al.: H-denseunet: hybrid densely connected unet for liver and tumor segmentation from CT volumes. IEEE Trans. Med. Imaging **37**(12), 2663–2674 (2018)
25. Seo, H., Huang, C., Bassenne, M., et al.: Modified u-net (mu-net) with incorporation of object-dependent high level features for improved liver and liver-tumor segmentation in CT images. IEEE Trans. Med. Imaging **39**(5), 1316–1325 (2019)
26. Moghbel, M., Mashohor, S., Mahmud, R., et al.: Automatic liver tumor segmentation on computed tomography for patient treatment planning and monitoring. EXCLI J. **15**, 406 (2016)

Weakly Supervised Optical Remote Sensing Salient Object Detection Based on Adaptive Discriminative Region Suppression

Xingyu Li[1], Jieyu Wu[1,2(✉)], Yuan Zhou[1], Jingwei Yuan[1], and Yanwen Chen[1,2]

[1] School of Computer Science and Technology, Anhui University, Hefei 230601, China
[2] Anhui Provincial Key Laboratory of Multimodal Cognitive Computation, Anhui University, Hefei 230601, China
jieyu_wuu@163.com

Abstract. Salient object detection in optical remote sensing images aims to detect attractive objects from optical remote sensing images, providing important prior information for many remote sensing tasks, which have received more and more attention in recent years. The existing convolutional neural network-based salient object detection networks mostly rely on pixel-level labelling. Although their detection accuracy is high, annotation cost for the data is high. In addition, it is always a difficult problem that the scales of salient objects in optical remote sensing images change significantly. To address these problems, a new weakly supervised salient object detection method for optical remote sensing images is proposed. Specifically, firstly, we introduce image-level labelling as the weakly supervised information for remote sensing image salient object detection, obtaining pseudo labels to train the saliency detection network. Secondly, we propose the Local Activation Suppression module, including the Discriminative Region Suppression module and Receptive Field Block, which can effectively spread the high response region of the object to the neighbouring low response region, improving the quality of large objects pseudo labels. Finally, the Adaptive Fusion module is proposed to raise the accuracy of pseudo labels of large and small objects, which aims to reduce the noise caused by small objects. Many experiments on a public dataset show that the proposed method is better than the existing weakly supervised learning methods for salient object detection, with better detection accuracy.

Keywords: Optical remote sensing image · Salient object detection · Weakly supervised learning · Image-level labelling

1 Introduction

Salient object detection(SOD) [16,27] methods aim to mimic the human visual attention mechanism to detect and segment attractive objects in images

---

X. Li and J. Wu—Contributed equally to this work.

© The Author(s), under exclusive license to Springer Nature Singapore Pte Ltd. 2024
L. Fang et al. (Eds.): CICAI 2023, LNAI 14473, pp. 364–375, 2024.
https://doi.org/10.1007/978-981-99-8850-1_30

accurately. The salient objects in optical remote sensing images(ORSI) have many categories and rich information. Recently ORSI SOD has been applied to many remote sensing vision tasks, such as ship detection, remote sensing scene classification and change detection.

However, there are still many challenges in ORSI SOD. For example, ORSI are taken by satellites or sensors at high altitudes, and the scale of salient objects varies greatly due to the variability of shooting altitudes and angles; since there are often multiple objects in remote sensing images, it is difficult to detect multiple objects more accurately; ORSI is easily affected by weather and environment when they are taken, so the background of ORSI is often complex and noisy.

Most of the existing deep-learning-based methods for ORSI SOD are strongly supervised methods that rely on many pixel-level annotations and are costly. To weaken the reliance of method models on accurate pixel-level annotations and reduce the cost of dataset construction, some low-cost annotations have been introduced for SOD, such as image-level or graffiti tagging. For example, Piao et al. [21] propose a multi-pseudo-label framework MFNet, which includes multiple directive filters, aiming to extract more comprehensive and accurate saliency cues from multiple pseudo labels and improve the accuracy of SOD by learning and integrating the resulting accurate cues.

Considering that image-level labelling of ORSI is simple and efficient, we use image-level labelling as weakly supervised information for ORSI SOD. We train the classification network using image-level labelling to obtain a class activation map(CAM) [34] that can locate the object's local regions and obtain pseudo labels through the post-processing process to train the saliency detection network. However, the CAM only focuses on the most discriminative region. It cannot cover the whole object, while the remote sensing image changes at a large scale, leading to a sparse CAM for large objects. Thus, in this paper, we design the Local Activation Suppression module(LAS), including the Discriminative Region Suppression (DRS) [10] and the Receptive Field Block (RFB) [31]. DRS suppresses the high response in the CAM and spreads it to adjacent regions, activating more regions and thus expanding the segmentation area. RFB is used to expand the receptive field and improve the quality of large object pseudo labels, enhancing the effectiveness of classification network detection. Therefore, introducing RFB and DRS modules will result in more accurate localization of large objects in the saliency maps. For the problem that small objects will activate the background region and thus introduce much noise, we introduce the Adaptive Fusion (AF) module [15]. This module learns a set of reliable weights for the features before and after suppression, thus adaptively performs feature selection and obtains fused features, improving the pseudo labels accuracy of both large and small objects. The comparison and ablation experiments reveal that the method in this paper outperforms existing weakly supervised methods of SOD.

The contributions of our work are as follows: We introduce a new model (denoted as ADRS) for weakly supervised ORSI SOD, which introduces image-level labeling as the weakly supervised information. We design the LAS module and the AF module to simultaneously improve the pseudo labels accuracy of both small and large targets. Extensive experiments on a public dataset demonstrate the superiority of our method.

2 Related Work

2.1 Salient Object Detection in Optical Remote Sensing Images

In recent years, deep learning-based approaches methods have achieved great progress in the field of computer vision [5,8,9,30]. The research of ORSI SOD has also attracted remote sensing scholars' attention and in-depth study. Li et al. [14] propose a two-stream pyramid module to extract a set of complementary multiscale information. The encoder-decoder module with nested connections concatenates the multiscale features to predict the salient maps. Li et al. [13] propose a novel parallel down-up fusion network for ORSI SOD to identify salient objects of different sizes and eliminate background confusion. Tu et al. [25] propose a joint learning framework to simultaneously optimize multi-scale salient regions and boundary features to generate exact saliency maps.

2.2 Weakly Supervised Salient Object Detection

Although the fully supervised methods have shown some performance improvement, these methods still rely on pixel-level annotations, which is expensive. Many recent studies have used weakly supervised information for object localization [18,33]. For SOD, Wang et al. [26] pioneer a network using image-level labels. It uses the joint training strategy consisting of a foreground inference network and a fully convolutional network. Pinheiro et al. [23] propose a weakly supervised segmentation model, which puts more weight on pixels which are important for image classification during training. Tian et al. [24] use complementary image-level labels to train the SOD network by weakly supervised learning. It detects target boundaries and locates instance prime centres through collaborative learning.

3 Method

3.1 Overall Structure

To better mine the saliency cues in pseudo labels, this paper uses MFNet [21] as the baseline. The architecture consists of a classification and SOD networks, as shown in Fig. 1. In the initial phase, we label the dataset at the image level and train the model for classification using a network architecture, as shown in Fig. 2. Using the classification network, class activation maps are acquired to determine the initial regions of salient objects within the image, and after postprocessing, the class activation maps are converted into pseudo labels. We use

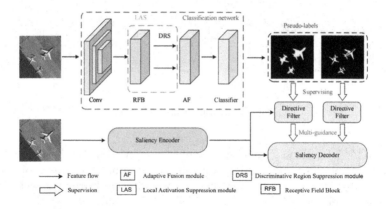

Fig. 1. The overall structure of the ADRS

the proposed LAS and AF to train the classification network better so that the CAM locates more salient regions and thus obtains high-quality pseudo labels. In the second stage, we use the pseudo label to train the sali network, which includes a saliency encoder-decoder and two directive filters. The directive filters are utilized to extract and refine highly accurate saliency cues from the noisy pseudo labels, effectively enhancing the quality and reliability of the extracted information. The accurate saliency cues are passed to the saliency decoder using the multicollinearity loss function to produce the final saliency map.

3.2 Local Activation Suppression Module

In the initial stage, classification networks are employed to generate CAM, which are subsequently processed to derive pixel-level pseudo-labels. The CAM can only provide discriminative regions of each target, which are usually very sparse and cover only a small part of the object. The application to remote sensing images will lead to the problem that the CAM can only recognise the local part of the object and produce the missing information of a large target pseudo label. Therefore, we improve the classification network by designing a local activation suppression module (LAS), which is used to expand the sensory field and suppress the CAM's very high local response to extend the target's activation region. This module consists of two parts, DRS [10] and RFB [31], to generate dense localisation maps simply and efficiently.

DRS aims to suppress discriminative regions, spread attention to neighbouring non-discriminative regions, effectively extend the target region, and produce a dense localisation map. DRS consists of three components: a maximum element extractor, a suppression controller, and a suppressor. Let $P \in M^{W \times H \times N}$ be the input feature map.

The maximum element extractor uses global max pooling to extract maximum values from each channel in the intermediate feature map P. Finally, N maximum values are obtained, and the output composition vector is noted as

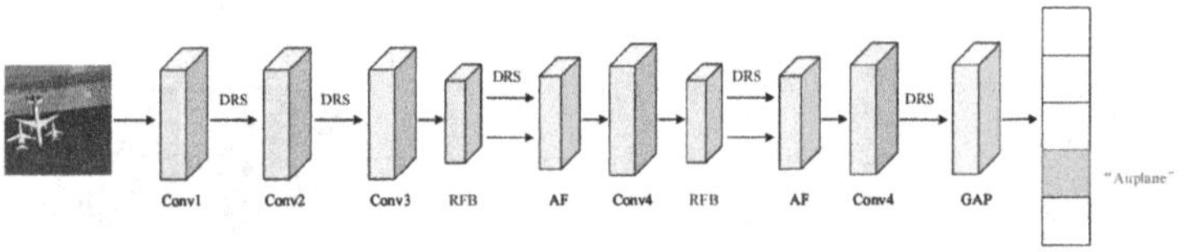

Fig. 2. Classification network

$P_{max} \in M^{1 \times 1 \times N}$. These N maximal elements are used as the basis for the discriminant region. The suppression controller determines the degree of suppression of the discriminant part. It generates an inhibition factor for each channel in P, which results in N inhibition factors that form vector $Q \in [0,1]^{1 \times 1 \times N}$. The suppressor uses N maxima and N control factors to suppress the discriminative region, specifically, Multiplying Q element by element. The upper limit of the pixel value for each channel is obtained:

$$\delta = P_{max} \times Q \in M^{1 \times 1 \times N} \tag{1}$$

The part above this upper bound is the discriminant region to be suppressed. The suppression controller in this paper uses an unlearnable controller with no additional training parameters, and each element in Q is set to a constant value of 0.55. Next, the suppressor expands δ from $M^{1 \times 1 \times N}$ to $M^{W \times H \times N}$. After developing the upper bound δ to P, an element-by-element minimum operation $\tilde{P} = \min(P, \delta)$ applies to P and δ to suppress the discriminant region such that the value of P at each pixel point does not exceed the value of the corresponding end of δ.

Large convolution kernels effectively capture larger targets, whereas small convolution kernels are more suitable for smaller targets. However, employing a single-scale kernel is suboptimal in the case of objects with various types and scales in ORSI. Dilated convolution with different dilation rates can expand the perceptual field and extend the discriminative region to adjacent uncertain areas. Therefore, this paper introduces RFB in the classification network to obtain multi-scale information. As shown in Fig. 3(a), the module incorporates a multi-branch architecture comprising convolutional kernels of diverse sizes and convolutional layers with varying dilation rates. Ultimately, the outputs from multiple layers are fused to combine multi-scale features and expand the activation region, resulting in dense predictions.

The feature vector generated by convolution is passed through the sensory field module RFB to develop a new feature vector, denoted as $\tilde{M}$. The feature vector generated by the discriminative region suppression module DRS immediately afterwards is noted as $\hat{M}$.

3.3 Adaptive Fusion Module

With the introduction of the judgment suppression region module, the localisation effect of large targets is improved; however, small marks activate the background region and introduce a lot of noise information. Therefore, AF [15] is presented in this paper, as shown in Fig. 3(b). The input of the AF module is the feature vector $\tilde{M}$ output from the RFB module and the feature vector $\hat{M}$ generated by the DRS module, and they are concatenated in the channel dimension, noted as M.

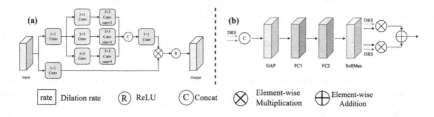

Fig. 3. Receptive Field Block and Adaptive Fusion Module

The global information is first compressed onto a one-dimensional vector using global average pooling (GAP). Then the compressed features are passed through two fully connected layers FC1 and FC2 to learn the non-linear interactions between channels, thus obtaining a feature vector $x \in 1 \times R^{2c}$ on a channel.

$$V = FC_2(FC_1(GAP(M))) \tag{2}$$

where FC is the fully connected layers, after the feature vector is obtained, it is mapped between 0 and 1 by the softmax function, transforming them into a weighted feature map.

$$S = softmax(V) \tag{3}$$

Finally, the weighted feature map is split into vectors S_1 and S_2 by channel dimension. The two attention vectors are multiplied and summed with the two feature vectors $\tilde{M}$ and $\hat{M}$ entered at the beginning of the module. The final feature map F is obtained:

$$F = S_1\tilde{M} + S_2\hat{M} \tag{4}$$

In conclusion, the adaptive fusion module can effectively suppress background noise while improving the localization of large and small targets in the CAM, improving the accuracy of pseudo labels.

3.4 Multi-filter Directive Network

After obtaining the class activation maps in the first stage, we use two different refinement algorithms, including pixel-level [4] and superpixel-level [17], to synthesize two different pseudo labels that provide a more comprehensive cue to supervise the training of the second stage saliency network. The saliency network consists of two directive filters and an encoder-decoder saliency prediction network. Both directive filters and decoders use a U-Net-type jump-connected structure. The primary objective of the two directive filters is to extract and refine highly accurate saliency cues from the respective pseudo-labels. Utilizing the features of the shared encoder as input, saliency cues are extracted from the pseudo-labels using multiple convolutional layers supervised by the pseudo-labels. Simultaneously, the convolutional layers within the two directive filters gradually rectify the cues present in the pseudo-labels. The corresponding loss functions L_1 and L_2 of the two directive filters are described as follows [21]:

$$L_m(P_m, Q_m) = -\sum_i q_{mi} * \log p_{mi} - (1 - q_{mi}) * \log(1 - p_{mi}), m = 1, 2 \quad (5)$$

where P_m and Q_m denote the directive filter prediction and its pseudo-label, respectively. We transmit these filtered saliency messages to the decoder via multicollinearity loss L_{mg} [21]:

$$L_{mg}(P_s, Q_s) = -\sum_i (1 - q_i) * \log(1 - p_{si}) - q_i * \log p_{si} \quad (6)$$

where P_s and Q_s are the decoder prediction and the average prediction of the two filters refined by the pixel level.

Furthermore, a self-supervised strategy is used between the two filters, prompting the two filters to extract similar saliency cues, resulting in more accurate saliency information. The loss L_{ss} [21] of the self-supervised term is defined as:

$$L_{ss}(P_1, P_2) = -\sum_i (p_{1i} - p_{2i})^2 \quad (7)$$

The final loss function, denoted as L, is derived by integrating the aforementioned individual loss functions:

$$L = L_1 + L_2 + L_{mg} + \delta L_{ss} \quad (8)$$

where δ is a hyperparameter that controls the weights of the self-supervised terms.

4   Experiments

4.1   Implementation Details

The network uses DenseNet-169 as the backbone, like the latest work MFNet [21]. The network is trained on two TITAN Xp using a two-stage training approach. The input ORSI size is set to 256 × 256. We use the Adam optimization algorithm [11] to optimize the network parameters. The learning rate and batch size are set to $1e^{-4}$ and 12.In the inference phase, the CAM is generated using a multi-inference strategy according to the settings of AffinityNet [3]. Specifically, the input image is flipped and adjusted to four scales. The final output cam is the average of the corresponding eight CAM. For the SOD network, we only take the images and the corresponding pseudo labels for training. The learning rate and the maximum number of iterations are set to $3e^{-6}$ and 26000.

4.2 Datasets and Evaluation Metrics

To validate our method denoted as ADRS, a series of experiments are conducted on the ors-4199 dataset, which contains 4199 images with different scenes and their truth values: the training set contains 2000 samples from the dataset.

For quantitative evaluations, three widely used SOD evaluation indicators are used in this paper, including mean absolute error(MAE [20]), maximum F-measure(MaxFm [1]), and S-measure(Sm) [7] for comparison.

4.3 Comparison with State-of-the-Art Methods

Table 1. Quantitative Comparison

methods	MAE	MaxFm	Sm
CPD	0.0391	0.8616	0.8562
JRBN	0.0391	0.8631	0.8596
MINet	0.0378	0.8640	0.8595
SCRN	0.0368	**0.8743**	0.8632
GCPANe	**0.0340**	0.8727	**0.8624**
MSW	0.0957	0.5664	0.6951
NSALWSS	0.0937	0.6220	0.6856
MFNet	0.0641	0.7231	0.7702
Ours	**0.0589**	**0.7409**	**0.7758**

As shown in Table 1, we compare our method with eight state-of-the-art SOD models, including five fully supervised methods: CPD [28], JRBN [25], MINet [19], SCRN [29], GCPANet [6], and three weakly supervised methods: MSW [32], NSALWSS [22], MFNet [21]. Our method consistently outperforms other weakly supervised methods under the three evaluation metrics compared. Specifically, compared to the sub-optimal method [21], our method improves MaxFm 1.78%. These results further validate our method has higher accuracy and stability than other weakly supervised methods. This indicates that our method has great potential to solve the weakly supervised SOD problem.

The visualization comparison is shown in Fig. 4. By comparing the visualization results, we can observe our method's superior performance on the SOD task. Compared with other weakly supervised methods, the method of this paper can accurately capture the objects in the image and effectively separate them from the background. In contrast, other methods have some limitations in extracting salient objects. For example, NSALWSS [22] misclassifies the backgrounds as salient objects and accurately outlines the boundaries of objects; MFNet [21] loses a part of the object in the large target challenge.

Image   GT   MFNet   MSW   NSALWSS   Ours

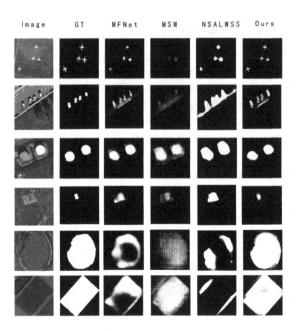

Fig. 4. Visual comparisons between our results and other methods

4.4 Ablation Studies

We apply both pixel-level and superpixel-level approaches, specifically PAMR [4] with CRF [12] and SLIC [2] with CRF [12] to refine the class activation maps and generate two different pseudo-labels. As shown in Table 2, our method performs better in all evaluation metrics. After introducing the LAS module, the experimental results show a slight decline compared to the baseline [21] due to the activation of background regions by small objects, which introduces noise. To improve the accuracy of the pseudo labels, we incorporate the AF module to eliminate the noise information, resulting in improvements in all metrics. Specifically, compared to using PAMR with CRF post-processing, our method improves the MAE metric by 14.7%, the MaxFm metric by 4.4%, and the Sm metric by 3%. For SLIC with CRF, the improvement is 24.7% on the MAE metric, 7% on the MaxFm metric, and 13.0% on the Sm metric, further demonstrating the effectiveness of our method.

Figure 5 shows a visual comparison between the original CAM and the CAM obtained by the method of this paper. From the results, compared to the original CAM, our method can cover a complete range of target regions instead of focusing only on the most discriminative regions, possessing a more accurate localization capability and effectively improving the problem of sparse large target CAM. It also shows the pseudo labels obtained in both post-processing processes, and it can be seen that our method achieves better results than the baseline [21] and obtains higher-quality pseudo labels, especially in large target localization.

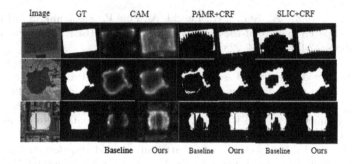

Fig. 5. Visual comparison of CAM and pseudo labels

Table 2. Comparison of pseudo labels

methods	PAMR+CRF			SLIC+CRF		
	MAE	MaxFm	Sm	MAE	MaxFm	Sm
Baseline	0.0572	0.7618	0.7856	0.0838	0.6988	0.6885
+LAS	0.0928	0.6851	0.7464	0.0886	0.6295	0.6995
+LAS+AF	**0.0488**	**0.7955**	**0.8095**	**0.0631**	**0.7488**	**0.7777**

5 Conclusion

This paper introduces image-level annotation as weak supervision for ORSI SOD, and the adaptive discriminative region suppression model is proposed. In the proposed network, considering the problem that the class activation maps of large targets are very sparse, we design the local suppression activation module and the adaptive fusion module in the classification network to effectively enhance the semantic information of pseudo labels of large targets while improving the pseudo labels accuracy of small targets, which overcomes the problem of large target scale variation. Quantitative and qualitative experimental results on publicly available datasets show that this method outperforms existing related methods for weakly supervised salient object detection.

Acknowledgement. This work was supported in part by the Natural Science Foundation of Anhui Higher Education Institution of China under Grant KJ2020A0033, in part by Anhui Provincial Natural Science foundation under Grant 2108085MF211, in part by University Synergy Innovation Program of Anhui Province under Grant GXXT-2022-014.

References

1. Achanta, R., Hemami, S., Estrada, F., Susstrunk, S.: Frequency-tuned salient region detection. In: 2009 IEEE Conference on Computer Vision and Pattern Recognition, pp. 1597–1604. IEEE (2009)

2. Achanta, R., Shaji, A., Smith, K., Lucchi, A., Fua, P., Süsstrunk, S.: SLIC super-pixels compared to state-of-the-art superpixel methods. IEEE Trans. Pattern Anal. Mach. Intell. **34**(11), 2274–2282 (2012)

3. Ahn, J., Kwak, S.: Learning pixel-level semantic affinity with image-level supervision for weakly supervised semantic segmentation. In: Proceedings of the IEEE Conference on Computer Vision and Pattern Recognition, pp. 4981–4990 (2018)

4. Araslanov, N., Roth, S.: Single-stage semantic segmentation from image labels. In: Proceedings of the IEEE/CVF Conference on Computer Vision and Pattern Recognition, pp. 4253–4262 (2020)

5. Chen, S., et al.: Transzero++: cross attribute-guided transformer for zero-shot learning. IEEE Transactions on Pattern Analysis and Machine Intelligence (2022)

6. Chen, Z., Xu, Q., Cong, R., Huang, Q.: Global context-aware progressive aggregation network for salient object detection. In: Proceedings of the AAAI Conference on Artificial Intelligence, vol. 34, pp. 10599–10606 (2020)

7. Fan, D.P., Cheng, M.M., Liu, Y., Li, T., Borji, A.: Structure-measure: a new way to evaluate foreground maps. In: Proceedings of the IEEE International Conference on Computer Vision, pp. 4548–4557 (2017)

8. Jin, L., Wang, X., Nie, X., Liu, L., Guo, Y., Zhao, J.: Grouping by center: predicting centripetal offsets for the bottom-up human pose estimation. IEEE Trans. Multimed. **25**, 3367–3374 (2022)

9. Jin, L., et al.: Single-stage is enough: Multi-person absolute 3d pose estimation. In: Proceedings of the IEEE/CVF Conference on Computer Vision and Pattern Recognition, pp. 13086–13095 (2022)

10. Kim, B., Han, S., Kim, J.: Discriminative region suppression for weakly-supervised semantic segmentation. In: Proceedings of the AAAI Conference on Artificial Intelligence, vol. 35, pp. 1754–1761 (2021)

11. Kingma, D.P., Ba, J.: Adam: A method for stochastic optimization. arXiv preprint arXiv:1412.6980 (2014)

12. Krähenbühl, P., Koltun, V.: Efficient inference in fully connected CRFs with gaussian edge potentials. In: Advances in Neural Information Processing Systems, vol. 24 (2011)

13. Li, C., et al.: A parallel down-up fusion network for salient object detection in optical remote sensing images. Neurocomputing **415**, 411–420 (2020)

14. Li, C., Cong, R., Hou, J., Zhang, S., Qian, Y., Kwong, S.: Nested network with two-stream pyramid for salient object detection in optical remote sensing images. IEEE Trans. Geosci. Remote Sens. **57**(11), 9156–9166 (2019)

15. Li, X., Wang, W., Hu, X., Yang, J.: Selective kernel networks. In: Proceedings of the IEEE/CVF Conference on Computer Vision and Pattern Recognition (2019)

16. Li, Z., et al.: Dense attentive feature enhancement for salient object detection. IEEE Trans. Circuits Syst. Video Technol. **32**(12), 8128–8141 (2021)

17. Liu, N., Han, J.: DHSNet: deep hierarchical saliency network for salient object detection. In: Proceedings of the IEEE Conference on Computer Vision and Pattern Recognition, pp. 678–686 (2016)

18. Meng, M., Zhang, T., Yang, W., Zhao, J., Zhang, Y., Wu, F.: Diverse complementary part mining for weakly supervised object localization. IEEE Trans. Image Process. **31**, 1774–1788 (2022)

19. Pang, Y., Zhao, X., Zhang, L., Lu, H.: Multi-scale interactive network for salient object detection. In: Proceedings of the IEEE/CVF Conference on Computer Vision and Pattern Recognition, pp. 9413–9422 (2020)

20. Perazzi, F., Krähenbühl, P., Pritch, Y., Hornung, A.: Saliency filters: contrast based filtering for salient region detection. In: 2012 IEEE Conference on Computer Vision and Pattern Recognition, pp. 733–740. IEEE (2012)
21. Piao, Y., Wang, J., Zhang, M., Lu, H.: MFNEt: multi-filter directive network for weakly supervised salient object detection. In: Proceedings of the IEEE/CVF International Conference on Computer Vision, pp. 4136–4145 (2021)
22. Piao, Y., Wu, W., Zhang, M., Jiang, Y., Lu, H.: Noise-sensitive adversarial learning for weakly supervised salient object detection. IEEE Trans. Multimed. **25**, 2888–2897 (2022)
23. Pinheiro, P.O., Collobert, R.: From image-level to pixel-level labeling with convolutional networks. In: Proceedings of the IEEE Computer Vision and Pattern Recognition, pp. 1713–1721 (2015)
24. Tian, X., Xu, K., Yang, X., Yin, B., Lau, R.W.: Learning to detect instance-level salient objects using complementary image labels. Int. J. Comput. Vision **130**(3), 729–746 (2022)
25. Tu, Z., Wang, C., Li, C., Fan, M., Zhao, H., Luo, B.: ORSI salient object detection via multiscale joint region and boundary model. IEEE Trans. Geosci. Remote Sens. **60**, 1–13 (2021)
26. Wang, L., et al.: Learning to detect salient objects with image-level supervision. In: Proceedings of the IEEE Computer Vision and Pattern Recognition, pp. 136–145 (2017)
27. Wang, W., Lai, Q., Fu, H., Shen, J., Ling, H., Yang, R.: Salient object detection in the deep learning era: An in-depth survey. IEEE Trans. Pattern Anal. Mach. Intell. **44**(6), 3239–3259 (2021)
28. Wu, Z., Su, L., Huang, Q.: Cascaded partial decoder for fast and accurate salient object detection. In: Proceedings of the IEEE/CVF Computer Vision and Pattern Recognition, pp. 3907–3916 (2019)
29. Wu, Z., Su, L., Huang, Q.: Stacked cross refinement network for edge-aware salient object detection. In: Proceedings of the IEEE/CVF International Conference on Computer Vision, pp. 7264–7273 (2019)
30. Xiao, Y., et al.: QueryPose: sparse multi-person pose regression via spatial-aware part-level query. Adv. Neural. Inf. Process. Syst. **35**, 12464–12477 (2022)
31. Yu, F., Koltun, V.: Multi-scale context aggregation by dilated convolutions. arXiv preprint arXiv:1511.07122 (2015)
32. Zeng, Y., Zhuge, Y., Lu, H., Zhang, L., Qian, M., Yu, Y.: Multi-source weak supervision for saliency detection. In: Proceedings of the IEEE/CVF Conference on Computer Vision and Pattern Recognition, pp. 6074–6083 (2019)
33. Zhao, F., Li, J., Zhao, J., Feng, J.: Weakly supervised phrase localization with multi-scale anchored transformer network. In: Proceedings of the IEEE Conference on Computer Vision and Pattern Recognition, pp. 5696–5705 (2018)
34. Zhou, B., Khosla, A., Lapedriza, A., Oliva, A., Torralba, A.: Learning deep features for discriminative localization. In: Proceedings of the IEEE Conference on Computer Vision and Pattern Recognition, pp. 2921–2929 (2016)

SPCTNet: A Series-Parallel CNN and Transformer Network for 3D Medical Image Segmentation

Bin Yu, Quan Zhou, and Xuming Zhang[(⊠)]

Department of Biomedical Engineering, College of Life Science and Technology,
Huazhong University of Science and Technology, Wuhan, China
zxmboshi@hust.edu.cn

Abstract. Medical image segmentation is crucial for lesion localization and surgical navigation. Recent advancements in medical image segmentation have been driven by Convolutional Neural Networks (CNNs) and Transformers. However, CNNs have limitations in capturing long-range dependencies due to their weight sharing and localized receptive fields, posing challenges in handling varying organ shapes. While Transformers offer an alternative with global receptive fields, their spatial and computational complexity is particularly high, especially for 3D medical images. To address this issue, we propose a novel series-parallel network that combines convolution and self-attention for 3D medical image segmentation. We utilize a serial 3D CNN as the encoder to extract multi-level feature maps, which are fused via a feature pyramid network. Subsequently, we adopt four parallel Transformer branches to capture global features. To efficiently model long-range information, we introduce patch self-attention, which divides the input into non-overlapping patches and computes attention between corresponding pixels across patches. Experimental evaluations on 3D MRI prostate and left atrial segmentation tasks confirm the superior performance of our network compared to other CNN and Transformer-based networks. Notably, our method achieves higher segmentation accuracy and faster inference speed.

Keywords: Deep learning · 3D Medical image segmentation · Transformer

1 Introduction

Medical image segmentation plays a vital role in computer-aided lesion localization, treatment planning, and surgical navigation. Accurate delineation of structures in medical images is essential for tasks such as quantitative analysis and personalized intervention [1]. However, the complexity, variability, and noise inherent in medical images pose significant challenges for achieving accurate and robust segmentation.

Over the past decade, deep learning (DL) has revolutionized medical image analysis by addressing the limitations of traditional segmentation methods [1, 2]. Unlike traditional approaches that heavily rely on manual feature engineering and heuristic algorithms like region growing, watershed and active contour [3–5], these DL-based methods employ automatic feature extraction from raw image data. The dominant paradigm

© The Author(s), under exclusive license to Springer Nature Singapore Pte Ltd. 2024
L. Fang et al. (Eds.): CICAI 2023, LNAI 14473, pp. 376–387, 2024.
https://doi.org/10.1007/978-981-99-8850-1_31

in medical image segmentation has been U-shaped fully convolutional neural networks (CNNs) since the inception of U-Net [2, 6–9]. The architecture enabling effective feature fusion across different semantic levels [2]. Attention U-Net [6] extends this concept by employing attention modules to dynamically focus on relevant image regions, thereby facilitating capture of intricate details in complex segmentation scenarios. To further increase U-Net's representation capability, researchers have introduced progressive feature fusion methods. U-Net++ [7] integrates dense skip connections and multi-scale feature aggregation to ensure better integration of contextual information at different scales. Furthermore, to enhance feature extraction capabilities or improve the interconnections within the U-shaped architecture, several variants such as Res-UNet [8] and UNet3+ [9] have been proposed.

Despite the improved efficiency and accuracy of medical image segmentation achieved by CNN-based methods, their ability to capture long-range information remains limited due to localized receptive fields [10]. This limitation is particularly critical in the segmentation of anatomically diverse organs and tumors. Recently, Transformer [11] has emerged as a compelling alternative due to its achievements in natural language processing and computer vision. Chen et al. [12] have designed TransUNet, which incorporates Transformer to capture global contexts by encoding tokenized CNN feature maps. These encoded features are later fused with detailed CNN feature maps in the decoder module. Similarly, UNetR [13] utilizes a Transformer encoder to tokenize the image patches and performs upsampling and feature fusion at different layers using CNN blocks. Despite the improved performance of TransUNet and UNetR over the traditional CNN methods, the standard self-attention mechanism poses significant computational challenges, especially in 3D image. To reduce the computational and spatial complexity, Xie et al. [14] have introduced a deformable self-attention mechanism into Transformer, focusing on a limited number of key points in the sequence. This attention mechanism effectively improves efficiency while maintaining performance. Inspired by Swin Transformer [15], Swin-Unet [16] has combined the hierarchical Transformer blocks within the U-Net framework. Nonetheless, more in-depth research is required to explore the effective strategies for enhancing feature interaction and optimizing the fusion of convolution and self-attention mechanisms.

In this paper, we propose a series-parallel CNN and Transformer network (SPCTNet) that combines convolution and self-attention for volumetric segmentation. Specifically, we utilize a serial 3D CNN structure to extract multi-level feature maps in the encoder. The extracted features are preliminarily fused through the feature pyramid network (FPN) [17], enhancing the encoder's capacity to learn features across multiple levels. These features are then fed into parallel Transformer blocks, enabling the network to capture global context. Inspired by MobileViT [18] and Swin Transformer, we introduce patch self-attention (PSA) to realize the 3D image segmentation. Similar to window attention [15], PSA partitions the image into non-overlapping patches, computes attention between corresponding pixels across patches. This approach significantly reduces the computation of Transformer so that it can process feature maps at higher resolutions.

Our method has been extensively evaluated on three 3D medical image datasets, including the ProstateX Challenge dataset [21], Atrial Segmentation Challenge dataset [22] and a private prostate dataset from Zhongnan Hospital of Wuhan University. By leveraging the series-parallel architecture, multi-scale feature fusion, and patch self-attention mechanism, our method exhibits higher segmentation accuracy compared to existing algorithms. Additionally, the parallel computing mechanism employed in our method enables faster inference speed.

2 Method

2.1 Architecture

The overall framework of the proposed SPCTNet is shown in Fig. 1. SPCTNet consists of three primary components: a serial CNN encoder, parallel Transformer blocks, and a segmentation head. The encoder utilizes 3D ResNeXt [19], a highly effective network architecture for extracting features from the input 3D volume. Specifically, we denote the features from the last four residual blocks as $\{X_1, X_2, X_3, X_4\}$, corresponding to conv1, conv2, conv3, and conv4 layers with respective strides of $\{4, 8, 16, 32\}$. Notably, conv0 is excluded from the feature pyramid to prevent memory overflow.

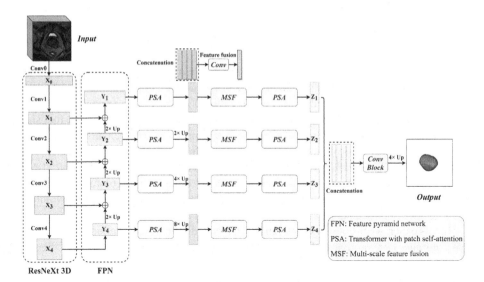

Fig. 1. Network architecture of SPCTNet.

To optimize the interaction of features across various scales and semantic levels, we utilize a feature pyramid network (FPN), incorporating a top-down pathway to upsample higher-level semantic features to align with the resolution of lower-level features. Lateral connections are utilized to fuse the $\{X_1, X_2, X_3, X_4\}$ with the corresponding lower-level ones. The preliminary fused feature maps $\{Y_1, Y_2, Y_3, Y_4\}$ that capture multi-scale information are obtained via FPN. These feature maps are then fed in parallel to the Transformer blocks, enabling the model to learn long-range dependencies and model complex relationships between different regions of the input.

Additionally, the pixel attention [6] is employed between two Transformer blocks to selectively enhance multi-scale contextual information. Following the first Transformer block, the feature maps from different branches are upsampled to a unified resolution. Next, these features are concatenated and processed through a convolution module to generate a fused feature representation. We selectively enhance the features from the four branches with the fused feature via pixel attention. The features are further processed by the second Transformer block, producing outputs denoted as $\{Z_1, Z_2, Z_3, Z_4\}$. The outputs are then concatenated and passed through a cascaded convolution block before undergoing trilinear upsampling to obtain the final prediction. To incorporate deep supervision, we also perform upsampling on $\{Z_1, Z_2, Z_3, Z_4\}$ to obtain the auxiliary predictions.

2.2 Transformer Block

Although FPN is capable of integrating features from different receptive fields, it is limited by the inherent locality of convolution operations. To address this constraint, we propose the patch self-attention (PSA) module for efficient modeling of long-range contextual dependencies.

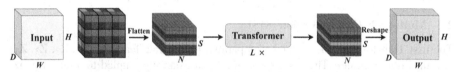

Fig. 2. The structure of the Transformer block with the patch self-attention. The volume is flattened and reshaped at the input and output. Here, the patch size is $2 \times 2 \times 2$, and self-attention is computed within pixels of the same color across different patches.

As illustrated in Fig. 2, the feature tensor $I \in \mathbb{R}^{H \times W \times D \times C}$ with (H, W, D) spatial dimensions and C channels is flattened and reshaped at the input and output. Specifically, the input is divided into non-overlapping patches, where each patch has a resolution of (ph, pw, pd). However, unlike previous approaches [13] that directly represent these patches as tokens, we flatten them into a 3D tensor, $I \in \mathbb{R}^{H \times W \times D \times C} \rightarrow I' \in \mathbb{R}^{S \times N \times C}$, where $S = ph \times pw \times pd$ represents both the volume of a patch and the number of subsequences, $N = H \times W \times D/S$ is the length of each subsequence. Self-attention is computed within pixels across different patches. In our task, the patch sizes for the first four PSA blocks are $4 \times 4 \times 4$, $2 \times 2 \times 2$, $2 \times 2 \times 2$, and $1 \times 1 \times 1$ while the patch size for the remaining four blocks is consistently set to $4 \times 4 \times 4$. The Transformer blocks are computed as:

$$\begin{aligned} \hat{z}^i &= PSA(Norm(z^{i-1})) + z^{i-1} \\ z^i &= MLP(Norm(\hat{z}^i)) + \hat{z}^i \end{aligned} \tag{1}$$

The output features of the PSA and the MLP block for layer i are denoted as $\hat{z}^i$ and z^i, , respectively. Layer normalization (Norm) is applied, and the MLP module consists of two linear layers with non-linear activation functions.

A PSA block is composed of S parallel self-attention submodules which can effectively learn long-range dependencies within a three-dimensional space with a receptive field of the entire image. The computation method for self-attention remains unchanged and can be formulated as:

$$\text{Attention}(Q,K,V) = \text{Softmax}(QK^T/\sqrt{d})\, V \tag{2}$$

where Q, K, V $\in \mathbb{R}^{S \times N \times d}$ are the query, key and value matrices; d is the dimension of key. Positional encoding is not utilized in the sublayer due to the inherent characteristics of zero padding, which is used in the convolutional layers to maintain the consistent feature map dimensions.

The computational complexity of the global MSA and PSA modules is:

$$\begin{aligned} \Omega(MSA) &= (H \cdot W \cdot D)^2 C, \\ \Omega(PSA) &= (H \cdot W \cdot D)^2 C/(ph \cdot pw \cdot pd) \end{aligned} \tag{3}$$

By setting the patch size as $ph = pw = pd = 2$, the computational complexity of the PSA becomes only 1/8 of that of the multi-head self-attention (MSA) [11]. Moreover, our model effectively learns image representations across multiple feature spaces without the need for artificial partitioning in the MSA mechanism.

2.3 Multi-scale Feature Fusion (MSF)

The first Transformer block operates in parallel to generate features $\{Z_1, Z_2, Z_3, Z_4\}$ at four different scales. These scale-specific features are upsampled to a uniform size and concatenated along the channel dimension. Subsequently, a refinement process is performed by passing the concatenated features through a convolutional module with $1 \times 1 \times 1$ and $3 \times 3 \times 3$ kernels, resulting in a refined fused feature representation denoted as Z_f. To compute the pixel-wise attention as shown in Fig. 3, Z_f is individually used in conjunction with each of four scale-specific features.

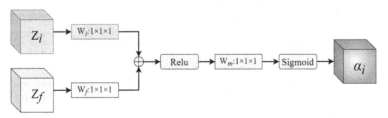

Fig. 3. Scheme of the pixel attention module. By applying convolution, fusion, and activation functions, the module generates attention weight α_i for each pixel.

The pixel-wise attention is given by:

$$\alpha_i = \text{Sigmoid}(W_m(\text{Relu}(W_i Z_i + W_f Z_f))) \tag{4}$$

where W_i, W_f are $1 \times 1 \times 1$ convolutions used to align Z_i and Z_f in channels, and W_m is a $1 \times 1 \times 1$ convolution that reduces the channels to 1. These operations adapt the feature maps for the pixel attention mechanism. α_i is the attention coefficient selectively enhancing the feature responses of Z_i with respect to Z_f.

Next, the attention coefficient α_i is multiplied with Z_f in an element-wise way, resulting in a weighted fusion of the refined feature. This fused representation is then concatenated with Z_i along the channel dimension, yielding an integrated feature representation. By incorporating the pixel attention, our method adaptively adjusts the contribution of each scale in Z_i based on its relevance to Z_f.

2.4 Loss Function

We utilize a hybrid of loss functions to reduce training time and optimize the segmentation accuracy. The Dice loss [20], commonly used for evaluating the overlap between predictions and labels, captures fine-grained details and ensures spatial consistency. Additionally, the incorporation of cross-entropy loss encourages pixel-wise classification. To further enhance learning and address the vanishing gradient problem, we introduce deep supervision by calculating the loss between the four intermediate feature representations. The loss function is computed as:

$$\ell = 1 - \frac{2}{M} \sum_{j=1}^{M} \frac{\sum_{i=1}^{N} P_{i,j} G_{i,j}}{\sum_{i=1}^{N} P_{i,j}^2 + \sum_{i=1}^{N} G_{i,j}^2} - \frac{1}{N} \sum_{j=1}^{M} \sum_{i=1}^{N} G_{i,j} \log P_{i,j} \qquad (5)$$

where M is the num of classes and N is the number of voxels in the input volume; At voxel i, $P_{i,j} \in [0.0, 1.0]$ is the network's prediction for class j, while $G_{i,j} \in \{0.0, 1.0\}$ is corresponding segmentation label. The deep supervision loss is calculated as the summation of losses from both the segmentation head and the four parallel branches:

$$\ell_{total} = w_f \ell_f + \sum_{i=1}^{n} w_i \ell_i \qquad (6)$$

where ℓ_f and ℓ_i represent the losses of the segmentation head and the i-th branch, w_f and w_i are denote the corresponding weights. To ensure a balanced contribution from each branch during the learning process, we set the weights $(w_f, w_{i=1,2,3,4})$ as $(1.0, 0.2, 0.3, 0.4, 0.5)$ according to experience.

3 Experiments

3.1 Datasets

We have selected two public datasets and one private dataset for experiments, including the SPIE-AAPM-NCI ProstateX Challenge dataset [21], the 2018 Atria Segmentation Challenge dataset [22], and a private prostate MRI dataset from Zhongnan Hospital of Wuhan University. The ProstateX Challenge dataset consists of multiparametric magnetic resonance imaging (mpMRI) data and clinical information of patients suspected of prostate cancer. For the mpMRI data, we employ a subset of the dataset containing 914 cases of T2-weighted imaging (T2WI) with a size of $256 \times 256 \times 60$ and a resolution of

$0.66 \times 0.66 \times 1.50 \, \text{mm}^3$. Among the dataset, we randomly partitioned the data into training, validation, and test sets, consisting of 639, 137, and 138 cases, respectively. The atrium dataset includes 154 gadolinium-enhanced magnetic resonance imaging scans with a resolution of $0.625 \times 0.625 \times 0.625 \, \text{mm}^3$. We use 100 scans for training and 27 scans each for validation and testing. Additionally, our in-house prostate MRI dataset reviewed by the Ethics Committee of Zhongnan Hospital. The dataset consists of 200 3D scans with a size of $320 \times 320 \times 24$ and a resolution of $0.56 \times 0.56 \times 3.00 \, \text{mm}^3$. We split it into140 cases for training and reserve 30 cases each for validation and testing.

3.2 Experimental Settings and Evaluation Metrics

In our experimental setup, we use common online data augmentation methods including random flipping, rotation, and cropping. The ProstateX and in-house prostate datasets are randomly cropped to sizes of $192 \times 192 \times 48$ and $256 \times 256 \times 24$, respectively. Similarly, for the left atrium dataset, we choose a crop size of $128 \times 128 \times 80$. The framework is based on MindSpore Lite tool [23]. In order to accelerate training process, NVIDIA GeForce A100 GPU with 40 GB memory is used. The network is optimized using AdamW with a weight decay of 0.01. The learning rate is initialized at 0.001 and changes to 0.0001 using the cosine decay during the training. Our method is trained on the ProstateX, the atrium and our in-house prostate datasets for 90, 60, 60 epochs, respectively. Following the reference [24], we utilize a sliding inference technique with a stride of $16 \times 16 \times 4$ to segment the entire image for model testing.

To evaluate the efficacy of our method and enable comparative analysis, we adopt four quantitative metrics, i.e., Jaccard index (Jaccard), Dice coefficient (Dice), 95% Hausdorff Distance (95HD), and average symmetric surface distance (ASD) [25, 26].

3.3 Ablation Study

We conduct ablation experiments to examine the individual contribution of patch self-attention (PSA) and multi-scale fusion (MSF) in our network. Table 1 presents Jaccard and Dice of our network with/without PSA and MSF on the ProstateX dataset. Clearly, after removing the MSF component (Model 2), the Jaccard of our method decreases by 0.97%. To ensure fairness in terms of parameters, we replace the PSA module with two convolution layers during its removal (Model 1) and the corresponding Jaccard shows a reduction of 2.57%. Ablation results clearly demonstrate the significant impact of both MSF and PSA on the performance of our network.

Table 1. Ablation experiments on ProstateX dataset.

Methods	PSA	MSF	Jaccard(%)	Dice(%)
Model 1	✗	✗	82.61	90.37
Model 2	✓	✗	84.21	91.32
SPCTNet	✓	✓	85.18	91.92

3.4 Quantitative Evaluation

To validate the superiority of the SPCTNet, we perform a quantitative evaluation with six CNN and Transformer-based segmentation approaches: 1) U-Net; 2) Attention U-Net; 3) TransBTS [27]; 4) Swin-UNETR [28]; 5) CoTr [14]; 6) nnFormer [29]. As U-Net is originally designed for 2D segmentation, we have modified its architecture to enable 3D segmentation. Table 2, Table 3 and Table 4 represent the quantitative results on the three datasets. On the ProstateX dataset, our method achieves a Jaccard index of 85.18% and a Dice coefficient of 91.92%, which are higher than other methods. As regards inference time, our method achieves the fastest inference speed.

Similarly, on the private prostate, our method outperforms the most competitive method with a 1.73% higher Jaccard index, 1.11% higher Dice coefficient, 0.39 lower 95HD, and 0.23 smaller ASD. On the left atrium dataset, our method outperforms other methods with at least a 1.08% higher Jaccard index.

Table 2. Quantitative results of different methods on the ProstateX dataset.

Methods	Jaccard(%)	Dice(%)	95HD(voxel)	Inference Time(s)
U-Net	83.49	90.91	3.33	6.24
Attention U-Net	83.64	91.10	3.37	6.41
TransBTS	83.88	91.14	3.07	8.45
Swin-UNETR	84.30	91.39	2.98	12.81
CoTr	83.97	91.20	3.41	10.72
nnFormer	84.12	91.28	3.02	12.51
SPCTNet	**85.18**	**91.92**	**2.88**	**5.52**

Table 3. Quantitative results of different methods on the in-house prostate dataset.

Methods	Jaccard(%)	Dice(%)	95HD(voxel)	ASD(voxel)
U-Net	64.85	77.89	6.35	1.94
Attention U-Net	66.00	78.72	5.80	1.99
TransBTS	66.77	79.24	9.76	2.52
Swin-UNETR	67.59	79.98	4.21	1.16
CoTr	66.91	79.56	3.84	1.37
nnFormer	68.43	80.71	3.92	1.34
SPCTNet	**70.16**	**81.82**	**3.53**	**1.11**

3.5 Qualitative Evaluation

In Fig. 4, we present the 2D and 3D views of segmented results for the various methods on the two prostate datasets. Our method provides more consistent segmented results with the segmentation ground truths compared with other methods. The superiority of our method may stem from its successful integration of deep supervision loss and the efficient utilization of multi-feature interaction fusion. The former can facilitate capturing more discriminative features across different depths by introducing intermediate supervision signals at multiple layers. The latter can facilitate capturing and integrating information from multiple scales to provide more comprehensive representations of prostate structure and enhanced boundary localization.

Table 4. Quantitative results of different methods on the left atrium dataset.

Methods	Jaccard(%)	Dice(%)	95HD(voxel)	ASD(voxel)
U-Net	82.94	90.67	4.36	1.57
Attention U-Net	84.33	91.45	5.40	1.46
TransBTS	83.59	91.06	5.83	1.62
Swin-UNETR	85.19	91.94	4.66	1.40
CoTr	84.50	91.60	4.58	1.23
nnFormer	84.90	91.77	4.82	1.39
SPCTNet	**86.27**	**92.63**	**4.58**	**1.19**

To further validate the efficacy of our proposed MSF, the attention maps in Fig. 5 provide valuable insights into the allocation of attention within the fused feature for each layer. Clearly, the attention is concentrated in regions close to the prostate contours, aligning with the observations in Fig. 4. This indicates that our method effectively concentrates

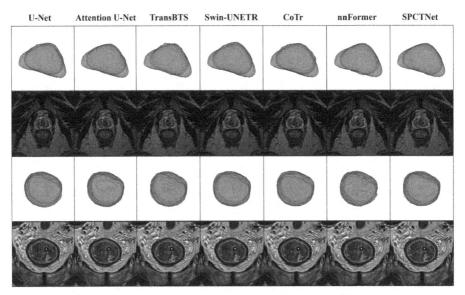

Fig. 4. Segmented results of various methods on ProstateX (top) and private datasets (bottom). Green color represents ground truths and red color represents predictions.

on relevant information within the fused feature, leading to improved representation of individual layers and enhanced segmentation accuracy.

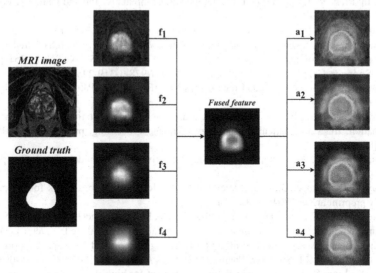

Fig. 5. The visualization of the multi-scale feature fusion block. Feature maps $\{f_1, f_2, f_3, f_4\}$ are upsampled to a consistent size and fused together. Pixel attention maps $\{a_1, a_2, a_3, a_4\}$ are calculated using the fused feature and the former feature maps.

4 Conclusion

In this paper, we have introduced SPCTNet, a series-parallel network that combines CNN and Transformer for volumetric segmentation. Distinctively, the presented method extracts multi-scale features effectively using 3D CNN and captures global information using Transformer. The integration of the patch self-attention mechanism, multi-scale information, and deep supervision loss contributes to improved segmentation result. Indeed, the SPCTNet can deliver superior segmentation performance by effectively leveraging the strengths of both CNN and Transformer. Extensive evaluations on three MRI datasets have confirmed its advantage over six baseline approaches in Jaccard, Dice, 95HD, and ASD. Future directions include exploring its applicability to other segmentation tasks and extending our method to additional medical modalities.

Acknowledgment. This work is sponsored by the National Natural Science Foundation of China (Grant No. 61871440), China Postdoctoral Science Foundation (Grant No. 2023M731204), and CAAI-Huawei MindSpore Open Fund.

References

1. Long, J., Shelhamer, E., Darrell, T.: Fully convolutional networks for semantic segmentation. In: Proceedings of the IEEE Conference on Computer Vision and Pattern Recognition, pp. 3431–3440 (2015)
2. Ronneberger, O., Fischer, P., Brox, T.: U-Net: convolutional networks for biomedical image segmentation. In: Navab, N., Hornegger, J., Wells, W.M., Frangi, A.F. (eds.) Medical Image Computing and Computer-Assisted Intervention — MICCAI 2015. LNCS, vol. 9351, pp. 234–241. Springer, Cham (2015). https://doi.org/10.1007/978-3-319-24574-4_28
3. Adams, R., Bischof, L.: Seeded region growing. IEEE Trans. Pattern Anal. Mach. Intell., 641–647 (1994)
4. Beucher, S., Meyer, F.: The morphological approach to segmentation: the watershed transformation. In: Mathematical Morphology in Image Processing, pp. 433–481. CRC Press (2018)
5. Kass, M., Witkin, A., Terzopoulos, D.: Snakes: active contour models. Int. J. Comput. Vis., 321–331 (1988)
6. Oktay, O., Schlemper, J., et al.: Attention U-Net: learning where to look for the pancreas. arXiv preprint arXiv:1804.03999 (2018)
7. Zhou, Z., Rahman Siddiquee, M.M., Tajbakhsh, N., Liang, J.: Unet++: a nested U-Net architecture for medical image segmentation. In: Stoyanov, D., et al. (eds.) Deep Learning in Medical Image Analysis and Multimodal Learning for Clinical Decision Support. LNCS, vol. 11045, pp. 3–11. Springer, Cham (2018). https://doi.org/10.1007/978-3-030-00889-5_1
8. Xiao, X., Lian, S., Luo, Z., et al.: Weighted res-unet for high-quality retina vessel segmentation. In: 2018 9th International Conference on Information Technology in Medicine and Education (ITME), pp. 327–331. IEEE (2018)
9. Huang, H., Lin, L., et al.: UNet 3+: a full-scale connected U-Net for medical image segmentation. In: IEEE International Conference on Acoustics, Speech and Signal Processing (ICASSP), pp. 1055–1059. IEEE (2020)
10. Prajit, R., Niki, P., et al.: Standalone self-attention in vision models. arXiv preprint arXiv: 1906.05909 (2019)
11. Vaswani, A., Shazeer, N., Parmar, N., et al.: Attention is all you need. In: Advances in Neural Information Processing Systems, pp. 5998–6008 (2017)
12. Chen, J., Lu, Y., Yu, Q., et al.: TransUNet: transformers make strong encoders for medical image segmentation. arXiv preprint arXiv:2102.04306 (2021)
13. Hatamizadeh, A., Tang, Y., Nath, V., et al.: UNETR: transformers for 3D medical image segmentation. In: Proceedings of the IEEE/CVF Winter Conference on Applications of Computer Vision, pp. 574–584 (2022)
14. Xie, Y., Zhang, J., Shen, C., Xia, Y.: CoTr: efficiently bridging CNN and transformer for 3D medical image segmentation. In: de Bruijne, M., et al. (eds.) Medical Image Computing and Computer Assisted Intervention – MICCAI 2021. LNCS, vol. 12903, pp. 171–180. Springer, Cham (2021). https://doi.org/10.1007/978-3-030-87199-4_16
15. Liu, Z., Lin, Y., Cao, Y., et al.: Swin transformer: hierarchical vision transformer using shifted windows. In: Proceedings of the IEEE/CVF Conference on Computer Vision and Pattern Recognition, pp. 10224–10233 (2021)
16. Cao, H., Wang, Y., Chen, J., et al: Swin-Unet: unet-like pure transformer for medical image segmentation. In: Karlinsky, L., Michaeli, T., Nishino, K. (eds.) European Conference on Computer Vision, pp. 205–218. Springer, Cham (2022). https://doi.org/10.1007/978-3-031-25066-8_9
17. Lin, T.Y., Dollár, P., Girshick, R., et al.: Feature pyramid networks for object detection. In: Proceedings of the IEEE Conference on Computer Vision and Pattern Recognition, pp. 2117–2125 (2017)

18. Mehta, S., Rastegari, M.: MobileViT: light-weight, general-purpose, and mobile-friendly vision transformer. arXiv preprint arXiv:2110.02178 (2021)
19. Xie, S., Girshick, R., Dollár P., et al.: Aggregated residual transformations for deep neural networks. In: Proceedings of the IEEE Conference on Computer Vision and Pattern Recognition, pp. 1492–1500 (2017)
20. Yang, X., Bian, C., Yu, L., Ni, D., Heng, P.-A.: Hybrid loss guided convolutional networks for whole heart parsing. In: Pop, M., et al. (eds.) Statistical Atlases and Computational Models of the Heart. ACDC and MMWHS Challenges. LNCS, vol. 10663, pp. 215–223. Springer, Cham (2018). https://doi.org/10.1007/978-3-319-75541-0_23
21. Geert, L., Oscar, D., Jelle, B., Nico, K., Henkjan, H.: ProstateX challenge data. Cancer Imaging Arch. (2017). https://doi.org/10.7937/K9TCIA.2017.MURS5CL
22. Xiong, Z., et al.: A global benchmark of algorithms for segmenting the left atrium from late gadolinium-enhanced cardiac magnetic resonance imaging. Med. Image Anal. **67**, 101832 (2021)
23. MindSpore. https://www.mindspore.cn
24. Yu, L., Wang, S., Li, X., Fu, C.-W., Heng, P.-A.: Uncertainty-aware self-ensembling model for semi-supervised 3D left atrium segmentation. In: Shen, D., et al. (eds.) Medical Image Computing and Computer Assisted Intervention – MICCAI 2019. LNCS, vol. 11765, pp. 605–613. Springer, Cham (2019). https://doi.org/10.1007/978-3-030-32245-8_67
25. Chang, H.H., Zhuang, A.H., Valentino, D.J., et al.: Performance measure characterization for evaluating neuroimage segmentation algorithms. Neuroimage **47**(1), 122–135 (2009)
26. Litjens, G., Toth, R., et al.: Evaluation of prostate segmentation algorithms for MRI: the PROMISE12 challenge. Med. Image Anal. **18**(2), 359–373 (2014)
27. Wang, W., Chen, C., Ding, M., Yu, H., Zha, S., Li, J.: TransBTS: multimodal brain tumor segmentation using transformer. In: de Bruijne, M., et al. (eds.) Medical Image Computing and Computer Assisted Intervention – MICCAI 2021. LNCS, vol. 12901, pp. 109–119. Springer, Cham (2021). https://doi.org/10.1007/978-3-030-87193-2_11
28. Hatamizadeh, A., Nath, V., Tang, Y., et al.: Swin unetr: swin transformers for semantic segmentation of brain tumors in mri images. In: Crimi, A., Bakas, S. (eds.) International MICCAI Brainlesion Workshop, pp. 272–284. Springer, Cham (2021). https://doi.org/10.1007/978-3-031-08999-2_22
29. Zhou, H., Guo, J., Zhang, Y., et al.: nnFormer: interleaved transformer for volumetric segmentation. arXiv preprint arXiv:2109.03201 (2021)

LANet: A Single Stage Lane Detector with Lightweight Attention

Qiangbin Xie, Xiao Zhao, and Lihua Zhang$^{(\boxtimes)}$

Intelligent Perception and Autonomous Systems Laboratory (IPASS),
Academy for Engineering and Technology, Fudan University,
Shanghai 200433, China
21210860087@m.fudan.edu.cn, lihuazhang@fudan.edu.cn

Abstract. Currently, lane detection is one of the key tasks in autonomous driving. Numerous lane detection methods have achieved high accuracy. However, there is still ample room for improvement in developing techniques that can meet both the accuracy and real-time requirements of driving scenarios. In our work, we proposed an anchor-based deep lane detection method named LANet. It meets the needs of lane detection in the case of insufficient information, and achieves a balance between accuracy and efficiency. Since the feature extraction of slender lane is extremely challenging, obtaining enough lane information is crucial for accurate lane detection. Therefore, we propose to absorb the indirect learning surplus of lane representation, by analyzing the latent distribution of lane features in other insufficiently informative scenarios. At the same time, we also use a more lightweight attention mechanism to improve the co-detection ability of anchors. Our approach also yields promising outcomes on two publicly available datasets, striking a favorable balance between detection accuracy and efficiency, which is crucial for practical lane detection in driving scenarios.

Keywords: Lane detection · self-driving · attention

1 Introduction

The emergence of deep learning technology has promoted the development of many traditional computer vision. In the field of intelligent driving, many deep learning methods are used in its perception system [4,12]. Especially, it is crucial for vehicles to leverage mathematical modeling based on deep learning in order to perceive its surrounding environment. The initial work focused on solving simple scenarios such as highways. However, with the rapid development of road traffic, effectively dealing with the long-tail effect(such as severe shading, marking wear, extreme weather, etc.) in lane detection has become a more concerned issue [23].

Early work [5,27,28] relied on the assumption of parallel geometry between pairs of traffic lines, and employed handcrafted filters [2,6,10,17] to extract line segment features. These segments were then clustered into different traffic lines.

L. Fang et al. (Eds.): CICAI 2023, LNAI 14473, pp. 388–399, 2024.
https://doi.org/10.1007/978-981-99-8850-1_32

However, many recent works [14, 15, 19, 22] have adopted CNNs to implement the aforementioned two-stage solution. The current two-stage approach [2, 14, 15, 19, 22] is limited, and the clustering operation conducted during post-processing fails to preserve the global information of lanes. As a result, distinguishing between different lanes becomes challenging, particularly in scenarios involving shadows or severe occlusion.

The lane itself has strong shape characteristics, such as thin, long and straight. And it occupies only a few pixels in the overall driving image. For lane detection tasks, accurately capturing the valid information among the abundant interference information is crucial to improve efficiency. However, the majority of methods ignore it. In addition, when there exists a series of problems such as extreme lighting and occlusion, it makes more difficult to capture information. With this condition, model can't directly learn this lane representation from the information in this scenario. In some cases the local information may not be enough to predict the lane. Some work [24] propose to use self-attention for aggregate global information. However, the computational complexity of self-attention is quadratic and its scope is limited to a single self feature. Inspired by human perception, mining the potential correlations among frames can facilitate the model's collaborative prediction of lane, and enhances the model's robustness.

In this work, we present a method for lane detection that takes into account both efficiency and accuracy in a balanced manner, with a focus on lane feature detection based on strong shape priors of the lanes. In the particularly, we introduce deformable convolution operation in feature extraction to enhance the adaptive ability of the feature extraction network to lane shape. We employ a novel anchor-frame attention mechanism, which is more lightweight than conventional attention mechanism, to improve the generalization perception of model. Our method conducts extensive experiments on two public datasets, and makes a trade-off between accuracy and efficiency in the design details of the module. In summary, our main contributions are:

- A feature extraction network that is more suitable for lane tasks is introduced with deformable convolution, enabling the network to adapt better to object shape and extract more precise features;
- The independent memory unit is utilized to acquire the latent relationship between anchors and datasets, for the collaborative detection ability of the model in the lack of information;
- Our approach demonstrates excellent performance in terms of both speed and accuracy.

2   Related Work

In this section, we present the mainstream detection methods based on deep learning: classification-based [13, 19–21, 30], regression modeling-based [9, 25], and transformer architecture-based methods [3, 8, 11, 29].

Classification-Based Methods. Since the segmentation method is a two-stage method of pixel-level classification in nature, we consider it as a class of classification methods. For it, a segmentation map is generated from original pixel features. Then, it is decoded into distinct lane through post-processing steps. SCNN [19] exhibits strong spatial relationship for lane. However, its efficiency is weaken by repeated convolution operation. Later, SAD [13] incorporated self-attention distillation to significantly enhance detection speed. When it is faced with the dazzle environment, its performance is lacking. Another approach based on classification is through dividing the rows or columns of the input image into grids, and then classifies each grid cell. The concept was initially introduced in E2E-LMD [30]. In UFLD [20], the authors achieve fast detection speed with a loss of detection accuracy. However, the later version of UFLD (UFLD-V2) [21] improves this problem by adopting a mixed classification method based on both rows and columns. Nonetheless, their FDR and FNR are at a relatively high level.

Regression-Based Modeling Methods. PolyLaneNet [25] uses polynomial representation to fit the lane expression instead of a set of marked points. Since BézierLaneNet [9] considers polynomial coefficients difficult to optimize, it proposes to use third-order Bézier curves to fit the lanes globally. Bézier curve regression only needs a few control points to describe the curve.

Transformer-Based Methods. Benefiting from the vision transformer [3,8,18] on vision tasks, many work [11,26,29] start using it. RCLane [29] is compatible with the bifurcated lane locally, and considers the lane structure globally. Laneformer [11] puts the feature map into transformer-encoder and transformer-decoder, while using the information of object detection to capture the connection between the lane and the driving vehicle. They are excellent in detection accuracy. However, the use of a transformer results in a decrease in detection efficiency.

3   Proposed Method

LANet is a single-stage lane detection method that utilizes discrete ray points (referred to as anchors) for improved accuracy. Figure 1 provides an overview of the method, which takes RGB images ($F_{original} \in R^{3*H*W}$) captured by the front-facing camera as input and outputs precise boundary detection for lanes. Section 3.2 describes backbone and pooling. A neural network with both regular convolution and deformable convolution [7,31] is employed as the backbone. The resulting feature map is then used for subsequent feature pooling operation based on anchors that are discrete ray points. The pooled features will serve as query in our anchor-frame attention module (see Sect. 3.3), generating panoramic semantic that integrate both self-feature and collaboration-feature (referred to as co-feature). In Sect. 3.4, the panoramic features are fed into two fully connected layers to generate classification and localization prediction.

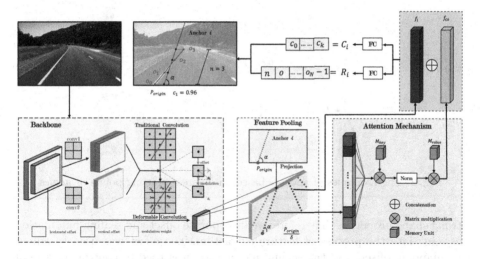

Fig. 1. Overview of the proposed method. A backbone generates feature maps from an input images. The anchor-frame attention is used for the anchor-based pooling feature to obtain the collaboration features. Finally, the panoramic features were used for classification and regression, which push the final prediction.

3.1 Anchor Representation

A lane is represented by a set of 2D coordinate points that are equidistant longitudinally and remain in a fixed and ordered sequence. For any point $P_i = (x_i, y_i)$ from that, its vertical coordinate y_i can be calculated as $i * \frac{H}{N_{strip}-1}$, where H represents the number of longitudinal pixels in the picture and N_{strip} represents the number of sampling strips. Assuming $Y = \{y_i\}_{i=0}^{N_{strip}-1}$ represents the sequence of ordinates, each x_i will have unique one y_i corresponding to it. Hence, a lane can be uniquely determined by its corresponding lateral coordinate sequence $X = \{x_i\}_{i=0}^{N_{strip}-1}$, as shown in Fig. 2. The majority of lane points are expected to appear a specific range on the vertical axis. Therefore, our method uses the starting and ending indices to define a continuous and valid sequence of lateral coordinates, thereby reducing unnecessary computations.

The concept of anchor line was initially proposed by Line-CNN [16]. Our method utilizes it during both inference and training. An anchor is a line segment of finite length that originates from a point P_{origin} on the boundary, and extends to the boundary of the image with a certain slope. The system allows for the multiple anchor based on various angles and starting positions, thereby catering to the vast majority of lane markings encountered in real-world scenarios.

3.2 Backbone and Feature Pooling

First of all, model extract high-level features from raw features. However, we observe that the feature distribution of lane across the entire image exhibits

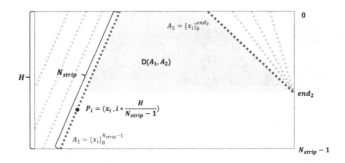

Fig. 2. The Examples of anchors based on different starting points or angles

strong shape properties. Therefore, we incorporate offset and scaling modulation mapping into the process of feature extraction. The offset was used to adjust the mapping offset, and the scaling modulation was used to control the size of the offset to prevent its offset from being too large. Finally, the regular-shaped convolution kernel was replaced with an adaptive one, to adapt to the elongated and straight shape characteristics of lane. The schematics of offset and scaling modulation are shown in "Backbone" from Fig. 1.

To avoid exploding caculation, we only use them into high-level semantic. In the offset process, the pixel point coordinates are transformed from an integers to an floats, requiring the use of bilinear interpolation to obtain feature values at these non-integer coordinates. So this stage generates the feature map $F_{backbone} \in R^{C'*H_F*H_F}$ from the original feature $F_{origin} \in R^{3*H*W}$. Moreover, we reduce the feature dimensionality of $F_{backbone}$, getting the final $F_{map} \in R^{C*H_F*W_F}$.

Feature pooling based anchors can facilitate feature utilization. For any point $P_F = (x_F, y_F)$ located on the feature map F_{map}, mapping based on P_{origin} and α, a unique x_F can be obtained for each value of y_F in the set $\{0, 1, 2, ..., H_F - 1\}$.

$$x_F = \left[\frac{x_{origin}}{\sigma} + \frac{y_F - \frac{y_{origin}}{\sigma}}{tan\alpha}\right] \tag{1}$$

The backbone produces an σ-fold downsize $F_{backbone}$ from F_{origin}. After mapping based on Eq. 1, an anchor-based feature vector $f_i \in R^{C*H_F}$ can be obtained. In cases where apart of the anchor is outside the boundaries of F_{map}, $f_i \in R^{C*H_F}$ is zero-padded. The vector will serve as the query for anchor-frame attention in the next stage.

3.3 Anchor-Frame Attention

The computational complexity of self-attention and its limitation between single self-feature show possibility of improvement. Therefore, our method proposes an anchor-frame attention mechanism that is linear complexity. Two shared external memory units is independent of feature information to capture potential collaborative relationships between different anchor and all of frame from datasets.

The anchor-frame attention can be formulated as:

$$F(key', query) * value' = attention\_feature \qquad (2)$$

where $F(key', query)_{i,j}$ is the similarity between the $i-th$ anchor and the $j-th$ row of $memory\_key$. Compared with the self-attention mechanism, the key and $value$ in anchor-frame attention are no longer generated by feature projection. Using two linear layers as memory units simplifies the computational complexity. Because external memory units is much fewer than input features. A separate $Softmax$ is generally used as the normalization layer, but it may lead to the corresponding co-feature being particularly large or small when self-feature value is particularly large or small, thereby compromising the original meaning of attention. So it is necessary to use a double normalization that adding an $L1$ norm after $Softmax$.

3.4 Prediction

For each predefined anchor, their feature vectors aggregated through anchor-frame attention and self-feature are fed into two parallel fully connected layers, one performing classification and the other performing regression, which together generate the final proposal. The classification layer is responsible for predicting the probability distribution ($K + 1$ confidence scores) of each anchor belonging to one of K lane types, denoted as $C_i = \{c_0, c_1, ...c_K\}$. The regression layer is responsible for predicting the horizontal offset of each point based on the current anchor and valid indexes. It includes the number of lane points and their corresponding horizontal offsets within a given range, denoted as $R_i = (n, \{o_0, o_1, ...\})$.

3.5 Non-maximum Supression (NMS)

In addition to using a substantial number of anchors as proposals for lane, we also incorporate deformable convolution and anchor-frame attention mechanism in the feature extraction and aggregation stages, respectively. Therefore, our method also requires NMS to filter most repeat detection. We utilize a distance metric (Line-CNN) to quantify the separation of common range between two anchors or anchors and a lane, as shown in Fig. 2. And the calculated metric is used in both training and testing phases. Anchor A_1 and A_2, for example, they can be respectively by the corresponding sequence of lateral coordinates to determine the abscissa, namely $A_1 = \{x_{1i}\}_{i=start_1}^{end_1}$, $A_2 = \{x_{2i}\}_{i=start_2}^{end_2}$. The start index of the common range is then defined as the larger of the two anchor's start indexes, while the end index is defined as the smaller of their end indexes. In other words, $start' = max(start_1, start_2)$ and $end' = min(end_1, end_2)$.

$$D(A1, A2) = \begin{cases} +\infty, & otherwise \\ \frac{1}{end'-start'+1} \sum_{i=start'}^{end'} |x_{1i} - x_{2i}|, & end' \geq start' \end{cases} \qquad (3)$$

3.6   Model Training

Based on the aforementioned lane distance metric, it is necessary to allocate positive and negative samples for the anchors. The distance between the anchors remaining after NMS filtering and the ground-truth is calculated one by one. Among them, anchors whose distance from the ground-truth is less than D_p are regarded as positive anchors, while anchors whose distance is more than D_n are negative anchors. Anchors that fall halfway between these two thresholds are disregarded as their contribution to the model's training for this task is negligible. The positive anchor A_P and negative anchor A_N will be utilized to compute the loss for classification and regression tasks, thereby guiding the model during training. The total loss function is defined as:

$$L(\{C_i, R_i\}_{i=0}^{A_{P\&N}-1}) = \lambda * Loss_{cls} + Loss_{reg} \tag{4}$$

$$Loss_{cls} = \sum_i FL(C_i, C_i^*), \qquad Loss_{reg} = \sum_i L1(R_i, R_i^*) \tag{5}$$

where C_i, R_i are the prediction results of classification layer and regression layer for $anchor_i$, and where C_i^*, R_i^* are the classification and regression targets of the model for $anchor_i$. The parameter λ is used to balance classification and regression for the total loss. Due to the imbalanced distribution of positive and negative samples in the datasets, Focal Loss is employed for loss calculation in classification tasks. For the regression task's loss calculation, $Smooth\ L1$ is utilized. It is worth noting that if $anchor_i$ is considered as a negative anchor during sample assignment, it will only be taken into account for the classification loss calculation. For positive anchors, the regression loss only calculates the error between each pair of horizontal offsets within the common index interval shared by both the predicted valid index range and ground truth index range.

4   Experiments

This section mainly describes the rules of the evaluation metrics and the details of the experiment execution. Our approach will be evaluated on two of the most widely used public lane detection datasetss. $Tusimple$ [1] is only contains highway scenes, $CULane$ [19] is divided nine categories, such as crowded, night, absence of visible lines, etc. Their main parameters are presented in Table 1. All of our experiments use default metrics set by the creators of the datasets. The two first subsection compare the method with the existing excellent methods (see Table 2 and Table 3), and the two final subsection conduct ablation analysis of the characteristic parts of this method.

The speed of detection is an important factor to judge the real-time performance of lane detection method. This method uses frames-per-second (FPS) to evaluate its speed of detection. Our method will pick 72 and 128 starting points from the left and right boundary and the bottom boundary, respectively, and then take 6 and 15 different angles based on them for anchors. But we picked out 1,000 of anchors that have a high frequency of being assigned as positive

Table 1. Detail of the datasets about Tusimple and CULane.

datasets	#Frame	Tra.	Val.	Test	Resolution	#Max	#Scenarios
Tusimple	6,480	3,268	358	2,782	1280×720	5	1
CULane	133,235	88,880	9,675	34,680	1640×590	4	9

samples in the training phase and the testing phase, for improving efficiency. The model parameters were $N_{strip} = 72, D_p = 15, D_n = 20, K = 1$.

By changing the number of doformable convolution and where they are used in our experiments, we found that using it only for high-level semantic features can play a great role. The last two layers are saturated with deformable convolutions, so we don't need to add them more than once. Otherwise, it will bring a large number of calculations and limit the detection speed. In anchor-frame attention mechanism, we set the dimension of the attention matrix of the memory unit to 64, and the performance improvement brought by continually adding the number of unit is actually not worth the loss.

Table 2. The results of mainstream methods on Tusimple. (* represents the Source-code is unavaliable)

Method	F1(%)↑	Acc(%)↑	FDR(%)↓	FNR(%)↓	FPS↑
Line-CNN [16]*	96.79	**96.87**	4.42	<u>1.97</u>	30
E2E [30]*	96.40	96.04	3.11	4.09	-
Laneformer [11]*	95.58	96.56	5.39	3.37	61
RCLane [29]*	**97.64**	96.58	**2.28**	2.27	43.8
SCNN [19]	95.97	96.53	6.17	**1.80**	7.5
ENet-SAD [13]	95.92	<u>96.64</u>	6.02	2.05	75
UFLD-V2 [21]	96.16	95.65	<u>3.06</u>	4.61	**330**
LaneATT [24]	96.77	95.63	3.53	2.92	<u>171</u>
BézierLaneNet [9]	95.03	95.41	5.30	4.60	-
LANet	<u>96.81</u>	95.59	3.41	2.98	105

4.1 Tusimple

Evaluation Metrics. On TuSimple, the three standard metrics are false discovery rate (FDR), false negative rate (FNR), and accuracy. The accuracy is defined as:

$$Acc = \frac{\sum_i C_{frame_i}}{\sum_i S_{frame_i}} \tag{6}$$

where C_{frame_i} is the number of lane points predicted correctly (the difference between the ground-truth point and the predicted point is less than 20 pixels) in the i-th frame, and S_{frame_i} is the total number of points in the i-th frame. For a lane prediction to be considered a true positive (for the FDR and FNR metrics), its number of correct predicted points has to be greater than 85%.

4.2 CULane

Evaluation Metrics. The only metric is the F1, which is based on the intersection over union (IoU) of lane areas. The datasets's official metric considers the lanes as 30-pixels-thick lines. If a prediction has an IoU greater than 0.5 with a ground-truth lane, it is considered a true positive (Fig. 3).

Table 3. The results of mainstream methods on CULane. (* represents the Source-code is unavaliable)

Category	E2E [30]*	Laneformer [11]*	RCLane [29]*	SCNN [19]	ENet-SAD [13]	UFLD-V2 [21]	LaneATT [24]	BézierLaneNet [9]	LANet
Normal	90.00	88.60	**93.59**	90.60	90.10	91.70	_92.14_	90.22	91.50
Crowded	69.70	69.02	**78.77**	69.70	68.80	73.00	_75.03_	71.55	74.02
Dazzle	60.20	64.07	**72.44**	58.50	60.20	64.60	_66.47_	62.49	64.87
Shadow	62.50	65.02	**84.37**	66.90	65.90	74.70	78.15	70.91	_79.12_
No-line	43.20	45.00	**52.77**	43.40	41.60	47.20	_49.39_	45.30	47.06
Arrow	83.20	81.55	**90.31**	84.10	84.00	87.60	88.38	87.16	_88.91_
Curve	_70.30_	60.46	**78.39**	64.40	65.70	67.70	67.72	58.98	63.29
Cross↓	2296	**25**	_907_	1990	1998	1998	1330	996	1170
Night	63.30	64.76	**73.96**	66.10	66.00	70.20	_70.72_	68.70	69.82
Total	70.80	71.71	**80.03**	71.60	70.80	74.7	_76.68_	73.67	75.59
FPS	-	61	43.8	7.5	75	**330**	_171_	-	105

Fig. 3. LANet qualitative results on TuSimple (the first row), CUlane (the second row). Blue lines are GT, while green and red lines are TP and FP, respectively. (Color figure online)

4.3 Ablation Study

This experiment evaluates the impact of each major part of the proposed method: deformable convolution and anchor-frame attention. The results are shown in Table 4. In the second row, the anchor-frame attention mechanism was removed. In the third row, the deformable convolution was replaced with conventional convolution. The drop of performance when anchor-frame attention mechanism is removing shows its importance of enhance collaborative detection ability. And it has little impact on FPS due to its linear complexity computation. The deformable convolution increase the model performance relatively small. However, our method achieves a balance between efficiency and accuracy, and does not compromise one with the other.

Table 4. Ablation study results on CUlane

Method	F1(%)	FPS
LANet	75.59	105
-anchor-frame attention	74.07	117
-deformable convolution	75.23	143

5   Conclusion

We proposed an anchor-based single-stage deep lane detection model to balance accuracy with efficiency. In order to balance them, we use an attention mechanism with linear complexity. On the one hand, we use the potential connections in different scenarios to collaborate with anchors for better lane prediction, and on the other hand, we control the computing cost of the attention mechanism to achieve the purpose of improving detection efficiency. In the phase of feature extraction and aggregation, our method makes full use of the strong lane shape prior condition that is ignored by most work, and improves the generalization ability of anchor in different scenes through a novel attention mechanism. The experimental results on two large public datasets show that our method achieved a high balance between accuracy and efficiency. However, due to the inherent characteristics of anchor itself, our method performs poorly in curved lane, bifurcating lane and high degree of freedom lane. This may be the next direction that anchor-based methods should strive for.

References

1. Tusimple benchmark (2017). https://github.com/TuSimple/tusimple-benchmark
2. Aly, M.: Real time detection of lane markers in urban streets. In: 2008 IEEE Intelligent Vehicles Symposium, pp. 7–12. IEEE (2008)
3. Ashish, V.: Attention is all you need. In: Advances in Neural Information Processing Systems, vol. 30, I (2017)
4. Badue, C., et al.: Self-driving cars: a survey. Expert Syst. Appl. **165**, 113816 (2021)
5. Bertozzi, M., Broggi, A.: Gold: a parallel real-time stereo vision system for generic obstacle and lane detection. IEEE Trans. Image Process. **7**(1), 62–81 (1998)
6. Chiu, K.Y., Lin, S.F.: Lane detection using color-based segmentation. In: IEEE Proceedings. Intelligent Vehicles Symposium, pp. 706–711. IEEE (2005)
7. Dai, J., et al.: Deformable convolutional networks. In: Proceedings of the IEEE International Conference on Computer Vision, pp. 764–773 (2017)
8. Dosovitskiy, A., et al.: An image is worth 16x16 words: transformers for image recognition at scale. arXiv preprint arXiv:2010.11929 (2020)
9. Feng, Z., Guo, S., Tan, X., Xu, K., Wang, M., Ma, L.: Rethinking efficient lane detection via curve modeling. In: Proceedings of the IEEE/CVF Conference on Computer Vision and Pattern Recognition, pp. 17062–17070 (2022)
10. Gonzalez, J.P., Ozguner, U.: Lane detection using histogram-based segmentation and decision trees. In: ITSC2000. 2000 IEEE Intelligent Transportation Systems. Proceedings (Cat. No. 00TH8493), pp. 346–351. IEEE (2000)
11. Han, J., et al.: Laneformer: object-aware row-column transformers for lane detection. In: Proceedings of the AAAI Conference on Artificial Intelligence, vol. 36, pp. 799–807 (2022)
12. Hong, Z., et al.: Semantic compression embedding for generative zero-shot learning. In: IJCAI, Vienna, Austria, vol. 7, pp. 956–963 (2022)
13. Hou, Y., Ma, Z., Liu, C., Loy, C.C.: Learning lightweight lane detection CNNs by self attention distillation. In: Proceedings of the IEEE/CVF International Conference on Computer Vision, pp. 1013–1021 (2019)
14. Huval, B., et al.: An empirical evaluation of deep learning on highway driving. arXiv preprint arXiv:1504.01716 (2015)
15. Lee, S., et al.: VPGNet: vanishing point guided network for lane and road marking detection and recognition. In: Proceedings of the IEEE International Conference on Computer Vision, pp. 1947–1955 (2017)
16. Li, X., Li, J., Hu, X., Yang, J.: Line-CNN: end-to-end traffic line detection with line proposal unit. IEEE Trans. Intell. Transp. Syst. **21**(1), 248–258 (2019)
17. McCall, J.C., Trivedi, M.M.: An integrated, robust approach to lane marking detection and lane tracking. In: IEEE Intelligent Vehicles Symposium, pp. 533–537. IEEE (2004)

18. Pan, W., Wu, H., Zhu, J., Zeng, H., Zhu, X.: H-ViT: hybrid vision transformer for multi-modal vehicle re-identification. In: Fang, L., Povey, D., Zhai, G., Mei, T., Wang, R. (eds.) Artificial Intelligence: Second CAAI International Conference, CICAI 2022, Beijing, China, 27–28 August 2022, Revised Selected Papers, Part I, pp. 255–267. Springer, Cham (2022). https://doi.org/10.1007/978-3-031-20497-5_21

19. Pan, X., Shi, J., Luo, P., Wang, X., Tang, X.: Spatial as deep: spatial CNN for traffic scene understanding. In: Proceedings of the AAAI Conference on Artificial Intelligence, vol. 32 (2018)

20. Qin, Z., Wang, H., Li, X.: Ultra fast structure-aware deep lane detection. In: Vedaldi, A., Bischof, H., Brox, T., Frahm, J.-M. (eds.) ECCV 2020. LNCS, vol. 12369, pp. 276–291. Springer, Cham (2020). https://doi.org/10.1007/978-3-030-58586-0_17

21. Qin, Z., Zhang, P., Li, X.: Ultra fast deep lane detection with hybrid anchor driven ordinal classification. IEEE Trans. Pattern Anal. Mach. Intell. (2022)

22. Revilloud, M., Gruyer, D., Rahal, M.C.: A lane marker estimation method for improving lane detection. In: 2016 IEEE 19th International Conference on Intelligent Transportation Systems (ITSC), pp. 289–295. IEEE (2016)

23. Romera, E., Alvarez, J.M., Bergasa, L.M., Arroyo, R.: ERFNet: efficient residual factorized convnet for real-time semantic segmentation. IEEE Trans. Intell. Transp. Syst. **19**(1), 263–272 (2017)

24. Tabelini, L., Berriel, R., Paixao, T.M., Badue, C., De Souza, A.F., Oliveira-Santos, T.: Keep your eyes on the lane: real-time attention-guided lane detection. In: Proceedings of the IEEE/CVF Conference on Computer Vision and Pattern Recognition, pp. 294–302 (2021)

25. Tabelini, L., Berriel, R., Paixao, T.M., Badue, C., De Souza, A.F., Oliveira-Santos, T.: PolyLaneNet: lane estimation via deep polynomial regression. In: 2020 25th International Conference on Pattern Recognition (ICPR), pp. 6150–6156. IEEE (2021)

26. Wang, Y., Qian, W., Li, M., Zhang, X.: A transformer-based network for deformable medical image registration. In: Fang, L., Povey, D., Zhai, G., Mei, T., Wang, R. (eds.) Artificial Intelligence: Second CAAI International Conference, CICAI 2022, Beijing, China, 27–28 August 2022, Revised Selected Papers, Part I, pp. 502–513. Springer, Cham (2022). https://doi.org/10.1007/978-3-031-20497-5_41

27. Wang, Y., Shen, D., Teoh, E.K.: Lane detection using spline model. Pattern Recogn. Lett. **21**(8), 677–689 (2000)

28. Wang, Y., Teoh, E.K., Shen, D.: Lane detection and tracking using B-Snake. Image Vis. Comput. **22**(4), 269–280 (2004)

29. Xu, S., et al.: RCLane: relay chain prediction for lane detection. In: Avidan, S., Brostow, G., Cissé, M., Farinella, G.M., Hassner, T. (eds.) Computer Vision-ECCV 2022: 17th European Conference, Tel Aviv, Israel, 23–27 October 2022, Proceedings, Part XXXVIII, pp. 461–477. Springer, Cham (2022). https://doi.org/10.1007/978-3-031-19839-7_27

30. Yoo, S., et al.: End-to-end lane marker detection via row-wise classification. In: Proceedings of the IEEE/CVF Conference on Computer Vision and Pattern Recognition Workshops, pp. 1006–1007 (2020)

31. Zhu, X., Hu, H., Lin, S., Dai, J.: Deformable ConvNets V2: more deformable, better results. In: Proceedings of the IEEE/CVF Conference on Computer Vision and Pattern Recognition, pp. 9308–9316 (2019)

Visible and NIR Image Fusion Algorithm Based on Information Complementarity

Zhuo Li and Bo Li[✉]

Beijing Key Laboratory of Digital Media, Beihang University, Beijing, China
{lizhuo320,boli}@buaa.edu.cn

Abstract. Visible and near-infrared (NIR) band sensors provide images that capture complementary spectral radiations from a scene. And the fusion of the visible and NIR image aims at utilizing their spectrum properties to enhance image quality. However, currently visible and NIR fusion algorithms cannot well take advantage of spectrum properties, as well as lack information complementarity, which results in color distortion and artifacts. Therefore, this paper designs a complementary fusion model from the level of physical signals. First, in order to distinguish between noise and useful information, we use two layers of the weight-guided filter and guided filter to obtain texture and edge layers, respectively. Second, to generate the initial visible-NIR complementarity weight map, the difference maps of visible and NIR are filtered by the extend-DoG filter. After that, the significant region of NIR nighttime compensation guides the initial complementarity weight map by the arctanI function. Finally, the fusion images can be generated by the complementarity weight maps of visible and NIR images, respectively. The experimental results demonstrate that the proposed algorithm can not only well take advantage of the spectrum properties and the information complementarity, but also avoid color unnatural while maintaining naturalness, which outperforms the state-of-the-art.

Keywords: Image Fusion · Near-Infrared · Low Light · Color Distortion · Signal Complementarity

1 Introduction

Recent studies have demonstrated various strategies for concurrently acquiring visible and Near-infrared (NIR) images, utilizing silicon-based sensors as imaging technology advances [14,18]. Especially for low-light enhancement, utilizing two image sensors with specialized optical components, one of which takes visible spectra while the other captures near-infrared spectra by adding near-infrared light correction, as shown in Fig. 1. The information of the two spectra can be combined by image fusion to generate high-quality images in various applications for night vision systems [1,13,31,32].

For combining NIR information with visible images, numerous image fusion techniques have been developed, including traditional [12,20,22,25] and deep-learning methods [14,17]. The traditional methods focus on the intensity channel

L. Fang et al. (Eds.): CICAI 2023, LNAI 14473, pp. 400–411, 2024.
https://doi.org/10.1007/978-981-99-8850-1_33

of the source images. The color information of visible spectra is retained by determining the chroma terms, finally used to reform the greyscale fused image into a color image.

(a)   (b)

Fig. 1. Visible and NIR image captured by adding near-infrared light compensation

In [21], bilateral and weighted least squares filters were employed by Sharma et al. to produce images that were upgraded with greater detail information and higher contrast. By taking into account the structural variations between visible and NIR images, Elliethy et al. [7] method maintained the essential detail and edge information of a visible image. [24] proposed a mapping model that maintains local contrast in the NIR image while changing the NIR image values to correspond to the visible image corresponding pixels in the luminance plane. In [23], the relative difference of the local contrasts in the visible and NIR image was used to estimate a fusion map initially. In order to create the enhanced fusion image, the approach first extracted spatial features from the NIR image. Then the details were weighted in accordance with the fusion map and combined with the visible image. Additionally, Connah et al. proposed the image fusion technique based on the Spectral Edge (SpE) [5] is a promising algorithm for combining images in the gradient domain. The kind of fusion method, however, requires a lot of computation and iteration.

Some data-driven methods were developed based on the deep learning theory [6,10,17]. For the fusion of visible and infrared images, Li et al. [10] suggested a deep learning system with an encoder, fusion layer, and decoder model. And the Dark Vision Net (DVN) [11], a near-infrared visible light fusion method based on Deep Structure and Deep Inconsistency Prior (DIP) was proposed. Deep Structure is used to extract structural information from multi-scale features of extracted depth, avoiding introducing a lot of noise directly from the original input. Then based on this structural information, DIP uses structural inconsistency to guide the fusion of visible-NIR. The above method based on deep learning has made remarkable achievements, but its defect is that it requires a large number of training samples and computing power. The quality of image fusion depends on the training label material, model capacity, loss function selection, super parameter selection, and many other aspects.

Overall, the above-mentioned schemes require a color compensation process to generate a natural color-looking image. For many applications, it is desirable to retain the characteristic colors of the scene. However, modifying the chroma terms often leads to undesirable false-color image renderings [29]. Therefore, we think more attention should be paid to the analysis of complementary at the level of image data, which is a display of physical signals. This paper designs a complementary fusion model from the level of physical signals. First, in order to distinguish between noise and useful information, we use two-scale image filters to obtain texture and edge layers, by the weight-guided filter and guided filter in proper order. Second, to generate the initial complementarity weight map, the difference maps of visible and NIR are filtered by the extend-DoG filter. After that, the significant region of NIR guides the initial complementarity weight map by the arctanI function. Finally, the fusion images can be generated by the complementarity weight maps of visible and NIR images, respectively. The experimental results demonstrate that the proposed algorithm can not only well take advantage of the properties of different spectra and the information complementarity, but also avoid color distortion while preserving chromaticity information of visible images, which outperforms the state-of-the-art.

The rest of this paper is organized as follows. The complementary theory and related work above the visible and near-infrared (NIR) are both covered in Sect. 2. The specifics of the proposed fusion algorithm are described in Sect. 3. Section 4 assesses both the objective and subjective performance of the suggested algorithm. Finally, Sect. 5 concludes the paper.

2   Related Work

As we have discussed in [16], each spectral band has different spectrum properties, providing different kinds of physical information. The similarity and difference between visible and NIR images have been addressed in [1,9]. The authors computed the correlation between visible and NIR gradients, and use the gradients of the visible image in reconstructing NIR only where the gradients are highly correlated. Meanwhile, many researchers often assumed that the high-frequency information of the visible-NIR channels is strongly correlated in [3,19].

Moreover, according to the theory of spectral reflection, the difference between visible and NIR spectra is the reflection-dependent molecular clusters [19,31]. The visible spectral reflection is based on the structural system in molecules called chromophores, therefore the visible images are colorful and suitable for human visual perception. However, the NIR spectral reflects the composition and molecular structure information of most types of organic compounds, namely NIR radiation is material dependent and with no color information.

It can be found that there are significant similarities between visible and near-infrared information that can be transformed, however, there are also some that cannot be obtained through transformation. In this paper, the information of one spectral cannot be transformed from the other one is called complementarity information. We think the color information of visible bands could not be replaced by NIR [8], therefore, the R, G, and B three bands of visible are combined with NIR band, respectively. Meanwhile, in low-light conditions utilizing two image sensors to capture visible spectra and near-infrared spectra by adding near-infrared light compensation, the NIR image contains a high signal-to-noise ratio, which can be supplemented for the visible image.

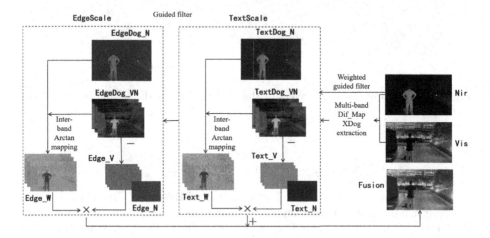

Fig. 2. The overall structure of the proposed fusion algorithm.

3 The Proposed Algorithm

3.1 Two-Scale Guided Image Decomposition

The proposed fusion algorithm is shown in Fig. 2, in order to better distinguish between noise and useful information, as well as maximize the utilization of high-frequency information, we use two-scale image filters to obtain texture layers and edge layers, by weighted guided and guided filter respectively. As shown in Fig. 3, we can see that the texture layer has more noise than the edge layer, which is more clear.

Considering the dark and uneven illumination conditions at night, the high-frequency noise of visible images in the texture layer is high. In order to distinguish noise and texture information in the first layer, we adopt the weight-guided filter (WGIF) proposed in [15], which can preserve sharp edges like the global filters, similar to the guided filter (GIF) in [22]. Besides that, the WGIF also avoids gradient reversal, therefore the halo artifacts can be avoided by the WGIF. After the first layer of filtering decomposition, the second layer filtered by the GIF will contain clear edge information. To some extent, the first layer of filtering can reduce the gradient of large-scale edges, which will also reduce the halo phenomenon of the second layer of filtering. The two-scale filters process is as follows:

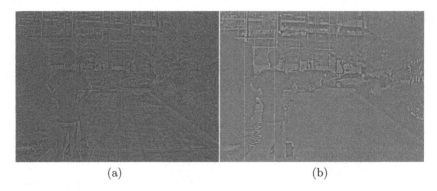

(a)   (b)

Fig. 3. The texture and edge layers of the Red channel of the visible image. (Color figure online)

$$R_p^1 = WGuidF_{\tau,\varepsilon}(R_p^0, R_p^0), \quad R_p^2 = GuidF_{\omega,\theta}(R_p^1, R_p^1) \tag{1}$$

where p represents the R, G, B channels of visible and NIR channel index, $p \in \{r, g, b, n\}$; R_p^1 are the first base layers calculated by the weight-guided filter; R_p^2 are the second base layers from the guided filter. The reason for using the weight-guided filter in the first layer is that it can better distinguish noise and preserve the gradients of edges. The τ, ε, ω, and σ are the parameters of the filter functions.

$$D_p^{i+1} = R_p^i - R_p^{i+1} \tag{2}$$

where D_p^{i+1} means the detail and edge layers of the image, p is the channel index, represents R, G, and B of visible and NIR channels, and i in this paper is $i = 0, 1$. That is to say, D_p^1 means the detail layer.

3.2   Inter-band Information Complementarity Map Estimation

The relationship between the visible and NIR spectral bands has been discussed in Sect. 2, particularly in the context of the reflectivity of vegetation and other natural scene features. It can be clearly seen that the original near-infrared is significantly different from all three original visible bands.

According to [30], the difference maps of visible and NIR images can include information from two modalities. The smaller the difference, the closer the indication is. The larger the difference, the more difficult. And it is also applied to the extraction of the DOG filter of difference maps. Therefore, We use the feature of difference maps to estimate the initial visible-NIR complementarity map, as well as add the significant region of near-infrared night-time compensation to guide the complementary information.

Additionally, the fundamental layer's potential texture and edge guide map are obtained using the extend-DoG ((XDog)) [2,27] method, the main goal of which is to expand the edge information. The edge line width of the generated edge graph is usually only 12 pixels, however, the general edges of images should not be so thin. The color weight map is obtained by using extend-DoG and the complementary information is obtained from the near-infrared light supplement area at night. The extend-DoG filter is applied to estimate the difference maps as the initial complementarity weight maps as follows:

$$RN_c^i = Normal(R_c^i - R_n^i), \tag{3}$$

$$dog_c^i = XDoG(RN_c^i), \quad dog_n^i = XDoG(R_n^i), \tag{4}$$

where $Normal()$ means the normalization processing of the base layers of the visible and NIR images processed by two-scale filters, $i = 0, 1$ represents the texture and edge layer, c is the R, G, and B of visible channels, n is the NIR channel.

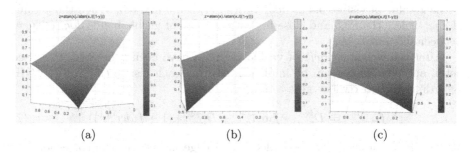

(a)   (b)   (c)

Fig. 4. The arctanI function used to fit the information complementary

3.3 Information Complementary Weight Model

Due to the low illumination data, when the brightness value in the image area is relatively low, the noise will be higher and the dog value will also be higher; So only when the brightness value of the image area is relatively high and the dog value is large, will useful information be obtained. So, we believe that the XDog value of an image, combined with its pixel value size, reflects whether it is a texture with a high signal-to-noise ratio or information with a low signal-to-noise ratio. As a preliminary estimate of fusion weights.

Considering that at night, the signal-to-noise ratio of near-infrared images that rely on supplementary lighting will be relatively high in the supplementary area, but the signal-to-noise ratio of areas that do not receive supplementary lighting is still relatively low. So, we use the extend-DoG filter and the value of near-infrared as a variable factor for adjustment.

Theorem 1. *When the signal-to-noise ratio of near-infrared is high, the weight value of R, G, and B of visible channels needs to be changed within a lower range based on the signal-to-noise ratio of visible light.*

Theorem 2. *When the signal-to-noise ratio of near-infrared is low, the weight value of R, G, and B of visible channels needs to be changed within a higher range based on the signal-to-noise ratio of visible channels.*

Inspired by [27], the arctanI function is used for adjustment to fit the information complementary between visible and NIR images as follows:

$$fuwt_c^i = arctanI(dog_c^i, dog_n^i) \tag{5}$$

where $arctanI$ is the function used to control the complementary based on the signal-to-noise of NIR, it is defined as follows:

$$arctanI(x, y) = \frac{atan(x)}{atan(\frac{x}{1-y}) + \alpha} \tag{6}$$

As shown in the Fig. 4, when the y value of NIR dog_n^i is a range of 0.5 approaches 1, the x value of visible bands dog_c^i varies between 0 and 0.5; When the y value of dog_n^i is less than 0.5 and close to 0, the x value of visible bands dog_c^i changes between 0.5 and 1.

After the weights $fuwt_c^i$ of visible channels have been generated, the fused detail and edge layers can be implemented from each visible channel and NIR according to their own weights as follows:

$$fuD_c^{i+1} = D_c^{i+1}. * fuwt_c^{i+1} + D_n^{i+1}. * (1 - fuwt_c^{i+1})) \tag{7}$$

Finally, combining the fused detail and edge layers and the correspondent base layer of RGB, the fusion F_c is defined as:

$$F_c = R_c^2 + fuD_c^2 + fuD_c^1 \tag{8}$$

4   Experimental Results

In this paper, by taking advantage of the spectrum properties and the information complementarity in fusion processing, the proposed fusion algorithm can not only improve image quality but also avoid color distortion while maintaining the natural color look. To verify the advantages of our fusion algorithm, We compare the proposed method with traditional state-of-the-art fusion methods including Joint Scale Map Restoration fusion (JSM) [28], Bilateral Filter fusion (BF) [12], Color Preserve fusion (CP) [1], Laplacian Pyramid fusion (Lap) [25] and Spectral Edge fusion (SE) [5]. And the group of test images is pairs of visible and NIR images captured by Hikvision Black Light Camera, which can simultaneously capture visible and NIR images with two CCDs through the same optical path. And we collected data on different conditions of lighting and noise, indoors and outdoors respectively.

Fig. 5. Qualitative comparison of the outdoor image (a) Visible image. (b) Near-infrared image. The fusion images are obtained by (c) BF [12] (d) CP [1] (e) JSM [28] (f) Lap [25] (g) SE [5] (h) our algorithm.

4.1   Objective Comparison

In our experiments, in order to value the authenticity and naturalness color of fusion images, we employ two metrics. To confirm the spectrum properties preservation as well as the chromaticity information of the visible image, the no-reference spectrum distortion index (SDI) is adopted [16], it is used to determine whether the correlation between visible and near-infrared spectra has changed.

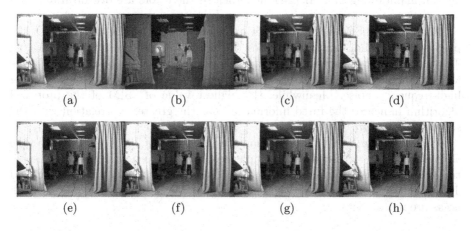

Fig. 6. Qualitative comparison of the indoor image. (a) Visible image. (b) Near-infrared image. The fusion images are obtained by (c) BF [12] (d) CP [1] (e) JSM [28] (f) Lap [25] (g) SE [5] (h) our algorithm.

Besides that, we also adopt a simple metric of color distance (CD) [4]. This metric is a combination of both weighted Euclidean distance functions, where the weight factors depend on how significant the "red" component of the color is. This formula has results that are more stable algorithms, the selection of the closest color is subjective. And the smaller both values of the two metrics are, the less the correlations between R, G, and B of visible and near-infrared bands have changed. And the CD is defined as follows:

$$r = \frac{C_{c,r} + C_{f,r}}{2},$$ (9)

$$R^{'} = C_{c,r} - C_{f,r}, G^{'} = C_{c,g} - C_{f,g}, B^{'} = C_{c,b} - C_{f,b},$$ (10)

$$CD = \sqrt{(2 + \frac{r}{256}) \times R^{'2} + 4 \times G^{'2} + (2 + \frac{255 - r}{256}) \times B^{'2}}$$ (11)

Meanwhile, to verify that the fused information comes from the original image, rather than artificially adding false information, we used SSIM [26] to measure the structural similarity between the source image and the fusion image. In addition, the peak signal-to-noise ratio (PSNR) is used to quantify the quality of the fusion image, as well as the visual information fidelity (VIF) [14] is used to measure information fidelity by calculating the distortion between the source image and the fusion image.

Table 1 demonstrates the comparisons of test images with corresponding algorithms, including 5 metrics. The greater value of the VIF, SSIM, and PSNR, the better the performance. As expected, the SE and Lap algorithms have high scores of SDI and CD, respectively. As shown in Fig. 5(g) the color is not real, as well as the other values of metrics are not well. These algorithms, in general, aim on maintaining more details, nonetheless, the colors are oversaturated and unrealistic.

Although the SE and JSM algorithms have lower values of SDI and CD, the proposed algorithm can have the best PSNR value and the second VIF value. That is to say, the proposed algorithm can not have a color appearance suitable for the human eye, but also ensure the clarity of the fusion image, avoiding high-frequency noise. Meanwhile, the highest value of SSIM of the proposed algorithm indicates the fused information has the greatest correlation with the source information.

With a comprehensive examination of indicator data, our algorithm can take advantage of the correlation and complementarity between visible and NIR spectra, resulting in a natural color look. While the color appearance of the SE and JSM algorithms is closest to the original viewable image, the edges and dark areas are not obvious.

4.2   Subject Comparison

As shown in Fig. 5 and Fig. 6, the fusion results with the SE, and the Lap algorithms all have color distortion, such as the clothes of people, and the areas

Table 1. Qualitative Comparision

Metrics	COMPARISION ALGORITHM					
	JSM [28]	SE [5]	Lap [25]	BF [12]	CP [1]	Ours
CD	0.98	5.00	5.72	1.11	0.76	0.73
SDI	0.0021	0.0777	0.0421	0.0321	0.0020	0.0018
VIF	0.41	0.38	0.36	0.39	0.57	0.46
SSIM	0.48	0.38	0.41	0.56	0.63	0.65
PSNR	39.83	37.46	27.07	37.46	37.88	40.93

of trees. Although the details in some dark areas can be seen with their algorithms, the color is unrealistic, such as the ground steps areas in Fig. 5. These algorithms, in general, emphasize maintaining more details, however, the colors are over-saturated and artificial, particularly in places with large variations between visible and NIR spectra. Furthermore, the noise on the black garments of the guy in the scene has been reduced in our fusion results. This demonstrates that our algorithm is capable of distinguishing useful information from meaningless noise input.

More importantly, due to overexposure, the details of the visual acuity chart in the visible image are invisible, which can be seen in the NIR image, as shown in Fig. 6. However, in the fusion images, our visual acuity chart features are the most evident, whereas the others are either indistinct or not visible. This comparison demonstrates that our algorithm can profit from the information complementarity between visible and NIR images, as well as distinguish valuable information from noise. Overall, our technology generates high-quality images with natural-looking color appearances.

5   Conclusion

In this paper, the fusion model based on the level of physical signals is proposed, with information complementarity between visible and NIR images. First, to distinguish between noise and useful texture and edge information, we use two layers of the weight-guided filter and guided filter to obtain texture and edge layers, respectively. Second, the extend-DoG filter is applied to estimate the difference maps as the Visible and NIR complementarity map. After that, to obtain the signal complementarity weight, the significant region of NIR nighttime compensation guides the complementarity map by the arctanI function we defined. Finally, the fusion images can be generated by the weights of three bands of visible and NIR images, respectively. Based on the physical optics imaging theory, the proposed algorithm analyzes the complementarity of physical information reflected in different light bands and designs a reasonable fusion model. Experiment findings show that our proposed fusion method outperforms state-of-the-art algorithms in both subjective and objective measures.

References

1. Awad, M., Elliethy, A., Aly, H.A.: Adaptive near-infrared and visible fusion for fast image enhancement. IEEE Trans. Comput. Imaging **6**, 408–418 (2020). https://doi.org/10.1109/TCI.2019.2956873

2. Boerner, H.: Feature extraction by grayscale morphological operations-a comparison to dog filters. In: International Workshop on Industrial Applications of Machine Intelligence and Vision, pp. 112–117 (1989). https://doi.org/10.1109/MIV.1989.40534

3. Brown, M., Süsstrunk, S.: Multi-spectral sift for scene category recognition. In: IEEE Conference on Computer Vision and Pattern Recognition (2011)

4. Chulhee, P., Kang, M.: Color restoration of RGBN multispectral filter array sensor images based on spectral decomposition. Sensors **16**(5), 719 (2016)

5. Connah, D., Drew, M.S., Finlayson, G.D.: Spectral edge image fusion: theory and applications. In: Fleet, D., Pajdla, T., Schiele, B., Tuytelaars, T. (eds.) ECCV 2014. LNCS, vol. 8693, pp. 65–80. Springer, Cham (2014). https://doi.org/10.1007/978-3-319-10602-1_5

6. Deng, X., Dragotti, P.L.: Deep convolutional neural network for multi-modal image restoration and fusion. IEEE (10) (2021)

7. Elliethy, A., Aly, H.A.: Fast near infrared fusion-based adaptive enhancement of visible images. In: 2017 IEEE Global Conference on Signal and Information Processing (GlobalSIP), pp. 156–160 (2017). https://doi.org/10.1109/GlobalSIP.2017.8308623

8. Fredembach, C., Süsstrunk, S.: Colouring the near-infrared. In: Proceedings IS T/SID 16th Color Imaging Conference (2008)

9. Helou, M.E., Sadeghipoor, Z., Susstrunk, S.: Correlation-based deblurring leveraging multispectral chromatic aberration in color and near-infrared joint acquisition. In: IEEE International Conference on Image Processing, pp. 1402–1406 (2017)

10. Jiang, J., Feng, X., Liu, F., Xu, Y., Huang, H.: Multi-spectral RGB-NIR image classification using double-channel CNN. IEEE Access **7**, 20607–20613 (2019). https://doi.org/10.1109/ACCESS.2019.2896128

11. Jin, S., Yu, B., Jing, M., Zhou, Y., Liang, J., Ji, R.: DarkVisionNet: low-light imaging via RGB-NIR fusion with deep inconsistency prior. CoRR abs/2303.06834 (2023). https://doi.org/10.48550/arXiv.2303.06834

12. Kumar, B.K.S.: Image fusion based on pixel significance using cross bilateral filter. Signal Image Video Process. **9**(5), 1193–1204 (2015)

13. Kwon, H.J., Lee, S.H.: Visible and near-infrared image acquisition and fusion for night surveillance. Chemosensors **9** (2021)

14. Li, S., Kang, X., Fang, L., Hu, J., Yin, H.: Pixel-level image fusion: a survey of the state of the art. Inf. Fusion **33**, 100–112 (2017)

15. Li, Z., Zheng, J., Zhu, Z., Yao, W., Wu, S.: Weighted guided image filtering. IEEE Trans. Image Process. **24**(1), 120–129 (2015)

16. Li, Z., Hu, H.M., Zhang, W., Pu, S., Li, B.: Spectrum characteristics preserved visible and near-infrared image fusion algorithm. IEEE Trans. Multimedia **23**, 306–319 (2020)

17. Lv, Y., Xiong, W., Zhang, X., Cui, Y.: Fusion-based correlation learning model for cross-modal remote sensing image retrieval. IEEE Geosci. Remote Sens. Lett. **19**, 1–5 (2022). https://doi.org/10.1109/LGRS.2021.3131592

18. Perconti, P.: Part task investigation of multispectral image fusion using gray scale and synthetic color night-vision sensor imagery for helicopter pilotage. In: Proceedings of SPIE - The International Society for Optical Engineering, vol. 3062, pp. 88–100 (1997)
19. Salamati, N., Süsstrunk, S.: Material-based object segmentation using near-infrared information. In: Proceedings 18th Color Imaging Conference (2010)
20. Sappa, A.D., Carvajal, J.A., Aguilera, C.A., Oliveira, M., Romero, D., Vintimilla, B.X.: Wavelet-based visible and infrared image fusion: a comparative study. Sensors 16(6), 861 (2016)
21. Sharma, V., Hardeberg, J., George, S.: RGB-NIR image enhancement by fusing bilateral and weighted least squares filters. J. Imaging Sci. Technol. 61 (2017). https://doi.org/10.2352/J.ImagingSci.Technol.2017.61.4.040409
22. Shutao, L., Xudong, K., Jianwen, H.: Image fusion with guided filtering. IEEE Trans. Image Process. 22(7), 2864–2875 (2013)
23. Son, C., Zhang, X.: Near-infrared fusion via color regularization for haze and color distortion removals. IEEE Trans. Circuits Syst. Video Technol. 28(11), 3111–3126 (2018). https://doi.org/10.1109/TCSVT.2017.2748150
24. Son, C.H., Zhang, X.P.: Near-infrared coloring via a contrast-preserving mapping model. IEEE Trans. Image Process. 26(11), 5381–5394 (2017)
25. Vanmali, A.V., Gadre, V.M.: Visible and NIR image fusion using weight-map-guided Laplacian-Gaussian pyramid for improving scene visibility. Sādhanā 42(7), 1063–1082 (2017)
26. Wang, Z., Simoncelli, E., Bovik, A.: Multiscale structural similarity for image quality assessment. In: The Thrity-Seventh Asilomar Conference on Signals, Systems Computers, vol. 2, pp. 1398–1402 (2003). https://doi.org/10.1109/ACSSC.2003.1292216
27. Winnemöller, H., Kyprianidis, J.E., Olsen, S.C.: XDoG: an extended difference-of-Gaussians compendium including advanced image stylization. Comput. Graph. 36(6), 740–753 (2012). 2011 Joint Symposium on Computational Aesthetics (CAe), Non-Photorealistic Animation and Rendering (NPAR), and Sketch-Based Interfaces and Modeling (SBIM)
28. Yan, Q., et al.: Cross-field joint image restoration via scale map. In: 2013 IEEE International Conference on Computer Vision, pp. 1537–1544, December 2013. https://doi.org/10.1109/ICCV.2013.194
29. Yang, W., Cai, J., Zheng, J.: Solving the out-of-gamut problem in image composition. In: 2010 IEEE International Conference on Image Processing, pp. 3977–3980 (2010). https://doi.org/10.1109/ICIP.2010.5650293
30. Zhang, Y.: Understanding image fusion. Photogram. Eng. Remote Sens. 70(6), 657–661 (2004)
31. Zheng, Y.: An overview of night vision colorization techniques using multispectral images: from color fusion to color mapping. In: International Conference on Audio, pp. 134–143 (2012)
32. Zheng, J., Jung, C., Yu, S.: Low light image enhancement by multispectral fusion of RGB and NIR images. In: 2020 IEEE International Conference on Image Processing (ICIP) (2020)

Data Mining

End-to-End Optimization of Quantization-Based Structure Learning and Interventional Next-Item Recommendation

Kairui Fu[1], Qiaowei Miao[1], Shengyu Zhang[1(✉)], Kun Kuang[1,4(✉)], and Fei Wu[1,2,3]

[1] Institute of Artificial Intelligence, Zhejiang University, Hangzhou, China
{fukairui.fkr,qiaoweimiao,sy_zhang,wufei}@zju.edu.cn
[2] Shanghai Institute for Advanced Study of Zhejiang University, Shanghai, China
[3] Shanghai AI Laboratory, Shanghai, China
[4] Key Laboratory for Corneal Diseases Research of Zhejiang Province, Hangzhou, China
kunkuang@zju.edu.cn

Abstract. With the development of deep learning, more and more related techniques are used in recommender system, making it more effective and reliable. However, due to the various distribution of real-time data, those deep-learning-based methods can merely learn the correlation between data rather than the actual causal effect, decreasing the performance of recommenders when a distribution shift occurs. Therefore, causal structure learning, which has been proposed to search for causal relationships between variables, is applied in recommender systems. However, existing methods assume that the recommender system is a non-interventional environment, making the causal graph learned not entirely correct. In this paper, we propose to decouple the recommender module and the causal module to consider the intervention of recommender system when building a causal graph. We utilize vector quantization to learn a cluster-level graph rather than an item-level graph to guarantee an acceptable training time. With an adjustable number of clusters, our model can adapt datasets of any size and be trained within a certain period. We conduct extensive experiments on both real-world and synthetic OOD datasets to demonstrate that our model is more effective than other state-of-the-art sequential recommenders.

Keywords: Sequential recommendation · Causal structure learning · Vector quantization

1 Introduction

Due to the extraordinary ability of sequential recommendation to model user's long and short-term interests, many sequential recommenders [10,13,17,29,32, 33] have been proposed to dynamically and accurately capture user preferences, achieving remarkable success in many scenes.

© The Author(s), under exclusive license to Springer Nature Singapore Pte Ltd. 2024
L. Fang et al. (Eds.): CICAI 2023, LNAI 14473, pp. 415–429, 2024.
https://doi.org/10.1007/978-981-99-8850-1_34

Despite their astonishing performance, they all assume that the datasets are independent and identically distributed, while the actual scenarios are pretty different, reducing the effectiveness of these methods. We figure out that this is because the relation learned is just correlation, not causality. [6] As exampled in Fig. 1(d), users in the training set are mostly programmers who always purchase *office supplies*, *plaid shirts*, and *digital gadgets*. In contrast, users in the validation set contain those addicted to *games*. For these programmers who bought a *printer* before, he would buy a *ink cartridge* for the *printer*, and this is the expected causal relation. However, some sequential recommenders may tend to attribute the purchase of *ink cartridges* to the purchase of the *mouse*, then they will learn a spurious relation. Thus they will recommend the *ink cartridge* due to the *mouse* in history to those internet addiction teenagers, leading to a fallacious recommendation.

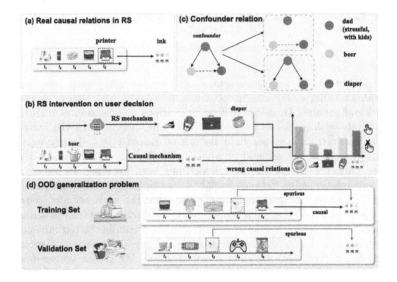

Fig. 1. (a) real causal relations in recommender systems. (b) causal structure learning under the intervention of recommender system. (c) confounder relations during causal structure learning. (d) spurious relationship in out-of-distribution environments.

Towards this end, we propose to learn the underlying causal graph, which reveals the data generation mechanism [2] and will always remain invariant in different environments [24]. However, applying causal structure learning in recommender system presents three main challenges: **i)** As illustrated in Fig. 1(b), user's mind would be changed due to the item list provided by recommender, prompting him to click the *diaper* rather than the *ink* he wishes to purchase initially. That is, the recommender intervention will change the user's mind and lead to a wrong causal graph where we try to model causal relations between origin interactions and *diaper*. **ii)** As shown in Fig. 1(c), the reason for this phenomenon is that the historical item *beer* and the target item *diaper* are both associated with a confounder C. Those newly married dads with child would buy *beer* and *diaper* simultaneously, thus constituting a confounder, making *beer* and *diaper* form a confounder relation, then changing user's mind. Our model must capture those relations properly. **iii)** We need to maintain massive causal functions whose quantity is equal to the number of items, denoted as n, whose time complexity is $O(n)$, and it will generate huge overhead for some e-commerce recommender systems with more than ten billion items. Apart from this, due to the long-tail item distribution in recommender, most items only appear a few times during user interaction sequences, making it a big problem to train satisfactory causal functions.

In our paper, we propose an end-to-end optimization of quantization-based structure learning and interventional next-item recommendation to address the abovementioned problems. For the first two challenges, we decouple the causal module and the sequential recommender to use the causal module to score if the user is not affected by the recommender else the recommendation module, thereby eliminating the effect of the intervention of recommenders and benefiting from the powerful sequential modeling capabilities of recommenders to learn the confounder relations when the causal relations are weak as exampled in Fig. 1(c). Another core idea for the third challenge in our paper is taking advantage of vector quantization [18] to build a cluster-level graph rather than the origin item-level graph, from which our model can: **i)** get a more beneficial alternative than the metadata in the dataset for training. **ii)** make the number of causal functions maintained adjustable with an adjustable number of meta-items, thereby decreasing time complexity from $O(n)$ above to $O(k)$ where $k \ll n$. **iii)** get enough data to train because each cluster corresponds to multiple items.

Overall, the main contributions of our paper are summarized below:

- We analyze the inconsistent distribution of users in recommender system and the difficulty in causal structure learning accompanied by the intervention of recommender system.
- We propose an effective method for end-to-end optimization of quantization-based structure learning and interventional next-item recommendation, improving the performance of the recommender.
- We conduct extensive experiments on three real-world datasets and their corresponding synthetic OOD datasets. The comparison with other models validates the effectiveness of our model.

2   Related Works

Sequential Recommendation. Owing to the effectiveness of capturing dynamic user preference through history interaction, various sequential recommendation methods have been proposed in industrial and research fields. Traditional methods include sequential pattern-based [9,20] and Markov chain-based models [7]. To learn complicated relations and long-term interests, deep learning methods are widely used to capture users' long and short-term interests.

RNN-based methods [10] leverages gate recurrent unit to capture the long-term dependencies in user interactions. Since each item in the historical sequence influences the target differently, some models [13,29,31] start exploiting the attention mechanism [19] in recommenders. CNN-based methods, like Caser and PAUP, have also been investigated to consider more sequential patterns [17,33]. Meanwhile, causal inference has also been used to improve the interpretability and reduce different kinds of bias [21–23,25–28].

Causal Structure Learning. Causal structure learning plays a vital role in understanding the underlying data generating process while learning from observational data is not easy. Existing methods mainly consist of two parts: score-based and constraint-based methods. The constraint-based method [12] will first utilize the independence test, learn the undirected graph of the causal relationship between variables, and then determine the direction of each causal edge based on the collision structure. But this method is hard to learn the directions of all edges in the causal graph, and only a set of Markov equivalence classes can be obtained in the end. The score-based method assigns a score to each edge of the causal graph, maximizing the obtained score while ensuring the directed acyclic property of the graph. Typical models include Notears [30] and graph-based approach [16], both solving this problem by converting it to a constraint continuous-optimization problem.

3   Methodology

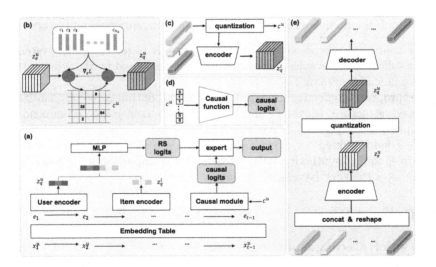

Fig. 2. The structure diagram of our method. (a): The overall architecture of the model. (b): Quantization module in the model. (c): Implementation process of the item encoder. (d): Implementation of the causal module. (e): Implementation process of user encoder

In this section, we will first give a brief problem formulation of sequential recommendation and then introduce our proposed method in detail. The model we propose is shown in Fig. 2:

3.1   Problem Formulation

In the setting of sequential recommendation, suppose we have an item set $I = \{i_1, i_2, ..., i_n\}$ and a user set $U = \{u_1, u_2, ..., u_m\}$. Our task is to predict the next clicked item $x_t \in I$ correctly for each user $u_i \in U$ with interaction sequence $(x_1, x_2, ..., x_{t-1})$ where $x_i \in I$ for any $i \in [1, t-1]$. Formally, the parameter θ in the model f is optimized by minimizing the following function:

$$L(\theta) = \sum_{i=1}^{i=m} \sum_{j=1}^{j=t-1} f(x_t | x_1, x_2, ..., x_{t-1}; \theta) \tag{1}$$

3.2   Causal Structure Learning in Recommendation

Due to decoupling the two modules, we should carefully select the causal or recommender module as the scoring source for each item. Because the intervention in recommender system is quite different from other fields like medical diagnosis, where the outcome of the intervention can be inferred from the patient's condition, we don't know whether the user is intervened successfully or not. The user will anyway click an item, and we have no idea about the source of the clicked item. In causal structure learning, a node given its parent nodes does not change and will always remain unchanged in the causal mechanism. Under this intuition, we choose to use causal mechanism if there is any parent node of the target node in the history interactions. We get a relatively good result from this approach compared to simply constant weighting shown in Sect. 4.3.

For each item x in the item set I, there is exactly one cluster c corresponding to it. Then the user interaction can be rewritten as $(c_1^u, c_2^u, ..., c_{t-1}^u)$, c_i^u is the corresponding clusters of x_i for each $i \in [1, t-1]$. When predicting the score of cluster c', we first filter out those less associated clusters in the sequence, that is, $(C \odot A')$, where C is a multi-hot vector of $(c_1^u, c_2^u, ..., c_{t-1}^u)$, c_i^u with length N_c. For each cluster, we train a causal function using a multi-layer perceptron, which accepts $(C \odot A')$ as input and outputs the predicted score of the cluster given its parents in the causal graph. Thus the ranking loss can be described as follows:

$$L_{ranking} = \sum_{i=1}^{i=m} \sum_{j=1}^{j=t-1} [p(x_t | x_1, x_2, ..., x_{t-1})^R \cdot f_{x_t} (\overrightarrow{C} \odot A_{c_u^t})^{1-R}] \tag{2}$$

where R describes whether there exists any parent node in history and is determined by the sample edges and the cluster that the target item belongs to.

3.3   Quantization-Based Structure Learning

In order to get a quantity adjustable and better input, we propose to learn the corresponding cluster for each item in the training phase and use the learned clusters as input for the causal module. We are inspired by VQ-VAE [18], which takes advantage of quantization to build an end-to-end discrete latent VAE model. By adding an item-quantization part, that is, for each item embedding i_e, find the nearest discrete latent representation c_i of it, we successfully get the meta-item and use it as the input of the causal part. During training, the meta-item of each item will gradually reach the optimum, and the causal function can then be optimized. Considering that the user embedding u may benefit from quantization, we also perform quantization for each user embedding i_u. The quantization process can be described as follows:

$$p(i = k|e) = \begin{cases} 1 & i = argmin_i \; dist(c_i, e) \\ 0 & otherwise \end{cases} \tag{3}$$

After applying quantization, we get latent representations c_i and c_u for each item and user representation, respectively. Then we concatenate all the three embeddings above and get the final representation e_{ui} for the feed-forward network.

3.4   End-to-End Optimization

Optimization of the Quantization Part. Although we have adopted vector quantization to do clustering ourselves, there are still deficiencies that gradients from e_{ui} can only backpropagate to the codebook while the item and user embeddings receive nothing useful, not conducive to parameter updates in the model. We fix this problem with the straight-through estimator used in the original paper, namely, adjust the concatenation embeddings c_i and c_u to propagate the gradient to the item embedding. Take the item embedding i_e as an example, we replace c_i with c_i':

$$c_i' = sg[c_i - i_e] + i_e \tag{4}$$

where sg stands for the stop-gradient method. Because the item embedding i_e is close to the latent representation c_i in the embedding space, we can simultaneously optimize the codebook by minimizing the distance between the item embedding and the latent representations. Thus, we get an extra objective loss:

$$L_{quantization} = \|sg[c_i'] - c_i\|^2 + \beta \cdot \|sg[c_i] - c_i'\|^2 \tag{5}$$

the second part is used to prevent items from fluctuating between each cluster, providing a stable input for the causal module.

Optimization of the Causal Module. Because our method decouples causal structure learning and sequential recommender, getting the causal graph through a single activation function is impractical. In that case, some causal functions won't be updated because the parameters in the graph are so small, and the recommender module results will be used to rate all items.

Therefore, we propose to sample each value in the causal graph G to overcome this problem and give each causal function a chance to update during training. For each edge A_{ij}, we sample it with probability p_{ij}:

$$A_{ij} = \begin{cases} 1 & Bernoulli(p_{ij}) = 1 \\ 0 & otherwise \end{cases} \tag{6}$$

Nevertheless, we can notice the sample operation is non-differential, and the graph can never be updated. To address this challenge, we utilize the Gumbel-Softmax trick and Straight-Through estimation method used in GDAS [4]:

$$A_{ij} = \mathbb{I}(\sigma(s + p_{ij}) \geq 0.5) + \sigma(s + p_{ij}) - sg[\sigma(s + p_{ij})] \tag{7}$$

where $\mathbb{I}$ is indicator function and σ is the sigmoid function. s is an independent sample from the standard Logistic distribution.

As for the directed acyclic graph constraints, we adopt the augmented Lagrangian in Notears [30] with a dual ascent method:

$$L_{DAG} = \frac{\rho}{2}|h(G)|^2 + \alpha h(G) \tag{8}$$

Until now, we have fixed all the optimization problems in our model. Then the log-likelihood loss function can be written as:

$$\begin{aligned} L &= L_{ranking} + L_{quantization} + L_{DAG} \\ &= \sum_{i=1}^{i=m} \sum_{j=1}^{j=t-1} [p(x_t|x_1, x_2, ..., x_{t-1})^R \cdot f_{x_t}(\boldsymbol{C} \odot A')^{1-R}] + \\ &\quad \|sg[c_i'] - c_i\|^2 + \beta \cdot \|sg[c_i] - c_i'\|^2 + \\ &\quad \lambda \|G\|^2 + \frac{\rho}{2}|h(G)|^2 + \alpha h(G) \end{aligned} \tag{9}$$

4 Experiments

To demonstrate the effectiveness of our method, we compare it with some sequential recommenders on three real-world datasets and corresponding synthetic OOD datasets. **All results are the average of five experiments.**

4.1 Experimental Setup

Datasets. We conduct experiments on three state-of-art benchmarks **Movielens1M**[1], **Netflix**[2] and **Amazon-Music**[3] and construct corresponding OOD datasets with the paradigm of DESMIL [15].

---

[1] https://grouplens.org/datasets/movielens/1m/.
[2] https://www.kaggle.com/code/laowingkin/netflix-movie-recommendation.
[3] https://nijianmo.github.io/amazon/index.html.

Baselines. For the implementation of our method, we choose YoutubeDNN [3] as the base model. We select **YoutubeDNN** [3], **Caser** [17], **AttRec** [29], **PAUP** [33], **GRU4Rec** [10], **NeuMF** [8], **SASRec** [13] and **FMLP-Rec** [32] as baselines.

Evaluation Metrics. The three evaluation metrics we used are the same as the framework in ComiRec [1]: Recall, Hit Rate, and NDCG. The higher the scores of the three indicators, the better the effect of the recommenders.
More details about the settings can be found in Appendix A.

4.2 Experiments Results

The results are displayed in Table 1, from which we can conclude that our model outperforms other models on almost all metrics. The metric Recall on Amazon is slightly worse than Caser. However, we find that our model is way ahead of Caser and other models on NDCG, a more convincing metric that still proves the effectiveness of our model. Regardless of the dataset, our model constantly significantly improved over the base model YoutubeDNN. Not surprisingly, among the other baselines, these models with self-attention mechanisms perform better in all three datasets compared to those without, which in line with that attention mechanism generalizes well in most deep learning tasks [11,19].

Table 1. Comparative performance between our model and the other baselines. We use bold font to denote the best-performing model and underline the next-best model.

Datasets	Movielens			Netflix			Amazon		
Metric	Recall	NDCG	Hit	Recall	NDCG	Hit	Recall	NDCG	Hit
YoutubeDNN	0.0878	0.1564	0.6510	0.2848	0.2241	0.5649	0.4100	0.4512	0.8536
GRU4Rec	0.0912	0.1440	0.6508	0.2895	0.1736	0.5827	0.2618	0.2246	0.5772
NeuMF	0.07927	0.1446	0.6268	0.2362	0.1767	0.4677	0.2208	0.2360	0.4684
SASRec	0.0909	0.1521	0.6661	0.3028	0.2287	0.6012	0.3494	0.3395	0.7382
Caser	0.0995	0.1474	0.6987	0.4818	0.3296	0.9550	**0.4276**	0.3751	0.9219
AttRec	0.0952	0.1169	0.6225	0.4460	0.3021	0.8843	0.4110	0.3502	0.8839
PAUP	0.0934	0.1644	0.6919	0.2804	0.2132	0.5591	0.3086	0.2603	0.6422
FMLP-Rec	0.0904	0.1533	0.6715	0.2698	0.2043	0.5378	0.2930	0.2332	0.6065
ours	**0.1051**	**0.1773**	**0.7098**	**0.4921**	**0.5713**	**0.9801**	0.4239	**0.5212**	**0.9556**
Improv	19.76%	13.40%	9.03%	72.78%	154.93%	73.51%	3.40%	15.50%	1.95%

4.3 Parameter Analysis

Influence of the Cluster Num. To further demonstrate the validity of the causal module in our model, we adjust the cluster num N_c used in our model. Logically, suppose we reduce the value to less than a certain degree. In that case, the performance between ours and the base model YoutubeDNN will be approximately 0 because, in that case the clustering information of the model will be rough, making the causal module invalid. We study its influence through tuning N_c in the range of [1, 2, 4, 8, 16, 32, 64, 128] and present the result in Fig. 3. We can conclude that our model performs almost identically to the base model when N_c equals 1. And the performance keeps increasing when we increase the value until a certain threshold is reached.

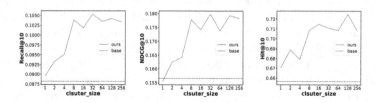

Fig. 3. Influence of the hyperparameter N_c on the model performance.

Influence of the Dynamic Selection. In this section, we replace this dynamic allocation with constant weighting to validate the necessity of our selective method mentioned in Sect. 3.2. Suppose we assign w_{RS} for recommendation module and w_{causal} for causal module, where $w_{RS} + w_{causal} = 1$. We tune the w_{RS} in the range of [0.25, 0.5, 0.75] and conduct experiments on Netflix and Amazon. We present the results in Fig. 4. For both datasets, our adaptive method can achieve the best performance than those with constant weighting. This agrees with our above analysis. By making choices adaptively, our model can better make better use of those strong causal relations and utilize the powerful sequential prediction capability when the causal relation is small.

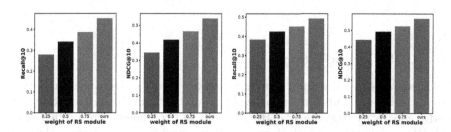

Fig. 4. performance comparison between our adaptive allocation strategy model and those with constant weighting.left panel: metrics comparison on Amazon dataset. right panel: metrics comparison on Netflix dataset.

4.4   Ablation Study

Since some datasets have their own category information, it is critical to conduct an ablation study to demonstrate the effectiveness of learned cluster information and the necessity of combining causal structure learning and recommender. The ablated models are as follows: **i) w.o. (without) causal** removes the causal module from our model, degenerating into the base model YoutubeDNN. **ii) w.o. RS** removes recommender from our model and will give the same logits to those items belonging to the same categories. **iii) w.o. quantization** removes vector quantization and uses the origin metadata as input of the causal module.

Relevant results are shown in Table 2, from which we can draw the following conclusions: **i)** Combining causal structure learning and recommendation is necessary for making the recommender works better, our model has relatively large improvements over models that only use a single module. **ii)** Simply using those semantic prior, namely, the original category information as input won't always improve our model. It can be inferred from the comparison between the base model and *w.o. quantization*, which makes use of the knowledge in the original dataset but gets worse results.

Table 2. Ablation studies on Movielens and Amazon.

Datasets	Movielens			Amazon		
Metric	Recall	NDCG	Hit	Recall	NDCG	Hit
w.o. causal	0.0878	0.1563	0.6510	0.4100	0.4512	0.8536
w.o. RS	0.0112	0.0232	0.1967	0.0100	0.0068	0.0267
w.o. quantization	0.0837	0.1289	0.6444	0.4096	0.4498	0.8536
ours	0.1051	0.1773	0.709	0.4239	0.5212	0.9556

4.5   OOD Generalization

In the above sections, we have demonstrated our model's effectiveness and understood the hyperparameter's influence by adjusting them through ablation study and comparative experiments. However, these experiments are carried out in the IID environment, which does not always hold in real scenarios. Hence we further investigate the OOD dataset to verify our model's stability under out-of-distribution environments. We use the same baselines and OOD datasets described in Sect. 4.1, and the results are shown in Table 3, from which we can observe that some methods, such as Caser and AttRec drop a lot in OOD environment while our model still gets the best results, proving the stability of our method.

Table 3. Comparative performance on OOD datasets between our model and the other baselines. We use the same symbols as in Table 1

Datasets	Movielens			Netflix		
Metric	Recall	NDCG	Hit	Recall	NDCG	Hit
YoutubeDNN	0.0931	0.1582	0.6634	0.3056	0.2354	0.5515
GRU4Rec	0.0814	0.1347	0.6114	0.1830	0.1053	0.3625
NeuMF	0.07911	0.1392	0.6079	0.2363	0.1737	0.4485
SASRec	0.0995	0.1552	0.6740	<u>0.3375</u>	<u>0.2430</u>	<u>0.5814</u>
Caser	0.0522	0.0932	0.490	0.1761	0.1185	0.3481
AttRec	0.0311	0.0584	0.3763	0.1038	0.0588	0.2038
PAUP	<u>0.0979</u>	<u>0.1662</u>	<u>0.6924</u>	0.2814	0.2131	0.5485
FMLP-Rec	0.0963	0.1594	0.6879	0.2672	0.1996	0.5221
ours	**0.1115**	**0.1824**	**0.7190**	**0.4470**	**0.4871**	**0.8224**
Improv	19.76%	15.30%	8.38%	46.27%	106.92%	49.12%

5   Conclusion

In our paper, we propose an end-to-end optimization of quantization-based structure learning and interventional next-item recommendation, which not only reconstructs the underlying causal graph in an interventional environment caused by RS but also adaptively allocate logits for each target item according to its parent node in the causal graph. Moreover, with an adjustable hyperparameter N_c, the time consumption can be guaranteed regardless of the size of the dataset. Extensive experiments conducted on three benchmark datasets and corresponding synthetic OOD datasets show that our method outperforms other sequential models by a large margin in all three metrics, validating the effectiveness and efficiency of our model. Additional parameter analysis and ablation study also prove the rationality of our method.

While an item exactly corresponds to a cluster, it can be extend to a more realistic scene where an item corresponds to many clusters with different weights. The distance between items and meta-items in the embedding space can be used as the weight criterion. We leave this as a future work to better improve the effect of the model.

Acknowledgement. This work was supported in part by National Natural Science Foundation of China (62006207, U20A20387), Young Elite Scientists Sponsorship Program by CAST (2021QNRC001), Zhejiang Province Natural Science Foundation (LQ21F020020), and the Fundamental Research Funds for the Central Universities (226-2022-00142, 226-2022-00051).

A   Appendix

A.1   Experimental Setup

Datasets. We conduct experiments based on the following benchmark datasets, of which the statistics are shown in Table 4:

- **Movielens-1M**[4] contains anonymous ratings of movies made by MovieLens users who joined MovieLens in 2000. Besides, it also includes the metadata of each movie, such as the categories it belongs to.
- **Amazon-Music**[5] is an e-commerce dataset collected from Amazon.com, which also includes the category information of a product.
- **Netflix**[6] is another movie rating file constructed to support participants in the Netflix Prize. In this experiment, We use the preprocessed dataset provided in NATR [5].

In order to keep dataset quality, We discard items with fewer than 20 related appearances, while for user filtering, we adopt 5-core settings for Amazon and Netflix and 20-core settings for Movielens due to their different sparsity.

For the three datasets above, we sort the user-item interactions in chronological order and divide the training and testing sets according to the ratio of 8:2. In our experiments, the validation set is consistent with the test set. For each interaction, We regard those feedback with positive ratings as positive.

OOD Datasets. Following the data splitting paradigm of DESMIL [15], we build the OOD datasets by adjusting the distribution of user groups in the training set and test set. We randomly select a user and calculate the Jaccard similarity[7] between other users and the selected user. Then we choose 80% users with the smallest similarity as the training set and use the whole dataset for testing, where the training set and testing set contain different user groups.

Table 4. Statistics of the datasets.

Dataset	#Users	#Items	#Interactions	#SeqLen	#Sparsity
Movielens	6,040	3,012	994,852	164.71	94.52%
Netflix	14,630	5,569	166,836	11.40	99.79%
Amazon	9,923	8,902	96,505	11.58	99.89%

Baselines. For the implementation of our method, we choose YoutubeDNN [3] as the base model, which is a classic deep learning recommendation system. Since our model is a sequential recommendation model, we ignore the graph

---

[4] https://grouplens.org/datasets/movielens/1m/.

[5] https://nijianmo.github.io/amazon/index.html.

[6] https://www.kaggle.com/code/laowingkin/netflix-movie-recommendation.

[7] https://www.learndatasci.com/glossary/jaccard-similarity/.

recommendation model and focus on the sequential recommendation model. As for those collaborative filtering (CF) recommendation models, we adjust them to apply the historical sequence to the model. The compared models are shown as the following:

- **YoutubeDNN** [3]. As one of the industry's most commonly used recommender systems, it represents each user with his historical interaction data and combines them to get the final predictive score.
- **GRU4Rec** [10]. GRU4Rec is a representative recommendation model in session based recommendation which adopts recurrent neural networks to train the relationship between target items and item sequences.
- **NeuMF** [8]. NeuMF combines traditional matrix decomposition and multilayer perceptron to extract both low- and high-dimensional features simultaneously.
- **SASRec** [13]. SASRec applies self-attention mechanisms in sequential recommendation to help learn more valuable information.
- **Caser** [17]. Caser is a state-of-the-art model that utilizes vertical and horizontal convolutional networks to extract short-term preferences from user interaction sequences.
- **AttRec** [29]. Similar to SASRec, AttRec makes use of self-attention mechanisms to capture long-term preference. Moreover, it uses metric learning to model the consequences of short-term interests versus long-term preferences.
- **PAUP** [33]. PAUP proposes a down-sampling convolution module and an unsymmetrical positional encoding strategy to effectively and efficiently capture both short- and long-term patterns.
- **FMLP-Rec** [32]. FMLP-Rec makes use of filtering algorithms in signal processing instead of the traditional transformer to relieve the noise in the original dataset.

Evaluation Metrics. The three evaluation metrics we used are the same as the framework in ComiRec [1]. In recommendation system, accuracy, that is, whether what the user wants to see is correctly recommended to the user, is crucial. Thus we use Recall and Hit Rate to evaluate the accuracy of a model. Another metric used in our experiment is NDCG(Normalized Discounted Cumulative Gain), which pays more attention to the ratings in the recommendation list of items desired by users and is more convincing than recall. The higher the scores of the three indicators, the better the effect of the recommendation model.

Implementation Details. For all the models mentioned above, we use Adam [14] as the optimizer and 0.001 as the learning rate. All of them are implemented with an item embedding with size $d = 64$. The number of horizontal and vertical convolution filters are 4 and 16 in Caser, respectively. For each sequence in Caser, AttRec, and SASRec, we randomly sample 10 items not interacted with by the user as negative samples. While for GRU4Rec, we follow the method used in the original paper, namely, using other items in the same batch except for the target item as negative samples. For the NeuMF baseline, we create an embedding for each user with the history of interactions over time to adapt sequential recommendations.

References

1. Cen, Y., Zhang, J., Zou, X., Zhou, C., Yang, H., Tang, J.: Controllable multi-interest framework for recommendation. In: Proceedings of the 26th ACM SIGKDD International Conference on Knowledge Discovery & Data Mining, pp. 2942–2951 (2020)
2. Chen, W., Wu, Y., Cai, R., Chen, Y., Hao, Z.: CCSL: a causal structure learning method from multiple unknown environments. arXiv preprint arXiv:2111.09666 (2021)
3. Covington, P., Adams, J., Sargin, E.: Deep neural networks for youtube recommendations. In: Proceedings of the 10th ACM Conference on Recommender Systems, pp. 191–198 (2016)
4. Dong, X., Yang, Y.: Searching for a robust neural architecture in four GPU hours. In: Proceedings of the IEEE/CVF Conference on Computer Vision and Pattern Recognition, pp. 1761–1770 (2019)
5. Gao, C., et al.: Cross-domain recommendation with bridge-item embeddings. ACM Trans. Knowl. Discov. Data (TKDD) **16**(1), 1–23 (2021)
6. Gao, C., Zheng, Y., Wang, W., Feng, F., He, X., Li, Y.: Causal inference in recommender systems: a survey and future directions. arXiv preprint arXiv:2208.12397 (2022)
7. He, R., Kang, W.C., McAuley, J.J., et al.: Translation-based recommendation: a scalable method for modeling sequential behavior. In: IJCAI, pp. 5264–5268 (2018)
8. He, X., Liao, L., Zhang, H., Nie, L., Hu, X., Chua, T.S.: Neural collaborative filtering. In: Proceedings of the 26th International Conference on World Wide Web, pp. 173–182 (2017)
9. Herawan, T., Noraziah, A., Abdullah, Z., Deris, M.M., Abawajy, J.H.: IPMA: indirect patterns mining algorithm. In: Advanced Methods for Computational Collective Intelligence, vol. 285, pp. 159–166 (2013)
10. Hidasi, B., Karatzoglou, A., Baltrunas, L., Tikk, D.: Session-based recommendations with recurrent neural networks. arXiv preprint arXiv:1511.06939 (2015)
11. Hu, J., Shen, L., Sun, G.: Squeeze-and-excitation networks. In: Proceedings of the IEEE Conference on Computer Vision and Pattern Recognition, pp. 7132–7141 (2018)
12. Kalisch, M., Bühlman, P.: Estimating high-dimensional directed acyclic graphs with the PC-algorithm. J. Mach. Learn. Res. **8**(3) (2007)
13. Kang, W.C., McAuley, J.: Self-attentive sequential recommendation. In: 2018 IEEE International Conference on Data Mining (ICDM), pp. 197–206. IEEE (2018)
14. Kingma, D.P., Ba, J.: Adam: a method for stochastic optimization. arXiv preprint arXiv:1412.6980 (2014)
15. Liu, Q., Liu, Z., Zhu, Z., Wu, S., Wang, L.: Deep stable multi-interest learning for out-of-distribution sequential recommendation. arXiv preprint arXiv:2304.05615 (2023)
16. Ng, I., Zhu, S., Chen, Z., Fang, Z.: A graph autoencoder approach to causal structure learning. arXiv preprint arXiv:1911.07420 (2019)
17. Tang, J., Wang, K.: Personalized top-n sequential recommendation via convolutional sequence embedding. In: Proceedings of the Eleventh ACM International Conference on Web Search and Data Mining, pp. 565–573 (2018)
18. Van Den Oord, A., Vinyals, O., et al.: Neural discrete representation learning. In: Advances in Neural Information Processing Systems, vol. 30 (2017)

19. Vaswani, A., et al.: Attention is all you need. In: Advances in Neural Information Processing Systems, vol. 30 (2017)
20. Wang, S., Cao, L.: Inferring implicit rules by learning explicit and hidden item dependency. IEEE Trans. Syst. Man Cybern. Syst. **50**(3), 935–946 (2017)
21. Wang, X., Zhang, R., Sun, Y., Qi, J.: Doubly robust joint learning for recommendation on data missing not at random. In: International Conference on Machine Learning, pp. 6638–6647. PMLR (2019)
22. Wang, Z., Chen, X., Dong, Z., Dai, Q., Wen, J.R.: Sequential recommendation with causal behavior discovery. arXiv preprint arXiv:2204.00216 (2022)
23. Xu, S., et al.: Causal structure learning with recommendation system. arXiv preprint arXiv:2210.10256 (2022)
24. Zhang, K., Glymour, M.R.: Unmixing for causal inference: thoughts on mccaffrey and danks. Br. J. Philos. Sci. (2020)
25. Zhang, S., et al.: Personalized latent structure learning for recommendation. IEEE Trans. Pattern Anal. Mach. Intell. (2023)
26. Zhang, S., et al.: Video-audio domain generalization via confounder disentanglement. In: Proceedings of the AAAI Conference on Artificial Intelligence, vol. 37, pp. 15322–15330 (2023)
27. Zhang, S., et al.: Devlbert: learning deconfounded visio-linguistic representations. In: Proceedings of the 28th ACM International Conference on Multimedia, pp. 4373–4382 (2020)
28. Zhang, S., Yao, D., Zhao, Z., Chua, T.S., Wu, F.: Causerec: counterfactual user sequence synthesis for sequential recommendation. In: Proceedings of the 44th International ACM SIGIR Conference on Research and Development in Information Retrieval, pp. 367–377 (2021)
29. Zhang, S., Tay, Y., Yao, L., Sun, A.: Next item recommendation with self-attention. arXiv preprint arXiv:1808.06414 (2018)
30. Zheng, X., Aragam, B., Ravikumar, P.K., Xing, E.P.: DAGs with no tears: continuous optimization for structure learning. In: Advances in Neural Information Processing Systems, vol. 31 (2018)
31. Zhou, G., et al.: Deep interest network for click-through rate prediction. In: Proceedings of the 24th ACM SIGKDD International Conference on Knowledge Discovery & Data Mining, pp. 1059–1068 (2018)
32. Zhou, K., Yu, H., Zhao, W.X., Wen, J.R.: Filter-enhanced MLP is all you need for sequential recommendation. In: Proceedings of the ACM Web Conference 2022, pp. 2388–2399 (2022)
33. Zhu, Y., Huang, B., Jiang, S., Yang, M., Yang, Y., Zhong, W.: Progressive self-attention network with unsymmetrical positional encoding for sequential recommendation. In: Proceedings of the 45th International ACM SIGIR Conference on Research and Development in Information Retrieval, pp. 2029–2033 (2022)

Multi-trends Enhanced Dynamic Micro-video Recommendation

Yujie Lu[1], Yingxuan Huang[2], Shengyu Zhang[3(✉)], Wei Han[4], Hui Chen[4],
Wenyan Fan[3], Jiangliang Lai[5], Zhou Zhao[3(✉)], and Fei Wu[3]

[1] University of California, Santa Barbara, USA
[2] The University of Hong Kong, Pokfulam, Hong Kong
[3] Zhejiang University, Hangzhou, China
zhaozhou@zju.edu.cn
[4] Singapore University of Technology and Design, Singapore, Singapore
[5] The Information Center of the Supreme People's Court of the People's Republic of China, Beijing, China

Abstract. The explosively generated micro-videos on content sharing platforms call for recommender systems to permit personalized micro-video discovery with ease. Recent advances in micro-video recommendation have achieved remarkable performance in mining users' current preference based on historical behaviors. However, most of them neglect the dynamic and time-evolving nature of users' preference, and the prediction on future micro-videos with historically mined preference may deteriorate the effectiveness of recommender systems. In this paper, we devise the DMR framework, which comprises: 1) the implicit user network module which identifies sequence fragments from other users with similar interests and extracts the sequence fragments that are chronologically behind the identified fragments; 2) the multi-trend routing module which assigns each extracted sequence fragment into a trend group and update the corresponding trend vector; 3) the history-future trend prediction module jointly uses the history preference vectors and future trend vectors to yield the final click-through-rate. We validate the effectiveness of DMR over multiple state-of-the-art micro-video recommenders on two publicly available real-world datasets. Relatively extensive analysis further demonstrate the superiority of modeling dynamic multi-trend for micro-video recommendation.

Keywords: Micro-video Recommendation · Multi-trend Routing · Personalization

1 Introduction

In recent years, the amount of searchable micro-videos has increased dramatically and exacerbated the need for recommender systems that can effectively mine users' preference and identify potentially interested micro-videos in a personalized manner. Due to the powerful representation learning capacity, the rapid

L. Fang et al. (Eds.): CICAI 2023, LNAI 14473, pp. 430–441, 2024.
https://doi.org/10.1007/978-981-99-8850-1_35

development of deep learning techniques has nourished the research field of recommendation [11,16]. Such a development also gives rise to diverse models for video recommendation, which can be roughly categorized to collaborative filtering [2,13], content-based filtering [8,10,18,19,23], and hybrid ones [5,6,22].

Recent years have witnessed much progress to confront the above challenges in this vein. THACIL [7] employs temporal block splitting and hierarchical multi-head attention to model diverse interests across blocks. ALPINE [15] models users' dynamic interests by constructing temporal behavior graph and devising the temporal graph-based LSTM. MTIN [14] considers personalized importance decay over time and diverse interests using item-level temporal mask and group routing mechanism, individually. In spite of the great advances of these works, we argue that solely modeling the historical behaviors deteriorates the capacity of user modeling capturing *diverse* and *dynamic* users' interests. For example, MTIN [14] assigns historically interacted items to one of six interest groups and accordingly updates the six interest vectors. Since users' interests are by nature dynamic, the interests learned from the logged data might be out-of-date or at least limited to the history, falling short to recommend fresh items and hurting the recommendation diversity. Therefore, capturing dynamic interest trends based on (but not limited to) historical items can be an indispensable function for high-quality recommender systems.

To this end, DMR framework makes predictions based on both the history interests implied by the historical behaviors as well as multi-trends implied in similar users, which helps to capture even more diverse and dynamic interests compared with existing micro-video recommenders. We validate the effectiveness of DMR on micro-video recommendation benchmarks. The substantial improvement over state-of-the-art comparison methods and in-depth model analysis demonstrate the superiority of modeling multi-trend for micro-video recommendation.

2   Our Approach

In this section, we first formulate the micro-video recommendation problem, and then introduce the proposed framework in detail. As illustrated in Fig. 1, our proposed DMR framework for dynamic micro-video recommendation mainly comprises of three modules: 1) Pearson Correlation Coefficient enhanced implicit user network module; 2) A history-future multi-trend joint routing module; 3) A multi-level time-aware attention module.

2.1   Problem Formulation

In a typical micro-video recommendation scenario, we have a set of users and a set of micro-videos, which can be denoted as $U = \{u_1, u_2, u_3, ..., u_{|U|}\}$ and $V = \{v_1, v_2, v_3, ..., v_{|V|}\}$ respectively. Let $I_u = \{x_1^u, x_2^u, ..., I_{|I_u|}^u\}$ represent the sequence of interacted micro-videos $x \in I_u$ of user $u \in U$, which is sorted in a chronological order according to the timestamp of each interaction, and x_t^u

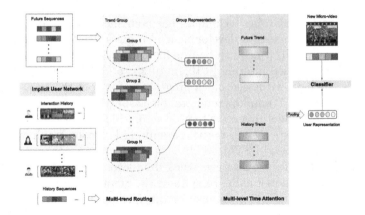

Fig. 1. Network Architecture of DMR. DMR is composed of an implicit user network module, a multi-trend routing module, a multi-level time attention layer and a prediction layer.

denote the micro-video that the user u has interacted with at timestamp t. The interaction sequence I_u is split into I_+ and I_- which represent the micro-videos clicked by the user and the ones not clicked respectively. Given the user's historical micro-video interaction behaviors, the investigated goal of the micro-video recommendation task in this paper is to predict the probability that the new candidate micro-video will be clicked by user u.

To model diverse user preferences dynamically, DMR learns a function f for mapping history trend set T_u^h and future trend set T_u^f into user representations, which can be formulated as $\overrightarrow{e_u} = f(T_u^h, T_u^f)$, where $\overrightarrow{e_u} \in \mathbb{R}^{d \times 1}$ denotes the representation vector of user u, d the dimension. Besides, the representation vector of target micro-video i is obtained by an embedding function g as $\overrightarrow{e_i} = g(A_i)$, where $\overrightarrow{e_i} \in \mathbb{R}^{d \times 1}$ denotes the representation vector of target micro-video i.

Based on the learned user representation vector and micro-video representation vector, the probability of candidate micro-video is calculated using the likelihood function P as $p(i|U, V, X) = P(\overrightarrow{e_u}, \overrightarrow{e_i})$, where $\overrightarrow{e_i}$ is the embedding of target item i from set of micro-videos V. Our framework outputs the click probabilities of the candidate micro-video to rank the personalized recommendation list. Then the system provide precise and diversified recommendation for each user, which entails potential preference of the specific user as they are most likely to interact with the recommended micro-videos.

The objective function for training our model is described in Sect. 2.6 We use the Adam optimizer to train our method.

2.2 Overview

The overall structure of our proposed framework DMR is illustrated in Fig. 1, which is composed of an implicit user network module, a multi-trend routing module, a multi-level time-aware attention module and a prediction layer. As the relative future sequence for current user is actually the history sequence for the neighbors, the multi-trend routing algorithm is applied on both the future and history sequences using shared parameters in parallel. The framework takes the user historical interactions set X as input. We use $X^u_{1,N-K}$ and $X^u_{N-K+1,N}$ to represent training and testing data of interactions sequence of user u respectively. N and K denotes the selected total length of interaction sequence of each user u and the length of training sequence respectively. For micro-videos from the set of $X^u_{1,N-K}$, embeddings are presented as $\overrightarrow{e}_{X^u_{1,N-K}}$.

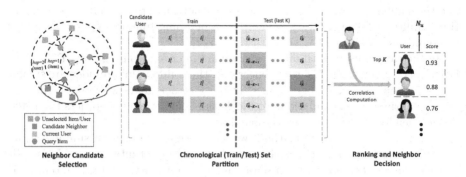

Fig. 2. Architecture of the implicit user network module. The leftmost part stands for the neighbor candidate selection process based on user-item graph with the interactions by edge, user and micro-videos by node. User behaviors of the selected neighbors are then split into train and test set to compare their similarity to the current user. The relative future sequence of the most similar users are utilized to generate the future sequence as the input of multi-trend routing module, which output the future trend representation.

2.3 Implicit User Network

As shown in Fig. 2, the implicit user network is constructed based on user-item heterogeneous graph, which contains both the user nodes and item nodes. The current user node is in the center, the linked nodes are query items, which extend to candidate neighbors based on the items' interaction records. The query items are selected in a multi-hop manner. The user nodes connected to the selected query items are considered as the candidate neighbor nodes of the current user. An edge in the graph represents the interaction between the user and the item. The weight of the edge indicates the temporal weight of each interacted item in a chronological order.

We compare the similarity among users via collaborative filtering implicitly based on the historical interactions with micro-videos. As the Pearson Correlation Coefficient (PCC) is a widely used similarity measure, we adopt Pearson Correlation Coefficient [4] to compute a linear correlation between the user and each candidate neighbor as:

$$s_{ij} = \frac{\sum\limits_{k \in I(i) \cap I(j)} (r_{ik} - \overline{r}_i) \cdot (r_{jk} - \overline{r}_j)}{\sqrt{\sum\limits_{k \in I(i) \cap I(j)} (r_{ik} - \overline{r}_i)^2} \cdot \sqrt{\sum\limits_{k \in I(i) \cap I(j)} (r_{jk} - \overline{r}_j)^2}} \tag{1}$$

where $I(i)$ is a set of micro-videos user i interacted with, r_{ik} and $\overline{r}_i$ represents the level (click or not click) of interaction of user i over micro-video k and the average level of action of user i. The user similarity s_i is ranging from $[-1, 1]$, and the similarity between users i and j is proportional to the value according to this definition. Following [17], we employ a mapping function $f(x) = (x + 1)/2$ to bound the range of PCC similarities into $[0, 1]$.

In the case of users with only one common micro-video in history, PCC similarity gets 1 when the users' preferences over the common micro-video are similar and -1 when not, which encourages diversity of neighbors while damaging the fairness of similarity calculation. To tackle this issue, we only kept less than 20% of such neighbor nodes to seek the balance.

In addition to the PCC method, we also design a filter with simple schema to extract similar users. For each user, if the historical interactions I_u is split into two pieces, $I_{1:t_1}^u$ for training data, and $I_{t_1:t_2}^u$ for testing data, the item $\hat{I}_k^u$ is defined as the last k micro-videos, k could be any value less than or equal to $|I^u|$, while in practice $k = 1$ can achieve good enough performance with simplicity. We extracted a list of neighbors $N = \{n_1, n_2, ..., n_{|N|}\}$ according to the query item. Furthermore, we constructed the future sequence of user u as:

$$F_u = \{n_f, n_f \in I^n, TI(n_f) \geq TI(I_{|I_u|-k}^u)\} \tag{2}$$

where Timestamp is denoted as TI and the query item is denoted as $I_{|I_u|-k}$. I_n represents the interaction set of neighbor n

2.4   Multi-trend Routing

To capture the trend information lies in both history sequence and future sequence, we devised a multi-trend routing module into a two-stage manner to generate trend represent parallelly. Specifically, we group each micro-video from both the user's historical sequence and extracted relative future sequence into diverse trends in the first stage. The micro-videos that are grouped into the same trend are considered to be similar according to users' interactions over them and their own basic features. In the second stage, the micro-videos from historical sequence and relative future sequence are utilized to generate the representation of history and future trend group in parallel.

Algorithm 1. Multi-trend Routing Algorithm

Require:

    User's historical interaction sequence I_u;

    Matching scores $P = \cup_{g=1}^{lo} P_j = p_{1 \leftarrow j}, p_{2 \leftarrow j}, ..., p_{s \leftarrow j}$;

    Iteration number δ;

Ensure:

    Interest groups $X = \cup_{g=1}^{s} g = \cup_{g=1}^{s} i_1^{(g)}, i_2^{(g)}, ..., i_l^{(g)}$;

  1: **for** each $i_j \in H_p os$ **do**

  2:    $S_j = -1, \epsilon_{S_j} \leftarrow \emptyset$

  3: **end for**

  4: **for** each iteration **do**

  5:    **for** each $i_j \in I_+$ **do**

  6:      $\varepsilon_g = \log_b(b + \max(avg_{\epsilon_g} - p_{g \leftarrow j}, 0)), g \in [1, s]$;

  7:      $p_{g \leftarrow j}^{(d)} = p_{g \leftarrow j} / \varepsilon_g, g^* = \arg\max_g(p_{g \leftarrow j}^{(d)})$;

  8:      **if** $g^* \neq S_j \wedge p_{g \leftarrow j}^{(d)} > \epsilon$ **then**

  9:        $\varepsilon_{S_j} \leftarrow POP(\varepsilon_{S_j}, i_j), S_j = g^*, \varepsilon_{g^*}) \leftarrow ADD(\varepsilon_{g^*}, i_j)$

10:      **end if**

11:    **end for**

12: **end for**

13: **return** $\varepsilon = \cup_{g=1}^{s} \varepsilon_g$

Based on the positive historical interaction sequence I_+ of user u, we represent each micro-video x in I_+ as an embedding vector $\vec{x} \in \mathbb{R}^d$, where d is the embedding size. And we initialize positive history trend group as $T_u^h \in \mathbb{R}^{s \times d}$ for user u, where s denotes the number of trend groups indicated from historical sequence and d denotes the embedding dimension of each history trend. Specifically, each trend embedding is represented as $\vec{t} \in \mathbb{R}^d$.

Similarly, based on the extracted future sequence F_+ from the implicit user network. The positive future trend group is denoted as $T_u^f \in \mathbb{R}^{s \times d}$ for user u, where s denotes the number of trend groups indicated from future sequence and d denotes the embedding dimension of each future trend.

In order to fine-tune the representation of each trend, we apply attention mechanism over each micro-video and the initialized trend group. Given the micro-video embedding $\vec{x} \in \mathbb{R}^d$ and the trend embedding $\vec{t} \in \mathbb{R}^d$, we calculate the weight between the micro-video and the trend based on a co-attention memory matrix. The micro-video from the history sequence and the future sequence are put into history trend and future trend separately. As the history sequence and future sequence is processed separately, our module is capable of capturing timeliness of trends which indicates evolved user interest.

2.5 Multi-level Time Attention Mechanism

As for the item-level, we use the weighted sum of historical micro-video features to obtain the current micro-video representation. Finally, we get the representation of each trend by attention mechanism on each micro-video in the trend group. As for the trend-level, we utilize the time-aware attention to activate the weight of diverse trends to capture the timeliness of each trend. Specifically, the attention function takes the interaction time of item i, the interaction time of trends and trend embeddings as the query, key and value respectively. We compute the final representation of trend representation future sequence of user u as:

$$HF_u = ATT(\overrightarrow{TI_i}, \overrightarrow{TI_{tr}}, \overrightarrow{t_u}) = \overrightarrow{t_u}\sigma(pow(\overrightarrow{TI_i}, \overrightarrow{TI_{tr}})) \tag{3}$$

where ATT denotes the attention function, σ denotes the softmax function, TI_i represents the interaction time of micro-video i, TI_{tr} represents the average interaction time of micro-videos related to the trend group, $\overrightarrow{t_u}$ represents the embedding of the specific trend group.

The trend group generated from the user's historical sequence and future sequence are then eventually updated by adding the corresponding trend group in T_u^h and T_u^f with the aggregation of history trend and future trend representation respectively.

2.6 Prediction

After computing the trend embeddings from activated trends through time-aware attention layer, we apply sumpooling to both history and future trend representations.

$$\begin{aligned} e_u^h &= sumpooling(T_u^{h_1}, ..., T_u^{h_s}), \\ e_u^f &= sumpooling(T_u^{f_1}, ..., T_u^{f_s}) \end{aligned} \tag{4}$$

And then we concatenate the history trend representation vector e_u^h and future trend representation vector e_u^f to form a user preference embedding $\overrightarrow{e_u}$ as:

$$\overrightarrow{e_u} = e_u^h \frown e_u^f \tag{5}$$

Given a training sample u, i with the user preference embedding $\overrightarrow{e_u}$ and micro-video embedding $\overrightarrow{e_i}$ as well as the micro-video set V, we can predict the possibility of the user interacting with the micro-video as

$$p(i|U, V, I) = \frac{exp(\overrightarrow{e_u}^T \overrightarrow{e_i})}{\sum_{v \in V} exp(\overrightarrow{e_u}^T \overrightarrow{e_v})} \tag{6}$$

In the same way, we calculate the prediction score $P(x|H_-)$ based on the negative interaction sequence, which aims to maximize the distance between the new micro-video embedding and user's negative trend embeddings.

The final recommendation probability $\hat{p}_{ij}$ is represented by the linear combination of $p(x|H_+)$ and $p(x|H_-)$. And the objective function of our model is as follows:

$$\mathbb{L} = -\sum_{i \in \mathbb{U}} \left(\sum_{i \in H_+} \log \sigma(\hat{p}_{ui}) + \sum_{i \in H_-} log(1 - \sigma(\hat{p}_{ui})) \right) \tag{7}$$

where $\hat{p}_{ui}$ denotes the prediction score of micro-video i for user u, σ represents the sigmoid activation function.

3 Experiments

3.1 Dataset

MicroVideo-1.7M [7] and KuaiShou were used as micro-video benchmark datasets in our experiments. Micro-video data and user-video interaction information can be found in each of these datasets. Each micro-video is represented by its features in these two datasets, and each interaction record includes the userID, micro-video ID, visited timestamp, and whether the user clicked the video.

Table 1. Overall Performance Comparision. The model performance of our model and several state-of-the-art baselines on two public datasets: MicroVideo-1.7M and KuaiShou-Dataset. The best results are highlighted in bold.

Model	MicroVideo-1.7M				KuaiShou-Dataset			
	AUC@50	Precision@50	Recall@50	F1-score@50	AUC@50	Precision@50	Recall@50	F1-score@50
BPR	0.583	0.241	0.181	0.206	0.595	0.290	0.387	0.331
LSTM	0.641	0.277	0.205	0.236	0.731	0.316	0.420	0.360
CNN	0.650	0.287	0.214	0.245	0.719	0.312	0.413	0.356
NCF	0.672	0.316	0.225	0.262	0.724	0.320	0.420	0.364
ATRank	0.660	0.297	0.221	0.253	0.722	0.322	0.426	0.367
THACIL	0.684	**0.324**	0.234	0.269	0.727	0.325	0.429	0.369
ALPINE	0.713	0.300	0.460	0.362	0.739	0.331	0.436	0.376
MTIN	0.729	0.317	0.476	0.381	**0.752**	0.341	**0.449**	**0.388**
DMR	**0.731**	0.323	**0.478**	**0.385**	0.742	**0.343**	0.442	0.386

Table 2. Effect analysis of Neighbors. The model performance with different Neighbor Number setting on two datasets: MicroVideo-1.7M and KuaiShou-Dataset. The metrics are @50. Here we set Neighbor Number to 5, 20, 50.

Model	MicroVideo-1.7M				KuaiShou-Dataset			
	AUC@50	Precision@50	Recall@50	F1-score@50	AUC@50	Precision@50	Recall@50	F1-score@50
DMR-N5	0.689	0.319	0.425	0.364	0.674	0.333	0.439	0.378
DMR-N20	**0.731**	**0.323**	**0.478**	**0.385**	**0.742**	**0.343**	**0.442**	**0.386**
DMR-N50	0.668	0.280	0.282	0.281	0.652	0.329	0.404	0.362

3.2 Implementation Details

We used TensorFlow on four Tesla P40 GPUs to train our model with Adam optimizer. The following are the hyper-parameters: The micro-video embedding is 512-dimensional vectors, while the user embedding is 128-dimensional vectors. The batch size was set to 32, the optimizer was Adam, the learning rate was set to 0.001, and the regularization factor was set to 0.0001. To find the user's similar neighbors, we used the Pearson Correlation Coefficient (PCC) described earlier. In the ablation analysis, we set neighbor numbers as 5, 20, and 50. As for the future sequences, we cut off each neighbor's at most 100 interacted micro-videos after the current user's query items.

3.3   Evaluation Metrics

To compare the performance of different models, we use **Precision@N**, **Recall@N**, **F1-score@N** and **AUC**, where N is set to 50 as metrics for evaluation.

3.4   Competitors

To validate the effectiveness of our proposed DMR framework, we conducted experiments on two publicly available real-world datasets. The comparision to other state-of-the-art micro-video recommenders (BPR [21], ALPINE [15], MTIN [14], etc.) are summarized in Table 1. To intelligently route micro videos to target users, ALPINE proposed an LSTM model based on a temporal graph, which is encoded by user's historical interaction sequence. And MTIN is a multi-scale time-aware user interest modeling framework, which learns user interests from fine-grained interest groups.

3.5   Results

The model performance on the two datasets is summarized in Table 1. We run experiments to dissect the effectiveness of our recommendation model. We compare the performance of DMR with several commonly used and state-of-the-art models: BPR, LSTM, CNN, NCF, ATRank, THACIL, ALPINE and MTIN. All these models are running on the two datasets introduced above: MicroVideo-1.7M and KuaiShou-Dataset. According to the results shown in Table 1, our model DMR achieve better performance on precision over KuaiShou dataset and performs better in terms of AUC, Recall and F1-score over MicroVideo-1.7M dataset.

We investigate the performance of our model DMR in different parameter setting by changing number of trends T. We set the two datasets setting T to 2, 6 and 12. Our model achieves improvements on T = 6 over T = 2, which may caused by insufficient trends for the dataset. However, it did not show much improvement when we change T from 6 to 12 showing clustering sequences to 12 trends in these datasets is redundant and to 6 trends is just suitable. Thus we fix T as 6 in our following experimental reports. We also compares the result of setting query item from the first to last item, the third to last item and the fifth to last one. The largest improvements appear on increasing K from 1 to 3. This demonstrates that by adding the number of query items, our model can capture more trend information and be more powerful to predict future sequences. Increasing query item number from 3 to 5 does not gain much improvement. This implies our model is efficient to capture much trend information by few historical items of the user. Thus we fix the last K number as 1 in our following experimental reports. Table 2 compares the result of different neighbor number setting of 5, 20 and 50. Considering more neighbors could result in more diversity, but too many neighbors would dilute interest trends' embedding. Our model achieves improvements on neighbor number equals 20 over 5. Besides, it shows reduction if setting neighbor number from 20 to 50. This means the number of neighbors also play a crucial part in model performance.

The computational complexity of sequence layer modeling user and neighbors is $O(knd^2)$, where k denotes the number of extracted neighbors, n denotes the average sequence length and d denotes the dimension of item's representation. Capsule layer's computational complexity depends on kernel size and number of trends. Average time complexity of capsule layer scales $O(nTr^2)$, where r denotes kernel size of capsule layer and T denotes the number of trends. For large-scale applications, our proposed model could reduce computational complexity by two measures: (1) encode neighbors with a momentum encoder [12].(2) adopt a light-weight Capsule network.

3.6 Recommendation Diversity

Aside from achieving high recommendation accuracy, diversity is also essential for the user experience. With little information of historical interactions between the users and the micro-videos, recommendation systems learned to assist users in selecting micro-videos that would be of interest to them. Recommender systems keep track of how users interacted with the micro-videos they've chosen.

Table 3. Model Recommendation Diversity Comparision on Micro-video Dataset.

MicroVideo-1.7M	THACIL	MTIN	DMR
Diversity@10	1.9112	1.9940	**1.9948**
Diversity@50	1.9104	1.9948	**1.9956**
Diversity@100	1.9436	1.9950	**1.9954**

Many research works [1,3,9,20] have been undertaken to propose novel diversification algorithms. Our proposed module can learn the diverse trends of user preference and provide recommendation with diversity. We define the individual diversity as below:

$$D@N = \frac{\sum_{j=1}^{N} \sum_{k=j+1}^{N} \delta(C(\hat{i}_{u,j}) \neq C(\hat{i}_{u,k}))}{N \times (N-1)/2} \tag{8}$$

where C represents the category of the item. $\hat{i}_u$ denotes item recommended for user u, j and k represents the order of the recommended items. $\delta(\cdot)$ is an indicator function.

Table 3 presents comparisons with THACIL and MTIN over the recommendation diversity metric on Micro-video dataset, which provides category information of micro-videos. We adopt the setting of six historical trend and six future trend evolved from 5 neighbors for our model. From the table, our module DMR achieve the optimum diversity metric indicating the recommendation it provide can effectively take neighbors' interests into account.

4 Conclusion

In this work, we propose to capture even more diverse and dynamic interests beyond those implied by the historical behaviors for micro-video recommendation. We refer to the future interest directions as trends and devise the DMR framework. DMR employ an implicit user network module to extract future sequence fragments from similar users. A mutli-trend routing module assigns these future sequences to different trend groups and updates the corresponding trending memory slot in a dynamic read-write manner. Final predictions are made based on both future evolved trends and history evolved trends with a history-future trends joint prediction module.

Acknowledgments. This work was supported Key R & D Projects of the Ministry of Science and Technology (2020YFC0832503).

References

1. Adomavicius, G., Kwon, Y.: Improving aggregate recommendation diversity using ranking-based techniques. IEEE Trans. Knowl. Data Eng. **24**(5), 896–911 (2012)
2. Baluja, S., et al.: Video suggestion and discovery for youtube: taking random walks through the view graph. In: Proceedings of the 17th International Conference on World Wide Web, WWW 2008, Beijing, China, 21–25 April 2008 (2008)
3. Boim, R., Milo, T., Novgorodov, S.: Diversification and refinement in collaborative filtering recommender. In: Proceedings of the 20th ACM International Conference on Information and Knowledge Management, CIKM 2011, pp. 739–744. Association for Computing Machinery, New York (2011)
4. Breese, J.S., Heckerman, D., Kadie, C.: Empirical analysis of predictive algorithms for collaborative filtering (2013)
5. Chen, B., Wang, J., Huang, Q., Mei, T.: Personalized video recommendation through tripartite graph propagation. In: Proceedings of the 20th ACM Multimedia Conference, MM 2012, Nara, Japan, 29 October–02 November 2012 (2012)
6. Chen, J., Song, X., Nie, L., Wang, X., Zhang, H., Chua, T.-S.: Micro tells macro: predicting the popularity of micro-videos via a transductive model. In: Proceedings of the 2016 ACM Conference on Multimedia Conference, MM 2016, Amsterdam, The Netherlands, 15–19 October 2016 (2016)
7. Chen, X., Liu, D., Zha, Z.J., Zhou, W., Xiong, Z., Li, Y.: Temporal hierarchical attention at category- and item-level for micro-video click-through prediction. In: 2018 ACM Multimedia Conference on Multimedia Conference, MM 2018, Seoul, Republic of Korea, 22–26 October 2018 (2018)
8. Cui, P., Wang, Z., Su, Z.: What videos are similar with you?: learning a common attributed representation for video recommendation. In: Proceedings of the ACM International Conference on Multimedia, MM 2014, Orlando, FL, USA, 03–07 November 2014 (2014)
9. Di Noia, T., Ostuni, V.C., Rosati, J., Tomeo, P., Di Sciascio, E.: An analysis of users' propensity toward diversity in recommendations. In: Proceedings of the 8th ACM Conference on Recommender Systems, RecSys 2014, pp. 285–288. Association for Computing Machinery, New York (2014)

10. Dong, J., Li, X., Xu, C., Yang, G., Wang, X.: Feature re-learning with data aug-mentation for content-based video recommendation. In: 2018 ACM Multimedia Conference on Multimedia Conference, MM 2018, Seoul, Republic of Korea, 22–26 October 2018 (2018)

11. Du, X., Wang, X., He, X., Li, Z., Tang, J., Chua, T.-S.: How to learn item rep-resentation for cold-start multimedia recommendation? In: MM 2020: The 28th ACM International Conference on Multimedia, Virtual Event/Seattle, WA, USA, 12–16 October 2020 (2020)

12. He, K., Fan, H., Wu, Y., Xie, S., Girshick, R.B.: Momentum contrast for unsuper-vised visual representation learning. CoRR, abs/1911.05722 (2019)

13. Huang, Y., Cui, B., Jiang, J., Hong, K., Zhang, W., Xie, Y.: Real-time video recommendation exploration. In: Proceedings of the 2016 International Conference on Management of Data, SIGMOD Conference 2016, San Francisco, CA, USA, 26 June–01 July 2016 (2016)

14. Jiang, H., Wang, W., Wei, Y., Gao, Z., Wang, Y., Nie, L.: What aspect do you like: Multi-scale time-aware user interest modeling for micro-video recommendation. In: MM 2020: The 28th ACM International Conference on Multimedia, Virtual Event/Seattle, WA, USA, 12–16 October 2020, pp. 3487–3495. Association for Computing Machinery, New York (2020)

15. Li, Y., Liu, M., Yin, J., Cui, C., Xu, X.-S., Nie, L.: Routing micro-videos via a temporal graph-guided recommendation system. In: Proceedings of the 27th ACM International Conference on Multimedia, MM 2019, Nice, France, 21–25 October 2019, pp. 1464–1472. Association for Computing Machinery, New York (2019)

16. Lu, Y., et al.: Future-aware diverse trends framework for recommendation. CoRR (2020)

17. Ma, H.: An experimental study on implicit social recommendation, pp. 73–82 (2013)

18. Mei, T., Yang, B., Hua, X.-S., Li, S.: Contextual video recommendation by multi-modal relevance and user feedback. ACM Trans. Inf. Syst. **29**(2), 1–24 (2011)

19. Park, J.: An online video recommendation framework using view based tag cloud aggregation. IEEE Multimedia (2010)

20. Premchaiswadi, W., Poompuang, P., Jongswat, N., Premchaiswadi, N.: Enhancing diversity-accuracy technique on user-based top-n recommendation algorithms. In: Proceedings of the 2013 IEEE 37th Annual Computer Software and Applications Conference Workshops, COMPSACW 2013, pp. 403–408. IEEE Computer Society, USA (2013)

21. Rendle, S., Freudenthaler, C., Gantner, Z., Schmidt-Thieme, L.: BPR: Bayesian personalized ranking from implicit feedback. CoRR, abs/1205.2618 (2012)

22. Yan, M., Sang, J., Xu, C.: Unified youtube video recommendation via cross-network collaboration. In: Proceedings of the 5th ACM on International Conference on Multimedia Retrieval, Shanghai, China, 23–26 June 2015 (2015)

23. Zhou, X., Chen, L., Zhang, Y., Cao, L., Huang, G., Wang, C.: Online video rec-ommendation in sharing community. In: Proceedings of the 2015 ACM SIGMOD International Conference on Management of Data, Melbourne, Victoria, Australia, 31 May–4 June 2015 (2015)

Parameters Efficient Fine-Tuning for Long-Tailed Sequential Recommendation

Zheqi Lv[1]📵, Feng Wang[2]📵, Shengyu Zhang[3(✉)]📵, Wenqiao Zhang[3]📵,
Kun Kuang[1(✉)]📵, and Fei Wu[1(✉)]📵

[1] College of Computer Science and Technology, Zhejiang University,
Hang Zhou, China
{zheqilv,kunkuang,wufei}@zju.edu.cn
[2] School of Software Technology, Zhejiang University, Hang Zhou, China
[3] DAMO Academy, Alibaba Group, Hang Zhou, China
{sy_zhang,wenqiaozhang}@zju.edu.cn

Abstract. In an era of information explosion, recommendation systems play an important role in people's daily life by facilitating content exploration. It is known that user activeness, *i.e.*, number of behaviors, tends to follow a long-tail distribution, where the majority of users are with low activeness. In practice, we observe that tail users suffer from significantly lower-quality recommendation than the head users after joint training. We further identify that a model trained on tail users separately still achieve inferior results due to limited data. Though long-tail distributions are ubiquitous in recommendation systems, improving the recommendation performance on the tail users still remains challenge in both research and industry. Directly applying related methods on long-tail distribution might be at risk of hurting the experience of head users, which is less affordable since a small portion of head users with high activeness contribute a considerable portion of platform revenue. In this paper, we propose a novel approach that significantly improves the recommendation performance of the tail users while achieving at least comparable performance for the head users over the base model. The essence of this approach is a novel Gradient Aggregation technique that learns common knowledge shared by all users into a backbone model, followed by separate plugin prediction networks for the head users and the tail users personalization. As for common knowledge learning, we leverage the backward adjustment from the causality theory for deconfounding the gradient estimation and thus shielding off the backbone

Z. Lv and F. Wang—These authors equally contributed to this study.

This work was supported in part by National Natural Science Foundation of China (62006207, 62037001, U20A20387), Young Elite Scientists Sponsorship Program by CAST (2021QNRC001), Zhejiang Province Natural Science Foundation (LQ21F020020), Project by Shanghai AI Laboratory (P22KS00111), Program of Zhejiang Province Science and Technology (2022C01044), the StarryNight Science Fund of Zhejiang University Shanghai Institute for Advanced Study (SN-ZJU-SIAS-0010), and the Fundamental Research Funds for the Central Universities (226-2022-00142, 226-2022-00051).

L. Fang et al. (Eds.): CICAI 2023, LNAI 14473, pp. 442–459, 2024.
https://doi.org/10.1007/978-981-99-8850-1_36

training from the confounder, *i.e.*, user activeness. We conduct extensive experiments on two public recommendation benchmark datasets and a large-scale industrial datasets collected from the Alipay platform. Empirical studies validate the rationality and effectiveness of our approach.

Keywords: Recommendation System · Long-tail · Gradient Aggregation · Collaborative Training

1   Introduction

With the rapid development of the Internet in recent years, recommendation systems play a vital role in people's daily life. Since users' behaviors naturally show chronological dependencies, many sequential recommendation algorithms have been proposed, including, but not limited to, GRU4Rec [4], DIN [30], SASRec [7], etc. One of the most enticing merits of sequential models is that we can dynamically update the recommendation list as long as users interact with new items. Many existing researches on recommender systems focus on personalization [12,13], disentanglement [26], Despite their great advances, we identify that existing methods still achieve less satisfied recommendation quality for non-active users. In industrial recommendation systems, it is known that user activeness tends to form a long-tail distribution. For example, as shown in Fig. 1, the majority of users have significantly less number of behaviors than head users. Apparently, to improve recommendation quality of most users, it is of paramount importance to pay attention to the tail users with low activeness.

Investigating long-tail distributions has gained much attention in the literature [27], especially in computer vision [5,22,29]. However, these methods cannot be directly applied to the recommendation domain due to its unique challenges. Specifically, in the recommendation system, the behaviors of tail users are quite limited, leading to less adequate preference understanding. Moreover, we identify that models are easily biased towards head users during joint training and thus make the problem even more severe.

As for separate training for tail users, we conduct an empirical study and find that the separately trained model still achieves inferior results due to the limited amount of data. At present, studying tail users in recommendation systems is still a nascent research field, such as Grad-Transfer [24]. Despite the performance improvement on tail users, most of them are at risk of sacrificing the performance of head users. Note that hurting the experiences of

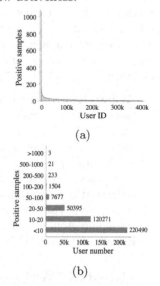

Fig. 1. The long-tail effect on Alipay dataset.

head users is less affordable in industrial environments due to the large amount of platform revenue contributed by active users. Another line of related works is cold-start recommendation [2,9,18], which aims to improve the performance of users that are not observed during training. We differ from these works fundamentally by improving the performance of observed tail users during joint training.

We argue that improving the model's performance on the tail user base does not necessarily degrade the model's performance on the short-head user base. Similar users (no matter how active they are) should all benefit from joint training through collaborative filtering. Besides these common knowledge shared by similar users, each user has their personalized preferences. Therefore, we argue that one possible solution is to extracting common knowledge that is shared by all users and is independent from user activeness while retaining the personalized information for different users. Upon the above analysis, we devise a gradient aggregation framework for long-tailed sequential user behavior modeling. To shield off the common knowledge learning from user activeness, we borrow back-door adjustment [16] technique from the causality theory and utilize it like [26]. In particular, we view the user activeness as a confounder and deconfound the model training via causal intervention. To instantiate back-door adjustment, a grouping strategy and a gradient aggregation strategy are proposed. We group each group of data according to the activity divided by the time window, and at the same time ensure that the amount of data in each group is as equal as possible. During training, we intervene the gradient estimation via back-door adjustment, leading to a activeness-independent training. Upon the causally learned trunk that encodes the common knowledge, we devise multiple plugin networks for group-specific personalization. Through the architecture of the trunk network and the plugin network, the model not only has strong general reasoning ability, but also has good individual reasoning ability. Moreover, we conduct extensive experiments on industrial datasets to demonstrate the effectiveness of our method. In this paper, our main contributions are as follows:

- We investigate how to improve the recommendation quality of tail non-active users without sacrificing the performance on active users. We identify disentangle the common knowledge learning and personalization is a plausible solution to the problem.
- We learn a trunk model that encodes the common knowledge via back-door adjustment borrowed from causality theory. With causal intervention, the estimated gradient should be independent from user activeness. Upon the trunk, we devise several plugin networks for group-specific personalization.
- We completed experiments on Movielens, Amazon, and Alipay datasets. Experiments show that our method is practical and effective.

2   Related Work

2.1   Long-Tail

Deep long-tail learning is one of the most challenging problems in deep learning, and its goal is to train well-performing deep learning models from data that follow a long-tailed class distribution. Long-tail class imbalance tends to limit the usefulness of deep learning-based models in real-world applications, as they tend to be biased towards dominant classes and perform poorly on tail classes. [27] In order to solve this problem, researchers have carried out a lot of research in recent years, and have made gratifying progress in the field of deep long-tail learning. Existing research on deep long-tail learning is mainly divided into three categories, namely class rebalancing [28,29], information augmentation [11, 22,24], and module improvement [5,17]. Although some other work is more or less related to the long tail, they cannot be directly transferred to the long tail learning [2,6,9,10,18,21,31].

2.2 Gradient Surgery

Gradient surgery is usually used in fields such as multi-task learning and domain generalization. It can use the knowledge learned on one task during the training process to improve the generalization performance of the model on other tasks. To achieve this, GradNorm [1] dynamically scales the gradients to ensure that the gradients produced by each task contribute similarly to model training. PCGrad [25] achieves soft fusion of two gradients with conflicting components by projecting between gradients of different tasks. GradVac [23] sets a separate gradient similarity objective for each task pair, making better use of inter-task correlations through adaptive gradient similarity. Agr-Rand [14] solves domain generalization through gradient surgery. It determines how gradients are updated by comparing the sign bits between gradients across domains.

3 Method

In this paper, we focus on the problem of long-tail distribution in recommendation in real industrial applications. To address this problem, we propose a novel framework to disentangle the common knowledge learning and personalization for improving the recommendation quality of the tail non-active users without sacrificing the performance on the head active users. Figure 2 shows the architecture of our proposed method. Next, we will detail each component of the proposed method.

3.1 Preliminaries

The sequence recommendation model can generally be expressed as: supposing we have a user set $U = \{u_1, u_2, ..., u_n\}$, and an item set $I = \{i_1, i_2, ..., i_m\}$. The click sequence $S = \{s^{u_1}, s^{u_2}, ..., s^{u_n}\}$ represents the L items that the user u has clicked recently so far. We randomly select some user-item pairs and the corresponding user behavior sequence S^u from the data set and put them into the model to get a prediction score $\hat{y}_{u,i}$ between 0 and 1, that is,

$$\hat{y}_{u,i} = f(u, i, s^u | \theta) \tag{1}$$

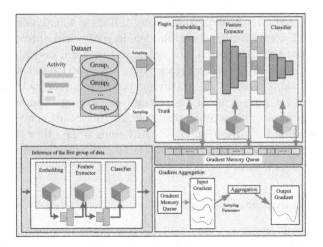

Fig. 2. Architecture of the proposed method. (1) During training, our method consists of two stages. The first stage is to use all of the data for training and aggregate the gradients of each group to obtain a trunk network that can extract generalization information. The second stage is to insert the plugin network into the trunk network. The plugin network for each group is trained using only the data of this group. At the same time, the trunk network is still undergoing updates similar to the first stage. In general, the trunk network extracts the common information of all groups, and the plugin network extracts the personalized information of each group. (2) During inference, the plugin network is plugged to the trunk network to realize the fusion of general information inference and individual information inference.

$f(\cdot)$ denotes the forward propagation function and θ represents the parameters of the model. The ground-truth $y_{u,i} \in \{0, 1\}$ is a binary variable, so we can use the binary cross entropy loss as the loss function which is commonly used in binary classification problems to calculate the loss. We use $\mathcal{D}$ to represent the entire dataset, then we can get the loss function $\mathcal{L}$ by

$$\mathcal{L} = -\frac{1}{|\mathcal{D}|} \sum_{i=1}^{|\mathcal{D}|} y_i \log \hat{y}_{u,i} + (1 - y_i) \log(1 - \hat{y}_{u,i}) \tag{2}$$

Then, we backpropagate the loss and update f, repeat several times to obtain the optimal parameter θ, and finally a sequential recommendation model can be obtained.

$$\theta = \arg \min_{\theta} \mathcal{L} \tag{3} \quad .$$

3.2 Gradient Aggregation

In the recommendation system, although the difference in user activity also affects the model's judgment of their preferences, users with different activity levels also have a lot of common information that can be extracted by the model.

These common information can not only help the model perform better on the tail user group, but also help the model to better learn the preferences of high-active users. Since the common information is implicit and highly entangled with personalized information, it is hard to identify and extract them directly. To bridge the gap, we borrow the back-door adjustment technique [16] from the causal literature and deconfound the model training. Deconfounding means shielding the model training/prediction from possible confounders. Since the major focus is user activeness, i.e., the number of users' behaviors, we regard it as the confounder. Formally, by the Bayes rule, the original training gradients can be obtained by:

$$P(g \mid u, i, y_{u,i}) = \sum_z P(g, z \mid u, i, y_{u,i}) \tag{4}$$

$$= \sum_z P(g \mid u, i, y_{u,i}, z)\underline{P(z \mid u, i, y_{u,i})}, \tag{5}$$

where g denotes the model gradients. z denotes the confounder which is user activeness here. $P(\cdot)$ denotes the forward function that takes u, i as the input and a deterministic backward function that estimates the gradient based on the prediction of the model and the ground-truth $y_{u,i}$. In the language of causality, the gradient estimation is confounded by the user activeness, leading to biased training that is favor of active users. Backward adjustment deconfounds the estimation by blocking the direct effect $z \rightarrow u, i, y_{u,i}$:

$$P(g \mid do(u, i, y_{u,i})) = \sum_z P(g|u, i, y_{u,i}, z)\underline{P(z)} \tag{6}$$

where the proof can be found in [3,19,20]. In practice, the essence of the above adjusted equation is to estimate the gradient $P(g|u, i, y_{u,i}, z)$ for each z value, and sum all gradients from different z values with the prior probabilities.

To estimate the gradients per z value, we divide users into n groups according to the level of activeness. During training, each batch can be divided into n mini-batches. When the j-th mini-batch in the b-th batch is trained with the data from the j-th group, we can get the gradient $g_{i,j}^{|k|}$ produced by this mini-batch at the k-th layer of the model. Similarly, when we train all mini-batches in this batch, we can get a gradient set $G_i^{|k|} = \{g_{i,2}^{|k|}, g_{i,2}^{|k|}, \ldots, g_{i,n}^{|k|}\}$. When a mini-batch in a batch completes backpropagation, we do not directly update the gradient generated by the mini-batch but put the gradient into a gradient memory queue $Q^{|k|}$. After all mini-batches in this batch have completed backpropagation, we aggregate these gradients using Eq. 6. The prior distribution of different z values is empirically set to a uniform distribution. This is because we divide the users into equally-numbered groups and different user groups are treated as equally important so as to deal with the long-tail problems. Formally, we obtain the deconfounded gradients as follows:

$$g_b^{|k|} = \frac{1}{n} \sum_{j=1}^n \frac{N}{n_j} g_{b,j}^{|k|}. \tag{7}$$

Among them, N represents the total number of samples in the dataset $\mathcal{D}$, n_j represents the number of samples in the j-th user group. We use $f_t(\cdot)$ denotes the forward propagation function.

3.3   Plugin Network

After gradient aggregation, we can obtain a trunk network containing the common knowledge of all user groups. However, the group-specific knowledge is less modeled, which may cause degraded performance. To alleviate the problem, we introduce the plugin network for each group to learn the personalized knowledge from the data of this group.

Naive Plugin Network. A naive method is training a plugin network of the same size as the trunk network for each user group, with its model parameters denoted $\Delta\boldsymbol{\theta}$. When predicting users belonging to the j-th group, it is necessary to add the plugin network parameters $\Delta\theta_j$ and the trunk network parameters θ dedicated to the j-th group. The forward propagation function is,

$$\hat{y}_{u,i} = f(u, i, j, s^u | \theta + \Delta\theta) \tag{8}$$

Furthermore, we split the model into embedding layers, feature extractors and classifiers. We use E to denote the parameters of the embedding layer in the trunk network. Since the parameters of the embedding layer are very sparse, only using the data of a certain user group for training will lead to inaccurate mapping of the data in the feature space, we remove the embedding layer from the plugin network. Therefore, we only update the parameters of the feature extractor $\Delta\Phi_j$ and the classifier ΔW_j when we train the plugin network for the j-th user group. Formally, we predict the user-item pair of the j-th user group as follows,

$$\hat{y}_{u,i} = f(u, i, j, s^u | E, \Phi + \Delta\Phi_j, W + \Delta W_j) \tag{9}$$

We compute the loss function as follows, where $\mathcal{L}_j$ denotes the data of the j-th group of users,

$$\mathcal{L}_j = -\frac{1}{|\mathcal{D}_j|} \sum_{i=1}^{|\mathcal{D}_j|} (y_i \log \hat{y}_{u,i} + (1 - y_i) \log(1 - \hat{y}_{u,i}))) \tag{10}$$

Then, we minimize the loss by,

$$\Delta\Phi_j, \Delta W_j = \arg \min_{\Delta\Phi_j, \Delta W_j} \mathcal{L}_j \tag{11}$$

Lightweight Plugin Network. The above plugin network is similar to the residual module in ResNet, the difference is that we use the residual of the network parameters instead of the residual of the feature. Such a method can stably extract the personalized information of each group into the residual parameters

$\Delta\Phi$ and ΔW. However, in order to avoid overfitting, the learning rate needs to be set very low, which leads to a stable effect but limited improvement. So we improve the plugin network. Specifically, we insert plugin networks between the embedding layer and the feature extractor and between the feature extractor and the classifier, whose parameters are denoted by Φ' and W', respectively. Specifically for the j-th user group, their parameters are Φ'_j and W'_j respectively.

$$\hat{y}_{u,i} = f(u, i, j, s^u | \theta, \Phi'_j, W'_j) \tag{12}$$

The loss function is same to Eq. 10. Then, we backpropagate the loss on the lightweight plugin network and minimize the loss by,

$$\Phi'_j, W'_j = \arg \min_{\Phi'_j, W'_j} \mathcal{L}_j \tag{13}$$

At the same time, we continue to update the trunk network using Eq. 7 with a lower learning rate. To summarize briefly, we update Φ'_j and W'_j immediately after the j-th mini-batch backpropagation of each batch. The trunk network is updated after all mini-batches of each batch have completed backpropagation. The plugin network can fine-tune the intermediate features inside the trunk network to meet the needs of model personalization. The trunk network with continuous gradient aggregation can not only continuously improve the trunk network's ability to capture common information, but also prevent the bias of the plugin network from being too large.

4   Experiments

In this section, we conduct extensive experiments to show the superiority of the proposed framework. Specifically, we will answer the following questions.

1. **RQ1:** How effective is the proposed method compared with the state-of-the-art (SOTA) competitors?
2. **RQ2:** Does the proposed method actually improve the performance of tail users?
3. **RQ3:** How do the gradient aggregation and plugin network affect the performance of the proposed method?
4. **RQ4:** Is the proposed method effective for other mainstream recommendation models?

4.1   Experiment Settings

Datasets. We conduct experiments on the following publicly accessible datasets: MovieLens, Amazon, and Alipay. Details can be referred to Appendix.

Evaluation Metrics. In the experiments, we use the widely adopted AUC, HitRate and NDCG as the metrics to evaluate model performance. They are defined by the following equations. Details can be referred to Appendix.

Baselines. To verify the applicability, the following representative sequential modeling approaches are implemented and compared with the counterparts combined with the proposed method. GRU4Rec [4], DIN [30], and SASRec [7] are three of the most widely used sequential recommendation models. Agr-Rand [14], PCGrad [25], and Grad-Transfer [24] are three gradient surgery methods. For details, please refer to the Appendix.

Table 1. Group level performance comparison on each group data.

Dataset	Group	DIN	Agr-Rand	Grad-Transfer	PCGrad	Ours
Movielens	Group 1	0.8262	0.8246	0.8443	0.8375	**0.8434**
	Group 2	0.9026	0.8828	0.9040	0.8964	**0.9131**
	Group 3	0.9072	0.8950	0.9133	0.9097	**0.9247**
	Group 4	0.9059	0.8899	0.9110	0.9033	**0.9227**
	Group 5	0.9105	0.8813	0.9094	0.9021	**0.9251**
Amazon	Group 1	0.9196	0.9139	0.9196	0.9205	**0.9233**
	Group 2	0.9218	0.9175	0.9211	0.9220	**0.9249**
	Group 3	0.9237	0.9192	0.9246	0.9247	**0.9261**
	Group 4	0.9240	0.9182	0.9240	0.9259	**0.9275**
	Group 5	0.9272	0.9212	0.9270	**0.9303**	0.9285
Alipay	Group 1	0.7253	0.6881	0.7159	0.7269	**0.7304**
	Group 2	0.7381	0.7045	0.7296	0.7390	**0.7432**
	Group 3	0.7508	0.7169	0.7415	0.7511	**0.7548**
	Group 4	0.7635	0.7297	0.7544	0.7625	**0.7658**
	Group 5	0.8025	0.7615	0.7889	0.8002	**0.8059**

4.2 Experiments and Results

Overall Comparison (RQ1, RQ2). The comparison between our model and three SOTA models on the group level and the user level are shown in Table 1 and Table 3, respectively.

Group-Level Analysis. We are interested in how different user groups with different activeness benefit from the propose technique. Towards this end, we explicitly present the performance of these groups across three datasets. Accordingly to the results in Table 1, we have the following observations:

– Overall, our technique yields the best performance across different datasets in most cases. Remarkably, the proposed method outperforms the best-performing SOTA by +.0091, +.0029, and +.0042 *w.r.t.* AUC on the Movie-Lens, Amazon, and AliPay datasets, respectively. Note that the improvement +.0042 AUC is significant for the large-scale industrial dataset, Alipay. These results demonstrate the merits of our technique for recommendation.

– Our method achieves consistent improvement across different user groups. Although many SOTA methods achieve performance gains on some user groups, they might fail to improve the base model in some other groups. For example, Grad-Transfer achieves significant performance gains on Group1 (+.0181, AUC), but achieves inferior results on Group5 (-.0011, AUC). These results demonstrate that some SOTA baselines might be at risk of hurting the experiences of some user groups. These results basically indicate the merit of our plugin components, which focus on learning personalized patterns and prevent over-correction for some users.

– The performance gain on tail user groups are larger than that of the head user groups in our method. Note that the major argument of this paper is that joint training in current recommendation models might be at risk of hurting head user groups. These results reveal that our method could offer all-user groups better recommendation quality that they deserve. Importantly, without sacrificing the recommendation quality of the others. These are notable merits in industrial environments where the non-active users might be potential loyal users and the active users currently contribute the most revenue.

User-Level Analysis. Note that the AUC in the above analysis is computed in the group level. To further reveal the performance gain in the user level, we compute the AUC metric for each user and take the average as the final performance. The results are shown in Table 3.

We observe that the proposed technique consistently outperforms the base model DIN and three SOTA methods. It is noteworthy that although the some baselines can achieve performance gains over DIN in the group-level, they cannot beat DIN in the user level in most cases. Remember that tail users are the majority in many recommender systems. These results basically indicate that these baselines are less optimal to deal with long-tail problems, and might fail to improve the average recommendation quality

Method	Movielens	Amazon	Alipay
DIN	0.8909	0.9165	0.6905
Agr-Rand	0.8728	0.9124	0.6754
Grad-Transfer	0.8958	0.9177	0.6853
PCGrad	0.8886	0.9177	0.6897
Ours	**0.9052**	**0.9202**	**0.6924**

Fig. 3. User level performance comparison on all data.

of all users. On the contrary, the consistent improvement of our technique further reveals the rationality and effectiveness of our problem analysis and model design for tail user behavior modeling.

Table 2. Performance comparison in terms of AUC to demonstrate the effects of gradient aggregation and plugin model.

Dataset	Group	GRU4Rec	+GA	+GA+PN	DIN	+GA	+GA+PN	SASRec	+GA	+GA+PN
Movielens	Group 1	0.8587	0.8595	**0.8633**	0.8262	0.8384	**0.8434**	0.8539	0.8591	**0.8638**
	Group 2	**0.9264**	0.9210	0.9250	0.9026	0.8977	**0.9131**	0.9242	0.9221	**0.9258**
	Group 3	0.9354	0.9338	**0.9385**	0.9072	0.9023	**0.9247**	0.9337	0.9345	**0.9393**
	Group 4	0.9379	0.9393	**0.9424**	0.9059	0.9017	**0.9227**	0.9360	0.9358	**0.9399**
	Group 5	0.9400	0.9371	**0.9425**	0.9105	0.8973	**0.9251**	0.9387	0.9355	**0.9408**
Amazon	Group 1	0.9306	0.9338	**0.9340**	0.9196	0.9198	**0.9233**	0.9287	0.9329	**0.9337**
	Group 2	0.9329	0.9366	**0.9367**	0.9218	0.9211	**0.9249**	0.9315	0.9353	**0.9357**
	Group 3	0.9381	0.9401	**0.9407**	0.9237	0.9216	**0.9261**	0.9367	0.9374	**0.9384**
	Group 4	0.9407	0.9438	**0.9452**	0.9240	0.9228	**0.9275**	0.9399	0.9412	**0.9417**
	Group 5	0.9479	**0.9487**	0.9470	0.9272	0.9270	**0.9285**	**0.9458**	0.9444	0.9421
Alipay	Group 1	0.7312	0.7318	**0.7372**	0.7253	0.7270	**0.7304**	0.7283	0.7313	**0.7353**
	Group 2	0.7432	0.7432	**0.7485**	0.7381	0.7397	**0.7432**	0.7411	0.7428	**0.7467**
	Group 3	0.7569	0.7565	**0.7620**	0.7508	0.7507	**0.7548**	0.7547	0.7558	**0.7609**
	Group 4	0.7700	0.7694	**0.7745**	0.7635	0.7622	**0.7658**	0.7674	0.7682	**0.7737**
	Group 5	0.8103	0.8081	**0.8135**	0.8025	0.7970	**0.8059**	0.8053	0.8067	**0.8125**

Ablation Study (RQ3, RQ4). We are interested in whether different building blocks all contribute to the proposed method. To have a comprehensive analysis, we progressively add the Gradient Aggregation component (GA) and the Plugin Network (PN) onto three base models (GRU4Rec, DIN, and SASRec) and test the constructed architectures on three datasets. The results are shown in Table 2, which also reveal the performance change on different user groups since it is one of the primary focuses in this paper. According to the results,

- The proposed technique (+GA+PN) demonstrates consistent performance improvement over different base recommendation architectures across different user groups and different datasets in most cases. These comprehensive results basically indicate that the effectiveness of the proposed method is model-agnostic and dataset-agnostic. These results again verify the merits of the proposed method in long-tail sequential behavior modeling with similar findings on five user groups to those illustrated in Section "Overall Comparison".
- Not surprisingly, the Gradient Aggregation (GA) module mainly improves the recommendation performance for tail user groups while achieving comparable or sometimes inferior results compared to the base model. For example, +GA achieves AUC +.0122 on Group1 and AUC -.0132 on Group5 compared to the DIN base model on the MovieLens dataset. These results are reasonable in the sense that GA might neglect the personalization by mainly

focusing on learning common information shared by all users. Nevertheless, learning common information boosts the performance on tail users, which is our primary focus, and lays the foundation for further group-specific personalization. These results basically reveal the rationality of our analysis and the effectiveness of the GA module.

– Based on the common information learned by the GA module, the PN module constructs an additional prediction network per group for group-specific personalization. PN achieves consistent performance improvement over different base models for five groups. These results demonstrate the necessity of personalization and the effectiveness of our design. Compared to GA, the PN component mostly improves the head users than tail users. For example, +GA+PN outperforms the +GA by AUC +.0278 and AUC +.005 on Group5 and Group1, respectively. These are reasonable results since tail users have significantly less number of interactions than head users. By jointly analyzing these results and those of GA, we can find that both GA and PN components are essential for bringing higher-quality recommendation to most users.

5   Conclusion

In this paper, we propose a gradient aggregation strategy. We group each data set according to activity. During training, the gradients generated by each group of data are aggregated to encourage the integration of knowledge from the perspective of optimization, and greatly improve the trunk model's ability to extract common information. In addition, we design the plugin network to guarantee the extraction of personalized information in each user group. Through the architecture of the backbone network and the plugin network, the model has both strong general reasoning ability and good individual reasoning ability. Experiments on real-world datasets demonstrate the effectiveness of the proposed method by comparing with state-of-the-art baselines.

A   Pseudo Code

The pseudo code of our proposed method is summarized in Algorithm 1.

Algorithm 1: Two-stage training strategy

Divide the dataset $\mathcal{D}$ into $\mathcal{D}_1 \sim \mathcal{D}_n$ according to the level of users' activeness.

Stage I: ▷ *Train the Trunk Network*

   1) Initialize **Trunk Network**.

   2) Feed each group of samples into Eq. (1) for forward propagation.

   3) Compute loss $\hat{y}_{u,i}$ via Eq. (2).

   4) Backpropagate via Eq. (3) and put the gradient into the gradient memory queue.

   5) Aggregate the gradients via Eq. (7) and update θ

Output the parameters θ of the **Trunk Network**.

Stage II: ▷ *Train the whole network*

   1) Initialize **Plugin Network** with small values.

   2) Feed each group of samples into Eq. (12) for forward propagation.

   3) Compute loss $\hat{y}_{u,i}$ via Eq.(10).

   4) Backward the loss in Eq. (10) and update $f_p(\cdot)$ and preserve the gradients on $f_t(\cdot)$.

   5) Backpropagate via Eq. (13), update $\Phi^{'}$ and $W^{'}$, put the gradient into the gradient memory queue.

   6) Aggregate the gradients via Eq. (7) and update θ

Output the parameters θ of the **Trunk Network** and the parameters $\Phi^{'}$ and $W^{'}$ of the **Plugin Network**.

B   Experiments

B.1   Experiments Settings

Datasets

Movielens[1]. MovieLens is a widely used public benchmark on movie ratings. In our experiments, we use movielens-1M which contains one million samples.

Amazon[2]. Amazon Review dataset [15] is a widely-known recommendation benchmark. We use the Amazon-Books dataset for evaluation.

Alipay. We collect a larger-scale industrial dataset for online evaluation from the AliPay platform[3]. Applets such as mobile recharge service are treated as items. For each user, clicked applets are treated as positives and other applets exposed to the user are negatives.

The detailed statistics of these datasets are summarized in Table 3.

---

[1] http://grouplens.org/datasets/movielens/.

[2] http://jmcauley.ucsd.edu/data/amazon/.

[3] https://www.alipay.com/.

Table 3. Statistics of the evaluation datasets.

Dataset	#Users	#Items	#Interactions	#Records/#user	#Records/#item	Density
Movielens	6,040	3,706	1,000,209	165.57	269.89	4.468%
Amazon	69,168	81,473	3,137,442	45.36	38.51	0.056%
Alipay	262,446	4,545	27,849,672	106.12	6,127.54	2.334%

Evaluation Metrics

$$\text{AUC} = \frac{\sum_{x_0 \in \mathcal{D}_T} \sum_{x_1 \in \mathcal{D}_F} \mathbb{1}[f(x_1) < f(x_0)]}{|\mathcal{D}_T||\mathcal{D}_F|},$$
$$\text{HitRate@}K = \frac{1}{|\mathcal{U}|} \sum_{u \in \mathcal{U}} \mathbb{1}(R_{u,g_u} \leq K), \tag{14}$$

where $\mathbb{1}(\cdot)$ is the indicator function, f is the model to be evaluated, R_{u,g_u} is the rank predicted by the model for the ground truth item g_u and user u, and $\mathcal{D}_T$, $\mathcal{D}_F$ is the positive and negative testing sample set respectively.

Baselines

GRU4Rec [4] is one of the early works that introduce recurrent neural networks to model user behavior sequences in recommendation.

DIN [30] introduces a target-attention mechanism for historically interacted items aggregation for click-through-rate prediction.

SASRec [7] is a representative sequential modeling method based on self-attention mechanisms. It simultaneously predicts multiple next-items by masking the backward connections in the attention map.

To evaluate the effectiveness on tail user modeling, the following competing methods are introduced for comparison.

Agr-Rand [14] introduced a gradient surgery strategy to solve the domain generalization problem by coordinating inter-domain gradients to update neural weights in common consistent directions to create a more robust image classifier.

PCGrad [25] is a very classic gradient surgery model that mitigates the negative cosine similarity problem by projecting the gradients of one task onto the normal components of the gradients of the other task by removing the disturbing components to mitigate gradient conflicts.

Grad-Transfer [24] adjusts the weight of each user during training through resample and gradient alignment, and adopts an adversarial learning method to avoid the model from using the sensitive information of user activity group in prediction to solve the long-tail problem.

Implementation Details

Preprocessing. On the Alipay dataset, the dates of all samples in the dataset are from 2021-5-19 to 2021-7-10. In order to simulate the real a/b testing environment, we use the date to divide the dataset. We take the data before 0:00 AM in 2021-7-1 as the training set, and vice versa as the test set. On Movielens and Amazon datasets, we treat the labels of all user-item pairs in the dataset as 1, and the labels of user-item pairs that have not appeared as 0. We take the user's last sample as the test set. On Movielens, we use positive samples in the training set: the ratio of negative samples = 1:4 to sample negative samples. In the test set, we refer to [8], so we use all negative samples of a user as the test set. In Amazon's training set, we sample negative samples with the ratio of positive samples: negative samples = 1:4, and this ratio becomes 1:99 in the test set. We also filter out all users and items in Amazon with less than 15 clicks to reduce the dataset. On Alipay and Amazon datasets, we group by the number of samples of users. On the Movielens dataset, we group by the length of the user's click sequence

Implementation. In terms of hardware, our models are trained on workstations equipped with NVidia Tesla V100 GPUs. For all datasets and all models, the batch size is set to 512. The loss function is optimized by the Adam optimizer with a learning rate of 0.001 for the gradient aggregation learning stage and 0.0001 for the plugin model learning stage. The training is stopped when the loss converges on the validation set.

B.2   Results

According to Fig. 4, the larger the group number, the more active the user is, that is, the first group is the least active user group, and the fifth group is the most active user group. Training the plugin network for relatively inactive groups of users requires only a small number of epochs to be optimal (such as groups 1 and 2). The training curve of the user group with relatively high activity level has a more stable upward trend with the increase of epoch (such as group 3, group 4 and group 5). This is mainly due to the difference in the

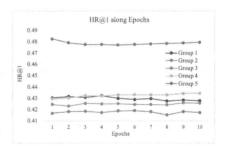

Fig. 4. Performance of Hit@1 on validation set with different epochs.

amount of personalized information in user groups with different levels of activity. For a user group with a large amount of data, more personalized information is required, and more epochs are needed to learn the personalized information. Otherwise, only a few epochs are required.

Toy Example. In Fig. 5, we give a toy example of long-tail effect of a real case in Alipay platform and show the improvement brought by our propose method.

In this case, there are two groups of women, one is young women with high activity and the other is middle-aged women with low activity. They have common preferences such as clothes and shoes but also some different preferences. Due to the long-tail effect, the preferences of low-activity women are difficult to capture, and the model will recommend some popular products for them.

To address this problem, we extract generalization information via the gradient aggregation module so that the model can recommend common preferences such as clothes and shoes to low-activity women, although sometimes not her favorite style. The model's recommendation for the high-activity women and the low-activity women are more similar, so the performance of the model on high-activity women has decreased. Next, we train a plugin

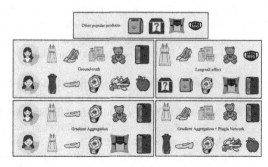

Fig. 5. A toy example of the long-tail effect and the improvement brought by our method.

network for each group of women. The plugin network captures the group-specific personalization information such as different styles of clothes and shoes and other unpopular preference.

References

1. Chen, Z., Badrinarayanan, V., Lee, C.Y., Rabinovich, A.: Gradnorm: gradient normalization for adaptive loss balancing in deep multitask networks. In: International Conference on Machine Learning, pp. 794–803. PMLR (2018)
2. Dong, M., Yuan, F., Yao, L., Xu, X., Zhu, L.: Mamo: memory-augmented meta-optimization for cold-start recommendation. In: Proceedings of the 26th ACM SIGKDD International Conference on Knowledge Discovery & Data Mining, pp. 688–697 (2020)
3. Glymour, M., Pearl, J., Jewell, N.P.: Causal Inference in Statistics: A Primer. Wiley, Hoboken (2016)
4. Hidasi, B., Karatzoglou, A., Baltrunas, L., Tikk, D.: Session-based recommendations with recurrent neural networks. In: International Conference on Learning Representations 2016 (2016)
5. Huang, C., Li, Y., Loy, C.C., Tang, X.: Learning deep representation for imbalanced classification. In: Proceedings of the IEEE Conference on Computer Vision and Pattern Recognition, pp. 5375–5384 (2016)
6. Huang, R., et al.: Audiogpt: understanding and generating speech, music, sound, and talking head. arXiv preprint arXiv:2304.12995 (2023)
7. Kang, W.C., McAuley, J.: Self-attentive sequential recommendation. In: 2018 IEEE International Conference on Data Mining (ICDM), pp. 197–206. IEEE (2018)
8. Krichene, W., Rendle, S.: On sampled metrics for item recommendation. In: Proceedings of the 26th ACM SIGKDD International Conference on Knowledge Discovery & Data Mining, pp. 1748–1757 (2020)

9. Lee, H., Im, J., Jang, S., Cho, H., Chung, S.: MeLU: meta-learned user preference estimator for cold-start recommendation. In: Proceedings of the 25th ACM SIGKDD International Conference on Knowledge Discovery & Data Mining, pp. 1073–1082 (2019)

10. Li, M., et al.: Winner: weakly-supervised hierarchical decomposition and alignment for spatio-temporal video grounding. In: Proceedings of the IEEE/CVF Conference on Computer Vision and Pattern Recognition, pp. 23090–23099 (2023)

11. Li, M., et al.: End-to-end modeling via information tree for one-shot natural language spatial video grounding. In: Proceedings of the 60th Annual Meeting of the Association for Computational Linguistics (Volume 1: Long Papers), pp. 8707–8717 (2022)

12. Lv, Z., et al.: Ideal: toward high-efficiency device-cloud collaborative and dynamic recommendation system. arXiv preprint arXiv:2302.07335 (2023)

13. Lv, Z., et al.: Duet: a tuning-free device-cloud collaborative parameters generation framework for efficient device model generalization. In: Proceedings of the ACM Web Conference 2023 (2023)

14. Mansilla, L., Echeveste, R., Milone, D.H., Ferrante, E.: Domain generalization via gradient surgery. In: Proceedings of the IEEE/CVF International Conference on Computer Vision, pp. 6630–6638 (2021)

15. McAuley, J.J., Targett, C., Shi, Q., Hengel, A.V.D.: Image-based recommendations on styles and substitutes. In: Proceedings of the 38th International ACM SIGIR Conference on Research and Development in Information Retrieval, Santiago, Chile, 9–13 August 2015 (2015)

16. Neuberg, L.G.: Causality: models, reasoning, and inference, by Judea Pearl, Cambridge University Press, 2000. Econom. Theory **19**(4), 675–685 (2003)

17. Ouyang, W., Wang, X., Zhang, C., Yang, X.: Factors in finetuning deep model for object detection with long-tail distribution. In: Proceedings of the IEEE Conference on Computer Vision and Pattern Recognition, pp. 864–873 (2016)

18. Pan, F., Li, S., Ao, X., Tang, P., He, Q.: Warm up cold-start advertisements: improving CTR predictions via learning to learn id embeddings. In: Proceedings of the 42nd International ACM SIGIR Conference on Research and Development in Information Retrieval, pp. 695–704 (2019)

19. Pearl, J.: Causal diagrams for empirical research. Biometrika **82**(4), 669–688 (1995)

20. Pearl, J.: Causality. Cambridge University Press, Cambridge (2009)

21. Tong, Y., et al.: Quantitatively measuring and contrastively exploring heterogeneity for domain generalization. In: Proceedings of the 29th ACM SIGKDD Conference on Knowledge Discovery and Data Mining (2023)

22. Wang, Y.X., Ramanan, D., Hebert, M.: Learning to model the tail. In: Proceedings of the 31st International Conference on Neural Information Processing Systems, pp. 7032–7042 (2017)

23. Wang, Z., Tsvetkov, Y., Firat, O., Cao, Y.: Gradient vaccine: investigating and improving multi-task optimization in massively multilingual models. arXiv preprint arXiv:2010.05874 (2020)

24. Yin, J., Liu, C., Wang, W., Sun, J., Hoi, S.C.: Learning transferrable parameters for long-tailed sequential user behavior modeling. In: Proceedings of the 26th ACM SIGKDD International Conference on Knowledge Discovery & Data Mining, pp. 359–367 (2020)

25. Yu, T., Kumar, S., Gupta, A., Levine, S., Hausman, K., Finn, C.: Gradient surgery for multi-task learning. arXiv preprint arXiv:2001.06782 (2020)

26. Zhang, S., Yao, D., Zhao, Z., Chua, T., Wu, F.: Causerec: counterfactual user sequence synthesis for sequential recommendation. In: SIGIR 2021: The 44th International ACM SIGIR Conference on Research and Development in Information Retrieval, Virtual Event, Canada, 11–15 July 2021, pp. 367–377. ACM (2021)
27. Zhang, Y., Kang, B., Hooi, B., Yan, S., Feng, J.: Deep long-tailed learning: a survey. arXiv preprint arXiv:2110.04596 (2021)
28. Zhang, Y., et al.: Online adaptive asymmetric active learning for budgeted imbalanced data. In: Proceedings of the 24th ACM SIGKDD International Conference on Knowledge Discovery & Data Mining, pp. 2768–2777 (2018)
29. Zhang, Z., Pfister, T.: Learning fast sample re-weighting without reward data. In: Proceedings of the IEEE/CVF International Conference on Computer Vision, pp. 725–734 (2021)
30. Zhou, G., et al.: Deep interest network for click-through rate prediction. In: Proceedings of the 24th ACM SIGKDD International Conference on Knowledge Discovery & Data Mining, pp. 1059–1068 (2018)
31. Zhu, D., et al.: Bridging the gap: neural collapse inspired prompt tuning for generalization under class imbalance. arXiv preprint arXiv:2306.15955 (2023)

Heterogeneous Link Prediction via Mutual Information Maximization Between Node Pairs

Yifan Lu[1], Zehao Liu[1], Mengzhou Gao[2(✉)], and Pengfei Jiao[2,3]

[1] Zhuoyue Honors College, Hangzhou Dianzi University, Hangzhou, China
{lyfcan,zehaoliu}@hdu.edu.cn
[2] School of Cyberspace, Hangzhou Dianzi University, Hangzhou, China
{mzgao,pjiao}@hdu.edu.cn
[3] Data Security Governance Zhejiang Engineering Research Center, Hangzhou, China

Abstract. Heterogeneous graphs (HGs), possessing various node and edge types, are essential in capturing complex relationships in networks. Link prediction on heterogeneous graphs has wide applications in real-world. Although existing methods for learning representations of HGs have made substantial progress in link prediction tasks, they primarily focus on the heterogeneous attributes of nodes when capturing the heterogeneity of heterogeneous graphs, therefore, it performs poorly in maintaining pairwise relationships in HG. To address this limitation, we propose a simple yet effective model for link prediction on HGs via Mutual Information Maximization between Node Pairs (MIMNP). We use an Multi-Layer Perceptron as a node encoder to learn node embeddings and maximizes the mutual information between node pairs. Our model effectively preserves the pairwise relationships between nodes, resulting in enhanced link prediction performance. Extensive experiments conducted on three real-world datasets consistently demonstrate that MIMNP outperforms state-of-the-art baselines in link prediction.

Keywords: Heterogeneous Graphs · Mutual Information Maximization · Link Prediction

1 Introduction

Heterogeneous graphs (HGs), also referred to as heterogeneous information networks (HINs), are extensively present in real-world scenarios, ranging from bibliographic networks [1], social networks [35] to recommendation systems [27]. Unlike homogeneous graphs, which contain only one type of node and edge, heterogeneous graphs encompass multiple types of nodes and edges, effectively capturing complex and diverse relationships within a given network. In heterogeneous graphs, nodes of diverse types can signify different entities or concepts, such as literature, authors, themes, among others. Edges represent associations between nodes, which may encompass various types of relationships like citation connections, author relationships, or thematic relationships. These different

L. Fang et al. (Eds.): CICAI 2023, LNAI 14473, pp. 460–470, 2024.
https://doi.org/10.1007/978-981-99-8850-1_37

types of edges encapsulate the diverse interconnections among different entities within the heterogeneous graph. Performing link prediction on heterogeneous graphs, with the aim of predicting whether a connection exists between a pair of nodes, constitutes an important task. The outcomes of link prediction can be leveraged for recommending relevant items [2], discovering new drugs [3], or detecting risks [5].

Many link prediction methods on HGs are based on heterogeneous representation learning [6–8], that is, they learn representations of HGs and determine the likelihood of link existence based on the similarity between nodes. Methods based on random walks [9,10] typically define a metapath and perform random walks based on the metapath to generate node sequences. These sequences are then used to learn node representations. Heterogeneous Graph Neural Networks (HGNNs) like R-GCN [11], HeteHG-VAE [23], HGT [12] amalgamate message-passing on HGs [34,35] with deep neural networks [33,36] to study node embeddings, and they have demonstrated outstanding performance in link prediction tasks. However, many representation learning methods may not be suitable for the task of link prediction. This is because these methods, in their attempt to capture heterogeneity in HGs, mainly focus on the heterogeneous attributes of nodes, thereby overlooking the importance of graph structure. For link prediction, similarity in graph structure is crucial, particularly the similarity between pairs of nodes, which indicates the probability of link existence. There have been relevant explorations of structural information learning in homogeneous graphs. Heuristic methods [14–17] represent a category of algorithms that are relatively simplistic, but nonetheless effective, in determining predefined graph structural data as nodal similarity indices, thereby establishing the probability of executing link prediction. Despite the acknowledged efficacy and impressive interpretability of heuristic methods, they frequently possess robust presuppositions about graph structures, which consequently limits their applicability across a broader spectrum of contexts [17,18]. SEAL [18] framework provides both a theoretical justification and empirical validation for the effectiveness of acquiring graph structural information by employing graph neural networks. N2N [19] learns node representations by maximizing the mutual information from nodes to their neighborhoods, thereby aggregating information from neighbors. However, as it is designed for node classification tasks, directly aggregating higher-order neighbor information for link prediction tasks can lead to link loss or confusion, thus reducing the effectiveness of link prediction. Moreover, these methods can only address homogeneous graphs and are unable to capture the rich semantics in HGs.

In this paper, we propose a simple yet effective model for link prediction on HGs via Mutual Information Maximization between Node Pairs, named MIMNP. We use an Multi-Layer Perceptron (MLP) as a node encoder to learn node embeddings and maximize the mutual information between nodes and their neighboring nodes. Then, we optimize the node embeddings specifically for link prediction, thereby further enhancing the performance of link prediction. By maximizing the mutual information between node pairs, we can maintain the pairwise structure of the graph, which is a key aspect in link prediction. Our model can achieve competitive results in link prediction on HGs without any special design. Our contributions are as follows:

- We introduce mutual information into heterogeneous graph learning, maintaining pairwise relationships of nodes by maximizing the mutual information between node pairs.
- We propose a simple yet effective model named MIMNP. It only uses MLP as node encoder and can handle link prediction in heterogeneous graphs without the need for specific heterogeneity design.
- We conduct extensive experiments on three heterogeneous graph datasets to validate our proposed model. Our model consistently outperforms state-of-the-art baselines in link prediction.

2   Related Work

In this section, we briefly review related work on Heterogeneous Graph Embedding and Link Prediction.

2.1   Heterogeneous Graph Embedding

The objective of heterogeneous graph embedding is to transpose nodes sourced from a HG into a corresponding vector space which has low dimension. Random walk-based techniques employ meta-path-based random walks to amalgamate structural and semantic information, as exemplified by methods like Metapath2vec [10], HIN2vec [9], and HeteEdgeWalk [13]. As Graph Neural Networks (GNNs) have advanced, numerous studies have employed them in the realm of HG embedding learning, such as HetGNN [8], HAN [6], MAGNN [7] and HDGI [20]. In the encoder-decoder-based technique, a neural network serves as the encoder to process node attributes, while a decoder is formulated to preserve the attributes of HGs, such as TaPEm [21], SHNE [22] and HeteHG-VAE [23]. However, all these methods lack attention to the pairwise relationships between nodes, thereby limiting the expressive capability of the model.

2.2   Link Prediction

Link prediction has garnered substantial scholarly interest, with an Multitude of methods being proposed by researchers in the field. Heuristic methods rely on structural information concerning pairs of nodes, including metrics like shortest path, degree, common neighbors, and more. Relevant works include Common Neighbors [14], Adamic-Adar [16], and Resource Allocation [15]. With the progression of Graph Neural Networks (GNNs), certain models have integrated them into link prediction tasks. For instance, GAE [24] and VGAE [25] employ autoencoders to learn node embeddings, leveraging GCN [26] as a foundation. SEAL [18] takes a different approach by extracting closed subgraphs around target links and aggregating node information to enhance link prediction performance. In the context of link prediction in HGs, the focus primarily revolves around heterogeneous representation learning. Several HG-based methods have been developed using GNNs, including R-GCN [11], HGT [12], and HERec [27]. However, these methods exhibit a deficiency in utilizing graph structural information, which subsequently impacts link prediction performance.

3   Preliminaries

Heterogeneous Graph. A HG is formally defined as $\mathcal{G} = (\mathcal{V}, \mathcal{E})$, where it comprises multiple types of nodes and edges. Here, $\mathcal{V}$ represents the set of nodes, and $\mathcal{E}$ represents the set of edges. Each edge, denoted as $e_{ij} = (v_i, v_j) \in \mathcal{E}$, signifies a connection between node v_i and node v_j. Additionally, a HG is equipped with two mapping functions, $\phi(v) : \mathcal{V} \to \mathcal{A}$ for nodes and $\varphi(e) : \mathcal{E} \to \mathcal{R}$ for edges. Here, $\mathcal{A}$ and $\mathcal{R}$ respectively denote the sets of node types and edge types, with the constraint that $|\mathcal{A}| + |\mathcal{R}| > 2$ to account for the heterogeneity in the graph. The adjacency matrix, denoted as $\mathbf{A}$, is defined as follows: $\mathbf{A}_{ij} = 1$ if the edge $e_{ij} \in \mathcal{E}$. The node features is defined as $\mathbf{X}$.

4   Methodology

Our model aims to learn node embeddings based on mutual information maximization between node pairs in a heterogeneous graph and apply it for link prediction. The overall framework is shown in Fig. 1.

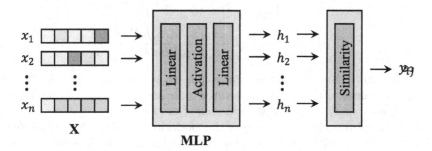

Fig. 1. The overall framework of our MIMNP. MIMNP first inputs the features of the nodes into an MLP, optimizing the model via mutual information maximization between node pairs during this process. Then, the learned node embeddings go through a similarity model to obtain the likelihood of links. In particular, rows of different colors in $\mathbf{X}$ represent different types of nodes.

MIMNP first inputs the node features $\mathbf{X}$ into an MLP, which is as follows:

$$\mathbf{H} = f(\mathbf{W} \cdot \mathbf{X} + \mathbf{b}) \tag{1}$$

where $\mathbf{H}$ is the learned node embeddings. $f(\cdot)$ is a non-linear activation function such as $ReLU(x) = max(0, x)$ or $Tanh(x) = \frac{2}{1+e^{-2x}} - 1$. $\mathbf{W}$ and $\mathbf{b}$ are the learned weight and bias. Each row of $\mathbf{H}$ represents the representation of each node, we use h_k to represent the embedding of the k−th node.

Then given a link (i, j), we calculate the similarity score $\hat{y}_{ij}$ between the node pair based on their embeddings:

$$\hat{y}_{ij} = Sim(h_i, h_j) \tag{2}$$

where the function $Sim(\cdot)$ is responsible for computing similarity scores, such as metrics like Euclidean distance and cosine similarity.

During the learning process of node embeddings, we optimize them by maximizing the mutual information between node pairs. N2N [19] introduces Probability Density Function into graph representation learning to obtain the mutual information between a node and its neighborhood through the node mapping function $H(\cdot)$ from x to h_i and the neighbor mapping function $S(\cdot)$ from x to s_i. The mutual information between the node representations and their respective neighborhood representations is defined as follows:

$$I(S(x); H(x)) = \int_D p(S(x), H(x)) \cdot \log \frac{p(S(x), H(x))}{p(S(x)) \cdot p(H(x))} dx \tag{3}$$

where D is the feature space. Then, to calculate mutual information in a high-dimensional and continuous space, MINE [28] convets converts mutual information maximization into minimizing the InfoNCE loss [29]:

$$\mathcal{L}_{InfoNCE} = -\mathbb{E}_{v_i \in \mathcal{V}} (\log \frac{\exp(Sim(s_i, h_i))/\tau}{\sum_{v_k \in \mathcal{V}} \exp(Sim(h_k, h_i))/\tau}) \tag{4}$$

In our paper, we extend the loss function to node pairs:

$$\mathcal{L}_1 = -\mathbb{E}_{v_i \in \mathcal{V}} (\log \frac{\exp(Sim(h_j, h_i))/\tau}{\sum_{v_k \in \mathcal{V}} \exp(Sim(h_k, h_i))/\tau}) \tag{5}$$

where the $exp(\cdot)$ function donates the exponential function, and τ is the temperature parameter. (h_j, h_i) is the positive pair and $(h_k, h_i)_{i \neq k}$ is the negative pair. Wherein, node j is the first-order neighbor of node i.

To further enhance the efficiency of the model in link prediction, we introduce a binary cross-entropy loss to optimize the model, and the loss function is as follows:

$$\mathcal{L}_2 = \sum_{(i,j) \in N} BCE(\hat{y}_{ij}, y_{ij}) \tag{6}$$

where y represents the existence label of edges derived from the adjacency matrix $\mathbf{A}$ of the heterogeneous graph. For a pair of nodes (v_i, v_j), if $e_{ij} = 1$, then $y_{ij} = 1$, otherwise, $y_{ij} = 0$.

Finally, the loss function in our proposed MIMNP can be represented as follows:

$$\mathcal{L} = \mathcal{L}_1 + \mathcal{L}_2 \tag{7}$$

Table 1. Statistics of Datasets.

Dataset	Node				Edge		
	$\mathcal{V}_1$	$\mathcal{V}_2$	$\mathcal{V}_3$	$\mathcal{V}$	$\mathcal{E}_1$	$\mathcal{E}_2$	$\mathcal{E}$
DBLP	P	A	V	18,405	P-A	P-V	33,973
	14,328	4,057	20		19,645	14,328	
IMDB	M	A	D	11,616	M-A	M-D	17,106
	4,278	5,257	2,081		12,828	4,278	
ACM	P	A	S	11,800	P-A	P-S	17,426
	4,057	7,723	20		4,019	13,407	

5 Experiments

5.1 Experiment Settings

Datasets. We evaluate the performance of MIMNP on three real-world datasets: DBLP, IMDB, and ACM. The details of the datasets are provided in Table 1.

- DBLP is a computer science bibliography network consisting of three distinct node types: paper (P), author (A), and venue (V). The authors within this network belong to four research domains, including Data Mining, Information Retrieval, Database, and Artificial Intelligence.
- IMDB is a network related to movies, which depicts user evaluations of movies and directors. It comprises three types of nodes: movie (M), actor (A), and director (D). In this network, movies are categorized into three genres: Action, Comedy, and Drama.
- ACM is a bibliographic network that encompasses papers published at conferences like KDD, SIGMOD, SIGCOMM, MobiCOMM, and VLDB. Within the network, there are three types of nodes: paper (P), author (A), and subject (S). The papers in this network are divided into three categories: Wireless Communication, Data Mining, and Database.

Baselines. We compare our MIMNP with eight baselines, including four methods for homogeneous graphs, and four methods for heterogeneous graphs:

- Methods for homogeneous graphs: GraphSAGE [30], node2vec [31], GAE [24], and DGI [32].
- Methods for heterogeneous graphs: Metapath2vec [10], R-GCN [11], HGT [12] and HeteHG-VAE [23].

Implementation Details. In our paper, we utilized the Adam algorithm for optimizing our model, with a learning rate set to 0.001. The relevant parameter settings in the paper are as follows: the temperature parameter τ is set to 5, and the final embedding dimension is 128. During the model training process, we randomly removed 20% to 80% of the edges as a test set, using the remaining edges for training. Additionally, we allocated 5% of the edges as a validation set to evaluate the model's performance. We employed the Tanh function as the non-linear activation function and used cosine similarity as the similarity metric. The meta-path configurations in our research are as follows: In the DBLP dataset, we employed APA and APTPA meta-paths. In the IMDB dataset, we utilized MAM and MDM meta-paths. In the ACM dataset, we used PAP and PSP meta-paths. For each different method, we conducted multiple experiments and selected the best-performing meta-path for that method. In this paper, we evaluate the link prediction performance of various models using standard evaluation metrics, including the AUC score (Area Under the Receiver Operating Characteristic Curve) and the AP score (Average Precision).

Table 2. Link prediction performances (%) of our MIMNP and baselines on three real-world datasets. **Bold** indicates the best performance.

Datasets	Metrics	Train	SAGE	nd2vec	GAE	DGI	Mp2vec	R-GCN	HGT	Hete-VAE	MIMNP
DBLP	AUC	20%	50.33	63.11	57.31	71.42	61.39	76.48	69.15	81.32	**84.31**
		40%	52.98	65.65	58.48	84.58	65.32	80.33	75.16	82.71	**85.31**
		60%	54.45	68.35	61.04	85.30	71.41	82.54	82.66	83.15	**86.21**
		80%	58.65	76.75	68.51	87.73	73.65	82.98	84.21	83.46	**87.88**
	AP	20%	50.61	61.27	59.77	73.65	60.81	76.65	70.36	82.37	**85.59**
		40%	50.91	64.82	61.89	86.04	64.74	81.33	76.84	83.56	**86.73**
		60%	52.69	64.29	65.02	87.01	70.69	82.93	81.63	84.26	**89.67**
		80%	55.95	71.19	72.14	89.61	71.51	83.52	85.93	85.39	**90.22**
IMDB	AUC	20%	55.22	53.77	56.38	73.80	52.77	64.02	55.36	54.21	**75.57**
		40%	58.31	59.26	60.21	75.20	51.94	64.31	55.81	60.33	**77.15**
		60%	60.09	63.82	65.52	77.03	53.84	65.27	57.32	54.53	**78.13**
		80%	69.01	69.21	74.29	76.56	53.28	65.89	56.19	61.32	**80.51**
	AP	20%	52.07	51.90	54.12	73.59	54.03	67.69	59.97	55.18	**74.38**
		40%	53.27	55.07	57.31	76.31	53.71	67.83	56.47	61.46	**74.96**
		60%	55.98	57.45	62.35	76.61	61.39	68.51	61.17	57.73	**76.89**
		80%	64.92	60.01	71.96	76.11	62.98	68.92	57.6	62.50	**78.75**
ACM	AUC	20%	61.52	55.49	64.29	74.20	51.56	60.27	53.59	65.54	**78.31**
		40%	63.17	57.34	66.87	74.33	51.90	61.39	52.22	69.98	**78.67**
		60%	65.30	58.69	67.35	74.92	53.24	61.94	54.93	66.72	**80.65**
		80%	67.34	63.14	68.79	74.94	52.47	61.73	52.59	70.39	**82.18**
	AP	20%	65.77	50.69	65.21	76.31	61.33	63.13	58.61	67.03	**75.28**
		40%	67.59	51.23	66.24	77.06	66.67	63.63	59.76	71.95	**75.43**
		60%	69.09	53.85	67.63	77.39	66.27	63.94	63.12	67.11	**82.45**
		80%	69.88	56.02	68.95	77.79	71.62	66.4	64.59	72.19	**83.55**

5.2 Results on Link Prediction

Table 2 shows link prediction performances (%) of our MIMNP and baselines on three real-world datasets. We can observe that MIMNP consistently achieve state-of-the-arts performance across all datasets. Compared to all baselines,

MIMNP improved the AUC scores by 3% to 27% and the AP scores by 3% to 21% on the three datasets. Especially, MIMNP show significant improvements on IMDB and ACM, where the improvements of MIMNP over the best baseline are 27% (AUC) and 12% (AUC), respectively. We noticed that DGI outperforms other baselines in link prediction, which is because DGI can effectively learn the structural information of the graph through the contrastive learning method based on mutual information. This further demonstrates the effectiveness of our designed method based on maximizing mutual information between node pairs. We can see that when only considering features, the performance of the methods for HGs is better than that of the methods for homogeneous graphs. This is because the methods for HGs can better learn the information of nodes and use it for link prediction.

5.3   Ablation Studies

We present ablation experiments to identify the beneficial components of MIMNP. We evaluate our MIMNP without the specially designed module for maximizing mutual information between nodes. Different from choosing neighbors with maximum mutual information, in the ablation study, we directly randomly select neighbor nodes adjacent to the node as positive samples. Table 3 demonstrates the effectiveness of the design of maximizing mutual information between node pairs.

5.4   Parameters Experiments

In this section, we explore the impact of varying the dimension of the node embedding H, and the results are illustrated in Fig. 2. It is evident that as the embedding dimension increases, performance initially improves before gradually declining. This behavior can be attributed to the fact that MIMNP necessitates an appropriate dimension to effectively encode semantic information, and an excessively large dimension may introduce redundancies.

Table 3. Ablation study analyzing the significance of MIMNP on the DBLP, IMDB, and ACM datasets for link prediction.

Dataset	MIMNP (w/ MIM)	MIMNP (w/o MIM)	Improve
DBLP	87.88%	84.37%	4.16%
IMDB	80.51%	75.35%	6.85%
ACM	82.18%	75.21%	9.27%

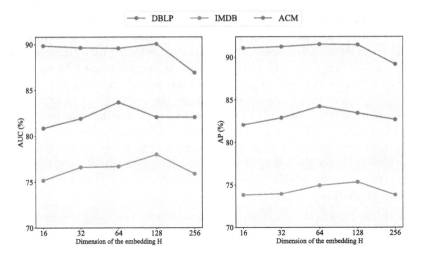

Fig. 2. The performance of various datasets at different embedding dimensions.

6   Conclusion

In this paper, we propose a simple yet effective model for link prediction on HGs via Mutual Information Maximization between Node Pairs, named MIMNP. We use an Multi-Layer Perceptron (MLP) as a node encoder to learn node embeddings and maximize the mutual information between nodes and their neighboring nodes. Extensive experiments conducted on three real-world datasets consistently demonstrate superior performance of our model. In future work, we intend to investigate better ways of generating graph structural information to enable the model to reach better performance. One promising application scene is the recommendation system.

Acknowledgement. This work was supported in part by the Zhejiang Provincial Natural Science Foundation of China under Grant LDT23F01015F01 and Grant LDT23F01012F01, in part by the Fundamental Research Funds for the Provincial Universities of Zhejiang Grant GK229909299001-008 and in part by the National Natural Science Foundation of China under Grant 62003120.

References

1. Tang, J., et al.: Arnetminer: extraction and mining of academic social networks. In: Proceedings of the 14th ACM SIGKDD International Conference on Knowledge Discovery and Data Mining (2008)
2. El-Kishky, A., et al.: Twhin: embedding the twitter heterogeneous information network for personalized recommendation. In: Proceedings of the 28th ACM SIGKDD Conference on Knowledge Discovery and Data Mining (2022)
3. Shao, K., Zhang, Y., Wen, Y., et al.: DTI-HETA: prediction of drug-target interactions based on GCN and GAT on heterogeneous graph. Brief. Bioinform. **23**(3), bbac109 (2022)

4. Jin, D., et al.: A survey of community detection approaches: from statistical modeling to deep learning. IEEE Trans. Knowl. Data Eng. **35**(2), 1149–1170 (2021)
5. Tao, X., et al.: Mining health knowledge graph for health risk prediction. World Wide Web **23**, 2341–2362 (2020)
6. Wang, X., et al.: Heterogeneous graph attention network. In: The World Wide Web Conference (2019)
7. Fu, X., et al.: MAGNN: metapath aggregated graph neural network for heterogeneous graph embedding. In: Proceedings of the Web Conference 2020 (2020)
8. Zhang, C., et al.: Heterogeneous graph neural network. In: Proceedings of the 25th ACM SIGKDD International Conference on Knowledge Discovery & Data Mining (2019)
9. Fu, T.-Y., Lee, W.-C., Lei, Z.: Hin2vec: explore meta-paths in heterogeneous information networks for representation learning. In: Proceedings of the 2017 ACM on Conference on Information and Knowledge Management (2017)
10. Dong, Y., Chawla, N.V., Swami, A.: metapath2vec: scalable representation learning for heterogeneous networks. In: Proceedings of the 23rd ACM SIGKDD International Conference on Knowledge Discovery and Data Mining (2017)
11. Schlichtkrull, M., Kipf, T.N., Bloem, P., van den Berg, R., Titov, I., Welling, M.: Modeling relational data with graph convolutional networks. In: Gangemi, A., et al. (eds.) ESWC 2018. LNCS, vol. 10843, pp. 593–607. Springer, Cham (2018). https://doi.org/10.1007/978-3-319-93417-4_38
12. Hu, Z., et al.: Heterogeneous graph transformer. In: Proceedings of the Web Conference 2020 (2020)
13. Liu, Z., et al.: HeteEdgeWalk: a heterogeneous edge memory random walk for heterogeneous information network embedding. Entropy **25**(7), 998 (2023)
14. Barabási, A.-L., Albert, R.: Emergence of scaling in random networks. Science **286**(5439), 509–512 (1999)
15. Zhou, T., Lü, L., Zhang, Y.-C.: Predicting missing links via local information. Eur. Phys. J. B **71**, 623–630 (2009)
16. Adamic, L.A., Adar, E.: Friends and neighbors on the web. Soc. Netw. **25**(3), 211–230 (2003)
17. Zhang, M., Chen, Y.: Weisfeiler-Lehman neural machine for link prediction. In: Proceedings of the 23rd ACM SIGKDD International Conference on Knowledge Discovery and Data Mining (2017)
18. Zhang, M., Chen, Y.: Link prediction based on graph neural networks. In: Advances in Neural Information Processing Systems, vol. 31 (2018)
19. Dong, W., et al.: Node representation learning in graph via node-to-neighbourhood mutual information maximization. In: Proceedings of the IEEE/CVF Conference on Computer Vision and Pattern Recognition (2022)
20. Ren, Y., Liu, B.: Heterogeneous deep graph infomax. In: Workshop of Deep Learning on Graphs: Methodologies and Applications co-located with the Thirty-Fourth AAAI Conference on Artificial Intelligence (2020)
21. Park, C., et al.: Task-guided pair embedding in heterogeneous network. In: Proceedings of the 28th ACM International Conference on Information and Knowledge Management (2019)
22. Zhang, C., Swami, A., Chawla, N.V.: SHNE: representation learning for semantic-associated heterogeneous networks. In: Proceedings of the Twelfth ACM International Conference on Web Search and Data Mining (2019)
23. Fan, H., et al.: Heterogeneous hypergraph variational autoencoder for link prediction. IEEE Trans. Pattern Anal. Mach. Intell. **44**(8), 4125–4138 (2021)

24. Schulman, J., et al.: High-Dimensional Continuous Control Using Generalized Advantage Estimation. CoRR abs/1506.02438 (2015)
25. Kipf, T.N., Welling, M.: Variational graph auto-encoders. In: NIPS Workshop on Bayesian Deep Learning (2016)
26. Kipf, T.N., Welling, M.: Semi-supervised classification with graph convolutional networks. In: International Conference on Learning Representations (2016)
27. Shi, C., et al.: Heterogeneous information network embedding for recommendation. IEEE Trans. Knowl. Data Eng. **31**(2), 357–370 (2018)
28. Belghazi, M.I., et al.: Mutual information neural estimation. In: International Conference on Machine Learning. PMLR (2018)
29. van den Oord, A., Li, Y., Vinyals, O.: Representation learning with contrastive predictive coding. arXiv preprint arXiv:1807.03748 (2018)
30. Hamilton, W., Ying, Z., Leskovec, J.: Inductive representation learning on large graphs. In: Advances in Neural Information Processing Systems, vol. 30 (2017)
31. Grover, A., Leskovec, J.: node2vec: scalable feature learning for networks. In: Proceedings of the 22nd ACM SIGKDD international conference on Knowledge Discovery and Data Mining (2016)
32. Veličković, P., et al.: Deep graph infomax. In: International Conference on Learning Representations (2018)
33. Jiao, P., et al.: Role discovery-guided network embedding based on autoencoder and attention mechanism. IEEE Trans. Cybern. **53**(1), 365–378 (2021)
34. Gao, M., et al.: Inductive link prediction via interactive learning across relations in multiplex networks. IEEE Trans. Comput. Soc. Syst. (2022)
35. Jiao, P., et al.: HB-DSBM: modeling the dynamic complex networks from community level to node level. IEEE Trans. Neural Netw. Learn. Syst. (2022)
36. Jiao, P., et al.: A survey on role-oriented network embedding. IEEE Trans. Big Data **84**, 933–952 (2021)

Explainability, Understandability, and Verifiability of AI

ADAPT: Action-Aware Driving Caption Transformer

Bu Jin[✉] and Haotian Liu

Institute for AI Industry Research (AIR), Tsinghua University, Beijing, China
jinbu18@mails.ucas.ac.cn

Abstract. Benefiting from precise perception, real-time prediction and reliable planning, autonomous driving systems have exhibited exceptional performance in research. However, the high complexity and opacity prevent its application in practice. To introduce a *user-friendly* autonomous driving system, we propose a driving captioner to generate real time description and explanation of self-driving systems in natural language. Specifically, we unify the end-to-end autonomous driving and video captioning tasks into a single yet effective framework by introducing an additional captioning head to describe the action of the vehicle and explain the reasons. Besides, we exploit an effective accelerating method to accelerate the inference process, which decreases the average inference time from 0.670 s to 0.298 s. Through extensive experiments on both simulation datasets and real-world datasets, we show the superior generalization ability and robustness of the proposed framework.

Keywords: Autonomous driving · Driving caption · Interpretability

1 Introduction

Autonomous driving has achieved significant success in research and development over recent years. Most state-of-the-art methods [4] decompose the autonomous driving task into a series of sub-tasks, including perception, prediction and planning. Despite their superior performance, the multifarious and intricate designing makes it too complicated for common passengers to understand, for whom the safety of such vehicles and their controllability is the top priority. How to explain the behavior of self-driving vehicles to passengers has been an increasingly important issue considering its industrial adoption in practice.

Currently, the interpretability of autonomous driving mainly focus on visual interpretation, like attention map [4] or cost volume [8]. Although such vision-based approaches provide promising results, the lack of linguistic interpretation makes them too complicated for passengers like the elderly to understand.

To bridge the gap, we propose an end-to-end driving caption framework named ADAPT (Action-aware Driving cAPtion Transformer), which unifies the

---

Supported by Institute for AI Industry Research (AIR), Tsinghua University.

L. Fang et al. (Eds.): CICAI 2023, LNAI 14473, pp. 473–477, 2024.
https://doi.org/10.1007/978-981-99-8850-1_38

two tasks of autonomous driving and textual generation. It empowers the model with the ability to both accurately predict the control signal of driving vehicles and provide sound descriptions and explanations of the action in natural language.

Specifically, ADAPT is a multi-task learning framework, which jointly trains the driving captioning task and control signal predicting task with a shared video representation to eliminate the discrepancy between two tasks. We argues that the cues from the other task help regularize the deviation of single task and improve the final performance of both. We demonstrate the robustness of ADAPT with extensive experiments on diverse domains, like different dataset styles, various weather et al.

The contributions are summarized as follows:

- We propose ADAPT, the first end-to-end action-aware driving caption transformer, which can provide linguistic interpretation for autonomous driving vehicles.
- We propose to unify the two pipelines of driving captioning and control signal predicting, which is beneficial to both tasks.
- Through extensive experiments on diverse driving scenarios, we demonstrate the effectiveness and robustness of ADAPT. With a fast inference time, ADAPT is feasible for applications in real-time autonomous driving system.

2   Method

2.1   Overview

As illustrated in Fig. 1, ADAPT comprises two distinct tasks: driving caption generation and control signal prediction. Specifically, a sequence of front-view frames are fed into the shared visual encoder. In driving caption generation task, the video features are passed as input to the language decoder, resulting in two natural language sentences: one describes the vehicle's action and another provides the underlying reasoning. The Control Signal Prediction task takes the same video features as input and produces a sequence of control signals, such as speed, course, or acceleration.

2.2   Model Design

Video Encoder. We employ Video Swin Transformer (Vidswin) [6] as our visual feature extractor. Specifically, for a front-view vehicular video, we perform uniform sampling to obtain T frames with size of $H \times W \times 3$. These frames serve as inputs to the Vidswin, resulting in video features F_V with size of $\frac{T}{2} \times \frac{H}{32} \times \frac{W}{32} \times 8C$. Note that C represents the channel dimension defined in Vidswin. The resulting video features are then fed into different prediction heads for the respective tasks.

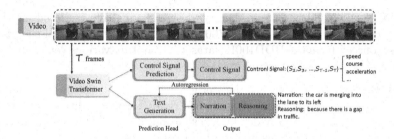

Fig. 1. Overview of the model framework. Input is a vehicle-front-view video, and outputs are predictions for the vehicle's control signals as well as description and explanation for the current action.

Text Generation Head. Text generation head aims to produce two sentences that describe the vehicle's action and the rationale behind it. With previous extracted video features, the video tokens are created by tokenizing along the channel dimension. Then the video tokens are utilized in a language decoder to generate words autoregressively.

Control Signal Prediction Head. The target of control signal prediction head is to predict the control signals based on the video frames. Given the previous extracted features, the prediction head generates a sequence of predicted control signals $\hat{S} = \{\hat{s_2}, ..., \hat{s_T}\}$. Note that each control signal s_i or $\hat{s}_i$ is an n-tuple, where n represents the number of sensor types utilized. The loss function in this process is defined as below:

$$\mathcal{L}_{CSP} = \frac{1}{T-1} \sum_{i=2}^{T} (s_i - \hat{s}_i)^2 \qquad (1)$$

Joint Training. In our work, we argue that the driving caption generation and control signal prediction are aligned on the semantic level of the video representation, and jointly training these tasks in a single network can improve performance by leveraging the inductive biases between different tasks. Thus during training, the two tasks are jointly performed, and the final loss function is obtained by adding the individual task losses, as follows:

$$\mathcal{L} = \mathcal{L}_{DCG} + \mathcal{L}_{CSP} \qquad (2)$$

3   Experiment

3.1   Implementation Details

Datasets. We conduct experiments on 3 autonomous driving datasets, detailed below.

BDDX. BDD-X [5] is a large dataset designed for driving-related captioning tasks, consisting of approximately 7000 videos paired with control signals. The videos, sourced from the BDD100K dataset [7], capture various vehicle behaviors and are annotated with textual explanations.

NUSCENES. NUSCENES [2] dataset is a collection of 1,000 scenes from different cities worldwide, featuring diverse road types, traffic conditions, and weather conditions. Each scene provides high-resolution 360-degree images, radar data, and precise vehicle positions and motion trajectories.

CARLA. CARLA [3] is an open-source simulator that offers a highly customizable virtual city environment for researchers and developers in autonomous driving, with a dataset providing detailed vehicle behavior information and simulation of diverse driving scenarios.

Specifically, We conduct experiments on videos that encompass multifarious scenarios, including various driving behaviors (e.g., stopping, turning, or merging), weather conditions (e.g., sunny, rainy, or snowy) or different time of day (e.g., daytime, dusk or nighttime).

3.2   Main Results

We show some qualitative results on three datasets (detailed in Demo). For BDD-X, our model's performance is impressive across various scenarios, including left/right turn, traffic light (red/green), stop sign, lane merging, pedestrian, and so on. Regardless of different weather conditions (sunny or rainy), the predictions of our model are aligned with the ground truth labels. Moreover, even in dark environment, our model can still produce sound predictions, indicating its effectiveness and robustness.

Furthermore, our model demonstrates excellent zero-shot performance on unseen datasets, like NUSCENES or CARLA. As is shown in our Demo, the selected NUSCENES data consists of videos captured in both sunny and rainy conditions, and the CARLA dataset includes videos from daytime and nighttime scenarios. The generated descriptions and explanations for these videos are essentially reasonable, highlighting the strong robustness of our model.

3.3   Accelerate the Inference Process

We utilize the Open Neural Network Exchange (ONNX) [1] to accelerate the inference process of our model. ONNX is an open format for deep learning models that allows model conversion between frames and enables inference on various platforms. We convert our model into the ONNX format to accelerate the inference process. The results show that the accelerated model decreases the average inference time from **0.670 s** to **0.298 s**, which suggests the possible applications of ADAPT on real-time autonomous driving system.

4   Conclusion

Linguistic interpretability is essential for the social acceptance of self-driving vehicles. We present ADAPT (Action-aware Driving cAPtion Transformer), a new end-to-end transformer-based framework for generating action description and explanation for self-driving vehicles. Through extensive experiments on diverse datasets, we show the superior generalization ability and robustness of the proposed framework. Effective accelerating methods enable the deployment of ADAPT in industrial practice.

References

1. Bai, J., Lu, F., Zhang, K., et al.: ONNX: open neural network exchange. GitHub repository, p. 54 (2019)
2. Caesar, H., et al.: nuScenes: a multimodal dataset for autonomous driving. In: Proceedings of the IEEE/CVF Conference on Computer Vision and Pattern Recognition, pp. 11621–11631 (2020)
3. Dosovitskiy, A., Ros, G., Codevilla, F., Lopez, A., Koltun, V.: CARLA: an open urban driving simulator. In: Conference on Robot Learning, pp. 1–16. PMLR (2017)
4. Kim, J., Canny, J.: Interpretable learning for self-driving cars by visualizing causal attention. In: Proceedings of the IEEE International Conference on Computer Vision, pp. 2942–2950 (2017)
5. Kim, J., Rohrbach, A., Darrell, T., Canny, J., Akata, Z.: Textual explanations for self-driving vehicles. In: Proceedings of the European Conference on Computer Vision (ECCV), pp. 563–578 (2018)
6. Liu, Z., et al.: Video swin transformer. In: Proceedings of the IEEE/CVF Conference on Computer Vision and Pattern Recognition, pp. 3202–3211 (2022)
7. Yu, F., et al.: BDD100K: a diverse driving dataset for heterogeneous multitask learning. In: Proceedings of the IEEE/CVF Conference on Computer Vision and Pattern Recognition, pp. 2636–2645 (2020)
8. Zeng, W., et al.: End-to-end interpretable neural motion planner. In: Proceedings of the IEEE/CVF Conference on Computer Vision and Pattern Recognition, pp. 8660–8669 (2019)

Structural Recognition of Handwritten Chinese Characters Using a Modified Part Capsule Auto-encoder

Xin-Jian Wu[1,2], Xiang Ao[1,2], Rui-Song Zhang[1,2], and Cheng-Lin Liu[1,2(✉)]

[1] State Key Laboratory of Multimodal Artificial Intelligence Systems,
Institute of Automation, Chinese Academy of Sciences, Beijing 100190, China
[2] School of Artificial Intelligence, University of Chinese Academy of Sciences,
Beijing 100049, China
{wuxinjian2020,aoxiang2017,zhangruisong2019}@ia.ac.cn,
liucl@nlpr.ia.ac.cn

Abstract. Handwritten Chinese character recognition has achieved high accuracy using deep neural networks (DNNs), but the structural recognition (which offers structural interpretation, e.g., stroke and radical composition) is still a challenge. Existing DNNs treat character image as a whole and perform classification end-to-end without perception of the structure. They need a large amount of training samples to guarantee high generalization accuracy. In this paper, we propose a method for structural recognition of handwritten Chinese characters based on a modified part capsule auto-encoder (PCAE), which explicitly considers the hierarchical part-whole relationship of characters, and leverages extracted structural information for character recognition. Our PCAE is improved based on stacked capsule auto-encoder (SCAE) so as to better extract strokes and perform classification. By the modified PCAE, the character image is firstly decomposed into primitives (stroke segments), with their shape and pose information decoupled. The transformed primitives are aggregated into higher-level parts (strokes) guided by prior knowledge extracted from writing rules. This process enhances interpretability and improves the discrimination ability of features. Experimental results on a large dataset demonstrate the effectiveness of our method in both Chinese character recognition and stroke extraction tasks.

Keywords: Handwritten Chinese character recognition · Structural recognition · Part-whole hierarchical relationship · Self-supervised learning · Modified part capsule auto-encoder

1 Introduction

Handwritten Chinese character recognition (HCCR) has been extensively studied in the field of artificial intelligence for many years and plays an essential

This work has been supported by the National Key Research and Development Program under Grant No. 2018AAA0100400, the National Natural Science Foundation of China (NSFC) grants 61836014 and U20A20223.

L. Fang et al. (Eds.): CICAI 2023, LNAI 14473, pp. 478–490, 2024.
https://doi.org/10.1007/978-981-99-8850-1_39

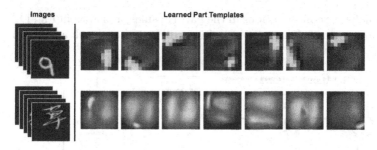

Fig. 1. The primitives discovered by SCAE [10] on digits and Chinese characters. Even though SCAE can capture primitives on simple digits, it tends to fail on more complicated objects like Chinese characters, learning holistic representations.

role in many applications. With over thousands of commonly used characters in the Chinese language, the ability to recognize and understand these characters is crucial for communication, education, business, and other areas of daily life. Traditional methods [3,12,15] on HCCR mainly rely on hand-crafted features and their performance is limited. With the rapid development of deep learning, the performance of HCCR has been promoted largely by using convolutional neural networks (CNNs) for end-to-end feature extraction and classification [4,11,24,25]. However, these end-to-end methods, based on feature vector classification, yield predictions with low interpretability, and with the inability to understand the character structure (stroke and radical composition).

Studies in cognitive psychology [1,4,14] reveal that humans have a natural ability to parse objects into their hierarchical component parts and consider their spatial relationships. Building on these findings, computer vision researchers have explored methods for HCCR based on their radicals [16,17] and strokes [9,15]. However, both radical-based and stroke-based methods rely on massive manual annotations, and the performance of stroke and radical extraction is still not satisfactory. To further enhance the hierarchical structure understanding of visual objects and align it with human intelligence, a promising approach is to learn parsing directly from data. The model is learned to discover visual part concepts with minimal human intervention while maintaining semantic consistency across different samples. Nonetheless, learning semantic parts in an unsupervised manner remains a challenging problem.

Capsule networks (CapsNets) were proposed as a promising alternative method for part detection and structural interpretability. CapsNets are specifically designed to achieve translation equivariance and model the part-whole hierarchical relationships of objects, making it feasible for our parsing tasks. Among the CapsNet variants proposed in recent years [6,7,10,13], the stacked capsule auto-encoder (SCAE) [10] is particularly well-suited for part-whole analysis, as it explicitly utilizes geometric relationships between parts to reason about objects in a self-supervised manner. However, SCAE is limited to learning a small number of simple objects such as handwritten digits. When applied to large-scale Chinese character datasets, SCAE fails to capture character primitives, generating pseudo-holistic representations in the part capsules, as shown in Fig. 1. And thus, the performance of character recognition will collapse in such a scenario.

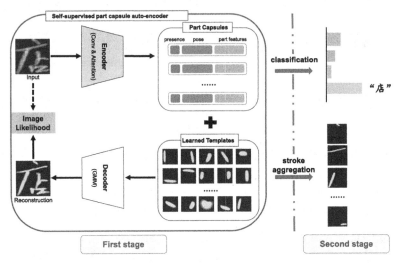

Fig. 2. Illustration of the proposed method. The model understands characters with two stages. The first stage learns the feature extractor and a set of primitives (stroke segments) in a self-supervised manner. The second stage performs post-processing to aggregate strokes and classification using a linear classifier.

In this paper, we find that using only the part capsule auto-encoder (PCAE) in SCAE for character primitive extraction results in better convergence. Motivated by this observation, to enhance the ability of primitive extraction, we enforce some modifications to the original PCAE: adjusting the backbone network architecture, constraining specific pose parameters, and eliminating redundant modules. To address the issue of lacking stroke-level labels, the PCAE is learned in a self-supervised manner: a set of primitives (stroke segment templates) shared across the entire Chinese character dataset are learned based on a reconstruction task. Based on primitive extraction, a post-processing merging algorithm is designed to aggregate transformed stroke segments and generate more complete strokes. The whole framework of the proposed modified PCAE-based method is shown in Fig. 2. Our approach has the potential to significantly improve stroke-based Chinese character recognition accuracy, particularly in scenarios where labeled data is limited.

The contributions of this work can be summarized as follows:

- We propose a method based on modified PCAE for stroke-based Chinese character recognition, which extends the application of CapsNets to large-scale Chinese character recognition problems.

- In our method, stroke segments are learned in a self-supervised manner by the modified PCAE, and a post-processing algorithm is designed to generate more complete strokes during the inference stage.
- Experimental results on a large dataset show that our method improves the interpretability of handwritten Chinese character recognition and yields competitive accuracy, particularly in scenarios where labeled data is limited.

2 Related Work

Chinese Character Recognition. HCCR has been studied since the 1990s intensively. Existing works can be divided into three groups: character based, radical based, and stroke based, corresponding semantic levels from high to low respectively. *Character based approaches* use hand-crafted features like Gabor features [15], directional features [8], vector features [2], and use different classifiers such as modified quadratic discriminate function (MQDF) [12]. Recent methods use DNNs such as CNNs to perform end-to-end feature extraction and classification, and have achieved high accuracies by training with large amounts of samples. ART-CNN [18] trains a relaxation CNN through alternative training and achieved first place in ICDAR2013 competition [20]. However, these methods overlook the structural information of characters and rely on massive training data. Traditional *radical based approaches* relied on hand-crafted rules for radical segmentation, while recent methods also resort to deep learning techniques. DenseRAN [16] treats the recognition task as image captioning by considering each character as a sequence of radicals. Based on DenseRAN, STN-DenseRAN [17] employs a rectification block for distorted character images. However, these methods still rely on radical definitions given by humans. *Stroke based approaches* usually rely on rule-based stroke extraction. In [9], the authors proposed a stroke-guided pixel matching method that can tolerate errors caused by stroke extraction. The stroke extraction method of [15] is based on a directional filtering technique. These rule-based methods are hard to extract complex strokes and achieve competitive recognition accuracy. Our method uses a PCAE to learn stroke primitives in an unsupervised manner and achieves significant improvement.

Capsule Networks. CapsNet [13] was first proposed to parse object parts with dynamic parse trees, inspired by the perception functions of the human brain. As a promising alternative model for improving the robustness and interpretability of CNNs, CapsNet is specifically designed to focus on translation equivariance and model the part-whole hierarchical relationships of objects. Architecturally different from CNNs, CapsNet replaces scalar neurons and pooling operations in CNNs with vector capsules and routing mechanisms, respectively. Over the past few years, a series of variants have been proposed to refine initial CapsNet [13]. EM-Routing CapsNet [7] modifies the capsule representation and proposes an improved routing mechanism based on the Expectation-Maximization algorithm. Self-routing CapsNet [6] further improves the performance by combining the

Mixture-of-Experts. The recent stacked capsule auto-encoder (SCAE) [10] was introduced as an unsupervised CapsNet that explicitly analyzes the hierarchical structure of objects. Although recent works have demonstrated the effectiveness of CapsNets in a various tasks [5, 19, 21–23], they were only evaluated on small-scale datasets, containing a small number of object categories. As the number of categories increases, CapsNets may suffer from catastrophic performance degradation. In this paper, we explore the application of CapsNets to large-scale Chinese character datasets.

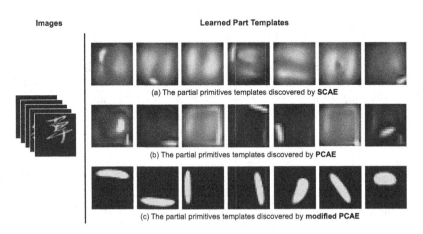

Fig. 3. The primitives discovered on Chinese characters by SCAE, PCAE, and modified PCAE respectively. The modified PCAE shows better performance in learning clear primitives.

3   Methodology

3.1   Overall Framework

The proposed method uses a PCAE based model to extract stroke segments from character images, aggregate the segments to complete strokes and extract features for classification. The PCAE model is learned in an unsupervised manner from a collection of characters images from a large dataset without stroke-level labels. The model contains three modules, *i.e.*, primitive extraction module, stroke aggregation module, and character recognition module. The overall framework is shown in Fig. 2. In training, the PCAE is trained to learn a set of fundamental stroke segments (primitives). In testing, based on the transformed primitives, the complete strokes are aggregated to give a better interpretation of character structure and a feature encoder extracts structural features from the primitives for classification.

3.2   Primitive Extraction

Primitives are a set of basic parts that make up objects. In the context of Chinese character etymology, primitives refer to strokes or stroke segments that form Chinese characters. Since Chinese characters are composed of many complex strokes, including curved and multi-line strokes, which are hard to extract directly, we choose to extract stroke segments as primitives using PCAE.

The recent SCAE [10] has shown potential in unsupervised part discovery, but it tends to fail on large-scale Chinese character dataset, as shown in Fig. 1. The main reason behind this is that the large number of categories poses a significant barrier to the convergence of the entire model. In contrast, using only the PCAE (a part of the SCAE) for part discovery, the model demonstrated better convergence. In addition, we proposed to modify the PCAE by substituting the feature encoder with more sophisticated CNN, eliminating noise in the part capsules, removing the alpha channel of the templates, and imposing constraints on the specific pose parameters. The modified PCAE demonstrates the ability to acquire sparse and well-defined part templates as illustrated in Fig. 3. Inspired by the observation, we design a Chinese character primitive extractor based on the modified PCAE.

The modified PCAE formulates the part discovery problem as auto-encoding: the encoder infers the part capsules which contain the presence probabilities $p_k \in [0,1]$, the poses $\boldsymbol{\theta}_k \in \mathbb{R}^{1 \times 6}$, and special features $\boldsymbol{f}_k \in \mathbb{R}^{1 \times d}$ of different parts. More formally, given an input image $\boldsymbol{I}$, the network initially employs a feature extractor to encode the image into K part capsules:

$$\mathcal{E}(\boldsymbol{I}) = \Theta_1, \Theta_2, ..., \Theta_K, \quad \Theta_k : \{p_k, \boldsymbol{\theta}_k, \boldsymbol{f}_k\}. \tag{1}$$

While the decoder learns a set of pixel-level primitive templates to reconstruct the input. Firstly, the learnable templates T are transformed by the parameters θ and the their gray level C is decoded from $\boldsymbol{f}$:

$$\hat{T}_k = \text{AffineTrans}(T_k, \boldsymbol{\theta}_k), \quad C_k = \text{MLP}(\boldsymbol{f}_k). \tag{2}$$

Then the transformed templates $\hat{T}$ are arranged in the image, and a spatial Gaussian mixture model is used to define the image likelihood. The model employs pixels of the transformed part templates as centers of isotropic Gaussian components with constant variance. The mixing probabilities of different components are proportional to the product of the presence probabilities of part capsules and the value of the template:

$$p_{k,i,j} \propto p_k \hat{T}_{k,i,j}, \quad \mathcal{L}(\boldsymbol{I}) = \prod_{i,j} \sum_{k=1}^{K} p_{k,i,j} \mathcal{N}(\boldsymbol{I}_{i,j} | C_k \cdot \hat{T}_{k,i,j}; \sigma^2), \tag{3}$$

where the (i, j) means the coordinates in image. This feature extractor and the primitive templates are learned by maximizing the image likelihood of $\mathcal{L}$.

3.3 Stroke Aggregation

As shown in Fig. 4, the part templates discovered by PCAE are primarily stroke segments (horizontal, vertical, left-slanted, and right-slanted), which coincides with many manually defined basic strokes [3,15], reflecting some extent the ability to understand the structure of Chinese characters. To extract more intuitive structural information from these fine stroke segments, we further aggregate them to obtain complete strokes. Specifically, we introduce certain writing rules of Chinese characters as priors. For example, a complete stroke should satisfy the **collinearity** rule. As a result, we systematically examine the continuity between neighboring stroke segments and merge the segments that should belong to the same stroke. This process allows us to extract higher-level complete strokes at the semantic level for the current input Chinese character, thereby enhancing the model's ability to understand the character's structure. Moreover, to avoid redundant computations during the continuity checking process, we adopt a greedy algorithm to optimize the entire stroke aggregation process. Algorithm 1 details the post-processing algorithm for stroke aggregation.

Algorithm 1. Post-processing algorithm for strokes aggregation

---

Input: A set of stroke segment images $\hat{T}_1, \hat{T}_2, ..., \hat{T}_K$
Output: A set of stroke images $S_1, S_2, .., S_M$
  for all $k \in \{1, 2, ..., K\}$ **do**
    calculates the center location of stroke segment m_k
    calculates the slope of stroke segment s_k
  end for
  $merge\_list = [\,]$ // store merged stroke segments
  for $i \in \{1, 2, ..., K-1\}$ and $i \notin merge\_list$ **do**
    for $j \in \{i+1, ..., K\}$ and $j \notin merge\_list$ **do**
      calculate the slope s_{ij} between m_i and m_j
      if $max(s_i, s_j, s_{ij}) - min(s_i, s_j, s_{ij}) < s_{th}$ **then**
        merge $\hat{T}_i$ and $\hat{T}_j$
        $merge\_list.append(j)$
      end if
    end for
  end for

3.4 Character Recognition

For character recognition, we train a linear classifier with supervision given the part capsules, which are encoded into a structural feature representation. This learns a $(K \times D) \times C$ weights and C biases without modification of the feature encoder, where K and D denote the number and the dimension of part capsules, respectively.

4   Experiments

4.1   Implementation Details

In our model, we replace the four-layer CNN in PCAE with a seven-layer CNN as the encoder, and the number of capsules is set as 40 considering that the primitives are stroke segments. For optimization, we employ the RMSProp optimizer with 3×10^{-4} learning rate. All the experiments are implemented on TensorFlow with a single NVIDIA TiTan Xp GPU, and the throughput of our model is 304 images/s with batch size fixed to 256.

4.2   Datasets

HWDB1.0-1.1. We train our model on the HWDB1.0-1.1 from CASIA-HWDB [12] datasets. It contains 2,678,424 offline handwritten Chinese character images in 3881 classes, collected from 720 writers. We use the samples of 3,755 GB level-1 Chinese characters in our experiments for training.

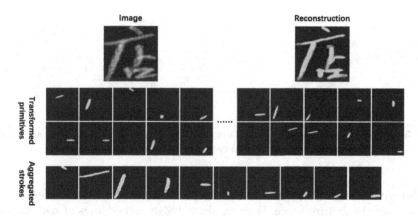

Fig. 4. The structural understanding of Chinese character by our framework. For each input image, the model automatically adjusts the basic stroke segments to describe current character and aggregates them to get more complete strokes with the stroke aggregation algorithm, constructing a bottom-up hierarchy.

ICDAR2013. We evaluate the performance of our model on the ICDAR2013 [20], which contains 224,419 offline handwritten Chinese character images in 3755 classes, collected from 60 writers.

4.3   Effects of Primitive and Stroke Extraction

For each input Chinese character image, the modified PCAE can encode character-aware part capsules. The parameters in these capsules can activate a subset of primitives and adjust their pose and shape to describe the current character. However, these fragmented stroke segments are not intuitive enough for understanding the structure of Chinese characters. The post-processing algorithm to aggregate complete strokes. Figure 4 shows the bottom-up hierarchical character strokes extraction by our model. It can be observed that our model effectively reconstructs the original images and parses them into strokes that are comprehensible to humans. This demonstrates its strong capability in understanding the structural aspects of Chinese characters.

4.4   Performance of Chinese Character Recognition

We test the classification performance of the model under different settings, including different numbers of categories, as well as a few-shot recognition scenario. We compared the performance of our model with the original SCAE and two popular DNN architectures: Conv-Auto-Encoders (Conv-AE) and CNN. For a fair comparison, the backbone of all models remains the same structure.

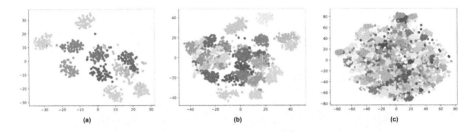

Fig. 5. TSNE Visualization of the feature distribution for different categories. Subfigures (a-c) correspond to the 10/20/100 categories samples from testset.

Different Category Numbers. We first investigate the distribution of part capsules in the feature space. Here we show TSNE embeddings of part capsules for 10/20/100 categories in Fig. 5. We can see that the feature distribution of samples belonging to the same class is relatively compact while those belonging to different classes are relatively scattered, indicating the separability of the learned features. The recognition accuracies on test dataset of different methods under different category numbers are shown in Table 1. With the category number increasing, the recognition accuracy of these models tends to decrease, while the SCAE even fails to converge during training. The performance of our modified PCAE is significantly better than that of other unsupervised feature extraction methods, but slightly inferior to CNN trained in a supervised manner.

Table 1. Accuracies (%) of Chinese character recognition under the different number of categories. HWDB-η means to test the accuracy with η categories.

Method	HWDB-10	HWDB-100	HWDB-3755
Conv-AE	97.6	88.1	43.8
CNN	99.8	97.7	91.7
SCAE	96.8	45.2	-
PCAE	98.4	93.6	62.5
Modified PCAE	99.7	95.8	74.7

Few-Shot Recognition. Considering that our model extracts features in a self-supervised manner, we further investigate its recognition performance in a scenario where the classifier is trained with a limited number of samples. As shown in Table 2, despite the decrease in classification accuracy caused by few-shot learning, our model exhibits better performance than other methods, demonstrating that the structural information extracted by our model has a stronger generalization ability in the few-shot scenario.

Table 2. Accuracies (%) of Chinese character recognition results with different numbers of labeled samples per class. HWDB-3755/ρ means ρ labels for each category of samples.

Method	HWDB-3755/1	HWDB-3755/10	HWDB-3755
Conv-AE	0.03	35.8	43.8
CNN	0.83	46.3	91.7
PCAE	8.4	40.6	62.5
Modified PCAE	10.73	48.6	74.7

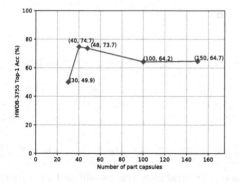

Fig. 6. Impact of the number of part capsules in our framework.

Table 3. Accuracies (%) of Chinese character recognition with different classification features selected from the parameters of part capsules.

Classification Features	Accuracy
presences	3.32
patches presences	64.3
pose	70.8
presences+pose	71.8
presences+pose+features	**74.7**

4.5   Ablation Study

We conduct ablation studies to explore the effectiveness of each component in our method.

Impact of Part Capsules Number. It is important to set an appropriate number of part capsules in PCAE. Insufficient number of capsules results in suboptimal reconstruction of input images, whereas an excessive number of capsules may lead to fragmented and repetitive primitive templates. As shown in Fig. 6, we observe the part capsule number is 40 leads to higher accuracy.

Effectiveness of Classification Features. We also investigate the impact of using different classification features on the performance of Chinese character recognition. The presence, pose, and features are decoupled parameters in part Capsules respectively, and the patches presences are enhanced presences features obtained by dividing the transformed primitive templates into blocks. As shown in Table 3, the integration of all these features gives optimal classification performance.

5   Conclusion

In this work, we bring a new perspective of primitive extraction for Chinese character recognition by modifying the PCAE and introducing a pose-processing stroke aggregation algorithm. Our method captures the structural information of Chinese characters by decomposing them into stroke segments based on a set of primitives and aggregating these segments into relatively complete strokes that align with human cognition. The PCAE is trained in an unsupervised manner to learn primitives, so, in addition to the stroke extraction ability, the model can generalize well even when a small number of samples are used to train the classifier. Our method performs comparably to CNN on medium/small-scale datasets and outperforms them in label-limited scenarios. The proposed method provides a potential solution to large-scale Chinese character recognition with structural interpretation. Our future work will seek better part capsule learning and feature encoding scheme to further improve the recognition performance.

References

1. Biederman, I.: Recognition-by-components: a theory of human image understanding. Psychol. Rev. **94**(2), 115 (1987)
2. Chang, F.: Techniques for solving the large-scale classification problem in Chinese handwriting recognition. In: Doermann, D., Jaeger, S. (eds.) SACH 2006. LNCS, vol. 4768, pp. 161–169. Springer, Heidelberg (2008). https://doi.org/10.1007/978-3-540-78199-8_10
3. Chiu, H.-P., Tseng, D.-C.: A novel stroke-based feature extraction for handwritten Chinese character recognition. Pattern Recogn. **32**(12), 1947–1959 (1999)
4. Cireşan, D., Meier, U.: Multi-column deep neural networks for offline handwritten Chinese character classification. In: 2015 International Joint Conference on Neural Networks (IJCNN), pp. 1–6. IEEE (2015)

5. Duarte, K., Rawat, Y., Shah, M.: VideoCapsuleNet: a simplified network for action detection. In: Advances in Neural Information Processing Systems, vol. 31 (2018)
6. Hahn, T., Pyeon, M., Kim, G.: Self-routing capsule networks. In: Advances in Neural Information Processing Systems, vol. 32 (2019)
7. Hinton, G.E., Sabour, S., Frosst, N.: Matrix capsules with EM routing. In: International Conference on Learning Representations (2018)
8. Jin, L.-W., Yin, J.-X., Gao, X., Huang, J.-C.: Study of several directional feature extraction methods with local elastic meshing technology for HCCR. In: Proceedings of the Sixth International Conference for Young Computer Scientist, pp. 232–236 (2001)
9. Kim, I.-J., Liu, C.-L., Kim, J.-H.: Stroke-guided pixel matching for handwritten Chinese character recognition. In: Proceedings of the Fifth International Conference on Document Analysis and Recognition, pp. 665–668. IEEE (1999)
10. Kosiorek, A., Sabour, S., Teh, Y.W., Hinton, G.E.: Stacked capsule autoencoders. In: Advances in Neural Information Processing Systems, vol. 32 (2019)
11. Lai, S., Jin, L., Yang, W.: Toward high-performance online HCCR: a CNN approach with DropDistortion, path signature and spatial stochastic max-pooling. Pattern Recogn. Lett. **89**, 60–66 (2017)
12. Liu, C.-L., Yin, F., Wang, D.-H., Wang, Q.-F.: Online and offline handwritten Chinese character recognition: benchmarking on new databases. Pattern Recogn. **46**(1), 155–162 (2013)
13. Sabour, S., Frosst, N., Hinton, G.E.: Dynamic routing between capsules. In: Advances in Neural Information Processing Systems, pp. 3856–3866 (2017)
14. Singh, M., Hoffman, D.D.: Part-based representations of visual shape and implications for visual cognition. In: Advances in Psychology, vol. 130, pp. 401–459. Elsevier (2001)
15. Yih-Ming, S., Wang, J.-F.: A novel stroke extraction method for Chinese characters using Gabor filters. Pattern Recogn. **36**(3), 635–647 (2003)
16. Wang, W., Zhang, J., Du, J., Wang, Z.-R., Zhu, Y.: Denseran for offline handwritten Chinese character recognition. In: 2018 16th International Conference on Frontiers in Handwriting Recognition (ICFHR), pp. 104–109. IEEE (2018)
17. Wu, C., Wang, Z.-R., Du, J., Zhang, J., Wang, J.: Joint spatial and radical analysis network for distorted Chinese character recognition. In: 2019 International Conference on Document Analysis and Recognition Workshops (ICDARW), vol. 5, pp. 122–127. IEEE (2019)
18. Wu, C., Fan, W., He, Y., Sun, J., Naoi, S.: Handwritten character recognition by alternately trained relaxation convolutional neural network. In: 2014 14th International Conference on Frontiers in Handwriting Recognition, pp. 291–296. IEEE (2014)
19. Xin, J., Wang, N., Jiang, X., Li, J., Gao, X., Li, Z.: Facial attribute capsules for noise face super resolution. In: Proceedings of the AAAI Conference on Artificial Intelligence, vol. 34, pp. 12476–12483 (2020)
20. Yin, F., Wang, Q.-F., Zhang, X.-Y., Liu, C.-L.: ICDAR 2013 Chinese handwriting recognition competition. In: 12th International Conference on Document Analysis and Recognition, pp. 1464–1470. IEEE (2013)
21. Yu, C., Zhu, X., Zhang, X., Wang, Z., Zhang, Z., Lei, Z.: HP-Capsule: unsupervised face part discovery by hierarchical parsing capsule network. In: Proceedings of the IEEE/CVF Conference on Computer Vision and Pattern Recognition, pp. 4022–4031 (2022)

22. Yu, C., Zhu, X., Zhang, X., Zhang, Z., Lei, Z.: Graphics capsule: learning hierarchical 3D face representations from 2D images. In: Proceedings of the IEEE/CVF Conference on Computer Vision and Pattern Recognition, pp. 20981–20990 (2023)
23. Zhang, X., Li, P., Jia, W., Zhao, H.: Multi-labeled relation extraction with attentive capsule network. In: Proceedings of the AAAI Conference on Artificial Intelligence, vol. 33, pp. 7484–7491 (2019)
24. Zhang, X.-Y., Bengio, Y., Liu, C.-L.: Online and offline handwritten Chinese character recognition: a comprehensive study and new benchmark. Pattern Recogn. **61**, 348–360 (2017)
25. Zhang, X.-Y., Yin, F., Zhang, Y.-M., Liu, C.-L., Bengio, Y.: Drawing and recognizing Chinese characters with recurrent neural network. IEEE Trans. Pattern Anal. Mach. Intell. **40**(4), 849–862 (2017)

Natural Language Processing

Sequential Style Consistency Learning for Domain-Generalizable Text Recognition

Pengcheng Zhang[1], Wenrui Liu[1], Ning Wang[1], Ran Shen[2], Gang Sun[2], Xinghua Jiang[3], Zheqian Chen[3], Fei Wu[1], and Zhou Zhao[1(✉)]

[1] Zhejiang University, Hangzhou, China
{zhangpengcheng1218,liuwenrui,ningxin99,zhaozhou}@zju.edu.cn,
wufei@cs.zju.edu.cn
[2] State Grid Zhejiang Electric Power Co., Ltd., Hangzhou, China
{shen_ran,sun_gang}@zj.sgcc.com.cn
[3] Yiwise AI Technology Co., Ltd., Hangzhou, China
{jiangxinghua,chenzheqian}@yiwise.com

Abstract. As a task aiming to recognize text from images, text recognition is of great significance in both industry and academia. The vast majority of existing text recognition methods use text images with the same styles as training and testing samples. However, when these models encounter images with new styles, their recognition accuracy will be significantly reduced. In this paper, we mainly explore Domain-Generalizable Text Recognition (DGTR), a challenging but meaningful setting focusing on enhancing the generalization ability of text recognition models. For this reason, we propose a practical framework called Sequential Style Consistency Learning (SSC), disentangling the style-specific and task-specific representation. Specifically, our SSC first constructs samples of augmented visual feature sequences, then disentangles the original and augmented feature sequences into style-specific features and task-specific features. To better separate the task-specific representation from the style-specific representation, the Style-Consistency Learning (SCL) is designed for learning the style consistency between original and augmented sequences. The disentangled module and style-consistency learning could provide complementary information for each other. Besides, our SSC is encouraged to meta-learn the style-specific and task-specific features during training based on text images with seen styles, generalizing better to text images with other styles. Numerous experiments and analyses conducted on the benchmark dataset MSDA have shown that SSC can achieve very competitive experimental results compared to state-of-the-art methods.

Keywords: Text Recognition · Domain Generalization · Style Consistency Learning

L. Fang et al. (Eds.): CICAI 2023, LNAI 14473, pp. 493–504, 2024.
https://doi.org/10.1007/978-981-99-8850-1_40

1   Introduction

As a task of reading text from natural images, text recognition has drawn the interest of many researchers. Numerous deep-learning-based text recognition models [2,4,10,25,31] have been proposed, and they have shown exciting performance on benchmark text recognition datasets [12,13,15,16,20,24,27,30].

These datasets usually consist of text images with only a few styles, and these text recognition models use text images with the same styles as training and testing samples. Unfortunately, when these models encounter images with new styles, such as different fonts, different angles, etc., their performance will deteriorate, which is also known as domain shift [23]. Obviously, these paradigms of text recognition research do not meet the needs of practical applications. A viable text recognition method should accurately recognize the text for images with unseen styles, instead of only images with specific styles.

In this paper, we mainly explore DGTR, a challenging but meaningful setting to enhance the generalizability of text recognition models. The previous methods [5,9,14,18,19,33,34] of domain generalization are mainly designed to eliminate the domain shift in image classification. However, text recognition is vastly different from image classification. Therefore, the above domain generalization methods are hard to be directly applied for text recognition. We argue that the sequentiality of text recognition must be considered to achieve DGTR. Motivated by the above considerations, we propose Sequential Style Consistency Learning (SSC), a practical framework for DGTR. Compared with original text recognition models, Our SSC has made several improvements in terms of deep architecture and training modes. Because style-specific information in the extracted visual feature sequence is trivial or even interferes with DGTR, style-specific and task-specific representation should be decoupled from the original representation. Specifically, our SSC first constructs a corresponding augmented feature sequence with our sequential augmentation methods for each extracted feature sequence. Then a disentangled module is implemented to decouple the style-specific and task-specific representation. Besides, we designed a style-consistency module for learning the style consistency between original and augmented samples to better separate the task-specific representation from the style-specific representation. We argue that both the sequential augmentation methods and the style-consistency module are designed to enhance the disentangled modules. As for the training mode, our SSC is encouraged to meta-learn the style-specific and task-specific features during training based on text images with seen styles, generalizing better to text images with other styles. We conducted numerous experiments on the dataset MSDA [26], and the analysis of experimental results show that our SSC can achieve very competitive experimental results compared to state-of-the-art methods. Specifically, Gulrajani et al. [11] stated in DomainBed that model selection is non-trivial for DG yet affects results. Following [11], we use training-domain validation as the mechanism in our experiments. In a word, the contribution points of our paper are summarized as follows:

- We propose domain-generalizable text recognition, a challenging but meaningful setting, enhancing the generalization performance of text recognition models. We are the first attempt to investigate the domain-generalizable setting of text recognition.
- We propose SSC for the challenging setting, disentangling style-specific and task-specific representation from the original representation.
- SSC constructs augmented visual features sequences, and both the original and augmented features are decoupled into style-specific and task-specific features. Besides, we design the style-consistency module to better separate the task-specific representation from the style-specific representation.
- Numerous experiments and comprehensive analyses on the text recognition dataset MSDA show that our SSC method can achieve very competitive experimental results compared to state-of-the-art text recognition methods.

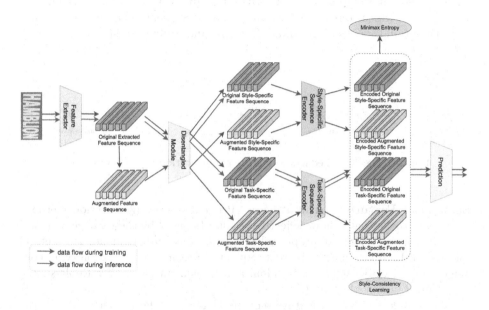

Fig. 1. Overview framework of our SSC.

2   Method

2.1   Base Network

Several methods for text recognition [4,10,25,31] have been proposed, which are mainly variants of [2]. In our paper, we focus on the general framework [2] and use it as the base network of our SSC. The framework [2] consists of the four stages:

1. *Transformation:* The input text image is standardized by a TPS transformation [28]. This stage is optional for a text recognition model.

2. *Feature extraction:* A CNN is utilized to extract the visual feature sequence of the text image. The quality of the extracted visual features has an essential impact on the effect of subsequent recognition.
3. *Sequence modeling:* This stage utilizes a Bidirectional LSTM (BiLSTM) to model the extracted visual feature sequence.
4. *Prediction:* At this stage, the model predicts the final character sequence based on the sequence-modeled feature sequence.

2.2 Sequential Style Consistency Learning

The visual feature sequences extracted in stage Feature extraction usually contain both style-specific and task-specific information in traditional models. To provide effective feature sequences containing only task-specific information to stage Prediction, we propose SSC for DGTR. Figure 1 presents the overall framework of SSC, which consists of three major parts: Sequential Feature Augmentation, Disentanglement and Minimax Entropy, and Style-Consistency Learning.

Fig. 2. Considered sequential feature augmentation types in our SSC.

Sequential Feature Augmentation. Previous data augmentation methods [1,7,8] for images have shown effective results. Inspired by these image augmentation methods [1,7,8], we propose the sequential feature augmentation method for DGTR. Figure 2 depicts different sequential feature augmentation types considered in our work, including Random Rearrangement (RR) Slice Replacement (SR) and Random Masking (RM).

The simple idea is if a feature sequence has a specific property (style), the augmented samples corresponding to this sequence should have the same property (style). Therefore, we construct an augmented sample for each visual feature sequence extracted in stage Feature extraction. Suppose the original visual feature sequence is denoted $S \in \mathbb{R}^{T \times d}$, we construct its augmented sample as $\tilde{S} \in \mathbb{R}^{T \times d}$, where T is the number of features and d is the dimension of features.

Disentangled Module and Minimax Entropy. The Disentangled Module is designed to decouple S into the task-specific feature sequence S_t and the style-specific feature sequence S_s by:

$$S_t = \alpha S, \quad S_s = (1 - \alpha)S \tag{1}$$

where $S_t \in \mathbb{R}^{T \times d}$ and $S_s \in \mathbb{R}^{T \times d}$. $\alpha \in \mathbb{R}^d$ is the weight used to calculate S_t and S_s. α is modeled as a two-layer perceptual structure:

$$\alpha = \sigma(W_2 ReLU(W_1 pool(S))) \tag{2}$$

where *pool* is the average pool operation along the time dimension, $W_1 \in \mathbb{R}^{d \times 2d}$ and $W_2 \in \mathbb{R}^{2d \times d}$ are learnable transformation weights.

Similarly, the augmented sample $\tilde{S}$ is disentangled into augmented task-specific feature sequence $\tilde{S}_t \in \mathbb{R}^{T \times d}$ and augmented style-specific feature sequence $\tilde{S}_s \in \mathbb{R}^{T \times d}$.

Inspired by the structure of existing text recognition models, we perform sequence modeling on these decoupled feature sequences, as shown in Fig. 1. Specifically, two BiLSTMs, Task-Specific Sequence Encoder and Style-Specific Sequence Encoder, are used to model task-specific and style-specific feature sequences, respectively. Let the encoded feature sequences corresponding to these disentangled feature sequences be denoted as $S'_t \in \mathbb{R}^{T \times d'}$, $S'_s \in \mathbb{R}^{T \times d'}$, $\tilde{S}'_t \in \mathbb{R}^{T \times d'}$ and $\tilde{S}'_s \in \mathbb{R}^{T \times d'}$, respectively, where d' is the dimension after sequence modeling. Note that only S'_t as the valid semantic representation is provided to the stage Prediction to predict the final character sequence.

To better disentangle S'_t, S'_s and $\tilde{S}'_t$, $\tilde{S}'_s$, we devise the Minimax Entropy strategy, employing label-based and entropy-based constraints. In detail, for style-specific information, S'_s and $\tilde{S}'_s$ are utilized to predict the corresponding style categories, which is simplified into a multi-class classification problem. The specific process is designed as follows:

$$p_s = softmax(W_3 pool(S'_s)), \quad \tilde{p}_s = softmax(W_3 pool(\tilde{S}'_s)) \tag{3}$$

$$\mathcal{L}_s = -\sum_{i=1}^{N} q_i log p_{s,i}, \quad \tilde{\mathcal{L}}_s = -\sum_{i=1}^{N} \tilde{q}_i log \tilde{p}_{s,i} \tag{4}$$

where q is the corresponding one-hot label, p_s and $\tilde{p}_s$ denote the probability distributions of all N style categories, $W_3 \in \mathbb{R}^{d' \times M}$ is a learnable transformation weight, $\mathcal{L}_s$ and $\tilde{\mathcal{L}}_s$ represent the cross-entropy loss function.

For task-specific information, an intuitive idea is that the corresponding style category should not be determined according to task-specific information. Therefore, we utility S'_t and $\tilde{S}'_t$ to calculate the probability distributions p_t and $\tilde{p}_t$ of all N style categories. Then we leverage reverse entropy loss to regularize S'_t and $\tilde{S}'_t$ to discard style discrimination, the process is as follows:

$$p_t = softmax(W_4 pool(S'_t)), \quad \tilde{p}_t = softmax(W_4 pool(\tilde{S}'_t)) \tag{5}$$

$$\mathcal{L}_t = \sum_{i=1}^{N} p_{t,i} log p_{t,i}, \quad \tilde{\mathcal{L}}_t = \sum_{i=1}^{N} \tilde{p}_{t,i} log \tilde{p}_{t,i} \tag{6}$$

where p_t and $\tilde{p}_t$ denote the probability distributions of all N style categories, $W_4 \in \mathbb{R}^{d' \times M}$ is a learnable transformation weight, $\mathcal{L}_t$ and $\tilde{\mathcal{L}}_t$ are the reverse entropy loss function which we need to minimize in our SSC.

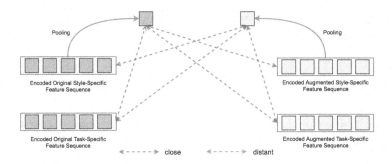

Fig. 3. Overall of our Style-Consistency Learning.

Style-Consistency Module. Style-consistency module aims to learn the style consistency between the original feature sequence and the corresponding augmented sample while reducing the correlation between the style-specific features and corresponding task-specific features, thereby decoupling better style-specific and task-specific features. As shown in Fig. 3, style-consistency learning is performed by maximizing the similarity between the pooling style features and style-specific feature sequences and minimizing the similarity between the pooling style features and task-specific feature sequences.

Inspired by [6], we first use a MLP to obtain the projected style-specific and task-specific features:

$$S_i^p = g(S_i') = \sigma(W_p(S_i')), \quad \tilde{S}_i^p = g(\tilde{S}'_i) = \sigma(W_p(\tilde{S}'_i)) \tag{7}$$

where $i \in \{s, t\}$ and $W_p \in \mathbb{R}^{d' \times d_p}$ is a learnable parameter.

Style-consistency learning is performed in two directions: original to augmented (o2a) and from augmented to original (a2o). The direction o2a is performed as follows:

We first define a feature set $S_{all} = \{\tilde{S}_s^p, S_t^p, \tilde{S}_t^p\} = \{s_1, \ldots, s_N\}$. And we calculate the pooling original style-specific feature s_p as follows:

$$s_p = pool(S_s^p) \tag{8}$$

where *pool* is is the mean pooling operation along temporal dimension.

The soft nearest neighbor $\hat{s}$ is defined as follows:

$$\hat{s} = \sum_{s_i \in S_{all}}^{N} \beta_i s_i, \quad \beta_i = \frac{exp(sim(s_p, s_i))}{\sum_{s_i \in S_{all}}^{N} exp(sim(s_p, s_i))} \tag{9}$$

where β_i is the the similarity distribution which signifies the proximity between s_p and each $s_i \in S_{all}$.

Then we utilize the style-pairs (s_p, s_j) between s_p and $\tilde{S}_s^p$ to apply with contrastive loss, which is defined similar to InfoNCE [22] as follows:

$$\mathcal{L}_{o2a} = -log \frac{exp(sim(s_p, s_j)/\tau)}{\sum_{s_i \in S_{all}}^{N} exp(sim(s_p, s_i)/\tau)} \tag{10}$$

Table 1. Comparison to recent DG methods for DGTR on MSDA.

Method	$\Omega \to$C		$\Omega \to$H		$\Omega \to$D		$\Omega \to$Sy		$\Omega \to$St		Average	
	WER	CER	WER	CER	WER	CER	WER	CER	WER	CER	WER	CER
ERM [29]	82.88	24.89	96.95	83.15	72.33	23.87	77.90	34.56	90.99	76.66	84.21	48.63
MLDG [17]	79.89	23.36	96.87	82.69	69.64	22.56	76.22	33.07	88.83	73.27	82.29	46.99
Reptile [21]	80.24	24.44	96.84	82.77	70.35	22.69	76.46	33.48	87.89	73.09	82.36	47.29
MetaReg [3]	80.03	24.37	97.02	82.55	69.86	22.03	76.84	32.99	89.02	74.01	82.55	47.19
MixStyle [34]	81.89	24.77	97.99	83.34	71.36	23.11	77.49	34.02	89.74	73.87	83.69	47.82
DTN [9]	80.17	23.85	96.90	83.02	69.71	22.17	76.83	32.46	88.61	72.99	82.44	46.90
SFA [18]	82.02	24.33	96.93	83.21	71.22	23.24	77.03	33.83	89.91	75.61	83.42	48.04
SSC	**78.51**	**22.54**	**96.45**	**81.71**	**67.57**	**20.00**	**74.07**	**31.27**	**85.92**	**71.99**	**80.50**	**45.50**

Minimizing $\mathcal{L}_{o2a}$ encourages the network to make the pooling original style-specific feature s_p close to $\tilde{S}_s^p$, and distant to S_t^p and $\tilde{S}_t^p$.

Similarly, we can obtain loss $\mathcal{L}_{a2o}$ for the direction a2o. Then we obtain the style-consistency learning loss $\mathcal{L}_{sc}$ as follows:

$$\mathcal{L}_{scl} = \mathcal{L}_{o2a} + \mathcal{L}_{a2o} \tag{11}$$

2.3 Training and Inference

Let the original loss function used for the base network of text recognition training be $\mathcal{L}_{base}$, and the final loss function $\mathcal{L}$ can be obtained by combining losses of the disentangled module and style-consistency module as follows:

$$\mathcal{L} = \mathcal{L}_{base} + \mathcal{L}_s + \tilde{\mathcal{L}}_s + \mathcal{L}_t + \tilde{\mathcal{L}}_t + \lambda\mathcal{L}_{scl} \tag{12}$$

where λ is a hyper-parameter.

Our method is encouraged to meta-learn the style-specific and task-specific features during training based on text images with multiple seen styles, generalizing better to text images with unseen styles.

As shown in Fig. 1, the data flow of our SSC model during training and inference is different, and the computational cost of our model during inference is much less than that during training.

3 Experiments

3.1 Dataset and Metrics

We evaluated our SSC method on the latest large-scale multi-domain text recognition dataset MSDA [26]. We utilize two commonly used text recognition metrics CER and WER. For both CER and WER, lower scores indicate better performance.

Table 2. Ablation studies of SSC for DGTR.

Method	$\Omega \to$C		$\Omega \to$H		$\Omega \to$D		$\Omega \to$Sy		$\Omega \to$St		Average	
	WER	CER	WER	CER	WER	CER	WER	CER	WER	CER	WER	CER
ERM	82.88	24.89	96.95	83.15	72.33	23.87	77.90	34.56	90.99	76.66	84.21	48.63
+D	82.03	24.01	96.94	82.04	72.20	23.92	77.24	33.63	90.27	75.03	83.74	47.73
+D,A	81.61	23.87	96.84	82.35	70.61	22.22	76.03	32.29	88.94	74.36	82.81	47.02
+D,A,S	80.04	22.82	96.85	82.01	69.43	21.24	75.24	31.88	87.61	72.90	81.83	46.17
SSC	**78.51**	**22.54**	**96.45**	**81.71**	**67.57**	**20.00**	**74.07**	**31.27**	**85.92**	**71.99**	**80.50**	**45.50**

Table 3. Experiment results of SSC with 3 different augmentation methods for DGTR.

Method	$\Omega \to$C		$\Omega \to$H		$\Omega \to$D		$\Omega \to$Sy		$\Omega \to$St		Average	
	WER	CER	WER	CER	WER	CER	WER	CER	WER	CER	WER	CER
ERM	82.88	24.89	96.95	83.15	72.33	23.87	77.90	34.56	90.99	76.66	84.21	48.63
with RR	78.84	22.84	96.68	81.87	68.33	20.11	74.21	31.83	86.44	72.81	80.90	45.89
with RM	79.35	23.03	96.90	82.14	68.22	20.32	75.31	31.64	87.03	72.67	81.36	45.96
with SR	78.51	22.54	96.45	81.71	67.57	20.00	74.07	31.27	85.92	71.99	80.50	45.50

3.2 Implementation Details

Our experiment is carried out on the PyTorch framework. We used a single NVIDIA GeForce GTX 1080Ti for training and inference. Following the work [2], we choose the AdaDelta optimizer [32], and the corresponding decay rate is set as $\rho = 0.95$. The training batch size in our experiment is set as 96, and the number of iterations is set as $300K$. We set the hyper-parameter $\lambda = 1.0$ in the Eq. 12 and $\tau = 0.1$ in the Eq. 10. The learning rates of meta-learning γ and η are set to $5e - 4$. Following [26], the TPS module is not used in our model. Other details of the network structure are the same as [2].

3.3 Model Selection

Gulrajani et al. [11] stated in DomainBed that model selection is non-trivial for DG yet affects results. Following the work [11], we use training-domain validation as the strategy in our experiments. Specifically, we use the 4 testing sets corresponding to the 4 training sets as the choose the model on the validation set for inference.

3.4 Comparison Baselines

We compare our SSC model with recent state-of-the-art domain generalization methods [3,9,17,18,21,34] that can be directly applied to text recognition. These DG methods include: ERM [29], MLDG [17], Reptile [21], MetaReg [3], MixStyle [34], DTN [9], and SFA [18]. For a fair comparison, we directly apply these methods to the same base text recognition network [2] as our SSC, and the model selection is also same as SSC.

Table 4. Experiment results of ablation studies on the disentangled module.

Method	Average	
	WER	CER
ERM	84.21	48.63
w/o. $\mathcal{L}_s$	81.47	46.22
w/o. $\mathcal{L}_s$ and $\tilde{\mathcal{L}}_s$	82.39	46.65
w/o. $\mathcal{L}_t$	81.73	46.61
w/o. $\mathcal{L}_t$ and $\tilde{\mathcal{L}}_t$	82.56	47.12
w/o. $\mathcal{L}_s$ and $\mathcal{L}_t$	82.33	47.35
w/o. $\tilde{\mathcal{L}}_s$ and $\tilde{\mathcal{L}}_t$	81.57	46.76
w/o. $\mathcal{L}_s$, $\tilde{\mathcal{L}}_s$, $\mathcal{L}_t$ and $\tilde{\mathcal{L}}_t$	83.61	47.81
w/o. $\mathcal{L}_{scl}$	81.97	46.66
Full Model	**80.50**	**45.50**

3.5   Comparison Results

Table 1 compares our SSC model with recent domain generalization models on the MSDA dataset. Obviously, our SSC outperforms these recent domain generalization methods on both metrics, WER and CER. Previous approaches (such as MLDG [17], Reptile [21], MetaReg [3], and DTN [9]) consider improving the generalization ability of the original model from the training mode, which is a common approach, but more specific designs are needed for specific tasks. Other DG methods (such as MixStyle [34] and SFA [18]) are only designed for image classification and do not take into account the properties of the sequence recognition task. When these methods are used directly for the text recognition task, their effect is not ideal. Comparatively, our proposed sequential style consistency learning method for DGTR, which disentangles the visual feature sequences and learns the style consistency between original and augmented samples. Our SSC method is designed for text recognition task, which also significantly improves the generalization ability of the text recognition method further.

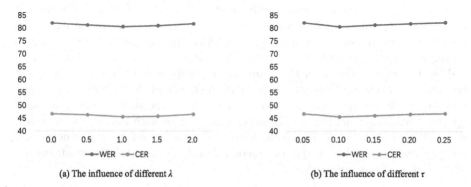

(a) The influence of different λ (b) The influence of different τ

Fig. 4. Experiment results of different hyperparameters λ and τ.

3.6   Ablation Studies

The Roles of Different Modules. Our SSC method can be divided into four different parts: the disentangled module, the sequential augmentation, style-consistency learning, and meta-learning. Table 2 shows the detailed ablation experimental result on these modules. As can be seen in Table 2, these four parts in SSC are all important, and it is the combination of these four parts that obtains the final effect of our SSC model.

The Influence of Different Augmentation Methods. As shown in Table 3, we conducted experiments with 3 different sequential augmentation methods. Compared to the baseline model, all augmentation methods are effective, and SSC model with SR performs the best.

The Role of the Specific Content of the Disentangled Module. As shown in Table 4, we remove the parts of the loss function $\mathcal{L}$ that are related to the disentangled module for experiments. As shown in Table 4, the performance of the SSC model is weakened when any part is removed. Specifically, as shown in Table 4, in the Minimax Entropy part, the loss function of the original sample and the augmented sample are complementary, and when the loss function of the original sample is removed, the loss function of the augmented sample can be supplemented to a certain extent.

The influence of different values λ and τ. As shown in Fig. 4, we also show the experiment results of influence of different values of hyper-parameters λ and τ on the average WER and CER. According to the results, we find $\lambda = 1.0$ and $\tau = 0.1$ are the relatively appropriate values.

4   Conclusion

In our paper, we propose domain-generalizable text recognition, a challenging setting, and we attack this setting with a novel framework called Sequential Style Consistency Learning (SSC). Since style-specific information in the extracted visual feature sequence is trivial, our model leverages a disentangled module to decouple the task-specific and style-specific feature sequences. Besides, sequential feature augmentation methods and style-consistency learning are designed to better separate task-specific features from style-specific features. As for the training mode, our SSC is encouraged to meta-learn the style-specific and task-specific features during training based on text images with multiple seen styles, generalizing better to text images with unseen styles. Extensive experiments and comprehensive analyses on the text recognition dataset MSDA demonstrate the effectiveness of our approach.

Acknowledgments. This work was supported in part by National Key R&D Program of China under Grant No.2022ZD0162000, National Natural Science Foundation of

China under Grant No. 62222211, National Natural Science Foundation of China under Grant No.61836002, and National Natural Science Foundation of China under Grant No.62072397.

References

1. Bachman, P., Hjelm, R.D., Buchwalter, W.: Learning representations by maximizing mutual information across views. In: Advances in neural information processing systems, vol. 32 (2019)
2. Baek, J., et al.: What is wrong with scene text recognition model comparisons? Dataset and model analysis. In: Proceedings of the IEEE/CVF International Conference on Computer Vision, pp. 4715–4723 (2019)
3. Balaji, Y., Sankaranarayanan, S., Chellappa, R.: Metareg: Towards domain generalization using meta-regularization. In: Advances in neural information processing systems, vol. 31 (2018)
4. Bhunia, A.K., Sain, A., Kumar, A., Ghose, S., Chowdhury, P.N., Song, Y.Z.: Joint visual semantic reasoning: multi-stage decoder for text recognition. In: Proceedings of the IEEE/CVF International Conference on Computer Vision, pp. 14940–14949 (2021)
5. Bui, M.H., Tran, T., Tran, A., Phung, D.: Exploiting domain-specific features to enhance domain generalization. In: Advances in Neural Information Processing Systems, vol. 34 (2021)
6. Chen, T., Kornblith, S., Norouzi, M., Hinton, G.: A simple framework for contrastive learning of visual representations. In: International conference on machine learning, pp. 1597–1607. PMLR (2020)
7. Chen, T., Kornblith, S., Swersky, K., Norouzi, M., Hinton, G.E.: Big self-supervised models are strong semi-supervised learners. Adv. Neural. Inf. Process. Syst. **33**, 22243–22255 (2020)
8. Chen, X., Fan, H., Girshick, R., He, K.: Improved baselines with momentum contrastive learning. arXiv preprint arXiv:2003.04297 (2020)
9. Du, Z., Li, J., Lu, K., Zhu, L., Huang, Z.: Learning transferrable and interpretable representations for domain generalization. In: Proceedings of the 29th ACM International Conference on Multimedia, pp. 3340–3349 (2021)
10. Fang, S., Xie, H., Wang, Y., Mao, Z., Zhang, Y.: Read like humans: autonomous, bidirectional and iterative language modeling for scene text recognition. In: Proceedings of the IEEE/CVF Conference on Computer Vision and Pattern Recognition, pp. 7098–7107 (2021)
11. Gulrajani, I., Lopez-Paz, D.: In search of lost domain generalization. In: International Conference on Learning Representations (2021)
12. Gupta, A., Vedaldi, A., Zisserman, A.: Synthetic data for text localisation in natural images. In: Proceedings of the IEEE Conference on Computer Vision and Pattern Recognition, pp. 2315–2324 (2016)
13. Jaderberg, M., Simonyan, K., Vedaldi, A., Zisserman, A.: Synthetic data and artificial neural networks for natural scene text recognition. arXiv preprint arXiv:1406.2227 (2014)
14. Jeon, S., Hong, K., Lee, P., Lee, J., Byun, H.: Feature stylization and domain-aware contrastive learning for domain generalization. In: Proceedings of the 29th ACM International Conference on Multimedia, pp. 22–31 (2021)

15. Karatzas, D., et al.: ICDAR 2015 competition on robust reading. In: 2015 13th International Conference on Document Analysis and Recognition (ICDAR), pp. 1156–1160. IEEE (2015)
16. Karatzas, D., et al.: ICDAR 2013 robust reading competition. In: 2013 12th International Conference on Document Analysis and Recognition, pp. 1484–1493. IEEE (2013)
17. Li, D., Yang, Y., Song, Y.Z., Hospedales, T.M.: Learning to generalize: meta-learning for domain generalization. In: Thirty-Second AAAI Conference on Artificial Intelligence (2018)
18. Li, P., Li, D., Li, W., Gong, S., Fu, Y., Hospedales, T.M.: A simple feature augmentation for domain generalization. In: Proceedings of the IEEE/CVF International Conference on Computer Vision, pp. 8886–8895 (2021)
19. Liu, C., Wang, L., Li, K., Fu, Y.: Domain generalization via feature variation decorrelation. In: Proceedings of the 29th ACM International Conference on Multimedia, pp. 1683–1691 (2021)
20. Mishra, A., Alahari, K., Jawahar, C.: Scene text recognition using higher order language priors. In: BMVC-British Machine Vision Conference. BMVA (2012)
21. Nichol, A., Achiam, J., Schulman, J.: On first-order meta-learning algorithms. arXiv preprint arXiv:1803.02999 (2018)
22. Van den Oord, A., Li, Y., Vinyals, O., et al.: Representation learning with contrastive predictive coding. arXiv preprint arXiv:1807.03748 (2018)
23. Pan, S.J., Yang, Q.: A survey on transfer learning. IEEE Trans. Knowl. Data Eng. **22**(10), 1345–1359 (2009)
24. Phan, T.Q., Shivakumara, P., Tian, S., Tan, C.L.: Recognizing text with perspective distortion in natural scenes. In: Proceedings of the IEEE International Conference on Computer Vision, pp. 569–576 (2013)
25. Qiao, Z., et al.: PIMNet: a parallel, iterative and mimicking network for scene text recognition. In: Proceedings of the 29th ACM International Conference on Multimedia, pp. 2046–2055 (2021)
26. Qiu, S., Zhu, C., Zhou, W.: Meta self-learning for multi-source domain adaptation: a benchmark. In: Proceedings of the IEEE/CVF International Conference on Computer Vision, pp. 1592–1601 (2021)
27. Risnumawan, A., Shivakumara, P., Chan, C.S., Tan, C.L.: A robust arbitrary text detection system for natural scene images. Expert Syst. Appl. **41**(18), 8027–8048 (2014)
28. Shi, B., Wang, X., Lyu, P., Yao, C., Bai, X.: Robust scene text recognition with automatic rectification. In: Proceedings of the IEEE Conference on Computer Vision and Pattern Recognition, pp. 4168–4176 (2016)
29. Vapnik, V.: Statistical Learning Theory. Wiley (1998)
30. Wang, K., Babenko, B., Belongie, S.: End-to-end scene text recognition. In: 2011 International Conference on Computer Vision, pp. 1457–1464. IEEE (2011)
31. Wang, Y., Lian, Z.: Exploring font-independent features for scene text recognition. In: Proceedings of the 28th ACM International Conference on Multimedia, pp. 1900–1920 (2020)
32. Zeiler, M.D.: ADADELTA: an adaptive learning rate method. arXiv preprint arXiv:1212.5701 (2012)
33. Zhang, G., Zhao, H., Yu, Y., Poupart, P.: Quantifying and improving transferability in domain generalization. In: Advances in Neural Information Processing Systems, vol. 34 (2021)
34. Zhou, K., Yang, Y., Qiao, Y., Xiang, T.: Domain generalization with mixstyle. In: International Conference on Learning Representations (2021)

MusicGAIL: A Generative Adversarial Imitation Learning Approach for Music Generation

Yusong Liao[1]([✉]), Hongguang Xu[1,2], and Ke Xu[3]

[1] Harbin Institute of Technology, Shenzhen, China
21s152107@stu.hit.edu.cn
[2] Peng Cheng Laboratory, Shenzhen, China
[3] Shenzhen Polytechnic, Shenzhen, China

Abstract. Deep learning based automatic music generation has received significantly attention and became an attractive research topic in recent years. However, most existing methods face three major challenges: (1) Models based on the Recurrent Neural Networks (RNNs) trained by Maximum Likelihood Estimation (MLE) suffer from the exposure bias problem, while some Generative Adversarial Networks (GANs) based methods have been proposed to alleviate it, they still suffer from the problems of reward sparsity and mode collapse. (2) Deep Reinforcement Learning (DRL) based models encounter the reward sparsity problem and it is impossible to manually specify a completely reasonable reward function. (3) Although Transformer can be used as an alternative to show the better parallelization and performance over the origin RNNs, it is still extremely difficult to optimize for the standard transformer structure in RL setting. In this paper, we propose MusicGAIL, a generative model for generating the online countermelody for folk melodies under the framework of generative adversarial imitation learning (GAIL) that directly learn the optimal policy from dataset without laboriously defining the reward. As the standard Transformer is hard to be applied in RL setting, we adopt Gated Transformer-XL (GTrXL) to stabilize the model training. Experimental results show that the melody pieces generated from MusicGAIL achieve better quality and diversity. Moreover, their subjective scores significantly higher than baselines in terms of melody, harmony, rhythm, folk style and emotion.

Keywords: Music Generation · GAIL

1 Introduction

As an important form of art to express human feelings and emotions, music has played an increasingly essential role in people's daily life. In recent years, with the advances of machine learning technology, deep learning and neural networks

This work is supported by the Major Key Project of PCL (PCL2021A03-1).

L. Fang et al. (Eds.): CICAI 2023, LNAI 14473, pp. 505–516, 2024.
https://doi.org/10.1007/978-981-99-8850-1_41

have been implemented in symbolic music generation domain. Most existing deep learning based generative model adopt the variants of Recurrent Neural Networks (RNNs) [1] such as Long Short-Term Memory (LSTM) [2] or Gated Recurrent Unit (GRU) [3], and are trained by Maximum Likelihood Estimation (MLE) [4] to learn the probability distribution of next note based on the previous note sequence.

However, generating a piece of reasonable music that have clear harmonic and rhythmic structure has always been an interesting and challenging task. These existing methods still face three major challenges.

Firstly, these autoregressive models trained by MLE are not always ideal since they suffer from the exposure bias problem [5] and mismatch problem between training criterion and generation objectives [6]. Meanwhile, MLE only focuses on the prediction of each note and greedily choose the note with the highest probability as the next prediction, but ignoring the long-term global consistency of the whole music. Therefore, the two major defects will significantly lower the quality of generated music. Although some Generative Adversarial Networks (GAN) [7] based methods have been proposed to alleviate the exposure bias problem, these adversarial models still suffer from the mode collapse problems [8], which means the distribution of generated music samples cannot cover the global distribution of expert samples, causing a lack of diversity and creativity for generated samples.

Secondly, some deep reinforcement learning (DRL) based models (e.g. [9–11]) are employed as an alternative to show the superior performance over most GAN based music generation models, among which RL-Tuner [9] is the first attempt to train model to generate monophonic melody by combining MLE and RL training. On this basis, Bach2Bach [10] adopt a two layers LSTM model with a convolutional kernel to generate polyphonic harmonies and achieve the superior performance than RL-Tuner [9]. However, they also encounter the reward sparsity problem similar to GAN, which makes the model training significantly difficult to converge. Sequence Tutor [11] adopt a pair of RNNs and manually define a domain-specific reward function to ensure the high-quality of generated melodies. These reward models manually specified in terms of a reward function as composition rules based on music theory in [9–11] have greatly limitations and it is almost impossible to manually specify a completely reasonable reward function for this complex task like music generation. While RL-Duet [6] used a set of neural networks to represent reward instead of manually specifying reward models based on composition rules and designed four types of reward models to achieve the global coherence in whole music pieces, it still has not completely got rid of its dependence on composition rules.

Thirdly, the original RNNs have poor performance in parallelization and are likely to suffer from vanishing or exploding gradients problem. One new network architecture Transformer [12] can handle longer temporal horizons better than RNNs. On this basis, MusicTransformer [13] modified the relative attention mechanism in Transformer and became the first successful case of using Transformers to generate music with long-term structure. Nevertheless, it is extremely difficult to optimize for the standard transformer structure in RL setting, which results in a number of transformers used in Natural Language Processing (NLP) domain still cannot be successfully applied to the RL setting.

To address these problems in existing music generation model, we propose using Generative Adversarial Imitation Learning (GAIL) [14] with high sample efficiency to directly learn the optimal policy for generating each note from giving expert musical pieces without laboriously specifying the reward function. Specifically, we design MusicGAIL based on [6,11,15], a novel model to generate the online countermelody for folk melodies via GAIL, which consists of a melodic generator, a style discriminator and a cooperation rewarder. To overcome the limitation that the standard Transformer is difficult to be applied to RL setting, a novel architectural variant, the Gated Transformer-XL (GTrXL), has been proposed in [16] to provide an easy-to-train alternative that improve the stability and learning speed of initial transformer. Therefore, MusicGAIL leverages guidance from GTrXL in our work.

To test and verify the MusicGAIL model, we compare it with three baselines: MLE, DuetLSTM and RL-Duet [6] and evaluate these models from the objective and subjective aspects. The experimental results of objective evaluation show that MusicGAIL model achieves significant improvement in performance, generates the more harmonious note sequences with reasonable intervals and imitate Chinese folk style better than baselines. The experimental results of user listening evaluation also show that the subjective scores of our proposed MusicGAIL are significantly higher than baselines in terms of melody, harmony, rhythm, folk style and emotion, especially folk style.

The main contributions of our work are summarized in: (1) We propose a generative adversarial imitation learning framework based music generation model MusicGAIL which directly learn the optimal policy from dataset without laboriously defining the reward. (2) Experimental results show that MusicGAIL can effectively alleviate the exposure bias problem in MLE and the mode collapse problem in most adversarial models to a certain extent. (3) The melody samples generated from MusicGAIL achieve better quality and diversity in objective evaluation and higher scores in subjective evaluation compared to baselines.

2   Musical Data Representation and Preprocessing

In order to make music data preprocessing more convenient and efficient, we implement it by an open source Python library MusPy [17] which has provided easy-to-use methods for data collection, data preprocessing and model evaluating in symbolic music generation system. In general, we pick up the required dataset from music database and filter out some music that have non-acceptable durations or cannot be successfully read by MusPy. In order to eliminate the influence of rhythm and tone on the music, we transpose music into C_{major}/A_{minor}.

2.1   Interactive Duet Model

It is extremely important to define the music representation for our subsequent work. According to RL-Duet [6], we take an interactive duet improvisation model as consisting of the human player part and the machine part. More specifically, denote the token representations of each music piece by

$$N_{1:K} = \begin{pmatrix} n_{1:K}^{(h)} \\ n_{1:K}^{(m)} \end{pmatrix} = \begin{pmatrix} n_1^{(h)} & n_2^{(h)} & \cdots & n_K^{(h)} \\ n_1^{(m)} & n_2^{(m)} & \cdots & n_K^{(m)} \end{pmatrix}, \tag{1}$$

where $n_{1:K}^{(h)} = \left[n_1^{(h)}, n_2^{(h)}, \cdots, n_K^{(h)} \right]$ represents the music melody which is composed by human player and the $n_{1:K}^{(m)} = \left[n_1^{(m)}, n_2^{(m)}, \cdots, n_K^{(m)} \right]$ represents the countermelody which is generated by machine. The $n_i^{(h)}$ and $n_i^{(m)}$ are the $i-th$ tokens in the human player part and machine part respectively.

2.2 Pitch and Duration Encodings

Following BachDuet [18], each token $n_i^{(\cdot)}$ encodes the pitch and duration information of a note. Pitch is encoded with the range of [36, 96] in MIDI number. The same as most of existing researches, we assume a 4/4-time signature and quantize music timing into 16th notes, which is the shortest duration of notes in this work. It means that each beat is subdivided into 4 equal parts. For those notes with longer duration, we use " _ " symbols for held notes. In this case, each note is represented by a pitch-onset token followed by some " _ " tokens. For example, a C4 quarter note can be represented as 4 time-steps: ["60", " _ ", " _ ", " _ "] (the MIDI number of C4 is 60). In addition, we use "R" symbol to represent rest.

In order to represent the rhythmic information of music and achieve a natural synchronization between human player part and machine part, we follow FolkDuet and adopt a subdivision $[b_1, b_2, \cdots, b_K]$ containing the within-measure position of each note to encode the beat information. Where b_i can be obtained by modulating the onset time t_i of each note by 16. However, this is not the final representation of music data and we are unable to feed non-numeric notes into a neural network. We need to convert these symbols to integers by constructing a mapping table from pitch and duration to integer numbers.

MusPy is used to extract the corresponding sequence of notes, which are applied to create mapping tables that map from each of possible pitches and durations to the unique integer. Since the pitch and duration sequences are all non-numeric, it is further necessary to convert these sequences into corresponding integer sequences based on the mapping tables. As shown in Fig. 1

3   Generative Adversarial Imitation Learning

In this work, we extend the generative adversarial imitation learning (GAIL) to music generation. This framework applies GAN to solving imitation learning problems and can directly learn a policy from giving dataset. Specifically, it consists of a generator G_θ which aims to generate note sequences similar to real note sequences and a discriminator D_ϕ which aims to distinguish the real note

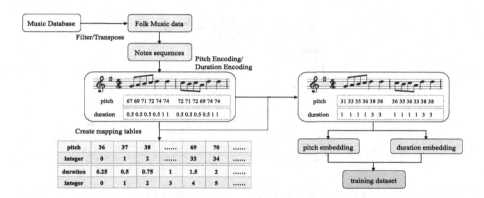

Fig. 1. Illustration of music data preprocessing procedure.

sequences from the generated sequences. They are parameterized with θ and ϕ, respectively.

What is more important, GAIL directly takes the optimal strategy as the learning objective, the strategy and reward function are represented by neural networks. Therefore, GAIL simplifies the steps of iterative training in IRL and more efficient than general IRL algorithm.

In GAIL, generator and discriminator satisfy the following objective function:

$$\min_{G} \max_{D} \mathbf{E}_{p_{\text{real}}}[D_{\phi}(s,n)] + \mathbf{E}_{G_{\theta}}[1 - D_{\phi}(s,n)], \tag{2}$$

where (s,n) denotes state-action pairs. n denotes each note generated from generator.

3.1 MusicGAIL Framework

For our task of music generation, we proposed MusicGAIL, a generative adversarial imitation learning framework base on the Sequence Tutor [11] proposed by Jaques, RL-Duet [6] and later expanded upon by Jiang's FolkDuet [15] model. Just like RL-Duet and FolkDuet, our framework consists of melodic generator, style-discriminator, cooperation-rewarder and critic-network. In order to apply the GAIL algorithm and achieve a globally coherent and rhythmic structure in music, we need to model generating corresponding machine counterparts according to human input as a RL problem. Figure 2 shows the overall framework of MusicGAIL. The novelty of our work is using GAIL algorithm to learn a policy from given expert demonstrations during the training process and adopt the Transformer [12], replacing the recurrent neural network most commonly used in music generative model. More specifically, our approach is that style-discriminator is trained to distinguish generated melody samples from the real expert samples and cooperation-rewarder in our model is the same as [15]. It is trained on two pre-trained models, Bach-HM and Bach-M [15], to make a judgement on the degree of interaction between human player and machine part, in

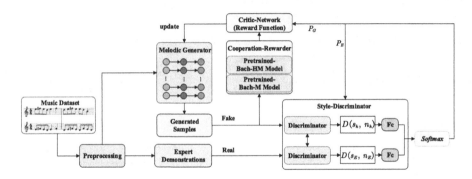

Fig. 2. GAIL framework for music generation.

this case the melodic generator is trained by the actor-critic algorithm with rewards provided by style-discriminator and cooperation-rewarder to learn an optimal policy to generate notes, which aims to generate melodies whose style is as similar as possible to the real melody samples. Critic network is a feedback network that can score each note generated by melodic generator and the reward function in critic network consists of the probability output of style-discriminator and output of cooperation-rewarder. The two training phases of melodic generator and style-discriminator are executed alternately. It is worth noting that during the training of melodic generator, cooperation-rewarder is fixed.

3.2   Melodic Generator

For the melodic generator, the probability of the note sequence is defined as the joint probability of all the tokens:

$$G_\theta\left(n_{1:K}\right) = \prod_{k=1}^{K-1} G_\theta\left(a_k = n_{k+1} \mid s_k = n_{1:k}\right), \tag{3}$$

where $n_{1:K}$ is the note sequence. a_k is the action to select the next note n_{k+1}, s_k is the state of the previous prediction $n_{1:k}$ and K is the length of sequence. We obtain the generated note sequence by sampling from the distribution. The melodic generator is trained by the Actor-Critic algorithm with generalized advantage estimator(GAE) [19] to learn a policy $\pi\left(n_k^{(m)} \mid S_k\right)$ and a value V_k to predict the next note, which aims to maximize the expected long-term discounted reward of note $n_k^{(m)}$.

$$R_k = \sum_{i=0}^{K} \gamma^i \left(R_{i+k}^{(s)} + \beta R_{i+k}^{(c)}\right), \tag{4}$$

where $R^{(s)}$ and $R^{(c)}$ are two rewards provided by style-discriminator and cooperation rewarder, γ is the discount factor, and β is the weight factor.

We randomly select one melody from training dataset as human player part $n_{1:K}^{(h)} = \left[n_1^{(h)}, n_2^{(h)}, \cdots, n_K^{(h)} \right]$ in each training iteration. The melodic generator acquired the observation of the current state s_k from the already played notes in the human player part $\left[n_1^{(h)}, n_2^{(h)}, \cdots, n_{k'-1}^{(h)} \right]$, the already generated machine part $\left[n_1^{(m)}, n_2^{(m)}, \cdots, n_{k-1}^{(m)} \right]$, and generate the new note n_k base on s_k.

In this work, GTrXL is used to form the melodic generator and discriminator, replacing RNNs. More details about GTrXL can be found in [16]. The main improvements of this architecture compared to the original transformer are as follows:

- Reordered the layer normalization modules in transformer block.
- The standard residual connections after Multi-Head Attention and Position-Wise MLP are replaced with gating layers.

3.3 Style-Discriminator

The purpose of the style-discriminator is to capture the style of folk melodies in expert samples and strive to classify the style between the real note sequences and the generated sequences from melodic generator. It takes the current state s_k, generated action a_k (i.e. state-action pairs (s_k, a_k)) and the state-action pairs of expert samples (s_E, a_E) as the input. The outputs of style-discriminator represent the probability of discriminator makes a judgment on (s, a) generated from the expert policy or agent policy, which satisfied the following expression:

$$P_G, P_E = \text{soft max} \left(W_t \left[D\left(s_k, a_k \right), D\left(s_E, a_E \right) \right] \right), \tag{5}$$

where W_t is the trainable weight matrix, P_E is the probability of judging note sequences are generated from the expert samples and it will be maximized during optimizing the style-discriminator with cross-entropy loss, P_G is the probability of judging note sequences are generated from the melodic generator and it can be interpreted as the reward function to provide the learning signal to train generator policy [14].

When the values of P_G and P_E approach 0.5, style-discriminator will not be able to distinguish between the generated samples and real expert samples. In this case, the samples generated by melodic generator can perfectly fit the real expert samples distribution (i.e. the style of the generated melodies are extremely similar to the real melodies).

4 Experimental Results

In the experiment section, we implemented the code of our MusicGAIL model for experiments by programming language Python 3.10 under the deep learning framework "Pytorch" and trained our model on a server with 40GB video memory NVIDIA A100 GPU. We used the default parameters in FolkDuet [15] and GTrXL [16]. After the training of MusicGAIL model, we can obtain some high-quality melody samples[1]

4.1 Dataset

In order to test and evaluate our MusicGAIL model better, folksong dataset in Essen Associative Code and Folksong Database[2] is employed on our experiment. It mainly consists of folksongs from Germany and China and their folksongs account for about 67% and 28% respectively. Due to the Chinese folksongs contained relatively complete information on area, style and phrase, we select the 2241 folksongs from China as our training dataset instead of Germany.

4.2 The Training Process of MusicGAIL

The training procedure of MusicGAIL consists of three main stages: First of all, we randomly select folksongs in training dataset, shuffle or randomly transposing pitch of each melody and take them as the corresponding countermelody to form fake duets, then warm up the melodic generator with fake duets. Next, we obtain the cooperation reward on Bach-HM and Bach-M. The melodic generator and style-discriminator are trained alternatively. Finally, we update style-discriminator and update the melodic generator respectively after normalizing all the rewards. It is worth noting that learning rate in our model will be updated every 10 training epoch. We repeat the aforementioned model training process until convergence.

4.3 Comparison and Evaluation

In this work, we compare the performance of our MusicGAIL model with three baselines: a maximum likelihood estimation (MLE) model, a DuetLSTM model and a RL-Duet [6] model. Among which, the DuetLSTM[3] model is our implementation of an open source project that generating melodies with LSTM network.

For a fair comparison between DuetLSTM model and our MusicGAIL model, DuetLSTM needs to be trained on the duets dataset and all settings should be the same as our MusicGAIL except LSTM network. On the other hand, following the previous work on music generation, we evaluate our MusicGAIL model from the subjective and objective aspects. Specifically, we implement it on quantitative metrics evaluation and user listening evaluation. It is noted that we only compare our model with MLE and DuetLSTM in the user listening evaluation since RL-Duet didn't publish their results in subjective evaluation.

---

[1] Melody samples are available at https://github.com/AcademicLoser/MusicProject.
[2] Database is available at http://www.esac-data.org.
[3] Code is available at https://github.com/musikalkemist/generating-melodies-with-rnn-lstm.

Quantitative Metrics Evaluation. We will evaluate the features of music generated from our model on several conventional objective metrics proposed in [20]: PC/bar, PI, IOI, NLH, PCH. These metrics can evaluate the generative model by comparing the statistical difference between the real dataset and the generated samples, the closer the values of these metrics are to the dataset, the more similar the style of generated melody is to Chinese folk style. Note that, for NLH and PCH, we adopt the earth moving distance between the generated melody and folk dataset in RL-Duet [6] to measure the similarity between the style of generated melody and Chinese folk style. We calculated the mean values and the standard deviations of these metrics on 10 runs.

Table 1. Results of quantitative metrics evaluation of MLE, DuetLSTM, RL-Duet and MusicGAIL. Results of RL-Duet with * are showed in [15].

	PC/bar	PI	IOI	NLH	PCH
Folk Dataset	3.97	2.86	2.41	–	–
MLE	4.36±0.14	**3.02±0.09**	2.91±0.09	0.032±0.009	0.015±0.001
DuetLSTM	3.34±0.17	3.16±0.11	3.05±0.07	0.068±0.001	0.021±0.002
RL-Duet	3.23±0.01*	4.02±0.01*	3.64±0.02*	0.055±0.002*	0.017±0.001*
MusicGAIL	**3.79±0.15**	2.64±0.08	**2.13±0.12**	**0.018±0.004**	**0.01±0.001**

We can observe in Table 1 that note sequences generated from MLE model are extremely messy and dense because of the exposure bias problem, its PC/bar is the highest, 4.36.

Furthermore, it is a challenging task for RL-Duet to imitate Chinese folk style due to it does not contain style information and its PI, IOI, NLH and PCH significantly deviate from the folk dataset. By contrast, these quantitative metrics of our model are closer to folk dataset than three baselines, which indicated MusicGAIL can generate the more harmonious note sequences with reasonable intervals and imitate Chinese folk style better.

Users' Evaluation. For the subjective evaluation, we recruited 215 volunteers from the Internet via our social circles to establish an expert review panel and conduct a listening test evaluation for the generated melody samples. Most of these volunteers have learned music theory or have learned to play at least one musical instrument. Following the previous work, we designed a simple online survey[4].

Specifically, we randomly select 4 music samples from each of the MLE, DuetLSTM, MusicGAIL and a piece of original music from dataset. Each volunteer needs to listen to the origin music and score the melody samples generated from different models in a range of 0 to 10, among which "0" means the worst

---

[4] The survey is available at https://github.com/AcademicLoser/MusicProject.

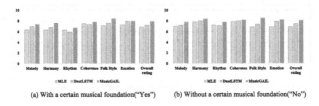

Fig. 3. The scores of subjective evaluation are divided into 2 groups based on question 1 in the survey: with (The selection in question 1 is "Yes") or without (The selection in question 1 is "No") a certain musical foundation.

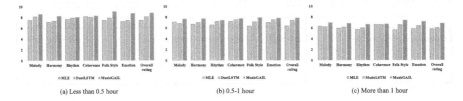

Fig. 4. The scores of subjective evaluation are divided into 3 groups based on question 2 in the survey: (a) less than 0.5 h of listening to music every day, (b) 0.5–1 hour of listening to music every day and (c) more than 1 h of listening to music every day.

and "10" means the best. Next, we collect the survey of all volunteers, filtered out outliers that are too high or too low scores compared to other scores and averaged all the scores. Figure 3 and Fig. 4 show the scores of subjective evaluation from 2 aspects: whether the volunteers have a certain musical foundation and how long they listen to music every day. In general, the subjective scores of MusicGAIL are significantly higher than baselines in terms of melody,harmony, rhythm, folk style and emotion, especially folk style. Interestingly, the subjective scores of the three models in coherence are very close. It indicated that although MLE and DuetLSTM are difficult to imitate the style of music due to their own defects, these defects do not directly affect the coherence of generated music. On the other hand, we can observe that the subjective scores from the group that listened to music for a longer time each day are lower overall. A potential reason may be that volunteers who listen to music for a longer time every day will have higher requirements for music quality and diversity, hence it is not surprising that they rate lower subjective scores.

However, it is reasonable for us to believe the melody sequences generated from MusicGAIL shows a clearer and more natural style and diversity, indicating that our proposed model is capable of capturing music style.

5   Conclusion

In this paper, we have designed a GAIL framework for generating the counter-melody for folk melodies based on the previous research, which avoids laboriously specifying the reward in RL based music generation models. We evaluate the MusicGAIL model from the objective and subjective aspects and the experimental results of objective evaluation show that MusicGAIL can generate the harmonious melody pieces with reasonable intervals and achieve better style imitation of Chinese folk than baselines. The volunteers' evaluation show that MusicGAIL obtain the significantly higher scores than baselines in terms of melody, harmony, rhythm, folk style and emotion, especially folk style. For future work, we would like to continue to explore and extend application scope of our model to other more styles of music.

References

1. Sperduti, A.: An overview on supervised neural networks for structures. In: International Conference on Neural Networks (1997)
2. Hochreiter, S., Schmidhuber, J.: Long short-term memory. Neural Comput. **9**(8), 1735–1780 (1997)
3. Cho, K., et al.: Learning phrase representations using RNN encoder-decoder for statistical machine translation. Comput. Sci. (2014)
4. Eck, D., Schmidhuber, J.: A first look at music composition using LSTM recurrent neural networks. Istituto Dalle Molle Di Studi Sull Intelligenza Artificiale (2008)
5. Bengio, S., Vinyals, O., Jaitly, N., Shazeer, N.: Scheduled sampling for sequence prediction with recurrent neural networks (2015)
6. Jiang, N., Jin, S., Duan, Z., Zhang, C.: RL-Duet: online music accompaniment generation using deep reinforcement learning. In: Proceedings of the AAAI Conference on Artificial Intelligence (2020)
7. Goodfellow, I.J., et al.: Generative adversarial networks (2014)
8. Bau, D., Zhu, J.Y., Wulff, J., Peebles, W., Torralba, A.: Seeing what a GAN cannot generate (2019)
9. Jaques, N., Gu, S., Turner, R.E., Eck, D.: Tuning recurrent neural networks with reinforcement learning (2016)
10. Kotecha, N.: Bach2Bach: generating music using a deep reinforcement learning approach (2018)
11. Jaques, N., Gu, S., Bahdanau, D., Hernández-Lobato, J.M., Turner, R.E., Eck, D.: Sequence tutor: conservative fine-tuning of sequence generation models with KL-control (2016)
12. Vaswani, A., et al.: Attention is all you need. arXiv preprint arXiv:1706.03762 (2017)
13. Huang, C., et al.: Music transformer (2018)
14. Ho, J., Ermon, S.: Generative adversarial imitation learning (2016)
15. Jiang, N., Jin, S., Duan, Z., Zhang, C.: When counterpoint meets Chinese folk melodies. In: Neural Information Processing Systems (2020)
16. Parisotto, E., et al.: Stabilizing transformers for reinforcement learning. In: International Conference on Machine Learning (2020)

17. Dong, H.W., Chen, K., Mcauley, J., Berg-Kirkpatrick, T.: MusPy: a toolkit for symbolic music generation (2020)
18. Benetatos, C., VanderStel, J., Duan, Z.: BachDuet: a deep learning system for human-machine counterpoint improvisation. In: Proceedings of the International Conference on New Interfaces for Musical Expression (2020)
19. Schulman, J., Moritz, P., Levine, S., Jordan, M., Abbeel, P.: High-dimensional continuous control using generalized advantage estimation. Comput. Sci. (2015)
20. Yang, L.C., Lerch, A.: On the evaluation of generative models in music. Neural Comput. Appl. **32**(9), 4773–4784 (2020)

Unsupervised Traditional Chinese Herb Mention Normalization via Robustness-Promotion Oriented Self-supervised Training

Wei Li[1]👤, Zheng Yang[2]👤, and Yanqiu Shao[1(✉)]👤

[1] School of Information Science, Beijing Language and Culture University,
Beijing 100081, China
{liweitj47,shaoyanqiu}@blcu.edu.cn
[2] School of Traditional Chinese Medicine, Beijing University of Chinese Medicine,
Beijing 100029, China
yangzheng@bucm.edu.cn

Abstract. Herbal prescriptions are a vital aspect of Traditional Chinese Medicine (TCM) treatment. The textual representations of herbs can vary significantly across various TCM documents and records. To enhance the utilization of this valuable knowledge in contemporary settings, we propose the objective of Traditional Chinese Herb Mention Normalization by associating them with standardized modern names. However, supervised approaches face the challenge of data sparsity, as they require a substantial amount of labeled data, which is particularly expensive to acquire in the context of TCM. Previous self-alignment methods solely focus on the mentions and names in the gazetteer, overlooking crucial contextual information. Drawing from the observation that mentions often exhibit shared characters with canonical names and possess similar contextual information related to the targeted symptoms and co-occurring herbs, we propose an unsupervised method focusing on promoting robustness. This is achieved by training the model with a self-supervised objective of recovering the original standard herb mentions from the perturbed ones, while leveraging a pretrained language model to capture context information. We argue that the model can develop the alignment ability by making the representation immune to the possible perturbations. To evaluate the effectiveness of the proposed method, we construct a dataset an ancient TCM record dataset. We then enlist TCM professionals to manually annotate the most prevalent aliases of the herbs. Our method achieves an accuracy of 89.79, which is practicable in the real-life scenarios. Extensive analysis further validate the efficacy of the proposed unsupervised method.

Keywords: Traditional Chinese Medicine · Mention Normalization · Self-supervised

---

W. Li and Z. Yang—Equal Contribution.

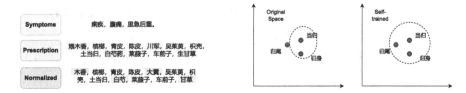

Fig. 1. An illustration of a prescription-symptom pair extracted from the TCM record in our proposed task of herb mention normalization.

Fig. 2. A preliminary depiction of the efficacy of the robustness-promotion method in the herb mention normalization task. Following self-supervised training, the semantic space of the herb expands to encompass its mentions.

1 Introduction

Traditional Chinese Medicine (TCM) holds a significant position within the medical system of China and its neighboring regions. One widely practiced TCM treatment involves the compositionally cooking of TCM soups with various herbal medicines. The TCM records from ancient documents contain numerous prescriptions and their corresponding targeted symptoms, serving as an invaluable knowledge source for TCM practitioners. However, one herb can exhibit various expression forms, related to factors such as historical background, place of production, and method of processing. This can lead to confusion for both machines and humans, impeding the utilization of historical TCM knowledge, particularly in situations where the names of the herbs have largely been standardized in modern TCM. Hence, there is significant value in normalizing the non-standard mentions of TCM herbs found in the TCM records to align with commonly used canonical names.

Figure 1 presents an example of the TCM record under study. The upper part displays the prescription, while the lower part exhibits the corresponding symptoms. The prescription comprises multiple herbs. Among them, the herb "roasted aucklandiae radix" (煨木香) should be normalized to "aucklandiae radix" (木香), and "raw Radix glycyrrhizae" (生甘草) should be normalized to "Radix glycyrrhizae" (甘草). These are instances where the same herb is represented with different processing methods. One challenging case involves the herb "byname of radix et rhizoma rhei" (川军), which literally translates to the "army of Sichuan province" in Chinese but refers to the herb "radix et rhizoma rhei" (大黄) within the TCM context. In such cases, the contextual information, including both the co-occurring herbs and the targeted symptoms, must be considered to determine the intended meaning.

Previous works on medical terminology normalization (medical entity linking) have predominantly employed supervised methods [1,13,19]. However, these supervised methods require a substantial amount of labeled data, which can be costly to acquire, particularly in specialized fields such as medicine. This issue is further exacerbated in the case of TCM scenario, as it not only demands expertise in TCM knowledge but also necessitates proficiency in reading ancient Chinese text. Liu et al. [10] propose a self-alignment pretraining method that leverages the aliases defined in UMLS[1], which, unfortunately, is not applicable to the TCM domain.

In the natural language processing (NLP) community, researchers aim to deceive the model by manipulating the input text in a way that remains recognizable to human beings [3,4], thereby identifying vulnerabilities in the targeted models. This process can be viewed, in our observation, as an inverse operation of aligning unseen mentions to their canonical names, because many of the mentions can be generated from the canonical names through text perturbation operations, such as flipping, mask insertion, and deletion. Furthermore, given the widespread use of pre-trained language models, perturbing the input embeddings is another promising method to deceive the model [6,8,15]. On the other hand, incorporating perturbed samples as augmented training data can enhance the model's robustness against unseen noise in the inference data [18], enabling the model to handle variations in the unseen representation forms of the same herb in our task.

Building upon the aforementioned observations, we propose a self-alignment method based on perturbation. This method involves creating pseudo positive samples by perturbing the canonical names found in the records. On one hand, the unaligned mentions can be considered as a variation of the perturbed (canonical) names, effectively simulating the potential mentions. On the other hand, the normalization operation serves to restore the canonical names from the perturbation. This transforms the objective of normalization into the goal of enhancing the model's robustness against perturbation. (Refer to Fig. 2 for an illustration.) By instructing the model on recovering the original canonical form from the perturbed form, we anticipate the model to acquire the capability to normalize unseen mentions. Additionally, as context information, encompassing co-occurring herbs and targeted symptoms, is valuable for accurate predictions, we propose a BERT-based model that treats the prescription text and the symptoms as a sequence pair. This enables the model to leverage the contextual information surrounding the target mention.

In order to evaluate the effectiveness of the proposed method, we create a dataset for TCM herb mention normalization using TCM records from ancient TCM books. A TCM professional is enlisted to label the mentions with their corresponding canonical herb names. The experimental results demonstrate that our proposed method achieves an accuracy of 89.79%, outperforming all baseline methods. Further analysis confirms the effectiveness of our proposed method.

We conclude our contributions as follows,

- We propose a Robustness-promotion Oriented Self-supervised Training method that learns the ability of TCM mention normalization in an unsupervised manner. The model is subjected to both text-level and embedding-level

---

[1] short for Unified Medical Language System, available at https://www.nlm.nih.gov/research/umls/index.html.

perturbation methods, with the expectation to learn the normalization ability by restoring the original names from their perturbed representations. The context of the target mentions is modeled using pretrained language models.

- We create a dataset for evaluating the normalization ability of TCM herb mentions, which includes labels provided by TCM professionals.
- Extensive experiments and analysis are conducted on the proposed method. We discover some intriguing and counter-intuitive findings. For example, despite the "flipping" operation being less similar to real mentions, it is more effective than other perturbation methods. This suggests that enhancing the model's robustness by appropriately expanding the semantic space can indeed improve herb mention normalization performance.

2   Approach

This section presents our proposed method, the Robustness-promotion Oriented Self-supervised Training. Our method comprises three components: the context-aware Pretrained Language Model (PLM) for TCM records, text-level perturbation, and embedding-level perturbation. The inference process relies on the restoration ability trained by our method.

Context-Aware Pretrained Language Model Framework

The context information, which includes both surrounding herbs and associated symptoms, serves as crucial indicators for predicting the correct herb. In fact, the model can occasionally predict the correct herb even without the mention text, resembling a fill-in-the-blank herb recommendation task. This objective closely aligns with the masked language model in BERT [2]. Hence, we propose using BERT as the backbone model to leverage the context information. To prepare the TCM record as input for BERT, we suggest converting the set of herbs into a sequence of characters, separated by commas, and concatenating it with the symptom text. To differentiate between symptoms and herbs, distinct segment IDs are assigned to the symptom sequence and herb sequence. Additionally, a special "[SEP]" token is inserted between the symptoms and the herbs.

Text Level Perturbation

Input perturbation techniques have been extensively utilized in the field of computer vision (CV) [7,17], where the pixel values of the input are subtly altered within an imperceptible range to deceive the model. In the task of TCM herb mention normalization, the perturbation operation serves to simulate various possible forms of herb mentions, while simultaneously expanding the semantic space of the herb. This expansion enables the herb representation to encompass unseen mentions, thereby enhancing the model's robustness (as depicted in Fig. 2). Drawing inspiration from similar endeavors in the field of NLP [3,4], we propose incorporating character-level perturbations to the canonical herb names

Fig. 3. Illustration of the text-level perturbation method, showcasing insertion masking and replacement masking on the left, and flipping on the right.

found in TCM records. Subsequently, the model is trained to be invariant to these perturbations through a self-supervised approach.

The perturbed names are considered as pseudo positive samples, with the objective of recovering the original standard herb names from the perturbed mentions. This approach allows us to train the model in a purely unsupervised manner, ensuring its invariance to unseen mentions that are simulated through the perturbation operations. Specifically, we propose the utilization of two types of character-level perturbations, namely masking and flipping. We refrain from employing cropping, a commonly used technique, due to the brevity of many herb names which consist of only two to three Chinese characters. Cropping such names would result in significant information loss. Figure 3 provides a visual representation of masking and flipping through a rough illustration.

While this approach deviates from the typical representation pattern of most mentions (as the forged names may not closely resemble actual herb mentions due to disorder), it expands the semantic space of the representation, thereby enhancing the model's robustness. In the experimental section, we will demonstrate that despite its seemingly less intuitive nature compared to masking, this method is highly effective.

Dynamic Perturbation Strategy. To introduce more variation in the perturbation patterns and ensure the model's invariance to different types of perturbations, we propose combining the masking and flipping strategies mentioned earlier with a dynamic random perturbation strategy. Specifically, for each mini-batch of record data, we randomly select a perturbation strategy from inserting masking, replacing masking, and flipping. To center the semantic space of a herb around its canonical name, we define a perturbation ratio ξ that determines whether the batch of data will be perturbed. If the ratio is met, the input text will be perturbed, requiring the model to predict the standard herb name given the correct standard herb names. Inspired by the masking strategy of Roberta [11] in comparison to the original BERT [2], we dynamically perturb the input text at each iteration, ensuring that each mini-batch encounters different perturbation methods.

Embedding Level Perturbation

Similar to CV, the embeddings in NLP can also be perturbed in the continuous space. In our study, we propose three embedding level perturbation methods: adversarial perturbation, dropout perturbation, and Gaussian perturbation.

Adversarial Perturbation. Taking inspiration from the successful FGSM method in CV [7], we propose to incorporate this gradient-based adversarial attack method into our perturbation approach. Given the target canonical herb denoted as y, the objective function of our PLM model as J, the model's parameters as θ, and the input embeddings as x, we introduce a small perturbation vector η that is added to the original input embeddings, calculated as,

$$\eta = \epsilon sign(\nabla_x J(x, y, \theta)) \tag{1}$$

where η acts as a perturbation vector that aims to push the model to a point where it would make incorrect predictions while incurring a small perturbation cost that is imperceptible to humans (the model makes correct predictions before the perturbation). The magnitude of the perturbation is restricted by the L2 norm of the noise $|\eta|$.

Dropout Perturbation. Inspired by the success of SIMCSE [5], which utilizes dropout [16] to generate positive samples for contrastive learning, we propose the incorporation of dropout as a perturbation technique applied to the embedding layer of the BERT model specifically designed for the TCM herb mention normalization task.

Gaussian Perturbation. Apart from the two perturbation methods above, we also propose to add random noise to the embeddings of the sequence. The random noise is sampled from the Gaussian distribution with an average of 0 and a standard deviation of ϵ. The purpose of introducing random noise is similar to that of dropout, aiming to expand the semantic space of herb representation.

Prediction Objective

To predict the specific standard herb from the perturbed herb representations, we propose to use the sum of the representation of the first and the last character of the herb from the last hidden layer of the PLM as the herb representation, which is then matched against the standard herbs after a linear transformation, calculated as,

$$h_{herb} = h_i + h_{i+k} \tag{2}$$
$$p = softmax(W_{out} h_{herb}) \tag{3}$$

where i indicates the starting position of the herb, k is the character-level length of the herb, $W_{out} \in (C \times H)$ is the parameters for the linear transformation, C is the size of the canonical herb list, while H is the dimension of the hidden vectors. The objective function used is cross entropy, which is minimized using the AdamW optimizer [12].

Inference

During inference, instead of using the perturbed herb name, we utilize the representations of the first and last characters of the actual mention (without perturbation) to predict the canonical herb name. The representation that corresponds to the highest probability is matched with the canonical herb, and this matched herb is chosen as the final prediction. In cases where the mention is infrequently encountered in the extensive record database used to train the PLM, the model may struggle to capture the relationship between the mention and its context. To address this, we draw inspiration from Kim et al. [9] and suggest integrating the Jaccard string matching method with our neural model. This integration involves combining the prediction probability from our model with the Jaccard matching score. By doing so, we aim to provide more reasonable responses when the confidence of the underlying deep learning model is low for a given mention.

Experiment

In this section, we introduce the experiment results.

Data and Setting

To evaluate the effectiveness of our proposed method, we enlisted the assistance of TCM professionals to annotate the frequently occurring herb mentions and associate them with their corresponding standard herb names. The test dataset consisted of 76,712 records, comprising 533 standard herb names and 1,469 non-standard mentions (each labeled with its corresponding standard herb name). We omit the records with no attached prescription, and construct regular expressions to extract herbs from the original records. We only consider the frequently seen mentions ($\geq$ 5 times) to mitigate the influence of noise from the automated regular expression extraction process.

We use guwen-bert[2] as the backbone model. The model is first pretrained with the MLM objective for 5 epochs and then trained with the proposed perturbation oriented objective for another 5 epochs. The dropout rate is set to 0.1. The batch size is set to 14 to accommodate the memory limitations of our GPUs, which are 2 Nvidia GTX 1080Ti. To ensure the model learns the fundamental prediction ability, we preserve 50% of the examples without perturbation. Following the approach of FGSM [7], we set ϵ to 1e-5. To mitigate the impact of randomness, we conduct each experiment five times and report the average accuracy and standard deviation. Accuracy serves as the primary evaluation metric to assess performance.

Baseline Methods

In this sub-section, we introduce the unsupervised normalization methods that we take as baselines. Because most of the previous works need labelled data, we

---

[2] GuwenBERT https://github.com/ethan-yt/guwenbert.

take the unsupervised method from Kim et al. [9] and Yan et al. [20], and adapt the supervised method from Mondal et al. [14] to the unsupervised setting.

- MARIE [9]: this method incorporates both string matching method (Jaccard, R/O or editdistance) and BioBERT to calculate the similarity between the candidate and standard herbs. We use the BERT trained on our TCM record instead of BioBERT.
- BEL [20]: a basic embedding based entity linking method that calculates the similarity between the candidate and standard herb names with average character embeddings.
- EMEL [20]: adapts multi-instance learning paradigm that applies BEL to detect potential positive candidates and then uses contrastive based multi-instance learning objective to make the representation of the mentions closer to the corresponding standard herb.
- TripletCNN [14]: this model adapts convolution based triplet network that applies contrastive learning to reduce the distance between the mention and its positive candidates, which are selected with Jaccard from the mention and the standard herb names. Either dynamic or static word2vec character embeddings are used by triplet network.

2.1   Overall Result

We present the overall results in Table 1. The findings demonstrate that previous unsupervised methods generally fail to achieve satisfactory outcomes, whereas our proposed method exhibits significantly improved results. Interestingly, among the baseline methods, the relatively straightforward BEL model outperforms others. This observation highlights the fact that the pseudo positive candidates obtained through heuristic matching methods are inadequate for guiding the model to learn the matching patterns between mentions and canonical herbs.

2.2   Ablation Study

we evaluate the accuracy of our proposed method by systematically removing each designed module in Table 2. It shows that all three modules contribute to the enhancement of prediction accuracy. Notably, the text level perturbation module exhibits the most substantial improvement, elevating the accuracy from 71.04 to 86.19. Moreover, without the text level perturbation module, the standard deviation across the five rounds significantly increases from 1.77 to 6.28. This indicates that the text level perturbation effectively stabilizes the representation, resulting in greater stability. Similarly, the embedding level perturbation module also contributes to stability. Although the accuracy improvement (from 86.19 to 87.03) achieved by the embedding level perturbation is not as significant as that of the text level perturbation, it significantly reduces the standard deviation from 1.77 to 0.31, thereby enhancing performance stability.

Table 1. Accuracy of the baseline methods and our proposed method.

Model	ACC
MARIE (Jaccard)	58.07
MARIE (R/O)	57.86
MARIE (Editdistance)	47.11
TripletCNN (dynamic)	55.59 ± 0.48
TripletCNN (static)	54.51 ± 0.87
BEL	79.58 ± 0.11
EMEL	22.95 ± 2.26
Proposal	89.79 ± 0.44

Table 2. Ablation study results. Accuracy and standard deviation are reported.

Method	Acc
Full	89.79 ± 0.44
w/o. Jaccard	87.03 ± 0.31
w/o. Embedding Level	86.19 ± 1.77
w/o. Text Level	71.04 ± 6.28

2.3 Analysis

Performance of Individual Perturbation Method. We show the accuracy of different perturbation methods for embedding and text levels in Fig. 4a. Observing the results, we find that the embedding level perturbation methods generally yield similar performance, with the widely-used dropout operation slightly outperforming the other two methods.

In contrast, the performance of text level perturbation methods exhibits larger variation. Intuitively, we initially expect that the "replace" and "insert" methods, which involve replacing a character in the canonical names with a mask token and inserting a mask token among the characters, respectively, would yield better results than flipping. This assumption is based on the notion that manipulating mask tokens on the herb characters aligns with the pattern of expected unseen mentions. However, surprisingly, the flipping operation actually achieves the best result. We postulate that this outcome arises because our model emphasizes the semantic space rather than the superficial text. The flipping operation can be viewed as an effective approach to expand the semantic space around the canonical name of the herb without significantly distorting the original meaning. This proximity of the expanded semantic space to unseen mentions contributes to the superior performance of the flipping operation.

Effect of Symptom Context. Figure 4b displays the accuracy comparison between inputs with and without symptoms as context under the text level perturbation scenario. The results clearly demonstrate that including symptoms as input significantly enhances the accuracy, improving it from 81.78 to 86.19. We posit that this improvement arises from the strong association between symptom text and the corresponding herb. A herb typically exhibits its own symptom matching pattern, which aligns with the targeted symptoms for the entire prescription. Consequently, incorporating the symptom information provides valuable context that aids in accurately predicting the associated herb.

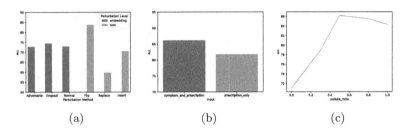

(a)   (b)   (c)

Fig. 4. (a) The accuracy of different perturbation methods (embedding level and text level). (b) The accuracy of input with and without symptoms as context. (c) The accuracy of different polluting ratios of text level perturbation. (Color figure online)

Effect of Polluting Ratio. In Fig. 4c, we present the accuracy results for different polluting ratios. We propose that preserving a portion of the canonical names from pollution helps maintain the semantic space of a herb centered around the original canonical name in the hyper-space. The experimental results corroborate this assumption, as the accuracy initially increases with the polluting ratio and then declines once the ratio exceeds 0.5. The initial increase can be attributed to the expansion of the semantic space around the herb through text level perturbation, facilitating the inclusion of unseen mentions within the herb's semantic space. However, beyond a certain pollution threshold, the centroid of the space becomes influenced by the perturbation, causing the canonical herb name to deviate from the centroid of the herb's semantic space. Consequently, this shift in the centroid adversely impacts the prediction accuracy.

3   Conclusion

In this paper, we introduce the task of herb mention normalization in TCM records and release a corresponding dataset to facilitate further research in this area. We propose a novel approach that leverages unsupervised learning and perturbation-based recovery to address this normalization task without the need for manual labeling. To capture the contextual information, including surrounding herbs and targeted symptoms, we employ a pretrained language model when processing the textual TCM records. Experimental results demonstrate the effectiveness of our method, achieving an accuracy of 89.79. Through extensive analysis, we uncover interesting findings, such as the surprising effectiveness of the "flipping" perturbation operation, which outperforms other methods despite not closely resembling real mentions. This highlights the importance of enhancing model robustness by appropriately expanding the semantic space, leading to improved herb mention normalization performance.

Acknowledgements. This research project is supported by National Key R&D Program of China (2020YFC2003100, 2020YFC2003102), Innovation Team and Talents Cultivation Program of National Administration of Traditional Chinese Medicine. (No: ZYYCXTD-C-202001), Science Foundation of Beijing Language and Culture University (supported by "the Fundamental Research Funds for the Central Universities") (No. 21YBB19)

References

1. Bhowmik, R., Stratos, K., de Melo, G.: Fast and effective biomedical entity linking using a dual encoder. In: Proceedings of the 12th International Workshop on Health Text Mining and Information Analysis, pp. 28–37 (2021)
2. Devlin, J., Chang, M., Lee, K., Toutanova, K.: BERT: pre-training of deep bidirectional transformers for language understanding. In: Burstein, J., Doran, C., Solorio, T. (eds.) Proceedings of the 2019 Conference of the North American Chapter of the Association for Computational Linguistics: Human Language Technologies, NAACL-HLT 2019, Minneapolis, MN, USA, June 2–7, 2019, Volume 1 (Long and Short Papers), pp. 4171–4186. Association for Computational Linguistics (2019). https://doi.org/10.18653/v1/n19-1423, https://doi.org/10.18653/v1/n19-1423
3. Ebrahimi, J., Rao, A., Lowd, D., Dou, D.: Hotflip: white-box adversarial examples for text classification. In: Proceedings of the 56th Annual Meeting of the Association for Computational Linguistics (Volume 2: Short Papers), pp. 31–36 (2018)
4. Gao, J., Lanchantin, J., Soffa, M.L., Qi, Y.: Black-box generation of adversarial text sequences to evade deep learning classifiers. In: 2018 IEEE Security and Privacy Workshops (SPW), pp. 50–56. IEEE (2018)
5. Gao, T., Yao, X., Chen, D.: Simcse: simple contrastive learning of sentence embeddings. In: Moens, M., Huang, X., Specia, L., Yih, S.W. (eds.) Proceedings of the 2021 Conference on Empirical Methods in Natural Language Processing, EMNLP 2021, Virtual Event / Punta Cana, Dominican Republic, 7–11 November, 2021, pp. 6894–6910. Association for Computational Linguistics (2021). https://doi.org/10.18653/v1/2021.emnlp-main.552, https://doi.org/10.18653/v1/2021.emnlp-main.552
6. Garg, S., Ramakrishnan, G.: BAE: bert-based adversarial examples for text classification. In: Webber, B., Cohn, T., He, Y., Liu, Y. (eds.) Proceedings of the 2020 Conference on Empirical Methods in Natural Language Processing, EMNLP 2020, Online, November 16–20, 2020, pp. 6174–6181. Association for Computational Linguistics (2020). https://doi.org/10.18653/v1/2020.emnlp-main.498, https://doi.org/10.18653/v1/2020.emnlp-main.498
7. Goodfellow, I.J., Shlens, J., Szegedy, C.: Explaining and harnessing adversarial examples. In: Bengio, Y., LeCun, Y. (eds.) 3rd International Conference on Learning Representations, ICLR 2015, San Diego, CA, USA, May 7–9, 2015, Conference Track Proceedings (2015). https://arxiv.org/abs/1412.6572
8. Jin, D., Jin, Z., Zhou, J.T., Szolovits, P.: Is BERT really robust? a strong baseline for natural language attack on text classification and entailment. In: The Thirty-Fourth AAAI Conference on Artificial Intelligence, AAAI 2020, The Thirty-Second Innovative Applications of Artificial Intelligence Conference, IAAI 2020, The Tenth AAAI Symposium on Educational Advances in Artificial Intelligence, EAAI 2020, New York, NY, USA, February 7–12, 2020, pp. 8018–8025. AAAI Press (2020). https://ojs.aaai.org/index.php/AAAI/article/view/6311

9. Kim, H.K., et al.: Marie: a context-aware term mapping with string matching and embedding vectors. Appl. Sci. **10**(21), 7831 (2020)
10. Liu, F., Shareghi, E., Meng, Z., Basaldella, M., Collier, N.: Self-alignment pretraining for biomedical entity representations. In: Proceedings of the 2021 Conference of the North American Chapter of the Association for Computational Linguistics: Human Language Technologies, pp. 4228–4238 (2021)
11. Liu, Y., et al.: Roberta: a robustly optimized BERT pretraining approach. CoRR abs/1907.11692 (2019). https://arxiv.org/abs/1907.11692
12. Loshchilov, I., Hutter, F.: Decoupled weight decay regularization. In: 7th International Conference on Learning Representations, ICLR 2019, New Orleans, LA, USA, May 6–9, 2019. OpenReview.net (2019). https://openreview.net/forum?id=Bkg6RiCqY7
13. Miftahutdinov, Z., Kadurin, A., Kudrin, R., Tutubalina, E.: Medical concept normalization in clinical trials with drug and disease representation learning. Bioinformatics **37**(21), 3856–3864 (2021)
14. Mondal, I., et al.: Medical entity linking using triplet network. In: Proceedings of the 2nd Clinical Natural Language Processing Workshop, pp. pp. 95–100 (2019)
15. Sato, M., Suzuki, J., Shindo, H., Matsumoto, Y.: Interpretable adversarial perturbation in input embedding space for text. In: Lang, J. (ed.) Proceedings of the Twenty-Seventh International Joint Conference on Artificial Intelligence, IJCAI 2018, July 13–19, 2018, Stockholm, Sweden, pp. 4323–4330. ijcai.org (2018). https://doi.org/10.24963/ijcai.2018/601, https://doi.org/10.24963/ijcai.2018/601
16. Srivastava, N., Hinton, G.E., Krizhevsky, A., Sutskever, I., Salakhutdinov, R.: Dropout: a simple way to prevent neural networks from overfitting. J. Mach. Learn. Res. **15**(1), 1929–1958 (2014). https://doi.org/10.5555/2627435.2670313, https://dl.acm.org/doi/10.5555/2627435.2670313
17. Szegedy, C., et al.: Intriguing properties of neural networks. In: Bengio, Y., LeCun, Y. (eds.) 2nd International Conference on Learning Representations, ICLR 2014, Banff, AB, Canada, April 14–16, 2014, Conference Track Proceedings (2014). https://arxiv.org/abs/1312.6199
18. Wang, Y., Bansal, M.: Robust machine comprehension models via adversarial training. In: Walker, M.A., Ji, H., Stent, A. (eds.) Proceedings of the 2018 Conference of the North American Chapter of the Association for Computational Linguistics: Human Language Technologies, NAACL-HLT, New Orleans, Louisiana, USA, June 1–6, 2018, Volume 2 (Short Papers), pp. 575–581. Association for Computational Linguistics (2018). 10.18653/v1/n18-2091, https://doi.org/10.18653/v1/n18-2091
19. Xu, D., Zhang, Z., Bethard, S.: A generate-and-rank framework with semantic type regularization for biomedical concept normalization. In: Proceedings of the 58th Annual Meeting of the Association for Computational Linguistics, pp. 8452–8464 (2020)
20. Yan, C., Zhang, Y., Liu, K., Zhao, J., Shi, Y., Liu, S.: Enhancing unsupervised medical entity linking with multi-instance learning. BMC Med. Inform. Decis. Mak. **21**(9), 1–10 (2021)

Feature Fusion Gate: Improving Transformer Classifier Performance with Controlled Noise

Yu Xiang and Lei Bai$^{(\boxtimes)}$

School of Information Science and Technology, Yunnan Normal University,
Juxian Street 768, 650500 Kunming, China
{xiangyu,bailey}@ynnu.edu.cn

Abstract. The pre-trained model based on the Transformer architecture is currently the most widely used model in the field of Natural Language Processing (NLP), and feature fusion technology is the process of aggregating features from different sources to form an augmented feature representation that contains more information. In multi-modal or multi-branch NLP models, feature fusion is a commonly used technique, but for models with only a single feature source, feature fusion technology can be difficult to apply. Therefore, this paper proposes a new probabilistic-controlled late fusion encoder-decoder architecture, called the Feature Fusion Gate (FFG), based on both feature fusion technology and Mixup technology to aggregate the feature representations from the last two layers of the NLP pre-trained model to better capture semantic information in samples. During the aggregation process, FFG utilizes controlled noise as a regularization technique to help the model achieve better generalization performance. Experimental results on eight NLP benchmark datasets show that FFG outperforms three other baseline methods and consistently achieves significant performance improvements across DistilBERT, BERT and RoBERTa.

Keywords: Feature Fusion · Controlled Noise · Mixup · Natural Language Processing · Transformer architecture

1 Introduction

In the field of deep learning, Feature Fusion Technology (FFT) can utilize the features extracted from multiple data sources for weighted combination to obtain more accurate prediction results [1]. In a multi-modal network model, the data of each modality, such as image, audio, text, etc., can be treated as an independent feature source after specific processing [2]. In a multi-branch (multi-stream) network model, each branch is usually an independent sub-network that can be used to process different types or formats of input data, thereby providing different feature information [3]. It is obvious that FFT plays a crucial role in the performance of these network models. How to adjust FFT properly according to specific needs to make it adapt to the structure of different network models is a

L. Fang et al. (Eds.): CICAI 2023, LNAI 14473, pp. 529–540, 2024.
https://doi.org/10.1007/978-981-99-8850-1_43

topic worthy of in-depth research and discussion. For example, in a multi-modal network model, commonly used feature fusion methods include element-wise addition, element-wise multiplication, and concatenation of modality features from different modules [4]. In multi-branch (multi-stream) network models, feature fusion methods generally involve weighted averaging, weighted voting, and concatenation of the feature data output from different feature extraction structures such as parallel branches, serial branches, or cascading branches [5]. It can be seen that the number of feature sources, the shape of features, and the specific location of feature extraction can all affect the model's choice of FFT.

On the other hand, for network models with only one feature source, if we want to use FFT to improve their performance, we first need to split or combine the input sample features from different perspectives to obtain multiple new features. Then, we can follow the ideas of multimodal and multi-branch models to feed these new features to specific modules or sub-networks, and finally fuse the output features [6]. The biggest drawback of this approach is that it adds a lot of additional computational overhead, while the improvement in model performance is very limited. Therefore, the starting point of this paper is to not change the structure of the backbone network, but to relatively simply process its output features, so that FFT can be seamlessly applied to various mainstream pre-trained transformer models [7]. In this way, we can expand the application scope of FFT as much as possible while minimizing the cost of computational resources.

The main contributions of this paper include the following four aspects: **First**, inspired by the gating structure of the LSTM network and the feature Mixup method, a feature fusion gate with adaptive weights named FFG is proposed. **Second**, based on the different ways of extracting sequence classification encodings from the pre-trained model under the transformer architecture, the model output is split and combined, and FFG is used for the initial Mixup to achieve feature augmentation. **Third**, inspired by the idea of Mixup technique, FFG is used for secondary fusion between different text feature sequences within the same mini-batch to augment the model's robustness to noise and reduce overfitting. **Fourth**, the proposed downstream decoder network can be seamlessly integrated with any transformer-based backbone network without the need for any adjustment or modification of their structure.

2   Related Works

2.1   The Gating Mechanism of LSTM

The LSTM network controls the transmission of information through three gates: the forget gate, the input gate, and the output gate [8]. These gates can be in one of three states - open, closed, or partially open - and the amount of information that can pass through the gates in each state can be precisely controlled by a probability σ. When σ is 0, the gate is closed and no information can pass through. When σ is 1, the gate is fully open and all information can pass through. When σ is between 0 and 1, the gate is partially open and information can pass through with a probability of σ [9].

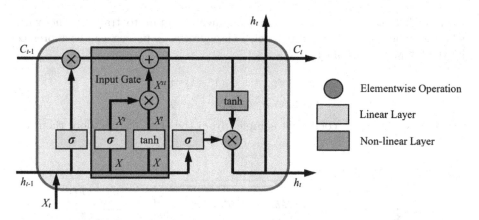

Fig. 1. The recurrent neural network structure of LSTM, where the three linear layers from left to right correspond to the probability control mechanisms of the forget gate, input gate, and output gate, respectively, and are marked as σ.

In neural networks, the output of the sigmoid non-linear function can be used to satisfy the requirements of σ, so it is introduced to implement the control process of information transmission. In the LSTM network structure shown in Fig. 1, taking the input gate as an example, a copy of the feature $X = cat(X_{t-1}, X_t)$ is sigmoid activated after passing through a fully connected layer σ and obtains X^s. Then another copy of X is also passing through a fully connected layer and activated by $tanh$, resulting in X^t. Thus, X^s and x^t are multiplied element-wise to implement the corresponding gate control. The formula for this probability control mechanism is shown below:

$$X^{st} = tanh(fc(X)) \otimes sigmoid(fc(X)) \tag{1}$$

2.2 Mixup

The standard Mixup method was first proposed in 2017 as a simple and effective image augmentation technique [10]. It aggregates the features of two images and their corresponding labels using linear interpolation to generate an augmented image and its pseudo-label. The main advantage of the standard Mixup method is that it generates beneficial noise by using the weighted average of features in the original samples, reducing the sensitivity of the model to harmful noise in the training samples and improving its generalization ability and robustness. Additionally, Mixup can aggregate different original sample pairs to generate augmented samples, even at high data augmentation magnitudes, without generating duplicate results. This greatly amplifies the diversity of training samples, effectively improving the model's prediction performance while reducing the risk of overfitting.

The basic idea of standard Mixup is to linearly aggregate two sample label pairs (x_i, y_i) and (x_j, y_j) in the training set D_{train}, to generate a new sample pseudo-label pair (x_{mix}, y_{mix}) as an augmented input to train the network, where x is the sample and y is its label. This aggregation process can be expressed by the following formulae:

$$x_{mix} = \lambda \cdot x_i + (1 - \lambda) \cdot x_j$$
$$y_{mix} = \lambda \cdot y_i + (1 - \lambda) \cdot y_j \tag{2}$$

where λ is the weight coefficient sampled from the Beta distribution, then $\lambda \in [0, 1]$ and $\lambda \sim Beta(\alpha, \alpha)$.

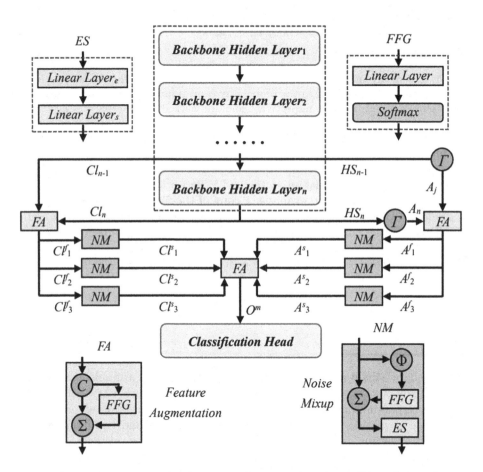

Fig. 2. A classification encoder-decoder architecture based on FFG and Transformer layer, which uses a three-level probability control gate mechanism. Additionally, both feature augmentation branches each generate three controlled noise Mixup branches, and these six feature branches are ultimately weighted and aggregated under FFG control and fed to the classification head. In general, it is a structure of 1-2-6-1.

3   Proposed Methodology

Our research approach is mainly to borrow the gating mechanism of the LSTM network to control the transmission of feature information. In addition, we also borrow the standard Mixup technique to perturb the feature information with beneficial noise. As shown in Fig. 2, to achieve these goals, we first constructed a simple FFG structure, consisting of one fully connected layer (In most cases, this layer has twice the number of neurons as the input feature dimension size.) and one softmax activation layer. It transforms the input feature tensor into a probability distribution used to control the proportion of feature information in Mixup, i.e. λ and $1 - \lambda$ in Formula 2, thereby achieving controlled noise perturbation of features. Secondly, we also constructed an ES module to rearrange the features after multiple Mixup operations. It consists of two fully connected layers (the first layer has 384 neurons and the second layer has 192 neurons) to achieve a certain degree of dimensionality reduction operation on the input feature vector.

For the Transformer-based NLP model, there are two ways to obtain the semantic encoding of the entire input sequence for downstream classification tasks. One way is to extract the feature vector Cl_n corresponding to the [CLS] token from the hidden state HS_n output by the last layer of the model. The other way is to obtain the sequence feature vector A_n by taking the average of HS_n along the sequence dimension by using the Γ operation, that is $A_n = \Gamma(HS_n, \ dim = 1)$, i.e., an average pooling operation over the sequence dimension. Therefore, in order to construct a dual-branch network structure, we extract the feature vectors Cl_{n-1} and A_{n-1} of the hidden state HS_{n-1} output by the second to last layer of the model, where $A_{n-1} = \Gamma(HS_{n-1}, \ dim = 1)$. Then, we concatenate them with their corresponding feature vectors Cl_n and A_n by the C operation. Finally, a copy of each of the concatenated vectors are fed into their respective FFGs to obtain two probability distributions $\{p_{Cl}, \ q_{Cl}\}$ and $\{p_A, \ q_A\}$. Next, we perform Mixup operation on the corresponding vectors separately in the two branches. Then, in order to accelerate the convergence of the model, the fused results are layer normalized to obtain the augmented feature vectors Cl^f and A^f. This process is denoted as Σ and is represented by the following formula:

$$
\begin{aligned}
Cl^f &= LayerNorm\left(p_{Cl} \cdot Cl_n + q_{Cl} \cdot Cl_{n-1}\right) \\
A^f &= LayerNorm\left(p_A \cdot A_n + q_A \cdot A_{n-1}\right)
\end{aligned}
\tag{3}
$$

In the next stage, three copies of both Cl^f and A^f are shuffled randomly across the mini-batch dimension to obtain Cl_i^f and A_j^f respectively, i.e. $Cl_i^f = \Phi\left(Cl_{ci}^f, \ dim = 0\right)$ and $A_j^f = \Phi\left(A_{cj}^f, \ dim = 0\right)$, where $Cl_c^f i$ is a copy of Cl^f, A_{cj}^f is a copy of A^f, and $i, j = 1, 2, 3$. Then Cl_i^f and A_j^f are fed into their corresponding FFGs and the probability distributions $\left\{p_i^{cf}, \ q_i^{cf}\right\}$ and $\left\{p_j^{Af}, \ q_j^{Af}\right\}$ are obtained. Using the strategy shown in Eq. 4, Mixup is performed between Cl^f and Cl_i^f, as well as between A^f and A_j^f, to obtain Cl_i^s and A_j^s respectively.

In this way, our method enhances the ability of the model to resist harmful noise by treating Cl_i^f and $A_j^f c$ as controlled noise and fusing them into Cl^f and A^f, while avoiding the introduction of out-of-domain noise during Mixup.

$$Cl_i^s = LayerNorm \left(p_i^{cf} \cdot Cl^f + q_i^{cf} \cdot Cl_i^f \right)$$
$$A_j^s = LayerNorm \left(p_j^{Af} \cdot A^f + q_j^{af} \cdot A_j^f \right) \tag{4}$$

In the third stage, all Cl_i^s and A_j^s are concatenated together after being processed by their corresponding ES modules to obtain the global feature representation O^w. As a result, a copy of O^w is fed into the last FFG for aggregating features to obtain the probability distribution $\{p_i, q_j | i, j = 1, 2, 3\}$, and the outputs of all six feature branches are fused under its control using formula 5 to derive the final feature vector O^m, which is subsequently fed to the classification head (It consists of two fully connected layers, with 96 and the number of classification categories neurons respectively.). Thus, the feature fusion under the probability control at three levels is proposed and shown as Algorithm 1, where the features output by the backbone network undergo a process of one-to-two splitting, followed by six-way splitting, and finally merging into one. Therefore, FFG can be regarded as an in-domain data augmentation technique in the mini-batch space [11,12].

$$O^m = LayerNorm \left(\sum_{i=1}^{3} p_i \cdot Cl_i^s + \sum_{j=1}^{3} q_j \cdot A_j^s \right) \tag{5}$$

4   Experiments and Results

4.1   Benchmark Datasets and Models

We conducted a detailed test of the effectiveness of FFG based decoder on eight NLP benchmark datasets using three different pre-trained backbone networks. The experimental results are shown in Table 1. These eight datasets include: SST-2 [13], SST-5 [13], TREC-Coarse [14], TREC-Fine [14], MRPC (Microsoft Research Paraphrase Corpus), RTE (The Recognizing Textual Entailment), SUBJ [15] and AG-News [16], all of which come from HuggingFace Datasets or the official website of the dataset. The three backbone network models include: DistilBERT-base-uncased [17], BERT-base-uncased [18] and RoBERTa-base [19], all of which come from the HuggingFace Model Hub. The reason for choosing these transformer-based pre-trained language models is that they have achieved remarkable success in various NLP tasks, and any performance improvement on them can result in significant gains [20,21]. Due to the lack of a dedicated test set in the RTE dataset, we randomly sampled 30% of the data from its training set to construct a test set.

Algorithm 1: FFG Aggregation Method Based on Controlled Noise

---

Input: Hidden states HS_n and HS_{n-1}
Output: Aggregated feature vector O^m

1 $Cl_n \leftarrow HS_n [0, :]$
2 $Cl_{n-1} \leftarrow HS_{n-1} [0, :]$
3 $A_n \leftarrow \Gamma (HS_n, \, dim = 1)$
4 $A_{n-1} \leftarrow \Gamma (HS_{n-1}, \, dim = 1)$
5 $\{p_{Cl}, q_{cl}\} \leftarrow FFG (C (Cl_n, Cl_{n-1}))$
6 $\{p_A, q_A\} \leftarrow FFG (C (A_n, A_{n-1}))$
7 $Cl^f \leftarrow \Sigma (Cl_n, Cl_{n-1}, p_{Cl}, q_{cl})$
8 $A^f \leftarrow \Sigma (A_n, A_{n-1}, p_A, q_A)$
9 **foreach** $i, j = 1, 2, 3$ **do**
10 $\quad$ $Cl^f_{ci} \xleftarrow{copy} Cl^f$
11 $\quad$ $A^f_{cj} \xleftarrow{copy} A^f$
12 $\quad$ $Cl^f_i \leftarrow \Phi \left(Cl^f_{ci}, dim = 0\right)$
13 $\quad$ $A^f_j \leftarrow \Phi \left(A^f_{cj}, dim = 0\right)$
14 $\quad$ $\left\{p^{cf}_i, q^{cf}_i\right\} \leftarrow FFG \left(C \left(Cl^f, Cl^f_i\right)\right)$
15 $\quad$ $\left\{p^{Af}_j, q^{Af}_j\right\} \leftarrow FFG \left(C \left(A^f, A^f_j\right)\right)$
16 $\quad$ $Cl^s_i \leftarrow ES \left(\Sigma \left(Cl^f, Cl^f_i, p^{cf}_i, q^{cf}_i\right)\right)$
17 $\quad$ $A^s_i \leftarrow ES \left(\Sigma \left(A^f, A^f_j, p^{Af}_j, q^{Af}_j\right)\right)$
18 **end**
19 $O^w \leftarrow C^3_{i,j=1} \left(Cl^s_i, A^s_j\right)$
20 $\{p_i, q_j | i, j = 1, 2, 3\} \leftarrow FFG (O^w)$
21 $O^m \leftarrow \Sigma \left(Cl^s_i, A^s_j, p_i, q_j | i, j = 1, 2, 3\right)$
22 **return** O^m

4.2   Baselines

In the experiments, we compared FFG with the following three baseline methods:

- **CLS**: The encoded sequence feature vector of the corresponding [CLS] token in the hidden state HS_n output by the last layer of the backbone network is directly fed to the classification head.
- **Mean**: the feature encoding of each token in the hidden state HS_n is averaged to obtain a feature vector for the entire sequence, which is then fed to the classification head.
- **S-Mixup**: Retaining the same downstream network structure as FFG, only performing Σ operations on the feature vectors with the same probability, which is equivalent to setting λ to 0.5 in Eq. 2.

4.3   Experimental Settings

To ensure consistency in the experimental environment, we only used AdamW [22] as the optimizer for the models, and introduced a cosine learning rate [23] with a warm-up step accounting for 10% of the total training steps [24]. The batch size was set to 32, the maximum learning rate was set to 3e-5, with ϵ set to 1e-8. In addition, all experiments were conducted on a computer with an NVIDIA RTX 4090 GPU. All pre-trained models were constructed and initialized using the default settings of the HuggingFace Transformers library [25], and during the training process of 30 epochs, their parameters were frozen, and only the downstream network parameters were updated, that is to say, we do not fine-tune the backbone network. Each experiment was repeated three times with 3 different random seeds (2, 42, and 882), and the average of the best performance from the three predictions was taken as the experimental result.

4.4   Overall Results

From Table 1, it can be observed that regardless of the backbone network used, FFG demonstrates significant performance improvements compared to the baseline methods across all datasets. Only in the case of using DistilBERT as the backbone network, FFG shows slightly lower performance compared to S-Mixup on the RTE dataset. This is because RTE does not provide a separate test set, and we had to randomly split 30% of the samples from the training set as the test set during the experiment. This resulted in a significant domain shift during training, and many out-of-domain features appeared during testing. As a result, the S-Mixup method, which has more intense feature perturbations during training, achieved the best adaptability. In addition, comparing CLS, Mean, and S-Mixup, FFG only increases the parameter size by 2.10%, 2.10%, and 0.28%, respectively. Therefore, the resource cost of FFG is quite limited, it is a high cost-effectiveness method to improve the prediction accuracy of the pre-trained language model.

To further investigate the impact of the number of controlled noise Mixup branches on model performance, we conducted detailed ablation experiments, and the results are shown in Table 2. In order to maintain the symmetry structure of the decoder network, the number of branches, denoted as b, was chosen to be even numbers between 2 and 12 in our experiments. It is evident from the results that b does have a noticeable impact on performance: as b increases, the model performance gradually improves. However, once b exceeds a certain threshold, which in our experiment is 6, the average performance gain diminishes, and in some datasets, it even decreases. Considering the relationship between b and the number of trainable parameters in the decoder, we ultimately used only 6 branches during the optimization of the decoder.

Table 1. Overall experimental results of different downstream aggregation methods on eight benchmark datasets. The values in the table represent the average prediction accuracy (%) and variance of the model after running three times with three different random seeds. The best result of the experiment is highlighted in bold.

backbone	dataset	CLS	Mean	S-Mixup	FFG
DistilBERT	SST-2	84.77 ± 0.04	85.06 ± 0.06	83.12 ± 0.86	$\mathbf{86.64 \pm 0.08}$
	SST-5	46.02 ± 0.01	46.85 ± 0.03	45.72 ± 0.14	$\mathbf{48.75 \pm 0.23}$
	TREC-Coarse	81.00 ± 0.28	87.73 ± 0.01	85.93 ± 0.25	$\mathbf{93.33 \pm 0.09}$
	TREC-Fine	55.33 ± 0.49	65.53 ± 0.65	72.87 ± 0.37	$\mathbf{82.87 \pm 1.85}$
	MRPC	70.36 ± 0.05	71.65 ± 0.13	72.00 ± 0.10	$\mathbf{72.73 \pm 0.12}$
	RTE	53.50 ± 7.00	54.80 ± 8.47	$\mathbf{58.05 \pm 1.94}$	58.01 ± 4.31
	SUBJ	95.28 ± 0.01	95.28 ± 0.01	92.32 ± 0.04	$\mathbf{95.28 \pm 0.00}$
	AG-News	90.49 ± 0.00	90.91 ± 0.03	88.47 ± 0.04	$\mathbf{92.91 \pm 0.02}$
	model size	66,438,628	66,438,628	68,609,764	68,641,274
BERT	SST-2	86.75 ± 0.12	87.08 ± 0.03	85.17 ± 0.15	$\mathbf{88.34 \pm 0.10}$
	SST-5	48.10 ± 0.04	48.01 ± 0.09	47.32 ± 0.06	$\mathbf{49.46 \pm 0.01}$
	TREC-Coarse	87.00 ± 0.28	86.80 ± 0.04	87.47 ± 1.21	$\mathbf{94.33 \pm 0.05}$
	TREC-Fine	60.07 ± 0.17	61.20 ± 0.52	73.73 ± 0.01	$\mathbf{83.33 \pm 0.09}$
	MRPC	73.58 ± 0.18	72.75 ± 0.20	73.60 ± 0.28	$\mathbf{73.99 \pm 0.09}$
	RTE	59.08 ± 8.97	56.40 ± 1.46	62.38 ± 4.96	$\mathbf{63.54 \pm 5.96}$
	SUBJ	95.62 ± 0.00	95.50 ± 0.01	93.05 ± 0.01	$\mathbf{96.08 \pm 0.37}$
	AG-News	89.93 ± 0.00	90.61 ± 0.00	87.57 ± 0.08	$\mathbf{92.67 \pm 0.07}$
	model size	109,557,988	109,557,988	111,729,124	111,760,634
RoBERTa	SST-2	84.02 ± 0.00	83.91 ± 0.02	83.42 ± 0.84	$\mathbf{88.32 \pm 0.03}$
	SST-5	40.59 ± 0.03	42.96 ± 0.38	45.69 ± 0.05	$\mathbf{49.53 \pm 0.18}$
	TREC-Coarse	56.40 ± 5.32	73.33 ± 1.05	78.00 ± 2.44	$\mathbf{91.67 \pm 0.01}$
	TREC-Fine	23.47 ± 1.21	46.73 ± 0.17	58.67 ± 0.69	$\mathbf{75.80 \pm 0.84}$
	MRPC	69.23 ± 0.02	70.65 ± 0.00	71.98 ± 0.04	$\mathbf{74.22 \pm 0.16}$
	RTE	54.53 ± 4.59	55.11 ± 8.64	56.72 ± 0.67	$\mathbf{59.04 \pm 4.59}$
	SUBJ	94.02 ± 0.00	94.06 ± 0.00	90.97 ± 0.09	$\mathbf{95.62 \pm 0.00}$
	AG-News	91.10 ± 0.00	91.39 ± 0.00	87.84 ± 0.01	$\mathbf{93.27 \pm 0.01}$
	model size	124,721,380	124,721,380	126,892,516	126,924,026

Table 2. The impact of different numbers of controlled noise Mixup branches in the text classification decoder on the accuracy (%) of the model. The random seeds in the experiment is fixed at 882, and other settings are unchanged. In addition, the trainable size represents the total number of trainable parameters (kilo) in the model, and the best result of the experiment is highlighted in bold.

backbone	dataset	b=2	b=4	b=6	b=8	b=10	b=12
DistilBERT	SST-2	86.45	86.66	**86.71**	**86.71**	86.45	86.55
	SST-5	**48.87**	47.83	48.73	47.96	48.64	48.01
	TREC-Coarse	92.60	93.60	93.60	**93.80**	**93.80**	93.40
	TREC-Fine	80.00	83.20	**84.40**	83.00	84.20	83.60
	MRPC	71.77	72.58	72.35	72.17	72.35	**72.64**
	RTE	**61.04**	60.24	60.11	60.51	59.84	60.51
	SUBJ	95.80	**96.10**	**96.10**	95.90	96.05	96.05
	AG-News	92.57	92.79	93.07	93.16	93.07	**93.18**
	average acc	78.64	79.12	**79.38**	79.15	79.30	79.24
BERT	SST-2	88.30	**89.02**	88.52	88.41	88.19	88.80
	SST-5	50.05	49.32	49.32	49.77	51.49	**50.41**
	TREC-Coarse	**94.40**	93.60	94.20	93.60	94.20	**94.40**
	TREC-Fine	81.00	82.00	83.60	82.00	82.80	**84.00**
	MRPC	73.86	**74.67**	74.32	74.15	73.80	73.74
	RTE	**67.34**	65.86	65.73	66.80	67.20	66.13
	SUBJ	96.20	96.45	96.40	96.35	**96.60**	96.45
	AG-News	91.92	92.36	92.47	92.84	**93.30**	93.03
	average acc	80.38	80.41	80.57	80.49	**80.95**	80.87
RoBERTa	SST-2	**88.63**	88.36	88.25	88.25	88.25	88.25
	SST-5	49.68	**50.00**	49.41	49.55	49.23	49.14
	TREC-Coarse	91.20	92.00	91.80	91.40	92.00	**92.20**
	TREC-Fine	73.40	73.60	76.00	**77.20**	76.00	76.20
	MRPC	74.09	74.03	**74.67**	74.20	74.55	74.44
	RTE	57.70	57.70	**58.37**	57.83	58.23	57.70
	SUBJ	95.17	95.17	**95.65**	95.17	95.08	95.17
	AG-News	92.67	92.99	93.37	93.38	93.20	**93.59**
	average acc	77.82	77.98	**78.44**	78.37	78.32	78.33
trainable size		776.8	1526.7	2278.2	3031.2	3685.8	4541.9

5   Conclusion and Future Work

In this paper, we focus on applying commonly used feature fusion techniques in multi-modal or multi-branch models to a network structure with only one modality and one main branch. To achieve this, we propose an encoder-decoder architecture that does not modify or adjust the structure of the pre-trained backbone network. Specifically, first, we split the outputs of the last two transformer layers of the backbone network into two feature branches using different sequence feature encoding methods. We then utilize probabilistic gating techniques for initial feature augmentation fusion. Next, we employ controlled noise to randomly augment the robustness of features in each feature branch within the mini-batch space using sequence Mixup method, resulting in six disturbed feature branches. Finally, we use probabilistic gating techniques again to fuse these branches into one aggregated outcome, which is fed into the classification head to complete the entire late fusion decoding process.

During the experimentation process, we also discovered some issues that are worth further investigation and discussion. In multi-classification tasks, for example, on Dataset TREC-Fine, RoBERTa exhibited a significant performance drop (below half of the normal value) when using traditional feature encoding output methods (CLS). This abnormal behavior was observed regardless of the random seed used for model initialization. Additionally, it would be interesting to explore whether ideas such as gated linear units (GLU) [26] can be introduced to optimize the component of FFG, upgrading the structure of its two fully connected layers and one non-linear $softmax$ activation layer to a more efficient form. Lastly, it would be valuable to assess whether FFG can achieve equally outstanding performance in computer vision classification tasks. In our future work, we will focus on addressing these specific questions.

References

1. Gao, J., Li, P., Chen, Z., Zhang, J.: A survey on deep learning for multimodal data fusion. Neural Comput. **32**(5), 829–864 (2020). https://doi.org/10.1162/neco_a_01273
2. He, X., Deng, L., Rose, R., Huang, M., Trancoso, I., Zhang, C.: Introduction to the special issue on deep learning for multi-modal intelligence across speech, language, vision, and heterogeneous signals. IEEE J. Selected Topics Signal Process. **14**(3), 474–477 (2020). https://doi.org/10.1109/JSTSP.2020.2989852
3. Li, C., Huang, X., Tang, J., Wang, K.: A multi-branch feature fusion network for building detection in remote sensing images. IEEE Access **9**, 168511–168519 (2021). https://doi.org/10.1109/ACCESS.2021.3091810
4. Domingues, I., Muller, H., Ortiz, A., Dasarathy, B.V., Abreu, P.H., Calhoun, V.D.: Guest editorial: information fusion for medical data: early, late, and deep fusion methods for multimodal data. IEEE J. Biomed. Health Inform. **24**(1), 14–16 (2020). https://doi.org/10.1109/jbhi.2019.2958429
5. Atrey, P.K., Hossain, M.A., El Saddik, A., Kankanhalli, M.S.: Multimodal fusion for multimedia analysis: a survey. Multimedia Syst. **16**(6), 345–379 (2010). https://doi.org/10.1007/s00530-010-0182-0
6. Ma, S., Shan, L., Li, X.: Multi-window Transformer parallel fusion feature pyramid network for pedestrian orientation detection. Multimedia Syst. **29**(2), 587–603 (2023)
7. Chen, S., et al.: TransZero: attribute-guided transformer for zero-shot learning. arXiv e-prints arXiv:2112.01683v1 (2021)
8. Zhao, F., Feng, J., Zhao, J., Yang, W., Yan, S.: Robust LSTM-Autoencoders for Face De-Occlusion in the Wild. arXiv e-prints arXiv:1612.08534v1 (2016)

9. Greff, K., Srivastava, R.K., Koutnik, J., Steunebrink, B.R., Schmidhuber, J.: LSTM: a search space odyssey. IEEE Trans. Neural Netw. Learn. Syst. **28**(10), 2222–2232 (2017). https://doi.org/10.1109/tnnls.2016.2582924

10. Zhang, H., Cisse, M., Dauphin, Y.N., Lopez-Paz, D.: Mixup: Beyond Empirical Risk Minimization. arXiv preprint arXiv:1710.09412 (2017)

11. Dong, Y., Hopkins, S., Li, J.: Quantum entropy scoring for fast robust mean estimation and improved outlier detection. In: Advances in Neural Information Processing Systems, H. Wallach, H. Larochelle, A. Beygelzimer, F. d'Alché-Buc, E. Fox, and R. Garnett (Eds.), Vol. 32. Curran Associates, Inc. (2019). https://proceedings.neurips.cc/paper_files/paper/2019/file/a4d92e2cd541fca87e4620aba658316d-Paper.pdf

12. Huang, Y., Zhang, Y., Zhao, Y., Shi, P., Chambers, A.J.: A novel outlier-robust kalman filtering framework based on statistical similarity measure. IEEE Trans. Autom. Control **66**(6), 2677–2692 (2021)

13. Socher, R., et al.: Recursive deep models for semantic compositionality over a sentiment treebank. In Proceedings of the 2013 Conference on Empirical Methods in Natural Language Processing, pp. 1631–1642, Seattle, Washington, USA (2013). Association for Computational Linguistics

14. Li, X., Roth, D.: Learning question classifiers. In: COLING 2002: The 19th International Conference on Computational Linguistics (2002)

15. Conneau, A., Kiela, D.: SentEval: An Evaluation Toolkit for Universal Sentence Representations. arXiv preprint arXiv:1803.05449 (2018)

16. Zhang. X., Zhao, J., LeCun, Y.: Character-level convolutional networks for text classification. In: Advances in Neural Information Processing Systems, vol. 28 (NIPS 2015)

17. Sanh, V., Debut, L., Chaumond, J., Wolf, T.: DistilBERT, a Distilled Version of BERT: Smaller, Faster, Cheaper and Lighter. arXiv e-prints arXiv:1910.01108 (2019)

18. Devlin, J., Chang, M.-W., Lee, K., Toutanova, K.: BERT: pre-training of deep bidirectional transformers for language understanding. arXiv e-prints arXiv:1810.04805 (2018)

19. Liu, Y.: RoBERTa: A Robustly Optimized BERT Pretraining Approach. arXiv e-prints arXiv:1907.11692 (2019)

20. He, P., Gao, J., Chen, W.: DeBERTaV3: Improving DeBERTa using ELECTRA-Style Pre-Training with Gradient-Disentangled Embedding Sharing. In: The Eleventh International Conference on Learning Representations (2023)

21. OpenAI. ChatGPT: Optimizing Language Models for Dialogue. Open AI, blog (2022)

22. Loshchilov, I., Hutter, F.: Decoupled Weight Decay Regularization. arXiv e-prints arXiv:1711.05101 (2017)

23. Shazeer, N., Stern, M.: Adafactor: adaptive learning rates with sublinear memory cost. In: International Conference on Machine Learning, PMLR, pp. 4596–4604 (2018)

24. Vaswani, A.: Attention Is All You Need. arXiv e-prints arXiv:1706.03762 (2017)

25. Wolf, T., et al.: HuggingFace's Transformers: State-of-the-art Natural Language Processing. arXiv e-prints arXiv:1910.03771 (2020)

26. Shazeer, N.: GLU Variants Improve Transformer. arXiv e-prints arXiv:2002.05202v1 (2020)

Multi-round Dialogue State Tracking by Object-Entity Alignment in Visual Dialog

Wei Pang[✉]

Beijing Information Science and Technology University, Beijing, China
pangweitf@bistu.edu.cn

Abstract. Visual Dialog (VD) is a task where an agent answers a series of image-related questions based on a multi-round dialog history. However, previous VD methods often treat the entire dialog history as a simple text input, disregarding the inherent conversational information flows at the round level. In this paper, we introduce Multi-round Dialogue State Tracking model (MDST), a framework that addresses this limitation by leveraging the dialogue state learned from dialog history to answer questions. MDST captures each round of dialog history, constructing internal dialogue state representations defined as 2-tuples of vision-language representations. These representations effectively ground the current question, enabling the generation of accurate answers. Experimental results on the VisDial v1.0 dataset demonstrate that MDST achieves a new state-of-the-art performance in generative setting. Furthermore, through a series of human studies, we validate the effectiveness of MDST in generating long, consistent, and human-like answers while consistently answering a series of questions correctly.

Keywords: Visual Dialog · Multi-round Dialogue State Tracking · Object-Entity Alignment

1 Introduction

Vision-language based multi-modal tasks have gained significant attention at the intersection of computer vision and natural language processing. Tasks such as Visual Question Answering (VQA) [2], and Visual or Video Dialogue [11, 18, 27] require the fusion of visual and textual information. Among these tasks, Visual Dialog (VD) [11] poses a unique challenge that goes beyond simple question answering grounded in an image. VD involves comprehending conversational language, navigating through multi-round dialog history, and reasoning based on visual and textual contents to generate coherent answers.

While previous methods in VD have made progress, they often overlook the inherent information flows and round-level interactions within the dialog history. Existing models [5, 7, 8, 12, 15, 20, 21, 28] commonly concatenate the entire dialog history into a single text sequence, lacking explicit focus on the most relevant

L. Fang et al. (Eds.): CICAI 2023, LNAI 14473, pp. 541–553, 2024.
https://doi.org/10.1007/978-981-99-8850-1_44

history clues. Although attention mechanisms, such as sequential attention [19], co-attention [1,31], dual-attention [9], and multi-view attention [25], have been proposed, they still treat each round of the dialog history independently.

To address these limitations, we propose the multi-round dialogue state tracking model (MDST) for Visual Dialog. Unlike prior work, MDST explicitly models the round-level interactions in dialog history. We define the dialogue state in VD as a 2-tuple of vision and language states, where vision states capture object-level representations and language states represent dialog entity-level representations.

In MDST, each round question from the dialog history is processed, grounding the question in the dialogue state to yield question-guided visual-textual clues. These clues are then used to decode accurate answers, while updating the dialogue states accordingly. Notably, vision states remain unchanged throughout the dialogue, while language states are updated in each round. We align the vision and language representations in dialogue states in an object-entity fashion, facilitating the grounding of follow-up questions.

Experimental results on the VisDial v1.0 dataset demonstrate that our proposed model achieves state-of-the-art performance in generative setting. Further examinations reveal that MDST consistently answers questions correctly, with a joint answer accuracy (JACC) of 79.8% in the generative setting. Moreover, MDST generates human-like responses, as validated through human studies. To summarize, our contributions are three-fold:

- We propose a novel multi-round dialogue state tracking model (MDST) for Visual Dialog. The MDST, including representations of image objects and representations of dialog entities, models the inherent interactions in dialog history at the round level.
- We achieve new state-of-the-art results on most evaluation metrics on VisDial v1.0, and find that the alignment of vision-language in dialogue states could improve the final performance significantly.
- We introduce JACC to evaluate the answer quality, and find that our MDST can continuously generate correct answers as proved by JACC of 79.8% that means about 8 rounds in 10 are correct on VisDial v1.0 val.

2   Related Work

Dealing with dialog history as a simple text input in Visual Dialog (VD) has been a prevailing practice since the works of LF [11], HCIAE [19], and LTMI [21]. However, recent research has highlighted the limitations of such approaches in explicitly capturing round-level interactions between dialog rounds [23,24]. Existing work can be categorized into three groups based on their handling of dialog history.

Firstly, attention-based models [1,9,11,13,17,19,22,25,29,30] typically encode each round of history separately to obtain a set of history embeddings. Sequential attention is applied in HCIAE [19] to attend to the history and image sequentially. MCA [1] leverages modular co-attention to fuse visual and textual modalities. DMRM [9] utilizes dual-attention mechanisms to resolve textual and visual co-references. MVAN [25] introduces multi-view attention to fuse the question and history at both the sentence and word level.

Secondly, graph-based models [6,14,32] construct a graph representation of the entire dialog history, where each node represents a question-answer (QA) pair. KBGN [14] and LTMI-GoG [6] establish edges between nodes to indicate coreference relations between QA pairs. However, these graph-based approaches can suffer from scalability issues as the graph size grows with the dialogue.

Thirdly, concatenation-based models treat the entire dialog history as a single sentence. DualVD [15] packs the dialog history into a long string encoded by an LSTM. UTC [5], ICMU [8], and LTMI [21] concatenate each QA pair as a text sequence, separated by a special token (e.g., [SEP]), and input them into a transformer encoder.

In summary, prior approaches for handling dialog history in VD have not explicitly modeled interactions at the round level of granularity. This limitation hinders their ability to capture the nuanced dynamics of multi-round dialogues.

3   Model

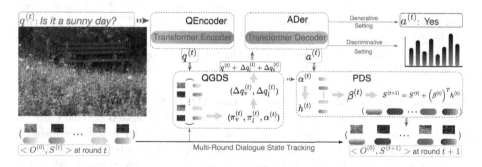

Fig. 1. Overall structure of our proposed MDST model for Visual Dialog.

Figure 1 presents an overview of our Multi-Round Dialogue State Tracking (MDST) model, which consists of four main modules: Question Encoder (QEncoder), Question Grounding on Dialogue State (QGDS), Answer Decoder (ADer), and Postdiction on Dialogue State (PDS). In the remainder of this section, we go into more detail on each module.

Problem Formulation. Given an image I and a multi-round dialogue history $H = C, (q^{(1)}, a^{(1)}), \ldots, (q^{(t-1)}, a^{(t-1)})$ up to round $t - 1$, where C represents the image caption and $(q^{(\cdot)}, a^{(\cdot)})$ denotes the previously experienced question-answer pairs, the dialogue agent aims to respond to the current question $q^{(t)}$ at round t. This response involve generating a free-form natural language answer in a generative setting.

We first extract object-level image features using Faster-RCNN [3]. For each image, we select the top-ranked N objects, each of them is of size 2048-dim and projected to low-dimension features with size d through a linear layer as:

$$O^f = \text{RCNN}(I), \tag{1}$$

$$O^{(0)} = \text{LayerNorm}(\text{ReLU}(W_o O^f + b_o)), \tag{2}$$

where LayerNorm is the layer normalization [4], W_o and b_o are learnable parameters, $O^{(0)} \in \mathbb{R}^{N \times d}$ represents a set of object-level image features. Furthermore, we insert two special pseudo-object features: NULL (ϵ) and ALL (χ), where NULL is a zero vector of size d, and ALL denotes the representation of the whole image by taking the mean of $O^{(0)}$. Thus, we get a new set of $N+2$ object features of $O^{(0)} \in \mathbb{R}^{(N+2) \times d} = O^{(0)} \cup \{\epsilon\} \cup \{\chi\}$. For clarity, we omit all the biases in the remainder of this section.

Let $<O^{(0)}, S^{(0)}>$ denote the initial dialogue state, where $S^{(0)} \in \mathbb{R}^{(N+2) \times d}$ is initialized as a set of zero vectors of the same size. In our approach, the image caption is treated as the zeroth round QA pair $C^{(0)}$, which serves as the initialization for $S^{(0)}$ at the beginning of the dialogue.

Question Encoder (QEncoder). For encoding both the question and the image caption, we employ a standard Transformer encoder [26]. This encoder generates contextual representations, denoted as $q^{(t)}$ and $C^{(0)}$, where l represents the length of the question or caption. It is worth noting that, for simplicity, we use the same symbol to represent both the textual string and its corresponding representation.

Question Grounding on Dialogue State (QGDS). QGDS aims to ground current question $q^{(t)}$ in dialogue state, yielding question-related textual clues on language states and visual clues on vision states. To better associate question with vision and language states, three probability distributions are designed: word-entity alignment between question words and language states, word-object alignment between question words and vision states, and switching probability. Before going into detail, we introduce a notation to express a non-linear transformation layer, to which dropout regularization and layer normalization are applied:

$$\text{MLP}(x) = \text{LayerNorm}(\text{Dropout}(\text{GELU}(Wx))), \tag{3}$$

where x is the input: a vector or a matrix, with learnable weight W of the size varying with the input.

Because many textual relations (e.g., co-reference) existing in question and previous history [11], our model will associate current question words with its most related dialog entities in language states using a learnable word-entity alignment distribution $\pi_l^{(t)} \in \mathbb{R}^{l \times N}$ in Eq. 4. To ground current question in an image, we then calculate a cross-modal matching as in Eq. 5,

$$\pi_l^{(t)} = \text{softmax}(\text{MLP}(q^{(t)}) \cdot \text{MLP}(S^{(t)})^T / \sqrt{d}), \qquad (4)$$

$$\pi_v^{(t)} = \text{softmax}(\text{MLP}(q^{(t)}) \cdot \text{MLP}(O^{(0)})^T / \sqrt{d}), \qquad (5)$$

where $\pi_v^{(t)} \in \mathbb{R}^{l \times N}$ represents word-object alignment distribution between question words and objects in vision states.

Switching probability is designed to 1) determine whether current question is related to previous dialog history; 2) provide a weight to fuse two alignment distributions because there is one-to-one correspondence (i.e., object-entity) between vision and language states:

$$\varphi^{(t)} = \text{sigmoid}(\frac{w(\text{MLP}(q^{(t)})\text{MLP}(S^{(t)})^T) \underset{l \to 1}{.mean}}{\sqrt{N+2}}), \qquad (6)$$

where $.mean$ takes the mean on the l dimension with trainable parameter $w \in \mathbb{R}^{(N+2) \times 1}$. $\varphi^{(t)} \in [0,1]$ is a weight measured the relationship between question and dialog history. The larger value of $\varphi^{(t)}$, the less relevant current question is to dialog history. Experiment shows introducing $\varphi^{(t)}$ can contribute to better the final performance.

The question-guided textual context $\Delta q_l^{(t)}$ is obtained by a weighted sum of language stats over both word-entity and word-object alignment distributions, as denoted in Eq. 7:

$$\Delta q_l^{(t)} = S^{(t)}(\pi_l^{(t)} + \varphi^{(t)} \pi_v^{(t)}), \qquad (7)$$

$$\Delta q_v^{(t)} = O^{(0)}(\pi_v^{(t)} + (1 - \varphi^{(t)})\pi_l^{(t)}), \qquad (8)$$

where $\Delta q_l^{(t)} \in \mathbb{R}^{l \times d}$ represents history context relevant to current question composed of two parts. The first part consists of an explicit history attention directly from question to language states, while the second part contains an aligned history attention indirectly from question, via vision states, to language states, weighted by switching probability. Similarly, the question-guided visual context is written as in Eq. 8, where $\Delta q_v^{(t)} \in \mathbb{R}^{l \times d}$ represents the focused visual regions relevant to current question from two parts, including an explicit visual attention from question to vision states and an implicit ones via the cross-modal alignment.

Finally, we use the sum of the three components to denote the final question representation as in $q^{(t)} + \Delta q_l^{(t)} + \Delta q_v^{(t)}$, which is decoded in next ADer module.

Answer Decoder (ADer). In ADer, we utilize a standard Transformer decoder as the backbone for the generative setting. It takes the final question representation, obtained by combining the question representation $q^{(t)}$ with the question-guided textual context $\Delta q_l^{(t)}$ and the question-guided visual context

$\Delta q_v^{(t)}$, as input. The decoder autoregressively generates the next word one by one until it encounters an end-of-sequence token, producing a free-form natural answer. Formally, the ADer module can be expressed as:

$$a^{(t)} = \text{Decoder}(q^{(t)} + \Delta q_l^{(t)} + \Delta q_v^{(t)}), \tag{9}$$

where $a^{(t)}$ represents the output of the decoder, which not only represents the free-form natural answer of length ℓ, but also denotes its contextualized representations over the words: $a^{(t)} \in \mathbb{R}^{\ell \times d}$. The decoder progressively generates each word based on the input representation.

In the discriminative setting, we encode each of the 100 candidate answers using another Transformer encoder. We score these candidate answers by computing the dot product similarity with the final question representation. The candidate answer with the highest score is selected as the response.

Postdiction on Dialogue State (PDS). PDS is responsible for updating the representation of previously experienced language states with the new question-answer (QA) pair. This module incorporates the new QA pair as new information into the dialogue history, refining the dialogue state representation. It's worth noting that the language states are updated from $S^{(0)}$ to $S^{(1)}$ with the image caption at the beginning, while the vision states remain unchanged throughout the dialogue.

The PDS module leverages an alignment distribution to fuse the QA pair and capture word-word interactions between the question and answer. The alignment distribution is defined as follows:

$$
\begin{aligned}
\alpha^{(t)} &= \text{softmax}(\text{MLP}(q^{(t)} + \Delta q_l^{(t)})\text{MLP}(a^{(t)})^T / \sqrt{d}), \\
h^{(t)} &= q^{(t)} + \alpha^{(t)} a^{(t)},
\end{aligned}
\tag{10}
$$

where $\alpha^{(t)} \in \mathbb{R}^{l \times \ell}$ represents the word-word alignment distribution between the question and answer. $h^{(t)} \in \mathbb{R}^{l \times d}$ denotes the final representation of the QA pair, which is used to update the previous language states, as follows:

$$
\begin{aligned}
\beta^{(t)} &= \text{softmax}(\text{MLP}(h^{(t)} + \Delta q_l^{(t)})\text{MLP}(S^{(t)})^T / \sqrt{d}), \\
S^{(t+1)} &= S^{(t)} + (\beta^{(t)})^T h^{(t)},
\end{aligned}
\tag{11}
$$

where $\beta^{(t)} \in \mathbb{R}^{l \times (N+2)}$ represents the assignment probability, indicating how the new QA information is distributed among the language states. It provides a word-entity alignment distribution for associating the new information with the language states. The language states are then updated to $S^{(t+1)}$ by adding the assigned new information to $S^{(t)}$. The updated dialogue states $<O^{(0)}, S^{(t+1)}>$ are used as input for the Question Grounding on Dialogue State (QGDS) module in the next round, and this process continues iteratively.

4   Experiment

Datasets and Evaluation. We conduct our experiments on the VisDial v1.0 dataset, which consists of a standard train/val/test split. To evaluate the performance, we employ NDCG and retrieval metrics, including MRR, Mean rank, and R@1, 5, 10, following the conventions of previous studies [5,8]. Additionally, we assess the quality of generated answers by generating 2064 dialogues for 10 rounds on the VisDial v1.0 validation set and calculating the following metrics: Joint Answer Accuracy (JACC) measures the percentage of correct QA pairs among all the generated QA pairs. It assesses whether the generated answers are correct given the corresponding images. Average Answer Length (AvgLen) calculates the average length of generated answers.

Implementation Details. We utilize a Transformer encoder-decoder architecture as the backbone. The encoder and decoder consist of 12 layers with 12 heads and 768 hidden states, respectively. For image features, we extract bottom-up features of 36 objects using Faster-RCNN. We employ the Adamax optimizer with an initial learning rate of 1e-3, which linearly decreases to 5e-5 following a scheduled warmup of 0.2. The model is trained for 20 epochs with a batch size of 32. The word embeddings, shared between encoders and decoders, are set to 768 dimensions. For training, we compute the negative log-likelihood of ground-truth and generated answer.

Comparison to State-of-the-Art Methods. We compare our approach to several state-of-the-art methods, categorizing them based on how they utilize the dialog history: 1) Attention-based models: MN [11], HCIAE [19], CoAtt [29], DAM [16], DMRM [9], ReDAN [13], SeqIPN [30], MVAN [25], and MCA [1]. 2) Graph-based models: KBGN [14], LTMI-GoG [6], and HKNet [32]. 3) Concatenation-based models: LateFusion [12], DualVD [15], LTMI [21], LTMI-LG [7], VDBERT [28], Visdial-BERT [20], ICMU [8], and UTC [5]. 4) Dialogue State Tracking (DST) based model: Our MDST model. It's important to note that our MDST model for VisDial v1.0 is trained from scratch, without relying on pretraining or fine-tuning on additional large-scale datasets.

Table 1. Comparisons on VisDial v1.0 val in the generative setting.

Model	MRR↑	R@1↑	R@5↑	R@10↑	Mean↓	NDCG↑
LateFusion	46.57	36.20	56.40	63.40	19.44	54.21
MN	47.83	38.01	57.49	64.08	18.76	56.99
HCIAE	49.07	39.72	58.23	64.73	18.43	59.70
CoAtt	49.64	40.09	59.37	65.92	17.86	59.24
DAM	50.51	40.53	60.84	67.94	16.65	60.93
DMRM	50.16	40.15	60.02	67.21	15.19	-
ReDAN	49.60	39.95	59.32	65.97	17.79	59.41
SeqIPN	47.86	38.16	57.08	64.89	15.27	60.72
SeqMRN	49.22	38.75	59.62	68.47	**13.00**	63.01
SKANet	45.53	36.17	55.05	61.41	19.79	-
KBGN	50.05	40.40	60.11	66.82	17.54	60.42
LTMI-GoG	51.32	41.25	61.83	69.44	15.32	62.63
LTMI	50.38	40.30	60.72	68.44	15.73	61.61
LTMI-LG	51.30	41.34	61.61	69.06	15.26	63.23
LTMI-LG*	51.43	41.68	61.96	**69.87**	14.89	63.53
UTC	52.22	**42.56**	62.40	69.51	15.67	63.86
MDST (Ours)	**53.49**	**42.56**	**62.47**	69.77	14.94	**65.03**

Table 1 presents the generative results on the VisDial v1.0 validation split. Our proposed MDST model outperforms all the comparison methods on 4 out of 6 metrics, establishing a new state-of-the-art. Specifically, we achieve an NDCG of 65.03, MRR of 53.49, R@1 of 42.56, and R@5 of 62.47. Notably, when compared to attention- and graph-based methods, our model shows significant improvements across all metrics, especially in NDCG and MRR. We improve NDCG by 2.02 points (65.03 vs. SeqMRN's 63.01) and MRR by approximately 2.17 points (53.49 vs. LTMI-GoG's 51.32). When compared to concatenation-based methods, our MDST model achieves similar or better results. Moreover, it surpasses the previous best-performing method, UTC, by approximately 1.27 points in MRR and 1.17 points in NDCG. It's important to note that UTC relies on ViLBERT pretraining and utilizes VQA datasets.

Table 2. Main comparisons on VisDial v1.0 test.

Model	MRR↑	R@1↑	R@5↑	R@10↑	Mean↓	NDCG↑
LTMI-LG	64.0	50.63	80.58	90.20	4.12	58.55
LTMI	64.08	50.20	80.68	90.35	4.05	59.03
VDBERT	65.44	51.63	82.23	90.68	3.90	59.96
LTMI-GoG	63.52	50.01	80.13	89.28	4.31	61.04
ICMU	**66.82**	53.50	83.05	92.05	3.59	61.30
UTC	66.27	52.25	83.55	92.23	**3.48**	62.65
MDST (Ours)	66.78	**53.58**	**83.69**	**92.62**	3.54	**63.18**

Table 3. Ablation study on VisDial v1.0 val in the generative setting.

#	Model	MRR	R@1	R@5	R@10	Mean	NDCG
1	MDST	53.49	42.56	62.47	69.77	14.94	65.03
2	-QGDS-PDS	50.80	40.55	60.79	67.46	15.73	61.15
3	$-\alpha^{(t)}$	52.79	41.65	61.43	69.05	15.20	63.64
4	-NULL-ALL	53.27	41.91	61.97	69.34	15.06	64.48

Table 2 displays the results on the VisDial v1.0 test split. Our MDST model achieves a NDCG value of 63.18, outperforming other methods across various metrics. Compared to UTC, MDST improves NDCG by 0.53 points. In summary, our MDST model, despite being simpler and not relying on larger pre-trained language models or extra datasets like UTC and ICMU, achieves significant improvements across most metrics, outperforming previous state-of-the-art models. These improvements highlight the effectiveness of the dialogue state tracking mechanism in VisDial.

Ablation Studies. Table 3 presents the results of ablation studies, which evaluate the importance of each module in the generative setting. The first row represents the performance of the full model, while the subsequent rows (2–4) indicate the effect of removing each module sequentially.

When removing the QGDS&PDS module (Row 2), we adopt a similar approach to previous work, where we directly use the question to attend to image features and original history embeddings. The fusion of the question, attended image features, and history features is then fed into the ADer module. The results show a significant drop in NDCG by -3.88 points, MRR decreases to 50.80 by -2.69 points, and R@1,5,10 exhibits a substantial decrease. These findings align with the previous comparisons and further demonstrate the effectiveness of the dialogue state tracking mechanism. It highlights the ability of the model to capture information flows in the dialogue history at the round level. It is important to note that utilizing PDS without QGDS or vice versa is meaningless since the dialogue states are updated in PDS but used in QGDS. The combination of the QGDS and PDS modules provides strong support for the tracking mechanism.

When removing the switching probability $\alpha^{(t)}$ in the QGDS module, we observe a significant decrease in overall performance. NDCG and MRR decrease by 1.39 and 0.7 points, respectively. This result underscores the importance of the switching probability in our model. Specifically, the switching probability plays a crucial role in associating the two alignment distributions ($\pi^{(t)}l$ and $\pi^{(t)}v$), facilitating the alignment of vision-language dialogue states. In other words, aligning vision-language states brings about a substantial improvement, which aligns with findings from previous studies [10,25].

Furthermore, when removing the two pseudo-object features, NULL and ALL (Row 4), we observe a slight decline in performance. This finding validates that both pseudo-objects carry useful information about the image. The inclusion of these pseudo-objects is valuable because the upcoming question may be unrelated to the input image or may involve the entire image.

#	Image & Caption	Ground-Truth Question	Ground-Truth Answer (Humans)	DST Answer (Ours)	LateFusion [Das et al. 2019]
1	a man talking to a giraffe in an enclosure	how many people are there?	1	1	2
		is it a male of female?	male	male	i can't tell
		is he outside?	yes	yes	yes
		what is he doing?	looking at the giraffe	he is just standing there	standing
		what color is the giraffe?	brown and tan	it is brown and white	brown and white
		is the man happy?	he's smiling so i would say yes	he looks like he is happy	can't tell
		is it sunny?	yes	yes, it is sunny	yes
		what color is his shoes?	i can only see chest up so i don't know	i can't see his shoes	brown
		what color is his shirt?	orange	his shirt is red	black
		is he white?	yes	yes, he is	no
	2 people are strolling on the sidewalk holding umbrellas walking past a street	are they male or female?	appears to be 1 of each	1 is female and the other is male	i can't tell
		is it raining?	yes	yes	no
		is there anyone else in the photo?	no	no	yes
		is there any cars?	no	no	no
		any road signs?	no	no	yes
		is the photo in color ?	yes	yes	yes
		what color are the umbrellas?	1 is black the other is red , white & blue	1 is black and 1 is red	black
		how old are the couple?	can't tell	i can't see their faces	i can't tell
		are they wearing rain boots?	no	no	yes
		are they wearing raincoats?	no	no, they are not	no
	a dog is catching a frisbee on the grass	is this outdoors?	yes , it is outdoors	yes	yes
		is it sunny?	it appears to sunny	yes	yes
		how many dogs are around?	there is only 1 dog	just 1	there are no people
		what color is the dog?	it is black and tan	the dog is brown and white	it is brown
		is it big or small?	it is a large dog	big	i ca n't tell
		what color is the frisbee?	the frisbee is yellow	the frisbee is yellow	red
		are there a lot of trees?	there are no trees visible	there are no trees	there are no trees
		are there people around?	there are no people	there are no people around	there are no people
		can you see the grass?	yeah , the grass is visible	yes, there are a lot of grass	no, i can not see the ground
		can you see any cars around?	there are no cars visible	there are no cars	no , i do not see any other animals

Fig. 2. Answers generated by our MDST model. The correct answers are highlighted in red, and blue highlights denote the incorrect answers. (Color figure online)

Human Studies. A series of human studies were conducted on VisDial v1.0 val to generate 2064 dialogues. The results are presented in Table 4, and we provide three examples of generated dialogues in Fig. 2. The findings reveal that our proposed MDST model demonstrates the ability to consistently provide correct answers throughout a series of questions, while generating more human-like responses. Specifically, MDST achieves a Joint Answer Accuracy (JACC) of 79.8% on VisDial v1.0 val split, indicating that approximately 8 out of 10 rounds yield correct answers. In comparison, LateFusion achieves a significantly lower JACC of 53.4%.

Table 4. JACC (%) and AvgLen on VisDial v1.0 val.

Model	#QA pair	Correct	InCorrect	JACC	AvgLen
MDST	1000	798	202	**79.8**	**3.57**
LateFusion		534	466	53.4	1.81
Human		–	–	–	3.11

In the first example, MDST generates 9 correct answers. Notably, in the 6th and 8th rounds, MDST produces reasonable responses: "he looks like he is happy" and "I can't see his shoes", which capture the semantics similar to the ground truth: "he's smiling so I would say yes" and "I can only see chest up so I don't know". In the second example, MDST provides correct answers in all 10 rounds, with the response "1 is female and the other is male" being as accurate and natural as the human-generated answer" appears to be 1 of each". The third example also showcases MDST's ability to correctly predict all 10 questions, with the response "the dog is brown and white" in the 4th round also deemed correct based on the image.

Interestingly, contrary to the human and LateFusion models, MDST tends to produce longer, more consistent answers. The average answer length (AvgLen) of MDST reaches 3.57, surpassing the human-generated answer length of 3.11 and LateFusion's length of 1.81. In terms of consistency, for the question "how many dogs are around?" in the second example, our model responds with an accurate answer "just 1", which aligns with dialog history (i.e., image caption). In contrast, LateFusion provides an inconsistent response of "there are no people", and in the last round, LateFusion produces a question-irrelevant answer.

5 Conclusions

In this paper, we introduce a novel approach called Multi-Round Dialogue State Tracking Network (MDST) for the task of Visual Dialog (VD). Unlike previous methods that treat dialog history as a simple text input, MDST tracks and updates dialogue states, which are 2-tuple aligned vision-language representations. By modeling the inherent interactions at the round level, MDST aims to capture dynamics of the conversation more effectively. Experimental results on VisDial v1.0 dataset demonstrate that MDST achieves state-of-the-art performance across most evaluation metrics. Additionally, extensive human studies further validate MDST can generate long, consistent, and human-like answers while maintaining the ability to provide correct responses to a series of questions. Overall, our proposed MDST framework represents a significant advancement in visual dialog systems, showcasing the importance of modeling dialogue states in capturing the complex nature of visual conversations.

Acknowledgements. We thank the reviewers for their comments and suggestions. This paper was partially supported by the National Natural Science Foundation of China (NSFC 62076032), Huawei Noah's Ark Lab, MoECMCC "Artificial Intelligence" Project (No. MCM20190701), Beijing Natural Science Foundation (Grant No. 4204100), and BUPT Excellent Ph.D. Students Foundation (No. CX2020309).

References

1. Agarwal, S., Bui, T., Lee, J.Y., Konstas, I., Rieser, V.: History for visual dialog: Do we really need it? In: ACL, pp. 8182–8197 (2020)

2. Agrawal, A., et al.: Vqa: Visual question answering. In: ICCV, pp. 2425–2433 (2015)

3. Anderson, P., et al.: Bottom-up and top-down attention for image captioning and visual question answering. In: CVPR, pp. 6077–6086 (2018)

4. Ba, J.L., Kiros, J.R., Hinton, G.E.: Layer normalization. arXiv preprint arXiv:1607.06450 11 (2016). https://doi.org/10.48550/arXiv.1607.06450

5. Chen, C., et al.: Utc: a unified transformer with inter-task contrastive learning for visual dialog. In: CVPR, pp. 18103–18112 (2022)

6. Chen, F., Chen, X., Meng, F., Li, P., Zhou, J.: Gog: relation-aware graph-over-graph network for visual dialog. In: Findings of ACL, pp. 230–243 (2021)

7. Chen, F., Chen, X., Xu, C., Jiang, D.: Learning to ground visual objects for visual dialog. In: EMNLP Findings, pp. 1081–1091 (2021)

8. Chen, F., Chen, X., Xu, S., Xu, B.: Improving cross-modal understanding in visual dialog via contrastive learning. In: ICASSP (2022)

9. Chen, F., Meng, F., Xu, J., Li, P., Xu, B., Zhou, J.: Dmrm: a dual-channel multi-hop reasoning model for visual dialog. In: AAAI (2020)

10. Chen, F., Zhang, D., Chen, X., Shi, J., Xu, S., Xu, B.: Unsupervised and pseudo-supervised vision-language alignment in visual dialog. In: ACM MM, pp. 4142–4153 (2022)

11. Das, A., et al.: Visual dialog. In: CVPR, pp. 326–335 (2017)

12. Desai, K., Das, A., Batra, D., Parikh, D.: Visual dialog challenge starter code. https://github.com/batra-mlp-lab/visdial-challenge-starter-pytorch (2019)

13. Gan, Z., Cheng, Y., Kholy, A.E., Li, L., Liu, J., Gao, J.: Multi-step reasoning via recurrent dual attention for visual dialog. In: ACL, pp. 6463–6474 (2019)

14. Jiang, X., Du, S., Qin, Z., Sun, Y., Yu, J.: Kbgn: Knowledge-bridge graph network for adaptive vision-text reasoning in visual dialogue. In: ACM MM (2020)

15. Jiang, X., et al.: Dualvd: An adaptive dual encoding model for deep visual under-standing in visual dialogue. In: AAAI, pp. 11125–11132 (2020)

16. Jiang, X., et al.: Dam: Deliberation, abandon and memory networks for generating detailed and non-repetitive responses in visual dialogue. In: IJCAI (2020)

17. Kang, G.C., Lim, J., Zhang, B.T.: Dual attention networks for visual reference resolution in visual dialog. In: EMNLP, pp. 2024–2033 (2019)

18. Le, H., Sahoo, D., Chen, N.F., Hoi, S.C.: Multimodal transformer networks for end-to-end video-grounded dialogue systems. In: ACL, pp. 5612–5623 (2019)

19. Lu, J., Kannan, A., Yang, J., Parikh, D., Batra, D.: Best of both worlds: transfer-ring knowledge from discriminative learning to a generative visual dialog model. In: NeurIPS (2017)

20. Murahari, V., Batra, D., Parikh, D., Das, A.: Large-scale pretraining for visual dialog: a simple state-of-the-art baseline. In: ECCV, pp. 336–352 (2020)

21. Nguyen, V.Q., Suganuma, M., Okatani, T.: Efficient attention mechanism for visual dialog that can handle all the interactions between multiple inputs. In: ECCV, pp. 223–240 (2020)

22. Niu, Y., Zhang, H., Zhang, M., Zhang, J., Lu, Z., Wen, J.R.: Recursive visual attention in visual dialog. In: CVPR (2019)

23. Pang, W., Wang, X.: Guessing state tracking for visual dialogue. In: 16th European Conference on Computer Vision - ECCV 2020, pp. 683–698 (2020)

24. Pang, W., Wang, X.: Visual dialogue state tracking for question generation. In: AAAI (Oral), pp. 11831–11838 (2020)

25. Sungjin, P., Taesun, W., Yeochan, Y., Heuiseok, L.: Multi-view attention network for visual dialog. Appl. Sci. 11(7) (2021). https://doi.org/10.3390/app11073009

26. Vaswani, A., et al.: Attention is all you need. In: NeurIPS, pp. 5998–6008 (2017)
27. de Vries, H., Strub, F., Chandar, S., Pietquin, O., Larochelle, H., Courville, A.: Guesswhat?! visual object discovery through multi-modal dialogue. In: CVPR, pp. 5503–5512 (2017)
28. Wang, Y., Joty, S., Lyu, M., King, I., Xiong, C., Hoi, S.C.: VD-BERT: a Unified Vision and Dialog Transformer with BERT. In: EMNLP, pp. 3325–3338 (2020)
29. Wu, Q., Wang, P., Shen, C., Reid, I., van den Hengel, A.: Are you talking to me? reasoned visual dialog generation through adversarial learning. In: CVPR, pp. 6106–6115 (2018)
30. Yang, L., Meng, F., Liu, X., Wu, M.K.D., Ying, V., Xu, X.: Seqdialn: sequential visual dialog networks in joint visual-linguistic representation space. In: 1st Workshop on Document-grounded Dialogue and Conversational Question Answering, pp. 8–17 (2021)
31. Yang, T., Zha, Z.J., Zhang, H.: Making history matter: history-advantage sequence training for visual dialog. In: ICCV, pp. 2561–2569 (2019)
32. Zhao, L., Li, J., Gao, L., Rao, Y., Song, J., Shen, H.T.: Heterogeneous knowledge network for visual dialog. IEEE Trans. Circ. Syst. Video Technol. (TCSVT), pp. 1–1 (2022). https://doi.org/10.1109/TCSVT.2022.3207228

Multi-modal Dialogue State Tracking for Playing GuessWhich Game

Wei Pang[1(✉)], Ruixue Duan[1], Jinfu Yang[2], and Ning Li[1]

[1] Beijing Information Science and Technology University, Beijing, China
{pangweitf,duanruixue}@bistu.edu.cn
[2] Beijing University of Technology, Beijing, China

Abstract. GuessWhich is an engaging visual dialogue game that involves interaction between a Questioner Bot (QBot) and an Answer Bot (ABot) in the context of image-guessing. In this game, QBot's objective is to locate a concealed image solely through a series of visually related questions posed to ABot. However, effectively modeling visually related reasoning in QBot's decision-making process poses a significant challenge. Current approaches either lack visual information or rely on a single real image sampled at each round as decoding context, both of which are inadequate for visual reasoning. To address this limitation, we propose a novel approach that focuses on visually related reasoning through the use of a mental model of the undisclosed image. Within this framework, QBot learns to represent mental imagery, enabling robust visual reasoning by tracking the dialogue state. The dialogue state comprises a collection of representations of mental imagery, as well as representations of the entities involved in the conversation. At each round, QBot engages in visually related reasoning using the dialogue state to construct an internal representation, generate relevant questions, and update both the dialogue state and internal representation upon receiving an answer. Our experimental results on the VisDial datasets (v0.5, 0.9, and 1.0) demonstrate the effectiveness of our proposed model, as it achieves new state-of-the-art performance across all metrics and datasets, surpassing previous state-of-the-art models.

Keywords: GuessWhich · Multi-Modal Dialogue State Tracking · Visual Dialogue

1 Introduction

In the future, visual conversational agents may engage in natural language conversations. Research in vision-language tasks is still in its early stages, progressing from single-round VQA [1] to multi-round Visual Dialogue and multi-modal multi-modal Video Dialogue [2,3,13,16]. Among these tasks, GuessWhich stands out as a two-player image-guessing game with a QBot and ABot. QBot aims to identify a hidden image by asking questions to ABot. While ABot has received attention, research on QBot is relatively limited, which is the focus of this paper.

L. Fang et al. (Eds.): CICAI 2023, LNAI 14473, pp. 554–565, 2024.
https://doi.org/10.1007/978-981-99-8850-1_45

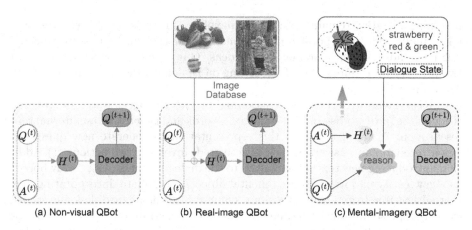

Fig. 1. Illustration of three types of QBot involving four components: question (Q), answer (A), history encoder (H) at round t, and Decoder for new question generation. Specially, a) Non-visual QBot, no visual information is provided to QBot. b) Real-image QBot, retrieves a real image per round from a pool to serve as visual information for Decoder. c) Mental-imagery QBot (Ours), explores visually related reasoning based on the QBot's mental model of the secret image.

QBot starts by receiving a caption and formulating the first question. Subsequent questions are generated based on the caption and dialogue history. Performing visual reasoning solely from textual information poses a challenge. Existing approaches, as illustrated in Fig. 1 (a) and (b), can be divided into non-visual methods [3,4,6,8,14,19,20] that rely on language-based models and real-image methods [21] that retrieve probable images as visual context. However, both approaches have limitations in visual reasoning.

Firstly, QBot needs to generate questions that pertain to the image, linking words to visual concepts, much like humans do [9]. Hence, QBot, which lacks visual information in its modeling, is inadequate for this purpose. Secondly, QBot samples a single real image from a large pool of images, often numbering in the thousands, e.g., 9,628 candidate images per round. This approach is unnatural in the context of a genuine game and introduces substantial sampling variance, rendering the model's reasoning process unstable.

Drawing on the Dual-coding theory [9], human cognition is based on two interconnected modes: words and images. Mental imagery plays a significant role in word comprehension. Building on this theory, we propose aligning dialogue entities with mental visual concepts in QBot, as depicted in Fig. 1(c). By constructing a mental model of the secret image through textual semantics, we establish a dialogue state consisting of representations of dialogue entities and mental objects denoted as ⟨words, images⟩ states.

As the game progresses, the dialogue state evolves, encompassing representations of mental objects in QBot's mind, and prompting QBot to pose visually related questions. To the best of our knowledge, the problem of modeling visual reasoning in QBot remains relatively unexplored. In this paper, we present a QBot model that incorporates mental imagery through dialogue state tracking (DST) to address the aforementioned ideas. Our model consists of a cycle of two primary procedures: Visual Reasoning on Dialogue State (VRDS) and State Tracking (STrack).

VRDS facilitates three-hop reasoning in the dialogue state, progressing through the path words→words→images→words and generating an internal representation. A decoder utilizes this representation to generate new questions. Upon receiving an answer, STrack is activated, involving two actions: 1) Addition, introducing new textual semantics to the dialogue states (e.g., "strawberry" as a new entity and its associated mental object). 2) Update, incorporating new textual features (e.g., colors, positions, counts) into the aligned dialogue states' existing representation. Experimental results demonstrate our model's superior performance, achieving a new state-of-the-art level. In summary, our contributions are three-fold:

- We propose a novel QBot agent that is capable of performing visually related reasoning based on mental imagery in one's mind in dialog.
- We present dialogue state tracking based QBot model (DST), which learns to form representations of mental imagery that support visually related reasoning. The dialogue states, composed of not only words states but also images states, are tracked and updated through dialoguing with ABot.
- Achieving new state-of-the-art results on the GuessWhich game underlying VisDial v0.5, v0.9 and v1.0 datasets. Compared with prior studies, this work takes a step towards mimicking humans playing a series of visual dialogue games (such as GuessWhich).

2 Related Work

Visual Dialogue is a key area of research in vision-language studies, with the aim of developing conversational agents capable of human-like interactions. Recent progress [10–12] has been made in various tasks, including GuessWhat!?, GuessWhich, and Visual & Video Dialogue. GuessWhich specifically involves the challenge of QBot finding an undisclosed image from a large pool without sharing it with ABot.

Existing QBot models can be categorized into non-visual and real-image approaches. Non-visual models, represented in Fig. 1(a), do not utilize visual information. For example, Das et al. [4] propose an encoder-decoder network with a feature regression network. They use a hierarchical encoder-decoder architecture to generate questions based on history. Murahari et al. [8] introduce a Smooth-L1 Penalty to mitigate repetitive questions. Zhao et al. [19] incorporate an Attentive Memory Network, and Li et al. [6] propose an information-theoretic model. These models solely rely on textual information.

Real-image models, shown in Fig. 1(b), provide physical images as input to the QBot decoder. Zhou et al. [21] introduce an image-guesser module into the

QBot model. While related works track real image objects, our approach focuses on constructing and tracking mental imagery representations during the dialogue.

3   Model

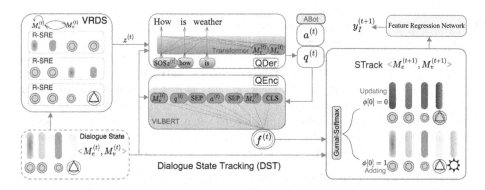

Fig. 2. Overall structure of the proposed DST model. The oblong colorful strips denote image state $M_v^{(t)}$, and the rounded circle are word state $M_e^{(t)}$.

The proposed Dialogue State Tracking based QBot (DST) model, depicted in Fig. 2, consists of five modules: Recursive Self-Reference Equation (R-SRE), Visual Reasoning on Dialogue State (VRDS), Question Decoder (QDer), QBot Encoders (QEnc), and State Tracking (STrack). Detailed explanations of each module will be provided in the subsequent sections.

Problem Setting. At the start of the game, QBot receives a caption C describing the target image I^* visible to ABot. This caption provides the initial textual information for QBot to generate its first question. In subsequent rounds, QBot generates questions $q^{(t)}$ based on the accumulated dialogue history H, which includes the caption C and previous question-answer pairs. QBot's goal is to use this information to guess the undisclosed image from a candidate pool.

We define an accumulated dialogue state $<M_e^{(t)}, M_v^{(t)}>$ at round t. The words state $M_e^{(t)}$ represents the textual representation of discussed entities, while the images state $M_v^{(t)}$ represents mental imagery information derived from the words in QBot's mind. The initial dialogue state $<M_e^{(1)}, M_v^{(1)}>$ is constructed using the caption C as input and the Adding action of the STrack module. Both $M_e^{(1)}$ and $M_v^{(1)}$ are $1 \times d$ matrices.

Recursive Self-Reference Equation (R-SRE). To capture visually related interactions within and between modalities in the dialogue state, we propose a recursive self-reference equation (R-SRE) denoted as $V' = \mathrm{R} - \mathrm{SRE}(Q, V)$. The R-SRE consists of two attention mechanisms that facilitate the update of the matrix V based on the guidance provided by another matrix Q. The equation is formulated as follows:

$$\alpha = \text{softmax}(w_\alpha Q), \tag{1}$$

$$q = \alpha^T Q, \tag{2}$$

$$\beta = \text{softmax}(w_\beta[\text{r}^{(k)}(q); \text{r}^{(k)}(q) \odot V; V]), \tag{3}$$

$$V' = \beta V, \tag{4}$$

where $Q, V \in \mathbb{R}^{k \times d}$ are two input data matrix, $w_\alpha \in \mathbb{R}^{d \times 1}$ and $w_\beta \in \mathbb{R}^{3d \times 1}$ are trainable projection matrices. $[;;]$ denotes the symmetric concatenation between bi-modalities as in [11,12], $\odot$ is the element-wise product. We define a repeat operation $\text{r}^{(k)}(q)$ that repeats q k times to form a matrix of size $k \times d$ with same dimension as V. Specially, a self-attention on Q is first performed and attention scores $\alpha \in \mathbb{R}^{k \times 1}$ is obtained, $q \in \mathbb{R}^{d \times 1}$ is the weighted sum of Q using α. Then, q is referred to as a key again to query V to get a $\beta \in \mathbb{R}^{k \times 1}$ over V. Finally, V is changed by multiplying the attention weight β to yield a new same-dimension representation V'. We omit bias where possible, for clarity.

Visual Reasoning on Dialogue State (VRDS). The VRDS process involves three-hops reasoning using the R-SRE operation. Firstly, a self R-SRE operation updates the words state (Eq. 5). Then, a cross-modal R-SRE operation generates a visually related context vector (Eq. 6). Iterative cross-modal R-SRE operations between the updated words state and the images state yield an intermediate textual context vector (Eq. 7). Finally, the visually and textually related context vectors are concatenated and processed by a linear layer to obtain the final context vector. Formally,

$$\widehat{M}_e^{(t)} = \text{R\,-\,SRE}(M_e^{(t)}, M_e^{(t)}), \tag{5}$$

$$\widehat{M}_v^{(t)} = \text{R\,-\,SRE}(\widehat{M}_e^{(t)}, M_v^{(t)}), a_v^{(t)} = \text{sum}(\widehat{M}_v^{(t)}), \tag{6}$$

$$\widetilde{M}_e^{(t)} = \text{R\,-\,SRE}(\widehat{M}_e^{(t)}, \widehat{M}_v^{(t)}), a_e^{(t)} = \text{sum}(\widetilde{M}_e^{(t)}), \tag{7}$$

$$z^{(t)} = \text{Dropout}(w_v[a_v^{(t)}; a_e^{(t)}]), \tag{8}$$

where $w_v \in \mathbb{R}^{2d \times d}$ are learnable projection matrixes, *sum* is operated on the k-dimension to compact the intermediate representation matrix to a vector, $z^{(t)} \in \mathbb{R}^d$ is the final context vector passed to QDer module.

From Eq. 5 to Eq. 8, VRDS performs textually and visually related interactions upon dialogue state. It models the cross-modal interactions between two states motivated from Dual-coding theory [9]: QBot can think with words as well as can think with images based on mental imagery representations in one's mind.

Question Decoder (QDer). We use a multi-layer Transformer decoder [15] and employs softmax on its output. It takes $z^{(t)}$ and dialogue states as input. The QDer module predicts next word by employing cross-attention with dialogue states as conditioning, continuing this process until an end-of-sequence token [EOS] is encountered. Formally,

$$h_{i+1}^{(t)} = \text{transformer\_decoder}(h_i^{(t)}, M_e^{(t)}, M_v^{(t)}), \tag{9}$$

$$w_{i+1}^{(t)} = argmax\ \text{softmax}(h_{i+1}^{(t)} w_{der}), \tag{10}$$

where $w_{der} \in \mathbb{R}^{d \times |V|}$ is trainable parameters, V is the number of vocabulary. $h_{i+1}^{(t)}$ denotes the representation of next token $w_{i+1}^{(t)}$, which is selected by the greedy algorithm. $h_0^{(t)}$ is initialized as the element-wise addition of the starting token [SOS] and $z^{(t)}$. We save a sequence of $w_{i+1}^{(t)}$ to produce a new question $q^{(t)}$.

QBot Encoders (QEnc). QEnc utilizes a pre-trained vision-linguistic model called ViLBERT [7]. The input to ViLBERT is structured as follows: [CLS] $q^{(t)}$ [SEP] $a^{(t)}$ [SEP] $M^{(t)}e$ [SEP] $M^{(t)}v$, with each segment separated by a [SEP] token. The output of [CLS] token is considered as the fact representation $f^{(t)} \in \mathbb{R}^d$, which captures the information from new question-answer pair.

State Tracking (STrack). STrack offers two actions: Adding and Updating. The decision between these actions is determined by a differentiable binary choice made using Gumbel-Softmax sampling [5]. This allows for end-to-end training. We introduce a two-layer feedforward network denoted as FFN($\cdot$), which incorporates GELU activation, Dropout, and LayerNorm. For clarity, we apply FFN($\cdot$) to the element-wise product of the fact representation $f^{(t)}$ and words state $M_e^{(t)}$. Subsequently, a Gumbel-Softmax operation is performed, yielding a probability distribution representing the action type.

$$\phi = \text{Gumbel}(\text{FFN}([r^{(k)}(f^{(t)}) \odot M_e^{(t)}])), \tag{11}$$

where $\phi \in \mathbb{R}^2$ is 2-d one-hot vector for discrete decision. According to predicted ϕ, one of the two actions is chosen for the STrack.

Adding Action on Words State. The Adding action is executed on the current words state if $\phi[0] = 1$. It takes the $f^{(t)}$ as input to FFN, resulting in a new textual representation $e^{(t+1)}a, w \in \mathbb{R}^d$. Subsequently, $e^{(t+1)}a, w$ is inserted into the set of words states, leading to a new set of words states $M_e^{(t+1)} \in \mathbb{R}^{(k+1) \times d}$:

$$e_{a,w}^{(t+1)} = \text{FFN}(f^{(t)}), \tag{12}$$
$$M_e^{(t+1)} = M_e^{(t)} \cup \{e_{a,w}^{(t+1)}\}, \tag{13}$$

where $\cup$ is an append operation. Note that the size of newly updated $M_e^{(t+1)}$ is increased to $k + 1$.

Adding Action on Images State. In the case of $\phi[0] = 1$, the adding action is performed on current images states. It produces a new mental object $o_{a,v}^{(t+1)} \in \mathbb{R}^d$, which denotes a new visual concept (e.g., "carpet"). We translate the fact representation into images with FFN network, and get a new set of images states $M_v^{(t+1)} \in \mathbb{R}^{(k+1) \times d}$, in which its size is increased to $k + 1$. Formally,

$$o_{a,v}^{(t)} = \text{FFN}(f^{(t)}), \tag{14}$$
$$M_v^{(t+1)} = M_v^{(t)} \cup \{o_{a,v}^{(t)}\}, \tag{15}$$

where fact representation $f^{(t)}$ is used for translation from words to images by FFN.

Updating Action on Words State. When $\phi[0] = 0$, the updating action is applied to the words state. It includes calculating an assignment distribution ψ that determines how much the new fact representation can be merged into the existing representation of the associated words state. This is achieved by passing $f^{(t)}$ and the current words state $M_e^{(t)}$ through a two-layer feedforward network and a softmax classifier.

$$\psi = \text{softmax}(\text{FFN}([\text{r}^{(k)}(f^{(t)}) \odot M_e^{(t)}])), \qquad (16)$$

$$M_e^{(t+1)} = M_e^{(t)} + \psi\text{FFN}_\psi(f^{(t)}), \qquad (17)$$

where $\psi \in \mathbb{R}^k$ is the assignment distribution, $\text{FFN}_\psi(\cdot) \in \mathbb{R}^d$ denotes another FFN network, $M_e^{(t+1)} \in \mathbb{R}^{k \times d}$ is the newly updated words states. Note that the number of words states in $M_e^{(t+1)}$ remains unchanged in this case.

Updating Action on Images State. If $\phi[0] = 0$, similar to the case of updating on words state, we compute an assignment distribution for associating current fact representation with previous images state. Formally,

$$\gamma = \text{softmax}(\text{FFN}([\text{r}^{(k)}(f^{(t)}) \odot M_v^{(t)}])), \qquad (18)$$

$$M_v^{(t+1)} = M_v^{(t)} + \gamma\text{FFN}_\gamma(f^{(t)}), \qquad (19)$$

where $\gamma \in \mathbb{R}^k$ is the assignment distribution, $\text{FFN}_\gamma(\cdot) \in \mathbb{R}^d$ is another FFN network different from in Eq. 18. It converts fact representation to visually related representation, which accumulates further visual attributes (such as object shape, color and position, e.g., a question "what color is the carpet?" with an answer "red") about the contents of the undisclosed image in the same representation in $M_v^{(t)}$. $M_v^{(t+1)} \in \mathbb{R}^{k \times d}$ is the newly updated images state, its size remains unchanged.

Model Training. Our model is optimized using supervised learning (SL) with three loss functions: Cross-Entropy (CE) loss, Mean Square Error (MSE) loss, and Progressive (PL) loss. The CE loss is computed based on ground truth questions, while the MSE loss is calculated using the feature regression network $f(\cdot)$ [4] to predict the image representation $y^{(t)}I$. The MSE loss compares the predicted representation $y^{(t)}I$ with the ground truth image representation $y_{I^*}^{(t)}$ obtained from VGG19.

$$\mathcal{L}_{\text{CE}} = -\frac{1}{l}\sum_{j=1}^{l}\log p_j; \mathcal{L}_{\text{MSE}} = -\frac{1}{T}\sum_{t=1}^{T}||y_{I^*}^{(t)} - y_I^{(t)}||_2^2, \qquad (20)$$

where l here denotes the total length of generated questions, T is the total dialog rounds, p_j is the probability of ground-truth word at step j in the dialogue.

Because of multi-round dialogue brings a series of MSE loss, we present a progressive loss that is defined as the difference of MSE loss in successive dialog rounds, which encourages Questioner to progressively increase similarity towards the target image, as written in: $\mathcal{L}_{\text{PL}} = -\frac{1}{T-1}\sum_{t=2}^{T}\mathcal{L}_{\text{MSE}}^{(t)} - \mathcal{L}_{\text{MSE}}^{(t-1)}$. Overall, the final loss for supervised learning QBot is a sum of three losses as mentioned above: $\mathcal{L}_{SL} = \mathcal{L}_{\text{CE}} + \mathcal{L}_{\text{MSE}} + \mathcal{L}_{\text{PL}}$.

4   Experiment and Evaluation

Dataset Our GuessWhich model is evaluated on three benchmarks: VisDial v0.5, v0.9, and v1.0. These datasets include various numbers of training, validation, and test images. VisDial v1.0 has 123,287 training images, 2,064 validation images, and 8,000 test images. VisDial v0.9 includes 82,783 training images and 40,504 validation images. VisDial v0.5 consists of 50,729 training images, 7,663 validation images, and 9,628 test images. Dialogues in these datasets contain a caption for the target image and multiple question-answer pairs. It's worth noting that only the test set of VisDial v1.0 has variable-length dialogues, while the other dataset splits have fixed 10-round dialogues.

Evaluation Metric. We follow the standard evaluation metrics [4,8] for QBot in two parts: image guessing and question diversity. At image guessing, we report retrieval metrics of target image, including mean reciprocal rank (MRR), Recall @k (R@k) for $k = 1, 5, 10$, mean rank (Mean) and percentile mean rank (PMR). At question diversity, we adopt six metrics like Novel Questions [8], Unique Questions [8], Dist-n and Ent-n [17], Negative log-likelihood [8], and Mutual Overlap [18].

Implementation Details. Our model architecture consists of a cross-modal Transformer decoder with 12 layers and a hidden state size of 768. It utilizes 12 attention heads. The base encoder is a pre-trained ViLBERT model with 12 layers and a hidden state size of 768. During training, we used a batch size of 64 and trained the model for 30 epochs. A dropout rate of 0.1 was applied after each linear layer. Early stopping was implemented on the validation split if the performance metric (PMR) did not improve for 10 consecutive epochs. We used the Adam optimizer with a base learning rate of 1e-3, which decayed to 1e-5 during training. For image representation, we used pre-extracted VGG19 features, where each image is represented by a 4096-dimensional vector.

Comparison to State-of-the-Art Methods. The comparing methods on QBot can be regarded to have three types: 1) Non-visual based models, like SL-Q [4], ReCap [14], ADQ [8], AMN [19], RL-Q [4], AQM+/indA [6], ReeQ-SL (trained in SL) [20] and ReeQ-RL (fine-tuned in reinforcement learning) [20]. 2) Real-image based methods, such as SL-Q-IG [21]. and 3) Mental-imagery based method: our DST.

Image Guessing. The results of image guessing are provided in Table 1. Our DST model achieves significant improvements over previous state-of-the-art models (SOTA) across all metrics and datasets. On the validation split of v1.0, DST outperforms ReeQ and establishes new SOTA with a PMR of 99.60 and Mean of 17.52. On the test split of v1.0, DST consistently outperforms other strong models, such as AMN, with a PMR of 98.10. Compared to the real-image based SL-QI-G on the v0.5 test, DST achieves a PMR of 98.69, demonstrating the inefficiency of image retrieval from larger pools. DST also performs well on the v0.9 validation split with a PMR of 98.02. The trends in PMR are consistent across all datasets, and only DST shows a continuous increase in PMR as the dialogue progresses, highlighting its robustness and effectiveness in different dataset settings.

Table 1. Result comparison of image guessing on VisDial datasets. Higher is better for MRR, R@k, and PMR, and lower is better for Mean. Note that † means we roughly estimated the value of Mean by an approximate evaluation: Mean $\simeq$ #Num of Image Pool $\times$ $(1.0 - \text{PMR})$ [14], and the results of $^\circ$ are cited from [19].

Model	MRR↑	R@1↑	R@5↑	R@10↑	PMR↑	Mean↓	Dataset	#Num of Image Pool
SL-Q [4]	–	–	–	–	91.19	848.2†	v0.5 test	9,628
RL-Q [4]	–	–	–	–	94.19	559.4†		
SL-Q-IG [21]	–	–	–	–	96.09	376.5†		
ReCap [14]	–	–	–	–	95.54	429.4†		
AQM+/indA [6]	–	–	–	–	94.64	516.1†		
DST (Ours)	6.25	2.59	8.31	13.14	**98.69**	**254.19**		
	8.73	3.55	10.49	15.96	98.76	184.65	v0.5 val	7,663
ADQ$^\circ$ [8]	–	–	–	–	94.99	400.8†	v1.0 test	8,000
RL-Q$^\circ$ [4]	–	–	–	–	93.38	529.6†		
AMN [19]	–	–	–	–	94.88	409.6†		
DST (Ours)	33.49	17.47	30.62	33.97	**99.44**	**161.19**		
SL-Q [4]	7.8	2.56	9.49	17.87	93.83	127.84	v1.0 val	2,064
ADQ [8]	10.73	3.39	14.82	25.29	95.73	87.92		
ReeQ-SL [20]	31.21	17.78	45.01	59.98	99.00	20.60		
ReeQ-RL [20]	33.65	19.91	48.50	62.94	99.13	18.05		
DST (Ours)	**34.01**	**24.99**	**49.49**	**63.92**	**99.60**	**17.52**		
	4.10	2.27	5.88	8.13	98.02	1195.43	v0.9 val	40,504

Fig. 3. Comparison of generated dialogs with ADQ [8] and humans on VisDial v1.0 val. Our QBot agent converses with SL-ABOT [8] for a fair comparison to ADQ model.

Ablation Studies. Ablation studies on the v1.0 validation set (Table 2) were performed to analyze the impact of each module. The full model's performance is reported in row 1, while subsequent rows correspond to the removal of specific modules to assess their significance.

Table 2. Ablation studies on major modules by removing it from the full model on VisDial v1.0 val.

#	Model	MRR↑	R@1↑	R@5↑	R@10↑	Mean↓	PMR↑
1	Full model	**34.01**	**24.99**	**49.49**	**63.92**	**17.52**	**99.60**
2	-VRDS	27.01	20.25	40.35	52.57	55.24	97.29
3	-STrack	25.45	19.08	38.47	49.82	75.80	96.40
4	-$\mathcal{L}_{\mathrm{MSE}}$	31.59	23.09	46.53	60.45	29.30	98.55
5	-$\mathcal{L}_{\mathrm{PL}}$	32.28	23.61	47.83	62.16	25.30	99.11

Removing the VRDS module resulted in a significant drop in PMR by 2.30 points, an increase in Mean by 37.72 absolute points to 55.24, and a decrease in MRR by approximately 7 points to 27.01. These findings highlight the importance of three-hop reasoning using the recursive self-reference equation (R-SRE) for accurate image guessing. The role of the R-SRE operation is indirectly verified as it enables visually related reasoning, providing more distinguishing clues for generating visually related questions (refer to Fig. 3 for details).

Removing the STrack module, which relies solely on the image caption at the 0th round, resulted in a decrease in PMR to 96.40, emphasizing the importance of caption information. The performance metrics of this configuration were lower than those of removing VRDS, indicating that the STrack module facilitates the incorporation of additional textual semantics and visual concepts into dialogue states. Additionally, the results from rows 4 and 5 demonstrate the effectiveness of both supervisions. Removing $\mathcal{L}_{\mathrm{PL}}$ led to a slight reduction in PMR, while removing $\mathcal{L}_{\mathrm{MSE}}$ decreased PMR by nearly 1 point, highlighting the efficacy of the combined $\mathcal{L}_{\mathrm{PL}}$ and $\mathcal{L}_{\mathrm{MSE}}$ in training the model efficiently.

Case Studies. In Fig. 3, a comparison with recent ADQ [8] reveals two key observations. Firstly, our model effectively avoids repetition over the 10 rounds by combining VRDS and STrack modules. This prevents repetitive context and ensures that context vector $z^{(t)}$ remains distinctive and informative, leading to non-repetitive questions generated. Secondly, our model generates a higher number of visually related questions. In the first example, it asks three color-related questions (highlighted in red), while [8] and humans ask questions that are not focused on color. In the last two examples, our model initiates the dialogue with four and five image-related questions, respectively. These findings indicate that mental model of the unseen image enables the generation of image-like representations, prompting QBot to ask visually related questions.

5   Conclusion

This paper proposes DST, a novel dialogue state tracking approach for visual dialog question generation in the GuessWhich game. DST maintains and updates dialogue states, including word and mental image representations, enabling mentally related reasoning. Unlike previous studies, DST performs visual reasoning using mental representations of unseen images, achieving state-of-the-art performance. Future work will focus on exploring and visualizing the image state in DST.

Acknowledgements. We thank the reviewers for their comments and suggestions. This paper was partially supported by the National Natural Science Foundation of China (NSFC 62076032), Huawei Noah's Ark Lab, MoECMCC "Artificial Intelligence" Project (No. MCM20190701), Beijing Natural Science Foundation (Grant No. 4204100), and BUPT Excellent Ph.D. Students Foundation (No. CX2020309).

References

1. Agrawal, A., et al.: VQA: visual question answering. In: ICCV, pp. 2425–2433 (2015)
2. Das, A., et al.: Visual dialog. In: CVPR, pp. 326–335 (2017)
3. Das, A., Kottur, S., Moura, J.M., Lee, S., Batra, D.: Evaluating visual conversational agents via cooperative human-AI games. In: HCOMP (2017)
4. Das, A., Kottur, S., Moura, J.M., Lee, S., Batra, D.: Learning cooperative visual dialog agents with deep reinforcement learning. In: ICCV, pp. 2951–2960 (2017)
5. Jang, E., Gu, S., Poole, B.: Categorical reparameterization with gumbel-softmax. In: ICLR (2017)
6. Lee, S.W., Gao, T., Yang, S., Yoo, J., Ha, J.W.: Large-scale answerer in questioner's mind for visual dialog question generation. In: ICLR (2019)
7. Lu, J., Batra, D., Parikh, D., Lee, S.: ViLBERT: pretraining task-agnostic visiolinguistic representations for vision-and-language tasks. In: NeurIPS (2019)
8. Murahari, V., Chattopadhyay, P., Batra, D., Parikh, D., Das, A.: Improving generative visual dialog by answering diverse questions. In: EMNLP, pp. 1449–1454 (2019)
9. Paivio, A.: Imagery and verbal processes (1971)
10. Pang, W.: Multi-round dialogue state tracking by object-entity alignment in visual dialog. In: CICAI (Oral) (2023)
11. Pang, W., Wang, X.: Guessing state tracking for visual dialogue. In: Vedaldi, A., Bischof, H., Brox, T., Frahm, J.-M. (eds.) ECCV 2020. LNCS, vol. 12361, pp. 683–698. Springer, Cham (2020). https://doi.org/10.1007/978-3-030-58517-4_40
12. Pang, W., Wang, X.: Visual dialogue state tracking for question generation. In: Thirty-Fourth AAAI Conference on Artificial Intelligence, pp. 11831–11838. AAAI (Oral) (2020)
13. Shuster, K., Humeau, S., Bordes, A., Weston, J.: Image-chat: engaging grounded conversations. In: ACL, pp. 2414–2429 (2020)
14. Testoni, A., Shekhar, R., Fernández, R., aella Bernardi, R.: The devil is in the details: a magnifying glass for the guesswhich visual dialogue game. In: Proceedings of the 23rd SemDial Workshop on the Semantics and Pragmatics of Dialogue, pp. 15–24 (2019)
15. Vaswani, A., et al: Attention is all you need. In: NeurIPS (2017)
16. de Vries, H., Strub, F., Chandar, S., Pietquin, O., Larochelle, H., Courville, A.: GuessWhat?! visual object discovery through multi-modal dialogue. In: CVPR, pp. 4466–4475 (2017)

17. Zhang, Y., et al.: Generating informative and diverse conversational responses via adversarial information maximization. In: NeurIPS (2018)
18. Zhang, Y., Galley, M., Gao, J., Schwing, A., Forsyth, D.: Fast, diverse and accurate image captioning guided by part-of-speech. In: CVPR, pp. 10695–10704 (2019)
19. Zhao, L., Lyu, X., Song, J., Gao, L.: GuessWhich? visual dialog with attentive memory network. Pattern Recogn. **114**, 107823 (2021)
20. Zheng, D., Xu, Z., Meng, F., Wang, X., Wang, J., Zhou, J.: Enhancing visual dialog questioner with entity-based strategy learning and augmented guesser. In: Findings of EMNLP, pp. 1839–1851 (2021)
21. Zhou, M., Arnold, J., Yu, Z.: Building task-oriented visual dialog systems through alternative optimization between dialog policy and language generation. In: EMNLP, pp. 143–153 (2019)

Diagnosis Then Aggregation: An Adaptive Ensemble Strategy for Keyphrase Extraction

Xin Jin[1,2], Qi Liu[1,2(✉)], Linan Yue[1,2], Ye Liu[1,2], Lili Zhao[1,2], Weibo Gao[1,2], Zheng Gong[1,2], Kai Zhang[1,2], and Haoyang Bi[1,2]

[1] Anhui Province Key Laboratory of Big Data Analysis and Application, University of Science and Technology of China, Hefei, China
[2] State Key Laboratory of Cognitive Intelligence, Hefei, China
{kingiv,lnyue,liuyer,liliz,weibogao,gz70229,sa517494, bhy0521}@mail.ustc.edu.cn, qiliuql@ustc.edu.cn

Abstract. Keyphrase extraction (KE) is a fundamental task in the information extraction, which has recently gained increasing attention. However, when facing text with complex structure or high noise, current individual keyphrase extraction methods fail to handle capturing multiple features and limit the performance of the keyphrase extraction. To solve that, ensemble learning methods are employed to achieve better performance. Unfortunately, traditional ensemble strategies rely only on the extraction performance (e.g., *Accuracy*) of each algorithm on the whole dataset for keyphrase extraction, and the aggregated weights are commonly fixed, lacking fine-grained considerations and adaptiveness to the data. To this end, in this paper, we propose an Adaptive Ensemble strategy for Keyphrase Extraction (AEKE) that can aggregate individual KE models adaptively. Specifically, we first obtain the multi-dimensional abilities of individual KE models by employing cognitive diagnosis methods. Then, based on the diagnostic abilities, we introduce an adaptive ensemble strategy to yield an accurate and reliable weight distribution for model aggregation when facing new data, and further apply it to improve keyphrase extraction in the model aggregation. Extensive experimental results on real-world datasets clearly validate the effectiveness of AEKE. Code is released at https://github.com/kingiv4/AEKE.

Keywords: Keyphrase Extraction · Ensemble Learning · Cognitive Diagnosis

1 Introduction

How to extract the needed information from the huge amount of unstructured knowledge is the fundamental problem in the field of natural language processing today [19,20,33]. Among the information extraction methods, keyphrase extraction (KE) has garnered significant attention [14,27,34] as it can enhance the efficiency of natural language processing and benefit numerous downstream tasks, such as information retrieval [14] and document summarization [25].

L. Fang et al. (Eds.): CICAI 2023, LNAI 14473, pp. 566–578, 2024.
https://doi.org/10.1007/978-981-99-8850-1_46

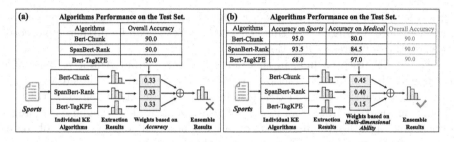

Fig. 1. Part (a) shows the traditional ensemble strategy based on *Accuracy*. Since the three methods perform consistently across the whole dataset, they are aggregated equally when encountering new data. However, part (b) shows that there are differences among the methods from a fine-grained perspective. When dealing with *Sports* news, more emphasis should be placed on the two methods (i.e. Bert-Chunk and SpanBert-Rank) that are more capable in *Sports*.

The goal of keyphrase extraction is to extract several keyphrases from documents that can represent the main information of the documents. For example, given a text document " *The authors had given a method for the construction of panoramic image mosaics with global and local alignment.* ", the keyphrase extraction method can identify *"panoramic image mosaics, global alignment, local alignment"* as the representative keyphrases. Finally, for evaluation, *Accuracy*, *Precision*, *Recall* and *F1-score* metrics are commonly employed to evaluate the performance of keyphrase extraction algorithms [10,29,32].

Despite previous approaches achieving promising results, when facing text with complex structure (e.g. long and difficult sentences) or high noise (e.g. text from different domains), these individual approaches fail to capture various features in the above text and have limited performance. To this end, a straightforward approach is to exploit the ensemble methods to aggregate different keyphrase extraction models to achieve better keyphrase extraction.

Figure 1(a) presents a traditional ensemble strategy that aggregates individual KE methods based on the *Accuracy*. However, unfortunately, in practice, the traditional methods can not always achieve satisfying results and even cause a negative impact on keyphrase extraction. Specifically, since SpanBert-Rank [28], Bert-Chunk, [28] and Bert-TagKPE [28] perform consistently in *Accuracy* on the overall dataset, we should aggregate these methods equally from the perspective of traditional ensemble strategy when facing new data about *Sports* topic. However, as shown in Fig. 1(b), from a more fine-grained perspective, both Bert-Chunk and Span-Rank outperform Bert-TagKPE on the *Sports* topic, while they perform poorly on the *Medical*. Therefore, when facing new *Sports* data, we should focus more on Bert-Chunk and SpanBert-Rank rather than dealing with all three methods equally during the model aggregation. In this paper, we define the extraction ability of the KE model for different topic domains as the multi-dimensional extraction ability of KE (See Sect. 3 for detail).

From the above observations, we can conclude that traditional ensemble methods fail to consider the multi-dimensional extraction abilities of individual models, and instead focus only on the performance of individual models with a single metric (e.g., *Accuracy*), degrading the performance of the ensemble. Therefore, we argue that this *"ensemble pattern"* can be further explored to improve the keyphrase extraction.

Along this research line, in this paper, we propose an **A**daptive **E**nsemble strategy for **K**eyphrase **E**xtraction (AEKE) based on the multi-dimensional abilities of individual keyphrase extraction models. Specifically, inspired by the psychometric theories [5,22] from human measurement, we first diagnose the multi-dimensional abilities of different keyphrase extraction models by means of cognitive diagnostic techniques. Then, based on the diagnostic abilities, we develop an adaptive ensemble strategy. The strategy will adaptively adjust the aggregation weights for different samples to achieve better ensemble performance. Finally, experiments over two datasets, including OpenKP [32] and Inspec [15], validate the effectiveness of our AEKE.

2   Related Work

Keyphrase Extraction aims to select a set of phrases that could summarize the main topics discussed in the document [14]. The algorithms in keyphrase extraction are commonly divided into supervised and unsupervised methods. Specifically, unsupervised methods [2,3,24] mainly used different features of the document such as topic features, phrase frequency and so on to make keyphrase extraction. In supervised methods [7,29], pre-trained language models have been exploited and achieved competitive performance with annotation of the corpus.

Ensemble Learning can fuse the knowledge of individual models together to achieve competitive performance via voting schemes based on some learned features, which is widely used in machine learning tasks [8,25]. Traditional voting schemes include unweighted averaging and weighted voting. Among them, unweighted averaging of the outputs of the base learners in an ensemble is the most followed approach for fusing the outputs [11]. It considers the output results of each learner equally but ignores the differences between learners. On the other hand, weighted voting methods [11] tend to assign different weights to different learners based on their unidimensional ability. Such ability is often assessed by a single traditional metric on the history datasets. But the weights are constant during the model aggregation. In ensemble strategies of keyphrase extraction, mainstream methods employed unweighted averaging and weighted voting methods to aggregate individual KE models. However, these methods still suffered from relying on the unidimensional ability (e.g., *Accuracy*, *Precision*) of individual KE models to achieve aggregation, resulting in limited performance in the ensemble. To solve that, we develop an adaptive ensemble strategy for keyphrase extraction from the perspective of multi-dimensional abilities.

Cognitive Diagnosis is a fundamental task in many real-world scenarios (e.g., business [17] and education [12,13,31]). The main goal of cognitive diagnosis is to measure learners' proficiency profiles of abilities to finish specific tasks from their observed behaviors [31]. For instance in education, it can be used to infer student (as *learner*) knowledge proficiency (as *ability*) by fully exploiting their responses of answering each exercise (as *task*). Most of the existing cognitive diagnosis models (CDMs) [5,12,22] are well designed from psychometric theories of human measurement. Among them, item response theory (IRT) [22] is the most classic CDMs which assumes the probability of the learner s_i correctly finishing a task e_j, i.e., $r_{ij} = 1$, increases with learner ability θ_i while decreasing with task difficulty β_j. Among them, the user ability and task difficulty are trainable unidimensional parameters [18]. A typical formulation of IRT is $P(r_{ij} = 1) = sigmoid((\theta_i - \beta_j) \cdot a_j)$, where a_j is an optional task discrimination item. Recently, some works extended the previous basic models to capture the more complex relationships among users, tasks, and abilities. The typical model is NeuralCD [31] which introduced neural networks $F(\cdot)$ to model high-level interaction between learners/abilities and tasks, i.e., $P(r_{ij} = 1) = F(\theta_i - \beta_j)$.

Inspired by the psychometric theories from human measurement, the multidimensional evaluation of KE algorithms can also benefit from the more fine-grained assessment of human learning performance.

3   Problem Definition

Cognitive Diagnosis for Keyphrase Extraction. Following the NeuralCD [31] which is a cognitive diagnostic model (CDMs), we introduce the definition of the cognitive diagnosis problem for keyphrase extraction algorithms. First, we denote the algorithms to be evaluated as learners and the CDMs as diagnosers. Then, with the diagnoser, we can evaluate the multi-dimensional abilities of learners on different skills, which are used to describe how well an algorithm performs on a particular category of samples.

Besides, in our work, since the topic of documents contains the main information and represents the specific textual features of keyphrase [23], we take the topics of documents as skills. For instance, topics on *Sports* and *Medical* convey a totally different message. Therefore, we define specific skills as specific topics of documents and one topic for one skill.

To design our diagnoser, we consider a well-trained learner set $S = \{s_1, ..., s_N\}$, a sample set $E = \{e_1, ..., e_M\}$ which is the dataset in our task, and a skill (topic) set $C = \{c_1, ..., c_P\}$. N and M denote the number of learners to be aggregated and samples in the dataset. P denotes the number of skills as a hyper-parameter in our task. Then the learner's output results on each sample as response logs R, which are denoted as a set of triplet (s, e, r_{ij}), where $s \in S$, $e \in E$ and r_{ij} is the score that learner i got on sample j. The top 5 results of keyphrase extraction are transferred to a score (0 or 1). We denote $r_{ij} = 1$ if learner i predicts more than one keyphrase correctly and $r_{ij} = 0$ otherwise. Meanwhile, an explicitly pre-defined sample-skill relevancy matrix Q should also be given. $Q = \{Q_{ij}\}_{M \times P}$, where $Q_{ij} = 1$ if sample e_i is related to skill p_j and $Q_{ij} = 0$ otherwise. Given the learner-sample response matrix R and the sample-skill matrix relevancy Q, we could estimate the multi-dimensional abilities of different learners on different skills through the diagnoser.

Adaptive Ensemble Strategy. Figure 1(a) illustrates the problems encountered with traditional ensemble strategies. They only focus on the performance of keyphrase extraction algorithms on a single metric, while ignoring the differences in multi-dimensional abilities. To solve that, from the perspective of the multi-dimensional abilities of the keyphrase extraction algorithms, we use the results of cognitive diagnosis to design adaptive ensemble strategies.

With the cognitive diagnostic module, we first obtain diagnostic results that include the multi-dimensional abilities of each algorithm and the characteristics (e.g., difficulty, discrimination, topic) of the data. Then, in the face of the new document n, we design the ensemble strategy of adaptive weight adjustment based on the above diagnostic results, including the multi-dimensional abilities, difficulty, discrimination, and topic. Among them, the multi-dimensional abilities represent the characteristics of the KE algorithms, while the difficulty, discrimination, and topic represent the characteristics of the samples. The goal of our strategy is to construct a relationship among diagnostic results and get more reasonable voting weights w for algorithms adaptively to get a better ensemble performance on every new document.

Problem Definition. *Given the multi-dimensional abilities of KE algorithms and features of the new document, our goal is to design an adaptive ensemble strategy to adjust the aggregation weights to improve the keyphrase extraction.*

4   Adaptive Ensemble Strategy via Cognitive Diagnosis

In this section, we present the details of AEKE for keyphrase extraction, which contains two stages. First, in the cognitive diagnostic stage, we follow NeuralCD [31] diagnostic approach and perform fine-grained diagnostics on the performance of various individual keyphrase extraction models to obtain their multi-dimensional abilities. In the ensemble stage, we design an adaptive ensemble strategy based on the diagnostic multi-dimensional abilities and document characteristics to get a better ensemble performance.

4.1   Cognitive Diagnose for Keyphrase Extraction Algorithms

Learner and Sample Factors. In our task, since we only focus on the ability of the different skills, each learner is represented with a one-hot vector $s_z \in \{0,1\}^{1 \times N}$ as input, where N denotes the number of learners to be evaluated. In the same way, we represent sample e_d input as one-hot vector $e_d \in \{0,1\}^{1 \times M}$.

Skill Factors. We want to make the topics as skills, as topic information is valuable in keyphrase extraction tasks. However, the published datasets do not contain topic labels for documents. To this end, in this paper, we employ the LDA [1] (Latent Dirichlet Allocation topic model) to obtain the topic labels by unsupervised clustering of the documents. Especially, LDA has better interpretability and the topical tokens for the clusters can be used as the explicit description for skills, which is great of importance for cognitive diagnosis.

After clustering the documents into P topics by LDA, we can obtain the sample-skill matrix $Q \in \{0,1\}^{M \times P}$. By this method, the topic label of each sample will be obtained.

Latent Factors. Following NeuralCD [31], with the model we can get the multi-dimensional abilities of the learner h_a and the difficulty h_d and discrimination h_d^{disc} of the sample. Among them, the h_a indicates the ability of the learner to process samples on different topics. The h_d represents the degree of difficulty the learner to solving the problem. Besides, the h_d^{disc} indicates the capability of samples to differentiate the proficiencies of learners. Samples with low discrimination mean that of low quality: they tend to have annotation errors or do not make sense.

Interaction and Prediction. Here, we exploit neural networks to model the relationship between learner ability factor h_a and skill difficulty factor h_d. The probability Y is defined as the ability compared with the sample in the covered topic as $Y = (h_a - h_d) \times h_d^{disc}$. Then, we use the full connection layers F to predict the score y of learner z on the sample d: $y = \sigma(F(Y))$. Finally, the whole objective of the diagnoser is defined with the cross entropy loss function:

$$\mathcal{L} = - \sum_i (r_i \log y_i + (1 - r_i) \log(1 - y_i)), \tag{1}$$

where r is the true score. Based on Eq. (1), we can get the multi-dimensional abilities of the keyphrase extraction algorithms.

4.2 Adaptive Ensemble Strategy

With the diagnostic module, we get the multi-dimensional abilities of each keyphrase extraction algorithm. Based on such diagnostic results, we propose an adaptive ensemble strategy to better aggregate the results of each extraction algorithm in the face of new test samples.

Inputs for Adaptive Ensemble Strategy. The inputs to the adaptive ensemble strategy include the abilities of individual KE algorithms and the features of the new sample. Among them, the KE algorithms' abilities are obtained from the previous diagnostic module, indicating the multi-dimensional abilities of the KE algorithms on different topics.

Features of the new sample contain information about the topic, difficulty and discrimination. Specifically, the topic information is associated with the diagnosed algorithm ability. The difficulty and discrimination information can reflect the implicit features of the algorithm in dealing with such problems to some extent. The information of the new sample is adequately represented by these three features.

To sum up, based on the topic model obtained in Sect. 4.1, the new sample is input and its distribution over each implicit topic is obtained as its topic information c_n. Each of its dimensions represents the probability of its distribution on that implicit topic.

Besides, since unseen samples are not used as input to the diagnostic module, the difficulty and discrimination of the samples cannot be directly obtained. To this end, we design a non-parametric module to predict the difficulty and discrimination. Specifically, as there is a close relationship between original texts and the factors of samples including the difficulty and discrimination, we choose to predict difficulty and discrimination based on semantic K-nearest neighbor [26] methods. Here, given the token sequence of original texts of keyphrase extraction samples $D^w = \{d_1^w, d_2^w, ..., d_n^w\}$, we map each word of D^w into word embedding by BERT [6], and get the document embedding by applying mean-pooling, where n_w is the length of the word sequence. We use the document embedding e_d as input representation for the new sample:

$$e_d = MeanPool(BERT([d_1^w, d_2^w, ..., d_{n_w}^w])). \tag{2}$$

Then, we match and retrieve the textual representations of the new samples with the representations of the samples entering in the diagnosis and find the K closest samples. These samples are able to get the corresponding difficulty $\{d_1, ..., d_k\}$ and discrimination $\{disc_1, ..., disc_k\}$ by diagnosis. Finally, we average the difficulty and discrimination retrieved as the difficulty d_n and discrimination $disc_n$ of the new sample.

Weight Prediction. After getting the above inputs, we need to get the most appropriate ensemble weights for each new sample. To ensure the interpretability of the weights, we design the ensemble strategy for the new samples by the following calculation:

$$w = SoftMax(h_a \cdot c_n \times d_n \times disc_n), \tag{3}$$

where $w \in \mathbb{R}^{N \times 1}$, $h_a \in \mathbb{R}^{N \times P}$, $c_n \in \mathbb{R}^{1 \times P}$, d_n and $disc_n$ are single numbers.

5   Experiments

5.1   Experimental Setup

Dataset Description. We conduct experiments on two common keyphrase extraction datasets, i.e., OpenKP [32] and Inspec [15]. OpenKP is an open-domain keyphrase extraction dataset with various domains. In our settings, we choose the valid set (6,600 documents) of OpenKP for experiments. Besides, Inspec consists of short documents selected from scientific journal abstracts which are labeled by the authors, we choose the test (500 documents) and valid (1,500 documents) sets in this paper. The detailed statistics of the datasets are shown in Table 1. In particular, in our task, it is necessary to divide the dataset into two subsets, one for the diagnostician module and the other for the ensemble experiments. Therefore, we split the two datasets according to 3:1.

Algorithms to be Aggregated. To better train the diagnoser module and obtain the multi-dimensional abilities of each KE algorithm, we select 24 representative KE algorithms as follows:

- **Unsupervised methods:** Firstphrase[1], YAKE [4], TextRank [24], SingleRank [30], TopicRank [3], TopicalPageRank [21], PositionRank [9], MultipartiteRank [2], SIFRank [29].
- **Supervised methods:** BERT-RankKPE [28], SpanBERT-Variants*5 [28], BERT-ChunkKPE [28], BERT-SpanKPE [28], BERT-JointKPE [28], BERT-TagKPE [28], RoBERTa-Variants*5 [28].

Among them, supervised methods are trained on the OpenKP training set (134k documents). We obtain the response logs of learners on all samples on the datasets. Following the past research [31], we split the response logs into the training set, validation set and test set as 7:1:2.

Table 1. Statistics of keyphrase extraction datasets.

Statistics	OpenKP	Inspec
Document Number	6,616	2,000
Document Len Average	900	128
Keyphrase Average	2.2	9.8
Keyphrase Len Average	2.0	2.5

Table 2. Evaluation of all diagnosers through predicting learner performance on samples.

Methods	OpenKP			Inspec		
	AUC	Accuracy	RMSE	AUC	Accuracy	RMSE
DINA	0.563	0.545	0.559	0.538	0.512	0.578
IRT	0.576	0.540	0.542	0.560	0.545	0.544
NeuralCD	**0.914**	**0.869**	**0.340**	**0.883**	**0.762**	**0.379**

Baselines. For the cognitive diagnosis, we evaluate the performance of NeuralCD with other well-known CDMs (i.e., IRT [22] and DINA [5]). Among them, IRT is the most popular cognitive diagnosis method, it models students' latent traits and the parameters of exercises like difficulty and discrimination with a logistic-like function. DINA is the first method to design the Q-matrix and it uses binary variables to represent mastery of skills. NeuralCD [31] is a neural cognitive diagnostic framework, which leverages multi-layers for modeling the complex interactions of students and exercises, aiming to diagnose students' cognition by predicting the probability of the student answering the exercise correctly.

For the ensemble learning strategy, we choose to compare our approach with the average strategy and the weighted voting strategy. The weights are constant based on the performance of the history dataset evaluated on the traditional metrics (e.g., *shape Precision*). We also choose several individual keyphrase extraction methods from the 24 representative KE algorithms described before as baselines.

Experimental Settings. In our experiment, we use the pre-trained uncased BERT-based [6] model with 768 dimensions hidden representation as our tool. In our experiments, we set $P = 10$ for both two datasets. As the number of topics P is the most important hyper-parameter in AEKE, we conduct sensitivity experiments on it in Sect. 5.3. To set up the training process for the diagnostic module, we initialize all network parameters with Xavier initialization. The Adam optimizer [16] is used in the experiment while the learning rate is set to

---

[1] https://github.com/boudinfl/pke..

0.0002. We train all diagnosers for 20 epochs and select the best model on the validation set for testing. All experiments are run on two NVIDIA A100 GPUs.

5.2 Evaluation Metrics

Learner Performance Prediction. Generally, the ground truth of the ability of learners can't be obtained, it's difficult to evaluate the performance of cognitive diagnosis models. In most works, the prediction of learners' performance is an indirect way of evaluating the model. Evaluation metrics including *Accuracy*, *RMSE* (Root Mean Square Error), and *AUC* (Area Under the Curve) are chosen. Among them, better predictions have higher values in *Accuracy* and *AUC*, while the lower *RMSE* value, the better the prediction is achieved.

Model Aggregation. We realize model aggregation based on each learner's proficiency in the topics. The aggregation is tested on both OpenKP and Inspec datasets with several traditional keyphrase extraction metrics including *Precision*, *Recall*, and *F1-score*.

5.3 Experimental Results

Learner Performance Prediction. The experimental results are reported in Table 2, we have several observations as follows. First, NeuralCD performs the best on both OpenKP and Inspec, demonstrating NeuralCD can effectively evaluate the ability of keyphrase extraction algorithms. Besides, the traditional models including IRT and DINA perform poorly, which reflects that the relationship between learners' ability and samples' features is too difficult to capture, and

Table 3. Model aggregation results of popular keyphrase extraction models. The top part lists some unsupervised methods, the middle part lists the supervised methods, and the bottom part lists the ensemble methods.

Methods	OpenKP			Inspec		
	P@5	R@5	F_1@5	P@5	R@5	F_1@5
Firstphrase	19.5	36.7	23.6	24.0	15.0	17.3
YAKE [4]	12.1	29.1	16.7	21.0	13.6	15.5
TextRank [24]	5.5	14.2	7.9	31.7	19.2	22.6
SingleRank [30]	14.4	34.5	19.7	33.0	20.2	23.6
TopicRank [3]	14.4	30.3	19.6	28.2	16.9	20.0
BERT-JointKPE [28]	22.7	57.1	30.3	37.9	24.3	27.9
SpanBERT-RankKPE [28]	23.2	61.8	33.9	38.7	24.9	28.6
RoBERTa-TagKPE [28]	23.0	58.9	31.8	36.9	23.7	27.2
Averaging	23.7	61.0	33.5	39.1	25.0	28.9
Weighted Voting (*Precision*)	24.0	61.4	33.7	39.7	25.2	29.4
AEKE	**24.5**	**62.0**	**34.1**	**40.3**	**25.8**	**29.8**

indirectly proves the effectiveness of neural networks. Through NeuralCD, we can obtain highly reliable diagnostic results to be applied in the ensemble stage.

Model Aggregation. We compare our AEKE with the traditional aggregation methods (i.e., weighted voting and averaging) to illustrate the efficiency of our method as presented in Table 3. Among them, weights for weighted voting are obtained based on the overall performance (*precision*) of the history datasets of each keyphrase extraction algorithm. Such weights are constant during the model aggregation. In general, firstly, compared to supervised and unsupervised methods, both AEKE and the baseline ensemble strategy perform better than individual methods, demonstrating the necessity of ensemble. Besides, our adaptive ensemble strategy outperforms the ensemble baseline on both datasets, indicating the effectiveness of aggregation according to multi-dimensional abilities.

Hyper-Parameter Sensitivity Study. In our work, the number of skills P is a hyper-parameter, which determines how well the topics are clustered and also influences the design of the assessment skills. Therefore, in this section, we investigate the sensitivity of P. Figure 2 shows the performance of AEKE with different topic numbers P on the OpenKP dataset. The experiment shows a rising trend followed by a falling trend in the effectiveness of the ensemble result as the number of P increases. 10 is the best topic clustering number for the OpenKP. Specifically, when P is small, the result of document topic clustering is poor, which further affects the cognitive diagnosis of multi-dimensional abilities and the ensemble procedure. While $P > 10$, the ensemble results tend to be stable. Therefore, in this paper, we set P to 10 for our experiments.

Case Study. In this section, to further illustrate the effectiveness of AEKE, we show a high-quality sample in OpenKP and the ensemble results of weighted voting and AEKE in Fig. 3. Specifically, we aggregate the extraction results of three KE methods (i.e. BERT-Chunk [28], RoBERTa-Rank [28] and RoBERTa-Span [28]) by our strategy and traditional weighted voting strategy, respectively. In Fig. 3(a), we illustrate a detailed procedure of our AEKE. First, the new sample is entered into the diagnosis module and we can obtain the corresponding diagnosis results. It is obvious that this sample is a shooting report, which belongs to

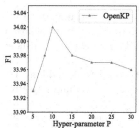

Fig. 2. Hyper-parameter Sensitivity Study.

Fig. 3. Visualized keyphrases extracted by AEKE (a) and traditional strategy (b).

the legal news topic. Its difficulty and discrimination indicate that this sample has high text quality. It also shows the ability of the three methods on legal news topics. Then, based on the diagnosis results, our AEKE can adaptively adjust the weights of different methods during aggregation to get good ensemble results. In Fig. 3(b), the traditional method relies on the evaluation result of the three methods on the history datasets evaluated on the single metric *Precision@5*, and since the overall results on *Precision@5* are similar, the same weights are constant for all new samples. However, such weights do not achieve satisfying ensemble results in this new sample. This case serves as a compelling demonstration of the remarkable flexibility and efficiency of AEKE.

It is worth noting that, unlike traditional methods whose ensemble weights are fixed during aggregation, the weights in AEKE are not constant. Specifically, the above case belongs to the *Legal* topic, and when facing with samples of other topics (e.g., *Sports*), AEKE will adjust the ensemble weights adaptively based on the multi-dimensional abilities of KE methods and features of new sample.

6   Conclusion

In this paper, we proposed an adaptive ensemble strategy (AEKE) based on cognitive diagnostic techniques in the keyphrase extraction task. To the best of our knowledge, this is the first attempt to aggregate machine learning algorithms from a cognitive diagnostic perspective. To be specific, we first carefully employed the NeuralCD to evaluate the multi-dimensional abilities of keyphrase extraction algorithms. Then, based on the diagnostic ability, we developed an adaptive ensemble strategy to aggregate individual keyphrase extraction methods. Experimental results on both OpenKP and Inspec datasets demonstrated the effectiveness of AEKE.

Acknowledgements. This research was supported by grants from the National Key Research and Development Program of China (Grant No. 2021YFF0901003).

References

1. Blei, D.M., Ng, A.Y., Jordan, M.I.: Latent dirichlet allocation. J. Mach. Learn. Res. **3**, 993–1022 (2003)
2. Boudin, F.: Unsupervised keyphrase extraction with multipartite graphs. In: Proceedings of the 2018 Conference of the North American Chapter of the Association for Computational Linguistics: Human Language Technologies, Volume 2 (Short Papers), pp. 667–672 (2018)
3. Bougouin, A., Boudin, F., Daille, B.: TopicRank: graph-based topic ranking for keyphrase extraction. In: International Joint Conference on Natural Language Processing (IJCNLP), pp. 543–551 (2013)
4. Campos, R., Mangaravite, V., Pasquali, A., Jorge, A.M., Nunes, C., Jatowt, A.: A text feature based automatic keyword extraction method for single documents. In: Pasi, G., Piwowarski, B., Azzopardi, L., Hanbury, A. (eds.) ECIR 2018. LNCS, vol. 10772, pp. 684–691. Springer, Cham (2018). https://doi.org/10.1007/978-3-319-76941-7_63

5. De La Torre, J.: Dina model and parameter estimation: a didactic. Journal of educational and behavioral statistics **34**(1), 115–130 (2009)
6. Devlin, J., Chang, M.W., Lee, K., Toutanova, K.: BERT: pre-training of deep bidirectional transformers for language understanding. arXiv preprint arXiv:1810.04805 (2018)
7. Ding, H., Luo, X.: AttentionRank: unsupervised keyphrase extraction using self and cross attentions. In: Proceedings of the 2021 Conference on Empirical Methods in Natural Language Processing, pp. 1919–1928 (2021)
8. Dong, X., Yu, Z., Cao, W., Shi, Y., Ma, Q.: A survey on ensemble learning. Front. Comp. Sci. **14**, 241–258 (2020)
9. Florescu, C., Caragea, C.: PositionRank: an unsupervised approach to keyphrase extraction from scholarly documents. In: Proceedings of the 55th Annual Meeting of the Association for Computational Linguistics (Volume 1: Long Papers), pp. 1105–1115 (2017)
10. Gallina, Y., Boudin, F., Daille, B.: Large-scale evaluation of keyphrase extraction models. In: Proceedings of the ACM/IEEE Joint Conference on Digital Libraries in 2020, pp. 271–278 (2020)
11. Ganaie, M.A., Hu, M., Malik, A., Tanveer, M., Suganthan, P.: Ensemble deep learning: a review. Eng. Appl. Artif. Intell. **115**, 105151 (2022)
12. Gao, W., et al.: RCD: relation map driven cognitive diagnosis for intelligent education systems. In: Proceedings of the 44th International ACM SIGIR Conference on Research and Development in Information Retrieval, pp. 501–510 (2021)
13. Gao, W., et al.: Leveraging transferable knowledge concept graph embedding for cold-start cognitive diagnosis. In: Proceedings of the 46th International ACM SIGIR Conference on Research and Development in Information Retrieval, pp. 983–992
14. Hasan, K.S., Ng, V.: Automatic keyphrase extraction: A survey of the state of the art. In: Proceedings of the 52nd Annual Meeting of the Association for Computational Linguistics (Volume 1: Long Papers), pp. 1262–1273 (2014)
15. Hulth, A.: Improved automatic keyword extraction given more linguistic knowledge. In: Proceedings of the 2003 Conference on Empirical Methods in Natural Language Processing, pp. 216–223 (2003)
16. Kingma, D.P., Ba, J.: Adam: a method for stochastic optimization. arXiv preprint arXiv:1412.6980 (2014)
17. Liu, C., Yang, L., Gao, W., Li, Y., Liu, Y.: MuST: an interpretable multidimensional strain theory model for corporate misreporting prediction. Electron. Commer. Res. Appl. **57**, 101225 (2023)
18. Liu, Q.: Towards a new generation of cognitive diagnosis. In: IJCAI, pp. 4961–4964 (2021)
19. Liu, Y., et al.: Technical phrase extraction for patent mining: a multi-level approach. In: 2020 IEEE International Conference on Data Mining (ICDM), pp. 1142–1147. IEEE (2020)
20. Liu, Y., et al.: TechPat: technical phrase extraction for patent mining. ACM Trans. Knowl. Disc. Data **17**, 1–31 (2023)
21. Liu, Z., Huang, W., Zheng, Y., Sun, M.: Automatic keyphrase extraction via topic decomposition. In: Proceedings of the 2010 Conference on Empirical Methods in Natural Language Processing, pp. 366–376 (2010)
22. Lord, F.: A Theory of Test Scores. Psychometric Monographs (1952)
23. Meng, R., Wang, T., Yuan, X., Zhou, Y., He, D.: General-to-specific transfer labeling for domain adaptable keyphrase generation. arXiv preprint arXiv:2208.09606 (2022)

24. Mihalcea, R., Tarau, P.: TextRank: bringing order into text. In: Proceedings of the 2004 Conference on Empirical Methods in Natural Language Processing. pp. 404–411 (2004)
25. Papagiannopoulou, E., Tsoumakas, G.: A review of keyphrase extraction. Wiley Interdisc. Rev. Data Min. Knowl. Disc. **10**(2), e1339 (2020)
26. Peterson, L.E.: K-nearest neighbor. Scholarpedia **4**(2), 1883 (2009)
27. Song, M., Feng, Y., Jing, L.: A survey on recent advances in keyphrase extraction from pre-trained language models. In: Findings of the Association for Computational Linguistics, EACL 2023, pp. 2108–2119 (2023)
28. Sun, S., Liu, Z., Xiong, C., Liu, Z., Bao, J.: Capturing global informativeness in open domain keyphrase extraction. In: Wang, L., Feng, Y., Hong, Yu., He, R. (eds.) NLPCC 2021. LNCS (LNAI), vol. 13029, pp. 275–287. Springer, Cham (2021). https://doi.org/10.1007/978-3-030-88483-3_21
29. Sun, Y., Qiu, H., Zheng, Y., Wang, Z., Zhang, C.: SIFRank: a new baseline for unsupervised keyphrase extraction based on pre-trained language model. IEEE Access **8**, 10896–10906 (2020)
30. Wan, X., Xiao, J.: Single document keyphrase extraction using neighborhood knowledge. In: AAAI, vol. 8, pp. 855–860 (2008)
31. Wang, F., et al.: Neural cognitive diagnosis for intelligent education systems. In: Proceedings of the AAAI Conference on Artificial Intelligence, vol. 34, pp. 6153–6161 (2020)
32. Xiong, L., Hu, C., Xiong, C., Campos, D., Overwijk, A.: Open domain web keyphrase extraction beyond language modeling. In: Proceedings of the EMNLP-IJCNLP 2019, pp. 5175–5184 (2019)
33. Yue, L., Liu, Q., Du, Y., An, Y., Wang, L., Chen, E.: DARE: disentanglement-augmented rationale extraction. In: Advances in Neural Information Processing Systems (2022)
34. Zhao, H., Lu, M., Yao, A., Guo, Y., Chen, Y., Zhang, L.: Physics inspired optimization on semantic transfer features: an alternative method for room layout estimation. In: Proceedings of the IEEE Conference on Computer Vision and Pattern Recognition, pp. 10–18 (2017)

Author Index

Printed in the United States
by Baker & Taylor Publisher Services